Change Management During Unprecedented Times

Kyla Latrice Tennin
College of Doctoral Studies, University of Phoenix, USA & Forbes School of Business, USA & World Business Angels Investment Forum (WBAF)-G20, USA & Lady Mirage Global, Inc., USA

IGI Global
PUBLISHER of TIMELY KNOWLEDGE

A volume in the Advances in Logistics, Operations, and Management Science (ALOMS) Book Series

Published in the United States of America by
IGI Global
Business Science Reference (an imprint of IGI Global)
701 E. Chocolate Avenue
Hershey PA, USA 17033
Tel: 717-533-8845
Fax: 717-533-8661
E-mail: cust@igi-global.com
Web site: http://www.igi-global.com

Library of Congress Cataloging-in-Publication Data

Names: Tennin, Kyla Latrice, 1982- editor.
Title: Change management during unprecedented times / edited by Kyla Latrice Tennin.
Description: Hershey, PA : Business Science Reference, [2023] | Includes bibliographical references and index. | Summary: "We will examine organizational change management through the lenses of research and innovative practices contained within the fields of leadership and organizational change. The benefit of the publication is to enlighten communities through the efforts of a research perspective that amplifies practice-based potentials in applying theory, models, and/or frameworks to real-time issues. Henceforth, solutions companies can implement to successfully solve a problem, move in a new direction, grow, innovate, and/or enter a new market"-- Provided by publisher.
Identifiers: LCCN 2022045609 (print) | LCCN 2022045610 (ebook) | ISBN 9781668475096 (hardcover) | ISBN 9781668475102 (paperback) | ISBN 9781668475119 (ebook)
Subjects: LCSH: Organizational change--Management.
Classification: LCC HD58.8 .C4543 2023 (print) | LCC HD58.8 (ebook) | DDC 658.4/06--dc23/eng/20221125
LC record available at https://lccn.loc.gov/2022045609
LC ebook record available at https://lccn.loc.gov/2022045610

This book is published in the IGI Global book series Advances in Logistics, Operations, and Management Science (ALOMS) (ISSN: 2327-350X; eISSN: 2327-3518)

British Cataloguing in Publication Data
A Cataloguing in Publication record for this book is available from the British Library.

Advances in Logistics, Operations, and Management Science (ALOMS) Book Series

John Wang
Montclair State University, USA

ISSN:2327-350X
EISSN:2327-3518

Mission

Operations research and management science continue to influence business processes, administration, and management information systems, particularly in covering the application methods for decision-making processes. New case studies and applications on management science, operations management, social sciences, and other behavioral sciences have been incorporated into business and organizations real-world objectives.

The **Advances in Logistics, Operations, and Management Science** (ALOMS) Book Series provides a collection of reference publications on the current trends, applications, theories, and practices in the management science field. Providing relevant and current research, this series and its individual publications would be useful for academics, researchers, scholars, and practitioners interested in improving decision making models and business functions.

Coverage

- Operations Management
- Services management
- Decision analysis and decision support
- Finance
- Computing and information technologies
- Networks
- Marketing engineering
- Production Management
- Risk Management
- Information Management

IGI Global is currently accepting manuscripts for publication within this series. To submit a proposal for a volume in this series, please contact our Acquisition Editors at Acquisitions@igi-global.com or visit: http://www.igi-global.com/publish/.

The Advances in Logistics, Operations, and Management Science (ALOMS) Book Series (ISSN 2327-350X) is published by IGI Global, 701 E. Chocolate Avenue, Hershey, PA 17033-1240, USA, www.igi-global.com. This series is composed of titles available for purchase individually; each title is edited to be contextually exclusive from any other title within the series. For pricing and ordering information please visit http://www.igi-global.com/book-series/advances-logistics-operations-management-science/37170. Postmaster: Send all address changes to above address.

Titles in this Series

For a list of additional titles in this series, please visit: http://www.igi-global.com/book-series/advances-logistics-operations-management-science/37170

Futuristic Technology Perspectives on Entrepreneurship and Sustainable Innovation
Sanjay Misra (Ostfold University, Norway) Amit Jain (Amity University, India) Manju Kaushik (Amity University, India) and Chitreshh Banerjee (Amity University, India)
Business Science Reference • © 2023 • 300pp • H/C (ISBN: 9781668458716) • US $250.00

Cases on Managing Dairy Productive Chains
Eduardo Guilherme Satolo (São Paulo State University, Brazil) and Priscilla Ayllen Bustos Mac-Lean (São Paulo State University, Brazil)
Engineering Science Reference • © 2023 • 320pp • H/C (ISBN: 9781668454725) • US $235.00

Perspectives and Strategies of Family Business Resiliency in Unprecedented Times
Hotniar Siringoringo (Gunadarma University, Indonesia) and Ravindra Hewa Kuruppuge (University of Peradeniya, Sri Lanka)
Business Science Reference • © 2023 • 300pp • H/C (ISBN: 9781668473948) • US $240.00

Moving From R&D Development to Production and Sales in Start-Up Companies
Amiram Porath (APC, Israel)
Business Science Reference • © 2023 • 181pp • H/C (ISBN: 9781799856856) • US $195.00

Advanced Research and Real-World Applications of Industry 5.0
Mahmoud Numan Bakkar (Abu Dhabi Vocational Education and Training Institute (ADVETI), Institute of Applied Technology (IAT), UAE) and Elspeth McKay (Cogniware.com.au, Australia)
Business Science Reference • © 2023 • 315pp • H/C (ISBN: 9781799888055) • US $250.00

Cases on International Business Logistics in the Middle East
Islam Abdelbary (Arab Academy for Science, Technology, and Maritime Transport, Egypt & University of Plymouth, UK) Sandra Haddad (Arab Academy for Science, Technology, and Maritime Transport, Egypt) and Ghada Elkady (Arab Academy for Science, Technology, and Maritime Transport, Egypt)
Business Science Reference • © 2023 • 342pp • H/C (ISBN: 9781668446867) • US $240.00

Examining the Vital Financial Role of SMEs in Achieving the Sustainable Development Goals
Dalila Taleb (University of Abou Bakr Belkaïd, Algeria) Mohammed El Amine Abdelli (University of Brest, France) Afef Khalil (University of Tunis, Carthage, Tunisia) and Asma Sghaier (University of Sousse, Tunisia)
Business Science Reference • © 2023 • 275pp • H/C (ISBN: 9781668448342) • US $250.00

IGI Global
PUBLISHER of TIMELY KNOWLEDGE

701 East Chocolate Avenue, Hershey, PA 17033, USA
Tel: 717-533-8845 x100 • Fax: 717-533-8661
E-Mail: cust@igi-global.com • www.igi-global.com

Editorial Advisory Board

Table of Contents

Foreword xvi

Preface xvii

Chapter 1
Managing Organizational Change During Turbulent Times: A Socio-Psychological Perspective 1
Filippo Ferrari, Independent Researcher, Italy

Chapter 2
Leading Change in an Unpredictable World: What Does Sustainable, Resilient Change Look Like?. 25
Jennifer Bryan, ABChange Consultancy, UK
John Higgins, The Right Conversation, UK

Chapter 3
The Challenges and Performance of Female-Owned Entrepreneurial Firms and Management Strategies 43
Raktima Bharadwaj, Queen's University, Belfast, UK
Rajoshi Das, Amity University, Kolkata, India
Anindita Majumdar, Woxsen University, Hyderabad, India

Chapter 4
The Change Potential of Social Media: Learning From Digital Business Cases 63
Silvia Fernandes, CinTurs, Faculty of Economics, University of Algarve, Portugal
Fatima L. Carvalho, CinTurs, University of Algarve, Portugal
Daniela Neves, Faculty of Economics, University of Algarve, Portugal

Chapter 5
Anxiety, Reactions, and Economic Expectations of University Students in the Effect of the COVID-19 Pandemic: Survey Evidence from Turkey 81
Ramazan Gökbunar, Manisa Celal Bayar University, Turkey
Füsun Küçükbay, Manisa Celal Bayar University, Turkey

Chapter 6
Can Change Management Be Disrupted Through Leadership Stretegies? Evidence From Start-Up Firms in Asia ... 100
Samrat Ray, Independent Researcher, India

Chapter 7
Building Change Maturity in Organisations ... 128
Isolde G. Kanikani, FUTURE:CM, The Netherlands

Chapter 8
Theories and Application of Organisational Change Management During the COVID-19 Era ... 155
Oindrila Chakraborty, J.D. Birla Institute, India

Chapter 9
A Play-Based Approach to Learning in Internationalizing Arab Family Businesses: Change as a Ludic Paradox ... 186
Edward Gonsalves, Cooplexity Institute, Spain
Rebecca Fakoussa, University of Northampton, UK

Chapter 10
A Dynamic Capability to Determine Business Performance in the Post-COVID-19 Era: Organizational Agility ... 206
Ibrahim Yikilmaz, Kocaeli University, Turkey

Chapter 11
Gender Differences in the Entrepreneurial Orientation Dimensions in the Middle East: Evidence From Palestine ... 228
Nidal A. Darwish, Al-Quds University, Palestine
Mohammed A. Bayyoud, Al-Quds University, Palestine

Chapter 12
Strategy Development With Future Scenarios: Brainstorming for the Future of a University ... 252
Mehmet Ertem, Yozgat Bozok University, Turkey

Chapter 13
Mastering the Chaos: Data-Driven and AI-Based Change Management as an Answer to Challenges in Unprecedented Times ... 266
Jens M. Sorg, CGI Deutschland B.V. & Co. KG, Germany
Karen Hodge Cunningham, CGI, Canada
Assia Stoyanova, CGI, USA

Chapter 14
Unleashed, Harnessed, and Empowered: The Potential of Women in the Change Management and Leadership of Crises ... 284
Catherine Hayes, University of Sunderland, UK

Chapter 15
Perspectives on Socio-Ecological Innovation Management Models 303
José G. Vargas-Hernandez, Instituto Tecnológico Mario Molina, Mexico
Teresa I. Salazar-Echeagaray, Universidad Autonoma de Sinaloa, Mexico
Omar C. Vargas-González, Tecnológico Nacional de México, Ciudad Guzmán, Mexico

Chapter 16
Understanding the Implementation of Lean Philosophy in Warehouse Management 323
Vanessa Amorim, ISCAP, Polytechnic of Porto, Portugal
Orlando Lima Rua, Center for Organisational and Social Studies (CEOS), ISCAP, Polytechnic of Porto, Portugal & Research Center of Business Sciences (NECE), Portugal
Bruno de Sousa Lopes, University of Aveiro, Portugal

Compilation of References 341

About the Contributors 402

Index 410

Detailed Table of Contents

Foreword xvi

Preface xvii

Chapter 1
Managing Organizational Change During Turbulent Times: A Socio-Psychological Perspective 1
Filippo Ferrari, Independent Researcher, Italy

During an organizational change, the main objective of change management actions is to generate and sustain a change commitment among the change recipients in order to increase the probability of success. This chapter therefore aims to present the antecedents, dynamics, and consequences of organizational change at a psychological and relational level, in a complex, uncertain, ambiguous, and unprecedented context. It focuses in particular on the organizational, interpersonal, and individual factors that favor coping with a turbulent scenario. This chapter shows how to develop organizational reliability, foster knowledge sharing, and adopt appropriate leadership models. Finally, the purpose of the chapter is to highlight the individual factors that favor or, conversely, hinder organizational change.

Chapter 2
Leading Change in an Unpredictable World: What Does Sustainable, Resilient Change Look Like?. 25
Jennifer Bryan, ABChange Consultancy, UK
John Higgins, The Right Conversation, UK

Both leadership and change are contested labels and there is no universal definition. What is usefully understood by leadership and change is specific to the unique nature of a particular change and the evolving context within which it is being carried out. By paying attention to what is specifically needed in the moment around leaders and leading, change leadership becomes an approach that is fit for a specific purpose and avoids becoming a generic approach which is incapable of adjusting to local realities. By noticing how the context of change is evolving and assumptions become validated and invalidated, the fitness of the chosen approach is also kept under constant review.

Chapter 3
The Challenges and Performance of Female-Owned Entrepreneurial Firms and Management Strategies 43
Raktima Bharadwaj, Queen's University, Belfast, UK
Rajoshi Das, Amity University, Kolkata, India
Anindita Majumdar, Woxsen University, Hyderabad, India

In India, society has set some unsaid rules. Some find it difficult to accept women in a work environment because of the patriarchy. Hence it becomes difficult for a woman to break the stigma and establish her own firm. The paper aims to look at the number of threats and challenges that female entrepreneurs face from both micro and macro perspectives. Covid has bought both temporary change (workplace change) and permanent change (shutting down a service/facility) in an organisation. A small new rising firm would not have the capacity to sustain during this time, and females who try to set up small businesses to run their families are mentally affected. This article is an extensive review from earlier works to understand the challenges faced by female owned entrepreneurial firms and their performance during the change brought by COVID times. This article explores the factors influencing the development of female entrepreneurs as well as measures required to enhance the scenario. This paper also aims to explore the psychosocial aspect of changes brought by female owned entrepreneurial firms.

Chapter 4
The Change Potential of Social Media: Learning From Digital Business Cases 63
Silvia Fernandes, CinTurs, Faculty of Economics, University of Algarve, Portugal
Fatima L. Carvalho, CinTurs, University of Algarve, Portugal
Daniela Neves, Faculty of Economics, University of Algarve, Portugal

This work results from an internship of two months at a new company of digital media, to evaluate its 'maturity' in terms of social media performance. For pursuing this objective, it is compared with its main competitors in the area as a panel of experts. Two methods of analysis addressed two main research issues: I1) which key performance indicators are mostly used in a sample of main firms in the area in Portugal; and I2) which new strategies came from their assessment in those firms? In the period considered, the company revealed a more adaptive strategy, missing some key indicators in the area. Its efforts may not be being directed at the greatest potential of social media. It can improve the performance of its social media by monitoring engagement what helps to preserve its reputation and give followers the answers they really want. A common aspect in the compared companies is the absence of outsourcing to digital influencers. However, this practice is growing because, with the demand and speed of response currently required, in-house digital marketing lacks the resources.

Chapter 5
Anxiety, Reactions, and Economic Expectations of University Students in the Effect of the COVID-19 Pandemic: Survey Evidence from Turkey 81
Ramazan Gökbunar, Manisa Celal Bayar University, Turkey
Füsun Küçükbay, Manisa Celal Bayar University, Turkey

The current survey study was designed to explore the mental health status, reactions, concerns, and expectations of university students during the COVID-19 pandemic, and the potential relationships between mental health and their reactions and macroeconomic expectations. The results show that the student's mental health worsened during Covid-19 which accelerated their pessimism, causing a decline in their academic success and purchases, and causing an increase in their negative expectations about macroeconomic indicators. The results also show that concerns about the economy, financial situation, and future are associated with mental deterioration. The analysis reveals that the most prevalent concern among the students is anxiety about the future. Moreover, gender, educational level, and income level also significantly impact the reactions and the macroeconomic expectations of the students.

Chapter 6
Can Change Management Be Disrupted Through Leadership Stretegies? Evidence From Start-Up Firms in Asia 100
Samrat Ray, Independent Researcher, India

The "change management" process is a helpful approach for changing the environment of business companies to go ahead in the upcoming days. It has been known that the employees are the main part of an organisation who has not accepted the changing process at first; and for that reason, the appropriate leadership strategy is required to bring the changes within. The start-ups of Asia have been explained in this study for improving the leadership techniques by which the leaders have enhanced their leadership qualities to accept the change management process. The analysis of the responses derived from the survey has been done using the statistical tool "SPSS," which has been chosen for its tools of descriptive and inferential statistics. The outcomes of the data analysis have been evaluated to depict the inference of the results of the correlation and regression of the data. Moreover, the results of the statistical analysis have been discussed in alignment with the hypotheses that have been formed using the independent and dependent variables.

Chapter 7
Building Change Maturity in Organisations 128
Isolde G. Kanikani, FUTURE:CM, The Netherlands

'Building change maturity in organisations' explores what change maturity looks like in practice and how increased maturity brings a myriad of benefits to the organisation investing in it. Building maturity of any kind is often seen as a luxury, and with the growing amount of change organisations contend with, this is no longer the case. It's becoming increasingly clear that if an organisation does not develop the capability to change effectively, it will metaphorically miss the boat. This tipping point is very real, making the subject of building change maturity a poignant one. The impact of change maturity is often seen via change management on the project or program levels, and ROI measurements don't often go beyond this focus. Building the capability at the organisational level might appear like a theoretical exercise for those managing change, but with the right mindset, change capability can already be built into the transformation projects already taking place.

Chapter 8
Theories and Application of Organisational Change Management During the COVID-19 Era 155
Oindrila Chakraborty, J.D. Birla Institute, India

Through the book chapter, the author would primarily explore the basic concept of change management and an overview of diverse fundamental theories of conventional organisational change management (OCM) models and approaches in human resource management, along with the application in several workplaces sector wise, during pandemic times with special reference to the organisational adaptation in structural and psychological aspects to combat the unfavourable situations. The chapter would fathom the needs, drives and ideal implementation plan of change management along with the practical implementation of the same. The chapter would also try to examine different group dynamics, Resistance, Intervention Instruments and success for organisational change management.

Chapter 9
A Play-Based Approach to Learning in Internationalizing Arab Family Businesses: Change as a Ludic Paradox 186
Edward Gonsalves, Cooplexity Institute, Spain
Rebecca Fakoussa, University of Northampton, UK

Arab family businesses (AFB) can be found across a richly diverse region with a myriad of unique cultures. As Arab family businesses worldwide become more sophisticated with ownership, succession and wealth planning changing, family business training and education need to rapidly evolve its support of family businesses. This chapter argues that in the MENA region, training and education approaches for family-owned businesses differ to others due to their environmental paradox. Given such differences, play could offer Arab family business leaders an alternative route to training and education, as executives increasingly encounter rapid and complex environmental, competitive, and internal changes. In particular, the chapter argues that AFB's which are internationalizing their markets and operations will be driven by changes that force breaks with traditional routines.

Chapter 10
A Dynamic Capability to Determine Business Performance in the Post-COVID-19 Era: Organizational Agility 206
Ibrahim Yikilmaz, Kocaeli University, Turkey

The Covid-19 pandemic has made the competition process even more difficult for businesses, changing the competitive dynamics. The already high level of VUCA (volatility, uncertainty, complexity, and ambiguity) has increased even more. To be successful in the new industry environment, businesses need to develop their skills in "speed, flexibility, resilience, responsiveness, cost, and efficiency." Adaptive, flexible, and resilient dynamic capabilities needed by businesses in the post-covid19 era are defined as organizational agility. In this context, the concept of organizational agility is discussed in detail. In the study, recommendations were made about what the new era brought in terms of businesses in the pandemic and post-pandemic era and how to increase organizational agility capabilities (responsiveness, competency, flexibility, speed, and proactiveness) to achieve sustainable competition and survive in the changing competitive dynamics of businesses.

Chapter 11
Gender Differences in the Entrepreneurial Orientation Dimensions in the Middle East: Evidence From Palestine.......... 228
Nidal A. Darwish, Al-Quds University, Palestine
Mohammed A. Bayyoud, Al-Quds University, Palestine

The research aims to explore and describe to what extent there is gender difference across the entrepreneurial orientation dimensions (risk-taking, innovativeness, proactiveness, competitiveness, and autonomy) in the Middle East. To achieve this goal, the authors employed a descriptive quantitative research design where 60 male and female entrepreneurs in Palestine were surveyed through a closed-ended questionnaire. The study findings indicate that males are more entrepreneurial-oriented than females, but to a relatively small extent. Moreover, the results showed that male entrepreneurs have a higher mean in risk-taking, competitiveness, and innovativeness, whereas females have a higher mean in proactiveness and autonomy. Additionally, the study showed that the traditions and customs prevalent in Palestine were the most critical restrictions for females to become entrepreneurs. Moreover, female entrepreneurs face different restrictions, including society's perception toward women, lack of funds, and legislation obstacles such as registration.

Chapter 12
Strategy Development With Future Scenarios: Brainstorming for the Future of a University.......... 252
Mehmet Ertem, Yozgat Bozok University, Turkey

In this chapter, a university's story of conducting a "brainstorming session for strategy development with future scenarios" process and the steps of this process are presented and examined, in detail. This chapter aims to help managers and scholars know how to conduct a brainstorming session for producing future scenarios for their organizations by explaining the process with a lived example. For this purpose, "Narrative Research Design," which is one of the qualitative research designs, is chosen for this research study. Consequently, a brief theoretical framework and a step-by-step guide are presented for the related parties.

Chapter 13
Mastering the Chaos: Data-Driven and AI-Based Change Management as an Answer to Challenges in Unprecedented Times.......... 266
Jens M. Sorg, CGI Deutschland B.V. & Co. KG, Germany
Karen Hodge Cunningham, CGI, Canada
Assia Stoyanova, CGI, USA

You know that change endeavors are highly complex. You know that decision-making can be extremely challenging. Today, change capacities are more important than ever. This holds even more true in unprecedented times. What if it is possible to handle change endeavors with +1000, +10.000, and even +5 million affected stakeholders and indefinite challenges? Sounds too good to be true? It is the sound of the future. CGI is harnessing the velocity of change and is making the complex simple. The authors will give insights into the current field of data-driven and AI-based strategic change management (SCM) consulting. The focus of the chapter is the challenges the authors currently facing in elaborating a data-driven and AI-based consulting approach for SCM.

Chapter 14
Unleashed, Harnessed, and Empowered: The Potential of Women in the Change Management and Leadership of Crises 284
Catherine Hayes, University of Sunderland, UK

This chapter provides an insight into the challenges faced specifically by women in relation to the agency they are afforded within the context of change management in crisis situations and responses. This is contextualised within global higher education and examined through theoretical perspectives such as neoliberalism, which have impacted so much on the context specificity of change management and the cultures within which it has influenced so greatly. The recent global COVID-19 pandemic is used as a vehicle by which to drive thinking around concepts, which have had such an impact on women during this time, such as emotional labour and inequality. The chapter concludes with a consideration of organisational structures and the agency that this has afforded women both historically and within the leadership challenges they currently face.

Chapter 15
Perspectives on Socio-Ecological Innovation Management Models 303
José G. Vargas-Hernandez, Instituto Tecnológico Mario Molina, Mexico
Teresa I. Salazar-Echeagaray, Universidad Autonoma de Sinaloa, Mexico
Omar C. Vargas-González, Tecnológico Nacional de México, Ciudad Guzmán, Mexico

This study has the aim to analyze the different perspectives on socio-ecological innovation management models. The analysis departs if socio-ecological innovation initiatives connect to resources and capabilities, culture, creativity, tacit, and formal knowledge between nurtured entrepreneurship and different domains of innovation management models that become supply factors to determine the production potential and based on this assumption to analyze the ability to economic growth. The method used is the meta-analytic reflection based on theoretical and empirical literature review. It is concluded that the socio-ecological thinking and collaborative knowledge production takes the natural environmental resources for socio-ecological management innovation relevant for the transition towards the analytical framework for innovation management models This is a crucial factor that contributes to economic development of the internal and external environments full of a range of threats and opportunities because the interactions of biological diversity.

Chapter 16
Understanding the Implementation of Lean Philosophy in Warehouse Management 323
Vanessa Amorim, ISCAP, Polytechnic of Porto, Portugal
Orlando Lima Rua, Center for Organisational and Social Studies (CEOS), ISCAP, Polytechnic of Porto, Portugal & Research Center of Business Sciences (NECE), Portugal
Bruno de Sousa Lopes, University of Aveiro, Portugal

The core of the lean concept is expressed not only in eliminating waste and losses but also in the pursuit of continual improvement and creating greater value. Although lean management is commonly linked with industrial production processes, this research illustrates the application of lean techniques to optimize warehouse management operations. In this context, the research in an SME of the Import and Export sector in Portugal intends to describe the use of lean tools in warehouse optimization. The outcomes of the lean tool deployment meet the specified objectives and emphasize the need to integrate various approaches to achieve a better pursuit of the optimization strategy. The organization can respond to customer needs more effectively and efficiently through improved warehouse flow and continuous improvement.

Compilation of References 341

About the Contributors 402

Index 410

Foreword

One of the revolutionary powers that keep us moving, elevate our perspectives, and transcends us from the darkness of uncertainty to opportunity is "Change." Having spent several years of professional life as a management consultant and change strategist in public, private and academic settings with executives engraving change management mindset, I have witnessed the upheaval battle leaders across various industries face to navigate change. With change happening at a transformational rate, we must take responsibility for building change leaders for the future.

I have known Dr. Tennin since 2022 and have participated in several webinars and initiatives. Her commitment and passion for bringing evidence-based research and application to change management to social causes impress me.

Dr. Tennin is a global thought leader with over 20 years of experience leading her global conglomerate firm (Lady Mirage Global Inc) to work with clients ranging from Fortune 500 companies to Fortune 100 companies. Dr. Tennin's professional assignments cover financial services, hospitality, restaurant, consumer products/beauty, and healthcare industries. Her charisma, hard work, and determination spread to the academic field, where she has written 18 books, acquired three patents, and nearly 85 research reports.

Dr. Tennin's book provides evidence-based research and insights into the concepts of change management, digital transformation, organizational change and dives into resilience attributes that today's leaders and clients need during these unprecedented times. The book strategically covers different change frameworks, methodologies and provides a way to apply the newly gained knowledge in a real life-changing business environment.

Dr. Tennin's work ethic, professionalism, academic accomplishments, and in-depth knowledge of the changing global market conditions provide credibility and promise that readers are well-equipped for the future.

This book is for everyone who is a leader: - running an enterprise, a business consultant providing consulting services to their client, an entrepreneur in the process of starting their own business, a naive change practitioner, to a graduate who wants to build change knowledge and desires to make a difference in the changing landscape by helping organizations around the world.

Rishwinder Sethi
BCLC, Vancouver, Canada

Preface

Change Management During Unprecedented Times discusses various crises in organizations around the globe. For instance, during the COVID-19 pandemic. To combat COVID-19 with change management. Yet, other examples of crises are listed in Table 1 by Tennin (2022).

Table 1. Past pandemics and epidemics and the year of occurrence

Crisis Name	Year	Pandemic, Endemic, or Epidemic
West Nile Virus	1999-2002	Seasonal Epidemic
Anthrax	2001	Epidemic
SARS-CoV	2003	Pandemic
Mumps	2006	Endemic in various nations
E. Coli and Salmonella	2006	Epidemic
Swine Flu	2009	Pandemic
Whooping Cough	2012	Epidemic
MERS-CoV	2012	Epidemic
Ebola	2014	Epidemic
Zika Virus	2016	Epidemic
COVID-19	2019	Pandemic

Note: This table demonstrates the names of past pandemics and epidemics, and year occurrences.

The publication covers a range of topics such as managing change in the workplace, change maturity, leading change, sustainable resilient change, change management and digital transformation, data-driven and AI-based change management, change management strategy, change in the import and export sector, change management theories, change management best practices, change management in times of crises, change management measurement, women entrepreneurship, business strategies for emerging markets, large scale to small change efforts (e.g. small firms compared to large firms – SMEs and 1,000 to even 5M organizational stakeholders), how to adapt in the face of change, successful transformation efforts, tools and methods to measure change success, organization design, ineffective change management, ADKAR Change Management Model, and the PROSCI Change Management Model. Other change management frameworks worth considering are the Burke-Litwin Change Model and Leavitt's Diamond Model.

The topic of Change Management for the publication fits in the world today because due to the COVID-19 pandemic, 41.3% of firms reported they shut temporarily because of the pandemic (Bartik et al., 2020). In the United Kingdom, 32.5% of entrepreneurs stated they were still able to work during the pandemic, in comparison with entrepreneurs in Norway (58.5%), Bosnia and Herzegovina (81.6%), North America (55%), and France (55.9%) (Stephan et al., 2021). Within a global survey for the World Economic Forum (2020), a variety of industries were surveyed, from entrepreneur startups to music festivals, manufacturing companies, and automotive enterprises. According to the World Economic Forum (2020), 70% of startups reported they had to terminate their full-time employees since the start of the COVID-19 pandemic. Only 40% of new enterprises reported they have sufficient earnings to endure three months of operations (World Economic Forum, 2020).

Meanwhile, Connley (2021) at *CNBC* advised, because of the pandemic, women lost 64 million jobs and $800 billion in earnings globally. To compare, Boesch and Phadke (2021) at the American Progress Report presented since the pandemic women lost nearly 5.4 million jobs while men lost 4.4 million jobs. From private experience, with consultation clients in almost 50 nations, working with investment forums, world leaders, presidents of nations, and business owners, Cuyper et al.'s (2020) claim closely resemble what various entrepreneurs stated, even though Bartik et al. (2020) and Stephan et al.'s (2021) claims are necessary too. Crises in economies possess the capability to bring on hardships to both businesses and markets, as well as develop additional institutional voids. For example, to clearly state the statistics abovementioned, Bartik et al. (2020) carried out a quantitative survey on the North American small business ecosystem within the Alignable Business Network of 4.6 million companies. Bartik et al. (2020) stated out of all the sample, 7500 businesses replied to taking the resilience survey, where 41.3% of firms, as abovementioned, reported they shut down temporarily because of the COVID-19 pandemic. However, from the sample, 1.8% stated they shut down permanently because of the pandemic, but more or less 55.5% advised they were still able to operate; found a way to stay open and in business (Bartik et al., 2020).

Yet, what about the other 42.7%? Nearly half of the businesses struggle with issues, resources, and a strategy on how to say open during unprecedented times is a major concern. Could aspects of change management be applied to assist? To help firms pivot, especially digitally, and whether large scale or small? Filing an application for funding to remain open by paying operating expenses and employees shouldn't be the only option for companies. What about applying change management strategies for the short-term to remain open, for the long-term to mitigate risk and proof the company against future catastrophes and unpreparedness, but also for the long-term because the length of a catastrophic economical event is typically unknown? Businesses help economies not only exist, but to survive and thrive. They also play a role in addressing global social, environmental, and economic issues. Hence, for many years small businesses have been claimed to be the driving force behind economies' existence and stability.

Gargi (2019) postulated entrepreneurship regards contributing to economies by employing people and is connected to new technologies and innovations that have the potential to create additional employment for markets. The new innovations and technologies also possess the ability to be profitable (Gargi, 2019). Conclusively, resilience, education, financial inclusion, digital transformation, strategic partnerships, and particularly change management are needed when crises occur, to save and advance organizational ecosystems and economies. Therefore, knowing about the ideation and processes of change management to improve company negative circumstances are crucial to know. To innovate, improve performance, execute strategy to increase revenue, address risk, implement new systems, processes, or digital transformation to scale, and help stop companies from closing and ultimately from filing for dissolution. As a result, the aim of this book is to provide scholars, leaders, practitioners, and even key stakeholders of economies with different avenues to addressing important challenges companies encounter that impact the global economic landscape. Particularly, to assess the role and effects of change management on institutions, during unprecedented times.

The objectives (benefits of the publication) are we examined organizational change management through the lenses of research and innovative practices contained within the fields of leadership and organizational change. The benefit of the publication is to enlighten communities through the efforts of a research perspective that amplifies practice-based potential in applying theory, models, and/or frameworks to real-time issues. Henceforth, solutions companies can implement to successfully solve a problem, move in a new direction, grow, innovate, and/or enter a new market.

The impact of the publication, why the publication should be published is the purpose of this book is to substantiate change management in organizations (specifically during unprecedented times where digital transformation is critical), discuss the practical experience of change implementation, and to measure the effectiveness of a change initiative implemented. Chapters to be hosted in this book are also intended to be used as part of course/training material in various professional development settings. Presenting resources, tools, scientific and methodological perspectives, and various change management models or frameworks organizations can apply to assist them with being effective during crises or unprecedented times.

Moreover, the value of the book or how the theme will impact our field of research is the book is aimed at professionals and professionals of organizations who want to improve their understanding of change management and its processes, the specifics of change management models, and the advantages of applying change management in organizations or entrepreneurship to survive challenging times. Or for general company transformation to scale, transition to new business models, processes, systems, or resources, successfully adopt or use some sort of change, or to remain competitive. Including while encountering unprecedented times. Yet, while also highlighting the challenges, solutions, and opportunities within change management.

The target audience for the book is a variety. This premier reference source is an essential resource for business leaders, executives, entrepreneurs, human resource managers, consultants, practitioners, organization behavior specialists, managers, economists, government officials, policymakers, lawmakers, librarians, students and faculty of higher education, scholars, researchers, and academicians.

Nevertheless, the book is divided into four sections. Section one contains chapters one, two, three, and four and is about managing change, leading change, management strategies challenges and performance, change potential, and digital businesses. Chapters five, six, seven, and eight comprise section two and regard change in universities and startup firms, dealing with change during economic uncertainty or crisis (e.g., COVID-19), building change maturity in organizations, and theories of organizational change management and their application. Section three encompasses chapters nine, ten, eleven, and twelve and discusses change as a play-based approach, organizational agility, considering gender differences in change management strategy, strategy development for managers and scholars. The final section is section four and includes chapters thirteen, fourteen, fifteen, and sixteen and is about data-driven and AI-based change management, women in leadership and change management, innovation management models, and implementation of lean philosophy.

For example, Dr. Filippo Ferrari of Bologna, Italy wrote Chapter 1 and discussed the antecedents, dynamics, and consequences of organizational change at a psychological and relational level, in a complex, uncertain, ambiguous and unprecedented context and adopt appropriate leadership models, highlighting individual factors that favor or hinder organizational change. Jennifer Bryan and John Higgins of London, England wrote Chapter 2 and talked about how for leaders leading change, "change leadership becomes an approach that is fit for a specific purpose and avoids becoming a generic approach which is incapable of adjusting to local realities". For Chapter 3, Raktima Bharadwaj, Rajoshi Das, and Dr. Anindita Majumdar of India conducted "an extensive review from earlier works to understand the challenges faced by female-owned entrepreneurial firms and their performance during the change brought by COVID times". In Chapter 4, Professor Silvia Fernandes, Professor Fatima L. Carvalho, and Dr. Daniela Neves of Portugal reviewed a digital media company and its maturity regarding social media performance, in the face of change. Ramazan Gokbunar and Fusun Kucukbay of Turkey explained the mental health status, reactions, concerns, and expectations of university students during the COVID-19 pandemic and the potential relationships between mental health, and their reactions and macroeconomic expectations study in Chapter 5.

Moreover, in Chapter 6 Samrat Ray of Pune, India discussed how "employees are the main part of an organisation who has not accepted the changing process at first and for that reason; the appropriate leadership strategy is required to bring the changes within the start-ups of Asia". In Chapter 7, Isolde Kanikani, Netherlands discussed "the impact of change maturity is often seen via Change Management on the project or program levels, and ROI measurements don't often go beyond this focus". Dr. Oindrila Chakraborty of India weighed in on various change management models and "different group dynamics, resistance, intervention instruments, and success for organisational change management" in Chapter 8. For Chapter 9, Mr. Edward Gonsalves of Barcelona, Spain and Dr. Rebecca Fakoussa of the United Kingdom talked about Arab family businesses and how as such family businesses internationalize, become more sophisticated and experienced in ownership, succession and wealth planning changes, their training and education will need to evolve rapidly. In Chapter 10, Dr. Ibrahim Yikilmaz of Turkey considered how organizations who already have a "high level of VUCA (volatility, uncertainty, complexity, and ambiguity) has increased even more. To be more successful in the new industry environment, businesses need to develop their skills in speed, flexibility, resilience, responsiveness, cost, and efficiency".

Meanwhile, for Chapter 1 and in considering the unprecedented times, Dr. Nidal A. Darwish and Mohammed A. Bayyoud of Palestine conducted a study on female entrepreneurs and found "female entrepreneurs face different restrictions, including society's perception toward women, lack of funds, and legislation obstacles such as registration". For Chapter 12, Mehmet Ertem of Turkey discussed strategy development for universities going through unprecedented times while Dr. Jens M. Sorg of Deutschland, Karen Hodge of Canada, and Assia Stoyanova of the United States of America talked about "how change endeavors are highly complex… and challenges the authors are currently facing in elaborating a data-driven and AI-based consulting approach for strategic change management (SCM) consulting". On the other hand, Professor Catherine Hayes of the United Kingdom talked about how women respond to change management in crisis circumstances in Chapter 14. Inclusive, she discussed "how the recent global COVID-19 pandemic is used as a vehicle by which to drive thinking around concepts, which have had such an impact on women during this time, such as emotional labour and inequality. The chapter concludes with a consideration of organisational structures and the agency that this has afforded women both historically and within the leadership challenges they currently face". For Chapter 15, Dr. Jose G. Vargas-Hernandez, Dr. Teresa I. Salazar-Echegaray, and Omar C. Vargas-Gonzalez of Mexico explained "nurtured entrepreneurship and different domains of innovation management models that become supply factors to determine production potential and based on this assumption to analyze the ability to provoke economic growth". And in Chapter 16, Vanessa Amorim, Professor Orlando Lima Rua, and Bruno de

Sousa Lopes of Portugal discussed SMEs in warehouse management operations within the import and export sector on "the need to integrate various approaches to achieve a better pursuit of the optimization strategy. The organization can respond to customer needs more effectively and efficiently through improved warehouse flow and continuous improvement".

In conclusion, the book impacts the fields of leadership, economic development, international business, multinational enterprises, management, and organization studies, like organizational culture, organization design, and organizational behavior. Inclusive, contributes to the *Change Management* subject matter because of the successful adoption and application of change management strategies within a business, during the unprecedented time. Hence, what a variety of organizations around the world in various industries are implementing to overcome challenges presented during times of crisis; COVID-19 as an example.

Kyla Latrice Tennin
College of Doctoral Studies, University of Phoenix, USA & Forbes School of Business, USA & World Business Angels Investment Forum (WBAF)-G20, USA & Lady Mirage Global, Inc., USA

REFERENCES

Bartik, A. W., Bertrand, M., Cullen, Z., Glaeser, E. L., Luca, M., & Stanton, C. (2020). The impact of COVID-19 on small business outcomes and expectations. *Proceedings of the National Academy of Sciences of the United States of America*, *117*(30), 17656–17666. doi:10.1073/pnas.2006991117 PMID:32651281

Boesch, D., & Phadke, S. (2021). *When women lose all the jobs: Essential actions for a gender-equitable recovery*. American Progress. https://www.americanprogress.org/article/women-lose-jobs-essential-actions-gender-equitable-recovery/

Connley, C. (2021). *In 1 year women globally lost $800 billion in income due to COVID-19 new report finds*. CNBC. https://www.cnbc.com/2021/04/30/women-globally-lost-800-billion-dollars-in-income-due-to-covid-19.html

Cuyper, L. D., Kucukkeles, B., & Reuben, R. (2020). *Discovering the real impact of COVID-19 on entrepreneurship*. World Economic Forum. https://www.weforum.org/agenda/2020/06/how-covid-19-will-change-entrepreneurial-business/

Gargi, B. (2019). Financial inclusion, women empowerment, and entrepreneurship: A special emphasis to India. *Malaysian E-commerce Journal*, *3*(3), 18–21. doi:10.26480/mecj.03.2019.18.21

Stephan, U., Zbierowski, P., Perez-Luno, A., & Klausen, A. (2021). *Entrepreneurship during the COVID-19 pandemic: A global study of entrepreneurs challenges, resilience, and well-being*. King's Business School. https://www.kcl.ac.uk/business/assets/pdf/research- papers/global-report-entrepreneurship-during-the-covid-19-pandemic-a-global-study-of-entrepreneurs'-challenges-resilience-and-well-being.pdf

Tennin, K. (2022). Entrepreneurship and organizational resilience: Responding to and recovering from crisis situations (COVID-19). In W. J. Aloulou (Ed.), *Handbook of Research on Entrepreneurship and Organizational Resilience During Unprecedented Times* (pp. 1–24). IGI Global. doi:10.4018/978-1-6684-4605-8.ch001

World Economic Forum. (2020). *Discovering the real impact of COVID-19 on entrepreneurship*. WEF. https://www.weforum.org/agenda/2020/06/how-covid-19-willchange-entrepreneurial-business/

Chapter 1
Managing Organizational Change During Turbulent Times:
A Socio-Psychological Perspective

Filippo Ferrari
Independent Researcher, Italy

ABSTRACT

During an organizational change, the main objective of change management actions is to generate and sustain a change commitment among the change recipients in order to increase the probability of success. This chapter therefore aims to present the antecedents, dynamics, and consequences of organizational change at a psychological and relational level, in a complex, uncertain, ambiguous, and unprecedented context. It focuses in particular on the organizational, interpersonal, and individual factors that favor coping with a turbulent scenario. This chapter shows how to develop organizational reliability, foster knowledge sharing, and adopt appropriate leadership models. Finally, the purpose of the chapter is to highlight the individual factors that favor or, conversely, hinder organizational change.

INTRODUCTION

Since the 1980s, scholars have shared the opinion that the organization of work has become extremely flexible, fragmented and individualized over time, generating difficulties both in terms of strategic planning and day-to-day management. The difficulties encountered within the world of organizations are best identified with the term VUCA (Bennis & Nanus, 1985). The acronym indicates an environment characterized respectively by;Volatility (V), where the context is characterized by continuous and sudden changes; Uncertainty (U), where the future is not predictable in a clear and precise way; Complexity (C) where the whole is difficult to analyse concretely, and finally, Ambiguity (A), where the incompleteness of information, for example, does not allow for adequately decoding a situation under examination, generating negative responses in the subject, (Peters & Mckewen, 2015).

DOI: 10.4018/978-1-6684-7509-6.ch001

BACKGROUND

The lock-down and other limitations due to the Covid-19 pandemic are a prime example of such a scenario.

A VUCA scenario is itself a source of change, with varying levels of predictability and intensity. Furthermore, the response to this scenario consists of frequent, continuous or discontinuous, radical or incremental organizational changes (Cummings & Worley, 2015; Senior, 2002). Organizations that want to deal with change successfully must therefore prepare for the change, developing management strategies based on reliability. They must also oversee change and its effects at *all* levels of organizational functioning (cultural, interpersonal, individual). A VUCA scenario therefore poses multiple challenges to changing organizations.

Managing the Impact on Strategy

Change management has been defined as "the process of continually renewing an organization's management, structure, and capabilities to meet the ever-changing needs of external and internal customers" (Moran & Brightman, 2001: 111). According to Burnes (2004), change is an ever-present feature of organizational life, both at an operational and strategic level. Therefore, no organisation should harbour doubt about the importance of its ability to identify where it needs to be in the future and how to manage the changes needed to get there. Consequently, organizational change cannot be separated/it is almost impossible to separate from organizational strategy, or vice versa (Burnes, 2004; Rieley & Clarkson, 2001).

Preparing for Constant Change

Early approaches to organizational change management and theories emerging from that research have suggested that organizations can not be effective or improve performance if they are in a state of constant change (Rieley & Clarkson, 2001). It has been argued that people need routines to be effective, and to be able to improve performance (Luecke, 2003). However, it has more recently been argued that it is vital for organizations that their population is able to effectively undergo constant change (Burnes, 2004; Rieley & Clarkson, 2001). While Luecke (2003) suggests that a state of constant change can become a routine in its own right, Leifer (1989) perceives change as a normal and natural response to internal and environmental conditions.

Ensuring Organizational Reliability

Although the planned approach to change is well established and has long been considered highly effective (Bamford and Forrester, 2003; Burnes, 2004), it has also been the subject of increasing criticism since the early 1980s (Kanter et al., 1992; Burnes, 1996). In response to this critique of the planned approach to organizational change, an emerging approach has gained ground. Rather than seeing change as driven from the top down, this approach tends to view change as driven from the bottom up (Bamford & Forrester, 2003; Burnes, 1996, 2004). Burnes (1996: 13) argues that "the success of change depends less on detailed plans and projections, than on achieving an understanding of the complexity of the issues at hand and identifying the range of options available." It can, therefore, be suggested that the emerging approach to change is more concerned with readiness for change and facilitating change, rather than providing specific pre-planned steps for each and every change project and initiative.

Preserving Knowledge

Park and Kim (2015) revealed that there is a lack of studies backing up, empirically as well as theoretically, the association between organizational change and knowledge sharing. Within the same context, Pemsel et al. (2014) argued that there is a lack of understanding of the knowledge exchange process; inducing researchers to highlight the way organization members participate in collective behavior (Acharya et al., 2018; Al Ahbabi et al., 2017). Madsen et al. (2005) found that the social relationships among employees at work are linked to their readiness for organizational change. This could be due, among other factors, to the sharing of organizational knowledge. For instance, Mattar (2021) showed how innovation/innovative implementation takes place during a crisis, when all organization members are quarantined, and when the knowledge exchange process is being carried out online. Designing and maintaining processes that allow the exchange, selection and development of knowledge collectively thus becomes a strategic objective for organizations exposed to a VUCA scenario.

The purpose of this chapter is to present the implications that a VUCA scenario has for the management of organizational change, in its antecedents, intervening factors and consequences, and the people involved in the change.

MAIN FOCUS OF THE CHAPTER

This chapter aims to provide a complete view of the socio-psychological factors that intervene and that must be considered during a change in turbulent times. Managing change, it is possible to focus on three levels in which the change takes place: organizational, interpersonal, individual. At each level, the specific focus is on the antecedents, characteristics and consequences of organizational change.

At organizational level, the chapter investigates the factors that favour organizational reliability, often jeopardized by changes. At this level, the focus is on knowledge sharing and organizational learning processes. At an interpersonal level, the focus of the chapter is on the interpersonal dynamics that are activated during a change: leadership, social influence, conformism, and their consequences on change commitment. Finally, at the individual level, this chapter highlights the characteristics of change recipients and change agents (both positive and negative) that influence the outcome of the change.

THEORETICAL DEVELOPMENT: STRATEGY AND CHANGE COMMITMENT

Senior (2002) suggests that the management of an organizational change should be *strategic*, that it ought to be based on the ability to identify; the type of change (rate of occurrence: continuous/discontinuous), how it comes about (planned/emergent), and the scale (level of impact: fine-tuning/corporate transformation). In fact, change processes are different, and literature suggests that the type of change resistance depends on the type of change (By, 2005). Indeed, many organizational change processes fail because the involved people are not adequately prepared for the specific type of change (Bovey& Hede, 2001).

Since the need for change is often unpredictable, it tends to be reactive, discontinuous, ad hoc and often triggered by a situation of organisational crisis (Burnes, 2004; De Wit & Meyer, 2005; Luecke, 2003; Nelson, 2003). Although the successful management of change is accepted as a necessity in order to survive and succeed in today's highly competitive and continuously evolving environment (Luecke, 2003;

Okumus & Hemmington, 1998). Dunphy and Stace, (1999) suggested that, in a turbulent environment, organizations which face the change as an open learning system rather than using detailed plans more likely succeed. Other authors (e.g. Burnes, 1996) underline that in a continuously evolving environment the employee's readiness to change becomes a strategic characteristic in order to ensure positive and enduring outcomes, rather than providing them with programs and procedures.

From a Strategic Human Resources Management point of view (Alvesson & Svengisson, 2015; Appelbaum et al., 2017; 2017a; 2017b) change appears to be the most critical event both on an individual and organizational level (Wuorinen et al., 2021; Devers et al., 2020). Fugate (2013), adopting a transactional perspective to change management, identifies three personal factors that can cause change to be perceived as a challenge, a threat or an opportunity. These antecedents are positive change orientation (Fugate et al., 2012); positive psychological capital (Avey et al., 2008); and employability (Fugate & Kinicki, 2008). However, to date empirical research has not adequately investigated the relationship between HRM practices and positive change orientation, which would make an important contribution to the literature (Ferrari, 2022; Kebede & Wang, 2022).

Changes at work can be emotionally intense. They often lead to burnout and put an insidious cycle into motion that leads to even greater resistance to organizational change. Improving employees' adaptability, (a critical aspect of emotional intelligence - EI competency), is key to breaking this cycle (Wiens & Rowell, 2018). Emotional intelligence is defined as 'the ability to perceive and express emotion, assimilate emotion in thought, understand and reason with emotion, and regulate emotion in the self and others" (Mayer, Salovey, & Caruso, 2000, p. 396). EI has shown links with organizational effectiveness, especially in challenging and uncertain contexts (Cherniss & Goleman, 2001). EI can be developed and learned, so it is an aspect to be carefully considered by those who govern organizational change, in particular regarding HRM in regards to training facilitation and recruitment. Furthermore, it is a personal characteristic suitable for generating organizational reliability.

In management and complex adaptive systems literature, *exploration* refers to the search for new, useful adaptations, and *exploitation* refers to the use and propagation of known adaptations (March, 1991; Mitchell, 1996). Hence, exploration seems to ensure more adaptive capabilities for organizations, from a long term perspective. However, during an organizational change 'lazy organizations' have often utilized exploitation due to immediate and certain return (Denrell & March, 2001), but then can go on to experience future failures and economic losses. Furthermore, exploitation could also even become an 'invisible trap' for these organizations: in fact, it is possible that the current situation could be appraised as profitable and, overall, as excellent by organizations in terms of effectiveness and efficiency, but at the same time neglecting reliability in the long term. As cited by Fang et al. (2010, 626), Holland (1992, p. 69) generalized such a dilemma as follows: "Deciding to what degree the present should be mortgaged for the future is a classic problem for all systems that adapt and learn." In such a situation where organizational change will increase ambiguity and insecurity, workers are exposed to a much higher level of stress (Smollan, 2015; Cameron & Green, 2015; Kiefer, 2005). In order to identify how to prevent undesired psychological outcomes, a set of studies considered the personal consequences that change had had for change recipients (Vakola et al., 2013; Piderit, 2000, Rafferty & Griffin, 2006) and for organizational resilience (Weick & Sutcliffe, 2005; Weick et al., 1999).

March (1991) suggests that the more immediate returns from exploitation tend to lead organizations to exhibit a myopic bias whereby exploitation is overemphasized at the expense of exploration (see also Denrell & March 2001). The utilization of existing knowledge, routines, and experience increases the likelihood that, during an organizational change, solutions will be found quickly and at reasonable costs.

As a consequence, adaptive processes can become self-destructive by leading the organization to become trapped in a suboptimal equilibrium.

More recent research (Fang et al., 2010, and references here cited) focuses on organizational structure in order to ensure a balance between exploration and exploitation. More specifically, the role of isolation and decentralization is emerging: to separate a unit from the rest of an organization could permit the exploration of a new approach for managing contingency. In this way, there is the possibility to add a contribution from the 'small worlds structure' approach (Schilling & Phelps 2007; Uzzi & Spiro 2005; Yayavaram & Ahuja 2008) to traditional contingency theories (Burns & Stalker 1961; Galbraith 1973; Lawrence & Lorsch; 1967). The result is a theoretical model which describes how, in particular conditions of the organization's internal or external environment, semi-isolated small groups can face contingency more profitably. According to this approach, during an organizational change conducted in conditions of uncertainty (or forced by unexpected events), organizations should therefore pay attention to how the change is *understood* and *applied* to all organizational levels, avoiding too/ over-centralized or top-down logic (Ferrari, 2017).

Finally, an important contribution comes from the *microfoundation* approach (Bonesso et al., 2014). The debate on the micro-level origins of a firm's capabilities (Felin et al., 2012; Foss, 2011), has shown that an individual's characteristics are important antecedents of the development of organizational capabilities, such as reliability. The *microfoundation* approach added an individual, psychological level of analysis to contingency theory, providing a more exhaustive model in order to analyse and monitor organizational resilience foundations. During a change, routines are challenged; furthermore, in a turbulent environment, following routines can be counterproductive for the organization. Change management is therefore called upon to accompany change recipients towards successfully adopting the new routines, and encouraging continuous learning to generate reliability.

Achieving these results is possible if the change management process generates an adequate level of change commitment (Meyer & Hamilton, 2013). Commitment in general is defined as '... a force (mentality) that binds an individual to a goal and / or a sequence of actions (course of action) relevant to that goal' (Meyer & Herscovitch, 2001); while *Change Commitment* is defined as ``... a psychological state that binds an employee to a course of action deemed necessary for the successful implementation of a change initiative.'' (Herscovitch, 1999, p. 17, in Meyer & Herscovitch, 2001, p.303). An employee's sense of belonging is usually on multiple levels, they may feel a part of the organization, organizational unit, tcustomer group, the order / project/ objective, etc. The various commitments are correlated but autonomous, therefore different types of change commitments should be considered separately.

According to Meyer and Allen (1991, p. 67), *affective commitment* is ``the employee's emotional attachment to, identification with, and involvement in the organization'', continuance commitment is ``an awareness of the costs associated with leaving the organization'' and normative commitment ``a feeling of *obligation* to continue employment''.

As suggested by Meyer and Hamilton (2001), the impact of *affective commitment* on compliance and discretionary support is known (Baraldi et al., 2010; Michaelis et al, 2009; Meyer et al. 2007); moreover, *affective commitment* is positively correlated with general compliance, but negatively with mere compliance (Meyer et al 2007). There is also a positive correlation between affective commitment and job satisfaction at the time of the change, and a negative correlation with Intention To Quit months after the change ((Rafferty & Restubog, 2010; Hinduan et al., 2009).

Normative commitment has been studied much less, but it seems to have similar consequences to *affective commitment*: improving compliance and discretionary support, and decreasing mere compliance and ITQ (Baraldi et al., 2010; Michaelis & Sonntag, 2010; Meyer et al. 2007). In particular, a positive correlation with individual learning during the change process has been described (Parish et al., 2008).

The *continuance commitment* is not correlated, or even negatively correlated, with the desired outcomes. A positive correlation with compliance is known, but a negative correlation with discretionary support (Meyer et al., 2002). An early continuance commitment generates a reduction in support for change up to eight months later (Meyer et al., 2007). Finally, there is evidence of a positive correlation with the intentions to quit - ITQ (Cunningham, 2006).

Change commitment is therefore the basis of desirable behaviours in change recipients, behaviors that can help the organization to face a turbulent scenario and a radical, and even unexpected, change. Given this theoretical scenario, it is hence possible to identify various factors that play a role in influencing organizational changes, and that favor reliability in a turbulent scenario on three levels: organizational, interpersonal, individual.

ORGANIZATIONAL FACTORS ACTIVE IN ORGANIZATIONAL CHANGE

Transferring, sharing and creating knowledge between people who are involved in succession plays a fundamental role in this delicate and uncertain process (Cabrera-Suarez, 2001; Cope, 2005; Koiranen & Chirico, 2006; Le Breton-Miller, 2004), but this knowledge transfer does not occur automatically (Boyd et al. 2015; Del Giudice, 2011; Ferrari, 2020; Konopaski et al., 2015). Indeed, an important reason for the failure of organizational processes to facilitate knowledge sharing is the lack of consideration for how the organizational and socio-cultural context influences knowledge sharing (Carter & Scarbrough, 2001; Voelpel, Dous, & Davenport, 2005).

Organizational Context: High Reliability Organizations

During an organizational change in conditions of uncertainty, the people involved appear to be/ are often neither critical nor enthusiastic without motivation. The literature in the HRO field suggests that it is necessary to develop an *attitude of wisdom* (Weick & Sutcliffe, 2005; Weick et al., 1999). This *attitude of wisdom* (Weick, 1993) should not be confused with wisdom itself (which is a type of knowledge derived from study): wisdom is knowing without excessive certainty and without excessive caution. Understanding the role of wisdom (Bigelow, 1992) as a source of resilience is a Socratic kind of knowledge (the operator knows he doesn't know), a kind of knowledge which is free of presumption on the one hand, and of excessive caution on the other. Various psychologists have attempted to define wisdom as a composite of personal qualities or abilities (Ardelt, 2005), as the final state of psychosocial development (Herickson, 1982), as a high level of cognitive reasoning (Kramer, 2000), or even as a way to live 'a good life' (Yang, 2013). Although this attitude is a personal trait, it has a socio-cultural basis, as it is founded on the *culture of error*. It has by now been proven (Weick & Sutcliffe, 2005) that organizational, managerial and training models that exploit rather than penalize error and failure incidents are correlations of reliability, and in particular of the *First HRO Principle: concern about critical events*. Wisdom is constructed by making mistakes and allowing mistakes to happen, as long as the situation does not affect the survival of the system: it must, of course, occur in a protected environment. The curve of the function that binds experience and wisdom has the form of an inverted "U": at first it increases with experience, to the point where wisdom begins to diminish from *overconfidence*.

Knowledge Sharing and Organizational Learning Processes

Organizational changes can make the intangible assets of the organization obsolete or scarcely fit for use. A strategic objective therefore becomes to preserve and disseminate organizational knowledge, making it available to all those involved in the change in order to create a widespread mechanism of exploration and exploitation of knowledge. Literature (Lave, 1993; Gherardi & Nicolini, 2004) suggests that the 'peripheral legitimated participation' of the employees ensures the best outcomes in terms of knowledge sharing and development, due to the Situated Learning process (Boyd et al. 2015; Hamilton, 2011; Lave, 1993). The ability to activate and maintain these learning processes is a fundamental factor in guaranteeing reliability and resilience for organizations during organizational changes. In other words, the *community of practice* must be preserved at the organizational level during organizational change (Lave & Wenger, 1991). Work practices are also social practices, as they always occur through interactions (direct or mediated) with other people. The cultural and situated perspective provides a strong construct for analyzing groups in their daily functioning: the community of practices, defined as "a set of lasting relationships between people, activities and the world, in communication and overlap with other communities of practice" (Lave & Wenger, 1991) or as "informal aggregations defined not only by their members, but by sharing operational modes and interpretation of events" (Eckert, 1993). The community of practice is the context in which learning and work take place: telling and sharing stories is the privileged way through which the specific professional competence of the community is built and distributed. The construct of community of practice is also useful for the study of the mechanisms of communication, formation and distribution of information, that is, of power within organizations (Ferrari & Emiliani, 2010). If it is true that the construction of competence is a social, narrative and collaborative phenomenon, then during an organizational change it is more important to support these mechanisms than, for example, to re-design work groups by planning their new required tasks. A large part of organizational knowledge is tacit, and this is the basis of organizational reliability.

In summary, a VUCA environment can be handled more successfully by a reputable organization. The unpredictability and complexity of the scenario that generates the change and, at the same time, the information uncertainty, highlight the need to activate mechanisms for social and community sharing of knowledge. Furthermore, at the organizational level, the *culture of error* should be fostered for the purpose of organizational development. Finally, the diffusion of the *attitude of wisdom* on a social basis allows the organization to be more effective in dealing with unforeseen events, which are inevitable in conditions of change.

INTERPERSONAL FACTORS ACTIVE IN ORGANIZATIONAL CHANGE

At this level it is possible to identify both the leadership dynamics that are activated in guiding change, the followership dynamics in influencing the behaviour of the change agent in a bottom-up manner, and finally the horizontal dynamics within the group subject to change. The change agent can activate different sources of power for leading change. These six-bases of power (coercive, reward, referent, expert, legitimate, informational) were identified by French & Raven in the early 1960's through a study they had conducted on power in leadership roles (French & Raven, 1959). The study showed how different types of power affected one's leadership ability and success in a leadership role.

Literature (Meyer & Hamilton, 2011) also shows leadership styles have a positive impact on change commitment. Burns (1978) distinguished between two types of leadership: *transactional* and *transformational*. Transactional leadership refers to the bulk of leadership models, which focus on the exchanges that occur between leaders and their followers. The exchange dimension of transactional leadership is very common and can be observed at many levels throughout all types of organizations. Transactional leadership (effective in ordinary contexts) is negatively correlated with Affective Change Commitment (Conway & Monks, 2008).

As its name implies, *transformational leadership* is a process that changes and transforms people. It is concerned with emotions, values, ethics, standards, and long-term goals and involves learning/personal development. It includes assessing followers' motives, satisfying their needs, and treating them as full human beings. Transformational leadership involves an exceptional form of influence that moves followers to accomplish more than what is usually expected of them. It is a process that often incorporates charismatic and visionary leadership. Transformational leadership (Herold et al., 2008) and charismatic leadership (Michaelis et al., 2009), on the other hand, correlate positively with Affective Change Commitment; cultural differences are evident in the reaction to leadership (Hinduan et al., 2009), which must be taken into account in leading change in multinational contexts. Although the transformational leader plays a pivotal role in precipitating change, followers and leaders are inextricably bound together in the transformation process.

Other interpersonal factors come to light during an organizational change. The principle of authority (Milgram, 1974) and the drive to conformism (Asch, 1951) emphasize the success of change; the importance of Social Identity is also noteworthy at the base of the ingroup vs. outgroup dynamics resulting from the change (Tajfel, Turner, 1979). The theory was originally developed to understand the psychological basis of intergroup discrimination. Tajfel et al (1971) attempted to identify the minimal conditions that would lead members of one group to discriminate in favor of the in-group to which they belonged and against another out-group.

The need to manage these potentially negative dynamics highlights the role played by managerial support in preparing and accompanying change (Armenakis et al., 1993, Holt et al., 2007). Seeing that many human emotions grow out of social interactions (Kemper, 1978), emotion is a pervasive influence in groups and is fundamentally linked to how group members interact and work together. The ability of a group to intelligently manage emotion arising from a change plays an important role in its interaction processes and effectiveness (Coleman, 1990).

As change agents spend most of the time interacting with other people, they must have strong interpersonal skills. According to Waddell et al. (2014) change agents must "create and maintain effective relationships with individuals and groups within the organization to help them gain the competence necessary to solve their own problems (Waddell et al., 2014, p. 73). The change agent has to listen actively to recognize the needs of the employees and the organization (Hutton, 1994), ask skillful and meaningful questions to determine the needs (Dunphy et al., 2007), and has to provide adequate feedback (Waddell et al., 2014).

INDIVIDUAL FACTORS ACTIVE IN ORGANIZATIONAL CHANGE

There is a large body of consolidated theoretical and, in part, empirical literature that highlights the role played by some personal characteristics of change recipients in the success of change. Change can be perceived as a challenge, opportunity or threat (Fugate et al., 2011), depending on different types of input; both person-related (positive change orientation: Frese et al., 2007; Fugate et al., 2012; positive psychological capital: Avey et al., 2008; and employability: Fugate & Kinicki, 2008), and context-related (change fairness: Colquitt et al., 2005; Fugate et al., 2012; trust in management: Mishra & Spreitzer, 1998; perceived organizational support: Self et al., 2007).

A growing body of literature has been investigating the difficulty of accomplishing organizational change, especially regarding the personnel's reaction to change as stress and change fatigue (Wanous, Reichers, & Austin, 2000). For example, research focused on withdrawal behaviours such as quitting intentions/ intention to quit *due to the change* (Daly & Geyer, 1994; Martin et al., 2005). Similarly, some studies also focused on staff turnover or intentions to leave the organization (Coch & French, 1948; Fried et al., 1996; Gardner et al., 1987; Schweiger & Denisi, 1991; for a review: Oreg et al., 2011). More recently, van Gilst et al. (2020) highlight that, during a change, organizations can, and must, take great care not to breach the psychological contracts they have with their members/employees.

Positive Factors: Change Self-Efficacy and Internal Locus of Control

The main positive personal factors influencing the reaction of change recipients are change Self-efficacy (Armenakis et al. 2007; Emsza et al., 2016; Roczniewska et al., 2020; Weiner, 2009) and Locus of Control (Wong-McDonald & Gorsuch, 2004; Robbins & Judge, 2013).

A key positive factor in Readiness To Change is Change self-efficacy (or Change Confidence - CC, according to other terminologies), known for its protective effect on individual well-being and for the positive impact on professional performance (Stajkovic & Luthans, 1998a; 1998b). Drawing from Bandura (1997), self-efficacy is "one's conviction (or confidence) about his or her abilities to mobilize the motivation, cognitive resources, and courses of action needed to successfully execute a specific task within a given context" (Stajkovic & Luthans, 1998b, p.66). In highlighting that Change Self-efficacy had been addressed by 29% of the studies about Readiness o Change (Armenakis et al. 2007b), Armenakis et al (2007a) posited that to be motivated to support a change, individuals must feel that success is possible. If a change is viewed as being personally or collectively impossible, or with dubious likelihood of succeeding, support will be scant. Weiner (2009) suggested change efficacy as one of the relevant dimensions for assessing readiness for change. Several other authors such as Choi et al., (2011; 2013; 2016), Judge et al. (1999), Meyer et al. (2002), and Neves (2009), concluded that individuals with more confidence in their ability to cope with organisational change (self-efficacy), are expected to have a stronger commitment to changes. Finally, Change Self-efficacy is positively correlated with active engagement in change, especially when change recipients are involved in multiple and overlapping changes (so-called change turbulence) (Hormung & Rousseau, 2007).

Locus Of Control – LOC is the general expectations that individuals have about the level of control they have over their own behaviour, and it is an important personality trait that affects organizational behaviour. Individuals differ from each other in terms of perceiving the causes of events that they experience (Forte, 2005). People also have different ways of thinking about how much control they have over the situations they encounter (Wong-McDonald & Gorsuch, 2004), and these thoughts affect how they behave. While some individuals believe that they dominate the results of the events they experience (*internal* LOC), others think that the results of the events are mainly influenced by factors such as luck and fate (*external* LOC) (Robbins & Judge, 2013). While people with an internal LOC are less socially oriented, they tend to be more task-oriented (Spector, 1982). The most suitable environments for individuals presenting an internal LOC are those in which they have control over events (Byrne, 2011). An adequate level of internal LOC in change recipients is an important factor because during an organizational change, it is positively associated with affective commitment and normative commitment, and negatively with continuance commitment (Chen & Wang, 2007).

Both Change Self-efficacy and internal Locus Of Control can be fostered by adequate levels of emotional intelligence. Although the empirical evidence in this regard is still limited, emotional intelligence can be a well-suited construct to complement the work by giving greater depth in self-awareness and self-management especially. Unlike cognitive skills, emotional competences seem to be successfully applicable to different contexts (Cherniss & Goleman, 2001).

In summary, the literature highlights a high failure rate in organizational change projects (Balogun & Hailey, 2004). It is worth mentioning that, to date, more attention has been paid to changing negative attitudes (e.g. disengagement or cynicism) and dysfunctional behaviours (e.g. deviance), neglecting the role that positivity (what works well) has in the organizational change (Avey et al., 2008). *Empirical* research has instead highlighted the advantages for organizations of enhancing (for example, through training activities) factors such as self-efficacy and the perception of control, rather than trying to remove obstacles to change (see de Jong et al., 2016).

Negative Factors: Change Cynicism, Change History and Change Anxiety

A growing number of researchers have focused particularly on *Change Cynicism* (CC) (Andersson and Bateman, 1997; Reichers et al., 1997; Stanley et al., 2005) – i.e. a "pessimistic viewpoint about change efforts being successful because those responsible for making change are blamed for being unmotivated, incompetent, or both" (Wanous, Reichers, & Austin, 2000, p. 133). Literature shows that CC plays a prominent role in change management failures (Bordia et al., 2011; Brown et al., 2017; Kroll & Pasha, 2019; Pettigrew et al., 2001; Wanous et al., 2000). As confirmed by recent literature (Ozcelik et al., 2020), employees' cynicism toward an organisation reduces their commitment, organisational citizenship behaviour and job satisfaction (Abraham, 2000; Grama & Todericiu, 2016). Employees who are cynical about organisational change are also more prone to grievances with their unions (Kim, 2009). Further empirical evidence suggests that CC increases job burnout (Sak, 2018) and constitutes one of the major causes of organisational change failure (Brown et al., 2017; Grama & Todericiu, 2016). Finally, Ouedraogo & Ouakouak (2020) found a direct, negative effect of CC on change success (-.0,261).

Organizational Change History (i.e. frequency and success of similar previous initiatives) and *Poor Change Management History* - PCMH (i.e. similar personal experiences in current or previous organizations) influence the levels of commitment (Rafferty & Restubog, 2010). Wanous, Reichers, & Austin (2000) noted that if employees felt that changes had occurred in the past, they were less cynical about organizational change. Bordia et al. (2011) developed and tested a model of the effects of PCMH on employee attitudes (trust, job satisfaction, intention to quit, change cynicism, and openness to change) and *actual* staff turnover. They found that PCMH, through PCMH beliefs, led to lower trust, job satisfaction and openness to change, and higher cynicism and intentions to quit. In addition, PCMH beliefs predicted employee turnover for up to over 2 years.

Anxiety is an unpleasant emotional arousal resulting from stressful demands or threatening stimuli, and research finds evidence that, in a work environment, perceived levels of support from, and consultation with, management reduce anxiety levels (Lazarus, 1991). During turbulent times especially, workers often show negative reactions, psychological distress and resistance to change (Astrachan, 2004; Schweiger.

& De Nisi, 1991). Mergers especially have been associated with increased employee job insecurity and uncertainty (Schweiger & DeNisi, 1991), separation anxiety (Astrachan, 2004), and feelings of threat and reduced control (Burlew, Pederson, & Bradley, 1994; Schweiger & DeNisi, 1991). In uncertain situations, organizational change can generate *anxiety* in change recipients due to the impact on their Change Confidence level in particular (Lazarus, 1991; Rafferty & Restubog, 2010). Finally, Rafferty and Restubog (2010) report that *change anxiety* correlates negatively with *affective commitment* and positively with *intention to quit* and actual organizational turnover.

LEADING CHANGE: THE ROLE OF THE CHANGE AGENT

During a change process, two groups of people can be classified: those people who are implementing the change within the organization and those who are expected to apply and support that change. Those people who implement the change are acting as so-called "change agents" in their organization, while the receiver is usually the employee (Gerwing, 2016; Barratt-Pugh, Bahn & Gakere, 2012). The role of change agent can be taken by managers, employees or even external consultants hired to facilitate change initiatives. Certainly internal change agents in the organization bring with them the benefit of knowledge of the company's history, operations and people, but on the other hand, external change agents can provide a fresh objective perspective without the influence of tradition and of the corporate culture. When an organization wants to make changes, there are 2 perspectives it should take into account: all those who hold a role relating to business management - i.e. all the professionals who work to ensure that there is the service and/or product that the final customer purchases from the organization, departments such as admin and operations, and anyone in a project or change management role as their role is to make business changes.

The first group includes all staff impacted by the change, whose priorities are to use existing working methods to meet current customer demand and achieve work objectives. In addition to this, when a change comes, these are the professionals who have to change the way they work. Furthermore, they have to convince colleagues and the team itself to participate in the change and ultimately integrate the change into the current way of working. This is the exact definition of change agent: a professional who has a specific role in an organization and who, in addition to her role, has the task of facilitating change. This means that a change agent can have a role in HR, Finance, Marketing, Sales, Operation, Administration, etc...

In the second group there are project and change management teams, whose priorities are to introduce new ideas, innovation and new working methodologies, identifying activities and tasks and structuring plans to implement the change. In addition, they can guide those selected as change agents to do their job in the best way. The role of change agents is becoming increasingly popular within organizations. Professionals may not be identified as change agents, but the point is that, beyond their day-to-day activities, they play the role of helping to bring about change and integrate changes into the current system of work.

SOLUTIONS AND RECOMMENDATIONS

In order to be successful, the change agents need to possess a wide range of personality traits, skills and knowledge (Cawsey, Deszca, & Ingols, 2012). Within a change environment, change agents "encourage people to collaborate, take risks, take responsibility and be accountable for the change process" (Moran & Brightman, 2000, p. 66). Therefore, change agents must have the requisite skills e.g. leadership, creativity and problem solving (Gerwing, 2016). Nikolaou et al. (2007) conducted intensive research and identified five personality traits as being important for an effective change agent: Self-efficacy (confidence), Locus Of Control (control over the environment), core self-evaluations (positive self-identity), openness to experience, and personal resilience. According to Gilley (2005) the change agent needs strategic knowledge to align the organization to its long-term direction and their vision, mission, values and goals.

Finally, the literature mentions a wide range of skills that change agents need to possess to be effective, the most important of which are communication skills (Cawsey et al., 2012; Waddell et al., 2014). Beside communication skills, the interpersonal skills are the most important to possess as an effective change agent (Gilley, 2005; Dunphy et al., 2007).

FUTURE RESEARCH DIRECTIONS

Information can help employees deal with change because uncertainty is detrimental to employee well-being (Elrod & Tippett, 2002). Literature suggests providing information during change programs is a common organizational strategy to manage change (Bordia et al., 2004), although researchers are yet to fully understand the impact of the *source* of the information on employee reactions to change. This study shows that since perceived Managerial Support especially seems to be a defensive factor against cynicism, HRM practices (training and other support activities) should be designed and implemented to support this dimension. In particular, literature posited (Ferrari 2017a; 2022) that it would be useful to provide *specific* and *effective* training activities, aimed at preventing skill shortage and reducing skill mismatch (see also Ferrari, 2019; 2019a). However, Brown et al. (2017) demonstrate that the information provided by HR has an impact on employee reactions to change, but findings are still inconclusive. Future research is called upon to empirically validate that currently suggested in the hypotheses.

CONCLUSION: FOSTERING AFFECTIVE CHANGE COMMITMENT IN TURBULENT TIMES

In situations where organizational change will increase ambiguity and insecurity, workers are exposed to much higher stress levels (Smollan, 2015; Cameron & Green, 2015; Kiefer, 2005). In order to identify how to prevent undesired psychological outcomes, a set of studies considered the personal consequences that change had for change recipients (Oreg et al., 2011; Piderit, 2000, Rafferty & Griffin, 2006). The management of organizational change requires a better understanding of the psychological aspects of change, especially the involved employees' reactions (e.g. Armenakis & Harris, 2009; Cummings & Worley, 2005; Liu & Perrewe, 2005; Oreg, Vakola, & Armenakis, 2011).

A change process cannot be successful without the commitment of the change recipients. Although empirical literature is not definitive in addressing change management design, a change management process should consider the different types of commitment (affective, normative, and continuative) and their specific consequences for change processes and change recipients. Literature (Meyer & Hamilton, 2001) suggests that mainly *affective commitment* is related to desired change outcomes, such as *change compliance* especially, i.e. follow the required directions and keep to the expected behaviour during the change. Maybe more important, compliance means: do not boycott change. Affective commitment cannot be just a facade ('mere compliance'), but must be a convinced and internalized adherence, which manifests itself in the *discretionary support*: actively and independently engaged in facilitating change.

REFERENCES

Abraham, R. (2000). Organizational cynicism: Bases and consequences. *Genetic, Social, and General Psychology Monographs, 126*(3), 269–292. PMID:10950198

Acharya, A., Singh, S. K., Pereira, V., & Singh, P. (2018). Big data, knowledge co-creation, and decision making in fashion industry. *International Journal of Information Management, 42*, 90–101. doi:10.1016/j.ijinfomgt.2018.06.008

Al Ahbabi, S., Singh, S. K., Gaur, S. S., & Balasubramanian, S. (2017). A knowledge management framework for enhancing public sector performance. *International Journal of Knowledge Management Studies, 8*(3–4), 329–350. doi:10.1504/IJKMS.2017.087076

Andersson, L. M., & Bateman, T. S. (1997). Cynicism in the workplace: Some causes and effects. *Journal of Organizational Behavior, 18*(5), 449–469. doi:10.1002/(SICI)1099-1379(199709)18:5<449::AID-JOB808>3.0.CO;2-O

Ardelt, M. (2005). How wise people cope with crises and obstacles in life. *ReVision, 28*(1), 7–19. doi:10.3200/REVN.28.1.7-19

Armenakis, A., Bernerth, J. B., Pitts, J. P., & Walker, H. J. (2007b). Organizational Change Recipients' Beliefs Scale: Development of an instrument. *The Journal of Applied Behavioral Science, 43*(4), 481–505. doi:10.1177/0021886307303654

Armenakis, A. A., & Harris, S. G. (2009). Reflections: Our journey in organizational change research and practice. *Journal of Change Management, 9*(2), 127–142. doi:10.1080/14697010902879079

Armenakis, A. A., Harris, S. G., Cole, M. S., Fillmer, J. L., & Self, D. R. (2007a). A Top Management Team's Reactions to Organizational Transformation: The diagnostic Benefits of Five Key Change Sentiments. *Journal of Change Management, 7*(3), 273–290. doi:10.1080/14697010701771014

Armenakis, A. A., Harris, S. G., & Mossholder, K. W. (1993). Creating Readiness for Organizational Change. *Human Relations, 46*(6), 681–703. doi:10.1177/001872679304600601

Asch, S. E. (1951). Effects of group pressure upon the modification and distortion of judgments. In H. Guetzkow (Ed.), *Groups, leadership and men; research in human relations* (pp. 177–190). Carnegie Press.

Astrachan, J. H. (2004). Organizational departures: The impact of separation anxiety as studied in mergers and acquisitions simulation. *The Journal of Applied Behavioral Science, 40*(1), 91–110. doi:10.1177/0021886304263850

Avey, J. B., Wernsing, T. S., & Luthans, F. (2008). Can Positive Employees Help Positive Organizational Change? Impact of Psychological Capital and Emotions on Relevant Attitudes and Behaviors. *The Journal of Applied Behavioral Science, 44*(1), 48–70. doi:10.1177/0021886307311470

Balogun, J., & Hailey, V. H. (2004), *Exploring Strategic Change*. Prentice Hall/Financial Times, Harlow.

Bamford, D. R., & Forrester, P. L. (2003). Managing planned and emergent change within an operations management environment. *International Journal of Operations & Production Management, 23*(5), 546–564. doi:10.1108/01443570310471857

Bandura, A. (1997), *Self-efficacy: The exercise of control.* W H Freeman/Times Books/ Henry Holt & Co.

Baraldi, S., Jawaid Kalyal, H., Berntson, E., Näswall, K., & Sverke, M. (2010). The Importance of Commitment to Change in Public Reform: An Example from Pakistan. *Journal of Change Management, 10*(4), 347–368. doi:10.1080/14697017.2010.516482

Barratt-Pugh, L., Bahn, S., & Gakere, E. (2012). Managers as change agents. Implications for human resource managers engaging with culture change. *Journal of Organizational Change, 26*(4), 748–764. doi:10.1108/JOCM-Feb-2011-0014

Bennis, W., Nanus, B. (1985). Leaders: Strategies for Taking Charge. Harper & Row

Bigelow, J. (1992). Developing managerial wisdom. *Journal of Management Inquiry, 1*(2), 143–153. doi:10.1177/105649269212008

Bonesso, S., Gerli, F., & Scapolan, A. (2014). The individual side of ambidexterity: Do individuals' perceptions match actual behaviors in reconciling the exploration and exploitation trade-off? *European Management Journal, 32*(3), 392–405. doi:10.1016/j.emj.2013.07.003

Bordia, P., Hobman, E., Jones, E., Gallois, C., & Callan, V. J. (2004). Uncertainty during organizational change: Types, consequences, and management strategies. *Journal of Business and Psychology, 18*(4), 507–532. doi:10.1023/B:JOBU.0000028449.99127.f7

Bordia P, Restubog, S.L.D, Jimmieson N.L., & Irmer, B.E. (2011). Haunted by the past: effects of poor change management history on employee attitudes and turnover. *Group & Organization Management, 36*, 191–222. doi:10.1177/1059601110392990

Bovey, W.H, Hede, A. (2001), Resistance to organisational change: the role of defence mechanisms, *Journal of Managerial Psychology, 16*(7), 534-548.

Boyd, B., Royer, S., Pei, R., & Zhang, X. (2015). Knowledge transfer in family business successions: Implications of knowledge types and transaction atmospheres. *Journal of Family Business Manage.*

Brown, C., Kulik, T., Cregan, C., & Metz, I. (2017). 5) Understanding The Change– Cynicism Cycle: The Role Of HR. *Human Resource Management, 56*(1), 5–24. doi:10.1002/hrm.21708

Burlew, L. D., Pederson, J. E., & Bradley, B. (1994). The reactions of managers to the pre-acquisition stage of a corporate merger: A qualitative study. *Journal of Career Development, 21*, 11–22.

Burnes, B. (1996). No such thing as . . . a "one best way" to manage organizational change. *Management Decision, 34*(10), 11–18. doi:10.1108/00251749610150649

Burnes, B. (2004). *Managing Change:A Strategic Approach to Organizational Dynamics* (4th ed.). Prentice Hall.

Burns, J. M. (1978). *Leadership*. Harper & Row.

Burns, T., & Stalker, G. M. (1961). *The Management of Innovation*. Tavistock.

By, R. T. (2005). Organizational Change management: A critical approach. *Journal of Change Management, 5*(4), 369–380. doi:10.1080/14697010500359250

Byrne, S. (2011). Does individual locus of control matter in a JIT environment? *Journal of Applied Management Accounting Research, 9*(1), 37–57.

Cabrera-Suarez, K., De Saa-Perez, P., & Garcia-Almeida, D. (2001). The Succession Process from a Resource- and Knowledge-based View of the Family Firm. *Family Business Review, 14*(1), 37–47. doi:10.1111/j.1741-6248.2001.00037.x

Caldwell, R. (2003). Change leaders and change managers: Different or complementary? *Leadership and Organization Development Journal, 24*(5), 285–293. doi:10.1108/01437730310485806

Cameron, E., & Green, M. (2015). *Making Sense of Change Management: A Complete Guide to the Models, Tools and Techniques of Organizational Change* (4th ed.). Kogan Page Publishers.

Carter, C., & Scarbrough, H. (2001). Towards a second generation of KM? The people management challenge. *Education + Training, 43*(4), 215–224. doi:10.1108/EUM0000000005483

Cawsey, T., Deszca, G., & Ingols, C. (2012): Organizational Change: An action –oriented toolkit. Sage Publications.

Chen, J., & Wang, L. (2007). Locus of control and the three components of commitment to change. *Personality and Individual Differences, 42*(3), 503–512. doi:10.1016/j.paid.2006.07.025

Cherniss, C., & Goleman, D. (2001). The emotionally intelligent workplace: how to select for, measure, and improve emotional intelligence in individuals, groups, and organizations. Jossey-Bass, NY.

Choi, M., & Ruona, W. E. A. (2011). Individual Readiness for Organisational Change and Its Implications for Human Resource and Organisation Development'. *Human Resource Development Review, 10*(1), 46–73. https://psycnet.apa.org/doi/10.1002/9781118326404.ch16. doi:10.1177/1534484310384957

Choi, M., & Ruona, W. E. A. (2013). Individual Readiness for Organizational Change. In Leonard, H. S., Lewis, R., Freedman A. M., and Passmore (eds.), The Wiley-Blackwell Handbook of the Psychology of Leadership, Change, and Organizational Development. J. John Wiley and Sons, Ltd.

Choi, Y., Kim, J. Y., & Yoo, T. (2016). 'A study on the effect of learning organisation readiness on employees' quality commitment: The moderating effect of leader–member exchange'. *Total Quality Management & Business Excellence, 27*(3-4), 325–338. doi:10.1080/14783363.2014.981072

Coch, L., & French, J. R. P. Jr. (1948). Overcoming resistance to change. *Human Relations, 1*(4), 512–532. doi:10.1177/001872674800100408

Coleman, J. S. (1990). *Foundations of social theory*. Harvard University Press, Belknap Press.

Colquitt, J. A., Greenberg, J., & Zapata-Phelan, S. P. (2005). What is organizational justice? A historical overview. In J. Greenberg & J. A. Colquitt (Eds.), *Handbook of organizational justice* (pp. 3–56). Erlbaum.

Conway, E., & Monks, K. (2008). HR practices and commitment to change: An employee-level analysis. *Human Resource Management Journal, 18*(1), 72–89. doi:10.1111/j.1748-8583.2007.00059.x

Cope, J. (2005). Towards a dynamic learning perspective of entrepreneurship. *Entrepreneurship Theory and Practice, 29*(4), 373–399. doi:10.1111/j.1540-6520.2005.00090.x

Cummings, T., & Worley, C. (2015). *Organization development and change* (10th ed.). Thomson/South-Western.

Cunningham, G. B. (2006). The relationships among commitment to change, coping with change, and turnover intentions. *European Journal of Work and Organizational Psychology, 15*(1), 29–45. doi:10.1080/13594320500418766

Daly, J. P., & Geyer, P. D. (1994). The role of fairness in implementing large-scale change: Employee evaluations of process and outcome in seven facility relocations. *Journal of Organizational Behavior, 15*(7), 623–638. doi:10.1002/job.4030150706

de Jong, T., Wiezer, N., de Weerd, M., Nielsen, K., Mattila-Holappa, P., & Mockałło, Z. (2016). The impact of restructuring on employee well-being: A systematic review of longitudinal studies. *Work and Stress, 30*(1), 91–114. doi:10.1080/02678373.2015.1136710

De Wit, B., & Meyer, R. (2005). *Strategy Synthesis: Resolving Strategy Paradoxes to Create Competitive Advantage* (2nd ed.). Thomson Learning.

Del Giudice, M. (2011). Knowledge Management and Family Business. In *Knowledge and Family Business. Innovation, Technology, and Knowledge Management* (Vol. 7). Springer.

Denrell, J., & March, J. G. (2001). Adaptation as information restriction: The hot stove effect. *Organization Science, 12*(5), 523–538. doi:10.1287/orsc.12.5.523.10092

Dunphy, D., Griffith, A., & Benn, S. (2007). *Organizational change for corporate sustainability. A guide for leaders and change agents of the future* (2nd ed.). Routledge.

Dunphy, D., & Stace, D. (1993). The strategic management of corporate change. *Human Relations, 46*(8), 905–918. doi:10.1177/001872679304600801

Eckert, P. (1993). *The school as a community of engaged learners*, [unpublished manuscript].

Elrod, P. D. III, & Tippett, D. D. (2002). The "death valley" of change. *Journal of Organizational Change Management, 15*(3), 273–291. doi:10.1108/09534810210429309

Emsza, B., Eliyana, A., & Istyarini, W. (2016). The relationship between self-efficacy and readiness for change: The mediator roles of employee empowerment. *Mediterranean Journal of Social Sciences, 7*(3), 201–206. doi:10.5901/mjss.2016.v7n3s1p201

Erikson, E. H. (1982). *The life cycle completed* (1st ed.). Norton.

Fang, C., Lee, J., & Schilling, M. A. (2009). Balancing Exploration and Exploitation Through Structural Design: The Isolation of Subgroups and Organizational Learning. *Organization Science, 21*(3), 625–642. doi:10.1287/orsc.1090.0468

Felin, T., Foss, N. J., Heimeriks, K. H., & Madsen, T. L. (2012). Microfoundations of routines and capabilities: Individuals, processes, and structure. *Journal of Management Studies, 49*(8), 1351–1374. doi:10.1111/j.1467-6486.2012.01052.x

Ferrari, F. (2017). Human Resource Management and Organizational Reliability: Coordination Mechanisms, Training Models, and Diagnostic Systems for Contingency Management. In B. Christiansen & H. Chandan (Eds.), *Handbook of Research on Industrial and Organizational Psychology in the Modern Workforce*. Igi-Global Publishing. doi:10.4018/978-1-5225-2250-8.ch003

Ferrari, F. (2017a). *The impact of skill-mismatch on readiness to change: empirical research in the Italian Bank sector*. WOA - XVII Workshop dei Docenti e dei Ricercatori di Organizzazione Aziendale.

Ferrari, F. (2019). Everything must change, because nothing changes. A history of organizational change in Italian bank sector, in Hamlin R.G., Ellinger A:D., & Jones J. (Eds). Evidence-Based Initiatives for Organizational Change and Development. IGI-Global Publishing.

Ferrari, F. (2019a). Facing organizational change. Seven challenges for practitioners, in Hamlin R.G., Ellinger A:D., & Jones J. (Eds). Evidence-Based Initiatives for Organizational Change and Development. IGI-Global Publishing. doi:10.4018/978-1-5225-6155-2.ch017

Ferrari, F. (2020). A Theoretical Approach Exploring Knowledge Transmission Across Generations in Family SMEs. In M. Khosrow-Pour D.B.A. (Eds.), Encyclopedia of Organizational Knowledge, Administration, and Technology (pp. 1531-1550). IGI Global. doi:10.4018/978-1-7998-3473-1.ch105

Ferrari, F. (2022). Skills mismatch and change confidence: the impact of training on change recipients' self-efficacy. *European Journal of Training and Development*. doi:10.1108/EJTD-06-2021-0072

Ferrari, F., & Emiliani, E. (2010), Lo sviluppo delle competenze. Fondamenti teorici ed esperienze pratiche per l'apprendimento di una professione, Roma: Carocci.

Forte, A. (2005). Locus of control and the moral reasoning of managers. *Journal of Business Ethics, 58*(1-3), 65–77. doi:10.100710551-005-1387-6

Foss, N. J. (2011). Why micro-foundations for resource-based theory are needed and what they may look like. *Journal of Management, 37*(5), 1413–1428. doi:10.1177/0149206310390218

French, J. R. P. Jr., & Raven, B. (1959). The bases of social power. In D. Cartwright (Ed.), Studies in social power (pp. 150–167). University of Michigan.

Frese, M., Garst, H., & Fay, D. (2007). Making things happen: Reciprocal relationships between work characteristics and personal initiative in a four-wave longitudinal structural equation model. *The Journal of Applied Psychology, 92*(4), 1084–1102. doi:10.1037/0021-9010.92.4.1084 PMID:17638467

Fried, Y., Tiegs, R. B., Naughton, T. J., & Ashforth, B. E. (1996). Managers' reactions to a corporate acquisition: A test of an integrative model. *Journal of Organizational Behavior, 17*(5), 401–427. doi:10.1002/(SICI)1099-1379(199609)17:5<401::AID-JOB774>3.0.CO;2-R

Fugate, M., Harrison, S., & Kinicki, A. J. (2011). Thoughts and Feelings About Organizational Change: A Field Test of Appraisal Theory. *Journal of Leadership & Organizational Studies, 18*(4), 421–437. doi:10.1177/1548051811416510

Fugate, M., Kinicki, A., & Prussia, G. (2008). Employee coping with organizational change: An examination of alternative theoretical perspectives and models. *Personnel Psychology*, *61*(1), 1–36. doi:10.1111/j.1744-6570.2008.00104.x

Fugate, M., Prussia, G. E., & Kinicki, A. J. (2012). Managing Employee Withdrawal During Organizational Change: The Role of Threat Appraisal. *Journal of Management*, *38*(3), 890–914. doi:10.1177/0149206309352881

Galbraith, J. R. (1973). *Designing Complex Organizations*. Addison- Wesley.

Gardner, D. G., Dunham, R. B., Cummings, L. L., & Pierce, J. L. (1987). Employee focus of attention and reactions to organizational change. *The Journal of Applied Behavioral Science*, *23*(3), 351–370. doi:10.1177/002188638702300305

Gerwing, C. (2016). *Meaning of Change Agents within Organizational Change, Journal of Applied Leadership and Management*. University of Applied Sciences. https://www.journal-alm.org/article/view/17107

Gherardi, S., & Nicolini, D. (2004). *Apprendimento e conoscenza nelle organizzazioni*. Carocci.

Gilley, A. (2005). *The manager as change leader*. Praeger.

Grama, B., & Todericiu, R. (2017). Change, Resistance to Change and Organizational Cynicism. *Studies in Business and Economics*, *11*(3), 47–54. doi:10.1515be-2016-0034

Hamilton, E. (2011). Entrepreneurial learning in family business: A situated learning perspective. *Journal of Small Business and Enterprise Development*, *18*(1), 8–26. doi:10.1108/14626001111106406

Herold, D. M., Fedor, D. B., Caldwell, S., & Liu, Y. (2008). The effects of transformational and change leadership on employees' commitment to a change: A multilevel study. *The Journal of Applied Psychology*, *93*(2), 346–357. doi:10.1037/0021-9010.93.2.346 PMID:18361637

Herscovitch, L. (1999). *Employee commitment to organizational change. Extension and evaluation of a three componente model.* [Unpublished master's thesis, University of Western Ontario].

Hinduan, Z. R., Wilson-Evered, E., Moss, S., & Scannell, E. (2009). Leadership, work outcomes and openness to change following an Indonesian bank merger. *Asia Pacific Journal of Human Resources*, *47*(1), 59–78. doi:10.1177/1038411108099290

Holland, J. (1992). Genetic algorithms. *Scientific American*, *267*(1), 66–72. doi:10.1038cientificamerican0792-66

Holt, D. T., Armenakis, A. A., Feild, H. S., & Harris, S. G. (2007). Readiness for Organizational Change: The Systematic Development of a Scale. *The Journal of Applied Behavioral Science*, *43*(2), 232–255. doi:10.1177/0021886306295295

Hornung, S., & Rousseau, D. M. (2007). Active on the job—proactive in change: How autonomy at work contributes to employee support for organizational change. *The Journal of Applied Behavioral Science*, *43*(4), 401–426. doi:10.1177/0021886307307555

Hutton, D. (1994). *The change agents' handbook. A survival guide for quality improvement champions*. ASQC Quality Press.

Judge, T. A., Thoresen, C. J., Pucik, V., & Welbourne, T. M. (1999). Managerial coping with organizational change: A dispositional perspective'. *The Journal of Applied Psychology, 84*(1), 107–122. https://psycnet.apa.org/doi/10.1037/0021-9010.84.1.107. doi:10.1037/0021-9010.84.1.107

Kanter, R. M., Stein, B., & Jick, T. (1992). *The Challenge of Organizational Change: How Companies Experience it and Leaders Guide it.* Free Press/Maxwell Macmillan Canada/Maxwell Macmillan International.

Kemper, T. D. (1978). *A social interactional theory of emotions.* Wiley.

Kiefer, T. (2005). Feeling bad: Antecedents and consequences of negative emotions in ongoing change. *Journal of Organizational Behavior, 26*(8), 875–897. doi:10.1002/job.339

Kim, T. Y., Bateman, T. S., Gilbreath, B., & Andersson, L. M. (2009). Top management credibility and employee cynicism: A comprehensive model. *Human Relations, 62*(10), 1435–1459. doi:10.1177/0018726709340822

Koiranen, M., & Chirico, F. (2006). *Family Firms as Arenas for Trans-generational Value Creation: A Qualitative and Computational Approach.* University of Jyvaskyla Press.

Konopaski, M., Jack, S., & Hamilton, E. (2015). How family business members learn about continuity. *Academy of Management Learning & Education, 14*(3), 347–364. doi:10.5465/amle.2014.0244

Kramer, D. (2000). Wisdom as a classical source of human strength: Conceptualization and empirical inquiry. *Journal of Social and Clinical Psychology, 19*(1), 1. doi:10.1521/jscp.2000.19.1.83

Kroll, A., & Pasha, O. (2019). Managing change and mitigating reform cynicism. *Public Money & Management.* Advance online publication. doi:10.1080/09540962.2019.1683982

Lave, J. (1993). The practice of learning. In *S. Chaiklin, J. Lave (1993), Understanding practice. Perspective on activity and context.* Cambridge University Press. doi:10.1017/CBO9780511625510.002

Lave, J., & Wenger, E. (1991). *Situated Learning: Legitimate Peripheral Participation.* Cambridge University Press. doi:10.1017/CBO9780511815355

Lawrence, P. R., & Lorsch, J. W. (1967). *Organization and Environment.* Harvard Business School Press.

Lazarus, R. S. (1991). *Emotion and Adaptation.* Oxford University Press.

Le Breton–Miller, I., Miller, D., & Steier, L. P. (2004). Toward an Integrative Model of Effective FOB Succession. *Entrepreneurship Theory and Practice, 28*(4), 305–328. doi:10.1111/j.1540-6520.2004.00047.x

Leifer, R. (1989). Understanding organizational transformation using a dissipative structural model. *Human Relations, 42*(10), 899–916. doi:10.1177/001872678904201003

Liu, Y., & Perrewé, P. L. (2005). Another look at the role of emotion in the organizational change: A process model. *Human Resource Management Review, 15*(4), 263–280. doi:10.1016/j.hrmr.2005.12.001

Luecke, R. (2003). *Harvard Business Essentials. Managing Change and Transition.* Harvard Business School Press.

Madsen, S. R., Miller, D., & John, C. R. (2005). Readiness for organizational change: Do organizational commitment and social relationships in the workplace make a difference? *Human Resource Development Quarterly*, *16*(2), 213–234. doi:10.1002/hrdq.1134

March, J. G. (1991). Exploration and exploitation in organizational learning. *Organization Science*, *2*(1), 71–87. doi:10.1287/orsc.2.1.71

Martin, A. J., Jones, E. S., & Callan, V. J. (2005). The role of psychological climate in facilitating employee adjustment during organizational change. *European Journal of Work and Organizational Psychology*, *14*(3), 263–283. doi:10.1080/13594320500141228

Mattar, D. M. (2021). An Organizational Change With Quarantined Members. *SAGE Open*, *11*(1). Advance online publication. doi:10.1177/2158244020988851

Meyer, J., & Hamilton, L. (2013). Commitment to organizational change: Theory, research, principles, and practice. In S. Oreg, A. Michel, & R. By (Eds.), *The Psychology of Organizational Change: Viewing Change from the Employee's Perspective* (pp. 43–64). Cambridge University Press. doi:10.1017/CBO9781139096690.005

Meyer, J. P., & Allen, N. J. (1991). A three-component conceptualization of organizational commitment. *Human Resource Management Review*, *1*(1), 61–89. doi:10.1016/1053-4822(91)90011-Z

Meyer, J. P., & Herscovitch, L. (2001). Commitment in the workplace: Toward a general model. *Human Resource Management Review*, *11*(3), 299–326. doi:10.1016/S1053-4822(00)00053-X

Meyer, J. P., Srinivas, E., Lal, J., & Topolnytsky, L. (2007). Employee commitment and support for an organizational change: Test of the three-component model in two cultures. *Journal of Occupational and Organizational Psychology*, *80*(2), 185–211. doi:10.1348/096317906X118685

Meyer, J. P., Stanley, D. J., Herscovitch, L., & Topolnytsky, L. (2002). Affective, Continuance, and Normative Commitment to the Organization: A Meta-analysis of Antecedents, Correlates, and Consequences. *Journal of Vocational Behavior*, *61*(1), 20–52. doi:10.1006/jvbe.2001.1842

Michaelis, B., Stegmaier, R., & Sonntag, K. (2009). Affective commitment to change and innovation implementation behavior: The role of charismatic leadership and employees' trust in top management. *Journal of Change Management*, *9*(4), 399–417. doi:10.1080/14697010903360608

Michaelis, B., Stegmaier, R., & Sonntag, K. (2010). Shedding light on followers' innovation implementation behavior: The role of transformational leadership, commitment to change, and climate for initiative. *Journal of Managerial Psychology*, *25*(4), 408–429. doi:10.1108/02683941011035304

Milgram, S. (1974). *Obedience to authority: An experimental view*. Harper & Row: New York.

Mishra, A. K., & Spreitzer, G. M. (1998). Explaining how survivors respond to downsizing: The roles of trust, empowerment, justice, and work redesign. *Academy of Management Review*, *23*(3), 567–588. doi:10.2307/259295

Mitchell, M. (1996). *An Introduction to Genetic Algorithms*. MIT Press.

Moran, J., & Brightman, B. (2000). Leading organizational change. *Journal of Workplace Learning, 12*(2), 66–74. doi:10.1108/13665620010316226

Moran, J. W., & Brightman, B. K. (2001). Leading organizational change. *Career Development International, 6*(2), 111–118.

Nelson, L. (2003). A case study in organizational change: Implications for theory. *The Learning Organization, 10*(1), 18–30. doi:10.1108/09696470310457478

Neves, P. (2009). Readiness for change: Contributions for employee's level of individual change and turnover intentions. *Journal of Change Management, 9*(2), 215–231. doi:10.1080/14697010902879178

Nikolaou, I., Gouras, A., Vakola, M., & Bourantas, D. (2007). Selecting change agents: Exploring traits and skills in a simulated environment. *Journal of Change Management, 7*(3-4), 291–313. doi:10.1080/14697010701779173

Okumus, F., & Hemmington, N. (1998). Barriers and resistance to change in hotel firms: An investigation at unit level. *International Journal of Contemporary Hospitality Management, 10*(7), 283–288. doi:10.1108/09596119810240906

Oreg, S., Vakola, M., & Armenakis, A. (2011). Change Recipients' Reactions to Organizational Change: A 60-Year Review of Quantitative Studies. *The Journal of Applied Behavioral Science, 47*(4), 461–524. doi:10.1177/0021886310396550

Ouedraogo, N., & Ouakouak, M. L. (2020). Antecedents and outcome of employee change fatigue and change cynicism. *Journal of Organizational Change Management, 34*(1), 158–179. doi:10.1108/JOCM-05-2019-0141

Ozcelik, S.K., Havva O., & Bahcecik A.N. (2020). Effects of organisational restructuring of hospitals on nurses. *Journal of Nursing Management, 28*(7), 1740-1747. doi:10.1111/jonm.13133

Parish, J. T., Cadwallader, S., & Bush, P. (2008). Want to, need to, ought to: Employee commitment to change. *Journal of Organizational Change Management, 21*(1), 32–52. doi:10.1108/09534810810847020

Park, S., & Kim, E.-J. (2015). Revisiting knowledge sharing from the organizational change perspective. *European Journal of Training and Development, 39*(9), 769–797. doi:10.1108/EJTD-06-2015-0042

Pemsel, S., Wiewiora, A., Muller, R., Aubry, M., & Brown, K. (2014). A conceptualization of knowledge governance in project-based organizations. *International Journal of Project Management, 32*(8), 1411–1422. doi:10.1016/j.ijproman.2014.01.010

Peters, A., McEwen, B. S., & Friston, K. (2015). Uncertainty and stress: Why it causes diseases and how it is mastered by the brain. *Progress in Neurobiology*. Advance online publication. doi:10.1016/j.pneurobio.2017.05.004 PMID:28576664

Pettigrew, A. M., Woodman, R. W., & Cameron, K. S. (2001). Studying organizational change and development: Challenges for future research. *Academy of Management Journal, 44*(4), 697–713. doi:10.2307/3069411

Piderit, S. K. (2000). Rethinking resistance and recognizing ambivalence: A multidimensional view of attitudes toward an organizational change. *Academy of Management Review*, *25*(4), 783–794. doi:10.2307/259206

Rafferty, A. E., & Griffin, M. A. (2006). Perceptions of organizational change: A stress and coping perspective. *The Journal of Applied Psychology*, *91*(5), 1154–1162. doi:10.1037/0021-9010.91.5.1154 PMID:16953776

Rafferty, A. E., & Restubog, S. L. D. (2010). The impact of change process and context on change reactions and turnover during a merger. *Journal of Management*, *36*(5), 1309–1338. doi:10.1177/0149206309341480

Reichers, A. E., Wanous, J. P., & Austin, J. T. (1997). Understanding and managing cyni cism about organizational change. *The Academy of Management Executive*, *11*(1), 48–59. doi:10.5465/ame.1997.9707100659

Rieley, J. B., & Clarkson, I. (2001). The impact of change on performance. *Journal of Change Management*, *2*(2), 160–172. doi:10.1080/714042499

Robbins, S. P., & Judge, T. A. (2013). *Organisational Behavior* (15th ed.). Pearson.

Roczniewska, M., Puchalska-Kamińska, M., & Łądka-Barańska, A. (2020). Facing education reform: Change-related self-efficacy is linked to job insecurity via appraisal. *Economic and Industrial Democracy*. Advance online publication. doi:10.1177/0143831X20975479

Sak, R. (2018). Gender Differences in Turkish Early Childhood Teachers' Job Satisfaction, Job Burnout and Organizational Cynicism. *Early Childhood Education Journal*, *46*(6), 643–653. doi:10.100710643-018-0895-9

Schilling, M. A., & Phelps, C. (2007). Interfirm collaboration networks: The impact of large scale network structure on firm innovation. *Management Science*, *53*(7), 1113–1126. doi:10.1287/mnsc.1060.0624

Schweiger, D. M., & Denisi, A. S. (1991). Communication with employees following a merger: A longitudinal field experiment. *Academy of Management Journal*, *34*(1), 110–135. doi:10.2307/256304

Self, D., Armenakis, A., & Schraeder, M. (2007). Organizational change content, process and context: A simultaneous analysis of employee reactions. *Journal of Change Management*, *7*(2), 211–229. doi:10.1080/14697010701461129

Senior, B. (2002). *Organisational Change* (2nd ed.). Prentice Hall.

Smollan, R. K. (2015). Causes of stress before, during and after organizational change: A qualitative study. *Journal of Organizational Change Management*, *28*(2), 301–314. doi:10.1108/JOCM-03-2014-0055

Spector, P. E. (1982). Behaviour in organizations as a function of employee's locus of control. *Psychological Bulletin*, *91*(3), 482–297. doi:10.1037/0033-2909.91.3.482

Stajkovic, A., & Luthans, F. (1998a). Self-efficacy and work-related performance: A meta analysis. *Psychological Bulletin*, *124*(2), 240–261. doi:10.1037/0033-2909.124.2.240

Stajkovic, A., & Luthans, F. (1998b). Social cognitive theory and self-efficacy. *Organizational Dynamics*, *26*(4), 62–74. doi:10.1016/S0090-2616(98)90006-7

Stanley, D. J., Meyer, J. P., & Topolnytsky, L. (2005). Employee Cynicism and Resistance to Organizational Change. *Journal of Business and Psychology, 19*(4), 429–459. doi:10.100710869-005-4518-2

Tajfel, H., Billig, M. G., Bundy, R. P., & Flament, C. (1971). Social categorization and intergroup behaviour. *European Journal of Social Psychology, 1*(2), 149–178. doi:10.1002/ejsp.2420010202

Tajfel, H., & Turner, J. C. (1979). An integrative theory of intergroup conflict. In W. G. Austin & S. Worchel (Eds.), *The social psychology of intergroup relations* (pp. 33–37). Brooks/Cole.

Uzzi, B., & Spiro, J. (2005). Collaboration and creativity: The small world problem. *American Journal of Sociology, 111*(2), 447–504. doi:10.1086/432782

Vakola, M., Armenakis, A., & Oreg, S. (2013). Reactions to organizational change from an individual differences perspective: A review of empirical research. In S. Oreg, A. Michel, & R. By (Eds.), *The Psychology of Organizational Change: Viewing Change from the Employee's Perspective* (pp. 95–122). Cambridge University Press. doi:10.1017/CBO9781139096690.008

van Gilst, E., Schalk, R., Kluijtmans, T., & Poell, R. (2020). The Role of Remediation in Mitigating the Negative Consequences of Psychological Contract Breach: A Qualitative Study in the Banking Sector. *Journal of Change Management, 20*(3), 264–282. doi:10.1080/14697017.2020.1737180

Voelpel, S. C., Dous, M., & Davenport, T. H. (2005). Five steps to creating a global knowledge-sharing system: Siemens' ShareNet. *The Academy of Management Executive, 19*(2), 9–23. doi:10.5465/ame.2005.16962590

Waddell, D., Creed, A., Cummings, T., & Worley, C. (2014). *Organizational change: Development and transformation* (5th ed.). Cengage Learning Australia.

Wanous, J. P., Reichers, A. E., & Austin, J. T. (2000). Cynicism about organizational change: Measurement, antecedents, and correlates. *Group & Organization Management, 25*(2), 132–153. doi:10.1177/1059601100252003

Weick, K. E. (1993). The collapse of sensemaking in organizations: The Mann Gulch disaster. *Administrative Science Quarterly, 8*(4), 628–652. doi:10.2307/2393339

Weick, K. E., & Sutcliffe, K. M. (2005). *Managing the unexpected. Resilient performance in an age of uncertainty*. Wiley.

Weick, K. E., Sutcliffe, K. M., & Obstfeld, D. (1999). Organizing for high reliability: Processes of collective mindfulness. In B. M. Staw & L. L. Cummings (Eds.), *Research in organizational behavior* (Vol. 21, pp. 81–123). JAI Press.

Weiner, B. J. (2009), A theory of organizational readiness for change, *Implementation science, 4*(1), 67. doi:10.1186/1748-5908-4-67

Wiens, K., & Rowell, D. (2018), How to Embrace Change Using Emotional Intelligence, *Harvard Business Review*. https://hbr.org/2018/12/how-to-embrace-change-using-emotiona l-intelligence

Wong-Mcdonald, A., & Gorsuch, R. L. (2000). Surrender to God: An Additional Coping Style? *Journal of Psychology and Theology*, *28*(2), 149–161. doi:10.1177/009164710002800207

Yang, S. Y. (2013). Wisdom and good lives: A process perspective. *New Ideas in Psychology*, *31*(3), 194–201. doi:10.1016/j.newideapsych.2013.03.001

Yayavaram, S., & Ahuja, G. (2008). Decomposability in knowledge structures and its impact on the usefulness of inventions and knowledge-base malleability. *Administrative Science Quarterly*, *53*(2), 333–362. doi:10.2189/asqu.53.2.333

ADDITIONAL READING

Bennis, W. (1993). *An Invented Life, Reflections on Leadership and Change*. Addison-Wesley.

Bridges, W. (2009). *Managing Transitions: Making the Most of Change*. Da Capo Press.

Lewis, L. (2011): *Organizational change – Creating change through strategic communication*. United Kingdom: A John Wiley & Sons, Ltd

O'Neill, M. (2007). *Executive coaching with backbone and heart – A systems approach to engaging leaders with their challenges* (2nd ed.). Jossey – Bass.

KEY TERMS AND DEFINITIONS

Change Agent: An individual who promotes and supports a new way of doing something within the company. This can be the use of a new process, the adoption of a new management structure or the transformation of an old business model to a new one.

Change Commitment: This refers to an intention to implement a change that is shared across members of an organization.

Change Cynicism: This is a construct that has two elements: a pessimistic outlook for successful change and blame placed on "those responsible" for lacking the motivation and/or the ability to effect successful change.

Change Recipients: An individual or group of people who the organization must influence to initiate change.

Intention To Quit: The desire is to stop working for an organization is what literature refers to as turnover intention or intention to quit (ITQ).

Organizational Reliability: The abilities to anticipate and explore potential and occurring hazards, prevent and resolve disruptions, and learn from the problems in order to maintain a proper organizational performance in both normal and abnormal situations.

Readiness to Change: The extent to which an individual or individuals are cognitively inclined to accept, embrace, and adopt a particular plans to purposefully alter the status quo.

Chapter 2
Leading Change in an Unpredictable World:
What Does Sustainable, Resilient Change Look Like?

Jennifer Bryan
ABChange Consultancy, UK

John Higgins
The Right Conversation, UK

ABSTRACT

Both leadership and change are contested labels and there is no universal definition. What is usefully understood by leadership and change is specific to the unique nature of a particular change and the evolving context within which it is being carried out. By paying attention to what is specifically needed in the moment around leaders and leading, change leadership becomes an approach that is fit for a specific purpose and avoids becoming a generic approach which is incapable of adjusting to local realities. By noticing how the context of change is evolving and assumptions become validated and invalidated, the fitness of the chosen approach is also kept under constant review.

INTRODUCTION

Praxis is an orientation that is hard to bring about when writing about change, it is much easier to stay fixed within either the strictly academic tradition and its membership rules or else embrace the purely pragmatic, the lists of 'how to' actions that meet the need for ready action popular with organizational leaders, developers, and their advisers. Praxis requires an epistemological promiscuity that doesn't fit easily with either tradition, and especially the academic one with its desire to locate arguments within established boundaries, hierarchies of truth and bodies of disputation.

In this chapter we look to bring together the worlds of practitioners, who are more focused on what works within the particular world they find themselves operating in, alongside that of a particular philo-

DOI: 10.4018/978-1-6684-7509-6.ch002

sophical tradition i.e., that of a critically subjective, participative and socially constructed approach to knowing and acting. The argument and advocacy that only by engaging with a dynamic, messy and situation-specific understanding of change can leaders create a sustainable and evolving (and so resilient) approach to leading organizational change.

BACKGROUND

Practitioner based, or practitioner inclusive, approaches to writing about change are inherently problematic. If writing from a purely academic perspective, what would follow at this point would be a comprehensive list of relevant academic articles that would position the authors within a specific school of argument. Practitioners are however less concerned about the niceties of academic schools and the professional distinctions that matter to those who have scholastic careers to establish, maintain and justify – and will tend to pick and mix from multiple sources of insight, often pushing at the boundaries of received wisdom in order to find the right combination of language and framings that will allow an organization to deal with the situation they are facing in the, often highly politicised and power saturated, here and now. Practice rarely follows espoused prescription.

However, this doesn't mean that anything goes; the eclectic reality of the practitioner approach to organizational change and leadership can be put into a conceptual framing by using John Heron's notion of an extended epistemology (Heron & Reason, 1997). The practitioner perspective allows for a constant cycling between its four forms, broadening and deepening the engagement with the experiential base in such a way that new forms of expressive, propositional and actionable knowing become possible, responding to and creating in turn new forms of organizational experience. This is why it underpins the practitioner focused Ashridge Doctorate and Masters in Organizational Consulting and Change (Critchley et al, 2007; King & Higgins, 2010; King & Higgins, 2014), which is also heavily informed by the relational shift in understanding psychological development (Gilligan, 1993) and a focus on inquiry over advocacy when it comes to organizational learning (Reason, 1988).

What this chapter also embraces, with its focus on 'what work's' and a dynamic flowing up and down the epistemological hierarchy of experiential and actionable knowing, is a focus of the qualities rather than the quantities of change. Within the discipline of organizational change, as with so much of the humanities and the social sciences, is an overdeveloped desire to privilege the scientific method and its truth traditions – a perspective which is rigorously critiqued, alongside other myths and paradoxes, in Cole & Higgins' (Cole & Higgins, 2022) and their examination of the frequently unexamined headwaters of management thinking which create the confusion of so much downstream understanding. A more populist critique which covered much of the same ground, with a particular focus on the institutional habits which sustain particular ways of organizational knowing, is covered in Martin Parker's work and his advocacy of the need to 'Shut down the business school' (Parker, 2018).

The remainder of this chapter explores the authors relationship with change through the lens of their personal perspectives, what they have found does and doesn't make a difference to how people understand and go about leading change in their particular worlds. The personal practitioner perspective is therefore foregrounded over the connection to specific academic debates, while at the same time making reference to those schools of thought that have most and least relevance to how they have and do go about their work.

MAIN FOCUS OF THE CHAPTER: THE PRAXIS OF CHANGE

Setting the Scene

What change means is constantly changing and when its meaning changes so what counts as useful and who's responsible changes. Within the business world it has shifted from being a discrete project, a separate event or programme at arms-length from the day-to-day, to being seen as an ordinary ingredient of business-as-usual. Every manager, so to speak, is a change manager.

In terms of how it is understood as an activity or process, its definition has been as varied as that for strategy and which is nicely overviewed in Strategy Safari (Mintzberg et al, 2008). Some have advocated that it is best understood not as evolution but revolution (Peters, 1982), an argument professional Historians have been having for centuries without either side being able to claim a definitive victory. Others have reframed it to be best understood as learning (Argyris 1999), with different types of change reflecting different forms and modes of learning, with connections into cybernetics and our relationship to information (Bateson, 1972).

The mainstream business change 'gurus' have seen some recommend the metaphor of military general-ship, with change being likened to an organised campaign, strongly directed from the top down (Kotter, 1995). Meanwhile as an antidote to this 'Great Leader' or 'Helmsman' school, those of a more democratic, emergent and opportunistic disposition are keen advocates of change as an inherently bottom-up experience (Beer, Eisenstat & Spector 1990), closely linked to the school of strategy that sees organisational life growing like weeds in a garden rather than hot-house flowers (Mintzberg et al, 2008).

This flux in meaning and understanding reflects both the emergence of the 'Change Management' industry and a business world in constant connection with the intended and unintended consequences of technical, social and political developments/upheavals, which have landed many executives with an all but impossible agenda to manage.

Change can never be a perfect process because it is dependent on human behaviour which is specific to particular individuals going about their lives in a specific time and place; it is inherently complex and multi-faceted because it is psychologically, historically and geographically constrained – a reality that is often wished away by people with a vested interest in promoting a more universalist (and so less realistic) world view. There is a huge range of future and current forces that act on life, society and business, with major implications for what counts as change, including internal organisational and personal change.

In the past, there has been a degree of confidence in being able to predict about how external and internal environments are evolving and hence giving clear direction on what paths to follow. A lot of this certainty being a manifestation of a dominant economic orthodoxy and a world of unipolar great power politics. Increasingly this degree of certainty has been eroded and the level of confidence and ability to predict has fallen, and yet there is still a degree of impetus to continue to do what has always been done, to set aside recent social and environmental upheavals as aberrations from a norm that will reassert itself.

That unfortunately puts people and organisations at a great risk; the old puzzle piece no longer fits at a time when people's anxiety, in the face of the overwhelmingly new, can lead them to seek out security wherever they can find it. Better to stay with what they know won't work but is familiar, than stepping into the world of the genuinely creative and novel (or stay stuck in what Watzlawick et al identified as Type 1 rather than embrace Type 2 change, where Type 1 change fits with the way things have traditionally been understood, and Type 2 change happens in a context where traditional ways of understanding have run out of road (Watzlawick et al, 2011). It is one of the reasons that people's insistence on things being practical can be both seductive and dangerous – because practical often means fitting within what has been tried and tested i.e. the old, Type 1, ways, when what is needed is something that doesn't make sense if looked at through that lens.

At the same time as having to grapple with an evolving and slippery understanding of what counts as change, we also have to contend with the fact that what is meant by leading and leadership is also contested. This contention co-exists with a growing gap between what is espoused and what is practiced when it comes to leadership, throwing up a smokescreen of confusion when it comes to understanding what is actually making a difference compared to what is claimed to be making a difference.

In terms of the evolving world of leadership studies, many theories continue to be discussed and debated. Whether, for instance, leadership is innate as stated in the trait (Grint 2000) and transformation theories (Bass & Aviolo, 1990) or situational (Tannerbaum & Schmidt, 1958, Lewin et al, 1939). Goleman states "great leadership works through the emotions… no matter what leaders set out to do – their success depends on how they do it." (Goleman 2002, pp. 3). McGregor (McGregor, 1960) believes behaviour in leadership will depend on a person's perceptions of people. The rate of development of new leadership perspectives and theories points to the same problem as with change – there is now an industry invested in creating ever-novel perspectives around leadership, with little incentive in staying focused on what it is that persists in human groups and how they come together to achieve collective goals in social contexts riven with power.

Experience from many years of practice and study illustrates that no one size fits all leadership or change, which begs the question, if that is the case, then how can people lead, manage and support others through change and in change? Is there a 'special ingredient' required for people to take on the position of leadership in change? Leadership could simply exert authority and power if they are in a position to do that, but that will immediately ensure they are cut off from the necessary collective wisdom that lies at the heart of successfully engaging with an unknowable future.

If there is a 'special ingredient' for leading change well that ingredient is integrity, a word and concept used in business without any real understanding of what it means beyond some bland statements, or a simplistic appeal to fiduciary or other legal duty. The Oxford dictionary defines integrity as meaning "the quality of being honest and having strong moral principles." But what does it really mean to be honest and have strong moral principles in business? Many companies have honesty as a core value, but what does it really mean? At a time, when people's distrust of organisations is at such a high level, the question of integrity and honesty is critical in the discussion of leading change. There can be in place all the communication and influencing skills in the world, but if people don't have faith in the integrity of leaders and managers, and the integrity of the interests served by the current habits of power, then change leadership will just be another one of those organisational rituals that generate a lot of heat and not much light. Or worse further fuel cynicism and disengagement.

But a focus on integrity is not of itself enough; there is also the need for leaders to be emotionally mature and sophisticated because leading people through change is an emotional experience, whereas most of the language used around it is notably rational and technocratic - or overuses terms like 'passion' to such an extent that they lose their power. Change gets to the guts of human emotions because there will be difficult conversations, established relationships will be broken and new ones needed. Telling people that what they want is not going to happen is never easy, or that the secure job they were anticipating - and underpinned their mortgage application - is now up for grabs and the security they hoped for is no longer there.

Stepping into new roles that put distance between management and people, who previously were close to each other, may make sense to an organigram, but the human heart has its own reasons and schedules. Recognising that everyone is, to varying degrees, outside of their comfort zone is needed when reviewing and understanding how to build sustainable and resilient change in organisations – and for the most powerful and well-resourced a capacity to understand what it feels like for others to be outside their comfort zone when they are not feeling powerful and well-resourced.

This chapter will continue by exploring how best to engage with a world that is going through one of its periods of messier-than-usual flux; where, for instance, the boundaries of business and social responsibility are once more up for grabs. The Friedmanites and the Chicago School, with their highly bounded "shareholder value" sense of corporate responsibility, once again doing battle with the more Galbraithian world of the good society (Galbraith, 1996), with its much more unbounded take on where corporate and institutional responsibility should end and how it should be exercised.

This exploration will consist of:

- How change is a'changing – and how businesses can position their understanding of change to be more sustainable and resilient
- How to engage with a less elite, expert and management-oriented understanding of change in order to engage with the collective wisdom of staff and customers
- How to get the right mix of activity and engagement – to achieve purposeful, collective, adaptive energy

How Change is A'changing

The changing nature of change presents in two ways – philosophically and then in terms of scope. Which means that what counts as change and how we think about change is a work in progress – something we're going to have to think about more than we've been used to in the recent past.

a) The changing nature of the philosophy of change

Philosophy is a pretty dirty word in the business and organizational world, frequently dismissed as academic, impractical and irrelevant to people who have to live in the real world and get things done. The bad news for 'real-world doers' is that they are living a life through the lens of philosophy whether they like it or not. Philosophy shows up in what people chose to see and not see, what gets valued and what doesn't and what assumptions are made about human nature.

The challenge for people tasked with leading change, and the people that get tasked with doing the change, is that they have to inhabit two world views – the one that says change is something mechanistic and controllable alongside one which treats change as emergent and negotiated. This is not a simple matter of finding the common ground, because there is no common ground between the two philosophical schools - it is about holding the tension between what are in theory incommensurable world views… that just so happen to co-exist in reality. The point of connection between the two being the human beings who have to live in workplaces where these very different experiences of life impact them at the same time.

Let's spell out the basic assumptions that have to be acknowledged and are in play in the world of work right now - both have to be engaged with if change work is to succeed. Within the dominant philosophy of change as practised, if not espoused, of the last few decades the following assumptions are either explicitly or implicitly made:

- Change is a phenomenon that exists apart from how things currently are and can be treated as a discrete activity apart from business as usual
- Change is in the gift of the formally powerful, who can direct change according to their superior wisdom and power
- Change can be understood and policed on the basis of a mechanistic model of cause and effect
- Change within an organization happens independently of how the external world is impacting how people think and feel about their lives

The evidence for the presence of this managerial model can be seen in the focus on measurability and the expectation that leaders will be able to demonstrate that they are in control of their organization. This control made visible through the achievement of published goals, milestones and improvements in performance, as set out in the annual plan and budget.

The emergent and negotiated philosophy of change, which has been much talked about within academic circles for years, and often best describes what happens on the ground if not what gets reported in the Management Information System, works from a very different set of assumptions:

- Change co-exists with continuity and is an already existing phenomenon of all social and workplace systems (and so is an inherently bound up with business as usual)
- Change is a systemic and group activity, riddled with conscious and unconscious behaviours, that is in itself an ongoing expression of attempts to shift or retain existing patterns of power
- Change is best understood as a political activity where success is defined by those who have most weight in defining the terms of debate

The evidence for this model exists in the messy world of organizational politics and the through-the-looking glass world where what is said to be done and what is done are not the same thing (beautifully encapsulated in Kegan and Lahey's observation that everybody at work is doing a second unpaid job, that of appearing to get the work done in the prescribed manner while doing the work in a way that suits (Kegan & Lahey, 2016)).

Traditionally the conversation about how to approach change has been to advocate one philosophy over another – our recommendation is one of radical pragmatism, where we seek to support people as they go about living with both. Which means in the following section our language will veer between the mechanistic and organic, the directive and the emergent. Change has to happen in both philosophical domains, which is why writing about it and recommending useful approaches is so difficult – because what makes sense in one world view makes none in the other.

Sustainable, resilient change has to deliver in both worlds – because that is the lived reality and how it is for people who are tasked with delivering it, taking part in it and managing its success!

b) The changing scope of change

Social norms are changing, as they always do, and both employees and customers are becoming more concerned about issues that have traditionally been seen as things you left at the office door. These range from the current Global North concerns around women's rights, racial equity and human rights in the global supply chain to the climate change agenda, which has an even more universal presence. It is in practice impossible to predict what will be an issue that organizations are expected to be mindful of, or quite where the balance of attention will be between traditional and emerging organizational agendas.

Does an organization respond defensively or openly to the emergence of an issue of potential significance to the corporate agenda? Does the organization need to change or not in what it sees as its responsibility and its priorities?

The defensive response works from the perspective that many of these activist concerns are more to do with fashion than with anything substantive – or are being promoted by groups that are still seen as outsiders to the mainstream of society, or are promoting their cause in such a way as to ensure that they are offensive to mainstream social opinion. If this is the case then those with power to prioritise the organizational agenda will take the view that the issues can be ignored, or responded to with lip service, or with the same minimum as competitors, or the law, requires.

The change agenda espoused by the organization may change in appearance (or not at all), but in substance it remains the same, or only slightly tips the balance of attention, but only at the rate of the mass (rather than minority) opinion. While the defensive response may be seen as the 'safe option', it still needs to be understood as an active choice, which may or may not serve the organization well in the long run. When it comes to activism, to take no action is in itself an action in the eyes of some.

The open response is much more dialogic and/or proactive. Rather than looking to ringfence, or ignore, certain concerns around issues traditionally seen as irrelevant to the corporate agenda, this response seeks to understand more about them, take a stand even. For many senior people this also means stepping out of their expert mode and into one of ignorance. This dialogic/proactive response requires organizations to engage with often over-looked voices, finding ways to include people and perspectives which will be novel to those in established positions of power and responsibility, which can often result in exposing some potentially shameful gaps in the world views of those at the top.

In the research data that underpins much of this debate (Reitz & Higgins, 2022) there was a fascinating divide between how open and how defensive different levels within organizations saw their organization when it came to responding to and engaging with activists - and the agendas for change they wished to promote. The more senior groups reported that they saw the organization response as being much more open than the more junior groups, who saw defensiveness in the organization response when the senior people saw open-ness. This finding is consistent with the finding that senior people consistently overrate how in touch they are with the zeitgeist and the experience of others.

From a change perspective this presents a knotty challenge for organizational leaders and managers – how do they challenge themselves to be less confident about their views and opinions? How do they find out whether their confidence is built on sand or on solid foundations, especially when it comes to engaging with issues that traditionally will have not been important to their success? And knottiest and trickiest of all, how do they know whether these novel views and opinions matter when it comes to the corporate change agenda?

How to involve and how to engage with people from throughout the organizational system is one of the red threads running through this chapter – because who gets heard, who has a voice, and who is at the heart of organizational culture, which is at the heart of organizational change. This will determine how change is perceived, communicated and in the end succeed (or not).

2. Engagement with collective wisdom

Many leaders and managers talk about the critical importance of culture change and are therefore acknowledging the need to put people at the heart of the dynamics of change – because culture is a human phenomenon, an active process through which people as a group create and sustain what counts as normal and what is seen as novel (Elias, 2000). Given this widely shared understanding, the implications are plain, namely that a people or human centric approach is critical and the most important element of any change programme.

Unfortunately, the reality of the behaviours exhibited by these leaders and managers is very different. They many times get caught by the glitter and gizmos of change and high desires to get things done, seeing people not as living, breathing beings, but as objects to be manipulated or used – a compelling point of view as it eliminates the need to take the time and effort required to actually implement a human centric change (especially when everyone around you speaks of the need to do things at pace and the world is seen through the metaphor of the machine, to borrow from the work of Gareth Morgan (Morgan, 1996)).

A human centric change requires joining people on a journey, not just to a destination but as an expedition in co-discovery, where what a senior leader thinks needs to happen from their point of view meets with the reality of other points of view, people who see the elephant of change quite differently, but often quite validly. To do this, there are two key steps necessary:

- Step into the "voice of the people"
- Really challenge and articulate the three basic questions of change

a) Step into the "voice of the people"

Many change projects and programmes start off either in the Board or Business Unit meeting room with an elite team of the usual suspects (and their usual advisers), trying to answer the question: "We need to do something to fix or improve or [insert verb] here." In doing so, the team members brainstorm or go away individually to think of 'an answer', or what they might well think is THE answer, and then report back to the same group of people and together they decide on not only what to do, but most of the time, how to do it as well.

One would think that at this time they would then go and test their theory with other employees, to get their opinion, before making the investment in the change, but rarely is that the case. Instead, they create, develop and typically implement their plans from the view of their 'ivory tower' and then wonder why the change did not stick, or get off the ground, or fail entirely, usually for very mundane reasons. One very prestigious financial institution went along with the ambitious growth plans its very prestigious advisers recommended for its Eastern European operations – right up until the moment that the local sales managers (overlooked until this point) noted that to meet the sales targets, given the rate of turnover in sales staff, would mean the company would be spending its entire time recruiting sales staff rather than selling to customers.

There are a number of different ways that can be used to gather this kind of intelligence – surveys, focus groups, team briefings, pilot/test groups and so on. The best approach for each organization being a mix of what works well within the existing cultural norm whilst also having enough that gives a taste of the cultural norm envisaged for the future. The critical element though in obtaining this information is to ensure it is coming from a wide sample group of the organisation – across different business areas as well as hierarchies, while paying acute attention to how truth gets spoken to power within the organization. What people say in the formal environment and/or are willing to say to their bosses tends to be what they believe the organization can bear to hear. Always remember the Alan Mulally at Ford story from the early 2000s, when every RAG report indicator was green, while the company haemorrhaged billions.

It doesn't have to be hundreds of people, but a reasonable sample group (which will depend on the size of the organisation) is highly recommended – and it is of the greatest importance that it doesn't simply consist of the usual suspects. Quality of response is more important than quantity – mass surveys are tempting because they generate large quantities of data that can be readily turned into numeric summaries, which results in all nuance and subjective judgements being airbrushed away. These days surveys can often have an unintended negative blowback, given how widely they've been used over the years and how little has happened as a result. People are also getting wise to the extent to which survey questions steer them into an already pre-thought answer, while being further reminded that a survey in itself is evidence of a lack of meaningful engagement between managers and staff.

Unfortunately, even if a team recognise that, in theory, they need to obtain the voice of the people, they will conduct these 'testing of the water' sessions with people who are from within the business area that is implementing the change. In other words, they are preaching to the already converted or those with relevant knowledge or skills. The problem with this is the results of the test will typically end up being a false positive, because the test is with people who already know in some way how the change needs to happen - rendering the exercise pointless. In recent times we've come across examples of technology vendors who, to stay within the terms of the original budget, have reduced the costs of user acceptance testing by avoiding getting actual users to fulfil this role – and instead getting the development teams to act as proxies for the users. The result was a change project that hit its budget and delivered very little real-world change.

Information needs to come preferably from the people who are the furthest from the decision-making room, who are often the ones who will live with the day-to-day realities of the change, rather than the idealised fantasy. This will give you a real test result that will create and build human centric change strategies, approaches, plans, tactics and methods that will meet the needs, expectations and demands of the people in the organisation. Afterall, as Jennifer has said and written on numerous occasions, "Change is about people not rocket science!", so understanding the potential impacts of the change from people across the business will play a major role in determining whether the change is successful or not. Once again, we cannot reiterate enough how easy it is for senior people to nod along to these comments, while in practice holding to the view that in their heart-of-hearts they know all the answers or remain blissfully unaware how out of touch they are. As research continuously confirms, senior people always over-estimate how in touch they are with what is going on at the sharp end of their business (Reitz & Higgins, 2019).

b) Really challenge and articulate the three basic questions of change:

1. Why is this change needed?
2. Why is this change needed now?
3. Why should the people care about the change (in terms that matter to them)?

Have you ever asked someone to do something, whether they be a toddler, teenager, parent or friend and when you do, they have asked 'why' in return? Or perhaps you knew they would ask that question, so you pre-empt it in the ask? Whichever the case may be, the same impetus and rule applies in the workplace. In order to influence another individual in anything, they need to know the why and have the chance to make sense of the why on their own terms. Tempting as it is, you can never make sense of something on their behalf.

The 'end person in mind' approach (Bryan, 2021), which Jennifer uses in much of her work, can help to identify the answers to this question. An easy way to do this is to create avatars, such as 'Sam' in Norwich or 'Jane' in Tay. These avatars need to represent the general person in the organisation that is nowhere near the implementation of the change. Thinking about 'Sam' or 'Jane', what they might potentially be feeling/thinking in general in this moment of time, much less than what they could think/feel/perceive of the change, can help answer the basic questions in a way that will help them be taken on the journey. The reason being that people in work are not isolated from the rest of the world – our environment externally and internally has an impact on whether we feel secure, confident, scared, anxious, in general and about life, which then influences how we may feel, think and respond to a workplace change.

For example, imagine you are a young person, leaving the home for the first time to go out into the world and make something of yourself, whether that is into a job or further education. If you are that young person, you may be feeling really excited and thrilled about the world around you and hence have positive thoughts and feelings and perceptions about change in general. Whereas, if you are the parent, watching your child leave the home for the first time and not be in your 'protective sphere', you may be feeling really sad, upset, anxious and worried about the world and hence have negative thoughts, feelings and perceptions of other changes that you face.

Reviewing and analysing this kind of information helps leaders understand the context of change, which feeds into the readiness levels of an organisation for change. It is an obvious insight that if an organisation is not ready for a specific change, then the likelihood of the change succeeding is very low. Whereas, if the organisation has a high level of readiness for change, then the success level is really quite high. This is why it is so important to put the work into change leadership in place prior to even starting the delivery of the change. Many organisations, and hence people, underestimate the amount of work that needs to go into place to get an organisation ready and they do so at their peril. The numbers of times a change manager is identified late on and brought onto the project team due to the fact that the team realises either things are going horribly wrong, or need to get a lot of communications out, is extraordinarily high.

Which brings us to another big pitfall with change – communication. To make it clear, change is not communication and lots of communication does not equate change. The two are not synonymous – they are two separate entities. With that said, organisational change does not happen without communication at different levels, but just because communication happened, does not mean that change will happen. We are not in the world of Star Trek where all that is needed is for a leader to say: "Make it so".

Getting the Right Mix of Activity and Engagement

Businesses typically focus on the formal tasks that are involved in change – creating a project plan, a communications programme, training suite and so on. The focus is on the tasks of getting things done and an 'if they build it, the people will come' belief. That might have been the case back in the industrial age, when being told what to do was not only imperative to completing a task, it was expected as a style of management in work. However, we are no longer in the industrial age, but in the digital and information age and the expectations in the workplace are very different. People's expectations have also changed, particularly post pandemic - people are reviewing how they work, want more balance and are demanding more flexibility and say in how things get done, hence the "great resignation." And that's just the tip of the ice berg.

A McKinsey report states that in 1958 the average life span of an organization was 60 years; now that is 12 years and in 2027, 75% of organizations listed will no longer exist – they will either be bought out, merged or gone bankrupt. This is a startling statistic that clearly illustrates that organizations need to change and adapt or die – it also raises tricky questions around how much an individual should invest in belonging to an organizational entity, when that psychological contract is becoming ever more short-lived and transactional. Leading change can be tricky and feel bewildering, particularly when faced with the degree of uncertainty that is indicative of the current world. On top of that, leading people to ensure they are confident and supported to take business to the next level can also both be and feel daunting.

Many leaders believe people do not like change. If you think about it, this is not possible, as people deal with change all the time – a child is sick, so they have to quickly review their diary, there is an accident on the road, so they have to change the route they were going to take to get to where they wanted to go. But it is possible to say that people do not like **being** changed. If you think about a change that has happened recently – did you make the decision to change or was it done to you? If you made the decision, then the likelihood of it happening was probably quite high, and very possibly actually happened. Whereas, if the change was done to you, how much of it did you adopt or accept? Did you resist as much as you could, until you couldn't anymore? Or did you make a public show of commitment, play the politics of the situation, while doing as little as possible to step out of a way of acting that has suited you just fine?

The exact same scenario happens with workplace change and should not be dismissed as 'people being difficult.' The behaviours are human and natural - an expression of the ordinary give and take of all human interaction. So, it is key to manage the change from the perspective of people in their own life-world to help them on the journey of change, because it is a journey not a destination. Part of people's 'natural' behaviours is also a well-deserved scepticism about the hype of change and who benefits – workplace change usually takes time (or certainly longer than advertised) and will involve short term disruption. People have to have a sense of continuity, to reap the benefits, if they are going to go through the inevitable short-term hassle and loss of the familiar.

A Toolkit of Activity and Engagement Approaches

A lot of people have heard the analogy that change is a story or a journey. But the real question to ask is, what story do you want to share and how do you want to travel. The word share is used deliberately, because change is not a solitary activity, it is a social process. It takes multiple teams and hence people to enable change – as well as some self-work.

In the diagram (Figure 1) below, leading sustainable change is presented along two orienting dimensions, both of which need to be present – there's got to be activity, because without activity nothing happens, and there's got to be engagement, because without engagement activity achieves nothing.

Figure 1. Leading Sustainable change with two orienting dimensions

People need to be sincerely motivated and participating in activities that consistently and regularly promote, encourage and embody the change required. In other words, give a lived and felt experience of what it is the change is about, not a conceptual representation of someone else's good idea.

If there is a high level of engagement but a low level of activity, then there is a risk of generating a frenzy of highly motivated people, buzzing with energy but with no focus or shared direction to engage their motivations. This can lead to frustration, disillusionment and cynicism with the change. If there is high activity but low engagement, then there can be a great deal happening but no one is either aware of the activity or inclined to actually get involved. This de-prioritises the change and ultimately leads to the change not happening – all talk and no action many times ends up being the mantra describing that change. If there is no engagement and no activity, then the change is at a stalemate and ultimately gets forgotten about and seen as either an empty promise or inconsequential organisational rhetoric.

To bring people on board, a clear vision, a purposeful focus, needs to be established to support the 'why' of the change we discussed earlier. When envisioning the change, people need to ask, 'what type of organization do you want to be, not now, but in 10 years – how do you want to be seen, perceived, thought of?'

This process needs to achieve two goals which underpin sustainable change. Firstly, it needs to be systemic, engage with the whole system within which the organization operates and which it in turn shapes. It has to be something that has meaning in the eyes of not only the leaders, but staff, customers/ clients, suppliers and regulators. A vision cannot have legs if it is simply the dream of the executive elite and their advisors. The second goal for a vision is to take people out of the day-to-day, which is why it starts from ten years out, providing a compelling possible future which can be reached for. Visioning that takes too short a time horizon will in all likelihood simply turn into an exercise of extrapolating current trends and situations as if they were eternal.

This act of exploring the future also brings people face-to-face with the extent to which things can't be known, inviting people to realise the inherently contingent nature of what they are planning. By forcing people to make explicit assumptions about the future, so people are sensitised to the inevitability of having to make decisions, now, which may have to change in the future - when things turn out differently to the assumptions the original choices were based on.

If things happen which take the organisation further away from the vision and the organisation still believes the vision is the right direction, then decisions can be made to manage the disruptive events with the aim of getting back to the vision. Whereas, if it is then decided the vision is no longer valid, then steps can be taken to develop a new vision fit for the world as it is now unfolding. A sustainable vision is an active thing, not something that gets fixed and lives apart from a world of constant flux.

Next, we need to really understand the level to which the organisation is ready to change. This, has to be a holistic approach, which takes into account the external and internal influencing factors on people, organisations and hence change. This can then be followed by the ABChange model (Bryan 2021), a highly pragmatic and non-prescriptive change framework that facilitates clear-sightedness rather than a cookie-cutter process of activity. It focuses on identifying what type of change leadership is needed rather than prescribing a universal approach.

The world is complex and multi-faceted with many factors impacting on organisational change, however small or large. This includes the political dynamics within an organisation as well as outside – the war in Ukraine, as well as the pandemic, illustrated clearly how Governmental politics and policies have a big impact on all our lives in different ways, generating a variety of emotions and circumstances that are complex and difficult to manoeuvre, wherever we sit in an organisation. In addition, there are the economic fluctuations that follow these situations and changes in societal norms and expectations that can arise from any number of situations. Who would have thought the murder of an ordinary, single man in the US would reverberate around the world in quite the way that George Floyd's death has.

To review the potential of these impacts we don't need to reinvent the wheel and can use the widely known and ubiquitous STEEP or PESTLE models, which helps everybody do two things. Firstly, from an external perspective these models provide a lens for identifying persistent, one-off and emerging factors which are shaping the context within which the organization lives. Once these factors have been identified they can be explored, understood and extrapolated by looking out for trends – both established and new. This analysis gives a clear picture of not only the current situation but potential future situations and hence create different scenarios for people to work with and use as a springboard for change opportunities. Secondly, from an internal perspective, the same review of influencing factors and trends analysis can take place using organisational development tools which explore the business in terms of its strategic arena, internal culture, policies, procedures, IT, teams and physical environment (Bryan 2021). Taken together this gives a big picture perspective to help define the type of change that is being planned and how to actually go about doing it.

Once the type of change is identified, the ABChange model outlines the leadership style and most important change skill that the leader(s) of the change need to demonstrate - with the rest of the change skills in order of importance. The pitfall that many leaders end up with is identifying the type of leadership style they think is needed rather than starting with the type of change. It is the type of change that defines the leadership style, not the other way round. The other big challenge with the holistic approach is time, or rather the decision to not make the time. Many leaders are very anxious to get started on delivering change and under-estimate the criticality of fully understanding the context of change and how this impacts the leading of it.

A holistic approach that takes outside and inside perspectives into consideration, not just on the impact of the change but also on the assumptions made on those potential impacts, allows for a more complete approach that brings the future context of change into focus. This information is then used to define and obtain a real understanding of the type of change being planned and the potential impacts it will have on the people and the organization itself.

The ABChange model then gives a clear direction on what is needed to lead people through that specific type of change. How to lead the change, specific to the change, needs to be incorporated into the full change plan. Too often only the 'things' that need to happen with a change i.e. create a communication plan, training strategy and so on are identified. Rarely are the critical activities associated with leading planned out, as they determine what communications need to be planned, to whom, when and how as well as the other elements in a change strategy. To not really understand and plan the leadership tasks of change, is to create a change plan that is generic and not necessarily applicable to the change at hand, thus increasing the potential risk of failure.

Being resilient is not about knowing exactly when or where the next disruption will come from, so it can fully be planned. It is about being able to understand all the different factors that could have an impact, so adjustments/amendments or completely new plans can be put in place quickly, to help people and organisations flex and adapt to changing environments. To sum it up, resilience is "not waiting for the storms to pass, but learning how to dance in the rain" (Vivian Greene, 2013).

FUTURE RESEARCH DIRECTIONS

The practitioner concern is always with what works in the world as it is, future research therefore needs to be focused on what new situations emerge as a result of the inevitable dynamics of an evolving world. Social norms change and what counts as good organizational practice will therefore have to change. In the judgement of the authors, the persistent challenge will be for all organizations to find ways to stay in touch with diverse opinions and perspectives, especially as the organizational hierarchy becomes more established and formal policies and procedures become a substitute for inter-personal connection.

When it comes to praxis, the challenge for future research remains the same as it has been for years, how to marry the insights of practitioners and academics in a way that is seen as mutually respectful and beneficial. This means finding new ways to cross epistemological traditions and bring together people whose world views and priorities tend to privilege one way of knowing change and leadership over another.

At a relational level, the challenge remains as to how the world rebalance its instrumentalist approach to human relating, how the shadow of an excess of I-It relating impacts the conversations people are able to have when there is a lack of an I-Thou orientation (Buber, 2004).

SOLUTIONS AND RECOMMENDATIONS: WHAT DOES SUSTAINABLE, RESILIENT CHANGE LOOK LIKE?

To rephrase a popular statement from the politics of the 1990s, "It's the people, stupid". Change is all about people, not the rocket science of the latest gizmo or business school theory. And as we have spelled out, it's the people who have to live with the mess of reality, not the experts of change.

Our three conclusions around what makes change sustainable and resilient are:

- It has to make sense in two often contradictory world views at the same time – one mechanistic and controllable and the other emergent and negotiated
- It has to allow room for people to make sense of change on their own terms
- It has to achieve a sufficient mix of activity and engagement, where neither become an end in itself and become busyness for busyness sake

The factors that impact and determine how the change will affect people as individuals and as an organisation whole are vast, ignoring them is not only detrimental to plans for change, but probably fatal in terms of the success of change. How change is perceived, felt, thought about and experienced determines whether the change is viewed as an enemy, friend or casual acquaintance people are not greatly invested in one way or another. This in turn impacts the potential for survival of an organisation in a time where there is a great deal of uncertainty and complexity, which is only going to persist as time goes on. Afterall, we don't have a crystal ball and hence cannot plan for every eventuality, but we can prepare for engaging with and managing uncertainty, whilst also planning for a future that will enable the organisation to thrive, rather than just survive change.

In terms of specific steps that an organization needs to take when it comes to leading change in uncertain times, we see these four as providing a good foundation:

1. Use a holistic approach to change for defining and constantly monitoring the external and internal factors that influence the organization and the validity of the change
2. Know the type of change that is being undertaken (every change has a unique character) so there is clarity about the scale and impact of the change on people and the organization from the perspective of multiple stakeholders
3. Know what type of leadership is fit for purpose for this specific change. Use the ABChange framework to plan how best to lead people throughout the transformation, including course corrections and adaptations
4. Create both a high level of activity and a high level of engagement, to develop purposeful commitment across the organization where people understand the need to adapt to the changing needs and environments of people and the business.

REFERENCES

Argyris, C. (1999). *On organizational learning*. Blackwell.

Bass, B. M., & Avolio, B. J. (1990). The Implications of Transactional and Transformational Leadership for Individual, Team and Organisational Development. In *Pasmore, W. A. and Woodman, R. W. Organisational Change and Development* (Vol. 4, pp. 231–272). JAI Press Inc.

Bateson, G. (1972). Steps to an ecology of mind. Chandler Publishing Company

Beer, M., Eisenstat, R. A., & Spector, B. (1990). *The Critical Path to Corporate Renewal*. Harvard Business School Press.

Bryan, J. (2021). *Leading People in Change: A Practical Guide*. Hero Publishing.

Bryan, J. (2022). Building workplace resilience in a changing environment. *Workplace Insight Magazine*. https://workplaceinsight.net/building-resilience-in-a-changing-environment/

Buber, M. (2004). *I and Thou*. Continuum.

Cole, M., & Higgins, J. (2022). *Leadership Unravelled: the faulty thinking behind modern management*. Routledge.

Critchley, B., King, K., & Higgins, J. (2007). *Organisational consulting: a relational perspective*. Middlesex University Press.

Elias, N. (2000). *The Civilizing Process*. Blackwell.

Galbraith, J. (1997). *The Good Society: The Humane Agenda*. Houghton Mifflin.

Gilligan, C. (1993). *In a different voice: Psychological theory and women's development*. Harvard University Press. doi:10.4159/9780674037618

Goleman, D. (2002). *The New Leaders: Transforming the Art of Leadership into the Science of Results*. Time Warner Books.

Greene, V. (2013). *Dancing in the Rain*. West Brow Press.

Grint, K. (2000). *The Art of Leadership*. Oxford University Press.

Heron, J., & Reason, P. (1997). A Participative Inquiry Paradigm. *Qualitative Inquiry*, *3*(3), 274–294. doi:10.1177/107780049700300302

Kegan, R., & Lahey, L. (2016). *An Everyone Culture: Becoming a Deliberately Developmental Organization*. Harvard Business Review Press.

King, K., & Higgins, J. (2010). *Organizational consulting @ the edges of possibility*. Faringdon: Libri.

King, K., & Higgins, J. (2014). *The change doctors: reimagining organisational practice*. Faringdon: Libri.

Kotter, J. P. (1995). Leading Change. *Why Transformation Effort Fail in Harvard Business Review*, *73*(March-April), 59–67.

Lewin, K., Lippitt, R., & White, R. K. (1939). Patterns of Aggressive Behaviour in Experimentally Created Social Environments. *The Journal of Social Psychology*, *10*(2), 271–299. doi:10.1080/00224545.1939.9713366

Sortino, J. (n.d.). *Lights in single direction: Joshua Sortino. Unsplash*. https://unsplash.com/@sortino

Zaidi, S. (n.d.). *Lines of light: Sohib Zaidi*. Unsplash. https://unsplash.com/@msohebzaidi

McGregor, D. V. (1960). *The Human Side of Enterprise*. McGraw-Hill Books Co.

McKinsey & Co. (2022). *Risk and Resilience*. McKinsey & Co. https://www.mckinsey.com/capabilities/risk-and-resilience/our-insights/covid-19-implications-for-business

Mintzberg, H., Ahlstrand, B., & Lampel, J. (2008). *Strategy Safari: The complete guide through the wilds of strategic management*. FT Publishing.

Morgan, G. (2006). *Images of Organization*. Sage.

Labrum, M. (n.d.). *Multiple candles: Mike Labrum*. Unsplash. https://unsplash.com/@labrum777

Parker, M. (2018). *Shut down the Business School*. Pluto Press. doi:10.2307/j.ctvqhtj8

Peters, T., & Waterman, R. (1982). *In search of excellence: Lessons from America's best-run companies*. Harper & Row.

Reason, P. (1988). *Human inquiry in action: developments in new paradigm research*. Sage.

Reitz, M., & Higgins, J. (2019). *Speak-up: say what needs to be said and hear what needs to be heard*. FT Publishing.

Reitz, M., & Higgins, J. (2022). Leading in an age of employee activism. *Sloan Review*. https://sloanreview.mit.edu/article/leading-in-an-age-of-employee-activism/

Tannenbaum, R., & Schmidt, W. H. (1958). How to Choose a Leadership Pattern. *Harvard Business Review*, (March-April), 162–180.

Watzlawick, P., Weakland, J., & Fisch, R. (2011). *Change: Principles of Problem Formation and Resolution*. WW Norton & Co.

ADDITIONAL READING

Bryan, J. (2021). *Leading People in Change: A Practical Guide*. Hero.

Burr, V. (2003). *Social constructionism*. Routledge.

Cole, M. (2020). *Radical organisation development*. Routledge.

Fenton-Jarvis, S. (2021). *Human-Centric Workplace*. LID.

Isaacs, W. (1999). *Dialogue and the art of thinking together*. Doubleday.

Reitz, M. (2015). *Dialogue in organizations: developing relational leadership*. Palgrave. doi:10.1057/9781137489128

Shotter, J. (1993). *Conversational realities: constructing life through language*. Sage.

KEY TERMS AND DEFINITIONS

Advocacy: Argument and learning through propositional knowing.
Change: A contested term about what constitutes an existing or to be created experience of life.

Extended Epistemology: An epistemological hierarchy that sees the world as having epistemological levels, starting with a base of experience, then working upwards through expressive knowing and then onto propositional and actionable knowing.

I-It: A form of relating that sees self and others as things to be used.

Inquiry: Learning and engagement through curiosity and attention to the world, others and habits of mind.

I-Thou: A form of relating privileging inter-personal connection and the valuing of self, other and the relationship as being of value in and of themselves.

Leadership: A contested term about what constitutes power, influence and authority in socially mediated/constructed settings.

Practitioner: A person concerned with making a difference happen within a specific situation.

Praxis: A way of knowing and being in the world that integrates and pays attention to both theoretical and lived/applied experience.

Relationality: An attention to the dyadic and group experience of the inter-personal rather than the sovereign individual.

Resilience: An individual and group capacity to retain and/or develop agency and liveliness in the face of evolving circumstances.

Sustainable: A way of being that can endure over a period of time.

Type 1 Change: Change that fits within the established way of understanding and acting in the world.

Type 2 Change: Change that does not fit within established ways of understanding and acting in the world.

Chapter 3
The Challenges and Performance of Female-Owned Entrepreneurial Firms and Management Strategies

Raktima Bharadwaj
Queen's University, Belfast, UK

Rajoshi Das
Amity University, Kolkata, India

Anindita Majumdar
Woxsen University, Hyderabad, India

ABSTRACT

In India, society has set some unsaid rules. Some find it difficult to accept women in a work environment because of the patriarchy. Hence it becomes difficult for a woman to break the stigma and establish her own firm. The paper aims to look at the number of threats and challenges that female entrepreneurs face from both micro and macro perspectives. Covid has bought both temporary change (workplace change) and permanent change (shutting down a service/facility) in an organisation. A small new rising firm would not have the capacity to sustain during this time, and females who try to set up small businesses to run their families are mentally affected. This article is an extensive review from earlier works to understand the challenges faced by female owned entrepreneurial firms and their performance during the change brought by COVID times. This article explores the factors influencing the development of female entrepreneurs as well as measures required to enhance the scenario. This paper also aims to explore the psychosocial aspect of changes brought by female owned entrepreneurial firms.

DOI: 10.4018/978-1-6684-7509-6.ch003

INTRODUCTION

A firm is clearly an engineering unit, that is, a unit that turns factors of production into products. Following Machlup (1967), it was about how production and cost functions interact with market demand. But the firm is also an institutional unit that deals with questions of fundamental definition, identity, internal structure, and external boundaries (Hodgson, 2002). It can also be referred to as a type of business organization that allows two or more people to do business together in the form of a joint venture. Members must contribute personal assets according to the terms of the deed of incorporation. Each member of the corporate body bears full responsibility for the future success of the business.

Women can differentiate their desire to start a business by behavioural and motivational factors, but these groupings are fluid and allow women to transition into different types of entrepreneurs. Their personal ambitions and domestic arrangements significantly affect how their business develops. The company's performance is then considered in terms of individual qualitative and quantitative success criteria. Initial success is not judged by the usual business criteria of profitability and pre-orders. No matter how old the company is, there are differences between current and future success criteria. Enterprise helps economies not only survive but also survive and thrive. They also play a role in solving global social, environmental and economic problems. It's evident from the reports that females devote more time to their families, which has a negative impact on their physiological, mental, emotional, and social work lives (Arathi & Rajkumar, 2015), making it a primary concern for female entrepreneurs. They struggle to balance their personal and professional life, which impacts their professional growth (Kelley, Singer & Herrington, 2016). Despite the drawbacks, they have demonstrated their capacity to manage not only small firms but also to transform them into extremely profitable large industries. Hence, initiatives to address changes in societal attitudes and mindsets should be one of the priorities. It is crucial to encourage female entrepreneurship in order to enhance the financial status of women. This can be accomplished with the help of education, as education is one of the significant instruments for developing entrepreneurship qualities in people. Furthermore, efforts should be made at all levels to motivate, inspire, and assist female entrepreneurs. The gender divide has been gradually narrowing across all age brackets. However, this reduction is attributed to fewer male self-employment rather than an increase in female entrepreneurship. However, this does not explain why female entrepreneurs are less entrepreneurial than male company owners. Studies found that there is no significant difference between male and female owned firms (Li et al, 2020) although the acuteness of the challenges faced may vary.

BACKGROUND FOCUS OF THE ARTICLE

History of Firm

The history of the Firm can be traced back to the concept of the Factory. The factory had replaced the "family business" craft-based display system. The craft workshop was run by a master craftsman with a few companions, apprentices, and domestic helpers. In the output system, the business enterprise would own raw materials, work-in-progress, equipment, tools, and subcontracted work for workers who normally worked from home. The factory then was a new form of organization: it was an enterprise, while the production system was a market-like organization based on market contracts.

The Industrial firms appeared only until after the beginning of the Industrial Revolution, in the second half of the 18th century in England and a little later, on the Continent and in America, when a new source of power, Newcomen's steam engine (1663 -1729), later improved by Watt (1736-1819), made it economically reasonable to arrange labor-intensive factories in one location. In the Middle Ages, industrial production essentially did not exist. Most of the population was rural (more than 90%) and produced goods for auto-consumption. Some craftsmen worked in the cities. The whole society is not based on free markets, free production and free trade. In addition, the only physical products constructed using manufacturing processes, as opposed to agricultural products, are stone for buildings, bridges and other monuments, and wooden parts for various constructions and some metal objects such as hoes, nails, and later the first clock. None of these factories are necessary for their production. Large ships were built in a shipyard controlled by the prince. In other words, recently industrial companies gather large quantities of production equipment and large workforces in one place. They were the result of the invention of the steam engine and other machines, themselves the result of protectionist laws (the Calico Act). The fence law also played a certain role.

Industrial companies brought great changes to British and later Western companies. Demographics and cities have changed. But the way workers were paid also changed: medieval craftsmen and industrial money were paid for what they produced; workers in large factories were paid for their time, no matter how much they produce. It also lead to big changes. From the three social classes of aristocracy, clergy and commoners, we have moved to the working class, capitalist and landlord class.

At the beginning of the 21st century, we live in a world that is changing very rapidly, and we take this pace for granted, but it has never happened in the past. Until the industrial revolution, men walked no more than 20 to 30 miles a day, since the dawn of time. We live in the age of the information revolution (computers, instant communication, information flooding).Every recent century has had its technological marvels and the revolutions they have brought: the first steam engines, as we have seen, appeared in the 18th century. The 19th century was improve them a lot. This gave birth to the new science of thermodynamics. The 19th century understood and began to use electricity and magnetism. Towards the end of the century, the first wireless communication technology appeared that did not use optics. The 20th century has created many new technologies: automobiles, airplanes, telephones, computers, nuclear power, etc.

Computers have profoundly changed many activities, accounting over the years. 1960s, production control in the 1970s, publishing, image processing, office work in the 1980s, as well as banking and financial exchanges, even the role and nature of money. It is likely that these changes will continue. Means of payment may still experience major changes. Paypal is one example, bitcoin is another - the author doesn't predict a great future for them, as long as they use so-called "blockchains" that are unwieldy and unreliable, but they are precursors of the invention of money in the future.

A characteristic feature of new technologies introduced in the 20th century is that most of them are understandable by the general public, at least in terms of their use (cars, telephones), if not in their fundamentals (quantum mechanics of integrated circuits, nuclear energy). On the other hand, the things introduced in the 21st century are even less: genetics or the latest computer prowess. A computer-based documentary is sure to include sequences of fireworks such as zeros and ones against a dark blue background hinting at mysterious - admittedly inexplicable processes. what. In this respect, science, after a century, from 1880 to 1980 approximately, a public instruction vector, once again became knowledge in the hands of the wizard Merlin.

The story of commercial enterprises was somewhat different. Modern commercial enterprises could be traced back to the merchants of the northern Italian cities, which emerged in the 12th century, when they gained independence from the Holy Roman Empire. It was also a time of peace in Western Europe, after all the barbaric invasions that incited and led to the fall of the Western Roman Empire, the last of the Normans. (The Mongols and Turks arrived later, but were stopped before Vienna.) Peace has always been conducive to economic activity, commerce, and prosperity. Hence the great growth of Western Europe, the increase in demographics, the universities, the great churches, the big businesses like the crusades (with such harmful and lasting consequences), etc. characteristic of the three centuries after the year 1000.

Business organizations should be seen as viable solutions to the economic problems of their time. Thus, none of them has an advantage over the others, meaning that each can have a comparative advantage depending on the characteristics of the technical-institutional environment. While the most favorable form always gains status, other forms, which existed before, have not completely disappeared; thus co-existing different corporate entities. It is clear that multi-division large enterprise has not collapsed and continues to thrive in many industries, while network and project-based businesses are mainly found in intensive industries. knowledge applications such as biotechnology and semiconductors (Powell et al., 1996). Besides that, of course there are many examples of highly centralized hierarchies, which today are the successors to the factory.

Coming to corporation's business activities that are usually conducted in the company name, the level of legal protection available to employees and owners varied depending on the ownership structure used to form the business. organize. Some types of organizations, such as corporations, provide greater legal protection than others. Companies can be classified in different ways based on their ownership structure:

1. **Sole proprietorship-** This type of firm is controlled by a single person who is responsible for all costs and liabilities and owns all assets. While it is rare for proprietary companies to operate as a business, it does happen.
2. **Corporation-** The financial statements of companies are separated from the financial statements of the owners. The owner of the company is not responsible for the costs, disputes or other obligations of the company. Individuals or governments can own the company. Companies, commercial entities, can act like humans. They can borrow money, sign contracts and pay taxes, among other things. Corporation is often used to refer to a business owned by more than one person.
3. **Partnership-** Two or more individuals owning the firm are in partnership.; The number of partners is unlimited. Each partner is personally responsible for all the debts of the business and collectively they control the assets of the business.
4. **Cooperative-** This type of firm is comparable to a corporation in that its owners have limited liability. However, investors have a say in how businesses operate.

Importance of Promoter in Firm

When an individual has an idea for a new business, he or she can interest others in the business and convince them to contribute capital to a company established for the purpose of continuing the business. The individual will then be considered the "promoter" of the business. In the 19th century, when the industrial revolution came and businesses flourished, the concept of promoter took on as much importance as no other profession, since there were no restrictions on advertising to the public, inviting them to stake in new projects, some promoters took advantage of their position and public sympathy and thus deceived the public to a large extent. The role of the promoter in starting a business changed dramatically in the 20th century. When then, people refused to buy shares in start-ups, due to an established gullible image. and therefore hesitant to invest in companies with no business history and thus few commendable business promoters will disappear. With the rise of the stock market and the role of sensitive promoters gone, what finally happened was an influx of promoters around the world to start trading again and their own improvement and that of other associates. Judging by their historical role, it is clear that business promoters play an integral role in establishing a business. A company is not born until it is incorporated. To form a company, various documents must be prepared and other procedures must be followed. All this work is done by the promoters.

Promoters have powers over the incorporation of the company. Interestingly, however, he (promoter) is neither the agent nor the trustee of the company he is forming. He is not an agent because there is no company yet, and he is not a trustee because there is no trust. However, this does not mean that the Promoter has no legal relationship with the Company. The promoter's legal status can be accurately described as having a relationship of trust with the company. In Erlanger vs. New Sombrero Phosphate Lord Cairns said: They have the establishment and organization of the company in their own hands. "They are concerned with how, when, in what form, under whose authority it is a commercial company." It has the power to determine how it is born and how it operates.

SOLUTIONS AND RECOMMENDATIONS

Challenges Faced by Female Entrepreneurs

The Vedic Rig Women in India had a high social status. This period (2000-500 BCE) is seen specifically as a 'Golden age' for women (Altekar, 1956). Women were adequately educated and had the ability to achieve high intellectual and spiritual standards. During this time, there were several female Rishis. There was no sati system, and there was no child marriage. Women were also free to choose their husbands. This system was termed "Swayamvar." Widows were allowed for remarriage. Women were treated as "Ardhanginis" and granted complete autonomy in family affairs. Vedic women also enjoyed economic independence. Some of them worked as teachers, while others indulged in sites of manufacturing at home such as clothing spinning and weaving. In agricultural purists, women also assisted their husbands. However, after having free and revered positions in Rig-Vedic society, women began to face discrimination in education and other rights and amenities beginning in the Later-Vedic period. The status of women kept deteriorating up until the modern era during the 19th century.

The British extended their rule in India, and modernization began in the nineteenth century. The condition of women in India at its lowest ebb at the time of British reign. Sati was clearly present. On Muslim women, purdah was rigidly enforced. Dancing females had profitable careers. Almost all Hindu temples publicly accommodated devadasis. No doubt, British control attempted to check all of these ill practices.

Indians began to be impressed by the British way of life. The British administration made major attempts to alter India's caste-based social system. Some educated Indians backed the British endeavor to alter India's harsh social structure. With the growth of technology in every industry. Women's roles in the twenty-first century have also shifted. They are no longer limited to cooking, cleaning clothing, performing housework, and caring for their children and families. Women now lead in every sector and society, including sports, business and industry, education, health, politics, technology, the navy, army, and agriculture (Agrawal, & Joglekar, 2013). Some ignorant women are still denied their human rights; they are humiliated by society, and they are yet to achieve their own status.

Females contribute for almost two-thirds of all "everyday labor" done worldwide. Despite this, girls face significant social and economic disadvantages when compared to their male colleagues. The majority of labor is done by a female within the home and is hence unpaid. Many women do not have the opportunity to work a second job. Globally, though, Females who enter the labor force are frequently paid 60 to 70 percent less than their male counterparts male partners, despite the fact that they are regularly subjected to prejudice, harassment, and other forms of abuse. Despite worldwide efforts to promote equality, there are still places that have lagged behind.

However, women are transforming and emerging as prospective entrepreneurs. Women's role modeling in non-traditional business sectors to break down barriers between men's and women's industries. In practically every country, women-owned businesses are driving economic growth. The increased understanding of the function and position of economic society has gradually altered women's hidden entrepreneurial potential. A primary reason for women in business is their skills, expertise, and flexibility to the economy. Women are entering the business world with ideas for small and medium-sized businesses. They are open to being motivated by role models, such as the experiences of other women in business.

According to the "2018 State of Women-Owned Businesses Report" commissioned by American Express, the number of women-owned businesses has increased nearly 3,000% since 1972. Not only that, but between 2017 and 2018, women in the United States started an average of 1,821 new businesses per day (Castrillon, 2019). Women now account for 40% of new entrepreneurs, indicating that more women than ever before are turning to entrepreneurship. However, these figures only depict a portion of the story. Women-owned businesses remain in the minority, and the challenges faced by them are plentiful and frequently very different from those encountered by their male counterparts.

Women's business efficiency is hampered by cultural limitations. In Africa, males or husbands are expected to provide for their families. A woman who demonstrates her entrepreneurial skills is assumed to desire to take over the leadership role of her spouse. According to a research conducted by (Barwa, 2003) on women entrepreneurs in Vietnam, women experience additional disadvantages as a result of persistent societal and cultural gender inequities and stereotypes. Despite tremendous progress toward sexual equality in sectors such as education and the job, women's role as the family mainstay in terms of parenting and homemaking remains remarkably unchanged (McGowan et al., 2012). Religion and tradition have a great influence on UAE society, particularly on women's roles in society, and certain orthodox sectors of the community still frown on female entrepreneurs. These ingrained cultural standards make it challenging for female Emiratis to leverage their entrepreneurial talents while also meeting the demands of their families and society (Preiss & McCrohan, 2006).

Other difficulties that women entrepreneurs have in obtaining finance from formal institutions are exacerbated by their restricted access to formal education, property ownership, and social mobility (Ayadurai, 1987). According to (Karim, 2001), the most common challenges encountered by women entrepreneurs in Bangladesh are financial problems, with limited financing ranking. Other studies discovered that women were more likely to close their enterprises due to financial restrictions rather than commercial failure (Boden & Nucci, 2000; Watson, 2003). (Ayadurai, 1987) adds to this viewpoint by adding that one of the difficulties women encounter in acquiring loans is their lack of expertise negotiating with banks and their lack of financial confidence to argue for what they are entitled to. Male members believe it is a major risk to finance women's ventures, and many financial institutions are skeptical of women's entrepreneurial potential. Bankers believe women's loans to be riskier than men's loans, so they use unrealistic and inappropriate collateral to make loans to women entrepreneurs.

According to a report by the United Nations Industrial Development Organization (UNIDO, 2003), despite evidence suggesting women's loan payback rates are greater than men's, women continue to experience more difficulty in receiving credit, sometimes due to discriminatory attitudes of banks and lending groups. According to (Starcher, 1996), women in underdeveloped countries have limited access to funds since they are concentrated in poor rural communities with little options to borrow money. Women entrepreneurs also face a shortage of external finance due to their inability to provide physical security, forcing them to rely on their savings and loans from relatives and friends.

According to (Garland, 2006), banks tend to overstate the likelihood of female entrepreneurs defaulting, resulting in unreasonably high collateral requirements and credit rationing. According to Indarti and Langenberg, (2005), multiple empirical research have indicated that potential entrepreneurs see a lack of access to money and credit schemes, as well as financial system limits, as major barriers to business innovation and development in emerging nations (Marsden, 1992; Meier & Pilgrim, 1994; Steel, 1994 cited by Indarti & Langenberg, 2005). Personal savings, extended family networks, community saving and credit systems, and financial institutions and banks are all potential sources of capital. (Robinson, 1993) discovered that informal sources of financing, despite having high interest rates, make significant contributions to business start-ups in poor nations.

Lack of Education: Seeking for possibilities, being able to evaluate and understand them, and developing a profitable firm around these chances are vital characteristics of an entrepreneur, and education is a significant part in achieving these goals. It has been observed that the female population in developed nations is better educated than their counterparts in developing countries (Lerner, Brush, & Hisrich, 1997). In India, 56% of the female population is literate, with the majority having no education beyond high school. As a result, women entrepreneurs are not fully qualified to keep up with technological or market advances, much alone be aware of new business prospects. As a result of this deficit, women entrepreneurs face a variety of challenges while establishing and maintaining their firms (Vijayakumar & Naresh, 2013).

Social Barrier: Gender discrimination, fear of societal response, family duties and commitments are some of the elements that combine to create a social barrier for women to pursue business. Women in India are viewed as subordinates and live as dependents on males; hence it is thought that entrepreneurship is not a subject for women and is entirely reserved for men. The duties, responsibilities, and commitments to family are thought to be a barrier to women starting their own businesses. According to several polls, this mindset is the consequence of pressures brought on by the conservative thinking of a conventional culture, since women are supposed to priorities delivering on the family front over any other activity (Khurana & Sharma, 2013). Women have been made to feel guilty if they fail to perform their domestic responsibilities, indicating a lack of family support and commitment to the advancement of women in society (Jamali, 2009). This also prevents a woman from establishing and running a business, visiting banks, able to attend entrepreneurship development training courses and workshops and meetings, attracting more customers, or looking for diverse suppliers.

Financial Problem: Businesses' financial problems are connected to a lack of enough financing, difficulty in obtaining credit from banks, a lack of cash for development, being ignorant of acceptable finance sources, a lack of collateral, complex and lengthy loan procedures, and so on. In India, women entrepreneurs are constantly hampered by insufficient and incorrect financial resources. Because women have relatively little property and bank balance in their names, they are unable to get funding from external sources such as formal financial institutions owing to low creditworthiness and a lack of correct collateral (Mahajan, 2013; Siddiqui, 2012) According to Robert's research in non-OECD and emerging nations, 59% of respondents expressed financial problems as a critical issue, with 41% having trouble securing a loan. Sandhu highlighted in his research that a bank official makes the final judgement on a loan application of a female entrepreneur when the female owner provides collateral and a letter of assurance from a blood related, spouse, or village head for the establishment of firms. It is commonly assumed that women of the feminist gender have a poor risk-taking capacity (Sandhu et al., 2012). Thus, due to unfavourable internal and external factors, women entrepreneurs start a firm with a very low level of capitalisation and loan finance and do not utilise significant private equity for business sustainability (Roomi, Harrison, & Beaumont-Kerridge, 2009). This financial isolation is the result of both voluntary and unintentional factors. Women entrepreneurs have actively excluded themselves from banking services owing to illiteracy as well as the difficult and time-consuming procedures of bank loans (Nehru & Bhardwaj, 2013). On the other hand, involuntary exclusion from financial services occurs because banks are unwilling to provide loan facilities due to high interest rates, a lack of credit worthiness, a lack of past credit history, a lack of credit bearing capacity, and an unhealthy relationship with banks when seeking bank credit (Roomi, Harrison, & Beaumont-Kerridge, 2009). Furthermore, women entrepreneurs are unaware of financial help, such as subsidies, incentives, tax breaks, and so on, given by financial institutions and the government, which leads to company failure (Nandy & Kumar, 2014). As a result, women become more reliant on their tiny savings and loans from family and friends for day-to-day operations.

Personal Barriers: Personal barriers are issues that women entrepreneurs face in their personal capacity, such as mental obstacles that prevent them from taking risks and launching firms. Furthermore, in the society, general assumptions about women's characteristics such as lack of entrepreneurial aptitude, lack of self-confidence and fear of failure, difficulty gaining trust and assistance from several other businesses, lack of participation with business associates, and so on act as individual barriers.

Self-confidence and fear of failure: In general, males are assumed to be more positive and confident than women when it comes to business possibilities and running a firm (Koellinger, Minniti,& Schade, 2008). One of the most important issues confronting women who wish to start micro and small businesses is a lack of self-confidence (Mundra & Sharma, 2013; Fielden, Davidson, Dawe, & Makin, 2003; Nandy & Kumar, 2014). Women are thought to have lower levels of self-confidence than other women. However, confidence levels vary from person to person and scenario to situation, therefore this may not be the case when it comes to self-confidence in conducting business activity (Rozier & Thompson, 1998). Female business owners, on the other hand, have a fear of failure, which has been linked to the social and economic problems they confront (Halkias et al., 2011). According to certain studies, women may be able to overcome this obstacle and boost their self-esteem by participating in different entrepreneurial training programmers, workshops, and seminars offered by the government and government departments.

Lack of entrepreneurial aptitude: One of the personal challenges to starting and growing a firm is a lack of entrepreneurial aptitude and behavior. In general, women are not raised as well as males in terms of business understanding, and as a result, they lack an entrepreneurial mindset despite engaging in a variety of entrepreneurship development initiatives and seminars, conferences, seminars, and so on. Only a few of the women establish and operate businesses after altering their gloomy attitude about entrepreneurship or coercion, as well as increasing their risk bearing capabilities and caliber.

Market Related Barrier: Marketing is an organizational function responsible for creating, communicating, and delivering value to customers (Kotler, Keller, Koshy, & Jha, 2013). However, severe competition, a weak marketing network, inadequate sales methods, client payment delays, a lack of marketing knowledge, and rapid changes in demand and technology all put pressure on women-owned businesses to adjust rapidly to changing market conditions (Jovanov & Stojanovski, 2012). In general, women-owned micro, small, and medium-sized businesses have faced severe competition from established firms and male entrepreneurs in terms of pricing, quality, standards, and fulfilling the changing demands of customers. Furthermore, male entrepreneurs have extensive expertise, market knowledge, and use cutting-edge technology in their manufacturing. However, when women start their businesses with minimal savings and investments, they do not have enough money to spend on advertising their products and services. Thus, female entrepreneurs have done minimal marketing operations, relying largely on middlemen such as distributors, retailers, and so on, who aim to capture a large portion of the margin, resulting in a lower profit for the business. As a result, less money is available for technological development and advancement. Inadequate and inefficient technology provides low-quality and more expensive products, rendering them uncompetitive in the market, which is one of the key reasons for business failure (Vijayakumar & Jayachitra, 2013). Networking through their own social media network is another technique to advertise things since it is less expensive and has an emotional touch. It would also provide them with access to data and make it simpler for women entrepreneurs to reach consumers, suppliers, and financial resources from nearby.

Operational Barriers: Women entrepreneurs receive equal training from EDPs, regardless of whether their business is new or established. As a result, there is a significant shortage of information for running a firm. Second-generation female entrepreneurs have prior business experience and hence require assistance and advice to manage the unanticipated scenario that may occur as a result of unexpected economic or political events (Vijayakumar & Jayachitra, 2013). One such example is demonetization, when currency was no longer available and hence people's purchasing power fell. Furthermore, while a number of agencies support business development projects during the start-up phase, once the firm is established, women entrepreneurs are left to operate in an environment that does not give an equal playing field (Roomi, Harrison, & Beaumont-Kerridge, 2009). Women entrepreneurs have little experience running a business; therefore counselling, advice, mentorship, and advisory services can assist them overcome the obstacles they confront when running a firm that was set up with a lot of hard work and ensure its success.

FUTURE RESEARCH DIRECTIONS

Mental Health and Wellbeing of Entrepreneurs

The World Health Organization (WHO) defines mental health as "a condition of well-being in which each individual fulfills his or her own potential, can cope with the usual demands of life, can work successfully and effectively, and is able to contribute to her or his community" (WHO, 2014). Mental health and well-being have traditionally been studied in psychology, medicine, and public health, but are gaining traction in other fields.

Just like mental health and well-being are essential for optimal human functioning, entrepreneurs are no different. Entrepreneurs frequently multitask among several responsibilities and are often frustrated due to a variety of variables such as customer loss, disagreements with partners, high competition, staffing issues, and so on, all while under pressure to produce money. As a result, it should come as no surprise that entrepreneurship is fraught with worry when compared to other occupations.

A survey report by Freeman (2019) investigated the prevalence and co-occurrence of five psychiatric illnesses. Researchers discovered that mental health abnormalities directly or indirectly affected 72% of the entrepreneurs, including those with a psychological history (49%) and familial history among the asymptomatic entrepreneurs (23%). Entrepreneurs reported higher rates of depression (30%), ADHD (29%), substance abuse (12%), and bipolar illness (11%). Furthermore, 32% of entrepreneurs had two or more mental health disorders, while 18% had three or even more mental health conditions (Freeman et al., 2019). Only 24% of the entrepreneurs were asymptomatic (they had no mental health difficulties) and had asymptomatic families.

Entrepreneurial personalities have attracted a lot of attention. Entrepreneurs tends to have characteristics such as high energy and excitement, and they feel all emotions intensely. The Big Five personality framework is key to these findings since it outlines a collection of overall personality traits made up of sub-traits (Leutner et al., 2014; McCrae & Costa 2008). The Big Five personality dimensions (openness, conscientiousness, extraversion, agreeableness, and neuroticism) are thought to have a biological basis and to be largely stable across time (Digman, 1990; McCrae & Costa 2008). Entrepreneurs have a distinct pattern of Big Five personality traits, which includes higher levels of extraversion, conscientiousness, and openness combined with lower levels of agreeableness and neuroticism (Brandstätter, 2011; Obschonka et al., 2013; Zhao et al., 2010).

Several significant investigations back up these conclusions. In one nationally representative study, 149 German self-employed people did not differ in prevalence of affective disorders, anxiety disorders, or alcohol misuse from their age- and gender-matched employed comparator participants (Stephan & Roesler, 2010). Entrepreneurs had fewer lifetime mental health diagnoses and higher life satisfaction than employed participants. Similarly, no disparities in sadness, anxiety, or rage were found in a study of 238 entrepreneurs and 288 managers in the United States (Rahim, 1996). According to a study of over 2700 US individuals, entrepreneurs had lower rates of emotional negativity and use constructive mood and problem-solving coping mechanisms more often than employees (Patzelt & Shepherd, 2011). A study of 235 Canadian entrepreneurs and matched employed controls discovered no significant differences in mental health or job satisfaction between these groups (Jamal, 1991; Jamal and Mitchell 1980).

According to a study of over 2700 US individuals, entrepreneurs had lower rates of emotional negativity and use constructive mood and problem-solving coping mechanisms more often than employees (Patzelt & Shepherd, 2011). A study of 235 Canadian entrepreneurs and matched employed controls discovered no significant differences in psychological health or job satisfaction between these groups (Jamal, 1991).

High mental health and wellbeing in entrepreneurs has been associated with persistence, or tenacity and grit (Wincent et al., 2008), which helps alleviate the damaging consequences of stress (Patzelt & Shepherd, 2011). Research of 688 self-employed workers and a matched sample of 688 employees, for example, investigated the health and wellness trade-offs associated with entrepreneurialism in (Cardon & Patel, 2015). In this study, entrepreneurs experienced more stress, which was related with higher rates of good affect and increased income. Positive effect has been demonstrated to minimise the detrimental impact of stress on the physical health of entrepreneurs. There is a favourable association between Profitable and beneficial and firm performance (Gorgievski et al., 2010).

Although few books have highlighted the mental health status of entrepreneurs yet there has been a dearth of researchers in the field of psychology and entrepreneurship. Articles have defined bipolar spectrum disorders (Gartner, 2008), obsessive-compulsive disorders, ADHD (Wiklud et al., 2020) and other significant problems among business titans, as well as political and military leaders (Ludwig, 1992).

Impact of Covid in Business

Financial performance is the primary measure used by investors around the world. However, the performance of any company is subject to a number of predicted and unanticipated factors. Unexpected factors are those beyond management's control, such as the Covid-19 pandemic, which has caused significant changes in how the company operates. A nationwide lockdown has affected all businesses. Hospitality and tourism industries, transportation and aviation were among the most affected businesses (Alsamhi et al., 2022). The (Covid-19) pandemic is known to impact business performance. Additionally, COVID-19 pandemic in India has forced business leaders and owners to mobilize quickly and make quick decisions. Decisions such as reducing industrial production or temporarily closing factories can have unforeseen long-term consequences. As result, lockdown policies or government orders could affect the financial performance of companies. Additionally, organizations should always have scalable and effective contingency plans in place to prepare for the unexpected. Additionally, the business has much to learn from this pandemic to deal with the future when something like this happens.

The rapid spread of the pandemic has severely impacted the global economy and financial markets(Chen & Chia-Wei, 2021). The whole world has been forced to contend with the COVID-19 pandemic, inevitably causing great disruption in all aspects from the economy to society (Chen & Chia-Wei, 2021; Piccarozzi et al., 2021). Businesses around the world have been impacted by the COVID-19 epidemic, affecting virtually all business sectors and industries (Islam et al., 2020; Xuet al., 2021). Lockdowns and social distancing restrictions are being rolled out as part of his policies and efforts to control the ongoing COVID-19 pandemic (Cheval et al., 2020; Zhao & Feng, 2020).

According to Trueman's theory, investors determine the value of a company based on an assessment of management's ability to adapt to the economic environment in which it operates (Trueman, 1986). In addition, the investor wants full disclosure of relevant Covid-19- information and how, from a stakeholder perspective, has impacted enterprises.(Elmarzouky et al. ., 2021). Khatib and Nour (2021) states that the COVID-19 pandemic has a huge impact on the characteristics of business, structure of governance, liquidity and leverage. However differences between the early and post-pandemic periods are not significant. Another study by Ahmed (2020) analyzed the impact of COVID-19 on Pakistan's stock market performance. This study used data on positive cases, deaths and recoveries associated with COVID-19.

Shen et al. (2020) investigated the impact of her COVID-19 on the corporate performance of listed companies in China. The results showed that COVID-19 distorted the impact on business performance. D'Orazio and Dirks (2020) found that the introduction of her COVID-19-related policies in the Eurozone from 1 January 2020 to 17 May 2020 had a significant negative impact on stock markets. Google Trends, Bond Yields, EU Volatility Index and Infectious Rate movements show the negative impact. Fiscal policy announcements had little impact, but health initiatives had big impact. Fu and Shen (2020) investigated the impact of COVID-19 on the performance of the energy industry and found that COVID-19 had a significant negative impact on the performance of energy companies. Goodwill impairment was introduced as a mitigating variable as the pandemic has had a greater impact on companies experiencing goodwill impairments. Therefore, decision makers at all levels should pay more attention to the impact of COVID-19 on energy companies and take steps to limit its impact on the energy industry. Islam et al. (2020) found a significant correlation between entrepreneurial self-efficacy, financial performance, and entrepreneurial resilience in SMEs. Furthermore, the study found a significant mitigating effect of innovative work behaviour on the relationship between financial performance and organizational effectiveness.

In addition, Rababah et al. (2020) found that small businesses have been hit or affected the most brutally by this pandemic. Furthermore, their findings showed that the most impacted locations and industries hit hardest by COVID-19 suffered greater losses in financial performance than other industries. The conclusions of this study have resulted in important policy implications on how banks, regulators, central banks and governments need to work together to address the financial and economic impact of the COVID-19 predicament. Shen et al. (2020) used financial data of listed companies in China to examine the impact of COVID-19 on business performance. It shows that COVID-19 is having a negative impact on business performance. COVID-19 has had a greater negative impact on business performance, the smaller the company's investment scale and sales.

Zou and Li (2020) found that the COVID-19 pandemic has affected nearly all aspects of the global economy and society. The study surveyed companies in Guangdong to determine the impact of the pandemic and propose public strategies to mitigate the negative impact. Companies in Guangdong are facing major obstacles due to the outbreak. Their manufacture and operation are restricted and subject to serious hazards. In order to weather this difficult period and gradually resume normal operations, it is necessary to adopt the regulation, which significantly reduces the production costs of companies. Xu et al. (2021) found that epidemic severity had a significant negative impact on import and export cargo throughput. Moreover, the impact of the pandemic on imports is more significant than on exports.

In the Indian context, Dash et al. (2021) found that deaths from infectious diseases are having a negative impact on the Indian aviation market. Inline, Kumar Das and Patnaik (2020) found that various industries such as telecommunications, tourism, aviation, the automotive sector, and transportation are the hardest hit sectors facing adverse effects from the current disaster. pointing out. Existing studies have analysed the relationship between COVID-19 and economic performance (Debata et al., 2020; Goswami et al., 2021). In contrast, there are no studies analysing the impact of COVID-19 on the performance of listed companies in various sectors in India.

The COVID-19 pandemic has had far-reaching effects at the industry level in 2020-2021. transportation and storage; lodging and catering services; arts, entertainment and recreation. and other services. These "high-touch" industries are heavily impacted by coronavirus regulations because they rely heavily on physical interactions. We see "low-contact" industries as other industries that rely less on face-to-face contact. The peak-to-valley drop in output produced in the 'high contact' industries was relatively large at 37.1L compared to 17.1L in the 'low contact' industries. 2021 also saw a strong recovery in the "high touch" industry. Similarly, there was a significant impact on employment in these "high-touch" industries, with peak-to-trough declines in full-time employment of 7.6% and 1.7% in high-touch "low-contact" industries. Additionally, high-touch industries typically had higher levels of furloughs, especially during times of heightened COVID-19 restrictions (*Effects of the Coronavirus (COVID-19) Pandemic on 'High-Contact' Industries - Office for National Statistics*, n.d.)

Wholesale and retail businesses were the least affected of the high-touch industries, recording the smallest initial sales decline of 26% in the first half of 2020 compared to pre-coronavirus pandemic levels. The wholesale and retail sub-industries have widespread implications due to the fact that some industries have essential retail and others are considered non-essential and are subject to coronavirus restrictions. Additionally, some retail subsectors are benefiting from the shift to online shopping. Retail of information and communication equipment in specialty stores (down 55%) and retail of other goods in specialty stores (down 44%) were the subsectors to record the biggest declines in the first half of 2020 – Industry Materials not considered - for example, television and video game retail sales, watches and jewellery. By contrast, retail sales at non-specialty stores, including grocers, fell the least at 7% in the first two quarters of 2020, shielded from closure orders during the first nationwide lockdown. Retailers outside of stores, stalls and markets are the only retailers to see an increase in store sales during the initial lockdown. The third quarter of 2021 (July-September) was above pre-coronavirus pandemic levels. The industry has benefited from record online sales during the coronavirus pandemic. Consumers switched from brick-and-mortar stores to online shopping, and businesses responded to growing demand by improving their online and delivery operational capabilities. Corporate sales of retail sales through stalls and market sub-industries increased significantly, up 43% from pre-coronavirus pandemic levels in Q3 2021. This may reflect the public's preference for outdoor retail as a way to prevent coronavirus transmission. In the second quarter of 2020 (April to he June), nearly four in 10 of her adults said they felt safe leaving home due to the coronavirus outbreak. By the third quarter of 2021, this means more than half of adults will be comfortable leaving their homes restrictions (*Effects of the Coronavirus (COVID-19) Pandemic on 'High-Contact' Industries - Office for National Statistics*, n.d.)

Impact of Covid on Female Entrepreneurs

Women entrepreneurs, especially those in low- and middle-income countries supported by the Shelley Blair Foundation for Women, face many complex challenges in starting, growing and sustaining a business. A range of obstacles, from gender stereotypes to lack of access to finance, poverty, political instability, high levels of insecurity, and even complex social threats such as war, can prevent women from thriving in business. Therefore, according to a new survey report, which draws on the responses of 125 female entrepreneurs in 32 countries, nearly 1 in 10 female entrepreneurs (9.2%) who responded said they were affected by her COVID-19 pandemic. was the most challenging they have ever faced(Network, 2021)

The majority of women from a survey (83.8%) said the pandemic had a negative impact on their business. This is devastating news and very real not only for emerging markets where around 30-37% of all SMEs are run by women, but also for female entrepreneurs who depend on their companies for revenue. has become a threat. Of those respondents who may close their businesses due to the pandemic, 43.8% of them said that doing so would make it difficult for families to feed and put children around the world at risk of falling into poverty(Network, 2021).As a result, many women entrepreneurs have had to completely transform their businesses to keep food on the table, especially since many governments in low- and middle-income countries were unable to financially compensate for the loss of income due to the pandemic. No. For example, Dafne, an entrepreneur from Mexico and a graduate of the Road to Growth program, ran a successful event management company before COVID-19. After the pandemic hit, Dafne completely reorganized her business and instead she started manufacturing and selling PPE gear(*Dafne's Story*, n.d.). Other entrepreneurs like Kenyan entrepreneur Wangari, who runs a soap manufacturing business and uses her skills in the app Her Venture, have started selling online to give customers secure access to their products(*Wangari's Story*, n.d.)

While many women's businesses are struggling to survive, we also recognize that many other women have had to become entrepreneurs because of the needs created by the pandemic. -The economic fallout of 19 has left many people out of work -40% of employed women worldwide work in the four sectors most affected by the coronavirus crisis, while men Many are experiencing unemployment - compared to 36.6% of those who accept income from other family members who have lost their jobs. Many women became first-time entrepreneurs this year because they needed an income to support themselves and their families: especially since most of these businesses are informal and can be assumed to be vulnerable. If these new entrepreneurs, like existing female entrepreneurs, have equal access to the knowledge, skills and resources that are more readily available to men, then the economic recovery post-pandemic societies sorely need. will be seen. A 2019 independent study by the Foundation in partnership with the Boston Consulting Group showed that closing the gender gap in entrepreneurship could bring up to $5 trillion to the global economy. At a time of enormous economic loss and uncertainty, the untapped potential of women entrepreneurs could be key to reviving economies around the world (*ILO Monitor: COVID-19 and the World of Work. Fifth Edition*, n.d.)

Governments and policymakers have an important role to play in ensuring that women entrepreneurs and their businesses stay here. First, it is critical that women entrepreneurs can survive and thrive during the COVID-19 pandemic through financial assistance packages specifically designed for women-led micro, small and medium enterprises. Putting women entrepreneurs at the centre of economic policy and ensuring equal access to funding from all available sources means removing discrimination from the process of applying for funding. Second, lawmakers need to urgently review and repeal policies and laws that discriminate against women entrepreneurs or hinder their business success. In conclusion, we urge governments to provide gender-disaggregated data on micro, small and medium enterprises (MSMEs) and entrepreneurship to ensure that laws, policies, support packages, financial products and services are taken into account.

Professor Margaret Cobia, Kenya's Chief Cabinet Secretary and Minister of Public Services and Equality, explains: But in areas where women do not participate, we also see communities suffering(Nunn,2020). Women are the backbone of communities around the world, and women's businesses strengthen families, communities and society as a whole. We take the need for a gender-sensitive business environment very seriously and, through the actions outlined above and recommended in the research report, Women Entrepreneurs: Living Through the Pandemic and Beyond. Supporting entrepreneurs for a fast, equitable and sustainable successful recovery (*Women Entrepreneurs*, n.d.)

CONCLUSION

Entrepreneurship has many ups and downs. On the one hand there is abundance and freedom, on the other there are many sleepless nights. The sleep cycles are interrupted, food habits are changed and one tries to push themselves to the edge to give their best output. The new business seems like a baby in her life and in order to develop that she sacrifices a lot. There are times when they run out of ideas and creativity seems to become a duty. The desire to make their dream come true becomes challenging and stressful. These are parts of the entrepreneurship process, but they cannot run away from this or stop living their dreams. A best way is to think that mental health is their business partner and that should also be taken care of, to boost oneself and the business.

The important steps that should be taken to support oneself and the business to flourish are:

Set Boundaries- It is important to understand where to say 'Yes' and where to say 'No' in a business. For example if we consider the 'YES' to receive and 'No' to preserve, so we must know where we lie on the spectrum before navigating. A 'Yes' to many things can be the source of burnout and hence that should be the time to preserve. On the other hand if it's a 'No' to a lot more things, due to fear, then it's time to say 'Yes' for a while. Moving on with new opportunities can be a source of fear or self-doubts, and that's absolutely fine. Sometimes these imbalances makes one discover the tools to create a balance in their life.

At times a 'No' is difficult, especially in case of a new business. One might think that this could be a hindrance to grow their business to the exponential rate they dream of. Hence a 'No' can be sometimes replaced with 'Not now'. The opportunity can be looked on to later when they become ready to deal with it.

Create Self Care Routine- Being a business owner it is difficult to find time for you own self, getting up with a long to do list in the morning. These stress throughout the day drains away ones energy and you find yourself falling asleep in front of the computer. It's important for the brain to rest. Creating a self-care routine apart from the work routine is very important. Create a routine for yourself so you can check in first thing in the morning. For some it could be a hot cup of tea or coffee and inhaling fresh air. For others it could be some movements or exercise that could keep them going throughout the day. Beyond that, create a little routine throughout your day so you can take a moment to check in on yourself. Perhaps combine the first point of setting boundaries with the second point of creating a routine.

Positive Self Talk- In life, things does not go the way its planned. Of course, one has to adapt and roll with the punches, but remember that there is more pressure when you are talking to yourself negatively about the inevitable than when you are talking positively about it. Change the attitude towards yourself. Be kind to yourself and life will be fine. You may be waiting for it to happen while you sing sweet blessings to your soul and eat cookies. Start by adding positive self-talk time to your day! Make it part of your daily routine. Write down a list of affirmations and decide when to recite them. You can choose every morning or maybe every night if the moon wakes you up more. Think about the words you want to hear and start saying them to yourself more often. Not only does it support your sanity, it also attracts more of what you say to yourself.

When faced with adversity, some people crack while others swing back, and this is what creates the variation among individuals, organizations, and nations surviving, adapting, and even succeeding in the face of the greatest unforeseen life adversities. Hence resilience can be taken into consideration while we talk about coping and the concept of positive psychology "Psychological Capital" can help the entrepreneurs towards being resilient. Psychological capital has a clear link with individuals innovative and positive activities while minimizing undesirable attitudes such as anxiety. Hence it is possible that psychological capital can reduce employee worry and stress while increasing staff productivity.

Finally, the coping can be separated into two major criteria: either triggering the individual to confront the problem or regulating the emotional emotions resulting from the difficulty at hand. While entrepreneurs use a variety of coping strategies to deal with stress, problem focused coping appears to be more effective in achieving entrepreneurial results.

Hence this paper adds to the entrepreneurship literature and address the wider research gap on mental health and effective coping strategies.

REFERENCES

Agrawal, A., & Joglekar, A. (2013). Role of Women in 21 st Century. *Age*, *18*(26, 40).

Alsamhi, M. H., Al-Ofairi, F. A., Farhan, N. H. S., Al-ahdal, W. M., & Siddiqui, A. (2022). Impact of Covid-19 on firms' performance: Empirical evidence from India. *Cogent Business & Management*, *9*(1), 2044593. doi:10.1080/23311975.2022.2044593

Altekar, A. S. (1956). *The position of women in Hindu civilization, from prehistoric times to the present day*. Motilal Banarsidass Publ.

Ayadurai, D. (1987). *The Employer, the Employee, and the Law in Malaysia*. Butterworth-Heinemann.

Barwa, S. D. (2003). *Impact of Start Your Business (SYB) training on women entrepreneurs in Vietnam*. ILO Office in Vietnam.

Boden, R. J. Jr, & Nucci, A. R. (2000). On the survival prospects of men's and women's new business ventures. *Journal of Business Venturing, 15*(4), 347–362. doi:10.1016/S0883-9026(98)00004-4

Brandstätter, H. (2011). Personality aspects of entrepreneurship: A look at five meta-analyses. *Personality and Individual Differences, 51*(3), 222–230. doi:10.1016/j.paid.2010.07.007

Cardon, M. S., & Patel, P. C. (2015). Is stress worth it? Stress-related health and wealth trade-offs for entrepreneurs. *Applied Psychology, 64*(2), 379–420. doi:10.1111/apps.12021

Castrillon, C. (2019). Why more women are turning to entrepreneurship. *Forbes*, (December), 20.

Chen, H. C., & Yeh, C. W. (2021). Global financial crisis and COVID-19: Industrial reactions. *Finance Research Letters, 42*, 101940. doi:10.1016/j.frl.2021.101940 PMID:34566533

Cheval, S., Mihai Adamescu, C., Georgiadis, T., Herrnegger, M., Piticar, A., & Legates, D. R. (2020). Observed and potential impacts of the COVID-19 pandemic on the environment. *International Journal of Environmental Research and Public Health, 17*(11), 4140. doi:10.3390/ijerph17114140 PMID:32532012

Dafne's story. (n.d.). Cherie Blair Foundation for Women. https://cherieblairfoundation.org/impact/her-stories/dafne-adapting-to-covid19/

Digman, J. M. (1990). Personality structure: Emergence of the five-factor model. *Annual Review of Psychology, 41*(1), 417–440. doi:10.1146/annurev.ps.41.020190.002221

Effects of the coronavirus (COVID-19) pandemic on 'high-contact' industries. (n.d.). Office for National Statistics. https://www.ons.gov.uk/economy/grossvalueaddedgva/articles/effectsofthecoronaviruscovid19pandemiconhighcontactindustries /2022-05-06

Fielden, S. L., Davidson, M. J., Dawe, A. J., & Makin, P. J. (2003). Factors inhibiting the economic growth of female owned small businesses in North West England. *Journal of Small Business and Enterprise Development, 10*(2), 152–166. doi:10.1108/14626000310473184

Freeman, M. A., Staudenmaier, P. J., Zisser, M. R., & Andresen, L. A. (2019). The prevalence and co-occurrence of psychiatric conditions among entrepreneurs and their families. *Small Business Economics, 53*(2), 323–342. doi:10.100711187-018-0059-8

Gartner, J. D. (2008). *The hypomanic edge: the link between (a little) craziness and (a lot of) success in America*. Simon and Schuster.

Gorgievski, M. J., Bakker, A. B., Schaufeli, W. B., van der Veen, H. B., & Giesen, C. W. M. (2010). Financial problems and psychological distress: Investigating reciprocal effects among business owners. *Journal of Occupational and Organizational Psychology, 83*(2), 513–530. doi:10.1348/096317909X434032

Halkias, D., Nwajiuba, C., Nicholas, H., & Caracatsanis, S. M. (2011). Challenges facing women entrepreneurs in Nigeria. *Management Research Review, 34*(2), 221–235. doi:10.1108/01409171111102821

Headings, S. (n.d.). *Unit-III-Women Entrepreneur: Nature, Definition, Features and in Indian perspectives.* CCS University.

ILO. (2020). *ILO Monitor: COVID-19 and the world of work.* ILO.

Islam, D. M. Z., Khalid, N., Rayeva, E., & Ahmed, U. (2020). COVID-19 and financial performance of SMEs: Examining the nexus of entrepreneurial self-efficacy, entrepreneurial resilience and innovative work behavior. *Revista Argentina de Clínica Psicológica, 29*(3), 587.

Jamal, M. (1991). Job stress, satisfaction, and mental health: An empirical examination of self-employed and non-self-employed Canadians. *Journal of Small Business Management, 35*(4), 48–58.

Jamali, D. (2009). Constraints and opportunities facing women entrepreneurs in developing countries: A relational perspective. *Gender in Management, 24*(4), 232–251. doi:10.1108/17542410910961532

Jovanov, T., & Stojanovski, M. (2012). Marketing knowledge and strategy for SMEs: Can they live without it? Thematic Collection of papers of international significance. *Reengineering and entrepreneurship under the contemporary conditions of enterprise business,* 131-143.

Khurana, K., & Sharma, S. (2013). A comparative analysis of association rule mining algorithms. International Journal of Scientific and Research Publications, 3(5), 0.

Koellinger, P., Minniti, M., & Schade, C. (2008). *Seeing the world with different eyes: Gender differences in perceptions and the propensity to start a business.* Research Gate.

Kotler, P., Keller, K. L., Koshy, A., & Jha, M. (2013). *Marketing management: a South Asian perspectives.* Scientific Research Publishing.

Lerner, M., Brush, C., & Hisrich, R. (1997). Israeli women entrepreneurs: An examination of factors affecting performance. *Journal of Business Venturing, 12*(4), 315–339. doi:10.1016/S0883-9026(96)00061-4

Leutner, F., Ahmetoglu, G., Akhtar, R., & Chamorro-Premuzic, T. (2014). The relationship between the entrepreneurial personality and the Big Five personality traits. *Personality and Individual Differences, 63*, 58–63. doi:10.1016/j.paid.2014.01.042

Ludwig, A. M. (1992). Creative achievement and psychopathology: Comparison among professions. *American Journal of Psychotherapy, 46*(3), 330–356. doi:10.1176/appi.psychotherapy.1992.46.3.330 PMID:1530096

Mahajan, S. (2013). Women entrepreneurship in India. *Global Journal of Management and Business Studies, 3*(10), 1143–1148.

McCrae, R. R., & Costa Jr, P. T. (2008). Empirical and theoretical status of the five-factor model of personality traits.

McGowan, P., Redeker, C. L., Cooper, S. Y., & Greenan, K. (2012). Female entrepreneurship and the management of business and domestic roles: Motivations, expectations and realities. *Entrepreneurship and Regional Development, 24*(1-2), 53–72. doi:10.1080/08985626.2012.637351

Mundra, S., & Sharma, J. (2013). A Comparative Analysis of the Status of Women Entrepreneurship: India Vs. Global. *Research Journal of Social Science & Management, 3*(4).

Nandy, S., & Kumar, S. (2014). Women Entrepreneurship in 21st Century India. *Global Journal of Finance and Management, 6*(9), 967–976.

Nehru, J., & Bhardwaj, S. (2013). Women Entrepreneurship in India: Issues & Problems "You can tell the condition of a Nation by looking at the Status of its Women". Spectrum. *Journal of Multidisciplinary Research, 2*(7), 8–16.

OECD Network.. (2021, March 31). *What impact has COVID-19 had on women entrepreneurs and what can governments and policy makers do to put gender equality at the heart of global recovery?* The OECD Forum Network. https://www.oecd-forum.org/posts/what-impact-has-covid-19-had-on-women-entrepreneurs-and-what-can-governments-and-policy-makers-do-to-put-gender-equality-at-the-heart-of-global-recovery

Obschonka, M., Schmitt-Rodermund, E., Silbereisen, R. K., Gosling, S. D., & Potter, J. (2013). The regional distribution and correlates of an entrepreneurship-prone personality profile in the United States, Germany, and the United Kingdom: A socioecological perspective. *Journal of Personality and Social Psychology, 105*(1), 104–122. doi:10.1037/a0032275 PMID:23586410

Patzelt, H., & Shepherd, D. A. (2011). Negative emotions of an entrepreneurial career: Self-employment and regulatory coping behaviors. *Journal of Business Venturing, 26*(2), 226–238. doi:10.1016/j.jbusvent.2009.08.002

Piccarozzi, M., Silvestri, C., & Morganti, P. (2021). COVID-19 in management studies: A systematic literature review. *Sustainability, 13*(7), 3791. doi:10.3390u13073791

Preiss, K. J., & McCrohan, D. (2006). *GEM global summary 2006: United Arab Emirates*. London School of Economics/Babson.

Rahim, A. (1996). Stress, strain, and their moderators: An empirical comparison of entrepreneurs and managers. *Journal of Small Business Management, 34*(1), 46.

. Rani, V.P. (2021). The Position And Role Of Women At Historic Society To Modern Society In India- A Sociological Study. *International Journal of Multidisciplinary Educational Research.*

Roomi, M. A., Harrison, P., & Beaumont-Kerridge, J. (2009). Women-owned small and medium enterprises in England: Analysis of factors influencing the growth process. *Journal of Small Business and Enterprise Development.*

Rozier, C. K., & Thompson, M. (1998). Female entrepreneurs in a female-dominated health profession: An exploratory study. *Journal of Developmental Entrepreneurship, 3*(2), 149.

Sandhu, N., Hussain, J., & Matlay, H. (2012). Barriers to finance experienced by female owner/managers of marginal farms in India. *Journal of Small Business and Enterprise Development, 19*(4), 640–655. doi:10.1108/14626001211277442

Siddiqui, A. B. (2012). Problems Encountered by Women Entrepreneurs in India. *International Journal of Applied Research & Studies*, *I*(II), 1–11.

Starcher, D. C. (1996). *Women entrepreneurs: Catalysts for transformation.* European Bahá'í Business Forum.

Stephan, U., & Roesler, U. (2010). Health of entrepreneurs versus employees in a national representative sample. *Journal of Occupational and Organizational Psychology*, *83*(3), 717–738. doi:10.1348/096317909X472067

Teacher, L. (November 2013). Role of Promoters in Company Establishment. *Law Teacher.* https://www.lawteacher.net/free-law-essays/business-law/role-of-promoters-in-company-establishment-business-law-essay.php?vref=1

United Nations Industrial Development Organization. (2003). *Developing Rural and Women Entrepreneurship.*

Vijayakumar, A., & Jayachitra, S. (2013). Women entrepreneurs in India-Emerging issues and challenges. *International Journal of Developmental Research*, *3*(4), 12–17.

Vijayakumar, T., & Naresh, B. (2013). Women entrepreneurship in India-Role of women in small and medium enterprises. [TAJMMR]. *TRANS Asian Journal of Marketing & Management Research*, *2*(7), 13–25.

Wangari's story. (n.d.). Cherie Blair Foundation for Women. https://cherieblairfoundation.org/impact/her-stories/hv-kenya-wangari/

Watson, J. (2003). Failure rates for female-controlled businesses: Are they any different"? *Journal of Small Business Management*, *41*(3), 262–277. doi:10.1111/1540-627X.00081

Wiklund, J., Hatak, I., Lerner, D. A., Verheul, I., Thurik, R., & Antshel, K. (2020). Entrepreneurship, clinical psychology, and mental health: An exciting and promising new field of research. *The Academy of Management Perspectives*, *34*(2), 291–295. doi:10.5465/amp.2019.0085

Wincent, J., Örtqvist, D., & Drnovsek, M. (2008). The entrepreneur's role stressors and proclivity for a venture withdrawal. *Scandinavian Journal of Management*, *24*(3), 232–246. doi:10.1016/j.scaman.2008.04.001

Women Entrepreneurs: Surviving the Pandemic & Beyond. (n.d.). Cherie Blair Foundation for Women. https://cherieblairfoundation.org/what-we-do/research/2020-annual-audit/

World Health Organization. (2014). Mental health: A state of well-being. WHO. https://www.who.int/features/factfiles/mental_health/en/

Zhao, H., & Feng, Z. (2020). Staggered release policies for COVID-19 control: Costs and benefits of relaxing restrictions by age and risk. *Mathematical Biosciences*, *326*, 108405. doi:10.1016/j.mbs.2020.108405 PMID:32565231

KEY TERMS AND DEFINITIONS

Coping Strategies: The various behavioural and cognitive techniques used to deal with difficult situations, solve problems, crisis intervention or to manage stress are known as the coping strategies.

Female entrepreneurs: The women who establish, organise, manage, and drive an enterprise or a business, are the female entrepreneurs.

Management Strategies: The methods and techniques implemented in business ventures to plan, set, manage, and execute goals and targets are known as management strategies.

Psychosocial Aspect: Psychosocial aspect pertains to those contexts which determine the impact of the social factors upon an individual's mind, body, and behaviour, and vice-versa. There exists an inter-relation between the two variables, and hence, often the term is used in a conjoined manner to denote relational integration.

Societal Stigma: Social stigma or societal stigma refers to the discrimination directed to any specific person, gender, or group on the basis of certain pre-conceived notions and/ or perceived characteristics. This often leads to prejudice and biased attitude toward the person, gender or group who becomes subject to this kind of distinction.

Chapter 4
The Change Potential of Social Media: Learning From Digital Business Cases

Silvia Fernandes
CinTurs, Faculty of Economics, University of Algarve, Portugal

Fatima L. Carvalho
CinTurs, University of Algarve, Portugal

Daniela Neves
Faculty of Economics, University of Algarve, Portugal

ABSTRACT

This work results from an internship of two months at a new company of digital media, to evaluate its 'maturity' in terms of social media performance. For pursuing this objective, it is compared with its main competitors in the area as a panel of experts. Two methods of analysis addressed two main research issues: I1) which key performance indicators are mostly used in a sample of main firms in the area in Portugal; and I2) which new strategies came from their assessment in those firms? In the period considered, the company revealed a more adaptive strategy, missing some key indicators in the area. Its efforts may not be being directed at the greatest potential of social media. It can improve the performance of its social media by monitoring engagement what helps to preserve its reputation and give followers the answers they really want. A common aspect in the compared companies is the absence of outsourcing to digital influencers. However, this practice is growing because, with the demand and speed of response currently required, in-house digital marketing lacks the resources.

DOI: 10.4018/978-1-6684-7509-6.ch004

INTRODUCTION

Today there is an increased use of online platforms for purchasing products/services, and also answering to new preferences (Cardoso, 2020). To catch this wave, digital marketing has created innovative communication channels, providing customers with high interactivity and personalization. Thus, it is imperative to manage and integrate the various channels (or touchpoints) the customers are using today (Youtube, Google Play, Instagram, etc.). Besides a company's website, social networks (SN) are key elements of its digital marketing strategy (DMS). Companies should base their DMS on the content of their business goals, aligned with the needs of target market.

Using SN, companies can approach their customers in a more natural and informal way, for a more authentic branding (Sormaz et al., 2019). Entrepreneurs are increasingly aware of this role in order to gain as much economic value as possible. The latest trends in digital marketing and business communication indicate that the impact of SN is continuous. For example, if an ad is placed in a newspaper, it is difficult to estimate how many people really turned to a page and paid attention to it. However, digital marketing helps to know the reach of a product/service as it engages the customers with the firm/brand in a personalized way.

After considering these issues, the question is how to use SN to take advantage of their whole potential. It is important to consider their future, as they are a vital channel of marketing and communication for organizations. They are increasingly significant since they have become, for many, the primary domain where to receive and share important information to reach the world. This is due to the continuous innovation that occurs, both on the technological side (platforms that add new features and services), as well as on the consumer side (people and brands that find new uses of SN).

Main Trends: Engagement/Co-Creation

Nowadays, it is very important for entrepreneurs to focus on the factors involved in the attitude of customers. For instance, they now actively create content about a brand, something that previously was solely controlled by the firm (Chu, 2011). Therefore, the engagement marketing is gaining ground as an effort of a brand to motivate and measure customer contribution.

The use of visual SN has increased and influenced the marketing of customer engagement. Recent research highlights the relevance of consumer contributions to these platforms. Likes and comments are metrics directly related to the content of the messages and readily available to brand managers, providing immediate feedback on their posts (Rietveld et al., 2019; Rudd et al., 2017). In visual SN, such as Instagram, likes and comments are understood as an affective expression on the content. This is the largest and most growing network on a visual basis, due to the number of its active users. However, more metrics are needed such as conversions, for helping firms to create and retain their value.

SN, especially of visual kind, have allowed brands to demonstrate the benefits of product characteristics in a creative way (Rietveld et al., 2019). In addition, customer service tends to become more personalized and ubiquitous, i.e., customers are able to engage with brands anywhere and anytime. Solutions to customer needs will be even more accessible and immediate. Therefore, new metrics of SN performance will help to answer the customer before he realizes a problem or has a question (Appel et al., 2020). In today's world, decisions are no longer guided just by hypotheses and past experience. Influential marketing ideas can be now determined by analytics and big data. Predictive analytics can help businesses provide insights that lead to more agile solutions.

It is essential to take advantage of the wealth of social media, to derive a greater return from it. This work intends to bring up the hidden value of SN, through comparing a set of innovative digital marketing firms. Lessons could be learnt from observation, document analysis, questionnaire to specialists in the area, and measures of SN performance. This issue is so important today that firms should identify their key performance indicators (KPI) to drive their business strategy.

Thus, the main two research issues to be addressed are: I1) which KPI are mostly used in a sample of main firms in the area in Portugal (Algarve); and I2) which new strategies came from their assessment in those firms.

This work is then structured as follows: section 3 acknowledges the main performance indicators for social media evaluation; section 4 presents the research framework which includes data collection and methodology around a quantitative assessment, followed by a qualitative analysis; section 5 highlights another innovative trend which is the sensory; and section 6 presents the final considerations and implications.

Social Media Performance Indicators

KPI are the critical indicators of progress toward an intended result. They provide a focus for strategic and operational improvement, creating an analytical basis for decision making on what matters most. Good KPI provide objective progress toward achieving a desired result and help compare the degree of performance change over time (KPI.ORG, 2022). The use of KPI includes setting targets (desired level of performance) and tracking progress against that target. This often means working to improve leading indicators that will later drive lagging benefits. They can track efficiency, effectiveness, quality, governance, compliance, behavior, performance, etc.

The metrics of digital performance vary in type and period. Considering the type, they evaluate quantitatively or qualitatively. Quantitative metrics can include sales volume and revenue increase/decrease, while qualitative criteria can include brand awareness, image, and customer relationship (Desai, 2019). As for the period, interim metrics can be used as those that give some insight during a trip, and final metrics as those that inform whether the trip was successful or not. Most social media indicators such as likes, actions and comments can be classified as interim metrics.

Today, it is not enough for a company to make a brief analysis using only simple metrics (such as likes, comments or shares). It is essential to use indexes that can measure the engagement effectiveness of campaigns and product launches, such as: conversion rate, amplification rate, applause rate, economic value, social value, involvement rate, percentage of influencers, among other. Also, companies need to explore the dynamism and heterogeneity of metrics over time (Sudarsanam, 2017). For this author, the best social media metrics are:

Conversion Rate

It can be measured for any social network, and it is the percentage of visitors that complete a goal, such as a purchase, out of total number of visitors. A high conversion rate (CR) is indicative of successful marketing and web design because people really get what is offered. To achieve a higher CR, organizations need to understand the target audience, brand attributes, and added value to followers.

Amplification

This is measured through the content viewed and shared by a follower on his networks. Once followers find the shared content valuable, they will share it through their networks and the content will reach a larger group of customers.

Applause

This is measured by the number of likes in a publication. It helps organizations discover what social media users like or dislike to view.

Economic Value

It is the sum of long-term and short-term revenues and cost savings. Organizations use tools to measure macro and micro conversions in different channels. An example is Google's analysis that helps capture the economic value metrics of all participating social networks.

Organizations need to investigate and develop guidelines for defining SN KPI. They need to associate business goals with those metrics and measure their success. This will harness the power of social media in order to help them grow faster and outperform the competition (Sudarsanam, 2017). Companies need more and more to assess the quality of their content (dynamic and nondynamic) and measure its effectiveness (Grave, 2019).

Research Framework

Data Collection

Many researchers on the area defend the notion that managers primarily rely on easily quantifiable and readily available KPI. This choice is reasonable, but it minimizes the effort required to evaluate engagement marketing campaigns. According to Grave (2019), the preference for the *sentiment* metric (sum of positive comments minus negative) may arise. Positive net sentiment is the desired result in such a way that marketers strive for more positive comments and are willing to pay for it. Based on these aspects, this work discusses the following metrics: Reach, Likes, Shares, Comments, and Visits. And the following KPI were calculated: Audience growth rate, Post reach, Applause rate, Average engagement rate, Amplification rate and Comment conversation rate.

Data collection is from a sample of main Portuguese firms in the digital marketing sector. The technique used includes data from their websites and social networks. Also, the internal information of one of the firms was crucial (which is Growme, where the first author of present work developed a two-month internship). The websites and social networks consulted are from Growme's competitors in order to assess their publication reach and feedback. A questionnaire was sent (through email) to this joint panel of experts, targeting the person in charge for the area in each firm. The main goal was to assess and compare their social media performance, whose analysis together with the aforementioned technique, helped to settle important lessons for companies in this area.

Within the scope of social networks' potential, in digital marketing and in business, key performance indicators were analyzed. Such measures reflect data on online actions, helping to understand the behavior and preferences of users, market trends, among other aspects. Thus, a first quantitative assessment of those metrics was done, followed by a qualitative analysis. This integrated approach intends to address the main two referred research issues: I1) which KPI are mostly used in a sample of main firms in the area in Portugal (Algarve); and I2) which new strategies came from their assessment in those firms.

Quantitative Assessment

I1) which KPI are mostly used in a sample of main firms in the area in Portugal (Algarve)?

The following KPI were calculated to reflect on the performance of Growme's social media. The first one analyzed is the audience growth rate, which identifies the number of new followers of a certain platform (in percentage).

Table 1. Audience growth rate

Kpi / SN	Facebook	Instagram
Audience growth rate	40/235×100 = 17,02%	339/439×100 = 77,22%
Analysis	On Facebook, in the two months analyzed, there was an increase of 17.02%. This is positive for the company meaning it can get the message out to a wider audience	On Instagram, this metric was higher reaching 77%. Both social networks have different audiences, complementing each other

Another is the post reach, which measures the number of people that have seen a publication. Despite the number of followers achieved, not everyone sees the published content.

Table 2. Post reach

Kpi / SN	Facebook		Instagram	
	1st month	2nd month	1st month	2nd month
Post reach	106/235×100= 45,11%	49/235×100= 20,85%	302/439×100= 68,79%	319/439×100= 72,67%
Analysis	For each Facebook post, about 45% of followers viewed the new post	There was a decrease, due to type of shared content (no paid publications or current news)	The content here is reaching more than half of the followers (content attracts the audience)	Favorable increase (positive for the company, demonstrating a growth)

The applause rate measures how many people are 'applauding', i.e., liking the content over total followers.

Table 3. Applause rate

Kpi / SN	Facebook		Instagram	
	1st month	2nd month	1st month	2nd month
Applause rate	2/235×100= 0,85%	3/235×100= 1,28%	15/439×100= 3,42%	14/439×100= 3,19%
Analysis	The number of likes per publication is low	It increased, meaning a greater involvement	Higher for Instagram followers	Despite a slight decrease, public is gradually involved

The average engagement rate measures the audience engagement through likes, comments, and shares (calculated by adding total likes, comments, and shares of a publication).

Table 4. Average engagement rate

Kpi / SN	Facebook		Instagram	
	1st month	2nd month	1st month	2nd month
Average engagement rate	(2+0+0)/235×100= 0,85%	(3+0+0)/235×100= 1,28%	(15+0+1)/439×100= 3,64%	(14+0+1)/439×100= 3,42%
Analysis	Low value (few interactions through likes, comments and shares)	It increased (higher interest of interacting with content)	Higher than in Facebook (due to more likes and shares)	Similar value as the previous month

The amplification rate shows how followers share the content created by the company. The more followers share their interest in the brand, the higher this rate is. When someone shares a post, it is like a personal recommendation of its content.

Table 5. Amplification rate

Kpi / SN	Facebook		Instagram	
	1st month	2nd month	1st month	2nd month
Amplification rate	0/235×100= 0%	0/235×100= 0%	1/439×100= 0,23%	1/439×100= 0,23%
Analysis	No shares here	No shares (issue to be considered by the company)	Low value	Same as the previous month

Having comments on the published content is a great sign it draws attention. Creative and relevant content is more likely to generate a comment.

Table 6. Comment conversation rate

Kpi / SN	Facebook		Instagram	
	1st month	2nd month	1st month	2nd month
Comment conversation rate	0/235×100= 0%	0/235×100= 0%	0/439×100= 0%	0/439×100= 0%
Analysis	in both months there were no comments (the company has not achieved the necessary involvement with the public)		same reason for this network	

The metrics *applause rate*, *average engagement rate*, *amplification rate* and *comment conversion rate* have much lower results, compared to the first two, *audience growth rate* and *post reach*. This is due to Growme's recent adherence to the comparative management of SN. It is organically growing what will generate leads (interactions without effective return/ sales such as a contact form filled in).

These results reveal that current news have great potential, causing high interest and attention by the public. Thus, they must be part of the content used on Facebook. Also, results for Instagram were higher in every KPI. In this network, inspirational sentences related to business success and digital marketing seem to be relevant to the public as they had higher reach, likes and shares. But more important than likes or comments are the conversions such as orders, sales, and shares. At Growme, followers still ask questions about products through email or website, as the publications have a link to company's website for more information.

KPI and their relation are an essential tool for an effective digital marketing strategy. They contribute to measure social media performance and establish a standard to be reached. However, there is a need for analyzing data from more months/years. Increasingly activities are developed online, and technology is turning contactless. Therefore, users' perceptions and choices must be listened to regularly in order to carry out the necessary product innovation.

The results here obtained were then compared with the answers to a related questionnaire by a group of specialists in the area. These have served as an expert panel, which included the staff in charge for the area at Growme and at its main competitors.

The Panel of Experts

A brief questionnaire (table 7) was designed and sent by email to that group of entrepreneurs, in order to act as an expert panel. The main objective is to compare the results obtained from the indicators with what these entrepreneurs know/expect in terms of their social media performance.

Table 7. Questions (and sub-questions) considered

1) a) From the behaviors heard on social networks, did you make changes to the products and services? b) Why? c) Which ones?
2) a) In addition to likes and clicks, were there conversions, that is, did they sell more? b) In which situations? c) How much did your return increase (%)?
3) a) Do you analyze user perception patterns regarding your digital marketing actions? b) Which KPI do you now focus on from this knowledge?
4) a) What % of marketing outsourcing do you ask to influencers? b) Has it increased?
5) a) Do you integrate channels (Youtube, Instagram, Facebook, website…) to capture *touch points* the customer has used? b) What strategies do you have on this issue?

This research technique is usually applied in psychology, and social sciences in general, especially in investigations that include more than one technique. It intends to show the importance of including the view of specialists in studies of multidetermined phenomena (Pinheiro et al., 2013). The specialist represents a specific perspective on the subject, to be integrated with other views. In the period from May 19 to July 31 2020, 7 responses were obtained from these companies: Growme (3 experts answered), Dengun, Algardata, Visualforma, and VAN. The company Made2web did not answer the questionnaire on time. Table 8 resumes the results obtained where columns represent the variables analyzed through the main five questions asked:

Table 8. Resume of answers (as topics) to the questionnaire used

firms/ questions	changing products from listening to social networks	conversions (sales, orders)	social media KPI	outsourcing of digital influencers	Channel integration
Growme	cheaper web design solutions; adaptation of the language used	low	click-through rate, average visit duration, cost per click, leads, number of visited pages	low	yes, to increase user's perception of online presence of the brand
Dengun	changes in the strategies implemented, meeting the new market needs	fewer campaigns related to tourism and hotels, but increased conversions from e-commerce platforms	engagement rate, reach, leads, *marketing qualified leads*, *sales-accepted leads*, *sales-qualified leads*, CPL (*cost per lead*), CPC (*cost per conversion*)	—	yes, they do customer journey mapping using platforms like Hubspot
Algardata	focus on the products that received most attention	especially in products to respond to the pandemic (sales >10%)	campaign clicks, shares	—	yes, especially LinkedIn and Youtube
Visualforma	meeting the market needs	leads generation (sales >10%)	common KPIs (did not specify)	—	not yet
VAN	meeting the market needs	sold more (>20%)	focus on reach, average interaction, % monthly growth	some	yes (did not specify)

I2) which new strategies came from this quantitative assessment of the KPI used?

It appears that Growme shows a lower *maturity* in terms of its social media performance and return. It has a more *adaptive strategy* and does little to exploit certain key indicators. Thus, measures that increase conversions, relevant to the commercial realization of digital marketing initiatives, go unnoticed. Other respondent firms present a greater number and variety of social media metrics explored, such as Dengun and Algardata. This table also shows that most mature companies in terms of social media are further ahead in the integration of digital channels (touchpoints) to follow/support the customer, resulting in a better consumer experience. So they are more likely to follow a *proactive digital strategy*. A common aspect is the low (or absent) outsourcing to digital influencers, a practice that has recently increased. Facing the level of demand and response speed currently required in the area, internal digital marketing is lacking pace and resources.

The comparison of the KPI used with the answers from the experts has revealed the still low maturity of Growme in terms of social media performance. This company can take more advantage from social media marketing by knowing how to relate more effectively with the target audience to deliver the desired value. Thus, assessing the right social media KPI has become a strategic goal. By focusing on the most relevant ones – or the *smart* KPI - the company will be able to better track what is wrong and work better in its campaigns (Lyfe, 2019).

Smart KPI

Smart KPI will make it easier for an enterprise to work consistently toward its goals and audience over time. They will help to create specific and data-driven social media reports for all its social media activities. Some of these KPI are:

Customer Satisfaction Score

This metric shows how 'happy' followers are with the brand's products or services. This data can be collected through a Twitter poll or Facebook survey, asking a simple question such as: How would you describe your satisfaction with this product? Depending on how the poll is defined, respondents would rate their satisfaction either numerically or through descriptors.

Net Promoter Score

This metric measures followers' loyalty. Using a poll or survey on the firm's social networks, a question can be asked such as: How would you recommend this product to a friend? Again, this can be answered using a numerical scale or through descriptors.

Smart KPI involve using monitoring and analytical tools. This means resorting to tools as built-in analytics features of social media platforms. All major social networks have basic solutions for tracking social media performance. Thus, social media managers can use Instagram Insights, Facebook Insights, Twitter Analytics, LinkedIn Analytics and YouTube Analytics. Other tool refers to the customer report which involve compiling social media KPI into a single easy-to-read document for a team and its supervisors. A customer report requires the data collected across the firm's different social channels. It should be visual and understandable, including charts to demonstrate how it is meeting the brand's business goals.

Thus, if a firm's social media strategy involves managing multiple accounts on numerous platforms, it is increasingly relevant to use a social media management tool to track its KPI. An example is Hootsuite which tracks performance analytics for all social channels collectively (or individually) and organizes the data into comprehensive reports. Its interface is interactive, as one can simply drag and drop all of the elements to develop it, as a single dashboard.

Today, social media monitoring platforms strongly contribute to shape competitive digital businesses. Marketing, customer service and research teams from across the digital businesses industry are demanding the firms' services to create insightful social media reports and deliver better customer service on daily basis. The list of monitoring tools includes competitors such as Brandwatch, Simplify360, Radian6, Sysomos and Meltwater, which help digital businesses to understand their social reach through influencer partnerships and marketing efforts based on rich audience data. Brandwatch is a social intelligence company with tools such as conversation listening and sentiment analysis that collect data from over 80 million online sources (Brandwatch, 2022). The monitoring platform provides insights that can then be used to check the conformity of campaigns, develop more targeted marketing, and understand customer profiles, demographics, and social activity.

For instance, it recently issued a public report on the consumer packaged goods (CPG) sector with basis on how the conversation around products is shifting. With global inflation impacting buying habits for all areas of the CPG industry, understanding consumer sentiment towards different products is vital for brands. Also, with repeat custom sitting at the center of this industry, social data provides key insights into what drives a customer to repurchase.

These trends increasingly require the use of qualitative analysis due to the kind of this data (unstructured data). That is why a qualitative assessment followed the quantitative analysis.

Qualitative Assessment

It is essential to take advantage of the potential of social media for companies to derive a greater return on their marketing investments. Thus, with the idea of deepening the previous analysis, a qualitative assessment was developed. It is based on a content analysis of the answers to the questionnaire used. The objective is to compare what those leaders expect in terms of performance of their social networks, especially in the current context.

In the case of Growme, three employees responded because this work is centered on an internship report at this company. Thus, the questionnaire was given to two managing partners and a responsible for customer management. There were two main reasons for choosing the other companies (Algardata, Visualforma, Van, Dengun): 1) their proximity to the company where the internship took place; and 2) the popularity of these companies (market leading companies).

Codification of Answers

In Nvivo, a software used for qualitative analysis, encoding is one of several techniques to help make sense from available data. Manage coding depends on the research design used. Coding the sample content into topics (themes) produces the *nodes*. This is essential in most qualitative projects, as it organizes the material gathered into general themes. When opening a node in Nvivo, all its content is shown. It can include texts, audio, videos, images, etc. It can also be linked to a memo field that describes aspects to be analyzed there, or even be recoded into another node. On the other hand, the *cases* are the responses of the companies under study.

Regarding the expert panel, when asked about changes in their behaviors, the following chart shows the references they made to the questions sent (topics/nodes):

Figure 1. Number of references to the topics in the questionnaire

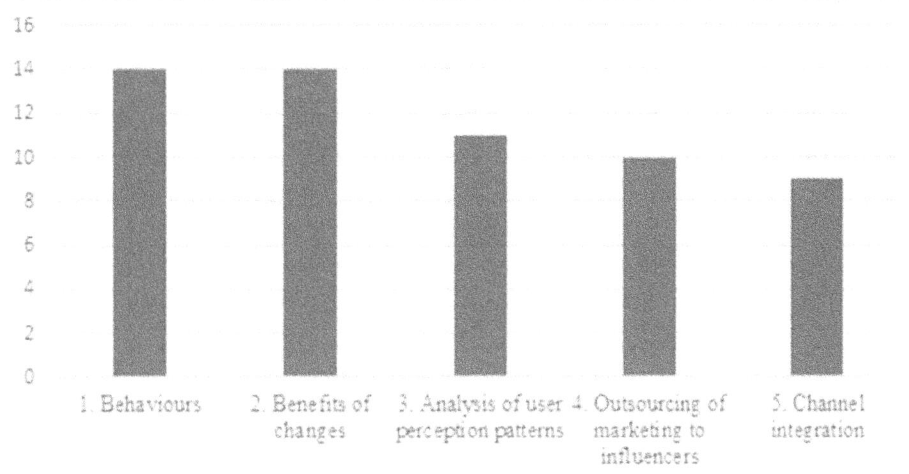

This figure shows that the highest number of references are related with, either changes in products/services, or benefits of changes (sales, feedback). Then comes the customer perception (reactions on social networks and KPI). Such references (i.e., number of respondents that referred a certain topic) do not mean that the respective companies do it in practice, but that they have talked about it and recognize its importance. Then the analysis continued in order to include more outputs, such as the word clouds and their comparison with respondents' answers.

Content Analysis

The word clouds obtained (table 9) reflect that Growme focused more on the role of digital marketing in sales and solutions; Algardata and Visualforma focused more on products and conversions; Dengun, besides conversions, on leads; and Van on products and behaviors.

Table 9. Frequency of terms in the word clouds

Respondent company	Higher (*lower*) frequencies of terms used
Growme (Cláudio Barbosa)	Marketing, increased, outsourcing, pandemic (*behaviors, conversions, analyze*)
Growme (Frederico Honrado)	Marketing, increased, services, customers, sales (*likes, conversions, analyze, listen*)
Growme (Ivo Pontes)	Marketing, increased, website, solutions (*behaviors, influencers, conversions, integration, leverage*)
Algardata (Juan Correia)	Marketing, increased, products, conversions, changes (*influencers, campaign, capture, indicators, channels, clicks*)
Dengun (Maxine Leal)	Marketing, increased, leads, journey, changes, conversions (*channels, campaign, capture, collaborate, commerce*)
Van (Pedro Rosa)	Marketing, increased, products, behaviors, changes (*channels, influencers, services, indicators, perception, integration, performance*)
Visualforma (Ana Parra)	Marketing, increased, products, channels, conversions (*perception, services, integration, indicators, performance, outsourcing, influencers*)

A common aspect is the fact that they all mention that their digital marketing has increased. Analyzing the experts' dialogues, more nuances could be detected:

Claudio Barbosa (Growme) agreed that there was a change in behavior on social media, which implied changes in products and services: "With the pandemic, we decided to put posts that demonstrate consumer behavior during this phase, and alert to the importance of digital marketing". Frederico Honrado (Growme) also noticed similar changes: "We created more economical web design solutions". The reason for such changes was: "We think that purchasing power may have been reduced. If there is a drop in income, we think that the money available for our services is less". Ivo Pontes (Growme) also observed changes in behavior on social networks: "Because we want to be in line with customer need, we adapted the language of the solutions so that people perceive us as specialists in certain areas".

Juan Correia (Algardata) considered that the changes were punctual and, therefore, depended on certain factors: "We made some changes, mainly focusing on the products that got the most attention". Maxine Leal (Dengun) also detected behavioral changes: "We essentially made changes in terms of strategies, meeting the new needs of the market". The representatives for Van and Visualforma also referred changes in the products adjusted to the current needs of customers.

Just like Mason's et al. (2021) study, the results obtained (considering table 9 of the most/least used terms and the experts' dialogues) show that consumers have increased their use of social media as a tool to find out about products' information, rate them and buy online. This determines a growing importance of digital marketing, what requires a more assertive strategy. This assertiveness can be nurtured by using smart KPI and qualitative assessments. Thus, this study has filled a gap in identifying either these two paths or purposing a research design/framework to do it.

Benefits of Changes

In the experts' dialogues, Claudio Barbosa (from Growme) detected that "There were more sales with the new website, but due to the pandemic, other customers end up canceling contracts". Thus, sales suffer a negative impact: "It turned out that there were no significant increases". Frederico Honrado, from the same company, noted that "The vast majority of our customers sold less". However, he recalled "a customer who has an online store of decorative wallpaper that increased its sales by about 100%". Ivo Pontes detected the benefits of the change in marketing, but he had no way of proving the improvement through concrete data.

Juan Correia (from Algardata) confirmed that "The conversions took place mainly in products to respond to the pandemic", and he quantified the improvement: "The percentage of increase in sales was approximately 10%". Maxine Leal (from Dengun) considered that the improvement in sales "depends on the business area"; he explained that "during the pandemic, we naturally felt a reduction in campaigns related to tourism and hospitality sectors. At the same time, we have seen an increase in conversions from e-commerce platforms".

Regarding KPI, Ana Parra (from Visualforma) states that "we use common KPI", without specifying which ones. And she adds "we don't do channel integration because we haven't connected them yet". For Van, Pedro Rosa says "we focus on reach, total interaction, average interaction per publication and gross % of growth each month".

Comparing these answers with the word clouds obtained, there is a higher "maturity" in Dengun and Algardata as they reflect the use of more KPI to quantify results in business. This can express a higher experience in SN performance. The use of more advanced metrics can help thinking of new digital strategies such as omnichannel, e-business, and influencer outsourcing. These practices have growing importance since, with the demand and speed of response currently required, in-house digital marketing is not sufficient.

The quantitative and qualitative assessments made reveal a different 'maturity level' in terms of social media performance. Compared to its competitors (market leaders in the area), Growme denotes a more *adaptive* strategy. The other companies analyzed (especially Dengun and Algardata) have a more *proactive* strategy. What does this mean?

Having thousands of likes or clicks can be irrelevant if the company does not engage through its brands and products. Its efforts have not been directed to their greatest potential. Better engagement indicators are shares, comments, leads and conversions as they make possible to move on to consume the related goods/services. Examples of conversions are sales, orders, reservations, etc. Monitoring this involvement, and the consequent product innovation, can help provide the answers that consumers are really looking for. These forms of active involvement will allow firms to have greater returns from their SN performance.

The present work helps to rethink the strategy companies apply to publish on their channels. Hence, there must be a digital marketing plan that includes specific metrics (Appel et al., 2020). Social media is truly a valuable, low-cost source of customer voice, allowing companies to fine-tune their digital marketing activities. They can be used as public relations and promotional tools, or as means that allow customers to personalize their online experience and the products they purchase. This is even more intensified through mobile media (mobile devices and related apps). Managers must be aware of this wellspring, and the underlying communication strategies, to improve their digital experience (Junusi, 2020). They need to rethink their business model in the face of these trends in order, not to be mere spectators, but effective agents of social/economic change.

Other Trends

Most social media posts (on Facebook, Twitter, etc.) were text before. Soon these platforms allowed the publication of photos and then videos. Separate platforms have dedicated to these last forms of media, such as: Instagram and Pinterest for photos; Instagram and Snapchat for short videos. Scholars suggest that image-based publications convey a greater social presence than just text (Pittman and Reich, 2016). High-quality shot pictures consistently lead to higher engagement on social platforms for most product categories. The presence of human face and image-text fit can induce higher user engagement (Li and Xie, 2019).

However, several new technologies on the market suggest that the future of social media will be richer in sensory. A notable technology that has already started to infiltrate social networks is augmented reality (AR). Examples of it are the Snapchat filters, which use a camera to create real-time visual and/or video overlays on a person's face. Other social media players quickly joined AR and VR (Virtual reality), such as Instagram (Rao, 2017). Besides AR technologies, which bring visual and interactive richness, other developments insert audible features. A new player - HearMeOut - recently launched a platform that allows users to share and listen to audio posts (Perry, 2018). The use of "hands-free" social networks not only allows us to interact in multitasking, but the voice also adds greater authenticity (Katai, 2018).

Future research will investigate how professionals can use such tools to improve their interactions with customers and their offerings (Shahid & Li, 2019). Significant challenges exist for organizations and marketers as they develop digital strategies and brand awareness within the modern era of social media communication (SMC). The opportunities of SMC give access to a wide and diverse customer base. Marketers need to develop their strategies alongside a deeper analysis of digital behaviors (Dwivedi et al., 2021). Also, the marketing function will have a more holistic customer experience and personalized customer journey, leading to greater brand engagement and return through increased sales and brand loyalty.

The use of AR-driven interaction offers significant advantages for marketers and increased scope for customer engagement. But the ethical dimension and subsequent trust from consumers are key issues in its wider use. Also, key aspects of privacy and security will be crucial for organizations in developing their digital media strategies (Mandal, 2019).

According to recent articles and reports (Social 2021; NBBJ, 2022) other social media trends are to: use short videos (ex: Tiktok; Youtube clips; Instagram reels) as strong engaging forms of content for a wider reach; follow influencers as they give insight into what trends are there; have understandable, compelling and dynamic content; be in the social platforms where the target audience is spending the majority of time; plan and build social media shopping/commerce because it is easier to purchase directly on these integrated platforms and there is a wider target audience (ex: Instagram shopping; Facebook Marketplace); incorporate marketing and advertising with AR/VR; use social platforms for social responsibility initiatives and for hybrid events (online/ offline); and also foresee the upcoming social media channels.

CONCLUSION

By bringing together findings from the current work and the views from reputable experts in the country, this research offers a reflection to practitioners in the form of opportunities, as well as questions, that can help researchers toward advancing knowledge in this domain.

Due to the pandemic, there is an increasing digital approach to activities and business. One challenge is to learn how to benefit from social media potential. For instance, it entails the 'wisdom of the crowd' which is driving major businesses and impacting the way of life. Social networks are privileged vehicles to generate rich data with multi-faceted insights to drive faster ideation and launching client-centric innovations (Bhimani et al., 2019). Research on social media adoption and the extent of its usage is still at its infancy (Bhimani et al., 2019; Barlatier and Mention, 2020).

The main goal of this work was to analyze and evaluate a company's social media performance, during an internship, with special focus on Facebook and Instagram. These are two major social networks, with thousands of fans. But other choice factors are the increasing value and complementarity of these visual-social platforms. The originality of this work is the systematic joint of most relevant social media performance metrics.

It appears that the company in study could enhance the performance of its social media and associated return. In the period considered for analysis, it has revealed a more adaptive strategy with low exploitation of relevant key indicators. A panel of experts, including main competitors in the region, ended up revealing that the company is missing measures that contribute to conversions (commercial realization of various initiatives). Having thousands of followers (through likes/clicks) can be irrelevant, if they are not engaged with the brand and its products.

In other words, the company's digital efforts may not be oriented to its greatest potential. Relevant engagement indicators are leads, shares, comments, among others. For instance, comments give a more assertive insight of what followers/visitors think about the firm and its services. Thus, if well explored, this indicator contributes to effectively purchase products/ services. And then this generates sales, orders, reservations, etc., depending on the sector. Also, monitoring this engagement helps to give followers the answers they really want what improves company's reputation. Conversions and other forms of active engagement with brands enable firms to achieve greater returns. Social networks are truly a valuable, low-cost live voice for customers, allowing companies to fine-tune their marketing activities. They can also be used as promotional tools, influential tools or tools that allow customers to personalize their online experience and the products they choose.

Portugal, whose business tissue is mostly composed of SME (small and medium-sized enterprises), should take advantage of what Borah, Iqbal and Akhtar (2022) observed, that social media usage can enhance their performance when mediated by innovation capabilities and digital leadership. Thus, the present work highlights the need to rethink the type of content firms publish on their social media channels. And monitoring them is crucial to rethink the objectives of their campaigns and what they seek to achieve. This can be further developed within mobile social media (mobile devices/apps). Mobile advertising is now imperative to reach the younger generation. This will lead to new ways of communicating and promoting products, services, and brands. In addition, robust social media analytics can help firms not only to build brand awareness, but also to create value and achieve competitive advantage (Akter et al., 2016).

Managers must be fully aware of these trends, and the underlying communication strategies, to engage customers and improve their digital presence. Many firms have already changed their business models to be social media agents, and not mere spectators. To do so, they have deepened the assessment of the referred social media trends.

REFERENCES

Akter, S., Bhattacharyya, M., Wamba, S., & Aditya, S. (2016). How does Social Media Analytics create value? *Journal of Organizational and End User Computing*, *28*(3), 1–9. doi:10.4018/JOEUC.2016070101

Appel, G., Grewal, L., Hadi, R., & Stephen, A. T. (2020). The future of social media in marketing. *Journal of the Academy of Marketing Science*, *48*(1), 79–95. doi:10.100711747-019-00695-1 PMID:32431463

Barlatier, P., & Mention, A. (2020). How social media can fuel innovation in businesses: A strategic roadmap. *The Journal of Business Strategy*, *41*(2), 11–18. doi:10.1108/JBS-12-2018-0197

Bhimani, H., Mention, A., & Barlatier, P. (2019). Social media and innovation: A systematic literature review and future research directions. *Technological Forecasting and Social Change*, *144*, 251–269. doi:10.1016/j.techfore.2018.10.007

Borah, P., Iqbal, S., & Akhtar, S. (2022). Linking social media usage and SME's sustainable performance: The role of digital leadership and innovation capabilities. *Technology in Society*, *68*, 101900. doi:10.1016/j.techsoc.2022.101900

Brandwatch. (2022). Buying habits and trends for the consumer packaged goods industry. *Brandwatch.* https://www.brandwatch.com/reports/cpg-consumer-trends/view/

Cardoso, S. (2020). *Google Ads - Adquira os clientes certos para o seu negócio.* Webinar organizado pela NEST - Centro de Inovação do Turismo.

Chu, S. (2011). Viral advertising in social media: Participation in Facebook groups and responses among college-aged users. *Journal of Interactive Advertising, 12*(1), 30–43. doi:10.1080/15252019.2011.10722189

Desai, D. (2019). Digital marketing: A review. *International Journal of Trend in Scientific Research and Development*, 196-200.

Dwivedi, Y., Ismagilova, E., Hughes, D., Carlson, J., Filieri, R., Jacobson, J., Jain, V., Karjaluoto, H., Kefi, H., Krishen, A., Kumar, V., Rahman, M., Raman, R., Rauschnabel, P., Rowley, J., Salo, J., Tran, G., & Wang, Y. (2021). Setting the future of digital and social media marketing research: Perspectives and research propositions. *International Journal of Information Management, 59*, 102168. doi:10.1016/j.ijinfomgt.2020.102168

Grave, J. (2019). What KPIs Are Key. Evaluating Performance Metrics for Social Media Influencers. *Social Media + Society, 5*(3), 1–9. doi:10.1177/2056305119865475

Junusi, R. (2020). Digital marketing during the pandemic period; A study of islamic perspective. *Journal of Digital Marketing and Halal Industry, 2*(1), 150–28. doi:10.21580/jdmhi.2020.2.1.5717

Katai, L. (2018). 3 Reasons why audio will conquer all social media. *Adweek.* https://www.adweek.com/performance-marketing/3-reasons-why-audio-will-conquer-social-media/

KPI.ORG. (2022). What is a Key Performance Indicator (KPI)? *KPI.* https://kpi.org/KPI-Basics

Li, Y., & Xie, Y. (2019). Is a picture worth a thousand words? An empirical study of image content and social media engagement. *JMR, Journal of Marketing Research, 57*(1), 1–19. doi:10.1177/0022243719881113

Lyfe. (2019). 12 Social media KPIs you should not ignore. *Lyfe Marketing.* https://www.lyfemarketing.com/blog/social-media-kpis/

Mandal, P. (2019). Public policy issues in direct and digital marketing - concerns and initiatives: Public policy in direct and digital marketing. *International Journal of Public Administration in the Digital Age, 6*(4), 54–71. doi:10.4018/IJPADA.2019100105

Martin, N. (2019). Why utilizing data in your digital marketing strategy is so essential. https://www.forbes.com/sites/nicolemartin1/2019/10/22/why-utilizing-data-in-your-digital-marketing-strategy-is-so-essential/?sh=4821dbedd525

Mason, A., Narcum, J., & Mason, K. (2021). Social media marketing gains importance after Covid-19. *Cogent Business & Management, 8*(1), 1870797. doi:10.1080/23311975.2020.1870797

NBBJ. (2022). *Social media is evolving quickly, and your business needs to also.* NBBJ. https://www.northbaybusinessjournal.com/article/industrynews/social-media-is-evolving-quickly-and-your-business-needs-to-also/

Perry, E. (2018). Meet HearMeOut: the social media platform looking to bring audio back into the mainstream. *HearMeOut.* https://tinyurl.com/y8yxbzah

Pinheiro, J., Farias, T., & Abe-Lima, J. (2013). Painel de especialistas e estratégia multimétodos: Reflexões, exemplos, perspectivas. *PSICO*, *44*(2), 184–192.

Pittman, M., & Reich, B. (2016). Social media and loneliness: Why an Instagram picture may be worth more than a thousand twitter words. *Computers in Human Behavior*, *62*, 155–167. doi:10.1016/j.chb.2016.03.084

Rao, L. (2017). Instagram copies Snapchat once again with face filters. *Fortune.* https://tinyurl.com/ybcuxxdv

Rietveld, R., Dolen, W., Mazloom, M., & Masoud, M. (2019). What You Feel, Is What You Like influence of message appeals on customer engagement on Instagram. *Journal of Interactive Marketing*, *49*(1), 20–53. doi:10.1016/j.intmar.2019.06.003

Rudd, J., Hooley, G., Piercy, N., & Nicoulaud, B. (2017). *Marketing strategy and competitive positioning*. Pearson.

Shahid, M. Z., & Li, G. (2019). Impact of Artificial Intelligence in Marketing: A Perspective of Marketing Professionals of Pakistan. *Global Journal of Management and Business Research*, *19*(2), 27–33.

Social (2021), Social media marketing trends for 2022. https://www.zoho.com/social/journal/social-media-marketing-trends-2022.html

Sormaz, J., Kuzmanovic, M., & Jeremic, V. (2019). Customer preferences towards digital marketing strategies. In *Economics of Digital Transformation*, 507-526.

Sudarsanam, S. K. (2017). Social media metrics. In R. Raghavendra (Ed.), *Social media listening and monitoring for business applications* (pp. 131–149). IGI Global. doi:10.4018/978-1-5225-0846-5.ch007

KEY TERMS AND DEFINITIONS

Change: It is the process that can alter the factors that highly influence an enterprise in terms of its offers, strategy, and innovation. The continual improvement of processes and/or technologies, and their diffusion, can nurture or stimulate a higher level of change.

Digital Business: It is a business model which keeps up with the latest updates and facts regarding digitalization. Some of the technologies that mostly support it are: Artificial Intelligence, Virtual Reality, Augmented Reality, Blockchain, Internet of Things (IoT), etc.

Digital Marketing: It is the field of marketing whose works evolve around the web (with website creation, social media, online ads, etc.). The transition to the online world has started this way of promoting brands' products and services.

KPI (Key Performance Indicators): These are the critical indicators of progress toward an intended result. They have a focus on what matters most in terms of improvement and create an analytical basis for decision making.

Social Media: It is the set of online communication channels dedicated to community-based interactions, content sharing, and collaboration. It is considered one of the most important ways for companies to achieve a high level of brand awareness and succeed with their customers.

Social Network: It is a website that allows people to come together and share information, photos, videos, etc. Some engage on social networking as a personal endeavor to interact or discuss their lives/ interests. Other use it for business purposes, especially marketing.

Value Creation: It is the process of turning resources into something that meets the needs/ interests of others (customers, investors, employees, etc.). In today's world, it is more related with intangible assets such as brands, ideas, people, and innovation. Therefore, it is a better management tool than mere financial measures.

Chapter 5
Anxiety, Reactions, and Economic Expectations of University Students in the Effect of the COVID-19 Pandemic:
Survey Evidence from Turkey

Ramazan Gökbunar
Manisa Celal Bayar University, Turkey

Füsun Küçükbay
Manisa Celal Bayar University, Turkey

ABSTRACT

The current survey study was designed to explore the mental health status, reactions, concerns, and expectations of university students during the COVID-19 pandemic, and the potential relationships between mental health and their reactions and macroeconomic expectations. The results show that the student's mental health worsened during Covid-19 which accelerated their pessimism, causing a decline in their academic success and purchases, and causing an increase in their negative expectations about macroeconomic indicators. The results also show that concerns about the economy, financial situation, and future are associated with mental deterioration. The analysis reveals that the most prevalent concern among the students is anxiety about the future. Moreover, gender, educational level, and income level also significantly impact the reactions and the macroeconomic expectations of the students.

DOI: 10.4018/978-1-6684-7509-6.ch005

INTRODUCTION

Covid-19 was first identified in China in the last months of 2019. Since then, it spread all over the world and caused several health problems, deaths, and several other problems. As Covid-19 spreads around the world, it is important to understand its impacts on young adults. However, the impacts worsened in many areas as the pandemic became a global threat.

Beyond the risk of getting sick or dying, the pandemic has consequences in many aspects, especially in psychological, social, and economic issues. Previous studies in the literature (Leduc & Liu, 2016), Born et al (2019) Beaudry & Portier (2006) have shown that new shocks will cause great fluctuations in economy. Unlike other crises, Covid-19 pandemic posed a sudden shock and spread rapidly. The fluctuations in economy caused shocking effects on individuals. Covid-19 pandemic is unprecedented and more global and more impactful compared to other crises such as 2008 economic crisis or flu pandemics. Therefore, the decision-makers, individuals, nor the governments have ever experienced such a health crisis. Several aspects of human concerns, belief, expectations, and reactions are updated in the unprecedented environment of Covid-19 pandemic. To understand the shock effects of pandemic on individuals is an important issue. This pandemic is unprecedented; however, new epidemics are expected from now on. Further, the pandemic is reaching new peak levels day by day and thus, the individuals are continuously exposed to further rising threats. In this study, we tried to collect data providing promising information to assess the mental health of the students, their concerns, reactions, and the macroeconomic expectations.

Determining the psychological anxiety levels, reactions, and macro expectations of the students during a health crisis might help in learning lessons from the pandemic and in avoiding losses. Covid-19 pandemic is an urgent problem. Therefore, this study wants to shed light to the mental health, concerns, reactions, and macroeconomic expectations of students during Covid-19 pandemic. This paper first investigates the mental health status of university students during the pandemic and describes the concerns of the students about their household finances, economy and about their future, as well as the effects of their concerns on their own mental health. The paper also tries to quantify the reactions and the macroeconomic expectations of the students, which are very important for the policymakers. The changes in their academic success and in their spending are evaluated to analyze the reactions of the students during Covid-19. Further, the expectations of the students on gross domestic product growth (GDP growth) and inflation are questioned in order to explore their expectations about macroeconomic issues. Lastly, this paper demonstrates how the students' characteristics and mental health affect their reactions and macroeconomic expectations.

The individuals are updating their beliefs, reactions, and expectations in the effect of this unprecedented pandemic. We must learn our lessons from this. The full impact of pandemic on the individuals is still unclear, but understanding the basis of mental health situation, reactions, and the macroeconomic expectations of the university students may shed some light on preparedness for the pandemic. The studies about the impacts of the pandemic assist us in terms of being more prepared to what lies ahead. Limited number of studies have been done with respect to Covid-19 pandemic. Some studies analyze the effects on the economy by presenting publicly available data (Özatay & Sak, 2020, Acar 2020, Telli, & Altun, 2020, Fernandes, 2020, Auray & Eyquem, 2020). Some research papers suggest several critical measures to consider in controlling its spread such as travel restrictions (Chinazzi et al, 2020), social distancing (Heymann & Shindo, 2020). Some studies provide an overall analysis of the Covid-19 pandemic such as preparedness of public health (Mustapha et al, 2020), trust in public health policies (Bargain & Aminjonov,

2020) or inequality in the impact of pandemic (Adams-Prassl et al, 2020) Some studies have analyzed the impact of the Covid-19 pandemic on economy or on firms by conducting survey analysis confined to countries such as USA and China (Binder, 2020, Dietrich et al, 2020, Knotek, et al., 2020, Zou, 2020, Altig et al 2020, Kim et al 2021). Some studies have only evaluated the mental health of individuals and their experiences (Bostan et al, 2020, Sayeed et al 2020, Qiu et al, 2020, Cao et al, 2020, Aucejo et al 2020, Vaterlaus et al, 2021, Li et al, 2021, Gittings et al 2021, Kiebler & Stewart, 2021). We employ a survey analysis to assess the mental health situation, concerns, reactions, and expectations of young adults who are exposed to traumatic change during covid-19 period. Understanding the perceptions and thoughts of young adults is important because they are among the most influential segment on the demand side of the country's economy. This study is confined to Turkey.

The remainder of the paper is organized as follows. The second section gives information about the method and the survey design. Third part is devoted to the survey results. The characteristics of the survey sample introduced, the mental health situation, concerns, reactions of the students, predictors of mental deteriorations, reactions and expectations are analyzed in this part. Fourth part discusses the results. The last part is devoted to the limitations and a conclusion of results.

BACKGROUND AND METHOD

Survey Description

The data of the study came from the survey of the university students in Turkey. Survey methods assist to describe the situation as it happens (Cohen et al 2007), thus it is a convenient method to understand the mental health situation, concerns, reactions, and expectations of the students.

In March 2020, the higher education institutions in Turkey announced that the studies would be held online in order to mitigate covid-19 pandemic. The survey has been informed to students through mails and messages, and they were invited to participate in an online survey.

We ran the survey on May 6 and May 11, 2021, to convey the demographics, psychological health, experiences, concerns, and expectations of the students in the influence of Covid-19 pandemic. It was created in Google Forms.

It is important to note that at the time we conducted the survey, the impacts of Covid-19 spread widely in Turkey and school closures, many businesses' closures and stay-at home orders were already in force. We are in the third wave of Covid-19 pandemic since March 2021. World Health Organization drew attention to increases of anxiety and stress within the context of Covid-19 pandemic (WHO, 2020). This conduces us to study the relationship between the mental health and the concerns & macroeconomic expectations of students.

Descriptive statistics are used to illustrate the demographic and other answers of the participants. An ordered probit regression is used to explore the relationship between demographic characteristics, their concerns with mental health and their mental health with their reactions and macroeconomic expectations in the influence of Covid-19. The ordered probit method is used when the dependent variable is ordered (Jeffrey, 2009).

Sample Size and Population

The sample population comprised of university students in Turkey. Data were collected through an online questionnaire. In the study, we tried to assess the mental health, concerns, reactions, and macroeconomic expectations of the students during Covid-19 pandemic. 2936 students who completed the questionnaires were accepted as a sample population (%100).

Questionnaire

The questionnaire of the study comprised of a structured format. The survey begins with the basic questions about education level, gender, household income and whether they have been infected by Covid-19 disease and how closely they follow the news about Covid-19.

The questionnaire was pretested to make all necessary adjustments. The purpose of the survey was informed to all participants in the beginning.

The students were inquired about their anxiety level, attention, concerns, reactions, and macroeconomic expectations during Covid-19 pandemic.

Their anxiety level is evaluated by using the 7-item Generalized Anxiety Disorder Scale (GAD-7). The 7- item Generalized Anxiety Disorder Scale inquires information about how much the respondents suffer from the seven core symptoms within the last 15 days. GAD-7 takes very little to answer and is easy to score. GAD-7 is available for free on www.phqscreeners.coms with about 70 translations. The scale consists of 7 symptoms and the participants answer 7 questions using a 4-item Likert scale. The 4-item Likert scale ranges from not at all (0) to almost every day (3). The sum of the answers varies between 0 and 21 points. The 5, 10 and 15 points are used for discrimination of mild, moderate, and severe anxiety levels (Spitzer et al., 2006).

The GAD-7 is an accepted instrument which has strong internal consistency (Cao et al, 2020). Cronbach's alpha coefficient is checked for the reliability analysis. According to the result of the reliability statistics, Cronbach alpha resulted a value of 0.922 which shows that GAD-7 scale was highly reliable (Kalaycı, 2016).

Many of the survey questions inquiring the attention, concerns, reactions and macroeconomic expectations of the students have been formed based on Dietrich et. al (2020), Binder (2020) and Aucejo et al (2020).

MAIN FOCUS OF THE CHAPTER AND RESULTS

The frequency distribution of selected characteristics and experiences of the sample are summarized in Table 1. 70,5% of the sample are undergraduate students; whereas, 24,4% are associate degree and 5,1% graduate level students. 57% of the sample is female. Big portion of the sample have a household income of below 10.000TL (45,9% below 3.000 and 48,9% between 3.000 and 10.000 TL).

Table 1. Frequency distribution of selected variables

Variable	N	%		N	%
1. Educational Level			**5. Have you been diagnosed with Covid-19 or have you ever been followed up?**		
Associate degree	716	24,4	Diagnosed with Covid-19	368	12,5
Undergraduate degree	2072	70,5	Followed up for contact with Covid-19 patient	404	13,8
Graduate degree	148	5,1	None	2164	73,7
2. Gender			**6. The effect of on-line learning on the student's academic success**		
Female	1683	57,3	Better	715	24,4
Male	1253	42,7	Same	964	32,8
			Worse	1257	42,8
4. Household income			7. **Have your or any family member experienced a job loss?**		
<3000 TL	1349	45,9	Yes	1327	44,9
3000-10.000TL	1435	48,9	No	1609	54,4
10.001-20.000TL	142	4,8	**6. Following the news about the Covid-19**		
>20.000TL	10	0,3	Not closely	144	4,9
			Somewhat closely	1256	42,9
			Very closely	1536	52,3

According to the results 12,5% of the sample is diagnosed with Covid-19 and 13,5% of the sample is followed up for the contact with Covid-19 diagnosed patient. 2164 students (73% of the sample) were neither diagnosed with Covid-19 nor followed up.

Since March 2020, the classes in universities are held online to mitigate covid-19 pandemic. The students were asked how their academic success has been affected from online education. 42,8% reported that they are negatively affected from online education.

The students were also asked how closely they have been following the news about Covid-19. Big portion (42,9% somewhat closely, 52,3% very closely) of the students stated to be following the news somewhat closely or very closely.

Anxiety Level of the Students

One of the most common mental disorders is the anxiety disorder. GAD-7 is the mostly used scale to diagnose anxiety levels in research (Toussaint et al., 2020). Table 2 shows the results of GAD-7 scale and provides information about the mental health of university students. 21,4% of the students do not show any symptoms of anxiety. The remaining of the sample has mild (27,1%), moderate (28,3%) and severe (23,1%) anxiety symptoms.

Table 2. Anxiety levels of the students

Anxiety Level	N	Ratio (%)
Normal	628	21,4
Mild	797	27,1
Moderate	832	28,3
Severe	679	23,1
Total	2.936	

This survey indicated that 78,5% of university students were afflicted with anxiety during the COVID-19 pandemic. 23,1% of those experienced severe anxiety, and 28,3% moderate anxiety. This might have been caused by absence of interpersonal relations because of quarantines, future employment concerns and physical health concerns (Xiao, 2020, Cao et al, 2020). World Health Organization (WHO) also warned about mental disorders as well as physical health concerns due to economical causes, homeschooling and lack of physical contact with people including even family members during the pandemic period (WHO,2020). Nergüz (2004) found a positive relationship between university students' anxiety levels and mental health deterioration.

One of the questions in the survey is as follows: 'How is your mental health compared to the period prior to Covid-19 (better, same, worse)'. Figure 1 shows students' mental health situation compared to pre-Covid-19 period'. Most (67%) of the students' mental health has worsened during the pandemic.

Figure 1. Mental health of students compared to pre-Covid-19 pandemic

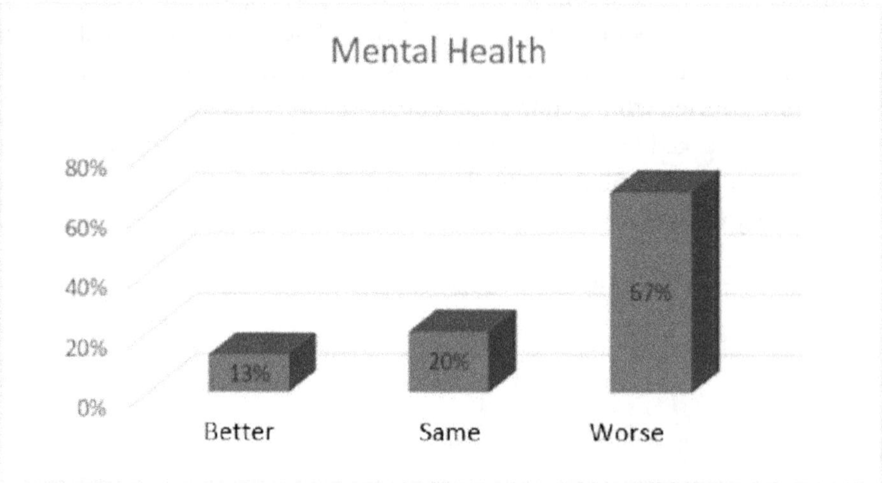

The results show that the students' mental health is affected from Covid-19 pandemic in a negative way. Barreira et al's study (2018) reveals that the students having goals to accomplish and those having the chance to make positive contributions to people and the ones having the feeling of being useful to others poses better mental health.

Advisors, who communicate with the students frequently and encourage them to be involved in meaningful activities can be assigned for each student in order to help them to mitigate effects of the pandemic.

Concerns and Reactions of Students Towards Covid-19 Pandemic

Figure 2 gives information about students' interest (the frequency of following the news about Covid-19 pandemic), concerns about the economy, household finance, future, and reactions (changes in academic success and changes in purchases) towards Covid-19 pandemic.

52,32% follow the news very closely and 43% somewhat closely. The majority (79,90%) of the students is very concerned about the economy whereas a smaller portion (40,19%) is very concerned for their household finances. The students are more concerned about the Turkish economy than their household finances.

Nearly all students (92,77%) are concerned in different levels about their future. Their future is the most prevalent concern among the students.

Zaleski (1996) refers the future concerns as "A state of fear and anxiety of an undesired situation expected to occur in the future.". Zaleski (1996) states that the future concerns are associated with the global conflicts which Covid-19 pandemic is a good example for. People tend to have higher future concerns in line with the increase in world problems. This is the result of a positive correlation between personal future concerns and pessimistic forecasts (Zaleski, 1996, Chlewinski, 1994).

Hammad (2016) states that the anxiety about the future increases in twenties which is the age of the university students. This result is due to the fact that at this age, people start to search for a job and are planning to have a family. Therefore, the students' high concern about their future during Covid-19 pandemic is consistent with recent research. Future anxiety of the students is associated with fears about the job and unclear future as a result of this unprecedented pandemic.

Further on the survey, students provide their reactions to Covid-19 pandemic. We posed the question: "Has there been a change in your purchases (more, same, less) and in your academic success (better, same, worse) in light of Covid-19 pandemic. 42,82% of the students declared a negative effect on their academic success compared to pre Covid-19 period. 56% of the students decreased their purchases during the pandemic. The reason of the decline in purchases and success might be the result of high future concerns and pessimistic forecasts. Previous studies reveal that there is a negative correlation between students' future concerns, academic achievement, and their motivation (Hammad, 2016).

Figure 2. The Students' Attention, Concerns and Reactions to Covid-19

Predictors of Deteriorations in Mental Health of University Students in Response to Covid-19 Pandemic

The ordered probit regressions have been applied to understand the factors of the deterioration in mental health of university students in response to Covid-19 pandemic. Table 3 conveys the predictors of the mental health of the students. University students concerned more about the economy, household finances and about future are experiencing worse mental health outcomes. This study indicates that concerns about the economy, financial situation and future are related to mental deterioration. More generally, students with higher levels of concern tend to have worse mental health (Jessop, 2020, Jessop et al, 2005).

Table 3. Predictors of deteriorations in mental health of university students

	Mental Health
Concern about Economy	0,14* (0,05)
Concern about Household Finances	0,30* (0,03)
Concern about Future	0,39* (0,02)
Not Diagnosed with Covid-19	-0,06** (0,03)
Not experiencing Job Loss	0,04 (0,04)
Following News	-0,01 (0,03)
N	2936
R^2 pseudo	0,08

*p<0,01, **p<0,05. Dependent variables in columns are ordinal variable (normal, mild, moderate, severe). Ordered probits model have been applied. Robust standard errors are in parentheses. Numbers not in parentheses are coefficients.

Like previous findings, students diagnosed with Covid or the ones who've had contact with a Covid patient tend to have worse mental health. (Cao et al 2020).

Following the news about the coronavirus or experiencing job loss does not statistically affect the mental health of the students. We are in a later stage of the pandemic, so it is acceptable that the pandemic news is accepted as a usual situation for the students. Students may not be affected by the news of Covid-19 as they are getting used to the related news on this topic.

To deal with unemployment, the Turkish government introduced stimulus packages such as short-term employment allowance, which is paid directly to employees. This incentive package is still ongoing. These types of employment-related measures may be helping the students to avoid deteriorations in their mental health concerning possible job loss.

Predictors of Reactions of The Students in Response to Covid-19 Pandemic

Table 4 conveys the predictors of the reactions of the students in response to Covid-19 pandemic. The ordered probit regressions have been applied to understand the predictors of the reactions.

Students with higher mental disorders tend to purchase less and experience a decline in their academic success compared to the period prior to the pandemic. More generally, students with higher mental disorders are more pessimistic both about financial situations and about how successful they are in their courses (Barreira et al, 2018, Hammad, 2016, Baldwin & Mauro, 2020).

Associate degree students are more likely to have less academic success compared to undergraduate and graduate students during Covid-19 pandemic. Consistent with previous studies (Binder, 2020), women are likely to make more purchases compared to men.

Students having higher household income have made more purchases and have better academic success compared to those having a lower income level. The negative correlation between income level and mental health support this result. Students with higher income level and a better mental health (low anxiety level) will be led to have better academic success (Barreira et al, 2018, Hammad, 2016, Baldwin & Mauro, 2020). Previous studies reveal that the individuals in a better financial situation are more optimistic (Meyler & Reiche, 2021). Similar to previous studies, students with higher income levels are more optimistic about the economy, allowing the students to make more purchases.

Table 4. Predictors of Reactions of Students during Covid-19 pandemic

	Purchases (1)	Success (2)
Mental Health	0,07* (0,02)	0,32* (0,02)
Education Level	0,01 (0,04)	-0,08** (0,04)
Female	-0,17* (0,05)	-0,01 (0,04)
Income	-0,37* (0,04)	-0,08** (0,04)
N	2936	2936
R^2 pseudo	0,02	0,05

*p<0,01, **p<0,05,. Dependent variables in columns are ordinal variables (changes in purchases and academic success). Robust standard errors are in parentheses. Numbers not in parentheses are coefficients.

Expectations

Students declare their expectations of GDP growth and inflation for the next year in the light of Covid-19 pandemic.

Figure 3. Macroeconomic Expectations during Covid-19 pandemic

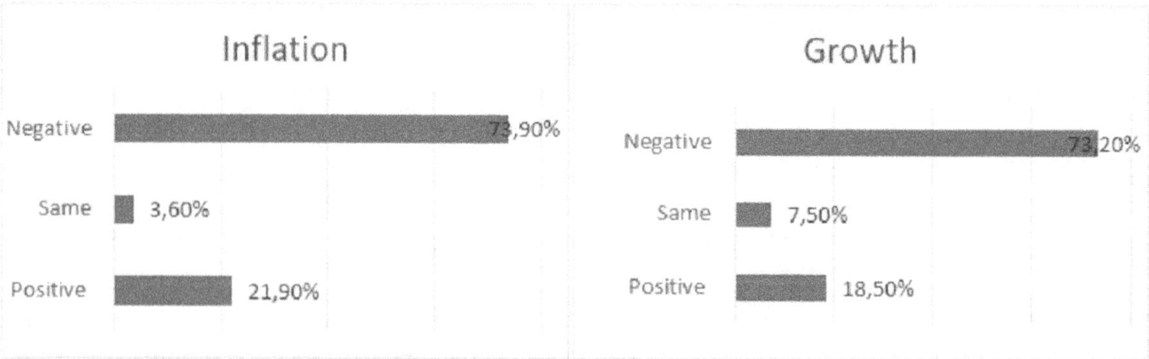

The students expect a negative during the Covid-19 pandemic on inflation and GDP growth. Alloy & Ahrens (1987) demonstrated that individuals with worse mental health will be more pessimistic about their forecasts. The covid-19 pandemic period caused mental distortions among the students. Students' negative forecasts about GDP growth and inflation reflect widespread pessimism.

Predictors of Expectations

Table 5 deploys the predictors of the macroeconomic expectations of the students considering the Covid-19 pandemic and important insights about different characteristics of the students and their macroeconomic expectations.

Previous studies demonstrate that individuals with worse mental health make more pessimistic forecasts (Alloy & Ahren, 1987, De Bondt & Thaler, 1995). This part of the study is designed to test a hypothesis stating that individuals with worse mental health endorse pessimistic forecasts about the future. The association between mental health and the macroeconomic expectations (inflation and GDP growth) of the students during the Covid-19 pandemic are statistically significant. The students with worse mental health make more negative forecasts for GDP growth and inflation. This result reflects the pessimism of the students with worse mental health.

Graduate students have more negative forecasts about GDP growth and inflation. Females think more negatively about inflation but are more positive about GDP growth compared to men.

Statistically, significant results are evaluated only in the result section. R^2 values are small for all probit ordered regressions. Thus, the predictors of mental health, the reactions and predictors of macroeconomic expectations may be idiosyncratic.

Table 5. Predictors of expectations

	GDP growth	**Inflation**
Mental Health	0,07* (0,02)	0,07* (0,03)
Education Level	0,50* (0,05)	0,14* (0,05)
Female	-0,24** (0,05)	0,11** (0,05)
Diagnosis	0,00 (0,04)	0,02 (0,04)
Income	0,03 (0,51)	0,07 (0,046)
News	0,06 (0,04)	0,04 (0,04)
Job Loss	0,08 (0,141)	-0,01 (0,05)
N	2936	2936
R^2 pseudo	0,04	0,008

*p<0,01, **p<0,05,. Dependent variables in columns are ordinal variables (macroeconomic expectations). Robust standard errors are in parentheses. Numbers not in parentheses are coefficients.

SOLUTIONS, RECOMMENDATIONS, AND DISCUSSION

Covid-19 pandemic affected people's mental and physical health negatively. Individuals are very concerned about the impacts of the pandemic on many issues. Despite the fact that very little study has been held about the impacts of Covid-19 on many aspects, there are even more limited studies that analyze the relationship between mental health and reactions and macroeconomic expectations of the young adults. Therefore, this study aims to shed light to the mental health situation, reaction, macroeconomic expectations of students and to explore the predictors of mental health and the relationship between mental health and other characteristics with their reactions and macroeconomic expectations during the Covid-19 pandemic.

Most of the students (67%) declared that their mental health is worse compared to pre-covid-19 pandemic consistent with other studies (Lie et al, 2020, Estaban, 2021, Lin, 2020). Most of the students reported that they afflicted with anxiety during the pandemic, consistent with previous anxiety research (Cao et al, 2020, Bostan, 2020).

Further, most of the students declare that they are concerned about economy, household income and about their future. The number of students concerned about the economy (79%) is higher than the number students concerned about their household income (40,19%). Further, nearly all, namely 92,77% of the students are very concerned, concerned, or somewhat concerned about the future. Thus, the anxiety about the future is the most prevalent concern among the students.

Indefinite future, unfavorable expectations, and uncertainty makes individuals unable to make plans. This ambiguity increases the future anxiety among individuals (Macleod et al, 1991, Karrie et al, 2000). Covid-19 pandemic is unprecedented. There have been financial crises such as 2008 financial crisis, 1994 Turkish economic crisis or flu pandemics., but the impacts of Covid-19 pandemic have a more global scope and are more dangerous than the precedent ones. These kinds of crises have not been contemplated or experienced by today's individuals. No one was prepared for such kind of a global health crisis.

The pandemic is spreading, and reaching new highs day by day; therefore, individuals are exposed to rising suspicions and uncertainty which increase the negative thoughts of the students. The results of this study are in line with previous studies demonstrating the relationship between uncertainty and anxiety levels. The results indicate that the students have high levels of concern about the future during the pandemic period. The student's anxiety regarding the future increases as they believe they will have difficulties in finding job opportunities (Bolanowski, 2005). A high percentage of the participants of this study are also concerned about the economy. Their rising belief in the difficulty of obtaining job opportunities and their negative thoughts about the economy are other sources of their high concerns about the future which is consistent with previous studies.

It has been posited that students in higher concerns may have worse mental health (Jessop, 2020, Jessop, 2005). A significant relationship between concerns on the economy, household finances and the future with worse mental health is defined in this study. It has been further posited that the case that an individual is diagnosed with Covid-19 or has had contact with someone infected may also have a negative impact on the individual's mental health (Madkor et al 2021, Cao et al 2020) which is consistent with the results of this study.

Within this study, there is a significant association between mental health, education level, gender, and income level with the reactions (change in their academic success and change in purchases) of the students. Greater anxiety levels are associated with the decline in academic success of the students. Schonwetter et al (1995) revealed that the anxiety impedes the academic success similar with the results of this study. This situation is explained with reduced mental ability, poorer study habits such as procrastination of study and reduced attention in following teaching activities (Schonwetter et al 1995, Rothblum et al 1986). The students with worse mental health decreased their purchases during pandemic period. In past crises such as the 2008 economic crisis, people preferred to postpone their purchases (Baldwin & Mauro, 2020). In making decisions, individuals usually use the availability heuristic. They find it relatively easy to recall previous crises (Tversky, Kahneman, 1973) which leads them to postpone their purchases. The reason of the decline in purchases might be the result of pessimistic forecasts experienced in previous crises.

Graduate students are more successful than undergraduate students who, in turn are more successful than associate degree students during Covid-19 period. This is perhaps caused by the fact that graduate students have higher levels of experience and greater academic ability compared to undergraduate and associate students (Nelson, 1983). The success of graduate students arises from their greater experience and academic ability which leads them to adapt more easily to online education compared to undergraduate and associate degree students.

Women tend to make more purchases compared to men during the pandemic period. Binder (2020) pointed out that this is due to the fact that women are more concerned and thus, they prefer to purchase more food and supplies.

Students having higher household incomes have made more purchases and have better academic success compared to students having lower income levels. Students holding higher income levels have low anxiety level which accelerates academic success. As previous research explored, low levels of anxiety help students to have better academic performance (Schonwetter et al 1995, Rothblum et al 1986). Having higher income levels allow the students to make more purchases during the covid-19 period.

People associate inflation and decline in GDP growth with stagflation and recessionary outcomes. Inflation and GDP growth expectations play an important role in decisions of purchasing, saving, and even in the price-setting process. The behaviors of young adults are an important determinant of future GDP growth and inflation rate. Therefore, understanding the expectations of young adults is crucial for policymakers (Meyler & Reiche, 2021, Kamdar& 2019). Many students in this study reported that they expect a negative impact of the pandemic on GDP growth and inflation; however, the survey was conducted later during the pandemic period. As the duration of the pandemic increases, the uncertainties brought about by the pandemic become more evident.

Within the sample, there was a significant relationship between mental health, education level and gender with macroeconomic expectations (GDP growth and inflation). Previous studies revealed that depressed individuals have more desperate forecasts. This relationship is the result of a significant association between pessimism and mental disorders (Alloy, 1987). The result of the study confirms previous findings in the literature that students with worse mental health are likely to have more pessimistic forecasts about inflation and GDP growth. Dietrich (2020) documents that individuals have negative forecasts which reflect widespread pessimism. This interpretation aligns with the result of this study.

Graduate students are more pessimistic about inflation and GDP growth. This is consistent with previous research demonstrating that students in later years are more likely to have high levels of depressive or anxious symptoms (Barreira et al 2018). High levels of anxiety cause more pessimistic forecast for macroeconomic indicators (Alloy, 1987). Women are more pessimistic about inflation expectation. In fact, they tend to be more pessimistic in many different aspects (Bryan & Venkatu, 2001, Binder, 2020, Meyler & Reiche, 2021). Different from previous studies, women are more optimistic about growth expectations.

Within the sample, there was not any significant relationship between following the news about Covid-19, having been diagnosed with Covid-19, income level, and experiencing a job loss with macroeconomic expectations of the students.

Students in the study showed to have worse mental health and being more pessimistic about the economy and giving worse reactions during the latter stage of the pandemic. Turkey has passed through a lot of lock-down until the research time. The studies conducted during the first periods of the pandemic show that generally, mental health is better (Recchi et al., 2020, Vaterlaus, 2021). Further research is necessary to better understand how the students' mental health, concerns, reactions, and macroeconomic expectations are impacted during and after Covid-19 pandemic.

Universities pay attention to how unprecedented change is understood by students and affects their decisions. Therefore, universities should have to identify what it needs to be in the future and how they can manage the changes needed to get there. Change management is important in universities as it is important in all organizations. Change management can be defined as the process to encourage continuous learning and the capability to meet the changing needs of stakeholders (Moran and Brightman, 2001).

Understanding the perceptions and thoughts of young adults in unprecedented times is also important for policymakers to increase the capability to meet the changing needs of young adults.

CONCLUSION AND LIMITATIONS

It is important to understand mental health and how young adults revise their reactions and economic expectations during a health crisis period such as Covid-19 pandemic. Understanding the predictors of the mental health, reactions and macroeconomic expectations will provide a way of dealing with unprecedented pandemic.

Results of this study give good insights into the effects on students during times of uncertainty. As a starting point, this survey methods study explores that the students' mental health affected from Covid-19 pandemic in a negative way. %78,50 of students is afflicted with anxiety during pandemic. Results also show that the students with higher level of concern about the economy, household finance and future and who are diagnosed with Covid-19 tend to have worse mental health. Worse mental health causes students to decrease academic success, decline purchases, and have more pessimistic macroeconomic expectations. The students belonging to higher income groups make more purchases and have better academic success during the pandemic. Females make more purchases and have more pessimistic forecasts about the inflation compared to men; whereas males have more pessimistic forecasts about GDP growth compared to women. Graduate students are more pessimistic about inflation and GDP growth but have better academic success during Covid-19. These results present important implications for both universities and policy makers.

The results show that change will increase ambiguity and anxiety among students so that students are exposed to more stress. Especially the students are most concerned about the future. In order to identify how to prevent worse mental health, change management can be held by universities and policymakers. Successful change management requires a better understanding of the psychological aspects of change, among young adults. So, the results of the study help in change management. Change management can be successful with the commitment of the individuals who are exposed to unprecedented times. The affective commitment may be possible by factors such as self-efficacy and the perception of control. The students may be convinced by actively and independently engaging in facilitating change (Meyer and Hamilton, 2001, Jong et al., 2016)

FUTURE RESEARCH DIRECTIONS

The study is cross-sectional. The main limitation of cross-sectional studies is the analysis of one-time horizon and the inability to make causal claims. Further research can be done, to mitigate the problem of cross-sectional studies and to fully understand the impact of the Covid-19 pandemic on students.

Future survey analysis will be needed to fully understand the impact of the Covid-19 pandemic on students' concerns, mental health, reactions, and macroeconomic expectations. Comparison between existing study and future studies will assist to understand whether there is a difference between the new shocks and the usual situations.

REFERENCES

Acar, Y. (2020). Yeni Koronavirüs (Covid-19) Salgını ve Turizm Faaliyetlerine Etkisi. *Güncel Turizm Araştırmaları Dergisi, 4*, 7–21. doi:10.32572/guntad.703410

Adams-Prassl, A., Boneva, T., Golin, M., & Rauh, C. (2020). Inequality in the impact of the coronavirus shock: Evidence from real-time surveys. *Journal of Public Economics, 189*, 104245. doi:10.1016/j.jpubeco.2020.104245

Alloy, L. B., & Ahrens, A. H. (1987). Depression and pessimism for the future: Biased use of statistically relevant information in predictions for self-versus others. *Journal of Personality and Social Psychology, 52*(2), 366–378. doi:10.1037/0022-3514.52.2.366 PMID:3559896

Aucejo, E. M., French, J., Araya, M. P. U., & Zafar, B. (2020). The impact of COVID-19 on student experiences and expectations: Evidence from a survey. *Journal of Public Economics, 191*, 104271. doi:10.1016/j.jpubeco.2020.104271 PMID:32873994

Auray, S., & Eyquem, A. (2020). The macroeconomic effects of lockdown policies. *Journal of Public Economics, 190*, 104260. doi:10.1016/j.jpubeco.2020.104260 PMID:32863463

Baldwin, R., & Mauro, B. (2020). *Economics in the time of COVID-19* (R. Baldwin & B. W. di Mauro, Eds.). CEPR Press.

Bargain, O., & Aminjonov, U. (2020). Trust and compliance to public health policies in times of COVID-19. *Journal of Public Economics, 192*, 104316. doi:10.1016/j.jpubeco.2020.104316 PMID:33162621

Barreira, P., Basilico, M., & Bolotnyy, V. (2018). *Graduate student mental health: Lessons from American economics departments*. Harvard University. https://scholar.harvard. edu/sites/scholar.harvard.edu/files /bolotnyy/files/bbb_mentalhealth_paper.pdf

Beaudry, P., & Portier, F. (2006). Stock prices, news, and economic ñuctuations. *The American Economic Review, 96*(4), 1293–1307. doi:10.1257/aer.96.4.1293

Binder, C. (2020). Coronavirus fears and macroeconomic expectations. *The Review of Economics and Statistics, 102*(4), 721–730. doi:10.1162/rest_a_00931

Bolanowski, W. (2005). Anxiety about professional future among young doctors. *International Journal of Occupational Medicine and Environmental Health, 18*(4), 367–374. PMID:16617853

Born, B., Mu¨ller, G. J., Schularick, M., & Sedlacek, P. (2019). The costs of economic nationalism: Evidence from the brexit experiment. *Economic Journal (London), 129*(623), 2722–2744. doi:10.1093/ej/uez020

Bostan, S., Erdem, R., Öztürk, Y. E., Kılıç, T., & Yılmaz, A. (2020). The Effect of Covid-19 Pandemic on the Turkish Society. *Electronic Journal of General Medicine, 17*(6), em237. doi:10.29333/ejgm/7944

Bozkurt, N. (2004). Bir Grup Üniversite Öğrencisinin Depresyon ve Kaygı Düzeyleri ile Çeşitli Değişkenler Arasındaki İlişkiler. *Eğitim ve Bilim, 29* (133), 1300-1337, http://egitimvebilim.ted.org.tr/index.php/EB/article/view/5095/1179

Bryan, M., & Venkatu, G. (2001). *The Curiously Different Inflation Perspectives of Men and Women.* Federal Reserve Bank of Cleveland.

Cao, W., Fang, Z., Hou, G., Han, M., Xu, X., Dong, J., & Zheng, J. (2020). The psychological impact of the COVID-19 epidemic on college students in China. *Psychiatry Research, 287*, 112934. doi:10.1016/j.psychres.2020.112934 PMID:32229390

Chlewinski, Z. (1994). PrzyszioSC swiata w aspekcie szans i zagrozen. Psychologiczne badania studentow: 1992 rok. [The future of the world in view of the chances and threats, Psychological research on students]. *Przegląd Psychologiczny, 37*, 51–63.

Cohen, L., Manion, L., & Morrison, K. (2007). Research Methods in Education (6th ed.). London and New York, NY: Routledge doi:10.4324/9780203029053

Jarrow, R. (Ed.), *Handbooks in Operations Research and Management Science, 9, 385–410*. Elsevier Science., . doi:10.4324/9780203029053

Dietrich, A. M., Kuester, K., Müller, G. J., & Schoenle, R. C. (2020). *News and uncertainty about Covid-19: Survey evidence and short-run economic impact.* Federal Reserve Bank of Cleveland, Working Paper No. 20-12. 1 doi:0.26509/frbcwp-202012

Fernandes, N. (2020). *Economic effects of coronavirus outbreak (COVID-19) on the world economy.* SSRN. https://papers.ssrn.com/sol3/papers.cfm?abstract_id=3557504

Gittings, L., Toska, E., Medley, S., Cluver, L., Logie, C. H., Ralayo, N., Chen, J., & Mbithi-Dikgole, N. (2021). 'Now my life is stuck!': Experiences of adolescents and young people during COVID-19 lockdown in South Africa. *Global Public Health: An International Journal for Research, Policy and Practice, 16*(6), 947–963. doi:10.1080/17441692.2021.1899262 PMID:33750269

Hammad, M. A. (2016). Future Anxiety and its Relationship to Students' Attitude toward Academic Specialization. *Journal of Education and Practice, 7*(15). https://files.eric.ed.gov/fulltext/EJ1103253.pdf

Heymann, D. L., & Shindo, N. (2020). Covid-19: What is next for public health? *The Lancet.*

Jeffrey, G. J., Stone, C. C., Zegeye, A., & Charles, T. A. (2009). How much math do students need to succeed in business and economics statistics? An ordered probit analysis. *Journal of Statistics Education : An International Journal on the Teaching and Learning of Statistics, 17*(3), 3. doi:10.1080/10691898.2009.11889532

Jessop, D., Reid, M., & Solomon, L. (2020). Financial concern predicts deteriorations in mental and physical health among university students. *Psychology & Health, 35*(2), 196–209. doi:10.1080/08870446.2019.1626393 PMID:31181966

Jessop, D. C., Herberts, C., & Solomon, L. (2005). The impact of financial circumstances on student health. *British Journal of Health Psychology, 10*(3), 421–439. doi:10.1348/135910705X25480 PMID:16238857

Jong, T., Wiezer, N., de Weerd, M., Nielsen, K., Mattila-Holappa, P., & Mockałło, Z. (2016). The impact of restructuring on employee well-being: A systematic review of longitudinal studies. *Work and Stress, 30*(1), 91–114. doi:10.1080/02678373.2015.1136710

Kalaycı, Ş. (2016). *SPSS Uygulamalı Çok Değişkenli İstatistik Teknikleri.*

Kamdar, R. (2019). The inattentive consumer: Sentiment and expectations, meeting paper from Society for Economic Dynamics. *Economic Dynamics.* https://economicdynamics.org/meetpapers/2019/paper_647.pdf

Karrie, J., Craig, K., Brown, J., & Andrew, B. (2000). *Environmental factors in the etiology of anxiety neuropsychopharmacology: The fifth generation of progress.* ANCP. http://www.acnp.org/g4/GN401000127/Default.htm

Kiebler, J., & Stewart, A. J. (2022, April). Student experiences of the COVID-19 pandemic: Perspectives from first-generation/lower-income students and others. *Analyses of Social Issues and Public Policy (ASAP), 22*(1), 198–224. doi:10.1111/asap.12288

Kim, D., Kim, M., & Shim, M. (2021). The macroeconomic consequences of stimulating offline consumption during COVID-19. *Global Economic Review, 50*(1), 20–42. doi:10.1080/1226508X.2021.1875868

Knotek, E. S., Schoenle, R. S., Dietrich, A. M., Kuester, K., Müller, G. J., Myrseth, K. O. R., & Webe, M. (2020). *Consumers and Covid-19: A real-time survey.* Federal Reserve Bank of Cleveland. doi:10.26509/frbc-ec-202008

Leduc, S., & Liu, Z. (2016). Uncertainty shocks are aggregate demand shocks. *Journal of Monetary Economics, 82*, 20–35. doi:10.1016/j.jmoneco.2016.07.002

Li, Y., Zhao, J., Ma, Z., McReynolds, L. S., Lin, D., Chen, Z., Wang, T., Wang, D., Zhang, Y., Zhang, J., Fan, F., & Liu, X. (2021). Mental health among college students during the COVID-19 pandemic in China: A 2-wave longitudinal survey. *Journal of Affective Disorders, 281*, 597–604. doi:10.1016/j.jad.2020.11.109 PMID:33257043

Lin, C.-Y. (2020). Social reaction toward the 2019 novel coronavirus (COVID-19). *Social Health Behavior, 3*(1), 1. doi:10.4103/SHB.SHB_11_20

MacLeod, A., Williams, J. M., & Bekerian, D. A. (1991). Worry is reasonable: The role of explanations in pessimism about future personal events. *Journal of Abnormal Psychology, 100*(4), 478–486. doi:10.1037/0021-843X.100.4.478 PMID:1757661

Madkor, O. R. E., Elsorady, K. E., Abdelhady, D. H., AbdulJawad, P., & Aly El Gabry, D. (2021). COVID-19 life events-anxiety inventory (C-19LAI): Development, reliability, and validity study on Egyptian population. *Middle East Curr Psychiatry, 28*(1), 21. doi:10.118643045-021-00101-z

Meyer, J. P., & Herscovitch, L. (2001). Commitment in the workplace: Toward a general model. *Human Resource Management Review, 11*(3), 299–326. doi:10.1016/S1053-4822(00)00053-X

Meyler, A., & Reiche, L. (2021). Making sense of consumers' inflation perceptions and expectations – the role of (un)certainty. *ECB Economic Bulletin*, https://www.ecb.europa.eu/pub/economic-bulletin/articles/2021/html/ecb.ebart202102_02~32e2ff1af1.en.html

Mihaylov, E., Mizen, P., Parker, N., Renault, T., Smietanka, P., & Thwaites, G. (2020). Economic uncertainty before and during the COVID-19 pandemic. *Journal of Public Economics, 191*, 104274. Advance online publication. doi:10.1016/j.jpubeco.2020.104274 PMID:32921841

Moran, J. W., & Brightman, B. K. (2001). Leading organizational change. *Career Development International, 6*(2), 111–118.

Mustapha, J. O., Adedokun, K. A., & Nasir, I. A. (2020). Public health preparedness towards COVID-19 outbreak in Nigeria. *Asian Pacific Journal of Tropical Medicine, 13*(5), 197–198. doi:10.4103/1995-7645.279650

Nelson, K. (1983). Differences in graduate and undergraduate performance in a core research course. *Journal of Education for Social Work, 19*(2), 77–84.

Özatay, F., & Sak, G. (2020). Kovid-19'un Ekonomik Sonuçlarını Yönetebilmek İçin Ne Yapılabilir? *Türkiye Ekonomi Politikaları Araştırma Vakfı,* https://www.tepav.org.tr/upload/files/1585023057-6.Covid_19un_Ekonomik_Sonuclarini_Yonetebilmek_Icin_Ne_Yapilabilir.pdf

Qiu, J., Shen, B., Zhao, M., Wang, Z., Xie, B., & Xu, Y. (2020). A nationwide survey of psychological distress among Chinese people in the Covid-19 epidemic: Implications and policy recommendations. *General Psychiatry, 33*(2), e100213. doi:10.1136/gpsych-2020-100213 PMID:32215365

Recchi, E., Ferragina, E., Helmeid, E., Pauly, S., Safi, M., Sauger, N., & Schradie, N. (2020). The "Eye of the Hurricane" paradox: An unexpected and unequal rise of well-being during the Covid-19 lockdown in France. *Research in Social Stratification and Mobility, 68*, 100508. Advance online publication. doi:10.1016/j.rssm.2020.100508 PMID:32834344

Rothblum, E. D., Solomon, L. J., & Murakami, J. (1986). Affective, cognitive, and behavioral differences between high and low procrastinators. *Journal of Counseling Psychology, 33*(4), 387–394. doi:10.1037/0022-0167.33.4.387

Sayeed, A., Kundu, S., Hasan Al Banna, M., Tasdik Hasan, M., Begum, R. M., & Shafiqul Islam Khan, M. (2020). Mental health outcomes during the COVID-19 and perceptions towards the pandemic: Findings from a cross-sectional study among Bangladeshi students. *Children and Youth Services Review, 119*, 105658. doi:10.1016/j.childyouth.2020.105658 PMID:33518861

Spitzer, R. L., Kroenke, K., Williams, J. B., & Löwe, B. (2006). A brief measure for assessing generalized anxiety disorder: The GAD-7. *Arch Intern Med. 22, 166*(10), 1092-1097.. doi:10.1001/archinte.166.10.1092

AERA. (n.d.). *Teaching Behaviors and Student Differences: Lecture Organization and Test Anxiety.* The Annual Meeting of the American Educational Research Association, San Francisco, CA.

Telli, S & Altun, D (2020). Coronavirüs ve Çevrimiçi (Online) Eğitimin Önlenemeyen Yükselişi. *Üniversite Araştırmaları Dergisi, 3*, 25-34

Science. (2020). The effect of travel restrictions on the spread of the 2019 novel coronavirus (Covid-19) outbreak. *Science, 368*(6489), 395-400.

Toussaint, A., Hüsing, P., Gumz, A., Wingenfeld, K., Härter, M., Schramm, E., & Löwe, B. (2020). Sensitivity to change and minimal clinically important difference of the 7-item generalized anxiety disorder questionnaire (GAD-7). *Journal of Affective Disorders, 265*, 395–401. doi:10.1016/j.jad.2020.01.032 PMID:32090765

Tversky, A., & Kahneman, D. (1973). Availability: A heuristic for judging frequency and probability. *Cognitive Psychology*, *5*(2), 207–232. doi:10.1016/0010-0285(73)90033-9

Vaterlaus, J. M., Spruance, A., & Patten, E. V. (2021). COVID-19 pandemic and social distancing in the United States: A mixed-methods study on lived experiences and well-being. *The Social Science Journal*, 1–13. doi:10.1080/03623319.2020.1852856

WHO. (2020b). *Mental health & COVID-19*. WHO/ https://www.who.int/teams/mental-health-and-substance-use/covid-19.

Xiao, C. (2020). A novel approach of consultation on 2019 novel coronavirus (COVID-19)- Related psychological and mental problems: Structured letter therapy. *Psychiatry Investigation*, *17*(2), 175–176. doi:10.30773/pi.2020.0047 PMID:32093461

Zaleski, Z. (1996). Future anxiety, concept, measurement, and preliminary research. *Personality and Individual Differences*, *21*(2), 165–174. doi:10.1016/0191-8869(96)00070-0

Zou, P., Huo, D., & Li, M. (2020). The impact of the COVID-19 pandemic on firms: A survey in Guangdong Province. China. *Global Health Research and Policy*, *5*(1), 41. doi:10.118641256-020-00166-z PMID:32885048

KEY TERMS AND DEFINITIONS

Ambiguity: A situation in which nothing is clear which causes confusion.

Anxiety: Having a sense of nervousness, panic, or restlessness.

Concern: Worried or panic feeling about something.

Gross Domestic Product: This measures the income earned for a certain amount of time or the total amount spent on final goods and services.

Inflation: Rise of the prices of goods and services for a certain time.

Mental health: Psychological wellbeing.

Chapter 6
Can Change Management Be Disrupted Through Leadership Stretegies?
Evidence From Start-Up Firms in Asia

Samrat Ray
Independent Researcher, India

ABSTRACT

The "change management" process is a helpful approach for changing the environment of business companies to go ahead in the upcoming days. It has been known that the employees are the main part of an organisation who has not accepted the changing process at first; and for that reason, the appropriate leadership strategy is required to bring the changes within. The start-ups of Asia have been explained in this study for improving the leadership techniques by which the leaders have enhanced their leadership qualities to accept the change management process. The analysis of the responses derived from the survey has been done using the statistical tool "SPSS," which has been chosen for its tools of descriptive and inferential statistics. The outcomes of the data analysis have been evaluated to depict the inference of the results of the correlation and regression of the data. Moreover, the results of the statistical analysis have been discussed in alignment with the hypotheses that have been formed using the independent and dependent variables.

INTRODUCTION

Change management is a process based on which the transformation processes of any organisation can be changed by implementing several technologies, processes, and goals. The main aim of change management is to apply several types of strategies to assist the people of the company in adopting changes and controlling changes. Leaders are considered as the power of an organisation that can create new plans. Leaders of companies have created many new plans and strategies to bring the change processes within the organisation, but sometimes they failed to adopt the changes. Different types of changes such

DOI: 10.4018/978-1-6684-7509-6.ch006

as changes in communication, innovation, and implementation plans have been done to bring changes within any kind of company. Communication is the driving factor based on which Asian companies can successfully meet their target on time. According to the findings of Alqatawenah (2018), the leaders of Tokopedia tried to implement innovation processes such as technology implementation but failed to change the mindset of old employees. In this way, the "change management" processes have been disrupted by poor leadership strategies. The balance between the engagement and the productivity of employees in Tokopedia has decreased due to the uncertainty processes of the "work from home" technique. The changes in technological aspects have not been done for this reason.

The main issue is the poor leadership techniques for which the processes of "change management" cannot be possible. It has been observed that the leaders have not motivated their employees and for this reason, they have not met the target and goals of their companies. Moreover, the communication gap between employees and leaders can affect the change management process. The leaders want to apply modern and advanced technologies but they have not convinced employees to adopt the changes and for this reason, change management processes have been disrupted. The leaders failed to meet the main goals of the companies and did not motivate and appreciate their employees to bring the change process. Moreover, financial issues are also a problem for which the implementation of technology cannot possible. Many experienced employees did not accept the changing process and this is the main reason for appearing the issue.

Figure 1. Reason for arriving issues in Indian start-ups
(Source: Statista.com, 2020a)

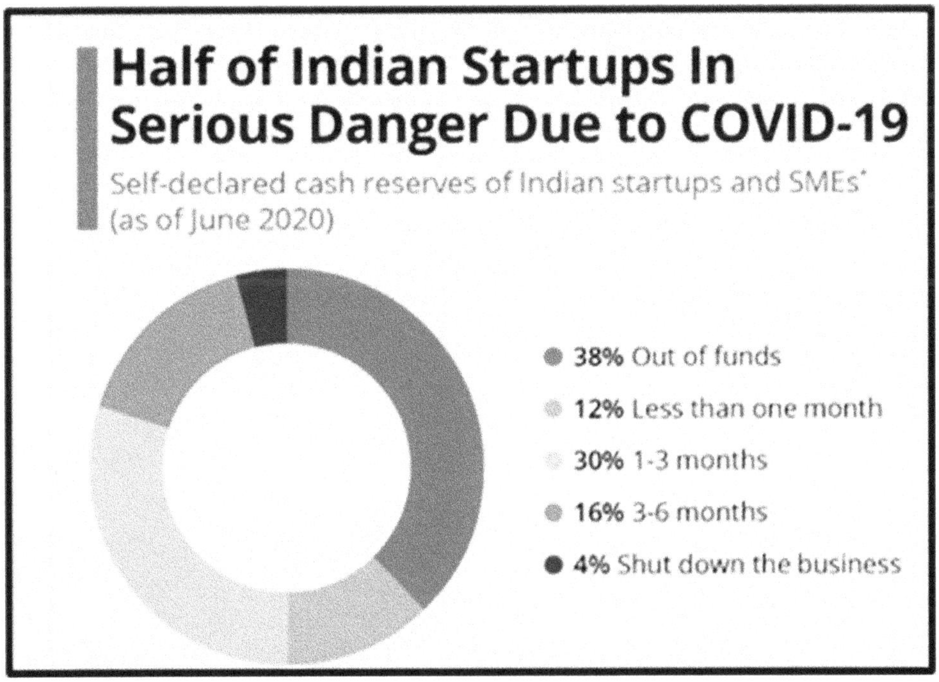

The issues are increasing in recent days for arriving the global pandemic. Many start-up companies in Asia have not had enough funds to implement modern technology for improving the overall function of companies. It has been seen that half of the start-ups in India are out of funds and for this reason, the leaders have not afforded much money to make the changes in the companies. Almost 38% of all the start-ups have faced issues of having a lack of money and for this reason; the employees have not obtained their salaries at that crisis time (Statista.com, 2020a). This research is focused on choosing the appropriate leadership strategies grounded on which the "change management" processes can be improved within Asian start-ups. Leadership strategies should be improved because the firms have suffered many issues for not adopting the "change management" techniques. The best leadership strategies can change the mindset of employees and for this reason; employees can do their best effort for the firm for reaching its goals.

The main objectives of this research are:

The aim of this research is to find out the best leadership strategies for improving the change management processes within start-ups in Asia.

- To know the concept of change management and leadership strategies
- To determine the impact of the change management process on Asian start-ups
- To identify challenges in bringing change management process
- To find some strategies for improving the leadership processes to adopt the change management processes

The importance of the research is to focus on improving the activities of leaders of start-ups in Asia so that they can successfully implement the "change management" process. In this way, the research has helped many business firms to enhance their business efficiency. The start-ups of Asia have faced many challenges during the global pandemic and they have obtained help from this research. In this way, the leaders of those firms have enhanced their business quality and thought differently to set up their plannings. Moreover, the satisfaction of consumers can be increased by implementing the "change management" process in the business.

BACKGROUND AND LITERATURE REVIEW

Theoretical Framework

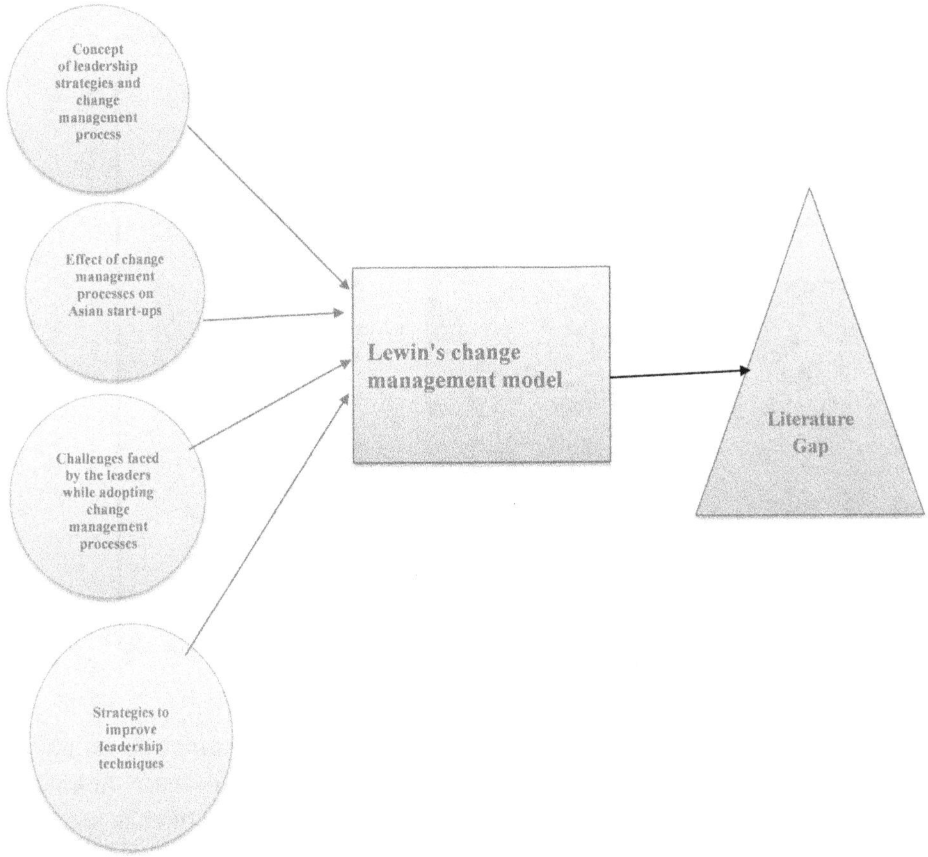

Concept of Leadership Strategies and Change Management Process

Figure 2. Change management in organisations based on project and culture
(Source: Statista.com, 2022a)

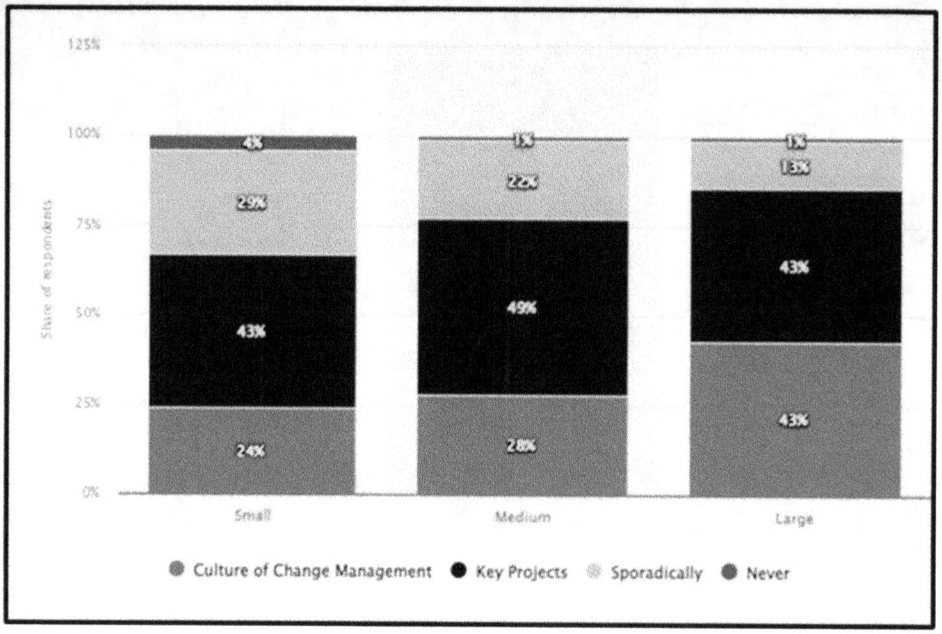

The "change management" process is mainly a planning procedure by which any company can implement and monitor the changing process in the organisation. This factor is essential because the change has helped business firms to operate their business activities smoothly. Several kinds of changes affect the performance of employees and they have not adopted the processes perfectly. It is important to create plannings and strategies for implementing plans in a different way so that the employees can adopt the positive changes. As per the thoughts of Mansaray (2019), developing plans to complete a task within time can bring positive change to any business company. The employees of Asian start-ups must are ready for adopting the change processes. Moreover, the leaders have created strategies to provide training to employees so that they can learn new knowledge about their daily tasks. On the other hand, Alqatawenah (2018) stated that leaders can define the meaning of organizational processes and provide their followers with directions for the kind of behaviour of employees. The leaders must listen to the suggestions and opinions of employees and in this way, they can apply their suggestions in the workplace to accept the changes. Around 55% of employees in reputed organisation feel that change management meet initial objectives but 25% feels that the growth gets sustained overtime (forbes.com, 2022).

The strategies of leadership are important factors for guiding the employees to accept the change process to improve the organisational culture. It has been observed that 24% of small-size organisation has implemented the "change management culture" to observe the positive changes within their firms (Statista.com, 2022a). The leaders have generated many new strategies to understand the employees that the change management process is very essential to see positive performance and gain the highest profit for the company. As per the opinion of Dzenopoljac, Alasadi, Zaim and Bontis (2018), leaders should appreciate the hard work of employees and in this way; the momentum of workers can be improved. Conflicts have been solved by the leaders for accepting the changing process.

Effect of Change Management Processes on Asian Start-Ups

Figure 3. Tech start-up business investment value from 2017 to 2020 in Southeast Asia
(Source: Statista.com, 2022b)

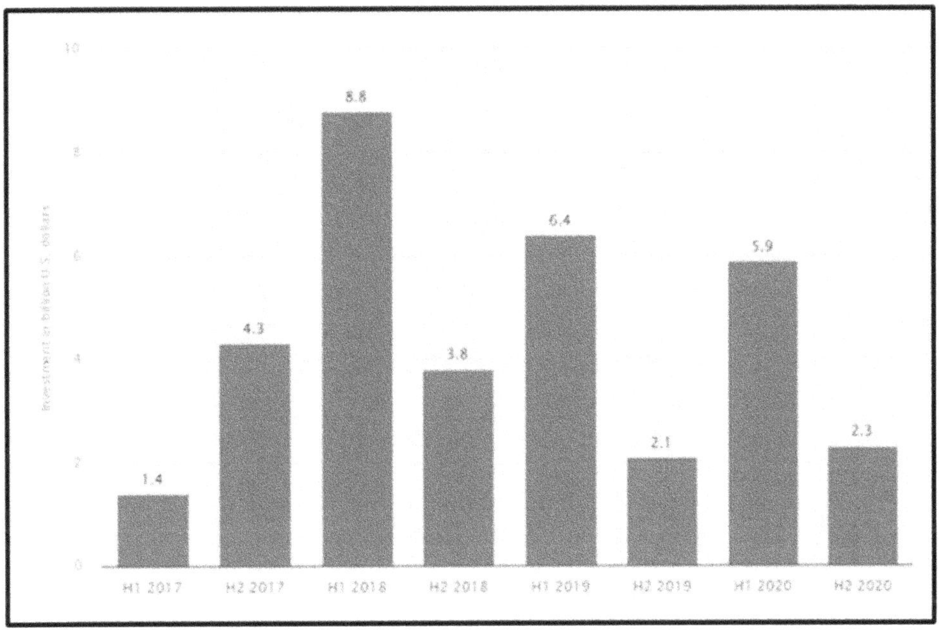

Change management processes are divided into many parts such as cultural, operational, technological, structural, adaptive, and so on. The impact of the "change management" process has been seen to be positive on the start-ups and many Asian start-ups have enhanced their efficiency of business by implementing the "change management" process. As per the thoughts of Jayatilleke and Lai (2018), "change management" can evaluate the improvement processes of any business firm so that the performance of companies can become positive. The productivity of businesses has been increased and for this reason, the companies have obtained the highest profit for expanding their business in the long run. Additionally, the leaders have made decisions in a perfect way so that the employees can follow their suggestion to make progress in their performance. On the contrary, Hechanova, Caringal-Go and Magsaysay (2018) argued that leaders avoid conflict among employees and create unrealistic expectations from employees, for which change management cannot be possible within an organisation. Leaders create many strategies and arrange reward systems for employees so that they can put their best effort to create a positive work environment. Asian start-ups have focused on their innovative behaviours to change the design of their organisational structure (Suoniemi et al., 2020). They have applied new ideas to increase the overall performance of companies and employees. In this way, they tried to satisfy their consumers by providing them with the best services.

It has been observed that in earlier five years, there is a numerous change in the organization and that are decreases gradually. The data has been found that there are more than ***70%*** of the organizations are undertaken to modifies the project of change management in the upcoming three years. The CEOs from various reputed companies of Asia approximately ***73%*** excluding the teams of corporate HR enhances the change which is most prominent in comparison to earlier three years (linkedin.com. 2022).

MAIN FOCUS OF THE CHAPTER

Transformational leaders know the significance of creating a fixed vision for taking decisions firmly and doing changes within organisations. According to the thoughts of Anwer, Wen and Wang (2019), the "change management" process can fall an impact on stakeholders, employees, and customers and in this way, the goals can be achieved on time (Ray, 2021). The communication between the leaders and employees has been seen to be clear and transparent and sometimes the communication gap has arisen between them for this reason, the change process has been delayed. It has been observed that many start-ups in Asia have invested more money than those recent years. Almost 8.2 billion U.S. dollars have been invested in the year 2018 by Asian start-ups but after the covid-19 pandemic, the start-ups have not afforded a huge amount of money in their business (Statista.com, 2022b). The external environment of Asian start-ups has been changed by meeting the goals of companies. Many training programs and the application of new technologies have also been included in the start-ups so that the employees have been satisfied and motivated.

Challenges Faced by the Leaders While Adopting Change Management Processes

Figure 4. Lack of knowledge and skills of leaders for handling technological application
(Source: Statista.com, 2022c)

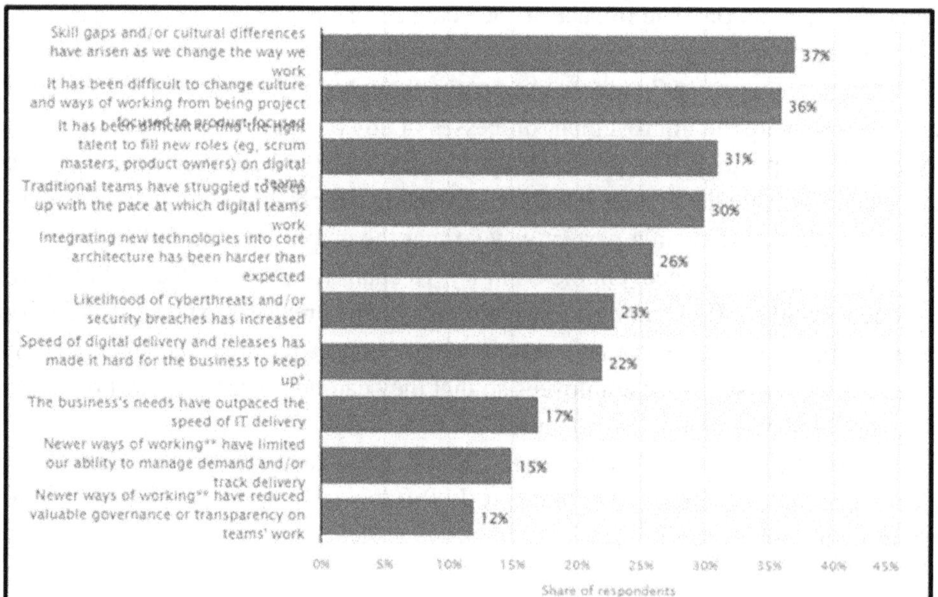

The leaders of the start-ups have not communicated with the employees in a good manner and for that reason; the workers have not understood the tasks. Moreover, communication issues have arrived during the time of the global pandemic since the employees have worked from home. Technological issues have arrived because the network connection was not good and many employees have not arranged the Wi-Fi connection. According to the thoughts of Ali and Anwar (2021), modern technologies are the most essential tools based on which leaders can bring positive changes within business organisations. The leaders have not planned well the process of implementing technologies and for this reason; the productivity of business has decreased. The leaders have not approached the implementation process for lack of money at the time of covid-19. It has been observed that 37% of leaders of start-ups do have not enough skills and knowledge about new and modern technologies and for this reason, they have not operated the advanced technologies (Statista.com, 2022c). The leaders have not provided the correct training to their employees for which the workers have not learned the modern application of the technologies. In this way, the profits and sales of start-ups in Asia have decreased. Around 87% employees feels that training would lead to change management in the organisation. But only 22% employees felt that training gave actual effective results (forbes.com).

Employees wanted to know the detailed procedures for the change processes and the leaders have not provided the detailed reason to the workers. In this way, the employees have faced problems and have not accepted the change process. According to the insights of Rosenbaum, More and Steane (2018), leaders should improve their communication skills and invest most of their time and effort in employees to bring changes to companies. If the workers have not properly understood the work process, the workflows and performance have been reduced. The daily tasks have been seen to be tough for the employees and they have not performed well for poor leadership strategies (Tawse, Patrick and Vera, 2019). They have not maintained their responsibilities well and for this, the change management process has not implemented in an exact way. In this way, the organisations have not benefited so much and the leaders failed to give the assurance to bring the "change management" process (Korchagina et al. 2022).

Strategies to Improve Leadership Techniques

Figure 5. Training for improving leadership
(Source: Weforum.org, 2022)

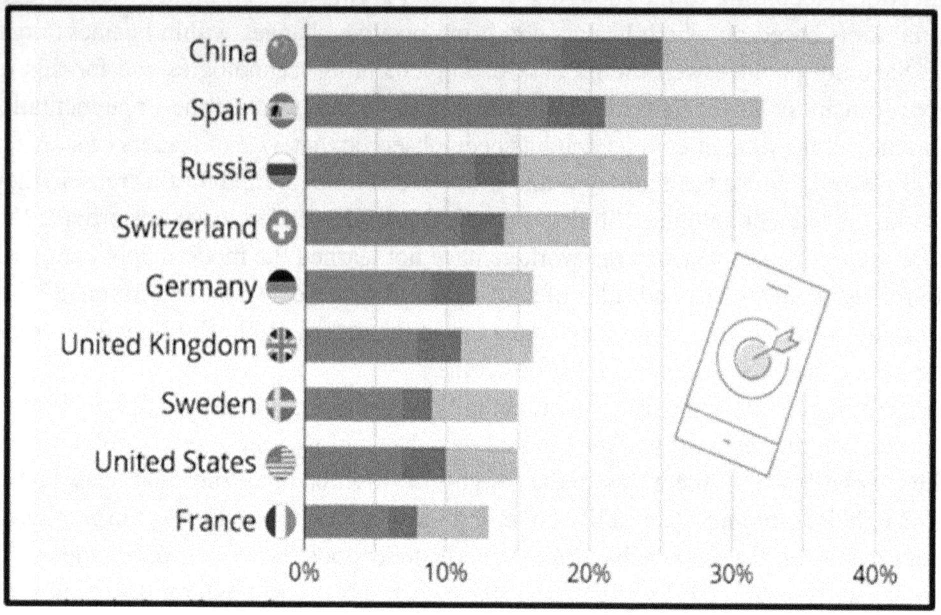

Leaders of Asian start-ups should arrange "training and development" programs so that the employees can learn new knowledge about their related fields. As per the views of Li, Sun, Tao and Lee (2021), a good leader can inspire others in the workplace so that they can put their best effort to reach the targets of companies. In this way, the leaders can assist the employees to identify their best areas so that they can understand their positive behaviour. Moreover, the leaders should listen to the employees' points of view carefully grounded on which they can experience some new changes in the workplace for improving the "change management" process. On the contrary, Mavrot, Hadorn and Sager (2019) stated that leaders should recognise the risk factors so that the challenges can be solved through transparent and open communication. They should celebrate the success of the companies and in this way, they can motivate the employees for successful implementation of change management processes.

The leaders should take care of employees' regular activities and should provide them with suggestions so that the mistakes cannot be repeated by themselves again. The leaders should analyse the important data and information perfectly and, in this way, they can change the progressing process of the organisation (Albukhitan, 2020). It has been observed that almost 20% of the start-ups in China focus on "online training courses" to bring and accept the changing process successfully (Weforum.org, 2022). Moreover, the plans should be done with experienced employees so that they can understand the overall process of new strategies. In this way, the employees can gather motivation grounded on which the performance can be obtained at the highest rate. According to thethougts of Ozkeser (2019), the main changes should be recognised by the leaders for setting the plans successfully for the "change management process". Additionally, the leaders should give examples of many business cases to the employees from which the workers can gather motivation. In this way, the employees can feel they can improve their efficiency in completing the tasks within time.

H_1: Leader's positive attitudes toward change management are positively related to the growth of business strategies of ASIAN start-ups

H_2: Inappropriate choices of leadership strategies affect the positive inclination of departmental and organisational change management

There exists a correlation between leadership strategies and disruption in "change management"

H_3: Communication strategies based on leadership have a positive effect on the transformation of strategic organisational change

Theory and Model

Leaders properly set up a standard vision or perspective and support their employees. Leaders make sure to achieve practical communication strategy and improve their skills that can thoroughly improve their change management. For instance, a ***"Lewin's change management model"*** clearly defines the improvement for leaders that they can enhance their change management.

Figure 6. Lewin's change management model
(Source: online.visual-paradigm.com, 2022)

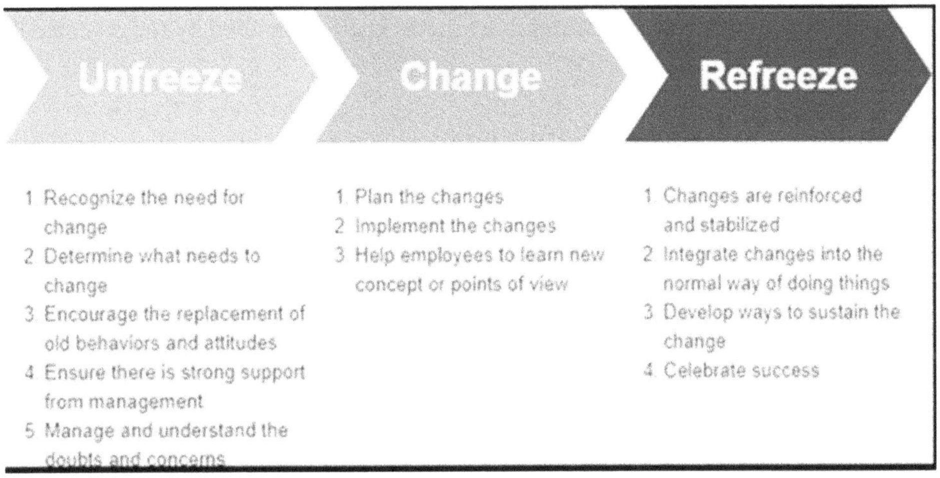

Lewin's Change Management Model

This model is the easiest way to understand in a better framework that can thoroughly change the entire process of the change management. This is the essential change that occurs by unfreezing the remaining statements and findings of the contemporary situation. This model helps in pointing out the supportive and reliable changes that make sure a proper support of the leadership is achieved.

On the other hand, this model helps in recognizing the attitude and manner of the human with reference to the respective changes. There are many distinctive steps in this model and these are ***"Unfreeze"***, ***"change,*** and ***"Refreeze".*** With the help of this theory, leaders thoroughly maintain to modify effectively in their change management. On the other hand, this theory assists the leaders to build up the corrective aims and objectives, properly train and motivates their team members, helps in encouraging the level of conversations and regularly communicates with their employees. In addition, this theory helps to increase the empowerment of the employees and selects a correct tool for communication. The strategy of communication helps the leaders to define and understand the main reason or consequences of the problems and also, helps in determining a standard solution of the particular problem (online.visual-paradigm.com, 2022). On the other side, this model helps in setting up many functional and operative changes for the organization, estimating a standard concept and action plan for transmission. It can help in changing the orthodox culture of the company and can improve many ineffective practices.

METHODOLOGY

Settings of the Study

The settings of the study mainly describe the place where the research has been conducted. The physical, social, experimental, and cultural factors have been determined by selecting the places of the research. The place has been selected as Asia to conduct the research work. The objectives and aims have been fulfilled by the research settings and the probs of the research work have also been solved by this process. The overall results and interpretation of the outcomes of the research work are fully dependent on the research settings and in this way, the research work has been completed by the research by choosing the proper places.

Data Collection Processes and Sampling

The "Cross-sectional quantitative" method has been utilized by the researcher for collecting data correctly. As per the thoughts of Hamilton and Finleyn (2019), data can be collected from several subjects of the research in a single time period for the "cross-sectional quantitative" study. Furthermore, the researcher has followed the "primary data collection" process so that the information can be gathered easily. The researcher formed the survey questionnaires at first and then they shared the questionaries through email. The questions have been sent to the employees of the Asian tech start-up companies. After that, the participants answered the questions and, in this way, the data have been collected.

The "Convenience sampling" technique has been chosen by the researcher to complete the research work successfully. According to the views of Covernton et al. (2019), the main advantage of "purposive sampling" is to save money and get the outcomes of research quickly. This sampling process is very easy to apply and for that reason, the researcher has utilized this sampling method. The employees of Asian tech start-ups are the samples of this research work and they have helped the researcher to conduct the study correctly.

Variables

Variables are the concept based on which the main topic and the significance of the research have been determined. As per the insights of Paddeu, Parkhurst and Shergold (2020), researchers can interpret the outcomes and analyse the results of the research by using the characteristics of variables. In this research work, the independent variable has been identified as "leadership strategies" and the dependent variable has been recognised as "change management process". Leadership strategies have been measured by seeing the overall performance of Asian start-ups. If the objectives and goals of the start-ups have been met on time, then it can be said that the leaders have managed the business process perfectly. Moreover, the good performance and the best workflows of employees can also evaluate the importance of leadership strategies. The evaluation of the "change management" process has been measured by seeing the number of employees participating in the training process. Additionally, the improvement of start-ups' performance and communication have also determined the significance of an effective change management process in this research.

Data Analysis

The data analysis in the study has been done using Excel as the database software for coding and the statistical analysis has been done using the "SPSS Statistical Tool". The statistical assessment of the responses to the survey has been done using "descriptive statistics" to derive the "mean, standard deviation, variance and Kurtosis statistics". Further, the correlation coefficient of the responses has been derived using the "Pearson's correlation coefficient" and the sum of squares. The tests of regression have been done using the "multilevel regression analysis" that has been facilitated to derive the intercept and residual values of the responses. This has been evaluated to derive the statistical significance of the responses by assessing the outcomes of the inferential and descriptive statistics and their relative values.

RESULTS

Descriptive Statistics

The quantitative analysis of the responses to the surveys has been derived for determining the outcomes of the leadership strategies for the change management of a startup using the "SPSS Statistical Tool". The responses to the survey have been procured from 62 employees of startups in Asia, where the leadership strategies have been considered for evaluating the success of the change management. Out of the participants, it has been found that 58% are males and 42% are females (SD = 0.497). Moreover, it has been found that more than 50% of the participants are of the age group of 20 to 30 years (SD = 1.027) and 25 participants have been found to be working less than 1 year (SD = 0.982). Since the participants of the survey are employees of startups, the age group and working tenure have been found to be less than 1 year.

Table 1. Descriptive Statistics

Descriptive Statistics									
	N	Minimum	Maximum	Mean		Std. Deviation	Variance	Kurtosis	
	Statistic	Statistic	Statistic	Statistic	Std. Error	Statistic	Statistic	Statistic	Std. Error
1. Whatisyourgender?	62	1	2	1.42	.063	.497	.247	-1.952	.599
2. Whatisyourage?	62	1	4	1.73	.130	1.027	1.055	-.033	.599
3. Sincehowmanyyearshaveyoubeeninyourstartup?	62	1	4	1.95	.125	.982	.965	-.468	.599
4. Doyouagreethatleadershipstrategiesarerequiredforchangemanagement?	62	1	5	1.84	.128	1.011	1.023	1.587	.599
5. Doyouagreethatappropriateleadershipstartegycandisruptchangemanagement?	62	1	5	1.98	.133	1.048	1.098	.802	.599
6. Doyouagreethattheleadershipstrategyinyourstartuphasmotivatedchangemanagement?	62	1	5	2.00	.151	1.187	1.410	.578	.599
7. Doyouagreethatdepartmentalchangemanagementcanbefacilitatedappropriatelybyagoodmanager?	62	1	5	2.05	.153	1.207	1.457	.277	.599
8. Howsatisfiedareyouwiththechangemanagementinyourorganizationordepartment?	62	1	5	2.05	.155	1.220	1.489	-.139	.599
9. Areyousatisfiedwiththeapproachofyourleaderforthechangemanagementinyourorganization?	62	1	5	1.87	.157	1.235	1.524	.414	.599
10. Areyousatisfiedwiththecommunicationstrategiesofthechangemanagementinyourstartup?	62	1	5	1.84	.161	1.270	1.613	.700	.599
Valid N (listwise)	62								

According to the findings of the descriptive statistics, the gender of the participants has the derivations (M = 1.42, SD = 0.497, Var = 0.247), that reflect more count of male participants. This is because a mean of 1.42 denotes more inclination towards the first option which is "male". Further, it has been found considering the demographics that the coefficient derived from the age group (M = 1.73, SD = 1.027, Var = 0.247) denotes that most of the participants are in the age group of 20 to 30 and 30 to 40 years. Considering the tenure of the participants working in the startups of Asia, it has been found that the output (M = 1.95, SD = 0.982, Var = 0.965) is inclined toward a tenure of less than 1 year to 2 years. This reflects that according to the demographics of the participants, the employees of the startups in Asia are mostly young and new in their organizations. Further, descriptive statistics have been derived for the survey questions based on the dependent variable and independent variable that has been considered in the study (Mishra et al., 2019).

It has been determined whether the employees agree with the fact that an appropriate leadership strategy is required for change management. In this respect, the output has been derived (M = 1.84, SD = 1.011, Var = 1.023) and reflects that the participants have responded by strongly agreeing with the fact. It has also been found that according to the derivations from the statistical coefficients of the Kurtosis, the responses are statistically significant with the correlation of the variables (Amrhein, Trafimow and Greenland, 2019). Considering the fact that the leadership strategy chosen has the potential to disrupt the change management being facilitated in the organization, the responses are similar. It has been found that the output (M = 1.98, SD = 1.048, Var = 1.098) has been derived at a positive relationship with the previous finding.

It has also been found that the participants believe that the leadership strategies in the startups where they work have somehow worked out well with the change management in their department or organization. This has been found by the output, where the "mean" has been derived at 2 (SD = 1.187, Var = 1.098, Kurt = 0.802), which reflects that there has been an inclination towards the options of "Neutral" and "disagreement". It has also been found from the output of descriptive statistics that the coefficient of the "Kurtosis statistic" is 0.802 which is close to 1. Further, it has also been found that the participants are not much satisfied with the change management that has been facilitated in the startups they work (Bono, Arnau, Alarcón and Blanca, 2019). It is also clear from the responses and their descriptive statistical output that the communication strategy and the approach of leadership implemented in the organizations are not appropriate. This is represented by the mean and the large standard deviation that has been derived from the outputs.

Correlations

Table 2. Correlation

Correlations											
		1. What is your gender?	**2. What is your age?**	**3. Since how many years have you been in your start up?**	**4. Do you agree that leadership strategies are require for change management?**	**5. Do you agree that appropriate leadership strategy can disrupt change management?**	**6. Do you agree that the leadership strategy in your start up has motivate change management?**	**7. Do you agree that department al change management can be facilitate appropriately by a good manager?**	**8. How satisfied are you with the change management in your organization or department?**	**9. Are you satisfied with the approach of your leader for the change management in your organization?**	**10. Are you satisfied with the communication strategies of the change management in your startup?**
1. What is your gender?	Pearson Correlation	1	-.092	-.058	.071	.013	-.167	.129	-.169	.170	-.073
	Sig. (2-tailed)		.476	.652	.581	.919	.196	.316	.189	.187	.574
	Sum of Squares and Cross-products	15.097	-2.871	-1.742	2.194	.419	-6.000	4.742	-6.258	6.355	-2.806
	Covariance	.247	-.047	-.029	.036	.007	-.098	.078	-.103	.104	-.046
	N	62	62	62	62	62	62	62	62	62	62
2. What is your age?	Pearson Correlation	-.092	1	.425**	-.027	.026	.040	-.240	-.225	-.235	.229
	Sig. (2-tailed)	.476		.001	.832	.839	.756	.060	.079	.066	.073
	Sum of Squares and Cross-products	-2.871	64.339	26.177	-1.742	1.726	3.000	-18.177	-17.177	-18.194	18.258
	Covariance	-.047	1.055	.429	-.029	.028	.049	-.298	-.282	-.298	.299
	N	62	62	62	62	62	62	62	62	62	62
3. Since how many years have you been in your start up?	Pearson Correlation	-.058	.425**	1	-.190	.190	.127	-.067	.057	.171	.164
	Sig. (2-tailed)	.652	.001		.140	.138	.327	.604	.662	.185	.201
	Sum of Squares and Cross-products	-1.742	26.177	58.855	-11.484	11.952	9.000	-4.855	4.145	12.613	12.516
	Covariance	-.029	.429	.965	-.188	.196	.148	-.080	.068	.207	.205
	N	62	62	62	62	62	62	62	62	62	62
4. Do you agree that leadership strategies are required for change management?	Pearson Correlation	.071	-.027	-.190	1	-.111	-.082	.020	-.126	.049	.030
	Sig. (2-tailed)	.581	.832	.140		.391	.527	.878	.328	.707	.814
	Sum of Squares and Cross-products	2.194	-1.742	-11.484	62.387	-7.161	-6.000	1.484	-9.516	3.710	2.387
	Covariance	.036	-.029	-.188	1.023	-.117	-.098	.024	-.156	.061	.039
	N	62	62	62	62	62	62	62	62	62	62

Continued on following page

Table 2. Continued

Correlations											
		1. What is your gender?	**2. What is your age?**	**3. Since how many years have you been in your start up?**	**4. Do you agree that leadership strategies are require for change management?**	**5. Do you agree that appropriate leadership strategy can disrupt change management?**	**6. Do you agree that the leadership strategy in your start up has motivate change management?**	**7. Do you agree that department al change management can be facilitate appropriately by a good manager?**	**8. How satisfied are you with the change management in your organization or department?**	**9. Are you satisfied with the approach of your leader for the change management in your organization?**	**10. Are you satisfied with the communication strategies of the change management in your startup?**
5. Do you agree that appropriate leadership strategy can disrupt change management?	Pearson Correlation	.013	.026	.190	-.111	1	-.158	-.012	-.012	-.116	-.248
	Sig. (2-tailed)	.919	.839	.138	.391		.220	.924	.925	.371	.052
	Sum of Squares and Cross-products	.419	1.726	11.952	-7.161	66.984	-12.000	-.952	-.952	-9.129	-20.161
	Covariance	.007	.028	.196	-.117	1.098	-.197	-.016	-.016	-.150	-.331
	N	62	62	62	62	62	62	62	62	62	62
6. Do you agree that the leadership strategy in your startup has motivated change management?	Pearson Correlation	-.167	.040	.127	-.082	-.158	1	-.137	.034	-.045	.228
	Sig. (2-tailed)	.196	.756	.327	.527	.220		.287	.793	.730	.074
	Sum of Squares and Cross-products	-6.000	3.000	9.000	-6.000	-12.000	86.000	-12.000	3.000	-4.000	21.000
	Covariance	-.098	.049	.148	-.098	-.197	1.410	-.197	.049	-.066	.344
	N	62	62	62	62	62	62	62	62	62	62
7. Do you agree that departmental change management can be facilitated appropriately by a good manager?	Pearson Correlation	.129	-.240	-.067	.020	-.012	-.137	1	.188	.070	-.166
	Sig. (2-tailed)	.316	.060	.604	.878	.924	.287		.144	.587	.197
	Sum of Squares and Cross-products	4.742	-18.177	-4.855	1.484	-.952	-12.000	88.855	16.855	6.387	-15.516
	Covariance	.078	-.298	-.080	.024	-.016	-.197	1.457	.276	.105	-.254
	N	62	62	62	62	62	62	62	62	62	62
8. How satisfied are you with the change management in your organization department?	Pearson Correlation	-.169	-.225	.057	-.126	-.012	.034	.188	1	.113	.248
	Sig. (2-tailed)	.189	.079	.662	.328	.925	.793	.144		.382	.052
	Sum of Squares and Cross-products	-6.258	-17.177	4.145	-9.516	-.952	3.000	16.855	90.855	10.387	23.484
	Covariance	-.103	-.282	.068	-.156	-.016	.049	.276	1.489	.170	.385
	N	62	62	62	62	62	62	62	62	62	62

Continued on following page

Table 2. Continued

Correlations											
		1. What is your gender?	**2. What is your age?**	**3. Since how many years have you been in your start up?**	**4. Do you agree that leadership strategies are require for change management?**	**5. Do you agree that appropriate leadership strategy can disrupt change management?**	**6. Do you agree that the leadership strategy in your start up has motivate change management?**	**7. Do you agree that department al change management can be facilitate appropriately by a good manager?**	**8. How satisfied are you with the change management in your organization or department?**	**9. Are you satisfied with the approach of your leader for the change management in your organization?**	**10. Are you satisfied with the communication strategies of the change management in your startup?**
9. Are you satisfied with the approach of your leader for the change management in your organization?	Pearson Correlation	.170	-.235	.171	.049	-.116	-.045	.070	.113	1	.039
	Sig. (2-tailed)	.187	.066	.185	.707	.371	.730	.587	.382		.765
	Sum of Squares and Cross-products	6.355	-18.194	12.613	3.710	-9.129	-4.000	6.387	10.387	92.968	3.710
	Covariance	.104	-.298	.207	.061	-.150	-.066	.105	.170	1.524	.061
	N	62	62	62	62	62	62	62	62	62	62
10. Are you satisfied with the communication strategies of the change management in your startup?	Pearson Correlation	-.073	.229	.164	.030	-.248	.228	-.166	.248	.039	1
	Sig. (2-tailed)	.574	.073	.201	.814	.052	.074	.197	.052	.765	
	Sum of Squares and Cross-products	-2.806	18.258	12.516	2.387	-20.161	21.000	-15.516	23.484	3.710	98.387
	Covariance	-.046	.299	.205	.039	-.331	.344	-.254	.385	.061	1.613
	N	62	62	62	62	62	62	62	62	62	62
**. Correlation is significant at the 0.01 level (2-tailed).											

The derivation from the correlation among the variables has been found to have a relationship in various aspects according to the effects that they pose on each other. The change management of the organization has been considered in the analysis depending on the role of the variables in the study. It has been found in the output that the participants who believe that appropriate leadership is required to facilitate change management also consider a good manager to be appointed to facilitate it successfully. This has been derived from the correlation coefficient that has been derived at 0.190 which is a positive correlation and is statistically significant. In this aspect, it has also been found that (Covar = - 0.080) there is a negative covariance and there is more significance between the two attributes. The correlation between the satisfaction of the employees with the change management of the organization and the appropriation of the leadership strategy has been found to be positively related.

The statistical significance of the variables has been found according to the correlation coefficient that has been derived at - 0.952 between the choice of a good manager and disruption of the change management strategy. This shows that the variables are inversely related to the attributes of the variables. The "sum of squares" of the variables has been found at - 12 in this case which reflects that there is an inverse relationship between the choice of good managers and the disruption of the approach of change management that has been facilitated in the departments and the organizations. Further, the correlation between the attributes of communication strategy and disruption of change management strategy has been found to be inversely related. This shows that if there is a good communication strategy implemented according to the leadership strategy, there will be no disruption in the change management process.

Multilevel Linear Regression

Table 3. Multilevel Linear Regression

Model Dimension[a]					
		Number of Levels	**Covariance Structure**	**Number of Parameters**	**Subject Variables**
Fixed Effects	Intercept	1		1	
Random Effects	Intercept[b]	1	Variance Components	1	@4.Doyouagreethatleadershipstrategiesarerequiredforchan * @7.Doyouagreethatdepartmentalchangemanagementcanbefacil
Residual				1	
Total		2		3	
a. Dependent Variable: 8. Howsatisfiedareyouwiththechangemanagementinyourorganizationordepartment?.					
b. As of version 11.5, the syntax rules for the RANDOM subcommand have changed. Your command syntax may yield results that differ from those produced by prior versions. If you are using version 11 syntax, please consult the current syntax reference guide for more information.					

Table 4. (continued)

Information Criteria[a]	
-2 Restricted Log Likelihood	201.539
Akaike's Information Criterion (AIC)	205.539
Hurvich and Tsai's Criterion (AICC)	205.746
Bozdogan's Criterion (CAIC)	211.761
Schwarz's Bayesian Criterion (BIC)	209.761
The information criteria are displayed in smaller-is-better forms.	
a. Dependent Variable: 8. Howsatisfiedareyouwiththechangemanagementinyourorganizationordepartment?.	

Table 5. (continued)

Type III Tests of Fixed Effects[a]				
Source	Numerator df	Denominator df	F	Sig.
Intercept	1	61	174.662	.000
a. Dependent Variable: 8. Howsatisfiedareyouwiththechangemanagementinyourorganizationordepartment?.				

Table 6. (continued)

Correlation Matrix for Estimates of Fixed Effects[a]	
Parameter	Intercept
Intercept	1

a. Dependent Variable: 8. Howsatisfiedareyouwiththechangemanagementinyourorganizationordepartment?.

Table 7. (continued)

Estimates of Covariance Parameters[a]			
Parameter		**Estimate**	**Std. Error**
Residual		1.489424	.269692
Intercept [subject = @4.Doyouagreethatleadershipstrategiesarerequiredforchan * @7.Doyouagreethatdepartmentalchangemanagementcanbefacil]	Variance	.000000[b]	.000000

a. Dependent Variable: 8. Howsatisfiedareyouwiththechangemanagementinyourorganizationordepartment?.

b. This covariance parameter is redundant.

Table 8. (continued)

Correlation Matrix for Estimates of Covariance Parameters[a]			
Parameter		Residual	Intercept [subject = @4.Doyouagreethatleadershipstrategiesarerequiredforchan * @7.Doyouagreethatdepartmentalchangemanagementcanbefacil]
			Variance
Residual		1	.
Intercept [subject = @4.Doyouagreethatleadershipstrategiesarerequiredforchan * @7.Doyouagreethatdepartmentalchangemanagementcanbefacil]	Variance	.	.[b]

a. Dependent Variable: 8. Howsatisfiedareyouwiththechangemanagementinyourorganizationordepartment?

b. The variance of this covariance parameter estimate is zero. Therefore, the correlations on this row and column are set to system missing.

The above table shows the outputs of the "Multilevel Linear regression" of the responses to the survey that have been evaluated to derive the statistical significance among them. It has been found that the outcomes of the components are applicable to the "mixed model of linear mixed-effects" (Pho, Ly, Ly and Lukusa, 2019). According to the output, the intercept that has been derived from the regression model is 1 in both the cases of "fixed and random effects" derived from the output. It has also been found that the residual total that is denoted by μ0j is 1, which is greater than 0.

According to the deliverables of the findings in the "mixed model of linear regression", if "μ0j < 0", it results in a residual which is lower than the average. On the contrary, if the "μ0j > 0", then the residual is above average than the anticipated outcomes (Sommet and Morselli, 2021). The statistical significance of the outcomes of the regression that is derived from the model is based on the derived "intraclass correlation coefficient (ICC)" that has resulted from the evaluation. It has been found that according to the value of the "Akaike's information criterion", the value has been derived above 200. This reflects that the model is acceptable and the deliverables of the data that have been considered for the analysis provide a statistically significant deliverable (Bhattacharya, Biswas, Nandi and Patra, 2020).

Moreover, the result of the "Hurvich and Tsai's Criterion", and the coefficient derived at 205.746 is also significant and derives a better model of regression considering the variables (DelSole and Tippett, 2021). Further, the results of the tests of fixed effects, show that the intercept of the "F-value" has been derived at 174.662, which is higher than 1 and depicts statistical significance among the variables.

DISCUSSION

The derivations from the results of the statistical analysis of the findings show that there is a relationship between the variables of change management and leadership strategy. This has been derived from the result that there is statistical significance among the considered variables (Cameron and Green, 2019). According to the outputs, it can be analyzed that as the choice of the leadership strategy alters according to the situational outcomes, there is an effect on the process of change management that has been implemented in the organization. These change management processes are implemented on the basis of the requirements on an overall aspect or on the basis of the individual components o the organization. The startups of Asia have undergone a vast change in their organizational structure and working approach after the pandemic (Ali and Anwar, 2021). In this context, it has been observed in many startups in Asia that an adverse choice of leadership strategy has led to a resultant outcome of the statistical analysis of the data. This reflects that the employees of the startups always desire a good manager or leader of any form so that the change management that has been facilitated in the department or organization is implemented in an appropriate manner.

The outcomes of the multilevel linear regression and the correlation coefficient show that there is a negative relationship between the attributes of communication strategy and disruption of the change management approach. According to this aspect, it can be reflected that if the communication strategy and leadership strategy go in a positive direction, there will be a beneficial effect on the change management (Luciano, Nahrgang and Shropshire, 2020). In this aspect, "hypothesis 3" can be accepted to be operational and statistically significant followed by the acceptance of "hypothesis 2". "Hypothesis 1" that has been considered is based on the positive attitude of the leadership, which has been denoted by the strategic approach of the choice of leadership and its responsibilities. In this aspect, the statistical significance of the preference of the employees on the strategic choice leads to acceptance of the hypothesis.

SOLUTIONS AND RECOMMENDATIONS

Strengths and Limitations

The outcomes of the study have an impact on the way in which the leadership strategies are chosen in an organization to facilitate the changes in the startups. There should be a choice of appropriate variables so that the management of the change is facilitated according to the requirements of the association (Amis and Greenwood, 2020). Moreover, the limitations of the study are based on the fact that the setting of the study has only been based on the Asian continent. The results of the study would be more beneficial and comprehensive if the employees would have been selected from all over the world. Further, the results of the study will also help the management of the startups to derive the approaches in which the outcomes of the change management approach would be affected (Harrison et al., 2021). Further, the limitations of the study have also been based on the choice of a number of employees that represent a small sample of the workforce of the startups.

Implications

The implications that have been derived from the outcomes of the study applicable in the future prospect of the area of study are relevant to the approach of the management of the startups to change their policies (Thakhathi, Le Roux and Davis, 2019). The startups in the technological industry that undergoes rapid change management processes should mostly align with the requirement of catering to the needs of changes with an appropriate leadership strategy. This will facilitate the smooth processing of the changes in the organizational setting of the startups according to the anticipations regarding the changes.

FUTURE RESEARCH DIRECTIONS

It has also been found that the results of the research will also help in finding the ways in which the strategies of the change management can be improved in association with the leadership strategies. This improves the approach of strategic management of the changes in the organization.

CONCLUSION

Thus, it can be concluded that there is a positive relationship between the independent and dependent variables of the study. It has been found that a positive attitude associated with the choice of strategic leadership in startups has a direct and positive impact on the change management process of the organizations. Further, it has also been found that there is a negative relationship between the communication strategies of the leader and the disruptions in the change management process facilitated by the leaders of the organizations. It is also derived that the effects of choosing a good leadership strategy are directly proportional to the approach of change management in tech startups.

REFERENCES

Albukhitan, S. (2020). Developing digital transformation strategy for manufacturing. *Procedia Computer Science, 170*, 664–671. doi:10.1016/j.procs.2020.03.173

Ali, B. J., & Anwar, G. (2021). The mediation role of change management in employee development. *Ali, BJ, & Anwar, G.(2021). The Mediation Role of Change Management in Employee Development. International Journal of English Literature and Social Sciences, 6*(2), 361–374. doi:10.22161/ijels.62.52

Ali, B. J., & Anwar, G. (2021). The mediation role of change management in employee development. *Ali, BJ, & Anwar, G.(2021). The Mediation Role of Change Management in Employee Development. International Journal of English Literature and Social Sciences*, *6*(2), 361–374. doi:10.1080/00031305.2018.1543137

Alqatawenah, A. S. (2018). Transformational leadership style and its relationship with change management. *Verslas: TeorijaIrPraktika/Business. Theory into Practice*, *19*(0), 17–24. doi:10.3846/btp.2018.03

Amis, J., & Greenwood, R. (2020). Organisational change in a (post-) pandemic world: Rediscovering interests and values. *Journal of Management Studies*. doi:10.1103/PhysRevD.101.055025

Amrhein, V., Trafimow, D., & Greenland, S. (2019). Inferential statistics as descriptive statistics: There is no replication crisis if we don't expect replication. The American Statistician, 73(sup1), pp.262-270. doi:10.3390ym12010019

Anwer, S., Wen, L., & Wang, Z. 2019. A systematic approach for identifying requirement change management challenges: Preliminary results. *Proceedings of the Evaluation and Assessment on Software Engineering*, (pp. 230-235). ACM. 10.1145/3319008.3319031

Bhattacharya, S., Biswas, A., Nandi, S., & Patra, S. K. (2020). Exhaustive model selection in b→ s $\ell\ell$ decays: Pitting cross-validation against the Akaike information criterion. *Physical Review. D*, *101*(5), 055025. doi:10.1103/PhysRevD.101.055025

Bono, R., Arnau, J., Alarcón, R., & Blanca, M.J. (2019). Bias, precision, and accuracy of skewness and kurtosis estimators for frequently used continuous distributions. *Symmetry, 12*(1), 19. 10.25/eydgfi201931.222

Cameron, E., & Green, M. (2019). *Making sense of change management: A complete guide to the models, tools and techniques of organizational change*. Kogan Page Publishers. doi:10.1103/PhysRevD.101.055025

Covernton, G. A., Pearce, C. M., Gurney-Smith, H. J., Chastain, S. G., Ross, P. S., Dower, J. F., & Dudas, S. E. (2019). Size and shape matter: A preliminary analysis of microplastic sampling technique in seawater studies with implications for ecological risk assessment. *The Science of the Total Environment*, *667*, 124–132. doi:10.1016/j.scitotenv.2019.02.346 PMID:30826673

DelSole, T., & Tippett, M. K. (2021). Correcting the corrected AIC. *Statistics & Probability Letters*, *173*, 109064. doi:10.1016/j.spl.2021.109064

Dzenopoljac, V., Alasadi, R., Zaim, H., & Bontis, N. (2018). Impact of knowledge management processes on business performance: Evidence from Kuwait. *Knowledge and Process Management*, *25*(2), 77–87. doi:10.1002/kpm.1562

Forbes.com. (2022). Why Change Management Fails. *Forbes*. https://www.forbes.com/sites/victorlipman/2013/09/04/new-study-explores-why-change-management-fails-and-how-to-perhaps-succeed/?sh=4daf34347137

Hamilton, A. B., & Finley, E. P. (2019). Qualitative methods in implementation research: An introduction. *Psychiatry Research*, *280*, 112516. doi:10.1016/j.psychres.2019.112516 PMID:31437661

Harrison, R., Fischer, S., Walpola, R. L., Chauhan, A., Babalola, T., Mears, S., & Le-Dao, H. (2021). Where do models for change management, improvement and implementation meet? A systematic review of the applications of change management models in healthcare. *Journal of Healthcare Leadership*, *13*, 85–108. doi:10.2147/JHL.S289176 PMID:33737854

Hechanova, M. R. M., Caringal-Go, J. F., & Magsaysay, J. F. (2018). Implicit change leadership, change management, and affective commitment to change: Comparing academic institutions vs business enterprises. *Leadership and Organization Development Journal*, *39*(7), 914–925. doi:10.1108/LODJ-01-2018-0013

Jayatilleke, S., & Lai, R. (2018). A systematic review of requirements change management. *Information and Software Technology*, *93*, 163–185. doi:10.1016/j.infsof.2017.09.004

Korchagina, E., Desfonteines, L., Ray, S., & Strekalova, N. (2022). Digitalization of Transport Communications as a Tool for Improving the Quality of Life. *In International Scientific Conference on Innovations in Digital Economy* (pp. 22-34). Springer, Cham. 10.1007/978-3-031-14985-6_2

Li, J. Y., Sun, R., Tao, W., & Lee, Y. (2021). Employee coping with organizational change in the face of a pandemic: The role of transparent internal communication. *Public Relations Review*, *47*(1), 101984. doi:10.1016/j.pubrev.2020.101984 PMID:36568504

Linkedin.com. (2022). *How to make change management work in Asia*. Linkedin. [https://www.linkedin.com/pulse/how-make-change-management-work-asia-anthony-liu]

Luciano, M. M., Nahrgang, J. D., & Shropshire, C. (2020). Strategic leadership systems: Viewing top management teams and boards of directors from a multiteam systems perspective. *Academy of Management Review*, *45*(3), 675–701. doi:10.5465/amr.2017.0485

Mansaray, H. E. (2019). The role of leadership style in organisational change management: A literature review. *Journal of Human Resource Management*, *7*(1), 18–31. doi:10.11648/j.jhrm.20190701.13

Mavrot, C., Hadorn, S., & Sager, F. (2019). Mapping the mix: Linking instruments, settings and target groups in the study of policy mixes. *Research Policy*, *48*(10), 103614. doi:10.1016/j.respol.2018.06.012

Mishra, P., Pandey, C. M., Singh, U., Gupta, A., Sahu, C., & Keshri, A. (2019). Descriptive statistics and normality tests for statistical data. *Annals of Cardiac Anaesthesia*, *22*(1), 67. doi:10.4103/aca.ACA_157_18 PMID:30648682

Online Visual Paradigm. (2022). *Understanding Lewin's Change Management Model*. Visual Paradigm Online. https://online.visual-paradigm.com/knowledge/business-design/understand-lewins-change-management-model/.

Ozkeser, B. (2019). Impact of training on employee motivation in human resources management. *Procedia Computer Science*, *158*, 802–810. doi:10.1016/j.procs.2019.09.117

Paddeu, D., Parkhurst, G., & Shergold, I. (2020). Passenger comfort and trust on first-time use of a shared autonomous shuttle vehicle. *Transportation Research Part C, Emerging Technologies*, *115*, 102604. doi:10.1016/j.trc.2020.02.026

Pho, K. H., Ly, S., Ly, S., & Lukusa, T. M. (2019). Comparison among Akaike information criterion, Bayesian information criterion and Vuong's test in model selection: A case study of violated speed regulation in Taiwan. *Journal of Advanced Engineering and Computation*, *3*(1), 293–303. doi:10.25073/jaec.201931.220

Ray, S. (2021). "Ifs" and "Buts" in Poverty and Developmental Economics. Perspectives of Entrepreneurial University Model in Counervailing Effects. *Beneficium*, (2 (39)), 55–60.

Rosenbaum, D., More, E., & Steane, P. (2018). Planned organisational change management: Forward to the past? An exploratory literature review. *Journal of Organizational Change Management*, *31*(2), 286–303. doi:10.1108/JOCM-06-2015-0089

Sommet, N., & Morselli, D. (2021). Keep calm and learn multilevel linear modeling: A three-step procedure using SPSS, Stata, R, and MPlus. *Revue Internationale de Psychologie Sociale*, *34*(1), 24. doi:10.5334/irsp.555

Statista.com. (2020). [Data Sett]. *Statista*. https://www.statista.com/chart/22027/startup-sme-financial-situation-india/

Statista.com. 2022a. *Change management in organisations based on project and culture*. Statista. https://www.statista.com/statistics/1085414/enterprise-change-management-worldwide/

Statista.com. 2022b. *Tech start-up business investment value from 2017 to 2020 in Southeast Asia*. Statista. https://www.statista.com/statistics/1251921/sea-value-of-tech-startup-funding/

Statista.com. 2022c. *Lack of knowledge and skills of leaders for handling technological application*. Statista. https://www.statista.com/statistics/1248921/challenges-to-technology-transformation-in-companies/#:~:text=Challenges%20of%20technology%20transformations%20in%20companies%202020&text=The%20majority%20of%20the%20surveyed,changing%20their%20technology%20operating%20models

Suoniemi, S., Meyer-Waarden, L., Munzel, A., Zablah, A. R., & Straub, D. (2020). Big data and firm performance: The roles of market-directed capabilities and business strategy. *Information & Management*, *57*(7), 103365. https://www.sciencedirect.com/science/article/am/pii/S0378720620303037. doi:10.1016/j.im.2020.103365

Tawse, A., Patrick, V. M., & Vera, D. (2019). Crossing the chasm: Leadership nudges to help transition from strategy formulation to strategy implementation. *Business Horizons*, *62*(2), 249–257. doi:10.1016/j.bushor.2018.09.005

Thakhathi, A., le Roux, C., & Davis, A. (2019). Sustainability leaders' influencing strategies for institutionalisingorganisational change towards corporate sustainability: A strategy-as-practice perspective. *Journal of Change Management*, *19*(4), 246–265. doi:10.1080/14697017.2019.1578985

Thakur, V., & Mangla, S. K. (2019). Change management for sustainability: Evaluating the role of human, operational and technological factors in leading Indian firms in home appliances sector. *Journal of Cleaner Production*, *213*, 847–862. https://pearl.plymouth.ac.uk/bitstream/handle/10026.1/14932/BDAJCPR203March2019+%20SKM.docx?sequence=2. doi:10.1016/j.jclepro.2018.12.201

Weforum.org. (2022). *Training for improving leadership*. WeForum. https://www.weforum.org/agenda/2021/06/which-countries-are-most-invested-in-professional-develeopment/ [accessed on: 15.09.2022]

APPENDIX 1: SURVEY QUESTIONNAIRE

1. What is your gender?
   Male
   Female
2. What is your age?
   a. 20 - 30
   b. 30 - 40
   c. 40 - 50
3. Since how many years have you been in your startup?
   a. 0 - 1
   b. 1 - 2
   c. 2 - 3
4. Do you agree that leadership strategies are required for change management?
   1. Strongly Agree
   2. Agree
   3. Neutral
   4. Disagree
   5. Strongly Disagree
5. Do you agree that appropriate leadership strategy can disrupt change management?
   1. Strongly Agree
   2. Agree
   3. Neutral
   4. Disagree
   5. Strongly Disagree
   6. Do you agree that the leadership strategy in your start-up has motivated change management?
      1. Strongly Agree
      2. Agree
      3. Neutral
      4. Disagree
      5. Strongly Disagree
   7. Do you agree that departmental change management can be facilitated appropriately by a good manager?
      1. Strongly Agree
      2. Agree
      3. Neutral
      4. Disagree
      5. Strongly Disagree
   8. How satisfied are you with the change management in your organization or department?
      1. Highly satisfied
      2. satisfied
      3. Neutral

4. dissatisfied
5. Highly dissatisfied

9. Are you satisfied with the approach of your leader for the change management in your organization?
    1. Highly satisfied
    2. satisfied
    3. Neutral
    4. dissatisfied
    5. Highly dissatisfied
10. Are you satisfied with the communication strategies of the change management in your startup?
    1. Highly satisfied
    2. satisfied
    3. Neutral
    4. dissatisfied
    5. Highly dissatisfied

Chapter 7
Building Change Maturity in Organisations

Isolde G. Kanikani
FUTURE:CM, The Netherlands

ABSTRACT

'Building change maturity in organisations' explores what change maturity looks like in practice and how increased maturity brings a myriad of benefits to the organisation investing in it. Building maturity of any kind is often seen as a luxury, and with the growing amount of change organisations contend with, this is no longer the case. It's becoming increasingly clear that if an organisation does not develop the capability to change effectively, it will metaphorically miss the boat. This tipping point is very real, making the subject of building change maturity a poignant one. The impact of change maturity is often seen via change management on the project or program levels, and ROI measurements don't often go beyond this focus. Building the capability at the organisational level might appear like a theoretical exercise for those managing change, but with the right mindset, change capability can already be built into the transformation projects already taking place.

INTRODUCTION

An organisation's change maturity will greatly impact its ability to transform at the speeds needed to stay relevant in these fast-moving times. By assessing an organisation's change maturity with a model gaging level of Change maturity 'as is' factors related to levels in the organisation and actionable growth areas, we can support organisations to understand their Change maturity level, and how to develop this alongside tailoring the approach to value creation for increased return on investment. Further still, a model that can be extended into a framework will be even more supportive to organisations seeking to effectively reaching strategic goals and outcomes.

This chapter explores the currently available best practice around the context of change maturity in organisations. A topic not widely developed beyond a simple matrix table and explanation, save a few that have indeed leapt within specific disciplines. With change being as abundant as it is in these times, increasing change maturity has become a pure necessity. The speed of technological advances

DOI: 10.4018/978-1-6684-7509-6.ch007

can leave an organisation unable to compete or give an advantage depending on it's ability to adopt new technology and the capabilities it brings. Pandemics, climate change and sustainability measures, risk and compliance, the list of changes that not only need attention but scream for it is ongoing. The choices around how much one can prepare and introduce measures depend very much on an organisation's ability to effectively manage change, and are certainly not restricted to the profession of Change management. Why does change need to be managed to meet countless requirements? Management can speed up the adoption of new behaviours and tools, improve the overall number of people who take part and proficiently use the new ways. A common approach builds a shared language and understanding of change where key stakeholders can actively participaterather than watch on the sidelines or actively oppose the changes as they happen to them. It is important to remember that change is not linear, nor can it be contained to a single part of an organisation. True change maturity will incorporate a mix of a systematic approach, standard practice and a high amount of changeability. Growing a mindset where change management disappears because the outcome of change maturity is 'change capable', a new normal that every employee embodies. We only need change managers because this capability doesn't exist yet.

These outcomes of change management support less impactful ways of carrying out more change in organisations. There are at least two understandings of 'managing change' emerging here. The one that manages 'the people side of change' is referred to as 'Change Management' within this text and is often related to change within projects. The Second holistically acknowledges all types of change occurring in organisations further referred to as ChangeOps or simply change maturity. ChangeOps is a strategic approach to different kinds of change, that will be the base of Change maturity building and a concept developed further within this chapter. A large amount of change needing to be implemented, put alongside the organisation's ability to implement change nearly always results in an answer of 'speed up so we can get more done', in a way where properly managed change of either kind can not occur. Many reasons exists, everything from ignorance, inability to understand the consequences of not changing, to having no personal vision or strategy when it comes to operational level management and company culture looking at this from a working environment perspective. This mentality is often driven by leaders who need to pivot their thinking toward the sustainability of their workforce, and understanding that speeding up mostly means surviving and then breaking rather than the desired business growth or other sustainable outcomes. Instead, shift to the concept of building change maturity in the first projects so an organisation can indeed hit the road running from survival mode to a c true thrive. Wait too long, and the crucial gaps will get too big to survive at all. The aim of this chapter is not to bring a doomsday message, but one to adapt now while the advancement gap is still small enough to avoid going beyond tipping points into a place of no return. Building change maturity alongside these vital projects to ensure that organisations can increase the effectiveness of those projects being carried out, make the most of the investment and shift mindset from maturity being a theoretical monster best left alone to an actionable think big start small strategy where value is delivered incrementally with every project that was going to take place anyway.

The combination of the general immaturity of organisation's when it comes to change, coupled with the lack of understanding around how to 'build change maturity' best practice and the organisation-wide benefit it brings gives rise to a clear need for further development. Making this an important area for further research and discovery.

What is Organisational Change Maturity?

Organisational change maturity can be defined in more ways. For alignment, we will use a working definition 'Change maturity is the state of an organisation when it effectively and sustainably manages organisational change in a manner that is adequately attuned to the needs of its owners, leadership, employees and customers while maintaining the thrive ability of the organisation as the system that delivers on those needs' (Sidhu et al., 2014) (Akhtar et al., 2021). There is a lot held in this statement that can be broken down into key focus points including: needs of the associated people, organisational structure and system of value creation, change that is effective and sustainable.

'Business enterprises are organs of society. They do not exist for their own sake, but to fulfil a specific social purpose and to satisfy a specific need of a society, a community, or individuals' (Drucker, 1993). With this in mind, it is often the fundaments of the organisation as well as the people that reside within the context of an organisation that are constantly required to change. Organisational structure shapes the people, and the people shape the organisational structures (Baligh, 2011), but for what purpose? Many would answer with profits or power, but essentially the effort boils down to building customers through value creation (Lim, 2020) (Esmanech, 2018). Sustainability should be designed into the system of value creation, and once implemented becomes a form of governance for the two other aspects mentioned above. These two aspects become potential approaches to build maturity, either through people or through the organisational structure and governance. These two aspects can be broken down into more specific factors which represent the 'as is' state and starting points for the growth of both maturity and the changes inherent in this process. With the speed of change needed at times, there are often decisions made that either focus on short term gains or have not taken the maintenance and updating of these factors into account. A state of change maturity promotes an organisational setup free of organisational debts and where value flows as an organisational capability through the organisation to customers.

Why is it Important and Why Now?

We are living in unprecedented times where VUCA elements are very relevant and building traction. VUCA is an acronym for Volatile, Uncertain, Complex and Ambiguous (Bennis & Nanus, 2003). BANI is another such model of extreme change outcomes describing four states namely Brittleness, Anxiety, Nonlinearity, and Incomprehensibility (Temmen, 2021) (Cascio, 2020). All 8 words relate to how each make us feel. A standard reaction to each is to resist, giving us time to process and find the correct course of action. Whether we take VUCA which is an outcome of the cold war situation or BANI shaped by climate and systemic change, dealing with these states created by mass change is an important aspect of building change capability and through this the elusive state of maturity. Instead of brittle we want agility, instead of expecting certainty get used to uncertainty and thrive from it. In a nutshell, we need to shift our mindset toward an image of life that we engage with every day.

The ability for organisations to change is no longer a nice to have, but a must-have to keep up and potentially conquer the massive advancement gaps grown in areas like technology in recent years. This may sound like the notorious burning platform of Kotter (Kotter, 2012, 21), but there is a very real tipping point of no return in multiple factor areas like technological advancement, organisational governance or security. An example is where an organisation is too slow to adapt to the technology needed to survive and the pace of technological advancement is increasing rather than slowing down (Cascio & Montealegre, 2019). There will come a point when the gap between the 'as is' and 'to be' states is too big to bridge as shown in Figure 9 and a theoretical basis for this was already laid in 1961 by M.V. Posner was examining the maturity of technology (Gandolfo, 1998). The tipping point is different in each industry and dependent on the amount of technology required for basic operations and the amount of technological advancement needed to not only survive but thrive (Kotter et al., 2021, 6-20). This tipping point is not only reserved for technology or one speeding-up scenario, but is an element of multiple organisational factors that can occur simultaneously.

The concept to manage change is relatively young, underdeveloped and possibly too focused on the people side as a reaction to an initial need that people were catered for within projects. This is a big statement, but one backed up by the interconnected reliance of factors: people, change and organisational governance. People are both enabled and blocked by governance, and governance can be poorly or well managed by people. So therefore the only way to support people in the process of change is to give the structural governance side of change attention too. A new generation of change managers are calling themselves 'Transformation Experts' or adding Organisational to their titles to show that they focus on both elements. It's also comparatively young to project management, leadership and management studies that saw an earlier start to the development. The available change management best practice is highly focused on change occurring during projects, along with scaled approaches for programs and portfolios. There is a clear relationship between project management and change management and a simpler situation to standardise. No one standard cohesively brings together best practices used across all organisational change management. It draws on theory, method and best practice across the board, spanning 60 years or more. In the background, all these methods have arisen from some pretty dated theory that while useful and even relevant, shouldn't fill the space of modern practice that brings together the knowledge we have available to us. Examples include the change curve by Elizabeth Kubler Ross (1969), and the three states of change reproduced by over 30 different parties including William Bridges (2009)(Bridges, n.d.) and Kurt Lewin (1947) (Lewin, n.d.). Why is all this important? There is a need to collect knowledge and experience in and around the topic of Organisational Change Management, centralising this into a body of knowledge that is truly able to support the building of change maturity in organisations.

Organisations like Prosci, the Association of change management professionals (ACMP) and the Change management institute (CMI) are beginning to create established bodies of general change management best practices. Others focusing on change at the leadership level will often use methods by AIM and Kotter, along with other disciplines that influence the leadership development circles. Organisation-wide change management is still emerging, relying on organisational development practices (OD), Systems theory, adaptive theories and more. Due to the naturally complex nature of organisation-wide change, practitioners tend to specialise in one area. Put this all together, there is a great amount of knowledge and best practices around change in the form of projects, but a big black hole when it comes to standardised approaches that cohesively bring it all together. We are only now experiencing times that call for a need to build change maturity and have the tools to build this body of knowledge. There is a knowledge and best practice gap, while a huge need for people who can build change maturity in organisations exists. We are living in a time where change doesn't wait for anyone, and where the capability to manage mass change has its tipping point.

The second answer to the question of why it is important and why now is the need to deal with what seems to be a sudden and growing amount of change from all areas including Politics, Economics, Social, Technology, Legal, Environmental and Ethical (PESTLE(E)). How can we prepare for uncertainty? Besides the search to build maturity, it is interesting to explore why we need change maturity at all. How can we innovate enough to thrive, with the growing amount of transformational change needed to remain modern and use up available resources? Getting rid of organisational debt resulting from short-term decision-making for short-term gains for strategically working with a 'think big, make small steps mentality'. Thinking small and acting small means we lose the bigger picture, we might or might not remain relevant but short-term gains are possible. Thinking big connects to the outward appearance of the last of any maturity model steps, where we keep checking our direction and strategic journey. Building value incrementally into this bigger picture allows us to regularly develop a value for the business, and mitigate the creation of wastes and systems we need to maintain but no longer deliver a benefit. There might even be a strategic value in advancing only to the second or third level of a five-step maturity. This is another case for becoming maturity aware, we create choices with insight. Currently, organisations are moving faster than their governance can keep up with, there is a need to move even faster still which creates a build-up of organisational debt. Building change maturity as a capability in organisations speeds up adoption, decreases debts and delivers incremental value. There is a potential moment coming when the low average organisational capability of change in organisations will limit investment in external factors like technology. But even here, the organisations with the highest degree of change maturity and capability are the ones that will remain the most competitive. The person or organisation with the most flexibility in a system will have the most influence.

Sustaining Change Maturity Level for Growth

The outputs of building change maturity would therefore be to increase value creation that further builds customers. An up-to-date governance that defines and maintains an organisation's purpose and value chain. Many of the changes we see organisations trying to implement are often seeking this precise outcome, but actual success varies and the greatest influences here are again organisational governance and people. If they are not aligned with business outcomes, then greater care is needed to get these internal transformation initiatives aligned. Not doing so can mean that delivered customer value is lost. This begs the question that if the project outcome doesn't fulfil the purpose of the organisation, uses limited resources and builds up the load of change on employees, why is it permitted to proceed? A short answer is that it should not, but an organisation often does not have the infrastructure to know or check or is loaded high with organisational debt so you can't see clearly past the simple maintenance of old procedures and ways. Business-orientated project management offices or a centralised transformation office can do wonders in prioritising change and aligning it to the strategic goals of the business (Cuellar et al., 2021) (Chauviere et al., 2016). 'We build the solution for the organisation, we support the people to adopt the solution' (Prosci, n.d.). Prosci's quote sums up the relationship between people, organisation and potential for value-creating solutions succinctly.

In a mature organisation, the approach to change needs to be effective while sustainable. The basis for effective change would be a standard approach, one that is used in every part of the organisation creating a shared purpose and language around change (Change Management Institute, 2014,). It's easy to want to apply a blanket approach to building change maturity in organisations, an approach many change managers have and still preach. But if we consider the purpose of the organisation, the limited resources it has to reach that purpose and the sheer fact that the people can only take so much change before becoming fatigued. A blanket approach to building change maturity is not effective because there is too much waste involved, while less value will be achieved in the areas where value can be quickly realised (Kanikani, 2022). Some parts of the organisation will realise far more value than others when a high level of change maturity is realised. If we tailor our change response to these parts of the organisation, we increase the return on investment (ROI) where it makes a difference (Goedhart et al., 2015) (Hall et al., 2012).

Sustainability is another interesting theme and refers to the journey of an organisation's people through changes. Everything from leadership's need for speed, and employees' need for attainable working conditions, to an organisation's need for maintenance of its governance and knowledge, are important aspects. Decreasing organisational debt by making decisions that are fit for the long term would be another. And of course … Building change maturity to balance these needs is a vital element. Leadership needs to pivot their thinking toward the sustainability of their workforce and the fact that speeding up means surviving and then breaking. Either from high percentages of attrition, organisational debt with its repercussions, to other aspects that can more often arise. Instead, shift to the concept of building change maturity in your first projects so you can indeed hit the road running from survival mode to a true thrive. This is possible because as an organisation's approach becomes more standardised, the impact of specific changes becomes less and as a consequence quicker to achieve. Wait too long, and the advances in technology, build-up of attrition and organisational debt will get too big to thrive at all.

This chapter will explore the currently available Change maturity best practices from different disciplines, explore practical method to building change maturity and use knowledge gained to create a Change maturity prototype that will already comprehensively support organisations with change maturity building.

BACKGROUND

Maturity Models and Frameworks:

The subject of building maturity is not a new one, while their maturity focus area is nuanced they have a lot they can lend to the search for building change maturity in organisations. There are many Maturity models and frameworks available from different disciplines currently used. Examples include the BABOK business analysis book of knowledge, the PMBOK, SAFe model, P3M3 and Prince 2 to name a few (Axelos, 2017) (IIBA, 2015) (PMI, 2013). With so many disciplines building maturity, it is maybe wise to question what the state of maturity looks like. For the sake of this text, maturity is the state of being fully developed, which implies a journey of growth. Mixed with the concept of an uncertain future which is a future that has not yet been determined, one that has not yet been captured in blueprints (Van der Duin & De Graaf, 2010), we rarely find the resting state of maturity because the goal posts keep moving with development. While the look of maturity remains elusive, the journey of growth to get there is more tangible and building change maturity is about focusing on this journey. We need to design a framework that supports the organisation and its people to agilely grow with the times while being standardised enough that change is a recognisable way of organising, regulating and communicating within the organisation.

Most maturity models available make actual maturity somewhat elusive, the last of the steps is a nice horizon but just a bit too out of reach for mere mortal organisations to achieve. This connects nicely with what has been written above about the flexibility of the end goal of maturity, as the organisational environment develops so too does the end state of maturity (Bruin, 2005). Organising capability in relation to good performance is often paired with operational efficiency when on the path to building maturity. Maintaining this good performance requires the organisation to continually change (Child, 1984). By building change maturity we give organisations the standard approach to change which makes it flexible to unprecedented future events, effective and efficient at organising the current state and the state of transitional change. This frees up resources for the organisation to invest in activities that increase profits, growth or innovation.

What are the core components of a change maturity model that will support value creation on the journey to becoming mature? The list gathered from different sources would suggest that a model is helpful to show the steps related to practical actions an organisation can take to grow maturity. Another addition would be an assessment of the 'as is' and 'to be' states to gauge where an organisation is on the maturity scale and what it needs to change. Within the 'as is' state it is important to recognise the current state and factors we want to change, conventionally this would be the governance, operations, adherence to compliance regulation, digital capability and the systemic ways of organising business-as-usual (BAU), important factors to include in the assessment. Then there is the 'journey' or transition with the structures and tools needed to effectively realise the change. This would include project frameworks, continuous improvement practices, ChangeOps and change capability. Besides this, digital maturity is becoming vital as organisations increasingly rely on and invest in technology (Kafel, 2021). Connecting strategic business goals with value-driven change that strategically flows through the organisation. A change maturity model is a great tool for becoming aware of the current maturity level but is missing out on a bigger invitation. Further developing the model into a change maturity framework that incorporates other maturity best practices enables organisations to make use of the existing best practices, some of which are already in use and combine them into a unified approach to building change maturity.

Exploration of Existing Maturity Models from Different Disciplines

One of the earlier maturity models is the Capability Maturity Model (CMM), a five-step development model created in 1986 after a study of data collected from organisation's that contracted with the U.S. Defense Department which can be seen in Figure 1 (Paulk et al., 1993). Built on an even earlier six-step maturity model created to manage information in organisations 'The stages of growth model created by Richard Nolan in 1973' (Favaretto & Meirelles, 2015). Both are still used widely, but the CMM model received an update from Carnegie Mellon University released in 2002 in the form of the Capability Maturity Model Integration in Figure 3 (CMMI) (Weber, 1995). There is a well-thought-out maturity assessment for CMMI (Erdogan & Yucalar, 2009), which helps to bring the discussion from possibly theoretical to very tangible. Many of the maturity models here have assessments that will be drawn on for the C+CMM, a new simple model shown later in this text. All in all, building capability of any kind has a lot to do with developing employees' ability to thrive during change (Osteen & Subramanian, 2013) and creating a supporting structure with process and technology that reinforce this ability.

Five appears to be the magic number of steps for many models and The Gartner Business intelligence model (2008) follows the same tradition with steps: Unaware, tactical, focused, strategic, and Pervasive (Thakur, 2022). This model is focusing on the trustworthiness of business information and the analysis of this to increase business outcomes. What is interesting is the core attributes of any given model rely more and more on the IT capability of the organisation making IT maturity an important factor of the 'as is' state and therefore an item to measure when it comes to change maturity. The IT-CMF or IT Capability maturity framework takes this view by providing an integrated management framework and set of tools for designing, deploying and operating information systems to deliver sustainable value and innovation (Craig, 2020) (Van Haren Publishing, 2017). There are five steps or levels of maturity in the IT-CMF model going from Initial through to Basic, Intermediate, Advanced and optimising. The feature

Figure 1. CMM steps, own elaboration (2022)

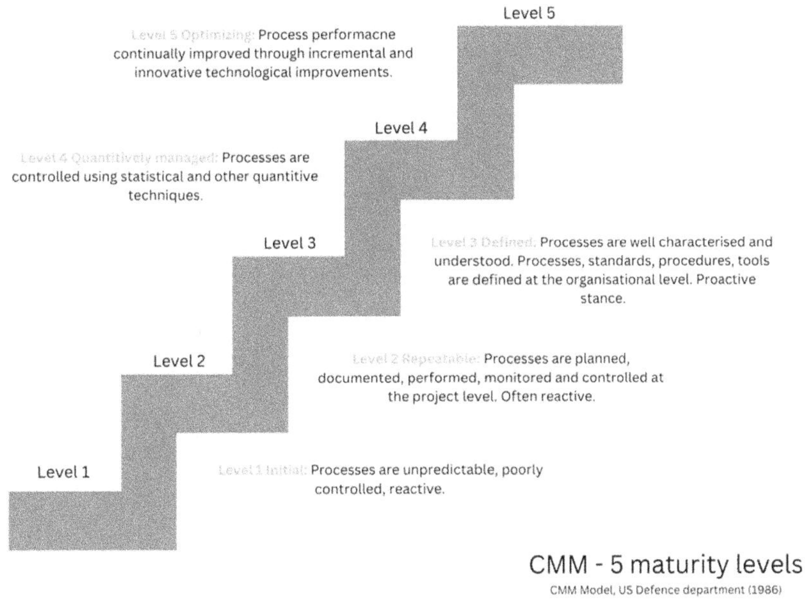

Figure 2. Nolan's Stages of Growth model, own elaboration (2022)

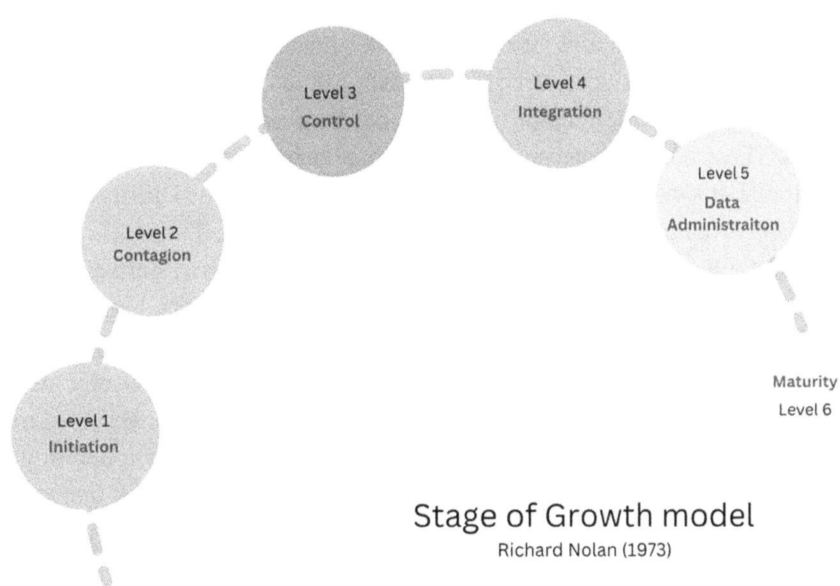

Figure 3. CMMI model (Carnegie Mellon University 2002), own elaboration (2022)

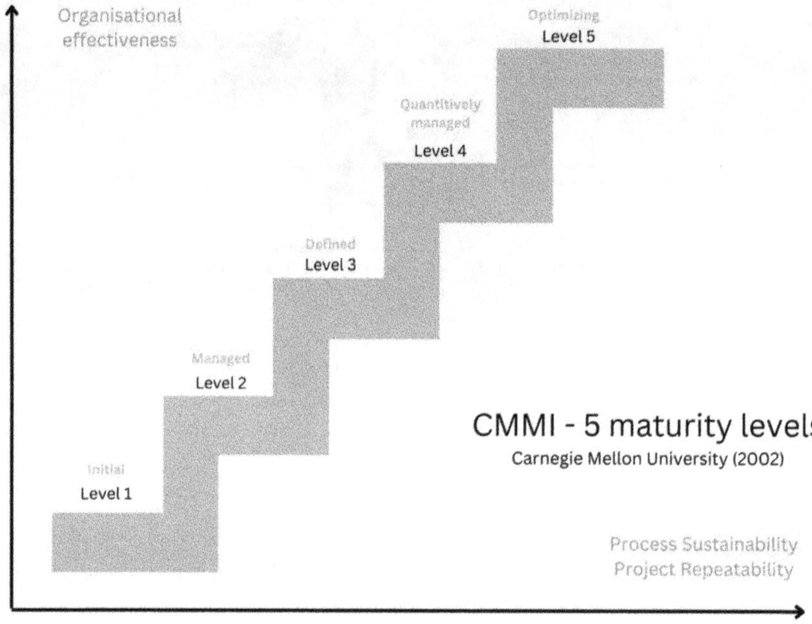

of 'five steps' is useful to keep in mind when considering a framework that could potentially combine with other maturity models out there.

While many of these models were originally tailored towards IT software, data and hardware, these days they have been developed to have a much broader application. The CMMI model is a good example here, with it's most recent rendition now having objectives for businesses that include enabling the organisation to: 'produce quality services or products, improve customer satisfaction, increase value for stockholders, achieve industry-wide recognition for excellence and grow market share' (Watts, 2020) (Shrum et al., 2003). These desired outcomes would also be on the list for a change maturity model 'as is' states to be developed. It's worth mentioning the Business Intelligence maturity model (Gartner 2008) and the Business analysis maturity model (BAMM), two models created to assess the level of Business analysis maturity (Hindle et al., 2014, 13). An 'as is' factor to incorporate within a change maturity model simply because we need to be able to assess where we are on the journey and keep outcomes related to strategic business goals. The same logic works when looking at project management maturity, there are various models here but one that has been developed with strategic business outcomes in mind is the OPM3 Project management maturity model (Fahrenkrog, n.d.). Project management maturity level is an important consideration due to project management being one of the main tools for change. There is an interesting invitation forming, one of building a change maturity framework that would unite many other best practices in such a way that an organisation could choose which types of maturity they want and need to build, much like COBIT does for governance.

Change maturity building brings value, and we can maximise this by connecting maturity building activities to areas of highest value creation. Each of the different maturity best practices out there can be combined to increase the benefits still further, theres no point to reinvent the wheel if the knowledge has already been tried and tested and found valuable. Therefore, it is advisable to focus development efforts where value is created, especially keeping in mind that every organisation has limited resources. Where there are models focused on building non-IT related maturity, they have become intrinsically linked to IT maturity for the sheer fact that in this day and age, technology is becoming the backbone that businesses are built. This fact is also one of the factors forcing organisations to change maturity due to the sheer speed of technological advancement, it is a do now or soon to be technologically redundant since not developing now means the technology gap is growing closer and closer to the point of no return. We can not be business minded without technology, we can nott have development of a technological environment that is not mindful of the business and the people who have to adopt the new 'to be' state being introduced. This brings us to the interconnectedness of the business culture of today with the People, Process Technology (PPT Model) view that succinctly clarifies the core relationship we could work with when building change maturity (March, 2015). Similar aspects show up in the KOPE Capability model by King published in 2006, complementing the PPT model by prompting us to think outside of the box with the same basic components (Change Management Institute, 2014, 117). The PPT model was first published in 1964 by Harold Leavitt and popularised by Bruce Schneier in the 1990s (People, Process, Technology: The PPT Framework, Explained, 2022). The process part of the equation was originally described as 'Tasks' and 'structure', clarified in Figure 5. Broken down in this way it is easier to see the core components where tasks would be done by either people or technology and structure can be associated with organisational governance, one of the basic aspects of the 'as is' state to be developed during change.

Figure 4.

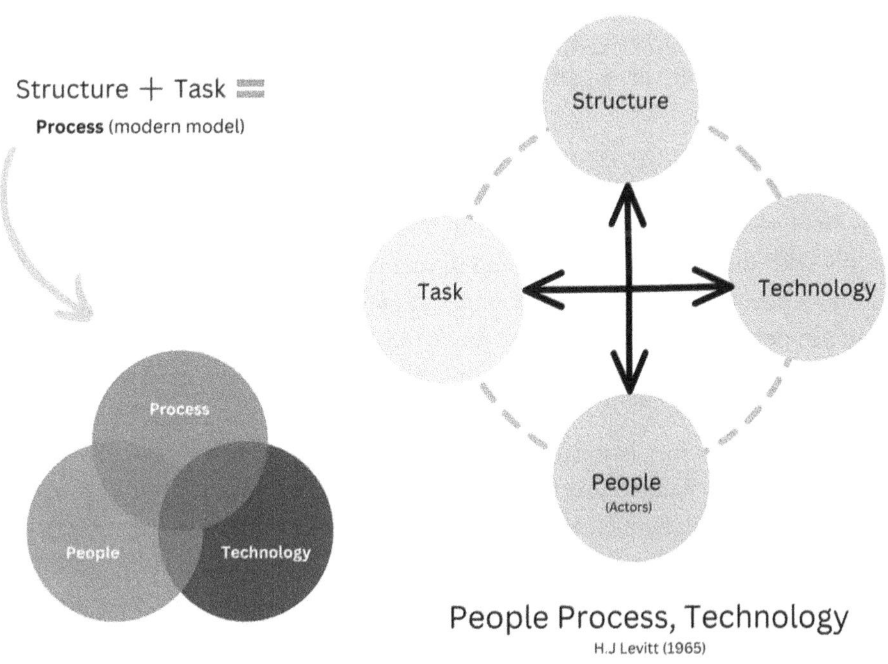

Figure 5. People process technology Levitt, own elaboration (2022)

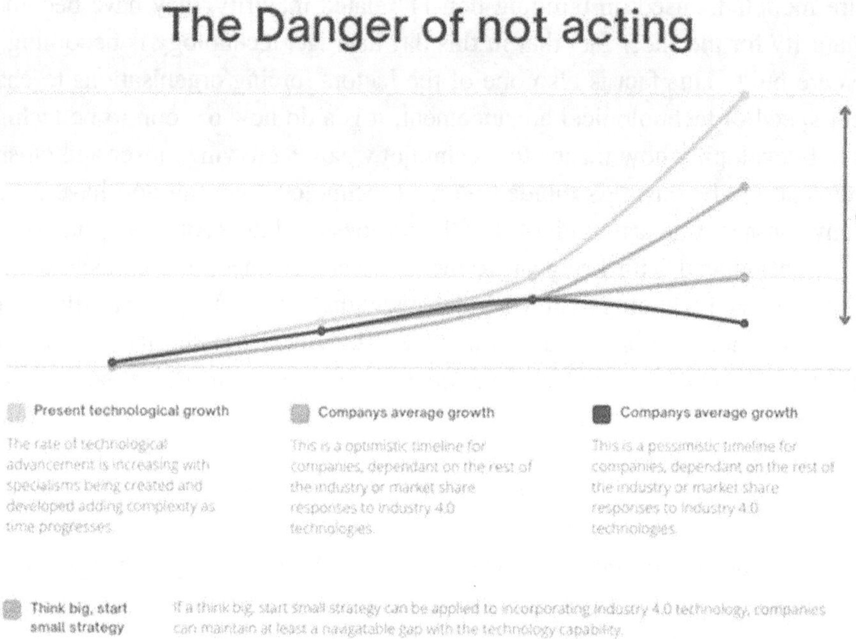

There is an abundance of material and inspiration to draw from when looking at the research, models, methods and approaches developed around the broader picture of building maturity. Many of the models looked at in this chapter have gone through an evolution, first being built with a specific type of maturity in mind, and then transitioning to a model that delivers both business value and builds maturity through a more tailored approach. There are models with only three steps and others with many more, but there seems to be a five-step sweet spot. Fewer steps mean a higher level approach and less detail, the more steps one has the more detail we can bring but at some point, we can lose sight of the destination. Couple this with the concept that the desired maturity level is a changing goal post due to many aspects of business developing at speed to counteract external influences. It would be good to keep in mind that to go too detailed would potentially place our focus on maturity development that is already outdated, creating a waste rather than create value. Working with a five or seven-step approach would hold these aspects in balance.

When developing our change Maturity model it will become more valuable if we take into account a broader number of 'as is' state factors that would include but are not limited to Governance, roles & responsibilities, employee behaviours, relationship and centricity of the customer, organisational design, information, knowledge and communication systems. These factors will need to go through a transformation to improve business value, the organising factor and performance. The way these factors will undergo change is also important because there is also a maturity level that can be attached to these. For example the maturity level of the project organisation or the continuous improvement practices and quality management systems in place. There are change maturity models out there that focus on the people side of transformation, we will look at these in the next part of this chapter. But if we combine some premises like change maturity being an organisational capability, that it relies on the maturity of many other aspects and that change maturity is more than people but incorporates Process and technology. Would it not be wise to take up the challenge of building a change maturity framework that unites these various factors and maturities based on what the organisation needs for value creation? This is a topic we will also develop further within this chapter. Last but not least, the ability to measure where we are on the scale of change maturity both at the beginning of the transformation journey and midway. With a moving end state, the importance of being able to celebrate progress is paramount to continued success, as are the important milestones defined by measurement.

'Every step is the journey, and the journey itself is home' Matsuo Basho

Existing Change Focused Maturity Models

While it has been hinted that maturity models focused specifically on building change management maturity are scarce, there are some notable models commonly found in the change managers toolkit out there. With a clear divide between those that cover organisational change maturity presented as a framework and those that are purely focused on building change Management maturity in an organisation and presented as a simpler model approach. One of which includes Prosci's five-step change Management maturity method and the change management institutes (CMI) change maturity model. There are also mentions of Change maturity in the Association of Change Management Professionals (ACMP) Standard but no formalised model exists (ACMP, 2019). A newcomer is a model fairly newly developed called the Org-CMF with a backbone of extensive research (Org-CMF). We will take a look at each of these models, exploring key takeaways for the further development of a framework for building change maturity in organisations.

This is where a key difference between a change maturity model and a change maturity framework can be clarified. The model can promote a more specific approach, usually presenting a situation more simply than it is in reality, an example of this could be the change maturity model by Prosci. The invitation of a framework is that many other methods and models could potentially be incorporated, building on the possibility of combining all sorts of Maturity best practices to meet the specific change maturity needs of any given organisation.

Prosci's change maturity model is a five-step model including the following five levels of maturity: Ad hoc or absent, Isolated projects, multiple projects, organisational standards, and organisational competency. These levels refer specifically to the level of change management maturity of an organisation rather than change maturity. It closely resembles the CMMI model (Five Levels of Change Management Maturity, n.d.) that has further influenced Microsoft's change management approach (Stephen, n.d.) (Delaini, 2022). This model is based on benchmarking research and is a great tool for building change management maturity. Combine this with a project management maturity model to optimise change carried out as projects, maximising success and project ROI.

The research effort to find fully developed change maturity models came with surprisingly few results. Change management is a relatively new profession in comparison with management generally or project management which both have a large number of developed best practice methods and frameworks. This might be one way to explain why there is a lack of highly developed best practices around change maturity. The reason for mentioning this is that the most recognisable change management happens alongside projects with several basic methods one can follow. While there are many practitioners out there who consider themselves seasoned change managers, it is harder to recognise a commonly shared best practices when it comes to building change maturity. This could be because it is not formalised yet, but it could also be a result of the overall maturity of the change management profession. Using Prosci's maturity levels, if change management practitioners are only at the level of maturity to be practised in Ad hoc and isolated change management delivery due to the average organisation's maturity levels (levels 1 & 2), then the natural focus of most practitioners would be to focus on the next level of shared method going across multiple projects. It is only the forward thinkers, big picture seekers and system theory believers who might search for maturity across a whole organisation before there is a tangible situation that calls for it. Understandable due to Organisational Change maturity often being seen as a luxury rather than the necessity that it is quickly growing into (Change Management Institute, 2014, 186), bringing a conclusion that development is slow in areas where there is not an understood need. With the growth of political, economic, health and climate instability we are facing a shake-up of this old status quo (Cameron & Green, 2012).

The change management Institutes Change Management maturity model works best around project level maturity but is certainly equipt to address upper levels of business and organisation. This maturity model breaks down into thirteen knowledge areas and the maturity of these is focused on the level of business worked with e.g. Project, Business or Organisation (Change Management Institute, 2014). It is an interesting model in that it uses a completely different format from the others found during research. The differentiation between levels is a useful reminder that all levels of the organisation are not the same and therefore need different approaches. Change management is a term with such a broad reach in terms of what this can mean professionally. As individual professionals there seems to be a tendency to first generalise and then specialise in one of the three areas. When looking at an organisation's change holistically we need to keep in mind all three aspects and more. There are different types of change occurring in organisations besides change happening at different levels and needing different approaches for each. Change can take the shape of projects, but also continuous improvement, quality management or even talent development activities. Clarifying this picture of different types of change in organisations and the flow of value creation can open up several strategic choices for building change maturity (Kanikani, 2022). ChangeOps is a model created in 2020 for building strategic choices around change and building maturity in the organisation.

ODTI's Organisation Maturity Index (OMI) is a Maturity Reference Model and related Body of Knowledge that represents the Key Capabilities and their respective Maturity Levels for any Organisation or Organisational Unit required to function, and to build Performance Advantage towards a Leadership position (Overview of the Organisation Maturity Index (OMI) — ODTI, n.d.). This is one of three main models that make up the Organisation Capability Maturity framework or Org-CMF for short. Another integral part of Org-CMF is the Dynamics Systems maturity theory which has been developed to understand and improve Organisation systems. Org-CMF has been developed by one of the same individuals who partly developed the IT-CMF discussed earlier in this chapter and draws from this model. So far the Org-CMF is one of the most actionable of the change management frameworks and has been developed with a lot of supporting research and further methods. It's good to mention though that it's a framework focused on Organisation capability maturity rather than the simpler change management Maturity models of CMI and Prosci.

Summing up the takeaways for already existing change maturity models, there are some interesting nuances to take into account when considering the creation of a new change maturity model. Some focus on actions and activities to achieve maturity which are actionable. If we combine both, we get a com-

Figure 6.

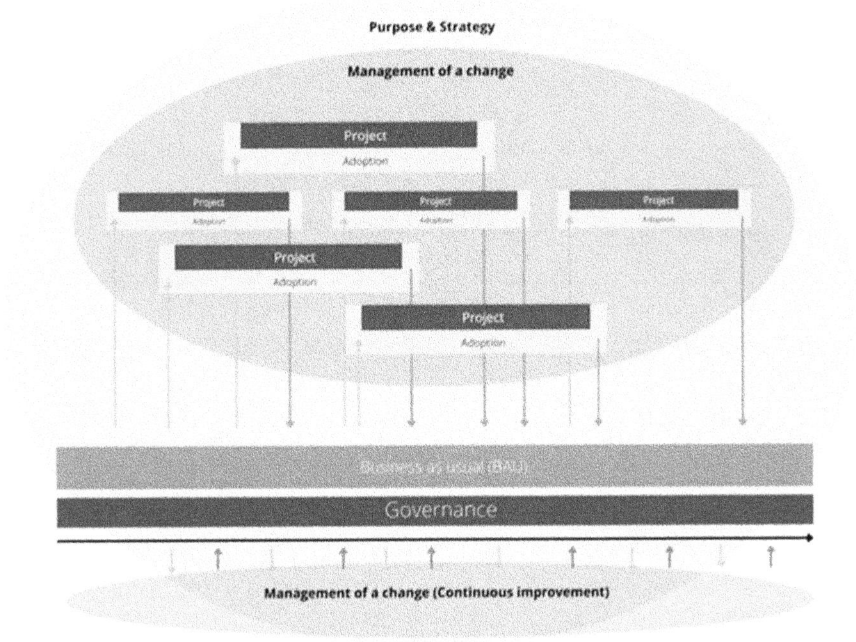

Figure 7.

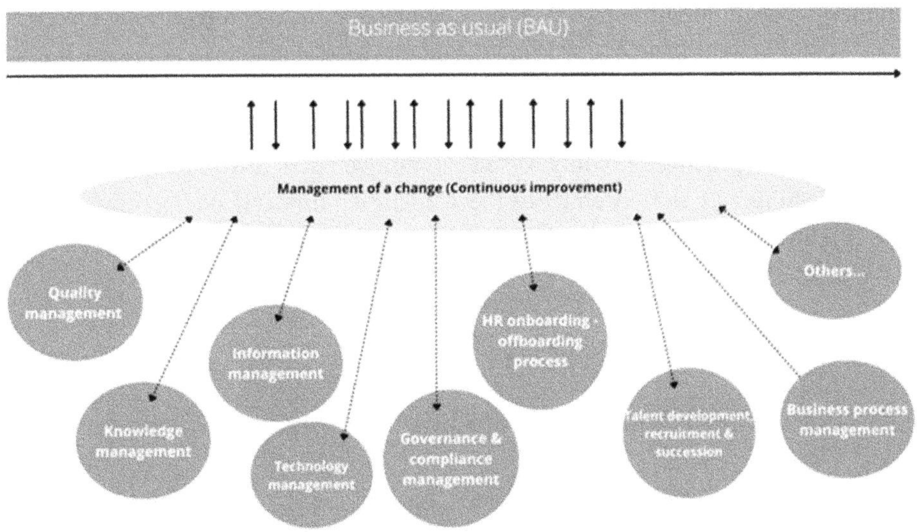

Figure 8. Technology gap, own elaboration (2019)

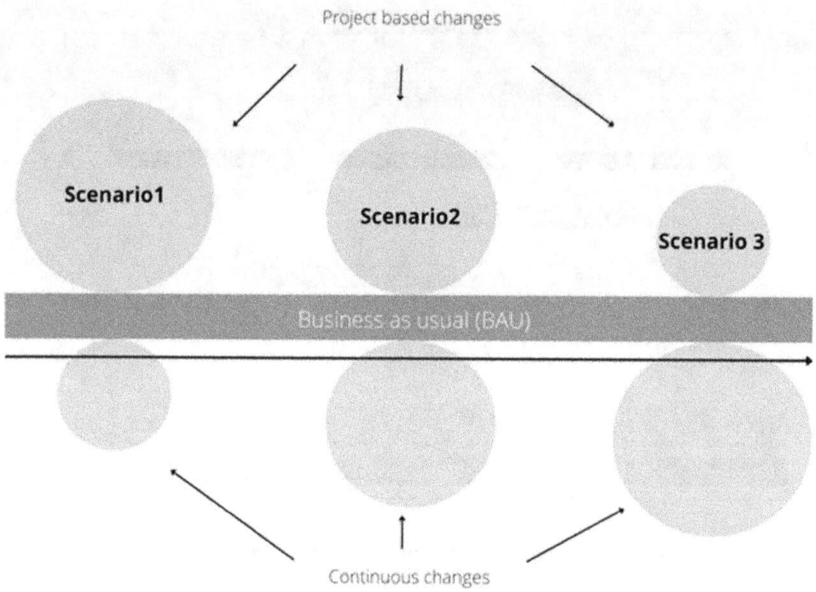

prehensive change maturity model, but does this help organisations grow maturity? How do we shift the mindset and focus away from the finished state of maturity to the journey and incremental growth? Are we looking for a model that builds change management maturity or organisational change maturity? A model is a great way to grow both, but a framework lends itself to being flexible enough to incorporate a lot of the other extremely relevant maturity best practices. How to connect change management maturity with that of projects, business intelligence, governance and any area that supports the business in achieving its purpose. Lastly, what about the nature of change itself and the fact that change can take many forms? A change maturity model that creates a holistic view of the change in an organisation, connecting this with other necessary best practices flexibly to suit the unique set of attributes of an organisation would be a huge asset in dealing with the extremity of these changing times. If such a framework were to exist, how would we persuade organisations that building change maturity capability is a worthy investment?

SOLUTIONS AND RECOMMENDATIONS

Strategically Harnessing the Power of Different Types of Change

Change can occur in many different circumstances, be it as a project, or as continuous improvement using kaizen principles or methods guided by other Agile frameworks. It can be radical which is harder to monitor and there is often more risk involved because outcomes are harder to predict. Usually, more investment is needed to ensure that we win the fight against inertia. It can be iterative, where the goals are easier to define, but significantly less change is realised in a short amount of time but more often a minimum viable product is available far sooner than larger more drawn-out projects. Change can be a problem to deal with in PRINCE2 and other project methods or something inevitable according to most change managers out there. The following definition of change will be used as a basis for discussion, 'We develop the solution for the organisation, we develop the people in the organisation for the solution

Figure 9.

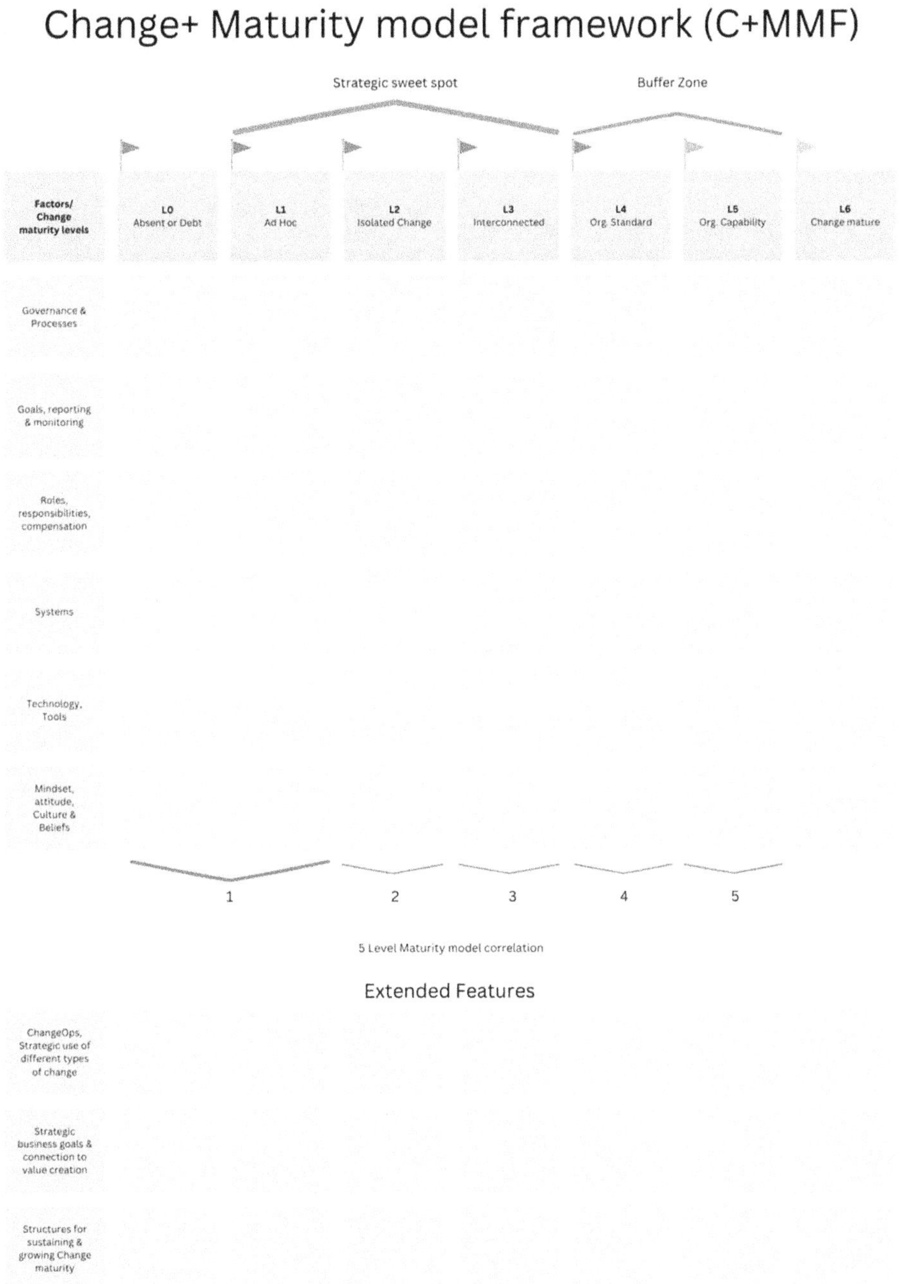

Figure 10. ChangeOps, governance and flow

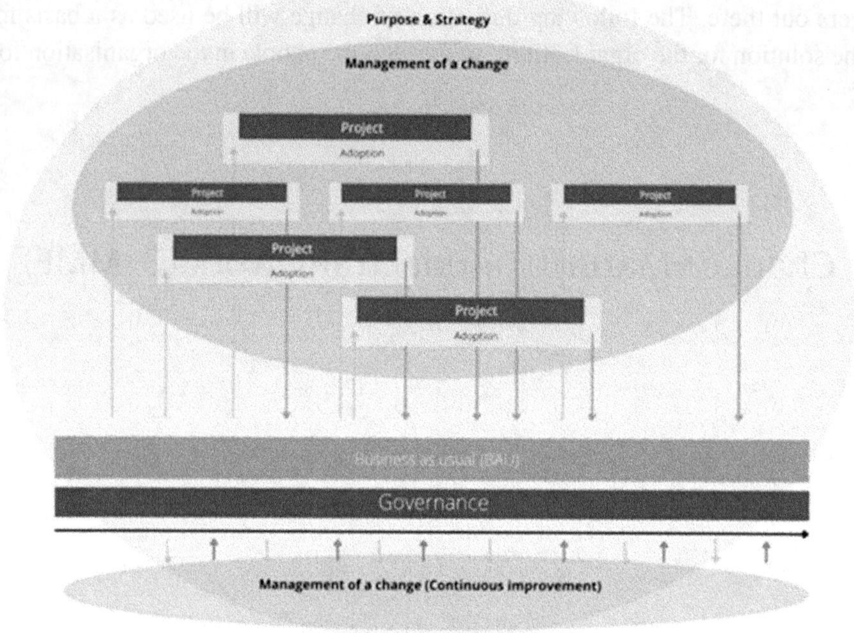

Figure 11. ChangeOps, continuous improvement and other forms of change

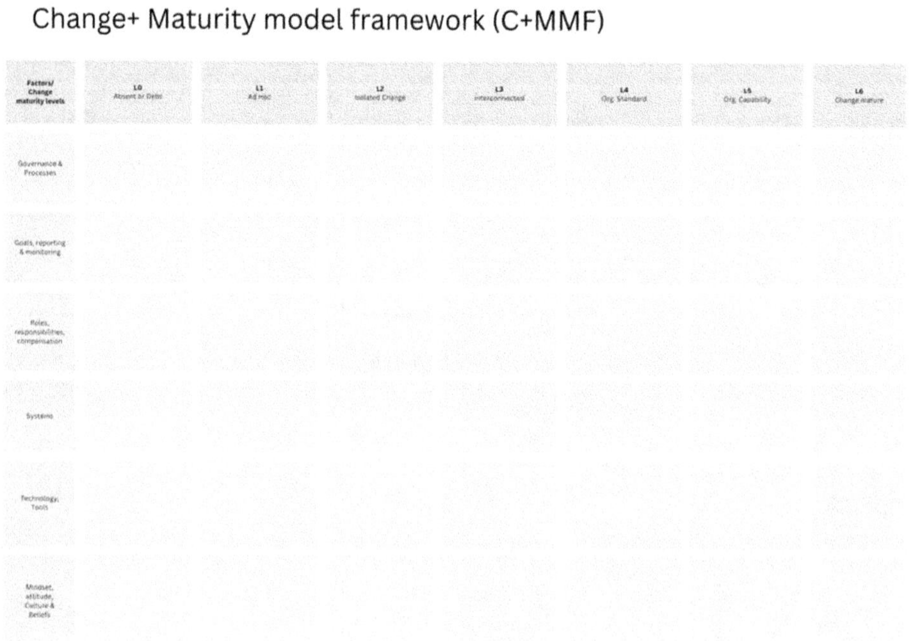

(Prosci, n.d.). The case of developing solutions for the organisation directly relates to improving the culture and governance structure factors. Keeping in mind that improving the organisation's ability for value creation is the primary goal here. This is not normally achievable without looking at the flow of day-to-day operations and the way value or work in progress (WIP) moves through the organisation.

Change takes many forms, and we tend to rely on only a few of the possible forms, theories and best practices available to us. There is also a tendency to rely on a radical change in the form of projects to change rather than more incremental approaches. Due to limits on time and a lack of resources, it is easier to stay with and perpetuate the known change pathways. Change as a project is probably one of the most established, yet we still rush the planning and do not leave enough time to properly integrate the outcomes of the change into business as usual (BAU) when we are done. Continuous improvement is another form of change that occurs more in the day-to-day running of the organisation and as a way to increase quality while reducing waste. Helping keep the standard way of working as up-to-date as possible, rather than relying on periodic radical change for this. The Toyota company has made many industry significant innovations within this field (Liker, 2004). Together in the coming pages, we will explore how change can take many forms, and how we can strategically make the most of the investments involved in getting people to intrinsically start the process of adapting behaviour to new situations. 'If a company has a strategic advantage, it has a particular characteristic or way of doing things that makes it more successful than others (Cambridge Dictionary, 2022). By combining different types of change while continually updating governance holistically, I propose that we can realise greater success, and through this create both competitive advantage and real value for stakeholders. ChangeOps is looking not only at the embedding of project change and continuous improvement into the governance bedrock as seen in Figures 10, 11 and 12, but also focusing on the connections that could be further developed

Figure 12. ChangeOps, Strategically harnessing different types of change in organisations

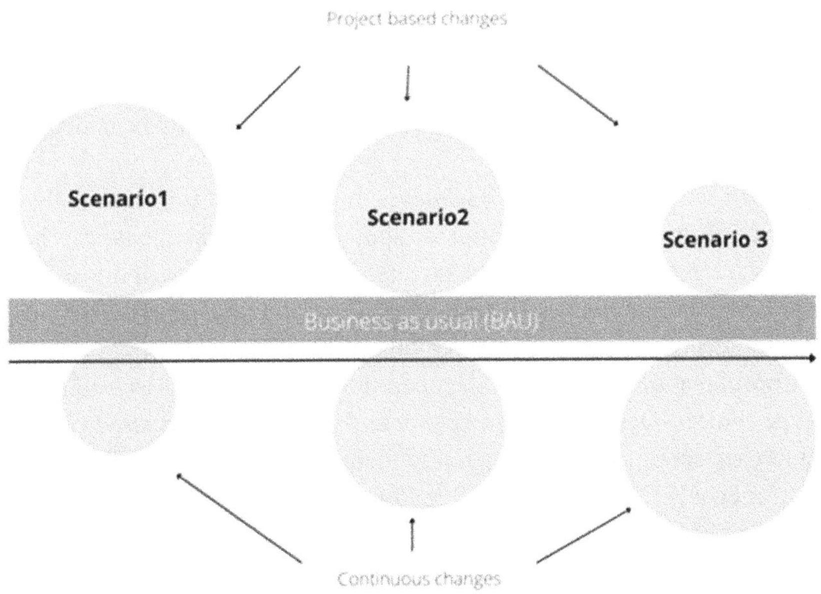

to support a holistic adaptive network of integrated change that fundamentally has the opportunity to grow beyond its parts. Besides this, automating and optimising core governance structure and repeatable processes allow an organisation's people to focus on the intrinsic value they can bring not simply being a machine or static resource. Last but not least, by thinking holistically about change and governance, there are new strategies and advantages to be realised, not to mention greater efficiency. Strategically using all forms of change requires both change capability and maturity. With attention to the organisational factors being interconnected with a sustainable flow of value first put in place, and second agility to be able to strategically switch the types of change utilised in tune with the strategic goals and needs of the organisation.

By assessing an organisation's change maturity with a model representing change maturity 'as is' factors related to levels in the organisation, we can support organisations to understand their change maturity level and how to develop this alongside tailored value creation at different levels of the organisation. Taking this further, a change maturity framework that is focused on creating a balance between the different aspects of the change maturity model as interconnected parts, the maturity best practice of influencing disciplines, built out with a holistic view of change that will enable an organisation to grow change maturity as a capability.

A Change Maturity Model with Framework Capabilities

The solution of a change maturity model with framework tendencies is an intriguing one and gives rise to many possibilities. Agility and flexibility to adapt key organisational factors and even the framework itself is important if we are to avoid the VUCA and BANI like characteristics associated with mass change. The presented model is a simple one, drawing together many different aspects of the models and frameworks found in available maturity best practice and research.

Design choices include building a seven level maturity model which provides more detail for change maturity development. Chosen because this type of maturity touches on many organisational factors, areas and disciplines, and therefore we need more detail to provide actionable steps towards viable outcomes. Many of the five step models can fit into the model-framework supporting the use of the abundant already tried and tested best practice out there, not to mention allow a nonlinear systematic approach to change maturity building. Business value creation, Strategic change use (ChangeOps) and change sustaining features can easily be assessed. Other aspects can easily be added giving the Model-framework a tailorable look and feel.

In Figure 13 you can see a description of each level in the topmost row of the table. The levels represent change maturity of the factors, the degree of strategic use of change types, the degree of value flow and the degree of interconnectedness of the factors. This row and descriptions are related to change maturity levels and Level 0 represents both states of non-existent change maturity and where there are forms of debt whether technical, organisational or otherwise. This debt acts as a negative in the level system due to the impact that this debt has on the operational effectiveness as well as the flexibility and strategic change type choices. Debt is a limiting factor and should not be ignored. The table is exploring the maturity level of each set of factors in relation to their agility and preparedness for change. In most cases, a healthy factor equals a higher change in maturity level. Factors can be rearranged or replaced according to the needs of the organisation and the organisational design. Some factors will have less importance in certain organisational governance structures, while other types will require a completely different set of factors. Think for example on the difference in design and factor priority between a 100 year old traditional, bureaucratic and highly hierarchical organisation compared to a network organisation or a helix organisational structure.

Figure 13. C+MMF model

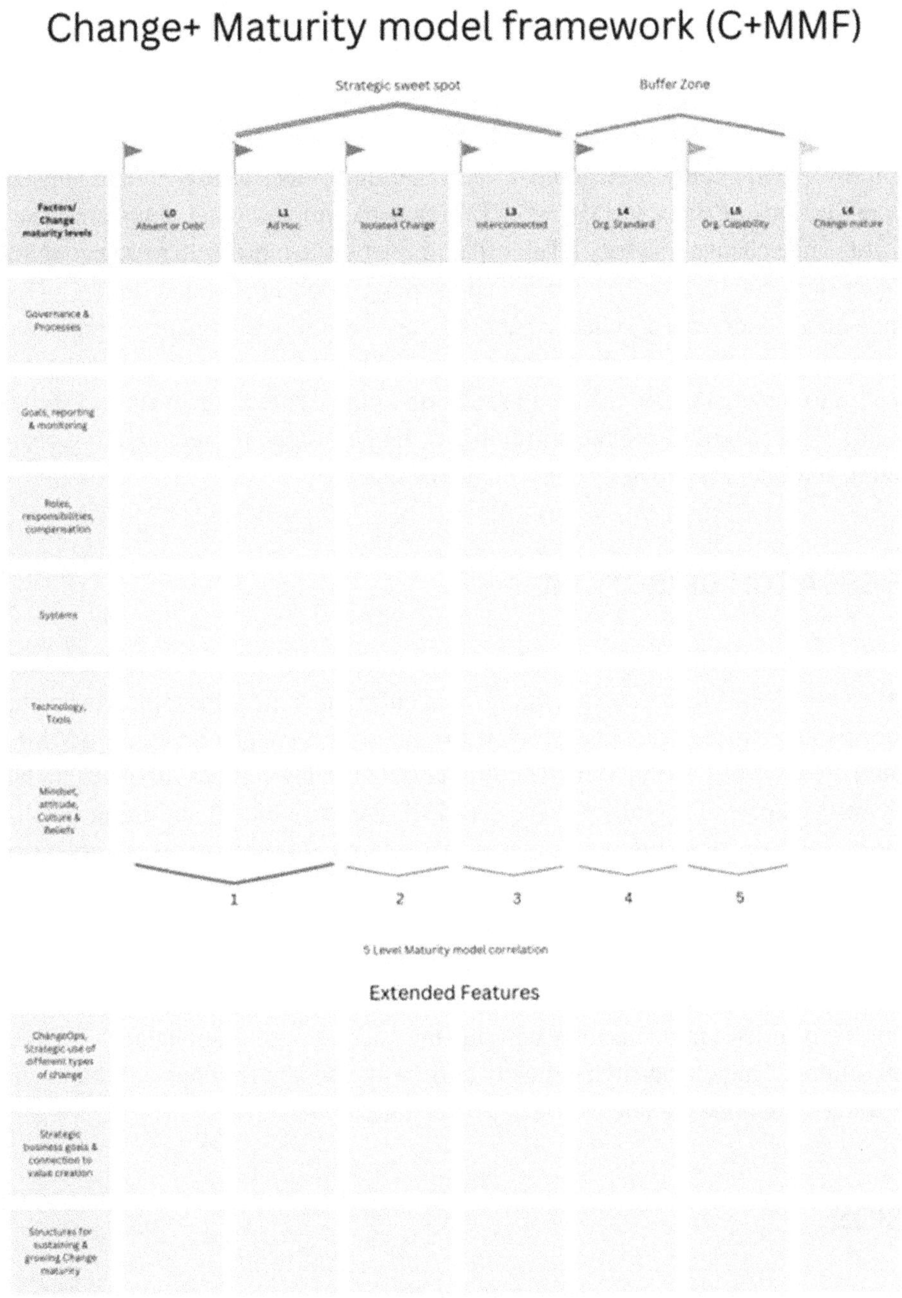

Above the table there is a 'Strategic sweet spot' mentioned, this is referring to the levels of maturity that if developed will bring the most impactful shift in change maturity and ROI for the organisation. There is also a buffer zone that supports the concept that building change maturity is a journey and that the end state of maturity will keep shifting. With this in mind, it becomes questionable whether it is worth investing in these maturity levels because in many cases the investment could outweigh the ROI. But this is a simple explanation and maturity level development should be assessed in relation to the organisation's strategic plans for growth. The extended feature section provides a simple way to achieve this either as an assessment itself or the collection point for a far more extensive investigation. At the bottom of the first section of the C+MMF model in Figure 13 you can see how the first two maturity levels can be combined into 1 level that conforms to many of the five step maturity models out there. This is a great way to take the best practices available in other maturity areas like project management, continuous improvement, quality management, and other disciplines used by the organisation.

Practical applications of the C+MMF model-framework are wide and abundant. The first step in many cases is to gauge change maturity level, often in relation to a particular project or solution being considered. Next steps can include creation of change playbooks, a dedicated Center of Excellence for growing change maturity or even a Transformation if one is wanting to organise change maturity on the organisational level. Each of these options has a very real business case and will bring a considerable amount of benefit to the organisation chosen in relation to the desired outcomes and strategic business goals (Kanikani). This maximises value and initiates the first steps towards making change maturity building a practical topic rather than a purely academic one.

FUTURE RESEARCH DIRECTIONS

Change maturity of organisations tends to end up being coined as a 'nice academic exercise'. Any topic can be made theoretical and put in the academic corner, but equally the same topic can be made so practical that it becomes industry best practice which is the aim of this chapter and the C+MMF framework. The model shared within this text is a simple culmination of many sources that have both inspired key elements or have been part of establishing the C+MMF maturity model and framework. An example is the five-step model being a common practice of maturity models and the systematic approach of 7-S inspiring the interconnectedness of 'as is' factors that allow value to flow with strategically connected change. The ChangeOps standpoint that connecting different types of change creates strategic choice which can lead to decreasing risk and overall impact felt by certain changes. The C+MMF framework is still only a prototype and the next step would be to build this into a fully fledged model and framework that comprehensively utilises more maturity best practices across organisational factors. Indeed a further research into building change maturity is already underway and key findings will be incorporated into the C+MMF framework once complete.

CONCLUSION

The biggest takeaway conveyed in this chapter is that building change maturity is one of the vital research areas of this time. Organisations are slow to realise the building need for change maturity so they can maintain the necessary pace of progress required to keep successfully serving customers. The end state of being mature is a moving goal post and there is a strategic choice created by assessing the current state of maturity. For each organisation, there will be a possible maturity they can reach and an intelligent level they should reach, determined by a whole host of factors to be considered. The point is that if the first step of establishing maturity level is not fulfilled, organisations can not benefit from it and close down further opportunities to be gained from strategic decision-making based on the outcomes of a maturity assessment.

There are two main ways we can understand building change maturity, one that focuses on the work of change managers and the other on a more holistic view that unites more disciplines, factors and types of change under one roof. Allowing us to see a bigger picture than simply enforcing the work of one profession that might not be needed anymore if this broader holistic view of change maturity is being grown in organisations. The role of a dedicated change manager potentially becomes redundant at a certain point of maturity due to an underlying aim of creating a mindset shift in all employees from a state where change is something negative to one of acceptance and prosperity, and importantly that all employees have the capability to manage change, not a select few. This systemic mindset shift is an intrinsic part of the model and further research on the topic will build it into the approach to each factor of the C+MMF framework and the relationships between factors.

There is a profound amount of research, development and innovation on the topic of building maturity capability in more disciplines. The available best practices within the change management toolkit are relatively simple and underdeveloped when compared with maturity models from other disciplines. There is no framework found to date that combines this into one change maturity-building strategy except the simple format of the C+MMF shared here. This is certainly a work in progress and one part of a growing change maturity building method that includes the ChangeOps strategy and assessments. In its current form, the C+MMF can already be used to combine more maturity models into one unified approach to change maturity building in organisations. With further development of the framework, organisations can tailor their focus on change maturity building that increases return on investment (ROI) and value creation while bringing a whole host of other benefits depending on the focus areas. Change maturity is not only practical but a vital competence of organisations in these times. Any organisation that invests in targeted change maturity building alongside strategically deploying all types of change will see both a short term impact on project outcomes and a cumulative effect that will mean continued ROI for years to come.

REFERENCES

ACMP. (2019, March). *Standard for Change Management.* Standard for Change Management© ACMP Change Management Code of Ethics. https://cdn.ymaws.com/www.acmpglobal.org/resource/resmgr/files/ACMP_Standard_2019_03_21.pdf

Akhtar, V., Gupta, G., & Kotter, J. P. (2021). *Change: How organisations achieve hard-to-imagine results in uncertain and volatile times.* Wiley.

Axelos. (2017). *Managing successful projects with PRINCE2.* TSO.

Baligh, H. H. (2011). *Organisation structures: Theory and design, analysis and prescription.* Springer.

Bennis, W. G., & Nanus, B. (2003). *Leaders: Strategies for taking charge.* HarperCollins.

Bridges, S. (n.d.). *Bridges Transition Model.* William Bridges Associates. https://wmbridges.com/about/what-is-transition/

Bruin, T. d. (2005). *Understanding the main phases of developing a maturity assessment model.* Academia. https://www.academia.edu/66533016/Understanding_the_Main_Phases_of_Developing_a_Maturity_Assessment_Model

Cameron, E., & Green, M. (2012). *Making Sense of Change Management: A Complete Guide to the Models, Tools, and Techniques of Organisational Change.* Kogan Page.

Cascio, J. (2020, April 29). Facing the Age of Chaos. We are in an age of chaos, an era that… | by Jamais Cascio. *Medium.* https://medium.com/@cascio/facing-the-age-of-chaos-b00687b1f51d

Cascio, W., & Montealegre, R. (2019, January 17). *How Technology Is Changing Work and Organizations.* Research Gate. https://www.researchgate.net/publication/299400943_How_Technology_Is_Changing_Work_and_Organizations .

Change Management Institute. (2014). *The Effective Change Manager: The Change Management Body of Knowledge.* Vivid Publishing.

Chauviere, K., Maritz, B., & van Halder, J. (2016, November 17). *The role of the transformation office.* McKinsey. https://www.mckinsey.com/capabilities/rts/our-insights/the-role-of-the-transformation-office

Child, J. (1984). *Organisation: A guide to problems and practice.* SAGE Publications. doi:10.4135/9781446280348

Craig, M. (2020, August 20). *IT capability maturity framework (IT-CMF) – Pittsburgh change ...* Pittsburgh Change Management Professionals. https://pitcmp.org/2020/08/20/it-capability-maturity-framework-it-cmf/

Cuellar, R., Augustine, S., & Scheere, A. (2021). *From PMO to VMO: Managing for value delivery.* Berrett-Koehler Publishers.

Delaini, S. (2022, June 27). *How Microsoft used change management best practices to launch a new business intelligence platform - Inside Track Blog*. Microsoft. https://www.microsoft.com/insidetrack/blog/how-microsoft-used-change-management-best-practices-to-launch-a-new-business-intelligence-platform/

Drucker, P. F. (1993). *Management: Tasks, responsibilities, practices*. HarperCollins.

Erdogan, S., & Yucalar, F. (2009, July). *A questionnaire based method for cmmi level 2 maturity assessment*. Academia.edu. https://www.academia.edu/16827112/A_questionnaire_based_method_for_cmmi_level_2_maturity_assessment

Esmanech, T. (2018, July 19). *The purpose of a business is to create and keep a customer*. LinkedIn. https://www.linkedin.com/pulse/purpose-business-create-keep-customer-tommaso-esmanech/

Fahrenkrog, S. L. (n.d.). *OPM3 - Successful execution of organisational strategies*. PMI. https://www.pmi.org/learning/library/organizational-strategies-outcomes-improvements-8398

Favaretto, J., & Meirelles, F. (2015, March). Nolan's stage level measurement of information and communication technology in modern organizations. *Research Gate*. https://www.researchgate.net/publication/311966074_Nolans_stage_level_measurement_of_Information_and_Communication_Technology_in_modern_organizations

Five Levels of Change Management Maturity. (n.d.). Prosci. https://www.prosci.com/resources/articles/change-management-maturity-model

Gandolfo, G. (1998). *International trade theory and policy*. Springer Berlin Heidelberg. doi:10.1007/978-3-642-61680-8

Goedhart, M., Levy, C., & Morgan, P. (2015, November 1). *A better way to understand internal rate of return*. McKinsey. https://www.mckinsey.com/capabilities/strategy-and-corporate-finance/our-insights/a-better-way-to-understand-internal-rate-of-return

Gonzalez, C., & Bush, R. O. (2020). *Instrument for the assessment of maturity in the digital economy*. Academia. https://www.academia.edu/85920803/Instrument_for_the_assessment_of_maturity_in_the_digital_economy

Hall, S., Lovallo, D., & Musters, R. (2012, March 1). *How to put your money where your strategy is*. McKinsey. https://www.mckinsey.com/capabilities/strategy-and-corporate-finance/our-insights/how-to-put-your-money-where-your-strategy-is

Hindle, K., Eva, M., Rollason, C., & Turner, P. (2014). Business analysis (D. Paul, J. Cadle, & D. Yeates, Eds.). BCS, The Chartered Institute for IT.

IIBA. (2015). *BABOK V3*. The international institute of business analysis.

Kafel, T. (2021). *Multidimensional public sector organisations digital maturity model*. Academia. https://www.academia.edu/88263663/Multidimensional_public_sector_organizations_digital_maturity_model

Kanikani, I. (2022, September 21). *ChangeOps*. LinkedIn. https://www.linkedin.com/post/edit/7000346460504358912/

Kanikani, I. (2022, October 25-10-22). *The change maturity report*. Linkedin. https://www.linkedin.com/pulse/draft/AgHwKO0tvNXsFwAAAYQplOQry0J7WDmNtjplc2tw2Pgrzfqlg_PCJHAWR2dAiP3r0laagtA

Kanikani, I. (2022). Whitepaper: Building change maturity. *Academia*. https://www.academia.edu/96126468/Whitepaper_Building_Organisational_Change_Maturity

Kotter, J. P. (2012). *Leading change*. Harvard Business Review Press.

Kotter, J. P., Akhtar, V., & Gupta, G. (2021). *Change: How organisations achieve hard-to-imagine results in uncertain and volatile times*. Wiley.

Lewin, K. (n.d.). *Frontiers in group dynamics*. Sage Journals. https://journals.sagepub.com/doi/10.1177/001872674700100103

Liker, J. K. (2004). *The Toyota way*. McGraw-Hill Education.

Lim, A. (2020, November 5). *The real purpose of business: Why does your business exist? | ariel lim consulting*. Ariel Lim. https://ariel-lim.com/blog/real-purpose-of-business-why-exist/

March, J. G. (Ed.). (2015). *Handbook of organizations*. Routledge.

Osteen, K., & Subramanian, R. (2013, September). *Assessment maturity model for competency mapping - A talent management enabler*. Academia.edu. https://www.academia.edu/5321331/Assessment_Maturity_Model_for_Competency_Mapping_A_Talent_Management_Enabler

Overview of the organisation maturity index (OMI) — ODTI. (n.d.). OrgCMF.

Paulk, M., Chrissis, M. B., Curtis, B., & Weber, C. (1993, August). Capability maturity model version 1.1. *ResearchGate*. https://www.researchgate.net/publication/3246910_Capability_Maturity_Model_Version_11

People, process, technology: The PPT framework, explained. (2022, March 8). Plutora. https://www.plutora.com/blog/people-process-technology-ppt-framework-explained

Peters, T., & Waterman, R. (2019, December 31). *Enduring ideas: 7-S Framework*. YouTube. https://www.mckinsey.com/capabilities/strategy-and-corporate-finance/our-insights/enduring-ideas-the-7-s-framework# PMI.

Primary sponsor's role and importance. (n.d.). Prosci. https://www.prosci.com/resources/articles/primary-sponsors-role-and-importance

Project management maturity model (PMMM) in educational organisations. (2010). Academia. https://www.academia.edu/42143101/Project_Management_Maturity_Model_PMMM_in_educational_organizations

Prosci. (n.d.). *What is change management and how does it work?* Prosci. https://www.prosci.com/resources/articles/what-is-change-management-and-how-does-it-work

Shrum, S., Chrissis, M. B., & Konrad, M. (2003). *CMMI: Guidelines for process integration and product improvement*. Addison-Wesley.

Sidhu, R., Smith, R., Skelsey, D., King, D., & APMG (Eds.). (2014). *The effective change manager's handbook: Essential guidance to the change management body of knowledge*. Kogan Page.

Stephen, E. (n.d.). *How microsoft uses the ADKAR model to improve customer success*. Prosci. Retrieved November 20, 2022, from https://www.prosci.com/blog/how-microsoft-uses-the-adkar-model-to-improve-customer-success

STRATEGIC ADVANTAGE | English meaning. (2022, November 16). Cambridge Dictionary. https://dictionary.cambridge.org/dictionary/english/strategic-advantage

Temmen, M. (2021, February 7). *BANI vs VUCA— a new acronym for a new world.* Marian Temmen. Retrieved November 23, 2022, from https://marian-temmen.medium.com/bani-vs-vuca-a-new-acronym-for-a-new-world-59c7be2dddce

Thakur, H. (2022, September 2). *Gartner business intelligence maturity model*. 121 Business Ideas. https://121businessideas.com/business-model/gartner-business-intelligence-maturity-model/

Understanding and using maturity driven improvement with the Org-CMF — ODTI. (n.d.). OrgCMF. https://orgcmf.com/en-gb/pages/knowledge/org-cmf/maturity/

Van der Duin, P., & De Graaf, R. (2010, August). The connection between innovation and the future. *Research gate*. https://www.researchgate.net/figure/The-connection-between-innovation-and-the-future_fig2_233527052

Van Haren Publishing (Ed.). (2017). *It-cmf: A management guide - Based on the it capability maturity framework*. Van Haren Publishing.

Watts, S. (2020, February 19). *CMMI: An introduction to capability maturity model integration*. BMC Software. https://www.bmc.com/blogs/cmmi-capability-maturity-model-integration/

Weber, C. V. (1995). *The capability maturity model: Guidelines for improving the software process* (M. C. Paulk, M. B. Chrissis, C. V. Weber, & B. Curtis, Eds.). Addison-Wesley.

KEY TERMS AND DEFINITIONS

Capability: The power or ability to do something

Change Management Maturity: The state of having Change management maturity, usually in the context of a project, department, business unit or organisation.

Change Management: The management and development of change within the context of a project, business, or organisation.

Change Maturity: The state of maturity when in the state of change or transformation.

ChangeOps: The holistic view of change in organisations that can be strategically harnessed to increase flow of value in organisations.

Continuous Improvement: Also known as Kaizen, is essentially an incremental approach to change and improvement strategy.

Framework: A supporting structure or platform that you can build others onto or into depending on context.

Governance: Governance refers to the structures, roles & responsibilities, processes designed to ensure that the organisations purpose is both defined and realised.

Maturity: The state of being mature, implying a journey to grow into maturity.

Organisational Change Management: The management and development of change within the context of a project, business, or organisation. In recent times, this term is used to differentiate between Change management carried out alongside projects and the enterprise-level management of change.

Chapter 8
Theories and Application of Organisational Change Management During the COVID-19 Era

Oindrila Chakraborty
J.D. Birla Institute, India

ABSTRACT

Through the book chapter, the author would primarily explore the basic concept of change management and an overview of diverse fundamental theories of conventional organisational change management (OCM) models and approaches in human resource management, along with the application in several workplaces sector wise, during pandemic times with special reference to the organisational adaptation in structural and psychological aspects to combat the unfavourable situations. The chapter would fathom the needs, drives and ideal implementation plan of change management along with the practical implementation of the same. The chapter would also try to examine different group dynamics, Resistance, Intervention Instruments and success for organisational change management.

INTRODUCTION

COVID-19 brought a host of uncertainties in every walk of lives. Work environment could not be an exception. The problem was initiated with the pandemic, inflicted by COVID-19 disease; causing a global health crisis and subsequently led to concerns for individualistic health, businesses, financial markets, and other fundamental elements of the global economy. COVID-19 unexpectedly emerged as a global issue, drawing the attention and solutions of decision-makers from all around the world. The government has adopted several policies, one of which is to advise individuals to stay back at home, and to continue working, learning, and even worshipping (social distancing norms had been practised in all prayer halls and shrines like Church, Mosque and Temples) within the four walls of home. It was quite evident that quarantine and social seclusion have been the main remedies as the lockdown was extended under vari-

DOI: 10.4018/978-1-6684-7509-6.ch008

ous terms and conditions. In the same vein, all businesses have made working from home mandatory for all employees, with the exception of the vital and emergency-based services like logistical services, medical and paramedical services, some of the IT and financial services.

Because of this series of situational complexity and uncertainty, the pandemic led to a host of diverse reactions in people. Some of which could be best described through following phrases: ***'sense of feeling left out'***; ***'uncontrolled behaviour'***, ***'Unexplainable anxiety and tension'***; ***'worry for one's own health and the family'***; and ***'negative speculations about one's financial security'***. Numerous organisations have set up wellness programmes and counselling hotlines for staff members and their families to help them get through this difficult time. The sudden shutdown of organisations, restrictive movements, stringent protocols, new strict government protocols, financial insecurities and shifting to virtual encounters made people completely devastated, leading to a confusing state of affairs. Dynamic leadership qualities and change management became the need of the hour, to combat psychological disturbances and related employee sentiments, as it could lead to behaviour issues, ultimately targeting organisational productivity and turn over.

As already described, to survive these uncertain circumstances, during COVID-19 driven pandemic, organisational change has undoubtedly been the most important and quintessential task. The thriving organisations, projecting the high rate of success to the outside world, were those, adapting quickly to the work- environment changes.

These observations called for certain ***research questions***:

1. What are the theories of change management?
2. Are the theories of change management actually implemented in work places?
3. To what extent has the change management inserted in the work places during COVID-19 pandemic?
4. Are the coping strategies adapted by organisations, adequate enough to handle the crisis?

Operational Definitions and Terms Used in the Chapter

Change: Any condition, different from the current condition; it may referrer to different context, unless specified.

Pandemic: An illness that spreads throughout the entire country or world.

COVID-19 (CORONA VIRUS DISEASE-19): A coronavirus-based Disease, caused by **SARS-CoV-2 virus**, is an acute human disease that is primarily characterised by fever and cough but has the potential to proceed to severe symptoms and, in some cases, death, particularly in elderly persons and those with underlying medical issues. It was first discovered in China in 2019, then it spread to other countries in 2020 and started being called as Pandemic due to its severely high mortality rates. Till date, many strains have been identified throughout the world with diverse pattern of symptoms and severity.

Coping Strategy: Coping mechanisms are behavioural and cognitive techniques used to deal with stressful situations, environments, and demands. It could be individualistic or organisational. Individualistic strategies could be coping strategies of employees to deal with the stress due to sudden changes in the work environment and personal life. Organisational stress is the overall stress, built up in the managerial position to deal with revenue models to minimise the loss.

Change Management-Definition and Related Strategies

The term **'change management'** may have diverse perspective based on various domains of usage. The change refers to a drastically dissimilar situation from the current static situation, which has been identified as part of invasive culture.

General Definition: In generalised manner, change management is a term best used to introduce a new practice, policy or environmental change like merger or acquisition. The meaning of change management is subtly different in different arena of work. There are many definitions of change management:

Project Management: Project management is one area where the word **'change management'** is popularly utilised. Sometimes a project makes good progress, but then it is important to adjust the original schedule, due to an anticipated or unforeseen occurrence. Therefore, change is quite frequent in project management based on need of the hour.

Information Technology: In Information Technology, when an improvement is required at some point in a software's life cycle, the change management process enables the use of an application or approach (such as ITIL).

Organisational Culture: The change management referred in this chapter, has got a different meaning, which is more congruent with the general definition of change management. It is mostly referring to the corporate change of policies and practices, rules and regulations and thereby the coping strategies adapted by the organisation to sustain the pressure of change for their employees and employers during the crisis.

Differentiation Between Change and Changing

The theories of change and the theories of changing are distinguished by **Bennis (1966)**. In general, while theories of changing deal with how changes might be generated and managed, theories of change concentrate on why and how organisations change. In every way, changes are vital processes. The earlier differentiated technique was further developed by **Porras and Robertson (1987, 1992)** and **Austin and Bartunek (2006)**.

In order to help the gradual team-transition from its current state to a better one, **Coffman and Lutes (2007)** claimed that change management is an organised strategy. According to **Nauheimer (2007)**, change management is a method, a methodology, and a tool that can be used to better execute change with the help of change agents, systems, and additional teams while also managing the process of change on the individual level. large. In its simplest form, change management refers to a structured and methodical effort and approach that aims to support individuals, teams, or organisations by applying the tools, resources, and knowledge to realise changes from adverse conditions to more favourable ones efficiently and effectively while minimising impacts. The practice of managing all the effects of changes in an organisation is known as "**change management**." In order to get the desired results and successfully implement change, change management is a tool, process, and approach for managing people in the change process. The fact that organisational structures, cultures, and routines frequently reflect the persistent and challenging "traces" of the past period, which are resistant to drastic changes even like the current context, makes significant and rapid organisational changes particularly challenging (**Christopher & Andras, 2013**). In order to make changes to a corporation, the process of change management employs a management strategy, including planning, organising, acting, and controlling. Through techniques for controlling the influence of change on individuals who are in it, change management is carried out to develop the business solutions required to be more successful in a way that is also more organised. After that, a new policy that was superior to the prior one was born as a result of this adjustment. Organizations struggle with change because system changes compel members to automatically adjust to ideas that may not be well received. Effective management on the part of a leader is therefore required. For the transition process to be successful, excellent management unquestionably needs an effective strategy. Change necessitates the creation of innovative ideas, which are of course inextricably linked to the organization's sustainability factors of planning, organising, actuating, and controlling.

According to **Davidson et al. (2005)**, the presence of cultural variations in an organisation will influence how well a change plan is prepared. The **Rational-Empirical Approach**, the **Normative Re-educative Approach**, the **Power-Coercive Approach**, and the **Environment-Adaptive Approach** are the four change management strategies that businesses can select from.

Figure 1. Change management strategies

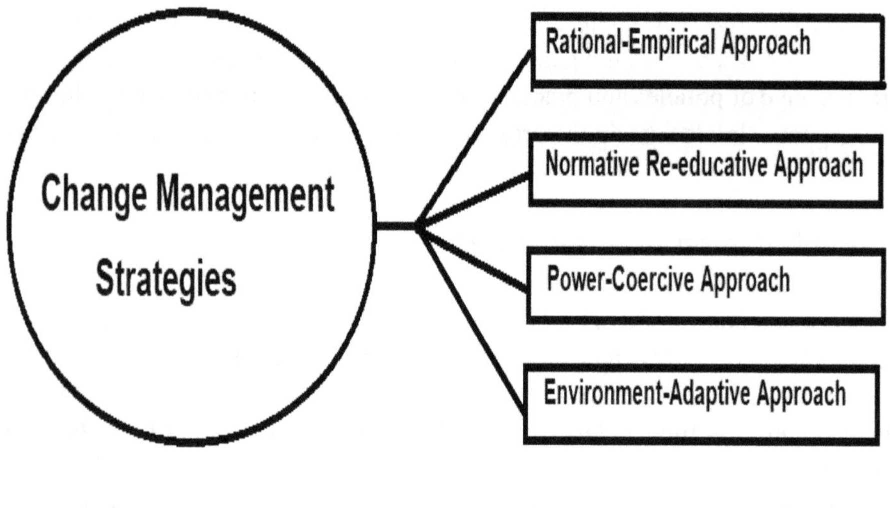

Most frequently happening when one member of the group embraces changes and upholds the group's values and beliefs. A rational-empirical approach, which is based on the idea that it is possible to forecast people's behaviour. An effective plan for the future will alter as a result of understanding these habits. Despite maintaining their rationality, these components would assume that every changing aim will be obscured by a variety of myths, ignorance, and falsehoods. When individuals receive more accurate & effective communication and incentives for change, that they deem more appropriate, they will adjust accordingly (Normative Re-educative Approach). Next comes the power-coercive strategy. This strategy forces change management to be carried out randomly by some parties and naively by others and it frequently ends up being the norm. The management approach's basic tenet is that because animals change according to instinct while also attempting to prevent any kind of loss, they are capable of adapting to a wide range of novel environments and circumstances. According to **Grundy**'s idea, there are three different kinds of change in an organisation depending on their nature. A succession of changes can be covered by smooth ***incremental change*** (static), which happens slowly, methodically, and reliably and has a tendency to happen at a consistent rate. A change that has a period of comparatively calm and is occasionally interrupted by an acceleration of the movement of change is known as a bumpy incremental change. This type of change can be brought on by changes in the organisational environment as well as from within, such as requests to boost productivity and enhance working practises. A quick alteration in structure, culture, strategy, or all three at once is referred to as a ***discontinuous change***. This transition is more rapid and revolutionary. A number of stages can be followed when putting change management into practise. According to **Haines et al., 2005**, it includes Positioning Value in Phase A (determining a strategic position). This phase of a system of thought is when the company's objectives or strategic position can be thoroughly described. This position will become available due to an organisational or business change. Goals and Measures in Phase B (measuring goals). At this stage, decisions will be made regarding the multiple metrics and procedures needed to assess whether the target has been accomplished. The assessment plan is Phase C. Policies will be created at this phase, which will also establish the distinction between the actual situation and the desired scenario, in order to better achieve all situations and conditions. Levels of Action in Phase D (***change activity***). The plan will be put into practise and justified during this phase, which will also include any interactions, activities, and revisions needed to fill in any gaps or achieve the objectives set forth in phase A. Phase E of the ***environment scan*** (identification of the external environment). The process of identifying the external environment that can influence transformation will be finished with this phase. The alterations that will be made and the course they should take will be determined by the identification's findings.

BACKGROUND

A) Overview of the COVID-19

In the month of December 2019, the COVID-19 driven pandemic began to spiral out of control in Wuhan, China. From there, it spread to all countries with equal ferocity, stopping life as usual in its tracks. Every nation received a warning to inform their citizens about the preventative measures needed to withstand the epidemic. Norms of social and physical segregation as well as various cleaning procedures, such as hand washing and the wearing of face shields or masks, were all included in the protective care. According to **Sintema (2020),** in order to prevent this tremendously harmful and uncontrollably contagious disease from spreading, it also included social gathering prohibitions. By causing significant disruptions, alienation, and a near breakdown of the on-going business scenario, the Covid 19 injected a catastrophic transformation into the global platform. A government announcement ordering the closure of academic, financial and other, business institutions was the culmination of the precautionary measures, which also included various social distance-building, protective measures, and cleaning standards. **(Pokhrel and Chhetri, 2021)** as the immediate effect of a highly contagious Novel Corona virus **(Dhawan, 2020)** exposing the globe to a never before problem. To deal with the competition and potential danger, the governments of the majority of the countries overnight changed the strategic paradigm from physical workplace scenario to digital (work from home) or phygital (hybrid work mode) **(Chaturvedi et al., 2020)**.

Figure 2. Work mode transformation due to covid driven pandemic

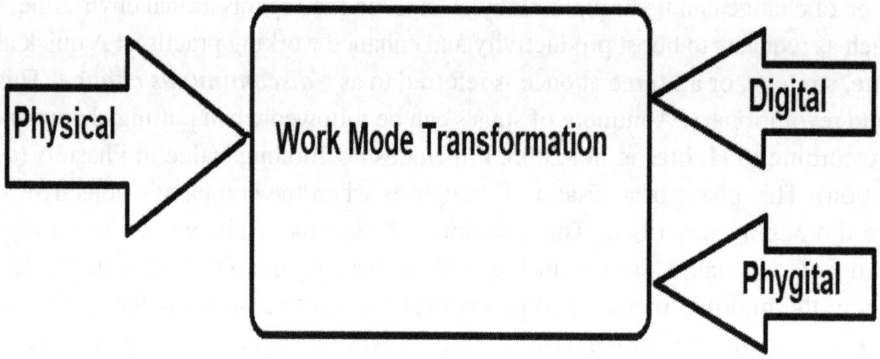

B) COVID-19 Impact in the Workplace

The world has been going through significant concerns over COVID-19. The COVID-19 pandemic would have terrible social and economic effects on everyone. Every nation in today's interconnected world has been affected by the pandemic's destruction. The COVID-19 is expected to have some long-lasting or permanent effects. By the time the pandemic is over, there would undoubtedly be significant economic and social destruction along with a new planet, new lexicon, and new social norm. As the COVID-19 outbreak expanded over the globe, hundreds of people began experiencing serious health problems, and rise in the fatality rate. All social and economic activity in the affected countries have to be suspended for an indeterminate amount of time in order to stop the pandemic from spreading. This prompted numerous nations to enact total lock-down, which is still in effect today. In such a case, all commercial operations in all sectors came to a full halt. Different industries were affected by the lock-down to varying degrees. For instance, the aviation industries, hospitality industries including hotel, and manufacturing industries have completely ceased operations for the majority of the time during lockdown and will take a very long time, if ever, to recover the loss. Millions of workers in these industries stand to lose their employment. Businesses were severely disrupted by the COVID-19 pandemic, and it will likely take years for them to fully recover. Due to the pandemic's financial losses and disruptions, many firms are likely to close permanently as a result of the disruption. Companies are attempting to manage offices and administrative positions through "Work from Home"(WFH) mode in an effort to overcome the existing scenario. Businesses have been utilising disruptive technologies and the idea of working from home to combat the economic turmoil brought on by COVID 19. Work from home was previously solely permitted in the IT and technology industries. Although WFH is an excellent business strategy, other industry sectors were hesitant to adopt it with apprehension of abnormal work culture and difficulty in controlling mechanisms. The biggest business change that could be observed in current scenario, as a result of the pandemic's global expansion, is the widespread adoption of work-from-home policies by businesses. Businesses have discovered the WFH to be quite beneficial during the past three years. Moving forward, the majority of businesses view WFH as a crucial component of their business model. In a limited fashion, the WFH mode aids several industries and functions in maintaining their operations. As a result of the COVID-19 problem, people who work from home are forced to live in social isolation and emotional distance (**Meenakshi Kaushik and Neha Guleria, 2020**). The WFH mode has diverse degrees, based on the convenience of the sector and the organisation. The pure work from home has been a choice for those companies, where physical evidences of customer encounter were not quintessential; the Phygital or Hybrid mode of work has been a chosen method where only extremely vital meetings have been conducted through physical and personal meetings, else virtual offices have been replacing to avoid any complications. Some of the unfortunate sectors could not introduce WFH, since it could have been their existential crisis.

Aim and Research Design of the Study

The study has primarily explored the research questions related to the relevant area of change management with the diverse theories of change management along with practical application of the concept in the field of organisational culture during COVID-19 inflicted pandemic. During this quest, the study has examined different significant work mode transformations, adapted by diverse workplaces. The primary research has mainly focused on the investigation of dynamic changes adapted by various sectors and coping strategies through an online survey and telephonic interview, maintaining anonymity of the respondents while recording responses in order to capture the truth. In the primary research, Information Technology, Finance (Banking, Insurance and Micro Finance), Retail (Life style and Daily Supplies), Hospitality industry (Hotel and medical care) and Academia have been explored. The employees have been selected from top-level and mid-level management mostly, keeping subaltern level at bay. The survey has been conducted from metropolitan cities across India, through **Snowball sampling** (**chain referral system**). The respondents were identified through their sources to avoid casual responses.

Figure 3. Research design

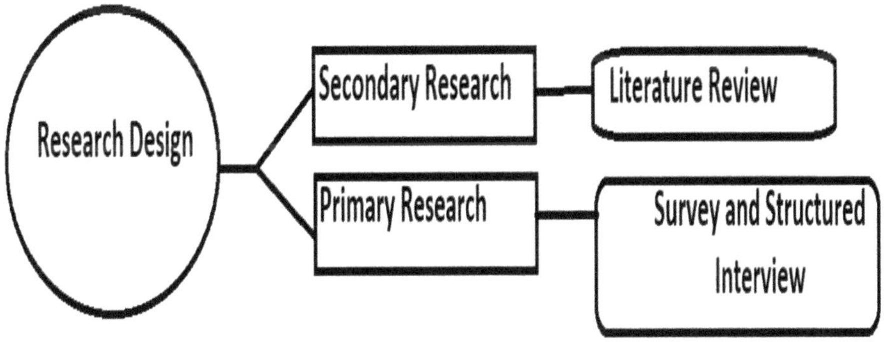

The primary research has recorded total 364 responses with maximum responses from financial sector with total 100 responses (27.47%), followed by 77 responses (21.15%) from Hospitality sector, 52(14.28%) from Academia,75(20.60%) from Retail and finally 60 (16.48%) from IT sector.

Table 1. Sample distribution over the different sectors for data collection.

Industry	Sub-section	Total Response sector wise
Information Technology		60
Finance	Insurance	30
	Micro Finance	25
	Banking	45
Retail	Life style	35
	Daily Supplies	40
Hospitality	Hotel	20
	medical care	57
Academia		52
Total Response		364

Figure 4. Graphical expression for sector wise responses

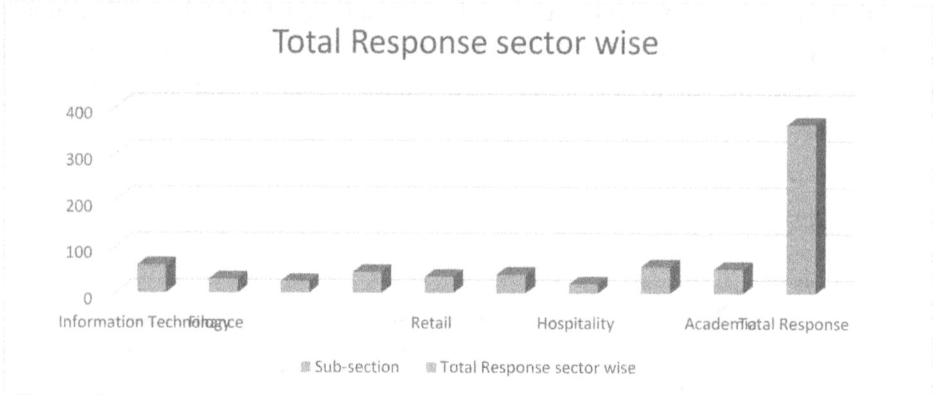

Table 2. Sample profiling for the respondents.

Sample Profile	Number of Individual
Male	198
Female	166
Total Response	364

Figure 5. Graphical expression of gender wise sample distribution

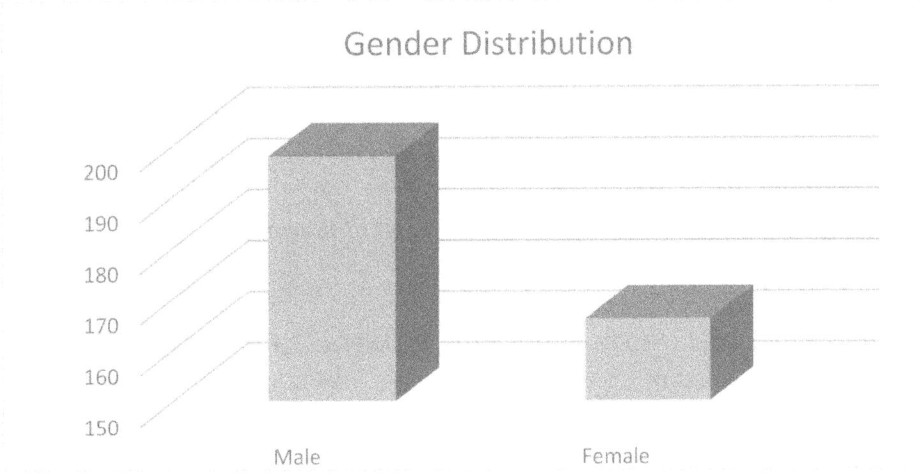

Literature Review on Adaptation, Changes of Organisational Culture and Norms During Covid -19 Pandemic

Theories of Change Management

Change process theory, according to **Porras and Robertson (1987, 1992)**, explains the dynamics of the change process. This strategy is focused on the various sorts of variables needed to achieve planned change. They defined implementation theory as the theory that focuses on activities change agents must conduct in accomplishing organisational transformation in contrast.

The System Theory

A) Basic Idea of The System Theory

First, it is necessary to define the term **"system"** for which **von Bertalanffy**'s definition from **1950** is used: "The **general systems theory** embraces all cybernetic theories that deal with systems of interacting components (e.g. human vs. environment), and studies the conclusions drawn about the relations between the structure and functions (e.g. behaviour) of subsystems, subject to the changing impacts of the various factors."

Systems theory is an interdisciplinary field of science:

*"The general systems theory is an approach rather than a rigid doctrine" (***Boulding,1969, p. 113***).*

The core idea of systems theory is that a system is an integrated whole (Gestalt) that exhibits a higher level of complexity than its constituent pieces; as a result, it has unique characteristics and can be viewed as a brand-new entity. The key ideas in systems theory are equilibrium and change, with the latter occurring as a result of interactions between subsystems and system components (**Boudon et al 1999**). It should be highlighted how much the aforementioned definition contributed to the growth of the

Gestalt method (e.g., Wertheimer, Köhler, Kofka, Lewin etc.). Undoubtedly, this strategy contributed to creating the groundwork for organisational development. At least three of the following statements apply to all systems:

a) ***"Systems are a set of interacting components."***
b) ***"One of the main features of all living systems is that they survive through constant change of their components."***
c) ***"Living systems sustain in a state of the highest level of improbability."***

(**von Bertalanffy, 1950**).

The last sentence might require some justification. Systems like to stay in an improbable condition because it costs the least amount of energy to maintain (i.e., disorder, entropy, chaos). Think of your workstation as a system: maintaining order (negentropy) on the desk needs energy, but allowing anarchy to take hold requires no effort.

Homeostasis (also known as **Morphostasis**), which describes a system's propensity to achieve equilibrium, is another idea that systems theory introduced. This propensity serves as a form of dynamic equilibrium. The system aims to maintain its comfort level, which it may do by using the least amount of energy while still achieving its objectives. In this context, manageability refers to the continual pursuit of the objective (Teleology: every system has a purpose) as well as the optimization of energy input. As per System theory, the change can be incorporated in various levels and scales from individual level to group level to social level or world at large.

Figure 6. The scalability of system model of change management

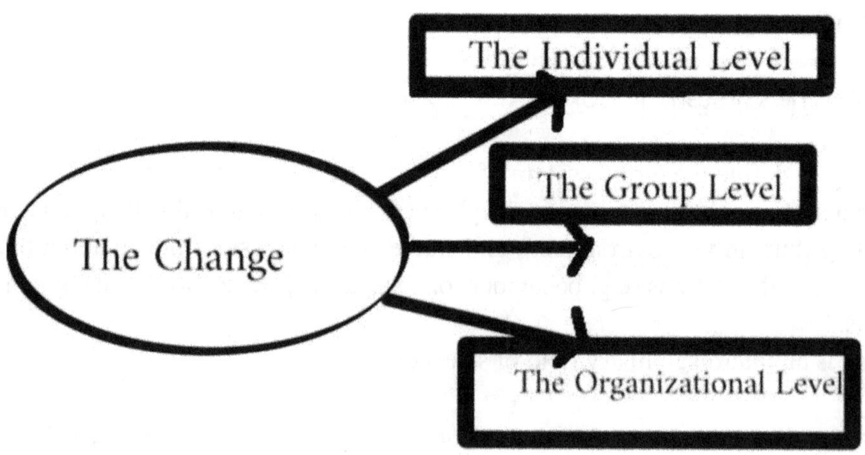

B) The Head of the System

Planning, organising, and controlling people, physical, financial, and information resources enables an organisation to formulate and realise its goals **(Pataki, 1999). Shearer et al**. assert in one of their articles that managers have the most formal and informal impact over change efforts (**Shearer et al, 2001**). They have a responsibility to do this since, at its core, leadership is about influencing how people behave in an organisation (**Pataki,1999**). How an organisation chooses its leaders affects how it interacts with its environment, how well it adapts, and how well changes in the organisation turn out. A leader can be proactive (acting before an anticipated change in the environment occurs) or reactive (passive, adapting, and responsive).

Leaders have the authority to legitimise a change since they serve as examples for the organization's members (**Schein, 1990**). The ability to impose new rules is essential to their declaration, regulation, and maintenance. The organization's members experience stress as a result of all changes. Legitimation reduces this tension.

C)The Forms of Changes

Changes can be **Incremental** (occurring gradually, step by step) or **Radical** (Sudden and drastic change), depending on their scope within a leadership-controlled organisation (**Dobák, 2002**).

Table 3. Comparison of incremental and radical changes

Domain of Change	*Incremental change*	*Radical change*
Scope	A or few significant organisational feature/ features change.	Most or all significant organisational features change
Extent	Almost no change in organisational features	Major changes in organisational features
Impact	Changes affect only a few organisational departments; sometimes only one.	The entire organisation is affected.
Level	Only in one or few organisational/ hierarchical positions or levels.	All hierarchical positions or levels would go through change.
Speed	Gradual and slow change	Fast, abrupt and robust changes.
Period/Tenure	Over a long period of time	Over a very short period of time
Essential Goal	The organization's ability to respond to external factors is facilitated, and/or internal alignment across subsystems, structures, and procedures is improved.	A new set of internal subsystems, structures, and procedures may be formed, or the organisation may be assisted in its external adaption.
Management	Managed by Ground Level or Front Level managers. Seldom Senior Executives of the organisation.	Managed by Senior Executives.

D) Field Theory

Lewin (1972) provided a framework of reference for the behaviour of a specific system when he described Field Theory. No entity (person, group, organization, or civilization) exists entirely in isolation, in accordance with his definition. Instead, a FIELD (the spatial, temporal and emotional stage of behaviour) with definite characteristics and force fields surrounds them. For instance, a person is a part of various groups (is embedded in them). These organisations are a part of a variety of cultures and subcultures that make up society at a more abstract level. Lewin was of the opinion that the field is ever-evolving. Despite the field's ongoing change, he also discussed the possibility of quasi-stationary equilibrium (however, one may be amazed with the fact that whether it is a perceived or an actual equilibrium). The salient features of Field Theory is given below:

1. ***Constructive:*** Scientific ideas frequently fall short of addressing the issue of people and individuality. The logic from generic discoveries to personal information cannot be reverse-engineered. This is precisely what psychology (social psychology and organisational psychology) aims to achieve in order to increase the predictability of human behaviour. It is possible to deduce one example from another by construction. The field itself is conceived of in Lewin's theory as a constellation of psychological forces. Since every building is a unique instance, prediction is possible.
2. ***Dynamic approach:*** It aims to pinpoint the driving reasons behind behaviour.
3. ***Psychological approach:*** It takes a psychological rather than a physical approach to examining the factors in the environment that influence how people behave.
4. ***Gestalt:*** The analysis first addresses the big picture before turning to the specifics to gather more data.
5. ***Behaviour as a Function of the Field:*** Only in respect to the current state of a particular area can behaviour be understood. Any change in the environment affects behaviour. Only how the past affected the field makes it relevant now.
6. ***Mathematical Representation:*** Quantitative analysis, topological mapping, and vectors affect changes.

On the basis of the aforementioned, it can be said that one particular field is where the goals of changes exist. The end outcome of the aims is some personal interest or want, to the extent that it can be represented by the actor (of the field) in the force field. Regardless of how good they are, the operational rules of the field are what determine whether ideas and thoughts survive. Change, as used here as a working hypothesis idea, denotes a change from a previous state of some aspects of the system under consideration. It seems realistic to employ such a broad term in this instance because organizational changes and the complexity of life cannot be adequately explained by a clear-cut definition.

Figure 7. Facets for field theory

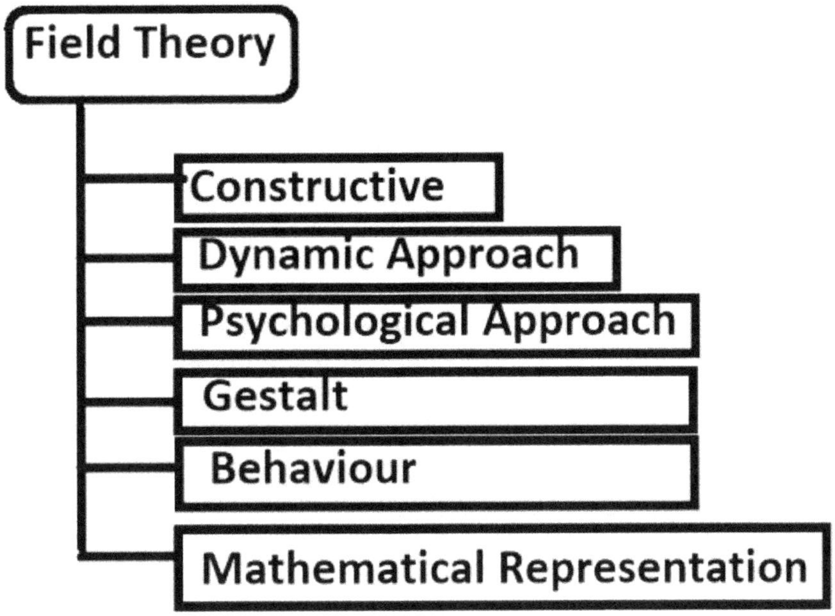

Theories of Change

Kurt Lewin's **Three-Step Change Model** serves as the foundation for all ideas relating to change. In the framework of individual and group learning, Lewin defined change **(1972,1975)**.

Figure 8. Three steps model of change management (Kurt Lewin)

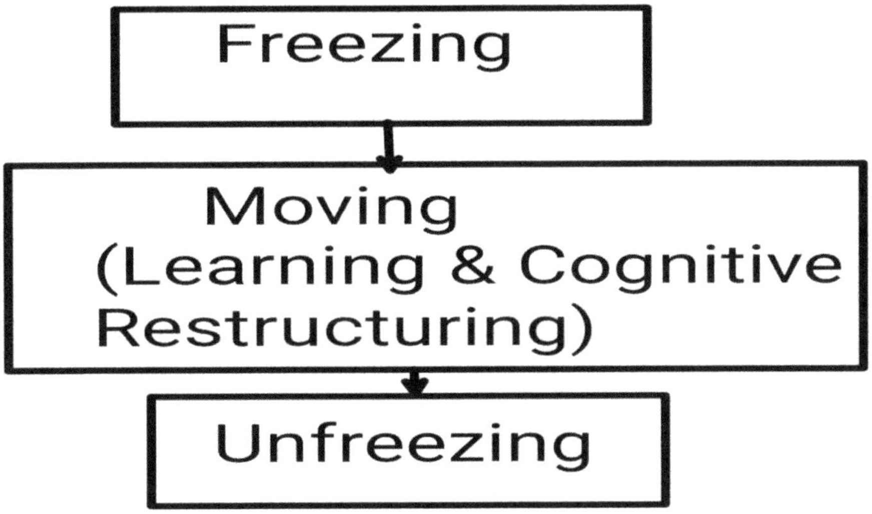

The same is true for organizations, although there are more steps in the process (**Weick and Quinn1999; Kotter 1999; Elrod II and Tippet, 2002**). This three-step procedure works together as a cohesive unit. According to **Van de Ven and Poole (1995)**, who examined 200 papers on change management, there are four main categories into which change-related theories can be divided. Based on what propels (facilitates, energizes, motivates, etc.) the change, a distinction is made to propose four model.

1. **The Teleological Motor** 2. **The Life-Cycle Motor** 3. **The Dialectical Motor** 4. **The Evolutionary Motor.**

Figure 9. Facets of change management

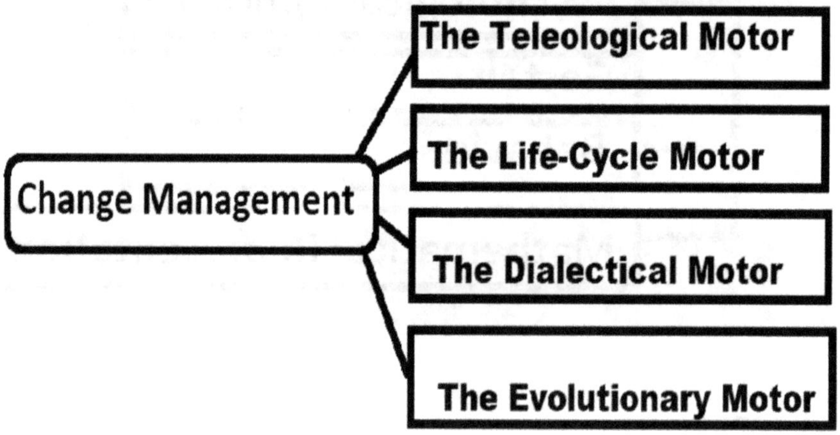

1.The Teleological Motor

Such changes are necessitated by the requirement to live up to the social structure that the organization's members are a part of. Development occurs through cycles that include setting, achieving, evaluating, and changing goals. This is the foundation of most change models.

Usually, a process of strategic change is goal-oriented. Since it refers to a planned and goal-oriented transformation that leaders started and oversaw, it falls under this category (**Rajagopalan and Spreitzer 1996**). A change in operations (daily production activities) as a result of changing goals may or should result in changes at the organizational level.

Change can also be described in terms of cognitive framing theories, which contend that the evolution of management's or managers' thinking, cognitive processes, worldview, etc. (i.e., a consistently cognitive approach) is the root cause of organizational changes. Reconciling preconceived notions about the world with the environment that is actually perceived is a repetitive process that leads to cognitive level changes in management (especially with regard to decision makers who have the ability to significantly alter the organizational system), which in turn results in changes in the organization (**Barret al 1992; Bartunek et al 1999; Weick 1995**).

The change momentum theories suggest that an organization must have sufficient momentum before changes may take place (energy). In an organization's life, momentum (having energy) and inertia (having less energy) always compete and alternate. A stage of life cycle known as inertia is characterized by a lack of (enough) energy. Another indication of it is the absence of goals, which may potentially be the root of this lack of motivation. It is known as indifference or, in severe situations, depression on an individual level. Additionally, these phenomena can be seen at the group and organizational levels.

Organizational researchers that study innovation theories aim to comprehend how unique innovation processes might take root in organizational life. How does an inventive and creative idea succeed in a dynamic system (organization), how is it enhanced, what resources does it rely on, etc.? Combining impulsive idea production with more deliberate and regulated processes organizations use to develop and implement ideas can lead to some interesting circumstances (**Orlikowksi and Hofman 1997**). Real idea-based development cannot occur unless these two strands are in sync. From an evolutionary perspective, ideas are crucial to how organisations adapt to their surroundings because spontaneous genetic changes have the ability to produce competitive advantages that guarantee the organization's survival and prosperity in the (ecological) niche in which it operates.

2. The Life-Cycle Motor

According to these views, change is a process that has clearly defined stages. The sequence of certain interdependent events that occur in order to reach the ultimate state determines and even necessitates them (**Van de Ven and Poole 1995**).

Punctuated balance. Numerous change theories that attempt to describe the dynamics of organizations, such as the idea of punctuated equilibrium, are built on the evolutionary and revolutionary framework theories of change developed by **Greiner (1972)**. According to the hypothesis of **Tushman and Romanelli 1985**, a number of small adjustments are being made within organizations, but even if they are noticeable, they do not have an impact on the system as a whole. For a while, these small changes are in a quasi-equilibrium state with continuity, but once they reach a critical mass, they cause significant systemic change. Management science took the idea from evolutionary biology.

3. The Dialectical Motor

Conflicts between different organizational units lead to organizational transformations, claims the dialectical motor method. The status quo is directly opposed by new ideas and principles. This is nothing more than the application of **Hegel**'s rules of evidence; theses and antitheses contend with one another in order to produce a potential synthesis that favours the preservation of the status quo. Some contend that enhancing an organization's capacity to create and resolve conflicts is more successful than a synthesis that starts the closure of a transformation **(e.g. Bartunek et al 2000).**

Schematic Changes

This hypothesis makes an effort to explain how individual cognitive processes (may) cause modifications to prevalent patterns (cognitive constructs). Patterns offer a cognitive framework that supports how we digest new information and serves as a frame of reference for how we see, think, decide, and act. In accordance with their nature, changes are divided into two categories. If a change inside a system does not impact the system as a whole, it is first-level or **Morphostatic**. When a modification also affects the system, it is referred to as second-level or **Morphogenetic (Watzlawick, 1974).**

Change management can be viewed as a second-level or morphogenetic management area that deals with the management of changes if the principles established in and the conclusions drawn from the previous chapters about managers and organization consultants being expected to intervene in order to support development are accepted **(Mink et al.,1993).**

People always attempt to fit new experiences into their preexisting routines. If they fail, they insert it into an existing cliché with the least amount of effort (which, because of the bias in perception, may cause problems in processing the information, which in turn may bias the response). Processing new information requires the adjustment of an existing pattern or procedure or the development of a new one that is appropriate for handling the information, therefore it is always a dynamic process. When we come across new items in our environment, we begin to form theories about how they function or what they resemble. This thesis serves as the foundation for how we interact with our surroundings, which in turn produces an antithesis in us.

These conflicts will have an impact on our individual clichés, which alter based on how the environment reacts. The learning theory enters the picture at this moment. In reaction to their responses, actors can gain approval from the system or punishment from it (the lack of an answer can also be understood as an affirmative answer, due to the lack of punishment). We either begin the creative cognitive process or simply put up with the responses depending on the intensity of these reactions and the effort needed to develop the novel pattern.

Communicative Changes

Interpersonal communication causes changes, according to the social interaction and social cognitive construct theories (**Berger and Luckmann 1966; Giddens 1984**). Most of the time, when we interact with others, we do it as representatives of particular social groupings rather than as lone individuals (**Wieman and Giles 1997**). A variety of diverse perspectives, attitudes, and ideas are conveyed within an organization, and these things are always changing depending on how much influence certain players have over the organization (in dynamic fields, thoughts are aligned along force fields). A new idea, or synthesis, may be the outcome. There is a fundamental struggle for attention, which is required for reception and, by extension, dominance.

As we continue to consider communication, the cognitive method comes up again. Language not only facilitates contact with the outside world but also shapes interior thought (**Vigotszkij, 1962**). It is a system of symbols that serves as one of the cornerstones of social life and is crucial to the advancement of society (**Mead, 1973**). The theories may be useful in understanding how language and culture interact. The notion of linguistic relativity, proposed by **Sapir and Worf in 1956,** contends that the language we use shapes the way we think. Simply put, we are unable to think about things we do not have words for. **Bernstein (1970)** concentrated on the vertical aspect of language instead of this horizontal distinction. He proposed that a given social group's language confines the group to a "cognitive universe," or limits thinking. Language gives us the chance to think in symbols and helps us to abstract from both current objects and people as well as from daily life. Without language, cultures could not be developed, maintained, or even described. G. H. Mead, Cooley, and Blumer, who are symbolic interactionism's representatives, stressed this.

4. The Evolutionary Motor

The process of evolution is based on a never-ending cycle of options, selection, and upkeep. The theories centre on how organizations react to environmental triggers. If the organization has the capability and expertise necessary to accomplish the change, we assume that someone will recognize changes in the environment and initiate change in accordance.

Internal Change Routines

This strategy examines how unique ideas for improvement are chosen and accepted by a company. According to **Nelson and Winter (1982)**, organizations should create a procedure, routine, or action pattern specifically intended to assist and facilitate the change process. A well-considered procedure (that can be sustained over the long term), according to **Lewitt and March (1988)**, may substantially aid organizations in adopting changes, regardless of their issue. A similar procedure, however, may also bring the organization's inertia to the surface, as **Kelly and Amburgey (1991)** point out.

Institutional Changes

This condition is more frequently linked to consistency than to change. It can be because anything becomes established once it is institutionalised. It should be emphasised that the theories of stability and change cover the same range of occurrences, as proposed by **Greenwood and Hinings (1996)**. In truth, in order to preserve stability in a dynamic environment, a system that makes every effort to stay the same (to maintain the status quo) is continually evolving. Any requirement for change that arises inside the organization is professionally handled through a focused, controlled, and managed process through the use of formal actors (regardless of whether triggered by internal or external factors).

Purpose of Change in Organization

Although it may appear simple, the solution is not. If we adopt the evolutionary viewpoint, which holds that all organizations desire to survive and prosper in a somewhat egotistical way, then all procedures ought to be directed toward achieving this objective (monitoring of the environment, detection of changes in the environment, generation of responses, implementation of responses, and repetition of this process in continuous cycles). Everything would be clear-cut, predictable, and reasonable in this scenario. Though it may sound cliche, life is trickier than that. In order to accomplish their own self-serving objectives, each subsystem, smaller group, and person (as autonomous entities) inside an organization adheres to a set of rules.

Trends and Success Rates of Different Adaptation and Coping Strategies

The level of workplace adaptation has been varied depending on the sectors and the convenience with the aforementioned self-interest and the desire to prosper in the future business scenario. Also, the adaptation has coaxed the organisation to design plethora of coping strategies during the pandemic to deal with the personal and professional change and pressure. The personal stress has been mainly due to financial and health wise losses along with orchestrating with the new work mode. Profession stress has been mainly due to disruptive changes and thereby the adaptations.

In Information Technology

In Information Technology sector, online/virtual workplace/WFH has been a chosen alternative during pandemic and continuing with the new-normal era. Only for extremely important matters like some of the meetings and client visits, the hybrid forms have been utilized. The kind of change, the employees have gone through, is of paramount importance. It was quite evident that employees have admitted of their psychological trauma and a state of being unwell, though the organisational initiatives were not adequate to embrace such trauma. The phase out of services were also adapted gradually, despite the fact, for a few new jobs, evolution of Job Nomenclature and Positions have been created. These job positions (like Business Analytics/Data Analytics and others) have been especially designed to cater to cross border projects and till now continuing for WFH format for the ease of the work space and time related complexities.

Table 4. Work mode status in it industry during pandemic time

Industry	Total Response sector wise	Work From Home	Phygital	Physical
Information Technology	60	52	8	0

Figure 10. Graphical expression of work mode in it industries during pandemic

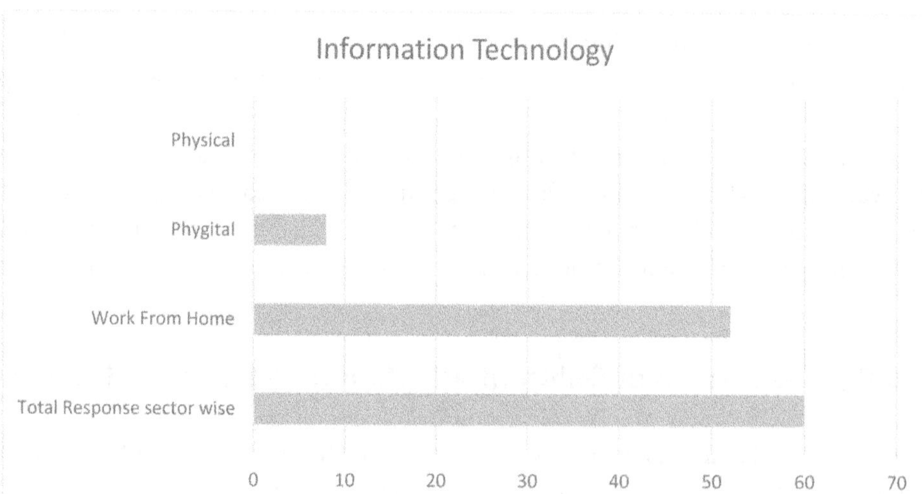

Table 5. Organisational change and adaptive strategies in it industries during pandemic

Information Technology		
Factor	**Number**	**Percentage**
Psychological Stress	**48**	**80**
Home	*12*	*25*
Work	*29*	*60*
Others	*7*	*15*
Anxiety	**55**	**92**
Depression	**33**	**55**
Financial Insecurity	**52**	**87**
Organisational Initiative to Solve	**35**	**58**
Counselling Sessions (By professionals or Bosses)	*24*	**69**
Motivational Webinar/ Seminar/ Workshop	*28*	**80**
Recreational Workshop/ Sessions	*12*	**34**
Virtual Get together/ Party	*16*	**46**
Gifts/ Incentives	*14*	**40**
Organisation being empathetic towards Employees	*2*	**6**
Work Related Stress	**56**	**93**

In Finance

For Financial Institutions

Table 6. Sector wise segregation in finance

Industry	Sub-section	Total Response sector wise
Finance	Insurance	30
	Micro Finance	25
	Banking	45

In Finance, three significant micro sectors like Insurance, Micro-Finance and Banking have been covered. In Insurance industry, almost no WFH has been incorporated except some insurance agents who are not under payroll. In Banking and Microfinance, barring some virtual meetings, mostly physical interface has been used, maintaining social distancing norms. The stress level was quite high though minimum initiatives have been taken by the institutions. Also, mostly the initiatives have been taken by reputed banks unlike the micro financial or insurance industry. The latter ones suffered a lot because of heavy death claims and less of sourcing from the customers. Within the spectrum of initiatives, incentives and virtual parties were some of the accepted norms.

Figure 11. Sector wise segregation in finance responses

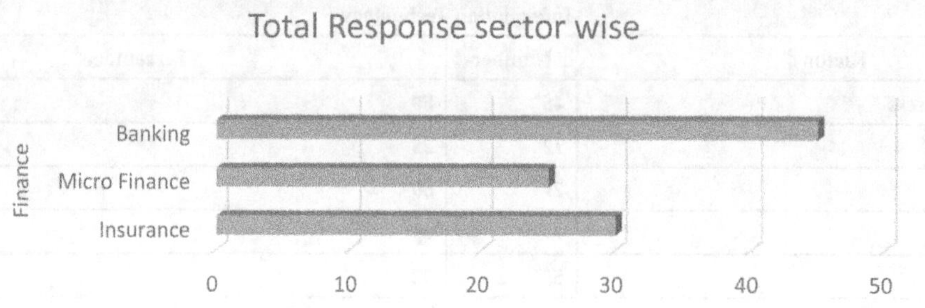

Table 7. Work mode status in insurance industry during pandemic time

Insurance	Work From Home	Phygital	Physical
30	0	5	25

Figure 12. Graphical expression of work mode in insurance industries during pandemic

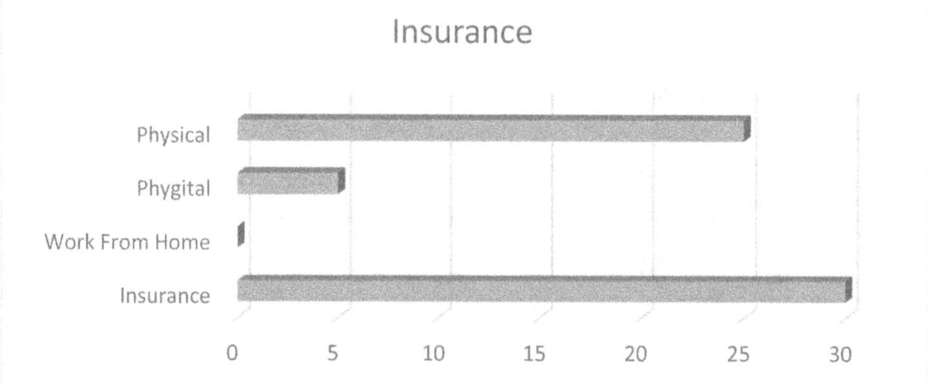

Table 8. Work mode status in micro finance during pandemic time

Micro Finance	Work From Home	Phygital	Physical
25	0	7	18

Figure 13. Graphical expression of work mode in micro finance industries during pandemic

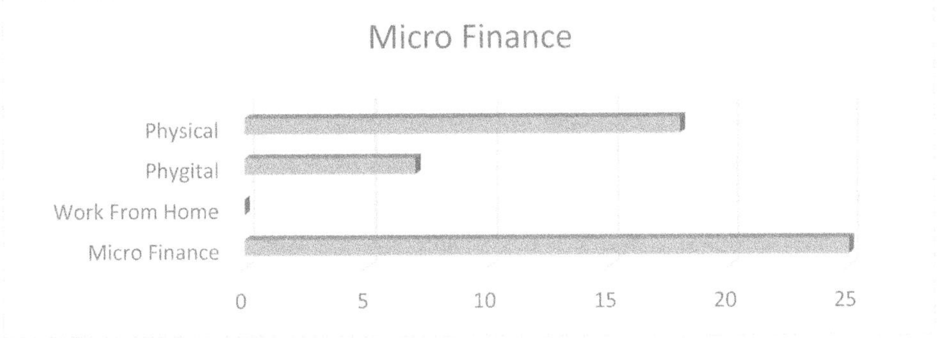

Table 9. Work mode status in banking industry during pandemic time

Banking	Work From Home	Phygital	Physical
45	7	26	12

Table 10. Organisational change and adaptive strategies in finance industries during pandemic

Finance		
Factor	Number	Percentage
Psychological Stress	62	62
Home	*26*	26
Work	*30*	30
Others	*6*	6
Anxiety	49	49
Depression	37	37
Financial Insecurity	39	39
Organisational Initiative to Solve	48	48
Counselling Sessions (By professionals or Bosses)	*8*	8
Motivational Webinar/ Seminar/ Workshop	*2*	2
Recreational Workshop/ Sessions	*0*	0
Virtual Get together/ Party	*23*	23
Gifts/ Incentives	*27*	27
Organisation being empathetic towards Employees	*12*	12
Work Related Stress	78	78

Figure 14. Graphical expression of work mode in banking industries during pandemic

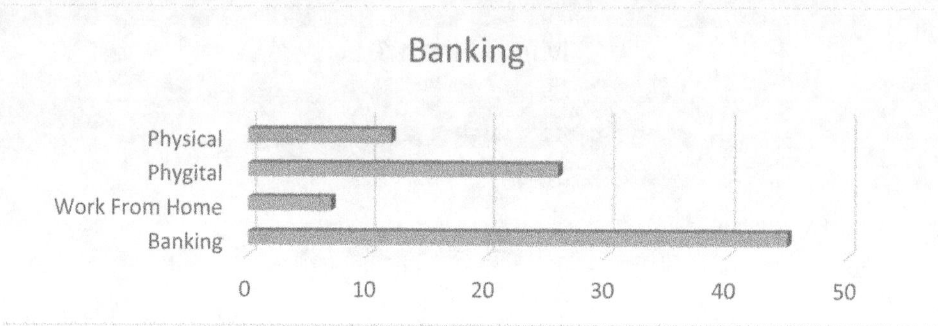

In Retail Industry

In retail industry, the weightage has been given on phygital/ hybrid mode, due to obvious reasons of pandemic. The stress level of the employees was undoubtedly very high, though the organisational initiatives to alleviate was not sufficient enough, except the informal counselling by bosses and some level of incentives.

Table 11. Sector wise segregation in retail

Retail	Life style	35
	Daily Supplies	40

Figure 15. Graphical expression of sector wise segregation in retail

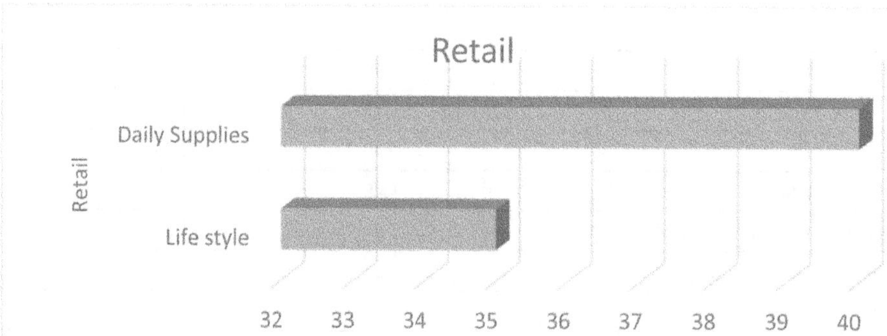

Table 12. Work mode status in retail industry during pandemic time

Retail	Work From Home	Phygital	Physical
75	0	67	8

Figure 16: Graphical expression of work mode in retail industries during pandemic

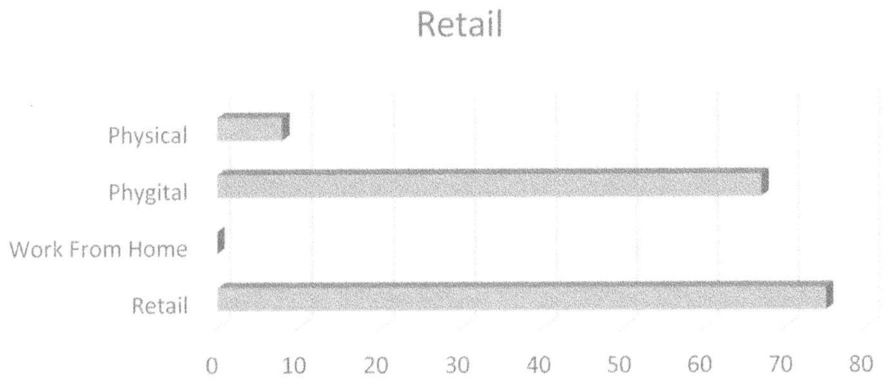

Table 13. Organisational change and adaptive strategies in retail industries during pandemic

Retail		
Factor	**Number**	**Percentage**
Psychological Stress	**70**	**93**
Home	*36*	**48**
Work	*68*	**91**
Others	*15*	**20**
Anxiety	**69**	**92**
Depression	**27**	**36**
Financial Insecurity	**72**	**96**
Organisational Initiative to Solve	**12**	**16**
Counselling Sessions (By professionals or Bosses)	*27*	**8**
Motivational Webinar/ Seminar/ Workshop	*0*	**2**
Recreational Workshop/ Sessions	*0*	**0**
Virtual Get together/ Party	*0*	**23**
Gifts/ Incentives	*29*	**27**
Organisation being empathetic towards Employees	*5*	**12**
Work Related Stress	**73**	**97**

In Hospitality Industry

For hotel industries, most of the activities were physical, except business development related meetings during the initial phase of pandemic and lock down. During Lock down phase, the staying facilities were almost closed except the quintessential operational execution. Some of the budget hotels temporarily converted into Quarantine Centre or Isolation Centre to accommodate the covid patients. In the medical fraternity, mostly it was either physical (direct contact) or Hybrid (online consultation and other paraphernalia) and less WFH for private chambers during the whole period of lock down or later. In hospitality, especially in medical fraternity, organisational initiatives like workshops, seminars, webinars were quite high compared to other sectors. Though the organisations were empathetic towards employees, but many doctors complained for excessive work pressure and extended hours of working for justifiable reasons.

Table 14. Sector wise segregation in hospitality industry

Hospitality	Hotel	20
	medical care	57

Table 15. Work Mode status in Hospitality Industry during Pandemic time

Hospitality	Work From Home	Phygital	Physical
77	20	22	35

Figure 17. Graphical expression of work mode in hospitality and medical fraternity during pandemic

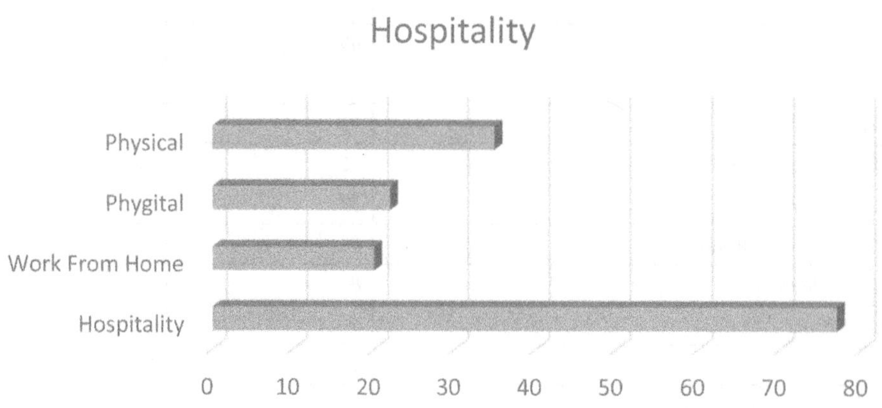

Table 16. Organisational change and adaptive strategies in hospitality industries during pandemic

Hospitality		
Factor	**Number**	**Percentage**
Psychological Stress	72	94
Home	*33*	43
Work	*70*	91
Others	*6*	8
Anxiety	75	97
Depression	57	74
Financial Insecurity	76	99
Organisational Initiative to Solve	38	49
Counselling Sessions (By professionals or Bosses)	*52*	68
Motivational Webinar/ Seminar/ Workshop	*14*	18
Recreational Workshop/ Sessions	*25*	32
Virtual Get together/ Party	*38*	49
Gifts/ Incentives	*27*	35
Organisation being empathetic towards Employees	*26*	34
Work Related Stress	75	97

Table 17. Work mode status in academia during pandemic time

Academia	Work From Home	Phygital	Physical
52	20	15	20

In Academia

In academia, it started with WFH mode and phased out to Phygital or hybrid teaching- learning to complete classroom interactions. The stress level of the teachers and administrative staffs were very high to cope up with the fast change of technology and to fit in the new age digital learning. But most of the organisations took nonmonetary initiatives like regular counselling and motivational sessions, meetings, webinars etc. to regularise the change

Figure 18. Graphical expression of work mode in academia during pandemic

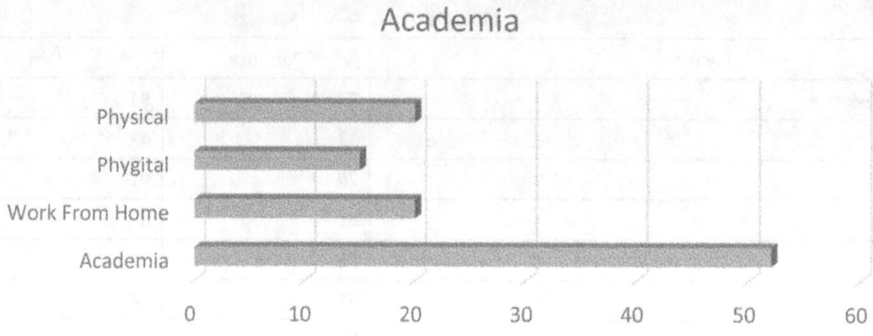

Table 18. Organisational change and adaptive strategies in academia during pandemic

Academia		
Factor	**Number**	**Percentage**
Psychological Stress	**48**	**92**
Home	*29*	**56**
Work	*49*	**94**
Others	2	**4**
Anxiety	**42**	**81**
Depression	**34**	**65**
Financial Insecurity	**50**	**96**
Organisational Initiative to Solve	**45**	**87**
Counselling Sessions (By professionals or Bosses)	*43*	**83**
Motivational Webinar/ Seminar/ Workshop	*32*	**62**
Recreational Workshop/ Sessions	*26*	**50**
Virtual Get together/ Party	*12*	**23**
Gifts/ Incentives	*2*	**4**
Organisation being empathetic towards Employees	*14*	**27**
Work Related Stress	**50**	**96**

Issues, Problems, and Challenges in Workplace During Pandemic

The issues, problems and challenges in workplace have been manifold during pandemic times; with various layers and dimensions. Also, it has two sides of the frame- one covering employee's perspective and the other covering the employers' perspective.

The employee's perspective has been consisting of mainly five areas, namely: ***1. Financial and job-related insecurity (pay cut and retrenchment), 2. Concern for health (self and family), 3. Mental stress of coping with changed work environment (professional work in presence of family members),***

4. Self-learning of digital platforms to cope with virtual workplace, 5. 24×7 work pressure to innovate disruptive methods for compensating commercial loss for corporate houses. These areas were evident from the telephonic conversation during the interview process (unstructured questionnaire).

The main challenges for employers have been the financial losses due to sudden closure of organisation and the new-normal work environment. Other than that, the psychological well-being of the employees has been a matter of concern for the organisations. Due to shut down of many logistics and channel of distribution, it became imperative for the Organizations to innovate new alternatives. This sudden increase in work pressure and upheaval in personal life (including personal loss) became the reason for under performance for many employees, culminating in less revenue generation. On one hand losing scope of business and on the other hand, under performance became an extraordinary burden for various organisations.

Discussion on the Research Questions

The first research question was related to the theories of change management and the first few modules of this chapter has done a justice to the query. The second and third questions were regarding the implementation of the theories in practice and to what extent. This became a bit vague while comparing with the actual scenario. Since the pandemic has brought a radical change, it could not follow a change momentum phase with a gradual transformation (TheTeleological Motor theory). To elaborate it further, under System Approach, Incremental theory could not be applied, instead Radical Changes were adapted based on the severity of the contamination and contagiousness of the disease. Under Field theory, Moving and Unfreezing have been practised without sufficient gap in between the stages to cope with the urgency, like implementing the Government protocol and to take necessary disruptive corporate strategies to stabilise it further. The Change Momentum Theories (under The Teleological Motor Theory) to pace up the status quo, could not be adapted, though change of goal for corporate world and government has been a regular affair based on the situation. The Lifecycle Motor theory was practised during phase out to demarcate different stages from online, hybrid to physical work mode. The Dialectical Motor theory explains the reasons behind the organizational stress (both employees' and employers' point of view), ultimately favouring the most convenient state of affair. The Schematic changes have also been reflected through the modification of cognitive learning through counselling sessions, motivational sessions / Webinars / Seminars, personal counselling through superior- subordinate interactions (Communicative Changes). The Evolutionary Motor Theories are also relatable to the adaptation and initiatives of the organisations at the basal level to try hardest to balance the phase, in turn the organisation got into experimentation with situation to strike a chord between the adverse scenario and organisational benefits (Internal Change Routine). The fourth question checked the adequacy of the coping strategies but failed to understand the depth of the appropriateness of the initiatives, as the study does not continue for a long run, neither respondents could share any valid response on the same.

CONCLUSION

The empirical study and meta-analysis across several industries have shown the use of Incremental method of organisational change rather than a Radical change except the drastic change of work mode due to government imposition. But during phase out of re- opening mostly Gradual change has been adapted to relieve employees of further mental shock. Though most of the organisations have been trying for coping strategies to balance the newly brought changes in the organisation, but these have been very superficially done without any deep intervention.

Limitations and Scope for Further Research

The main limitation and scope for further research is that this chapter does not hold any significant statistical test for the primary data. Therefore, the data could be subjected to adequate hypothesis testing to establish a statistically significant relationship between the set theories and the data.

REFERENCES

Austin, J. R., & Bartunek, J. M. (2006). Theories and practices of Organizational Development. Gallos, J. V (ed): Organization Development. San Francisco, CA. Jossey-Bass.

Barr, P. S., Stimpert, J. L., & Huff, A. S. (1992). Cognitive Change, Strategic Action and Organizational Renewal. *Strategic Management Journal*, *27*(S1), 489–510. doi:10.1002mj.4250131004

Bartunek, J. M., Krim, R., Necochea, R., & Humphries, M. (1999). Sense-making, Sense Giving and Leadership in Strategic Organizational Development. In J. Wagner (Ed.), *Advanced in Qualitive Organizational Research, 4,37-71.*

Bartunek, J. M., Walsh, K., & Lacey, C. A. (2000). Dynamics and Dilemmas of Women Leading Women. *Organization Science*, *11*(6), 589–610. doi:10.1287/orsc.11.6.589.12531

Bennis, W. G. (1966). *Changing Organizations.* McGraw-Hill.

Berger, P., & Luckmann, T. (1966). *The Social Construction of Reality.* Anchor Books.

Bernstein, B. B. (1970). A Socio-Linguistic Approach to Social Learning. Sebeok, T. (ed) Language and Poverty. Markham, London.

Boudon, R., & .... (1999). Szociológiai lexikon. *Budapest: Corvina.* 154-155, Boulding, K. E., (1969) 'A rendszerelmélet mint szemléletmód. In *Kindler J. -Kiss I. (szerk.), Rendszerelmélet* (pp. 113–130). KJK.

Boutaud, N., Agarwal, A., Postel, E. A., & Pericak-Vance, M. A. (2005). Complement Factor H Variant Increases the Risk of Age-Related Macular Degeneration. *Science*, *308*(5720), 419–421. doi:10.1126cience.1110359 PMID:15761120

Chaturvedi, S., Rizvi, I. A., & Pasipanodya, E. T. (2019). How Can Leaders Make Their Followers to Commit to the Organization? the Importance of Influence Tactics. *Global Business Review*, *20*(6), 1462–1474. doi:10.1177/0972150919846963

Coffman, K., & Lutes, K. (2007). Change Management: Getting User Buy-In. Management of Change, USA.

Davidson, R., Goodwin-Stewart, J., & Kent, P. (2005). Internal Governance Structures and Earnings Management. *Accounting and Finance*, *45*(2), 241–267. doi:10.1111/j.1467-629x.2004.00132.x

Dhawan, S. (2020). Online Learning: A Panacea in the Time of COVID-19 Crisis. *Journal of Educational Technology Systems, 49*(1), 5–22. doi:10.1177/0047239520934018

Dobák, M. (2002). *Szervezeti formák és vezetés*. KJK – Kerszöv.

Elrod, P. II, & Tippett, D. D. (2002). The death valley of change. *Journal of Organizational Change Management, 15*(3), 273–291. doi:10.1108/09534810210429309

Giddens, A. (1984). *The construction of society*. University of California Press.

Greenwood, R., & Hinings, C. R. (1993). Understanding Radical Organizational Change: Bringing Together the Old and the New Institutionalism. *Academy of Management Review, 21*(4), 1022–1054. doi:10.2307/259163

Greiner, L. (1972). Evolution and revolution as organizations grow. [Haines, J. L., Hauser, M. A., Schmidt, S., Scott, W. K., Olson, L. M., Gallins, P., Spencer, K. L., Shu, Y. K., Noureddine, M., Gilbert, J. R., Schnetz]. *Harvard Business Review*, (July-August), 37–46. PMID:10179654

Kaushik, M., & Guleria, N. (2020). The Impact of Pandemic COVID -19 in Workplace. *European Journal of Business and Management, 12*(5), 9–18.

Kelly, D., & Amburgey, T. L. (1991). Organizational Inertia and Momemtum: A Dynamic Model of Strategic Change. *Academy of Management Journal, 34*(3), 591–612. doi:10.2307/256407

Kotter, J. P. (1999) A Változások Irányítása Kossuth Kiadó, Budapest, Kotter, John P. Heskett, J. L.(1992). Corporate Culture and Performance, The Free Press, New York.

Kübler-Ross, E. (1969). *On Death and Dying*. Macmillan.

Lewin, K. (1972). *Mezőelmélet A Társadalomtudományban Gondolat*, Budapest, Lewitt, B.March, J. G (1988) Organizational Learning. *Annual Review of Psychology, 14*, 319–340.

Lcwin, (1975). *Csoportdinamika Közgazdasági és Jogi Kiadó*, Budapest, Lewin, K (1944). Problems of Research in Social Psychology. *D. Cartwright (Ed.) Field theory in social science*. London: Social Science Paperbacks.

Marquis, C., & Tilcsik, A. (2013). Imprinting: Toward a Multilevel Theory. *The Academy of Management Annals, 7*(1), 195–245. doi:10.5465/19416520.2013.766076

Mead, G. H. (1934). *Mind, Self and Society*. University Press.

Mink, O. G., Esterhuysen, P. W., Mink, B. P., & Owen, K. Q. (1993). *Change at Work*. Jossey-Bass.

Nauheimer, H. (2007). Change Management Toolbook. *Creative Commons Attribution-Share-Alike 3.0 Unported License.*

Nelson, R. R., & Winter, S. G. (1982). *An Evolutionary Theory of Economic Change*. Belknap Press.

Orlikowski, W. J., & Hofman, D. J. (1997). An Improvizational Model for Change Management: The Case of Groupware Technologies. *Sloan Management Review, 38*(2), 11–21.

Pataki, B. (1999). Technológiaváltások menedzselése – a változásmenedzsment alkalmazása a technológiamenedzsment területén. Műszaki Könyvkiadó, Budapest, Pokhrel, Sumitra., Chhetri, Roshan. (2021). A Literature Review on Impact of COVID-19 Pandemic on Teaching and Learning. *Higher Education for the Future*, *8*(1), 133–141.

Porras, J. I., & Robertson, P. J. (1987). Organization Development Theory: A Typology and Evaluation. In R. W. Woodman & W. A. Pasmore (Eds.), Research in Organizational Change and Development, Greenwich, CT: JAI Press, 1, 1–57.

Porras, J. I., & Robertson, P. J. (1992). Organizational Development: Theory, Practice, Research. In M. D. Dunnette and L. M. Hough (Eds.), Handbook of organizational psychology Palo Alto, CA: Psychology Press, 3, 719–822.

Quinn, R. E., Spreitzer, G. M., & Brown, M. V. (2000). Changing others through Changing Ourselves: The Transformation of Human systems. *Journal of Management Inquiry*, *9*(2), 47–164. doi:10.1177/105649260092010

Rajagopalan, N., & Spreitzer, G. M. (1996). Towards a Theory of Strategic Change: A Multi-Lens Perspective and Integrative Framework. *Academy of Management Review*, *22*(1), 48–79. doi:10.2307/259224

Shearer, C. S., Hames, D. S., & Runge, J. B. (2001). How CEOs Influence Organizational Culture following Acquisitions. *Leadership and Organization Development Journal*, *22*(3), 105–113. doi:10.1108/01437730110389256

Sintema, E. J. (2020). Effect of COVID-19 on the Performance of Grade 12 Students: Implications for Stem Education. *Eurasia Journal of Mathematics, Science and Technology Education*, *16*(7), 1–6. doi:10.29333/ejmste/7893

Tushman, M. L., & Romanelli, E. (1985). Organizational Evolution: A Metamorphosis Model Of Convergence And Reorientation. In: L Cummings – B. M. Staw (Eds) Research in Organizational Behavior Greenwich, CT:JAI Press, 7,171-222.

Van de Ven, A. H., & Poole, M. S. (1995). Explaining Development and Change in Organizations. *Academy of Management Review*, *20*(3), 510–540. doi:10.2307/258786

von Bertalanffy, L. (1979). *Adalék Egy Általános Rendszertanhoz: A Szervezet, Mint Rendszer Szerkesztő: Bleicher, Knut Dr*. Közgazdasági És Jogi Kiadó.

Vygotsky, L. S. (1962). *Thought and Language*. MIT Press. doi:10.1037/11193-000

Watzlawick, P., Weakland, J. H., & Fisch, R. (1974). *Change: Principles of Problem Formation and Problem Resolution*. W. W. Norton.

Weick, K. E. (1995). *Sensemaking in Organizations*. Sage.

Weick, K. E., & Quinn, R. E. (1999). Organizational Change and Development. *Annual Review of Psychology*, *50*(1), 361–386. doi:10.1146/annurev.psych.50.1.361 PMID:15012461

Wieman, J. M., & Giles, H. (1997): Az interperszonális kommunikáció In: Szociálpszichológia szerk.: Hewstone,-Stroebe,– Codol,– Stephenson. KJK, Budapest, 1997.221-244.

APPENDIX

Appendage for Revised Content based for evaluation comments: List of Response:

1. Alphabetical arrangement of the keywords done.
2. Copy editing for proof reading done to make it error free.
3. The background and the literature review have been organised and additional content has been supplemented to elaborate it further.
4. Research questions have been added in introduction part to elaborate the requirement of building up the objectives and there after the final discussion of the chapter.
5. The methodology part has been elaborated.
6. Limitations and Further scope for research have been added.
7. The objectives of the chapter are coherent with the objectives of the book (which should be the case ideally) but not same and hence are not changed.
8. Reference has been updated in APA 7th edition as per recommendation.
9. The common words like COVID-19 and others have been referred in similar manner throughout the text, to make it standardized and organised.
10. The ordering and captioning of the tables and figures have been made separately as per recommendations.
11. The key terms and Definitions have been added.
12. Hospitality has incorporated with hotel and medical services, since they belong to service industry.
13. Acronyms have been written in full.
14. Conclusion has been elaborated.
15. Discussion has been added.

Chapter 9
A Play-Based Approach to Learning in Internationalizing Arab Family Businesses:
Change as a Ludic Paradox

Edward Gonsalves
Cooplexity Institute, Spain

Rebecca Fakoussa
University of Northampton, UK

ABSTRACT

Arab family businesses (AFB) can be found across a richly diverse region with a myriad of unique cultures. As Arab family businesses worldwide become more sophisticated with ownership, succession and wealth planning changing, family business training and education need to rapidly evolve its support of family businesses. This chapter argues that in the MENA region, training and education approaches for family-owned businesses differ to others due to their environmental paradox. Given such differences, play could offer Arab family business leaders an alternative route to training and education, as executives increasingly encounter rapid and complex environmental, competitive, and internal changes. In particular, the chapter argues that AFB's which are internationalizing their markets and operations will be driven by changes that force breaks with traditional routines.

INTRODUCTION

Family businesses (FB) are found across the globe in different shapes and sizes, ranging from the local corner shop or bistro to national and international brands. FBs are of significant economic importance around the world, with 60%-90% of all businesses being family businesses (De Massis et al, 2015). Further, FBs have a significant impact on national economies as they contribute to job generation, GDP growth, innovation and philanthropy (Feliu & Botero, 2016).

DOI: 10.4018/978-1-6684-7509-6.ch009

Despite their economic importance there is still no agreement upon definition of the term 'family business' (Birdthistle, 2006; Chua, et al, 1999) and while academically FB definitions are varied (Diaz-Moriana et al., 2019), FBs fundamentally make up a significant proportion of businesses.

In the Arab world, more than 90% of businesses are family-run or family controlled (PWC, 2019), making family businesses central to Arab economies.

FBs given their long term outlooks across generations experience frequent and idiosyncratic changes in operational routines and strategic priorities across multiple dimensions (Miller et al., 2003). FBs, whether founders or successor generations, constantly seek out opportunities, intend to stay current and assume risks that further exacerbate the impact of changes on their businesses (Ward, 1997).

In these unprecedented times, change has become a constant, demonstrating that businesses, especially FBs due to their economic impact, need to adapt quickly to many situational unknowns. FBs need to be able to face the uncertainty of this ever changing macro context irrespective of their size, growth ambitions, competence acquisitions and legacy aspirations. Engaging with changes and the ability to learn is key for FBs to not only survive challenging times but to be able to evolve themselves across generations, transform their business models and leadership approaches in order to stay competitive. This chapter explores play as an approach to engaging with change in family businesses (Sandelands, 2010).

In addition to these external changes, FBs have an internal dimension to assimilate working, and sometimes living, with their family members. People they might have known all their lives, potentially from a different generation, spouses and partners; they make up the family business clan (Zabala, 2019). This makes FBs unlike non-FBs because of their pivotal and personal relationships. Internal family matters such as marriage, sibling rivalry, divorce, generational shifts all need to be navigated (Rutherford et al., 2006). Add the layer of internal business factors, including corporate culture, and FBs consistently face a range of evolving, volatile and ambiguous changes.

Comparative research into non-FBs versus FBs frequently report FBs outperforming non-family businesses across sectors, sizes and stock markets. Family businesses face different changes and more complex, non-economic challenges compared to their non-family business counterparts (Chrisman, et al., 2003; Lee & Rogoff, 1996; Steier, 2003), and without an understanding of these, comparisons between family and non-family businesses are understated. The chapter will explore the concept of play as a contemporary tool for family business training and education and a catalyst for executive decision-making in changing environments. Consideration is given to the challenging and changing nature of the decision making process in internationalizing Arab Family Businesses– and how training and education will need to develop innovative responses to AFB's emergent futures. As with entrepreneurs, educating and supporting family business experiences is complex given the myriad of skills, attitudes, and knowledge that are demanded in constantly evolving institutional and competitive landscapes (McCann et al., 2003; Sandhu et al., 2012).

FBs in the 'Arab world' constantly adapt to and reflect the wider societal changes and transformation that take place in their community and institutional settings (Barakat, 1987). The Arab World (Arabic-speaking countries) extends across 24 countries with differing political, socio economic territories and a population of some 325 million people stretched across more than 12.9 million square kilometres - an area larger than China, the United States or Brazil (Ambergh, 2020). This chapter will look closer at two commonly described regions; MENA (Middle east and North Africa) and within that, the GCC (Gulf Cooperation Council).

MENA, refers to Middle East and North Africa including the countries of Algeria, Bahrain, Djibouti, Egypt, Iran, Jordan, Kuwait, Lebanon, Libya, Mauritania, Morocco, Oman, Pakistan, Qatar, Saudi Arabia, Sudan, Syria, Tunisia, the United Arab Emirates, and Yemen(Worldbank, 2020).

The Cooperation Council for the Arab States of the Gulf or GCC are a subset of this region. The GCC, came into formal existence in 1981 and includes several monarchies: Bahrain, Kuwait, Oman, Qatar, Saudi Arabia, and the United Arab Emirates (constituted by seven emirates: Abu Dhabi, Dubai, Ajman, Fujairah, Ras al Khaimah, Sharjah and Umm al Quwain) (IMF, 2020). Further integrations such as the GCC's fully operational customs union in 2015 has increased equality among GCC citizens, and while some barriers still exist in the free movement of goods and services, the GCC have developed joint, strategic energy and transport projects.

Despite economic and regional convergences, and whilst most GCC and MENA countries speak a form of Arabic, nations vary significantly in socio-economic, and cultural norms. Family businesses in the region do, however, share the need to internationalize beyond their borders to pursue further growth opportunities (McNiff, 2013). This reflects the constantly transforming institutional, corporate and regional contexts, where AFBs need to adapt to local, national and international change. Therefore, the demand for a greater choice of change management tools that increase the likelihood of success in this environment has accelerated in recent years (Saleh, 2019).

AIM

This chapter posits the question: *How can leaders of internationalizing Arab Family Businesses (IAFBs) develop relevant training and education when faced with the challenges inherent in emergent strategic changes?*

Its aim is to consider the issues faced by internationalizing Arab family businesses as a sub-component of the wider international family business community; how can current and future generations of executives adopt new training and education tools for decision makers in uncertain and ambiguous environments that AFBs encounter in their emerging futures (Samara, 2021). The authors propose play as such a tool. This chapter will contribute to a growing body of work which explores internationalization of Arab family businesses, and how their decision-making processes adopt training and education innovations. Play as a learning response, in the context of changes faced by IAFBs is still largely underexplored in existing research and practice.

FAMILY VERSUS NON-FAMILY BUSINESSES DIFFERENCES

Family businesses differ from non-family businesses, in the ways that they evaluate, acquire, integrate and leverage their resources. This is frequently attributed to the involvement and legacy of either a founding or controlling family (Sirmon and Hitt, 2003). *Systems theorists* including Barnes and Hershon (1994), Hollander and Elman (1988) and McCollom (1988) recognize the individual importance of the family and business subsystems and claim that the two systems (family and business) can be effectively integrated. However, while some authors argue that family aims and values can be incorporated into a business's strategic aims and objectives, others such as Levinson (1971) claim that the family and business subsystems are so different that they cannot possibly co-exist, except in the most unusual situations.

These dualities are highlighted below by Collins (2012) (Table 1). Dualities may not synchronise across individual, family or business life cycles.

Figure 1. Family business
Dualities (Collins, 2012)

Family	Non-Family	Family	Non-Family	Family	Non-Family
Ownership	Management	Paternal	Leadership	Kinship	Professionalism
Nepotism	Equality	Life-style	Materialistic	Closed	Open
Tacit	Explicit	Vision	Mission	Values	Philosophy

The duality between family and business systems have been explored in various ways. Kets de Vries et al. (1993), Taguri and Davis (1996) and Gregory and Simmelkjaer (2002) all point to the strong identity and sense of unity which often characterize family firms, but, while such qualities may make it easier for these firms to implement long-term strategy, they can make it harder for them to develop professional leadership. The notion of duality has been used to support the idea that family and non-family dimensions of a family-owned business generate complex, contested and conflicting developmental priorities and therefore training, and education solutions should be customised and varied accordingly.

The chapter considers such duality to be even stronger in transforming AFBs, especially in the context of internationalization (Samara, 2020).

Sirmon & Hitt's (2003) definition of a family firm has been adopted for this study: *'a business firm may be considered a family business to the extent that its ownership and management are concentrated within a family unit.'* Furthermore, Poza (2010), suggests that *"Ownership structure aside, what differentiates family business from management controlled businesses are often the intentions, values and strategy-influencing interactions of owners who are members, and ownership subsystems to form an idiosyncratic family business system".* This not only highlights the emotional and value-based interactions of a family business but also notes the distinct structure of a family business as a system. Idiosyncratic relationships and interactions between family members and business systems have been recognised as key features distinguishing them from other businesses (Sharma, 2007). Lane et al. (2006) suggest that in family firms, accountability means making decisions that do not sacrifice long-term health for short-term personal or corporate gain. This infers that family businesses have differing aims, strategies and processes, which may depend on the complexity of the firm (generations and size) and family involvement (ownership, management and family roles) and can impact how and when they chose to internationalize.

Chrisman et al., (2005) argue that when a new generation joins a family business, it asserts its autonomy by generating new strategic actions. These may include 'starting a new venture or division of the business' (Barach, 1984) or 'internationalizing' (Gallo & Sveen, 1991). Developing an original entrepreneurial venture can be risky for the next generation (Pittino et al., 2018; Zahra, 2005); the would-be entrepreneur must take into account any potential strategic conflict between family and business aims. Sharma et al. (2007) suggests that: 'From a strategic management perspective, families are both a resource and a constraint' – particularly if the needs of the family system and the business system conflict. Several researchers indicate that 'family and nonfamily businesses differ in terms of goals (Lee & Rogoff, 1996), ethics (Adams, et al., 1996), size and ðnancial structure (McConaughy & Phillips, 1999; Romano, et al., 2001) and corporate governance (Randøy & Goel, 2003) and these differences or paradoxes can have an impact on internationalization. Various researchers argue that: 'Family and nonfamily ðrms differ in terms of strategies, structures, systems, processes, and governance mechanisms' (Chua, et al. 2009). Morris et al., 1997 emphasised the focus on the role of training and education in the above FB dynamics. The multidimensional changes facing AFBs (Barakat, 1987) as they internationalize throw into relief the urgency with which innovations in education and training must develop in the latter half of this decade.

Figure 2. Dynamics of family businesses

Preparation level of heirs	The relationship among family and business members	Planning and control activities
• Formal education	• Communication	• Succession planning
• Training	• Trust	• Tax Planning
• Work experience (outside firm)	• Commitment	• Use of outside board
• Entry-level position	• Loyalty	• Use of family business consultant / advisors
• Year working within firm	• Family turmoil	• Creation of a family council
• Motivation to join firm	• Sibling rivalry	
• Self-perception of preparation	• Jealousy / resentment	
	• Conflict	
	• Shared values and traditions	

FAMILY BUSINESS LIFE CYCLE: CONFLICTS AND ANOMALIES

Churchill and Hatten (1997) demonstrate family business succession at work and highlight conflicts and *anomalies* when prioritizing development processes across four stages. Their model aims "to aid the understanding of family business dynamics during the process of succession and transfer of power" (Burns, 2011) showing how each generation may have different difficulties. It adds the axis of the human lifecycle to the family and business system transitions. Predecessor and successor generations will be at different stages in their personal lives (for example, childhood, adolescence, education, marriage/ starting a family, retiring), while siblings might simultaneously experience similar life cycles. There are therefore intra-systemic differences to consider in addition to those presented by the anomalies present in the life cycles of business, ownership and family systems (Taguri and Davis, 1996). According to Churchill and Hatten (1997) "the model suggests that changes in management, strategy and control can be planned and executed but are shaped by family relationships and driven by the inexorable life cycle" (Burns, 2011). For this reason, it is important to consider the human lifecycle as an important factor in FB system dynamics because different generations are likely to project different attitudes, priorities, perceptions, communication styles and motivations into the experiences of an internationalizing AFB (IAFB).

In summary, the differing perspectives of family businesses as systems offer insights into the constantly diverging and converging priorities of IAFB stakeholders over the course of multiple lifecycles and distil a set of training and education challenges for providers of family business training and education. Family businesses from these perspectives come to be understood as diverse, dynamic, variable and adaptive sub-systems, in their demand for professional training and education. This is even truer in the context of AFBs. Most AFB members do not have the luxury of leaving work in the office; the Arab family business dynamic is an extension of the private sphere as well. The next sections argue the case for conceiving IAFBs as organizations that are particularly prone to increasing strategic complexity that is prevalent in international expansions, and ones that could benefit from adopting new models of training and education.

ARAB FAMILY BUSINESSES (AFBs)

ATKearney (2010) suggests that 'Family businesses account for three-fourths of the private-sector economy in the GCC. Most of these businesses are young — 60 percent were formed since the 1970s — and highly diversified, with more than half involved in trading, financial services, real estate and construction. Therefore, the continuity of these businesses is critical to the sustainability entrepreneurial ecosystem (Malecki, 2018). In the Gulf Cooperation Council (GCC) region, family businesses account for 80% of non-oil and gas GDP and more than 90% of the private sector, generating more than 70% of the employment (Carr, 2012; Sabi, 2015; Pierce, 2017). Further, within the UAE private sector, 90% are family-owned businesses (Strike, 2012; Farouk 2017). These statistics show the large presence of family businesses within the GCC and MENA economy and their contribution to employment, taxation, innovation and wealth creation. The evolution of the competitive landscape has accelerated to become even more cutting edge with political, economic and social factors influencing the markets, especially in the 'Arab world' (Fakoussa et al, 2020).

Alongside the significant economic role played by AFBs are paradoxes and uncertainties that emerge with economic growth and development. Such phenomena are reflected in a joint report by FBCG and PwC (cited in Mena Herald, 2019), which notes that across the Gulf and the Middle East, only 31% of businesses have a robust, documented succession plan in place, and only 33% have effective governance policies in place (Mena Herald, 2019). They suggest: "This absence of essential documentation can often leave room for ambiguity and complication for those looking to address challenges or conflicts in family dynamics." Demonstrating some of the challenges that will test the resilience of Arab entrepreneurial ecosystems. Basco (2017) suggests that Arab family businesses are characterized by paradoxes of conflict and peace, stability and instability, certainty and uncertainty, and modernity and tradition'.

PWC (2017) in its annual family business survey with senior executives from Arab family businesses (AFBs), in 50 countries worldwide, reported that 50% of the respondents attached a high value to leaving a positive legacy, compared to 25% globally. This reflects the incredible pressure put on the next generation (Fakoussa and Collins, 2017), not only to maintain the positive reputation of the company, family and predecessors but also to increase reputational collateral in order to establish permanent legacies.

In addition, AFB stakeholders' narratives of change are emerging that generate complex demands on the modern AFB. From employees to customers, from internal family members to external shareholders the demand for quicker decisions, access to information and results is universal. These emergent demands, characterised by uncertainty and paradox, require that educators and trainers offer innovative support for the next generation of AFB leaders to meet the strategic challenges prevalent in business scenarios characterised by emergent, volatile and ambiguous flux.

INTERNATIONALIZING ARAB FAMILY BUSINESSES (IAFB)

This chapter looks at growing Arab family businesses in the MENA region (Palaiologos & Khunaizi, 2017) and considers a different approach to capacity training and education (learning) when pursuing business growth and faced with the considerable flux experienced when internationalizing. The current generation of AFB successors more than their predecessors will need to adopt tools to lead their family businesses through internationalization (Jabeen et al., 2016). Internationalization, as a process driving change, is an area of interest for FB scholars.

As early as 2010, Kontinen and Ojala noted that:

The internationalization of family businesses (FBs) is developing into a significant research area. FBs have traditionally operated in domestic markets, but increasingly find themselves obliged to internationalize, in order to survive in a market that is becoming more and more globally competitive.

In the Arab world, internationalization-based uncertainty is considered a key dimension in IAFB behaviour that has a significant influence on strategic decision-making when implementing organizational changes (Samara, 2020). Strategic uncertainty is viewed as a situation that has limited or incalculable information about the predicted outcomes of internationalizing decisions, actions and behaviours of internal and external stakeholders.

The uncertainty of internationalization therefore refers to the degree to which the future states of the IAFB's environment cannot be accurately anticipated or predicted due to the imperfect information and decision processes brought on by the decision to internationalize. This occurs when something is doubtful or unknown, complicated, or unreliable; when information is inaccessible and inconsistent; and when the IAFB feels apprehensive about its state of knowledge while internationalizing (Basco, 2017).

This need becomes pronounced if we remind ourselves of the change-based anomalies presented in the previous arguments implicating the multiple life cycles and incongruent experiences of various parts of a family business in time (Basco, 2017).

THE NEED FOR NEW PERSPECTIVES ON TRAINING AND EDUCATION FOR IAFBs

The authors have identified 3 main types of family business training and education: Academic led, Practitioner led and Knowledge specific led. Some exceptions include for example Ernest Young's NextGen Academy training events designed for successors in family businesses. This program helps successors explore their potential and introduces them to the challenges of running a family business (EY, 2019), Tharawat (2019) and CFEG (2017). However, many of the techniques used are similar to historical traditions in training and education provision.

Historically, family business consultants were mainly drawn from professional services providers: lawyers, financial advisors, banks and accountants. Family businesses gained support, help and advice with anything from drawing up wills which helped with succession planning to having lawyers or financial advisers on the board to help with business decisions as trusted non-executives.

However, as the field has evolved and become more complex, a myriad of new family business consultants has emerged with their accompanying toolkits. Separate from professional service groups, they have instead prioritised either the family (soft skills) or business (business training). Family business consulting is a diverse industry with most countries offering family business consulting courses and certification in order to be able to cover the complexities and overlapping aims family businesses have (FBCG, 2022; EY, 2022; STEP, 2022).

Toolkits range from helping family businesses draw up family constitutions, wealth transfer agreements, creating next generation start-up options to financing a business. Reviewing some of the different consultation techniques over the last years, the techniques have not really changed. The style of a central trainer or moderator leading the way in education is changing to facilitation in which play can bring strategic interventions in family businesses professional development.

There has been an increasing awareness that emerging toolkits of intervention and development which acknowledge shifting challenges in the training and education of family businesses are required (Holt et al., 2018). Such challenges include the need for an emotional view of the firm (D'Allura, 2017), inside-out and inductive perspectives of family business development practice (Lansberg and Gersick, 2015) and participatory preferences by family businesses for managing multigenerational training and education (Konopaski et al., 2015), the reality of bifurcated experiences in human-resource practice in family businesses (Jennings et al., 2018) and the need to develop educational program resources beyond the traditional (De Massis & Kotlar, 2015).

Despite the seminal calls for changes in approach and the need for an expansive conception (Daniels et al., 2013) of family business training and education (Burch et al., 2015), and recent demands to develop deeper practice-based orientations (Sharma et al., 2007), there has been a very limited response from business faculty and family business consultants to the challenge of innovating in training and education for family businesses (Salvato et al., 2015).

The IAFB is not immune to this slow pace of development, which can be attributed to several interconnected reasons that include:

1. **Tradition:** Although many business-schools and consulting firms offer IAFBs training and education services today, most still suffer from a legacy of professors, facilitators and trainers steeped in the traditional management paradigms of the 1990s and early-2000s, with a focus on non-family businesses' training and education. This traditional model in program design has proven counterproductive as a response to the experiential solutions demanded by family businesses.
2. **Learning Resource Fragmentation:** Education resources that include local, national and international IAFB eco-systems, books, workshop materials, case studies and films. They remain highly variable, broadly disconnected and incoherently divergent. This may be rooted in the fact that most programs are individual-centric with no underlying model of the program participants who can vary from original founders, young next-generation successors, non-family professional managers. This despite the reality that family-owned businesses' units of learning are not just individuals but to the contrary they are immersed in communities of practice: the family, the generation, non-family versus family board members and family governance forums.
3. **Conflation:** Many family business training and education programs are conflated within entrepreneurship paradigms, with little distinction being made between enterprising families, founding family entrepreneurs and the next-generation's entrepreneurial capacity (Abdelgawad et al., 2013).

PLAY AND PLAYFUL TECHNIQUES AS ONE RESPONSE TO THE CHALLENGES OF IAFBS' FUTURE CHANGES

The authors suggest here and previously (Gonsalves & Zamora, 2017) (Gonsalves & Zamora, 2020) (Gonsalves & Fakoussa, 2018) that play-based programs offer family business educators and instructors a different way of perceiving and intervening in IAFB processes when facing the uncertainties of change experiences in internationalization (Wu et al., 2022). Play is not perceived as separate from business. Instead work, play and learning are synonymous. This is because play embraces uncertainty, ambiguity and resulting change dynamics. Playfulness might very well be the only way to reach an understanding with change, or at least more or less cope with it. It allows the development of IAFB decision-makers as they experience emergent tensions and unknown possibilities afforded to multiple-generations of an IAFB and found in the intra-system dynamic of such businesses.

The argument that the authors present here draws on traditions of serious play (Rieber, 2001) to conceptualise and operationalise family-businesses as paradox (Statler et al., 2011) (Schuman et al., 2010) and agents of significant change (Wu et al., 2022). This chapter draws on work developed for the training of family-businesses and senior executives using playful techniques (Gonsalves and Zamora, 2017) that are derived from activity theory (Vygotsky, 1967) and expansive learning theories in which:

[Playful] objects became cultural entities and the object-orientedness of action became the key to understanding the human psyche. (Engeström, 1999)

Consistent with this socio-cultural approach, it is argued that play is a transformative cultural experience designed to enhance IAFB's competences in increasingly uncertain environments (Gaver et al., 2004) (Basco, 2017).

Play is not perceived as separate from work. Instead work and play are synonymous. Play becomes a source not only for the IAFB decision-makers' happiness but also one that encourages increasingly creative and productive competencies (Holliday et al., 2007). In this way it can be understood that fundamental characteristic and apparent paradox in play, is its 'unserious seriousness'.

Play has existed as a field of study and practice and as a vehicle of creative endeavour for centuries; it is worth noting here some of the terminology associated with play as a serious form of activity relevant to family business work and learning.

An early analysis (Caillois, 1961) depicts four distinguishing characteristics of play. Briefly, these are:

- Agon: the competitive element in play that is regulated, defined and devoid of chance.
- Alea: the risk in play that is solely attributable to chance.
- Mimicry: activities in which there is pretend, imitation and role-play.
- Ilinx: activities that suspend reality, defy existing logics (individual or organisational) and create a sense of joy.

Caillois and Barash (1961) further placed most activities on a spectrum between pure creativity (paidia) and pure effort (ludus), thereby embedding play in work. The authors come to recognise that much of their work as family business training and education suppliers, is serious play (Rieber, 2001).

The perspectives presented here reject arguments that advocate the delivery of training and education programs based on the idea that because business life is hard, there is a need to lighten it by injecting fun and humour through play. This can be regarded as entertainment, the passive cousin of play (Okan, 2003).

To the contrary, play as proposed here, offers a serious mechanism for IAFBs to overcome obstacles and constraints when seizing opportunities in change. This will be a defining capacity of IAFB success, the ability to recognise and realise opportunity in change (Clampitt et al., 2000; Wiltbank et al., 2009) with real, anchored feelings of success and deep learning.

In other words, IAFB decision-makers actively play to work and work to change. In order to view play as change, Mainemelis et al. (2010) argue that:

Change can happen as play only in a reality open to fantasy; in a reality that is held lightly enough to be played-upon or played with. A light hold on reality enables unfreezing, which requires the alert acceptance of possibly dangerous consequences; promotes movement, which requires open-minded creativity in responding to difficult contingencies; and enables refreezing, which requires realistic acceptance of a new order of being.

The authors suggest that training and education programs offer such serious conditions and possibilities for IAFB learning and change. The irony is that many of educators and trainers are unwilling to accept the opportunity of *change as play* after the recent protracted global crises, wherein training tendencies are to:

Draw in the reins of the business and control its future … For example, how many managers would be willing to regard change as play in the midst of a larger downsizing?(Mainemelis et al., 2010)

The chapter countenances the view that much learning delivery and design can be invigorated if (serious) play is granted a prominent role in IAFB decision-makers' learning. This is pertinent because in many modern family-businesses the separation of work from the rest of life is increasingly ambiguous and impossible to implement. The following Fordist paradigm appears to be dissolving:

When we are at work, we ought to be at work. When we are at play, we ought to be at play. There is no use trying to mix the two (Ford & Crowther, 2014)

Play in one model, for example, involves distancing, pretending and active involvement, where stakes and risks are internal to play and in which family-business decision-making takes place under increasing complexity, uncertainty and change (Fig 3) (Gonsalves & Zamora, 2017).

Figure 3. Decision-Making for Complexity and Uncertainty in Change
(Gonsalves & Zamora, 2017)

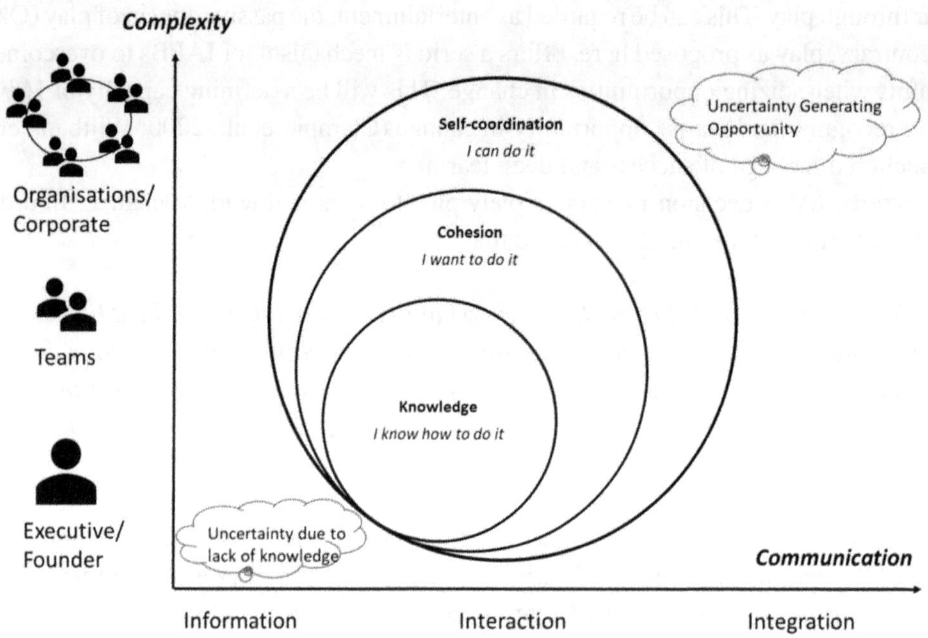

Play-based programs:

1. Embed learners in groups that may or may not evolve into executive teams.
2. Provide a dynamic and unpredictable social context for their efforts.
3. Offer a space for communicative rationality (Garland, 2014) to be established in which decision potentials are debated and produced.
4. Stimulate learning-logics like 'Ah, when we were right, it worked as we expected' and the corresponding reverse logics like 'Oh, that didn't work as we expected; how might we change for the next time?'
5. Permit repeated errors without condemnation of failure en-route to mastery.
6. Allow for entrepreneurial executives to be 'Always challenged, seldom overwhelmed'.

For IAFBs, there is the need to move away from a reliance on the problem-based, culturally unsympathetic approaches common in much family business education to approaches in which playful and experientially focused methods (Kets de Vries & Korotov, 2010) are paramount:

"The purpose of executive training is not to transfer truths ... but to motivate men and women to think (and act) in the presence of new situations. This requires a bifocal perspective: the ability to characterize quickly both the common and the distinctive elements of business issues." (Garvin, 2007)

Play-based learning in uncertain, international situations offers the AFB decision-maker the possibility that something unpleasant or unwelcome will happen. It stimulates exposure to chances of unknown dangers and reward. Despite the negative connotations of the concept, uncertainty is an attractive opportunity in many settings in which IAFBs can benefit from the internationalization process in long-term and unintentional ways.

The authors suggest that the role of play in supporting IAFB decision-makers' respond to uncertainty during internationalization is optimal when training and education programs:

1. are not focused on developing utilitarian skills aimed at satisfying basic business needs but rather activities focused on strategic and relational needs that do not block spontaneous exploration by family decision-makers.
2. do not build canonical templates, based on permanent action schemes which generate unchangeable circumstances, and constrain the decision-maker's ability to match his or her strategic actions to different internationalization stimuli.
3. are properly selected for their capacity to simulate a repertoire of situational stimuli, such that during independent explorations, the decision-maker embraces surprise and the procedures for rewarding the internationalizing team with the biggest reward being for the team's capacity to discharge the tension caused by the multi-dimensional uncertainties of internationalizing.
4. that simulate some difficulties for the decision-maker; with such problem stimulations originating from what the decision-maker perceives as an internationalization challenge for his/her family business, and the solution being what he/she independently develops to generate creative tension.

Play-based programs are 'as partial a representation of reality (as possible), that chooses crucial characteristics from a real situation and makes a replica of them within an environment essentially free from risk allowing the (IAFB) decision-maker to develop their strategies' (Saunders & Severn, 1999). However, play is a distinctive yet interrelated aspect of the IAFB decision-makers' experiences with the preceding design.

Play is:

An activity that works, entirely or partially, on the basis of the players' decisions. The simulation is an operative model that has the abstraction and the representation of a larger system (Tsuchiya, 1998).

Therefore, the chapter distinguishes between the simulation as a representational object and play as a (human) relational activity that only through experiential engagement gives meaning to the simulation's scope as the IAFB decision-makers' learning tool. This distinction is of special relevance because, from previous studies (Gonsalves & Zamora, 2017; Zamora, 2012), serious play generates the co-production of new and shared mental models by decision-makers.

Perhaps successor generations in IAFBs offer the best opportunity for developing play-based training and educational programs. This is especially true when the next generation is independent, creative and growth seeking, and where their participation is not only guided by the desire to get a reward, but the internal compulsion to internationalize.

It provides the opportunity to develop and enhance the next generation's strategic and relational competences in the process of internationalization. It also provides opportunities to develop competencies both for competitive survival in the early stage of internationalization (immediate benefits) and for handling important adaptive changes once the experience of internationalization is well underway (deferred benefits).

CONCLUSION

Internationalizing Arab family businesses are a complex and rich set of arrangements that face a duality of changes present in their societal and next-generation transformations. The decision to internationalize can be daunting to family businesses, therefore, this paper offers support that enriches IAFBs understandings and the consequential opportunities for change that they possess.

Facilitating AFB across generations with family-as-learners as opposed to individual learners using modern approaches to organizational change, creates a space where learning and play is possible (Hjorth, 2005). Current research suggests that using cross generational and family members, as opposed to 'just' solitary, individual learners, can support the IAFB's ability to manage the unprecedented changes that they face.

The authors have proposed a new way to approach IAFBs that integrates both the soft competences as well as hard business skills using play.

This chapter presents several avenues to support future research for change management scholars as well as openly inviting suggestions for new training and education approaches to support FBs and AFBs.

One of the unintended and deferred benefits of exposure to the changes presented by internationalization using play-based programs is that activities experienced by multiple generations of the IAFB can be foundational for understanding and coping with intra-family dynamics and priorities. Familiarity with such activities can be a platform for becoming constructively involved in innovative, conciliatory and inter-generational family business processes (including non-family/ family interrelationships) and increasing resilience.

REFERENCES

Abdelgawad, S. G., Zahra, S. A., Svejenova, S., & Sapienza, H. J. (2013). Strategic Leadership and Entrepreneurial Capability for Game Change. *Journal of Leadership & Organizational Studies*, *20*(4), 394–407. doi:10.1177/1548051813475484

Adams, J. S., Taschian, A., & Shore, T. H. (1996). Ethics in family and non-family owned firms: An exploratory study. *Family Business Review*, *9*(2), 157–170. doi:10.1111/j.1741-6248.1996.00157.x

Ambergh. (2020). The Arab world. *Ambergh.* http://www.ambergh.com/learn-arabic/the-arab-world

Aminova, M., Mareef, S., & Machado, C. (2020). Entrepreneurship Ecosystem in Arab World: The status quo, impediments and the ways forward. *International Journal of Business Ethics and Governance*, 1–13.

Barach, J. A. (1984). Is there a cure for the paralyzed family board? *Sloan Management Review*, *26*(1), 3–12.

Barakat, H. (1987). The Arab Family and The Challenge of Social Transformation. *Al-Raida Journal*, 6–7.

Barnes, L. B., & Hershon, S. A. (1994). Transferring power in the family business. *Family Business Review*, *7*(4), 377–392. doi:10.1111/j.1741-6248.1994.00377.x

Basco, R. (2017). Epilogue: The multiple embeddedness of family firms in the Arab world. In Family Businesses in the Arab World (pp. 247–256). Springer.

Bichler, B. F., Kallmuenzer, A., Peters, M., Petry, T., & Clauss, T. (2022). Regional entrepreneurial ecosystems: How family firm embeddedness triggers ecosystem development. *Review of Managerial Science*, *16*(1), 15–44. doi:10.100711846-020-00434-9

Birdthistle, N. (2006). Training and learning strategies of family businesses: An Irish case. *Journal of European Industrial Training*, *30*(7), 550–568. doi:10.1108/03090590610704402

Burch, J. J., Burch, G. F., Heller, N. A., & Batchelor, J. H. (2015). Rethinking family business education. *Journal of Family Business Management*, *5*(2), 277–293. doi:10.1108/JFBM-02-2015-0007

Burns, P. (2011). *Entrepreneurship and small business*. Palgrave Macmillan Limited. doi:10.1007/978-0-230-20848-3

Caillois, R. (1961). The definition of play. *The Game Design Reader: A Rules of Play Anthology*, 123–128.

Carr, R. (2012) Family Business: Setting a Benchmark. *Vision*. http://vision.ae/articles/ family_business_setting_a_benchmark

Chrisman, J. J., Chua, J. H., & Sharma, P. (2003). Current trends and future directions in family business management studies: Toward a theory of the family firm. *Coleman White Paper Series, 4*, 1-63.

Chrisman, J. J., Chua, J. H., & Sharma, P. (2005). Trends and directions in the development of a strategic management theory of the family firm. *Entrepreneurship Theory and Practice*, *29*(5), 555–576. doi:10.1111/j.1540-6520.2005.00098.x

Chua, J. H., Chrisman, J. J., & Bergiel, E. B. (2009). An agency theoretic analysis of the professionalized family firm. *Entrepreneurship Theory and Practice*, *33*(2), 355–372. doi:10.1111/j.1540-6520.2009.00294.x

Chua, J. H., Chrisman, J. J., & Sharma, P. (1999). Defining the family business by behavior. *Entrepreneurship Theory and Practice*, *23*(4), 19–40. doi:10.1177/104225879902300402

Churchill, N. C., & Hatten, K. J. (1997). Non-market-based transfers of wealth and power: A research framework for family business. *Family Business Review*, *10*(1), 53–67. doi:10.1111/j.1741-6248.1997.00053.x

Clampitt, P. G., DeKoch, R. J., & Cashman, T. (2000). A strategy for communicating about uncertainty. *The Academy of Management Perspectives*, *14*(4), 41–57. doi:10.5465/ame.2000.3979815

Coduras, A., de la Vega, I., & Salman, M. B. (2018). Entrepreneurial Ecosystems in Arabic Countries: A Recent Overview. In N. Faghih & M. R. Zali (Eds.), *Entrepreneurship Ecosystem in the Middle East and North Africa (MENA): Dynamics in Trends, Policy and Business Environment* (pp. 283–302). Springer International Publishing. doi:10.1007/978-3-319-75913-5_9

Collins, L., Grisoni, L., Seaman, C., Graham, S., Fakoussa, R., & Otten, D. (2012). *The Modern Family Business: Relationships, Succession and Transition*. Palgrave Macmillan. doi:10.1057/9781137001337

D'Allura, G. M. (2017). Bringing emotions into family firms: The business theatre as a tool for management coaching. *Academy of Management Proceedings*, *2017*(1), 11006. doi:10.5465/AMBPP.2017.11006abstract

Daniels, H., Edwards, A., Engeström, Y., Gallagher, T., & Ludvigsen, S. R. (2013). *Activity theory in practice: Promoting learning across boundaries and agencies*. Routledge. doi:10.4324/9780203609439

De Massis, A., & Kotlar, J. (2015). Learning resources for family business education: A review and directions for future developments. *Academy of Management Learning & Education, 14*(3), 415–422. doi:10.5465/amle.2014.0246

Diaz-Moriana, V., Hogan, T., Clinton, E., & Brophy, M. (2019). Defining Family Business: A Closer Look at Definitional Heterogeneity. In E. Memili & C. Dibrell (Eds.), *The Palgrave Handbook of Heterogeneity among Family Firms* (pp. 333–374). Springer International Publishing. doi:10.1007/978-3-319-77676-7_13

Eddleston, K. A., & Kellermanns, F. W. (2007). Destructive and productive family relationships: A stewardship theory perspective. *Journal of Business Venturing, 22*(4), 545–565. doi:10.1016/j.jbusvent.2006.06.004

Engeström, Y. (1999). Activity theory and individual and social transformation. *Perspectives on Activity Theory, 19*(38).

Ensley, M. D., Pearson, A. W., & Sardeshmukh, S. R. (2007). The negative consequences of pay dispersion in family and non-family top management teams: An exploratory analysis of new venture, high-growth firms. *Journal of Business Research, 60*(10), 1039–1047. doi:10.1016/j.jbusres.2006.12.012

Errington, E. (2003). *Developing scenario-based learning: Practical insights for tertiary educators.* Dunmore Press.

EY. (2022). EY NextGen. *EY.* https://www.ey.com/en_gl/next-generation Last accessed: 18.10.2022

EY. (2022). Family enterprise. *EY.* https://www.ey.com/en_vn/family-enterprise Last accessed: 22.10.2022

Fakoussa, R., & Collins, L. (2017). Socioemotional Approach: Exploring Women's Guilt in an All-Female Egyptian Family Business. In *Family Businesses in the Arab World* (pp. 107–130). Springer. doi:10.1007/978-3-319-57630-5_7

Fakoussa, R., O'Leary, S., & Salem, S. (2020). An exploratory study on social entrepreneurship in Egypt. *Journal of Islamic Accounting and Business Research, 11*(3), 694–707. doi:10.1108/JIABR-02-2017-0023

Fama, E. F., & Jensen, M. C. (1983). Separation of ownership and control. *The Journal of Law & Economics, 26*(2), 301–325. doi:10.1086/467037

Farouk, H. (2013). Cited in Grant Thornton: The Rules of Engagement for Family-Owned Businesses. *Grant Thorton.* http://www. grantthornton.ae/page/the-rules-of-engagement-fo r-family-owned-businesses

FBCG. (2022). Our work and your success begin with education *The FBG.* https://www.thefbcg.com/what-we-do/presentations-workshops/

Feliu, N., & Botero, I. C. (2016). Philanthropy in Family Enterprises: A Review of Literature. *Family Business Review, 29*(1), 121–141. doi:10.1177/0894486515610962

Ford, H., & Crowther, S. (2014). *My Life And Work.* CreateSpace Independent Publishing Platform.

Gallo, M. A., & Sveen, J. (1991). Internationalizing the family business: Facilitating and restraining factors. *Family Business Review, 4*(2), 181–190. doi:10.1111/j.1741-6248.1991.00181.x

Garland, P. (2014). What can the work of Habermas offer educational researcher development programmes? *Studies in Higher Education, 39*(1), 87–101. doi:10.1080/03075079.2011.644785

Garvin, D. A. (2007). Teaching executives and teaching MBAs: Reflections on the case method. *Academy of Management Learning & Education, 6*(3), 364–374. doi:10.5465/amle.2007.26361626

Gaver, W., Boucher, A., Pennington, S., & Walker, B. (2004). Cultural probes and the value of uncertainty. *Interactions-Funology, 11*(5), 53–56. doi:10.1145/1015530.1015555

Gonsalves, E., & Fakoussa, R. (2018). Playfulness - a novel approach to learning about family-owned business dynamics. In *Proceedings of 3E– ECSB Entrepreneurship Education Conference (vol. 7, pp. 43),* Gothenburg, Sweden: ECSB Press.

Gonsalves, E., & Zamora, R. (2015). RETS-MICA: An Entrepreneurial Learning workshop tool for MBA & MA programs. In *Proceedings of ABS Learning, Teaching & Student Experience Conference,* (vol. 4), York, UK.

Gonsalves, E., & Zamora, R. (2017). Ludic Executives: The Case For Play in Entrepreneurial Learning Design. In P. Jones & L. Pittaway (Eds.), *Entrepreneurship Education: New Perspectives on Research, Policy and Practice* (pp. 213–233). Emerald Publishing Ltd. doi:10.1108/S2040-724620170000007014

Gonsalves, E., & Zamora, R. (2020). Ludens Familias: Playful Learning for the Entrepreneurial Family. In A. O. Ayandibu (Ed.), *Reshaping Entrepreneurship Education With Strategy and Innovation.* IGI Global Publishing Ltd.

Harvey, M., & Evans, R. E. (1994). The Impact of Timing and Mode of Entry on Successor Development and Successful Succession. *Family Business Review, 7*(3), 221–236. doi:10.1111/j.1741-6248.1994.00221.x

Hjorth, D. (2005). Organizational Entrepreneurship: With de Certeau on Creating Heterotopias (or Spaces for Play). *Journal of Management Inquiry, 14*(4), 386–398. .

Hjorth, D., Strati, A., Drakopoulou Dodd, S., & Weik, E. (2018). *Organizational creativity, play and entrepreneurship: Introduction and framing.* SAGE Publications.

Hollander, B. S., & Elman, N. S. (1988). Family-owned businesses: An emerging field of inquiry. *Family Business Review, 1*(2), 145–164. doi:10.1111/j.1741-6248.1988.00145.x

Holliday, G., Statler, M., & Flanders, M. (2007). Developing practically wise leaders through serious play. *Consulting Psychology Journal, 59*(2), 126–134. doi:10.1037/1065-9293.59.2.126

Holt, D. T., Pearson, A. W., Payne, G. T., & Sharma, P. (2018). Family Business Research as a Boundary-Spanning Platform. *Family Business Review, 31*(1), 14–31. doi:10.1177/0894486518758712

Jabeen, F., Ahmad, S. Z., & Alkaabi, S. (2016). The Internationalization Decision-Making of United Arab Emirates Family Businesses [Chapter]. Handbook of Research on Impacts of International Business and Political Affairs on the Global Economy. IGI Global.

Jennings, J. E., Dempsey, D., & James, A. E. (2018). Bifurcated HR practices in family firms: Insights from the normative-adaptive approach to stepfamilies. *Human Resource Management Review, 28*(1), 68–82. doi:10.1016/j.hrmr.2017.05.007

Kets de Vries, M. F. R., & Korotov, K. (2007). Creating transformational executive education programs. *Academy of Management Learning & Education*, *6*(3), 375–387. doi:10.5465/amle.2007.26361627

Kets de Vries, M. F. R., Miller, D., & Noël, A. (1993). Understanding the leader-strategy interface: Application of the strategic relationship interview method. *Human Relations*, *46*(1), 5–22. doi:10.1177/001872679304600102

Konopaski, M., Jack, S., & Hamilton, E. (2015). How Family Business Members Learn About Continuity. *Academy of Management Learning & Education*, *14*(3), 347–364. doi:10.5465/amle.2014.0244

Kontinen, T., & Ojala, A. (2010). The internationalization of family businesses: A review of extant research. *Journal of Family BusinessStrategy*, *1*(2), 97–107. doi:10.1016/j.jfbs.2010.04.001

Lane, S., Astrachan, J. H. H., Keyt, A., & McMillan, K. (2006). *Guidelines for family business boards of directors. Family Business Review, 19(2), 147-167. Lawrence, P., & Lorsch, J. (1967). Organization and its Environment*. Harvard University Press.

Lansberg, I., & Gersick, K. (2015). Educating Family Business Owners: The Fundamental Intervention. *Academy of Management Learning & Education*, *14*(3), 400–413. doi:10.5465/amle.2014.0254

Lee, M. S., & Rogoff, E. G. (1996). Research note: Comparison of small businesses with family participation versus small businesses without family participation: An investigation of differences in goals, attitudes, and family/business conflict. *Family Business Review*, *9*(4), 423–437. doi:10.1111/j.1741-6248.1996.00423.x

Levinson, H. (1971). Conflicts that plague family businesses. *Harvard Business Review*, *49*(2), 90–98.

Mainemelis, C., Altman, Y., & Sandelands, L. (2010). The play of change. *Journal of Organizational Change Management*. 23(I 1), 71-86

Malecki, E. J. (2018). Entrepreneurship and entrepreneurial ecosystems. *Geography Compass*, *12*(3), e12359. doi:10.1111/gec3.12359

McCann, G., DeMoss, M., Dascher, P., & Barnett, S. (2003). Educational needs of family businesses: Perceptions of university directors. *Family Business Review*, *16*(4), 283–291. doi:10.1177/089448650 30160040601

McCollom, M. E. (1988). Integration in the family firm: When the family system replaces controls and culture. *Family Business Review*, *1*(4), 399–417. doi:10.1111/j.1741-6248.1988.00399.x

McConaughy, D. L., & Phillips, G. M. (1999). Founders versus descendants: The profitability, efficiency, growth characteristics and financing in large, public, founding-family-controlled firms. *Family Business Review*, *12*(2), 123–131. doi:10.1111/j.1741-6248.1999.00123.x

McNiff, J. (2013). Becoming cosmopolitan and other dilemmas of internationalisation: Reflections from the Gulf States. *Cambridge Journal of Education*, *43*(4), 501–515. doi:10.1080/0305764X.2013.831033

MenaHerald. (2019). Family Business Council – Gulf and PwC publish a guide on managing shareholder exits in family businesses. *MenaHerald.* https://www.menaherald.com/en/business/events-services/family-business-council-%E2%80%93-gulf-and-pwc-publish-guide-managing-shareholder

Miller, D., Steier, L., & Le Breton-Miller, I. (2003). Lost in time: Intergenerational succession, change, and failure in family business. *Journal of Business Venturing*, *18*(4), 513–531. doi:10.1016/S0883-9026(03)00058-2

Morris, M. H., Williams, R. O., Allen, J. A., & Avila, R. A. (1996). Correlates of success in family business transitions. *Journal of Business Venturing*, *12*(5), 385–401. doi:10.1016/S0883-9026(97)00010-4

Okan, Z. (2003). Edutainment: Is learning at risk? *British Journal of Educational Technology*, *34*(3), 255–264. doi:10.1111/1467-8535.00325

Palaiologos, G., & Khunaizi, Z. A. (2017). Growing the Arab Family Business (1): Hybrid Organizational Arrangements. *Journal of Entrepreneurship and Business Innovation*, *4*(1), 25. doi:10.5296/jebi.v4i1.10819

Pierce, C. (2016) What's Holding Back Family Businesses in the GCC? *Gulf News.* https://gulfnews.com/business/sme/what-s-holding-back-family-businesses-in-the-gcc-1.1870272

Pittino, D., Visintin, F., & Lauto, G. (2018). Fly Away From the Nest? A Configurational Analysis of Family Embeddedness and Individual Attributes in the Entrepreneurial Entry Decision by Next-Generation Members. *Family Business Review*, *31*(3), 271–294. doi:10.1177/0894486518773867

Poza, E. J. (2010). *Family Business.* Thomson South-Western.

PWC. (2017) *Global Family Business Survey.* PWC. https://assets.kpmg/content/dam/kpmg/bh/pdf/gcc-family-business-survey-2017.pdf html Last accessed: 25.10.2022

Randerson, K., Dossena, G., & Fayolle, A. (2016). The futures of family business: Family entrepreneurship. *Futures*, *75*, 36–43. doi:10.1016/j.futures.2015.10.008

Randøy, T., & Goel, S. (2003). Ownership structure, founder leadership, and performance in Norwegian SMEs: Implications for financing entrepreneurial opportunities. *Journal of Business Venturing*, *18*(5), 619–637. doi:10.1016/S0883-9026(03)00013-2

Rieber, L. P. (2001). Designing learning environments that excite serious play. *Annual Meeting of the Australasian Society for Computers in Learning in Tertiary Education,* Melbourne, Australia.

Romano, C. A., Tanewski, G. A., & Smyrnios, K. X. (2001). Capital structure decision making: A model for family business. *Journal of Business Venturing*, *16*(3), 285–310. doi:10.1016/S0883-9026(99)00053-1

Rutherford, M. W., Muse, L. A., & Oswald, S. L. (2006). A New Perspective on the Developmental Model for Family Business. *Family Business Review*, *19*(4), 317–333. doi:10.1111/j.1741-6248.2006.00079.x

Sabi, A. (2015) The Succession Challenge in GCC Family Business. http: //globalriskinsights.com/2015/11/the-succession-challenge-in-gcc-family-businesses/ .

Saleh, M. A. K. (2019). Review of the challenges facing family businesses in the Arab Region. *Next Generation Tools: Future Roadmap for Business and Industry.* https://www.academia.edu/44467706/Review_of_the_challenges_facing_family_businesses_in_the_Arab_Region

Salvato, C., Sharma, P., & Wright, M. (2015). From the guest editors: Learning patterns and approaches to family business education around the world—Issues, insights, and research agenda. Academy of Management Briarcliff Manor, NY.

Samara, G. (2020). Family businesses in the Arab Middle East: What do we know and where should we go? *Journal of Family Business Strategy, 12*(3), 100359. doi:10.1016/j.jfbs.2020.100359

Samara, G. (2021). Family businesses in the Arab Middle East: What do we know and where should we go? *Journal of Family Business Strategy, 12*(3), 100–359. doi:10.1016/j.jfbs.2020.100359

Sandelands, L. (2010). The play of change. *Journal of Organizational Change Management, 23*(1), 71–86. doi:10.1108/09534811011017216

Sandhu, N., Hussain, J., & Matlay, H. (2012). Entrepreneurship education and training needs of family businesses operating in the agricultural sector of India. *Education + Training, 33*(4), 727–743. doi:10.1108/00400911211274855

Saunders, D., & Severn, J. (1999). *Simulation and games for strategy and policy planning, The International Simulation and Gaming Research Yearbook* (Vol. 7). Psychology Press.

Schuman, A., Stutz, S., & Ward, J. (2010). *Family business as paradox.* Springer. doi:10.1057/9780230291768

Sharma, P., Hoy, F., Astrachan, J. H., & Koiranen, M. (2007). The practice-driven evolution of family business education. *Journal of Business Research, 60*(10), 1012–1021. doi:10.1016/j.jbusres.2006.12.010

Sirmon, D. G., & Hitt, M. A. (2003). Managing Resources: Linking Unique Resources, Management, and Wealth Creation in Family Firms. *Entrepreneurship Theory and Practice, 27*(4), 339–358. doi:10.1111/1540-8520.t01-1-00013

Statler, M., Heracleous, L., & Jacobs, C. D. (2011). Serious play as a practice of paradox. *The Journal of Applied Behavioral Science, 47*(2), 236–256. doi:10.1177/0021886311398453

Steier, L. (2003). Variants of agency contracts in family-financed ventures as a continuum of familial altruistic and market rationalities. *Journal of Business Venturing, 18*(5), 597–618. doi:10.1016/S0883-9026(03)00012-0

STEP. 2022. Advanced Certificate in Family Business Governance Accessed online: https://www.step.org/qualifications-courses/advanced-certificate-family-business-governance. Last accessed: 22.10.2022

Strike, V. M. (2012). Advising the family firm: Reviewing the past to build the future. *Family Business Review, 25*(2), 156–177. doi:10.1177/0894486511431257

Tagiuri, R., & Davis, J. (1996). Bivalent attributes of the family firm. *Family Business Review, 9*(2), 199–208. doi:10.1111/j.1741-6248.1996.00199.x

Tsuchiya, S. (1998). Simulation/gaming as an essential enabler of organizational change. *Simulation & Gaming, 29*(4), 400–408. doi:10.1177/104687819802900403

Vygotsky, L. S. (1967). Play and its role in the mental development of the child. *Social Psychology, 5*(3), 6–18.

Ward, J. L. (1997). Growing the Family Business: Special Challenges and Best Practices. *Family Business Review, 10*(4), 323–337. doi:10.1111/j.1741-6248.1997.00323.x

Wiltbank, R., Read, S., Dew, N., & Sarasvathy, S. D. (2009). Prediction and control under uncertainty: Outcomes in angel investing. *Journal of Business Venturing, 24*(2), 116–133. doi:10.1016/j.jbusvent.2007.11.004

Wu, H., Xu, Z., & Skare, M. (2022). How do family businesses adapt to the rapid pace of globalization? A bibliometric analysis. *Journal of Business Research, 153*, 59–74. doi:10.1016/j.jbusres.2022.08.022

Zabala, R. A. (2019). The family business as a clan: Resources and uniqueness. *Dimensión Empresarial, 17*(4), 9.

Zabit, M. N. M. (2010). Problem-Based Learning on Students' Critical Thinking Skills in Teaching Business Education in Malaysia: A Literature Review. *American Journal of Business Education, 3*(6), 19–32. doi:10.19030/ajbe.v3i6.436

Zahra, S. A. (2005). Entrepreneurial Risk Taking in Family Firms. *Family Business Review, 18*(1), 23–40. doi:10.1111/j.1741-6248.2005.00028.x

Zamora, R. (2012). *A model of collaboration in complexity for management in times of uncertainty and change*. Lulu Press.

Chapter 10
A Dynamic Capability to Determine Business Performance in the Post-COVID-19 Era:
Organizational Agility

Ibrahim Yikilmaz
Kocaeli University, Turkey

ABSTRACT

The Covid-19 pandemic has made the competition process even more difficult for businesses, changing the competitive dynamics. The already high level of VUCA (volatility, uncertainty, complexity, and ambiguity) has increased even more. To be successful in the new industry environment, businesses need to develop their skills in "speed, flexibility, resilience, responsiveness, cost, and efficiency." Adaptive, flexible, and resilient dynamic capabilities needed by businesses in the post-covid19 era are defined as organizational agility. In this context, the concept of organizational agility is discussed in detail. In the study, recommendations were made about what the new era brought in terms of businesses in the pandemic and post-pandemic era and how to increase organizational agility capabilities (responsiveness, competency, flexibility, speed, and proactiveness) to achieve sustainable competition and survive in the changing competitive dynamics of businesses.

INTRODUCTION

The Covid-19 pandemic is considered to be the biggest crisis experienced on a global scale since the Great Depression (Elali; 2021). The COVID-19 pandemic, which started in China and affected the world in a short time, has already caused approximately 400 million cases and 6 million deaths (https://www.worldometers.info/coronavirus). The pandemic, which is not limited to the field of health, has deeply affected all the dynamics of social life practice. All kinds of crises experienced in the historical process

DOI: 10.4018/978-1-6684-7509-6.ch010

have deeply affected the survival of organizations (Doern, Williams & Vorley, 2019). However, among these crises, the COVID-19 pandemic has triggered a radical paradigm shift in businesses, especially digital transformation (Verma & Gustafsson, 2020; Yıkılmaz, 2021b).

The COVID-19 pandemic, which has left deep traces in the socioeconomic field, has brought radical changes in many areas from doing business to processes and even the interaction with employees, businesses, and customers (Ivanov, 2020; Moon, 2020;Yıkılmaz, 2021a; Yıkılmaz, 2021b). It has further increased the level of VUCA (volatility, uncertainty, complexity, and ambiguity), which businesses are already struggling with. The uncertainty and unpredictability created by the increasing VUCA have brought about significant changes in the production and service delivery processes, the expectations of internal and external customers, and the dynamics of competition within the industry in an intense industrial environment. Businesses that have the proper skill set to adapt to these changes are successful in this process. In addition, the conditions created by the Covid-19 pandemic have also paved the way for businesses to gain important lessons in terms of the supply chain, production and service delivery processes, and resource agility (Nandi et al., 2021, 2020; Yıkılmaz, 2021b). In this context, the subject of organizational agility, which is the ability to properly interpret the threats and opportunities developing in their environment and to respond at the right place and time, within this radical change process in which businesses are involved, has been discussed within the scope of the study. Organizational agility is an important dynamic capability that will prevent the extinction of businesses and help them sustain their competitive advantage in today's challenging industrial environments (Tilman, 2019). Organizational agility is an important dynamic capability for businesses to properly interpret environmental changes, meet efficiency and productivity concerns, and offer innovative solutions for diversified customer expectations. Many studies emphasize that capabilities such as ***"speed, cost, resilience, flexibility"*** will play a critical role in the success of businesses in the post-pandemic period. In many respects, it is clear that organizational agility capabilities will make significant contributions to businesses adapting to newly developing situations and turning threats into opportunities in the post-pandemic era. Although arrows point to a detailed examination of organizational agility capabilities, most businesses have not yet started a comprehensive change process in this regard. In the studies, it is seen that the companies that started the agile change process by realizing the importance of the situation are around 14% (Aghina, Handscomb, Salo & Thaker, 2021). With this aspect, the subject requires more studies to be done to create the awareness it deserves.

The concept of organizational agility, which is an important dynamic capability for businesses to survive in today's industry environment with uncertainty and turbulence, and to establish an effective competitive advantage, will be discussed in detail in the following sections. The literature on the concept of organizational agility is summarized. In addition, in the conclusion part, suggestions were made on how companies can create a more agile business by following an effective management practice in the post-pandemic era. It is considered that the study will contribute to the literature in terms of examining organizational agility and the post-pandemic era together while increasing awareness of organizational agility, which is the fundamental skill that businesses will need in post-pandemic era.

BACKGROUND

Impact of Covid-19 Pandemic on Businesses

With the Covid-19 Pandemic, the socio-economic field has been significantly affected. Many negative situations have come to the fore in businesses that are the main subject of this effect. In a study conducted on 7511 companies in the USA, it was determined that especially SMEs were significantly affected by the pandemic and they have been financially fragile. In addition, it was shared that 43% of businesses closed and employment decreased by 40% (Bartik et al.,2020). The crisis created by the pandemic has prevented businesses from properly managing their supply chain, causing significant delays in product and service delivery and difficulties in supplying raw materials. The Bureau of Labor Statistics report, which examines the negative situation created by these effects, stated that the hospitality and food sector is the most affected sector, while the finance and insurance sector is the least (Stang, 2021). In the report, it was also shared that the highest rate of transition to the telework system was in the education sector and the least in the hospitality and food sector. Again, in a global study conducted by The World Bank (2021), it was determined that the sales of the enterprises decreased significantly (27%) and that many enterprises had difficulty in making the salaries and side payments of the employees. In addition, it was shared that 34% of businesses increased their use of the internet and digital platforms to overcome the crisis created by the pandemic, and 17% had to invest in new software and digital product and service solutions.

During and after the pandemic period, some lockdown practices and measures restricting social life have made it necessary for individuals to stay away from business and economic life. This situation firstly led to the transfer of consumer behavior to digital platforms, the development of a more internet and media-oriented consumption approach, and even shopping activities without having almost any physical interaction (Yıkılmaz, 2021a). While all this was going on, most brands and stores went bankrupt (Tucker, 2020). Many activities were blocked, from airlines to sports events, accommodation, and cultural events. The companies and employees serving in these areas have suffered significant damage from this situation. While these tragic events were developing, many areas, from ordinary consuming habits, current ways of doing business, to the interaction we have with each other, were moved to digital platforms. The demands and expectations of consumers have changed according to the opportunity and situation offered by this new platform. This new dynamic ecosystem, which is changing and developing, has shown us in a short time that while many companies and markets are shrinking, some are reborn and growing (Donthu & Gustafsson, 2020). The concept of hoarding, the trend of shopping through digital platforms and virtual applications, the adoption of more minimal and modern approaches in events such as weddings and ceremonies, the increase in expectations for online services have been the first dynamics of the new normal that has emerged since the first days of the pandemic (Sheth, 2020; Yıkılmaz, 2021b).

In addition to consumer habits, the pandemic also affected the workforce, which is among the most strategic resources of businesses. Social understanding in the workplace environment was interrupted for a while. Afterward, mostly communication and interaction continued through digital platforms. The boundaries of work and family life are blurred. For now, the diversified expectations of the existing human resources and their motivation to serve the goals of the business are among the main issues on the agenda of top management (Carnevale & Hatak, 2020).

The pandemic has created an even more uncertain and complex industry environment for both employees and businesses (Sharma et al., 2020). As employees display a more skeptical and reserved approach to their workplaces, the same situation has begun to develop among businesses within the industry ecosystem. The "foggy" environment created by uncertainty negatively affected both the decision-making processes of enterprises and the processes of managing the crisis. Negative economic conditions fueled by uncertainty further increased uneasiness and turbulence.

Pantano et al. (2020) listed the important factors for businesses to establish an effective competitive advantage in the pandemic environment and shared that businesses should develop new dynamic capabilities. It is necessary to develop new ways of acting in line with the expectations of diversified customers and regulatory authorities. The need for companies that prioritize the customer and have developed digital service delivery capacity has increased.

The pandemic has had a significant impact on the strategy and trends of businesses. Eggers (2020), who specifically addressed this situation on entrepreneurial and market orientation, emphasized that businesses should develop a hybrid strategy both during and after the crisis, that is, they should carry out both entrepreneurial and market orientation together. In this regard, it was shared that businesses should constantly look for new opportunities and use their resources in accordance with these situations. In addition, the necessity of gaining a management approach that focuses on the customer, improves the value delivery process and accepts risk as the new normal has been emphasized.

The pandemic has required businesses to offer significantly innovative products and services. In this context, Wang et al. (2020) examined what kind of understanding companies have to develop for innovation during the pandemic period in China. Within the scope of the study, it was stated that having two basic competencies, especially in the innovation process, is considered the key to success. The first of these is that businesses have the motivation to examine and innovate by correctly addressing the expectations of the market. Secondly, with this motivation, it is emphasized that it is necessary to establish collaboration to meet complex requests at the right place and time.

Asian countries, like the rest of the world, have important economies affected by the pandemic. Sonobe et al. (2021), examining 8 countries in Asia, reveal what kind of changes the pandemic has caused in businesses. The first of the results of the study revealed that there is a negative correlation between the use of technological platforms and unemployment. This shows that an unplanned change in service and product offering will negatively affect unemployment and common economic welfare. Therefore, it is clear that an integration capability is needed in change and development.

As mentioned in various studies, the pandemic has had significant effects on businesses. Among these effects, the points repeated in the studies can be summarized as follows:

- A financially fragile structure
- Uncertainty in employment and increasing anxiety
- Breaks in the supply chain
- Important problems in the supply of raw materials
- Trouble adapting to alternative business platforms
- There are inadequacies in digital product and service development in some sectors.

In addition, the changes that come with the pandemic are as follows:

- Differences experienced in consumers' shopping tendency
- Changes in the way businesses interact and do business
- Diversified demands and expectations of consumers

- The expectation of digital platform-based communication and interaction rather than physical interaction
- Higher VUCA
- Resistance to change
- Increasing need for dynamic talent that can turn change into opportunity
- The need for more digital products and services
- The obligation to determine the market and entrepreneurial orientation to be both a playmaker and a good player in the market
- Increasing expectation of innovation and compulsory transition to a business approach based on collaboration

As can be seen, the current way of doing business of enterprises has had to change significantly with the effect of the pandemic. This change has a parallel direction with the need to survive and have a competitive advantage rather than a choice. Therefore, there is a need for a dynamic capability that can respond to many of the above-mentioned change factors. The organizational agility capability, which is considered to improve the existing capabilities of the businesses and make significant contributions to turning the threats that occur in the post-covid era into opportunities, is discussed in this study. Detailed information on organizational agility capabilities, which offer continuous improvement and awareness in terms of diversified expectations and changing business platforms, is explained in detail in the next section.

Organizational Agility as a Dynamic Capability

Although change is expected in the socio-economic field in the historical process, its acceleration has become unprecedented in the recent period (Brosseau, Ebrahim, Handscomb, & Thaker, 2019). So much so that now, in planning processes, shorter-term goals are directed rather than medium and long-term goals, and strategic approaches that can adapt to developing sudden situations have begun to be applied (Blackburn, LaBerge, O'Toole, & Schneider, 2020). One of the factors that triggered this situation is the increase in competition conditions with the effect of globalization and the expectation of more specific and personalized products and services from all internal and external stakeholders and customers. These factors make the competitive environment in which businesses are more complex (Vinodh et al., 2010a; Vinodh 2010b). In such a complex environment that requires the management of various factors, organizations that can manage the current chaos and adapt survive. Businesses that cannot keep up with the requirements of this environment, unfortunately, fall behind in the competitive process very quickly and disappear. Businesses that perceive change quickly and accurately identify opportunities in an environment of uncertainty come to the fore with some of their abilities. For businesses to be successful in an industry environment where competition is intense and unpredictable, they need to properly interpret the emerging opportunities and develop the appropriate response. For this, they need to have a more agile and flexible dynamic capability (Aghina, De Smet, Lackey, Lurie, & Muraka, 2018). Organizational agility is the most inclusive one among the dynamic capabilities that offer flexibility and adaptation that organizations are expected to have. The concept of organizational agility was first mentioned in the early 1990s, in the process of examining the economy and production philosophy of Asian countries, which grew rapidly compared to Western countries. The concept was put forward with the expectation that a new production and management approach would be developed by western countries, as large

Asian companies, which have a share from European and US companies in almost every market, in their production processes and in meeting the quality expectations of their customers, can better analyze the changing situations. Since then, the concept has developed in the process of meeting even more complex expectations and has been studied on various platforms. Knowing the characteristics of the period in which the concept of organizational agility was introduced is important to compare it with the characteristics of today's period.

At the beginning of the 1990s, radical changes in political and economic terms and some changes on a global scale occurred in the world. Long-term large enterprises and production facilities routinely continued their administrative activities (Kidd, 2000). Understanding in competitive and industry environments did not require much change of conditions and adaptation to them. Many problems that businesses may encounter usually come with macro traces and there was time to develop the appropriate course of action. However, technological developments have affected the functioning of both businesses and large corporate structures and have built the very fast and volatile managerial atmosphere we are in (Hagel & Brown, 2003). Internet and ICT technologies, leading the technological developments, have made the parties on a global scale closer and more related than ever before in the historical process. This factor gave the environment a radical and more complex state. In the midst of the diversified and complex logistics and supply understanding, the boundaries of activities in businesses expanded and the need for high coordination came to the fore (Klapwijk, 2004; Bradley & Nolan, 1998). The communication between the businesses that produce goods and services and the end consumer has taken a different form with the current technologies. In addition to all these developments, after the collapse of the Union of Soviet Socialist Republics on the world stage, more nation states and large global companies from countries emerged. The new regulations brought by the state and various global actors emerged as an important factor in the complex stakeholder demands. All these developments have become more uncertain with many crises and wars on a global scale (Afghanistan, Iraq, Iran, etc.). As can be seen, technological developments, regulations of major global actors and governments, technological advances, wars and crises, in general terms, have taken a position that determines the competitive standards of businesses. These situations necessitated a business and management approach that exhibits a more proactive attitude and foresees change. At this point, it has been determined that a new management approach is necessary, especially with the attacks of the US car manufacturers, which have a high market share on a global scale, and Asian manufacturers, which have started to take a significant share of their market share. As a matter of fact, the DNA of competition began to change significantly, necessitating an effective situation analysis regarding this situation. The report on this due diligence is "Twenty-First Century Manufacturing Enterprise Strategy (Goldman etal., 1991)"which was created by the gathering of various stakeholders. It was decided that an agile business management approach was the most appropriate production and service delivery model in the industry environment where change and uncertainty increased. In this context, organizational agility has been defined in various perspectives since then. Organizational agility is defined as the ability of businesses to quickly identify some opportunities offered by the market (Sambamurthy, Bharadwaj & Grover, 2003). In addition, it is the process of developing the necessary response of the enterprises beyond detecting these opportunities and threats that develop in the industrial environment. Also the emphasises on definitions could be summarised as businesses can detect changes and develop the appropriate response (Overby et al., 2006; Holmqvist & Pessi, 2006), identify opportunities to create innovation (Liang et al., 2017; Queiroz et al., 2018), adapt to unforeseen changes (Sarker & Sarker, 2009; Ren et al., 2009; Zelbst et al., 2011) propose a new paradigm and solution in a changing environment (Sherehiy et al., 2007).

The fact that the market requires some changes in the industry environment, the diversification of customer expectations, the changes experienced in technology and social life dynamics push businesses to be agile (Sharifi & Zhang, 1999). Also, Oosterhout et al. (2006) grouped the situations that require organizational agility under 6 headings. Firstly, making of some legal regulations in the social and legal field, environmental changes, and the development of events such as disasters. In this case, it can be evaluated that socially, for example, the requirements of the Paris agreement for the adoption of a more environmentally friendly approach or events such as the covid pandemic experienced on a global scale will push businesses to agility. The relationship between businesses and their networks is decisive at this point. The combination of some competitors in the market, merger or acquisition processes force the business to change and adapt in terms of structure and network. The cost pressures of the companies in the competitive environment, the product life cycle and the threat of new players entering the market are decisive at this point. One of the most important factors is customer demands. Meeting the diversified expectations of customers, the speed of product offering, and changes in product quantity can be a driving factor. The change of technology, digital platforms and the formation of consumer tendency through this channel necessitate change and development on businesses. Internal factors, the need to adapt to the new culture and way of doing business created by mergers or acquisitions, and the use of new IT technology can be considered under this factor.

Along with organizational agility, it has come to the fore that basically four elements are a strategic issue (Goldman et al., 1995). The first strategic advantage is to provide detailed information about the product and service in a way that responds to the expectations of the customer. The second strategic issue is the establishment of a close relationship and cooperation with other stakeholders outside our own business. The third point is that businesses must now accept change and develop their organizational structures for a more flexible and sustainable innovation. Finally, it is to establish a balanced relationship between the organization (employee)-technology-innovation by posing as an effective learning organization. It is aimed to build an agile organizational structure that considers sustainable competition and customer satisfaction by considering these four issues.

A snapshot of Googltrends shows that there is increasing interest in an agile company transformation. It is seen that the rate of examination of the concept is quite high, especially between 2019-2022 (https://trends.google.com.tr). This situation shows that the answer to the need for dynamic capability in organizations is beginning to be understood. With organizational agility, the dynamic capability that businesses need can be established. The elements of organizational agility as a dynamic capability are gathered under 5 dimensions. These capabilities are important in terms of accurately reading the opportunities and developing the appropriate response in the industry environment that forces organizations to be agile.

Figure 1. Dimensions of organizational agility
(Source: Sharifi and Zhang (1999;2007)

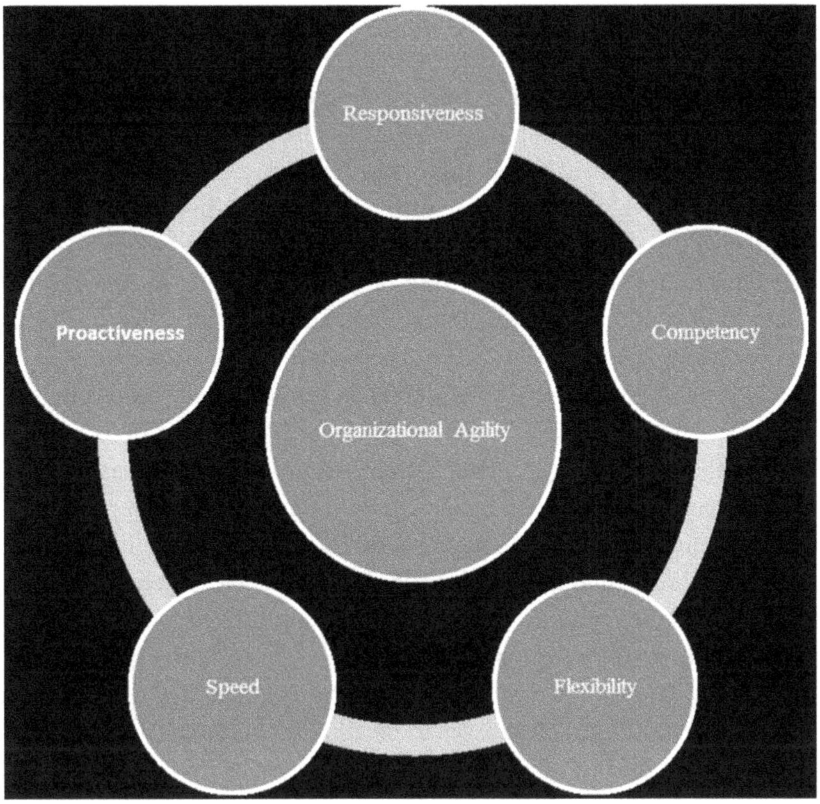

Businesses can develop a response to change in line with their 5 capabilities listed above in figure 1. Therefore, it would be appropriate to explain what these capabilities are and what they mean in the business. These capabilities can be explained as follows:

- **Competency**: Competence comes first among the organizational agility capabilities of the enterprise. This ability is a measure of the performance of the enterprise in the process of providing goods and services. In other words, it is related to how effectively and efficiently the company can use its existing resources and interaction with all its stakeholders in the value delivery process. As a matter of fact, the efficiency of resources and business processes is now an issue on the agenda of managers in every sectors. A business that adopts an efficient value delivery model can offer the product or service to the customer at the expected quality and time. In this context, businesses should be aware of their level of competence and constantly make due diligence on their level. Competence is the ability of an organization to realize its main goals and objectives in the fight against change and uncertainty. When organizations determine their competency levels accurately and objectively, they can determine their strengths and weaknesses in operational processes, and how well they adapt to their environment. In addition, the most important feature of competence that distinguishes it from other agility dimensions is the indicator of the level of speed and responsiveness that the organization needs (Sharifi & Zhang, 1999).

- **Responsiveness:** Businesses are constantly faced with new situations both in their close and macro environment. These situations encountered in business processes have gained even more dramatic momentum recently. Developing suitable solutions for unexpected situations experienced by businesses in their environment is considered as responsiveness. Businesses can develop a response proactively or reactively. As a result of the process of perceiving and predicting change, businesses should be able to develop their strategic responses to the requirements of change. As a matter of fact, the development of the appropriate response contributes to the development and continuity of the enterprise, while also supporting the increase in product and service quality.
- **Flexibility:** The only thing that does not change for businesses is adapting to change and updating the current understanding and situation of the business according to new developing situations. Businesses should be able to develop some flexible structural and managerial practices to meet environmental expectations. To meet these expectations in an environment of uncertainty, the company's reorganization of its existing resources in terms of expectations expresses the flexibility level of the business (Oosterhout, Waarts & Axelsson, 2007:59). For example, the ability of an enterprise to meet the demand for a sudden increase in production amount expresses its flexibility in volume of production. Again, when faced with a more complex project, the ability to adapt the existing human resources to this situation correctly refers to the flexibility of the human resource. Therefore, it is closely related to its flexibility ability to perceive the change and expectation in the market correctly, to develop it by diversifying the amount and form of the product and service it offers, and to gain competitive advantage.
- **Speed:** The dynamic behind change and uncertainty is speed. The turbulence created by rapidly shaped expectations obliges businesses to be agile in the provision of products and services. Although you are successful in offering products and services to a certain extent, if you do not keep up with the pace of change, your strategic superiority begins to make no sense after a while. Therefore, you should have both the skills required for agility and the ideal speed to respond to the needs of change at the right time with these skills. Therefore, no matter how important the reaction to change is, being quick in this regard has even more decisive importance. The success of a fast business in managing change is inevitable in business processes, administrative mechanisms and the correct processing of information. Therefore, speed is a capability that needs to be emphasized in meeting the new demands and expectations developing in the industry environment, in the delivery of the product and in the operational processes for production.
- **Proactiveness**: Proactiveness, which also supports the speed capability, is about taking the necessary precautions by evaluating the threats or opportunities developing around the business with a high foresight. At this point, the company closely monitors its internal and external stakeholders. It tries to determine in advance the expectations and future expectations and tendencies of the customers or partnerships. In this way, it takes the necessary foresight from the new situation that has occurred or will occur and starts to take action for it. It tries to anticipate the expectations and demands of each network in the value chain. This helps the business develop a rapid response to opportunities and threats. In this way, an agile and competitive business approach is developed.

It is important for businesses to have these capabilities to manage environmental change and maintain their competitive advantage. In order for businesses to develop these skills, 8 factors should be emphasized (Zhang & Sharifi, 2007):

- ***Relationship established with suppliers / customers / competitors:*** *Businesses should focus on the relationship they have established with their internal and external stakeholders (suppliers, customers, competitors ....). In this way, it can both determine the expectations of the stakeholders and establish the necessary information flow for innovation.*
- ***Technology****: The technique that the business uses in the service or product delivery constitutes its technology. Having a sufficient level of structure in this regard gives the business an advantage. Close monitoring of technology during product and service delivery provides flexibility in responding to changing expectations.*
- ***Integration:*** *Businesses express a dynamic system consisting of many sub-systems within itself. Just like the engine of a car, timing and harmony are the prerequisites for effective management in the interaction of each part. In this context, the interaction that develops in various departments of the enterprise should have a high level of integration with each other. This integration provides the managerial efficiency necessary for the business to maintain its sustainable competitive advantage. High integration of the unit with each other at various strategic levels in achieving the goals set by the business ensures that the right response is developed at the right time and place, that is, it is an agile business (Ricciardi, Zardini, & Rossignoli, 2018)*
- ***Organization****: The enterprise expresses a whole with all kinds of formal or informal components and networks. Bringing together all kinds of resources required within this whole to achieve the goals of the enterprise refers to the "organization". The correct analysis of the organizational structure of the enterprise and the design of it in a more organic or mechanical manner in accordance with industry requirements are decisive in achieving its goals. In today's conditions, it is important to determine an organic organizational structure to develop a more agile and rapid response. Leadership style, which is one of the main component of organization, is also an important issue for the organization to gain an agile structure (Watter, 2020). The leader takes important decisions regarding the resource allocation and structural processes of the enterprise. For an agile business structure, it is vital having for an agile organization to adopt a proper leadership approach that can develop the required response by accurately analyzing the expectations of internal and external factors. As a matter of fact, although a business may seem like an organization or systems that are interconnected with some technological software and business solution tools, it is actually a structure that can be successful to the extent of human factors and abilities. At this point, in the establishment of agility, both the leader and the quality of the leader member exchange play a role in creating a proactive organizational climate.*
- ***Human Resources****: Human resources are one of the most strategic resources in providing the necessary innovative solutions in today's industrial environments. The capacity of the human resources has a decisive effect on the agile capacity of the enterprises, their ability to adapt to change and to develop a quick response. In this context, it is necessary for agility to correctly analyze the existing structure and capacity of the human resources of enterprises, and to have proper the skills set suitable for proactive strategies. Management mechanisms should focus on this strategic resource.*
- ***Innovation****: Basically, the agility of the business is based on the understanding of adapting to new situations and developing the required response. This innovation climate necessary for expected response makes possible for enterpirises to offer new products and services. In this case, it makes it possible for the business to establish sustainable competition. Businesses with high innovation capacity can quickly respond to changing situations in competitive conditions.*

- ***Information and communication system (ICT):*** *ICT systems enable more rational and rapid response development in the management of more complex business processes and unexpected situations. For the operational excellence of the business, ICT provides a significant advantage (Roldán, José, Leal-Rodríguez, Antonio & Felipe, 2015). In this respect, ICT have a special place in acquiring agility skills. As a matter of fact, it is important to have an effective information flow to monitor the internal and external environment of the enterprise and to examine the developments. In this context, the fact that enterprises benefit from the operational and managerial opportunities offered by up-to-date ICT contributes to taking proactive measures.*

In the postcovid era, where change and uncertainty prevail, it is important to evaluate the above issues in detail to gain the agility capabilities.

MAIN FOCUS OF THE CHAPTER

Issues, Controversies, Problems

Increasing uncertainty and crisis conditions have been added to the intense competition atmosphere that businesses have been exposed to for a while with the COVID-19 pandemic. These conditions have radically affected the service or product supply chains of the enterprises, the business-customer-supplier interaction and the established way of doing business. As a matter of fact, the pandemic experienced on a global scale, lockdowns and dramatic changes in the functioning of daily life have shaken all businesses. Before the extent of this shock was understood, it was necessary to react for the continuity of socio-economic life, and some businesses that were relatively ready managed this situation well. While the pandemic brought about a financially fragile structure and uncertainty in employment, it had effects that required a paradigm shift in the supply chain and product/service delivery understanding. The flow of life has been interrupted by the pandemic, and the building blocks of the interaction between the individual and the business have changed with both health concerns and legal regulations. First of all, the shopping event, which is a social interaction process, has been moved to more virtual platforms. There have been significant changes in the daily needs and expectations of individuals who have to spend relatively more time at home due to lockdowns and health-themed regulations. These changes have made it necessary to analyze the needs and expectations of consumers from the beginning and in a comprehensive manner. Not only the customer-business relationship, but also the interaction between businesses has changed. Developing an interaction on a more digital basis, from payment methods to order and supply flow, has come to the fore. Although this situation causes everyone in the value chain to reconsider the network interaction with each other, most businesses have not been successful at this point. So, significant supply chain problems are still experienced. A study conducted by Ernst & Young LLP on 200 companies on a global scale revealed that 72% of companies still have significant supply chain problems (Harapko, 2021). In the study, it was shared that among the things to be done regarding the solution, the priority is to meet the efficiency and productivity concerns. It was emphasized that "resiliency and responsiveness" capabilities should be increased in the supply chain process, and that a more sustainable and digitally capable supply chain understanding should be developed. Again, in a study by McKinsey, it is emphasized that 93% of businesses, especially in the field of supply chain, should develop resilence (Alicke, Gupta & Trautwein, 2020). BCG consulting company shared that the main concern of businesses during and post-pandemic era should focus on "***cost, speed, and resilience***" and the solution will be possible if they have agility capabilities (Danoesastro et al.,2020). Also Forbes emphasizes that with the effect of the pandemic, external factors have become even more uncertain and the dynamics of competition in the industry is changing dramaticly. Forbes mentioned that organizational agility plays an even more vital role in meeting diversified customer expectations and providing "resilience" in competitive advantage in this environment of uncertainty (Roskil, 2022).

It is clear that businesses are experiencing significant difficulties with the pandemic. To be successful in the post covid-19 era, it is seen that businesses need to have a more resilient capability that can quickly control social and environmental changes and respond to diversified customer expectations. Organizational agility is defined as the ability to develop an appropriate response to changing conditions at the right place and time. In this context, it is clear that awareness of organizational agility and agile transformation should be handled quickly by both academicians and top managers. In this respect, organizational agility as the skill set needed by businesses in the post-pandemic era was discussed in the study and suggestions were made on how to be more agile in the next section.

SOLUTIONS AND RECOMMENDATIONS

Managing change for businesses should be considered as the basic reflex of survival rather than a choice. In this context, the first thing to do after the acceptance of change is to bring organizational agility, which is the ability to adapt to this change, to the enterprise. As a management philosophy and paradigm shift, a business's agility capabilities require agile transformation. Bringing some information technologies to the organizational environment does not make an organization agile in one aspect. Or the agility of a particular department does not make the business agile. Therefore, a radical transformation process must be initiated and a continuous improvement and development approach must prevail.

Significant results were obtained in a study conducted with the participation of 2190 senior executives on the acquisition of agile capabilities in the enterprise and how agile transformation should be (Aghina, Handscomb, Salo & Thaker, 2021). In the study, first of all, it is shared that the enterprises are basically gathered in two groups. Those who are in agile transformation and are not… Unfortunately, it is seen that only 14% of them are involved in some activities to gain agility capabilities at the enterprise level. The majority of businesses consider the introduction of certain ICT technologies in certain departments, especially in IT departments, as an agility process. However, this is an incomplete approach. In the study, it was shared that the majority of the enterprises that did not consider any agile transformation had other priorities (52%), their resources were not sufficient for transformation (29%), and the senior management had a resistance to agile approach (19%). Also, companies that have developed agile understanding have three times more competitive advantage than their competitors. In adopting the agile approach, it was shared that top management should have both knowledge and determination on this issue. It has been determined that Businesses that perform successful agile transformations have a significant advantage over other enterprises on achieving customer satisfaction (30%), increasing operational efficiency (30%), managing change and developing appropriate response (5 to10 times), innovation, employee engagement and empowerment (30%), and most importantly, efficiency (30%). Therefore, it has been empirically demonstrated that improving the organizational agility capabilities of enterprises contributes significantly to their competitive advantage.

As emphasized in other parts of the chapter, organizational agility needs to be developed for the flexibility, high responsiveness, high adaptability and firm performance required by the enterprise. In this context, it is considered important for businesses to follow these steps to gain a more agile. First of all, it is considered that it would be appropriate for businesses to follow the these stages:

- The agile transformation process should be started with the senior management and employees taking a determined stance to gain organizational agility.
- It should be ensured that the employees understand that the change is owned by the top management.
- In order for the agile change process to run smoothly, a senior manager responsible for change should be appointed with the skills and knowledge to carry out the change process. In addition, consultancy services can be obtained from an external source for the healthy functioning of the change process.
- The team responsible for change should conduct a comprehensive analysis of the current agility capabilities of the business. As a result of this analysis, a current situation analysis is made about the level of the enterprise in the 5 basic agility capabilities.
- After the current situation analysis, the skills that need to be developed are determined.

In the agile change process to develop capabilities, the current situation of the business in the "***strategy, structure, processes, people and technology***" factors should be redesigned in accordance with an agile management approach (Aghina, Handscomb, Ludolph, Róna, & West, 2020). These 5 domains are key elements that should be emphasized in decision mechanisms.

1. Strategy: It is important to define a clear strategy that will serve the vision and mission of the business. This strategy, which will include agile transformation, will guide the decisions and steps to be taken.
2. Structure: An organizational structure should be built in which the structure of the business is more accountable, measurable, flat and employees are empowered.
3. Process: By developing a performance and efficiency-oriented understanding of the way things are done, a business culture should be developed that can make quick decisions at all levels and enables continuous organizational learning.
4. People: Human resources should be put at the center as the main actor of the transformation, it is important to establish a human resource that adopts an entrepreneurial and innovative orientation, that employees have a team perspective on work processes and roles, and that adopts a culture based on shared change and agility.
5. Technology: By bringing the latest and user-friendly technologies together with competent human resources, digital product and service delivery should be strengthened.
    - It is a critical issue to share the added value of agility and how important it is for the future of the enterprise, to managers and employees at every level. In this way, while resistance to change is prevented, organizational agility can be adopted as a value shared by the business.
    - Consultancy services can be obtained for the analysis of business processes and the optimization of these processes. In addition, the presence of representatives from various departments at the beginning of the change process is important in the success of the process.
    - The change process always encounters resistance. As a matter of fact, researches reveal that there is a significant resistance to agile transformation. In this context, it will be beneficial

to keep the communication channels between the employee and the company at the highest level in every step and innovation.

- Agile transformation necessitates the development of some established decision and business processes for businesses in terms of hosting a paradigm shift for the general functioning of the business. In this context, it should be re-determined at every stage, by correctly addressing all kinds of resources of the enterprise, which agility capabilities need to be developed.
- Strategies should be determined to improve the current agility capability level. During the determination of the strategies, the following points should be emphasized. Firstly, the relationship established with the supplier / customer / competitors should be examined in detail, and the expectations of all stakeholders and the necessary innovative capacity should be determined. The appropriate service and product technology should be provided by benchmarking. Also it should not be forgotten that ICT has important contributions in the successful agile transformation process. Interdepartmental communication and integration into the agile transformation process should be ensured at a high level. A more organic and flattened organizational structure should be determined, and a leadership style that is open to communication and prone to empowering employees should be adopted. In the process of agile transformation, the hesitations of the existing human resources should be eliminated, and the necessary resources should be allocated in order for them to both be given a role in the transformation and acquire new capabilities. To increase the innovation capability, colloboration should be provided with internal and external resources.

With the capabilities to be developed at the end of all these steps, change and uncertainty are brought under control, while at the same time a sustainable competitive advantage is achieved.

The change and agile transformation process for businesses will definitely encounter some difficulties. More than 11,500 employees of BCG consulting companies examined the employees' view of the transformation process in businesses that prefer an agile transformation (Aliber et al., 2022). Within the scope of this study, it was shared that 3 subjects contributed to the success in the development of organizational agility. First of all, Learning organizations are successful in acquiring agility skills. The learning organization enables employees to produce new information, obtain it from internal and external sources, and effectively share the information among them in a way that integrates it into the processes of the enterprise. The other two aspects are the effective knowledge management process and the error-tolerant organizational culture. Strict standard procedures and control mechanisms prevent an agile management approach. As a matter of fact, in an environment where the severity and frequency of changing situations increase, it is essential to provide some managerial flexibility that allows the employee or manager to display a more courageous, entrepreneurial, and proactive attitude. Again, a study examining the barriers to the success of organizational agility on 637 top global leaders reveals striking results (Meythaler & Röber, 2020). It has been shared that the most important factor (70%) of the barriers to an effective agile transformation process is the managers with insufficient management skills in the agile transformation process, and mid-level managers (65%) are a significant barrier as resistance to change. Therefore, it is clear that qualified leaders are needed in the organizational agility and change management process.

FUTURE RESEARCH DIRECTIONS

Organizational agility triggers a continuous development and change process of enterprises. This situation makes it necessary for the organization and the individuals (employees) to implement ongoing change management in businesses. Although businesses are clearly in need of change and development, it is seen that the interest and awareness of an agile transformation at the organizational and individual (employee) level are still at a limited level. There seems to be a limited study in this area. In this context, it is essential to increase the number of academic studies on organizational agility for businesses to gain agile capabilities. In future studies, it will be appropriate to design reliable measurement tools that reveal the organizational agility capacity in detail on a sectoral basis (product-service, logistics, accommodation, etc.). In this way, businesses that can analyze the current situation can design development and change programs to improve their agile capabilities. Seeing organizational agility as the ability of only a team or department and allowing it to remain at this level creates an important risk situation for a sustainable competitive approach. As a matter of fact, it is vital to transform the agile philosophy into a competence that holistically covers the whole organization, by seeing the business and each element in the value chain as an interconnected sub-system element. At this point, with the support of various stakeholders, studies should be carried out on projects focusing on agile transformation and effective governance such as "*scrum, agile scaling, agile pilot application*...". In addition, it should not be forgotten that the main actor is human, whether change or development is in the technological or economic field. Human resources have a critical role in providing organizational agility. Human resources play an essential role both in the dissemination of corporate culture and in the development of agile understanding. At this point, it would be appropriate for future studies to focus on studies about the human sides of the organizational agility transformation process such as "c*apability accelerator, top team aspiration, adaptability, personal knowledge management and individual agility development*...". In this way, a detailed examination of both organizational and individual variables is considered to make significant contributions to increasing the dynamic capability of organizational agility, effective change management in an uncertain environment, and a better application of the concept.

CONCLUSION

Various factors require the business to be agile and are an important in sustainable competitive advantage and survival. These factors are various natural disasters, some social and legal regulations, the requirements in the merger or acquisition processes that develop in the business network, the change in the dynamics of competition within the industry, the diversifying and complex expectations of the customer, technological developments in the way of doing business, and new situations and practices occurring in the internal functioning of the business (Van Oosterhout, 2010:19). Among these factors, the recent Covid-19 pandemic, whose impact size is more extensive, is included. There have been radical changes in socio-economic life with the pandemic. While the expectations of all internal and external stakeholders have changed, it has started to transform into a virtual identity, including the environment in which the interaction is established. This situation has revealed new dynamics in competition dynamics and performance expectations. Companies that can manage these new factors and expectations, observe and respond quickly to changing issues in the environment, are ahead of the competition compared to others. Developing the necessary response by perceiving environmental change and expectations quickly and at the right time, namely organizational agility, has emerged as an vital dynamic capability. In this context, it is clear that businesses have to develop their organizational agility capabilities to be successful, especially in the postcovid era. Therefore, action should be taken to increase awareness on this issue and to adopt agility capabilities at the enterprise level. First of all, a comprehensive attitude and understanding towards agile transformation should be established in the top management. Subsequently, a transformation process should be initiated that includes organizational dynamics and managers, as well as professional support. In the agile transformation process of the business, a strategy should be determined and an organizational structure should be adopted in which organizational agility can be applied. All processes in the business and all stakeholders in the value chain should be examined in detail and it should be determined which agile capabilities of the business need to be developed. Then the necessary revisions on business processes and latest technology should be adopted. In transformation process, employees should not be abandoned and the skill sets necessary for an agile business should be gained to the employees. In this way, the agility capabilities of enterprises could be increased in a sustainable way. Thanks to the agile capabilities developed by transformation, businesses can properly evaluate new opportunities, diversified customer expectations and threats. By developing a proactive attitude at the right place and time in accordance with these evaluations, they can take the necessary successful actions within the industry and offer innovative solutions. This situation contributes to the sustainable competitive advantage and managerial efficiency of businesses in the uncertainty environment of the postcovid-19 era.

The pandemic has further increased the already intense competitive atmosphere and turbulence, and "cost, effectiveness, speed, responsiveness, flexibility and resilence" will become the main success factors in the survival of businesses in the post-pandemic era. It is clear that organizational agility will provide this adaptive and proactive capability that businesses need. In this context, for a successful business performance in the postcovid era, it would be appropriate for businesses to reconsider their current capabilities, and focus on agility capabilities that need to be developed to respond to environmental changes and expectations quickly.

REFERENCES

Aghina, W., De Smet, A., Lackey, G., Lurie, M., and Muraka, M. (2018). The five trademarks of agile organizations. *McKinsey & Company Report.*

Aghina, W., Handscomb, C., Ludolph, J., Róna, D., & West, D. (2020). *Enterprise agility: Buzz or business impact?* McKinsey. https://www.mckinsey.com/business-functions/people-and-organizational-performance/our-insights/enterprise-agility-buzz-or-business-impact

Aghina, W., Handscomb, C., Salo, O., & Thaker, S. (2021). *The impact of agility: How to shape your organization to compete* avaliable at: https://www.mckinsey.com/business-functions/people-and-organizational-performance/our-insights/the-impact-of-agility-how-to-shape-your-organization-to-compete# Aliber,M., Danoesastro, M., Kinderen,T., Djavdan,P., Hildebrandt,P. & Lenhard,E. (2022) *What 11,500 Employees Say About Agile Transformation.* BCG. https://www.bcg.com/publications/2022/what-employees-say-about-agile-transformations

Alicke, K., Gupta, R., & Trautwein, V. (2020) *Resetting supply chains for the next normal*. McKinsey. https://www.mckinsey.com/business-functions/operations/our-insights/resetting-supply-chains-for-the-next-normal

Bartik, A. W., Bertrand, M., Cullen, Z., Glaeser, E. L., Luca, M., & Stanton, C. (2020). The impact of COVID-19 on small business outcomes and expectations. *Proceedings of the National Academy of Sciences of the United States of America, 117*(30), 17656–17666. doi:10.1073/pnas.2006991117 PMID:32651281

Blackburn, S., LaBerge, L., O'Toole, C., & Schneider, J. (2020). *Digital strategy in a time of crisis*. McKinsey. https://www.mckinsey.com/business-functions/mckinsey-digital/our-insights/digital-strategy-in-a-time-of-crisis

Bradley, S. P., & Nolan, R. L. (1998). *Sense and Respond: Capturing Value in the Network Era*. Harvard Business School Press.

Brosseau, D., Ebrahim, S., Handscomb, C., & Thaker, S. (2019). *The journey to an agile organization.* McKinsey. www.mckinsey.com%2F~%2Fmedia%2FMcKinsey%2FBusiness%2520Functions%2FOrganization%2FOur%2520Insights%2FThe%2520journey%2520to%2520an%2520agile%2520organization%2FThe-journey-to-an-agile-organization-final.pdf&clen=1232003&chunk=true.

Carnevale, J. B., & Hatak, I. (2020). Employee adjustment and well-being in the era of COVID-19: Implications for human resource management. *Journal of Business Research, 116*, 183–187. doi:10.1016/j.jbusres.2020.05.037 PMID:32501303

Danoesastro, M., Rehberg, B., Ritter, D., Krishna, A., Hildebrandt, P., & Islam, M. (2020). *When the Ground Shifts, It Pays to Be Agile*. BCG.https://www.bcg.com/publications/2020/understanding-why-agile-will-help-move-the-needle-post-covid-19

Doern, R., Williams, N., & Vorley, T. (2019). Special issue on entrepreneurship and crises: Business as usual? An introduction and review of the literature. *Entrepreneurship and Regional Development, 31*(5-6), 400–412. doi:10.1080/08985626.2018.1541590

Donthu, N., & Gustafsson, A. (2020). Effects of COVID-19 on business and research. *Journal of Business Research, 117*, 284–289. doi:10.1016/j.jbusres.2020.06.008 PMID:32536736

Eggers, F. (2020). Masters of disasters? Challenges and opportunities for SMEs in times of crisis. *Journal of Business Research, 116*, 199–208. doi:10.1016/j.jbusres.2020.05.025 PMID:32501306

Elali, W. (2021). The importance of strategic agility to business survival during corona crisis and beyond. *International Journal of Business Ethics and Governance, 4*(2), 1–8. doi:10.51325/ijbeg.v4i2.64

Goldman, S., Nagel, R., & Preiss, K. (1995). *Agile Competitors and Virtual Organizations*. Van Nostrand Reinhold.

Goldman, S., Nagel, R., Preiss, K., & Dove, R. (1991). *21st Century Manufacturing Enterprise Strategy: An Industry Led View*. Iacocca Institute, Lehigh University.

Hagel, J. I., & Brown, S. (2003). *The agile dance of architectures—reframing IT enabled business opportunities*. SAP Design Guild, Edition on Composite Applications.

Harapko, S. (2021). *How COVID-19 impacted supply chains and what comes next.* EY. https://www.ey.com/en_gl/supply-chain/how-covid-19-impacted-supply-chains-and-what-comes-next

Holmqvist, M., & Pessi, K. (2006). Agility through scenario development and continuous implementation: A global aftermarket logistics case. *European Journal of Information Systems, 15*(2), 146–158. doi:10.1057/palgrave.ejis.3000602

Ivanov, D. (2020). Viable supply chain model: Integrating agility, resilience and sustainability perspectives-lessons from and thinking beyond the COVID-19 pandemic. *Annals of Operations Research.* doi:10.100710479-020-03640- PMID:32836614

Kidd, P. T. (2000). *Agile manufacturing enterprise strategy.* Cheshirenbury.

Klapwijk, H. P. (2004). *Economics Reconfigured - A vision on tomorrow's Value Chains.* (Inaugural Speech): University Nyenrode

Liang, H., Wang, N., Xue, Y., & Ge, S. (2017). Unraveling the Alignment Paradox: How Does Business-IT Alignment Shape Organizational Agility? *Information Systems Research, 28*(4), 863–879. doi:10.1287/isre.2017.0711

Meythaler, A., & Röber, B. (2020). *Organizational Agility as Competitive Factor.* Viewer. https://viewer.joomag.com/goetzpartners-publications-agile-performer-index-2/0283980001575907006?short

Moon, M. J. (2020). Fighting Against COVID-19 with agility, transparency, and participation: Wicked policy problems and new governance challenges. *Public Administration Review, 80*(4), 651–656. doi:10.1111/puar.13214 PMID:32836434

Nandi, S., Sarkis, J., Hervani, A. A., & Helms, M. M. (2021). Redesigning supply chains using blockchain-enabled circular economy and COVID-19 experiences. *Sustainable Production and Consumption, 27,* 10–22. doi:10.1016/j.spc.2020.10.019 PMID:33102671

Oosterhout, M. V., Waarts, E., & Hillegersberg, J. V. (2006). Change Factors Requiring Agility and Implications for IT. *European Journal of Information Systems, 15*(2), 132–145. doi:10.1057/palgrave.ejis.3000601

Oosterhout Marcel Van, Waarts Eric & Axelsson R. (2007). Business Agility: Need, Readiness and Alignment with IT Strategies, Agile Information Systems: Conceptualization. *Construction Manager, 44*, 52–69.

Overby, E., Bharadwaj, A., & Sambamurthy, V. (2006). Enterprise agility and the enabling role of information technology. *European Journal of Information Systems, 15*(2), 120–131. doi:10.1057/palgrave.ejis.3000600

Pantano, E., Pizzi, G., Scarpi, D., & Dennis, C. (2020). Competing during a pandemic? Retailers' ups and downs during the COVID-19 outbreak. *Journal of Business Research, 116*, 209–213. doi:10.1016/j.jbusres.2020.05.036 PMID:32501307

Queiroz, M., Tallon, P. P., Sharma, R., & Coltman, T. (2018). The role of IT application orchestration capability in improving agility and performance. *The Journal of Strategic Information Systems*, *27*(1), 4–21. doi:10.1016/j.jsis.2017.10.002

Ren, J., Yusuf, Y. Y., & Burns, N. D. (2009). A decision-support framework for agile enterprise partnering. *International Journal of Advanced Manufacturing Technology*, *41*(1-2), 180–192. doi:10.100700170-008-1443-3

Ricciardi, F., Zardini, A., & Rossignoli, C. (2018). Organizational integration of the IT function: A key enabler of firm capabilities and performance. *Journal of Innovation & Knowledge*, *3*(3), 93–107. doi:10.1016/j.jik.2017.02.003

Roldán. J. L., Leal-Rodríguez, A., L.& Felipe, C. (2015*)* Information systems capabilities and organizational agility: understanding the mediating role of absorptive capacity when influenced by a hierarchy culture. In *2nd International Symposium on Partial Least Squares Path Modeling - The Conference for PLS Users.*, Seville, Spain

Roskil, J. (2022) *Demonstrates Its Staying Power* available at: https://www.forbes.com/sites/forbestechcouncil/2022/01/14/2022-prediction-agility-demonstrates-its-staying-power/?sh=2e3
1f24f32c3

Sambamurthy, V., Bharadwaj, A., & Grover, V. (2003). Shaping agility through digital options: Reconceptualizing the role of information technology in contemporary firms. *Management Information Systems Quarterly*, *27*(2), 237–263. doi:10.2307/30036530

Sarker, S., & Sarker, S. (2009). Exploring Agility in Distributed Information Systems Development Teams: An Interpretive Study in an Offshoring Context. *Information Systems Research*, *3*(20), 440–461. doi:10.1287/isre.1090.0241

Sharifi, H., & Zhang, Z. (1999). A Methodology for Achieving Agility in Manufacturing Organizations: An Introduction. *International Journal of Production Economics*, *62*(1-2), 7–22. doi:10.1016/S0925-5273(98)00217-5

Sharma, P., Leung, T. Y., Kingshott, R. P., Davcik, N. S., & Cardinali, S. (2020). Managing uncertainty during a global pandemic: An international business perspective. *Journal of Business Research*, *116*, 188–192. doi:10.1016/j.jbusres.2020.05.026 PMID:32501304

Sherehiy, B., Karwowski, W., & Layer, J. K. (2007). A Review of Enterprise Agility: Concepts, Frameworks, and Attributes. *International Journal of Industrial Ergonomics*, *5*(37), 445–460. doi:10.1016/j.ergon.2007.01.007

Sheth, J. (2020). Impact of Covid-19 on consumer behavior: Will the old habits return or die? *Journal of Business Research*, *117*, 280–283. doi:10.1016/j.jbusres.2020.05.059 PMID:32536735

SonobeT.TakedaA.YoshidaS.TruongH. T. (2021). *The impacts of the Covid-19 pandemic on micro, small, and medium enterprises in Asia and their digitalization responses.* ADBI Working Paper 1241. https://ssrn.com/abstract=3912355 or doi:10.2139/ssrn.3912355

Stang, S. (2021). *Impact Of The Coronavirus Pandemic On Businesses And Employees By Industry*. BLS. https://www.bls.gov/spotlight/2021/impact-of-the-coronavirus-pandemic-on-businesses-and-employees-by-industry/home.htm

The World Bank. (2021). *How COVID-19 is Affecting Companies Around the World*. https://www.worldbank.org/en/news/infographic/2021/02/17/how-covid-19is-affecting-companies-around-the-world

Tilman, L. M. (2019). *Agility: How to navigate the unknown and seize opportunity in a world of disruption*. Missionday.

Tucker, H. (2020). Coronavirus Bankruptcy Tracker: These Major Companies Are Failing Amid The Shutdown. *Forbes*. https://www.forbes.com/sites/hanktucker/2020/05/03/coronavirus-bankruptcy-tracker-these-major-companies-are-failing-amid-the-shutdown/?sh=4882bad13425 URL1:https://trends.google.com.tr/trends/explore?date=all&q=agile%20transformation

Van Oosterhout, M. P. A. (2010). *Business Agility and Information Technology in Service Organizations (No. EPS-2010-198-LIS)*. Erasmus Research Institute of Management. http://hdl.handle.net/1765/19805

Verma, S., & Gustafsson, A. (2020). Investigating the emerging COVID-19 research trends in the field of business and management: A bibliometric analysis approach. *Journal of Business Research*, *118*, 253–261. doi:10.1016/j.jbusres.2020.06.057 PMID:32834211

Vinodh, S., Devadasan, S. R., Vasudeva Reddy, B., & Ravichand, K. (2010a). Agility index measurement using multi-grade fuzzy approach integrated in a 20 criteria agile model. *International Journal of Production Research*, *48*(23), 7159–7176. doi:10.1080/00207540903354419

Vinodh, S., Sundararaj, G., Devadasan, S. R., Kuttalingam, D., & Rajanayagam, D. (2010b). Amalgamation of mass customisation and agile manufacturing concepts: The theory and implementation study in an electronics switches manufacturing company. *International Journal of Production Research*, *48*(7), 2141–2164. doi:10.1080/00207540802456257

Walter, A. T. (2020). *Organizational agility: ill-defined and somewhat confusing? A systematic literature review and conceptualization*. Management Review Quarterly. doi:10.100711301-020-00186-6

Wang, Y., Hong, A., Li, X., & Gao, J. (2020). Marketing innovations during a global crisis: A study of China firms' response to COVID-19. *Journal of Business Research*, *116*, 214–220. doi:10.1016/j.jbusres.2020.05.029 PMID:32501308

Yıkılmaz, İ. (2021a). Digital transformation and organizational agility -Dijital dönüşüm ve örgütsel çeviklik. İ.Erdoğan Tarakçı& B. Göktaş (Eds.) in İşletmecilikte Dijital Dönüşüm (425-442). Efe Akademi,İstanbul.

Yıkılmaz, İ. (2021b). Covid-19 Pandemic As A Digital Transformation Catalyst. In M. Meciar & H. Şimşek (Eds.), *The Social And Economic Impact Of Covid-19* (pp. 119–138). IJOPEC Publication Limited.

Zelbst, P. J., Green, K. W., Sower, V. E., & Abshire, R. D. (2011, Fall). Radio Frequency Identification Technology Utilization and Organizational Agility. *Journal of Computer Information Systems*, 24–33.

Zhang, Z., & Sharifi, H. (2007). Towards theory building in agile manufacturing strategy-a taxonomical approach. *IEEE Transactions on Engineering Management, 54*(2), 351–370. doi:10.1109/TEM.2007.893989

ADDITIONAL READING

Akkaya, B., Gunsel, A., & Yikilmaz, I. (2021). Digital Management Towards Society 5.0: A Review of the Framework for Kurt Lewin Theory During COVID-19 Pandemic. In K. Sandhu (Ed.), *Emerging Challenges, Solutions, and Best Practices for Digital Enterprise Transformation* (pp. 120–137). IGI Global. doi:10.4018/978-1-7998-8587-0.ch007

Al-Omoush, K. S., Simón-Moya, V., & Sendra-García, J. (2020). The impact of social capital and collaborative knowledge creation on e-business proactiveness and organizational agility in responding to the COVID-19 crisis. *Journal of Innovation & Knowledge, 5*(4), 279–288. doi:10.1016/j.jik.2020.10.002

Batra, D. (2020). The impact of the COVID-19 on organizational and information systems agility. *Information Systems Management, 37*(4), 361–365. doi:10.1080/10580530.2020.1821843

Chen, X., & Siau, K. (2020). Business analytics/business intelligence and IT infrastructure: Impact on organizational agility. [JOEUC]. *Journal of Organizational and End User Computing, 32*(4), 138–161. doi:10.4018/JOEUC.2020100107

Ciampi, F., Faraoni, M., Ballerini, J., & Meli, F. (2022). The co-evolutionary relationship between digitalization and organizational agility: Ongoing debates, theoretical developments and future research perspectives. *Technological Forecasting and Social Change, 176*, 121383. doi:10.1016/j.techfore.2021.121383

Felipe, C. M., Roldán, J. L., & Leal-Rodríguez, A. L. (2016). An explanatory and predictive model for organizational agility. *Journal of Business Research, 69*(10), 4624–4631. doi:10.1016/j.jbusres.2016.04.014

Tallon, P. P., Queiroz, M., Coltman, T., & Sharma, R. (2019). Information technology and the search for organizational agility: A systematic review with future research possibilities. *The Journal of Strategic Information Systems, 28*(2), 218–237. doi:10.1016/j.jsis.2018.12.002

Walter, A. T. (2021). Organizational agility: Ill-defined and somewhat confusing? A systematic literature review and conceptualization. *Management Review Quarterly, 71*(2), 343–391. doi:10.100711301-020-00186-6

Yıkılmaz, İ. (2021a). Digital transformation and organizational agility -Dijital dönüşüm ve örgütsel çeviklik. İ. Erdoğan Tarakçı & B. Göktaş (Eds.) in İşletmecilikte Dijital Dönüşüm (425-442). Efe Akademi, İstanbul.

Yıkılmaz, İ. (2021b). Covid-19 Pandemic As A Digital Transformation Catalyst. In M. Meciar & H. Şimşek (Eds.), *The Social And Economic Impact Of Covid–19* (pp. 119–138). IJOPEC Publication Limited.

KEY TERMS AND DEFINITIONS

Agile human resources: Human resource that can detect change in the right place and time and update their skill sets and value creation process.

Agile transformation: It is the change process that covers the organization carried out in order to gain the agility capabilities that businesses need.

Change management: Change management is a systematic approach that an organization implements by developing new strategies to adapt its existing technology and processes to changing conditions.

Competitive advantage: The ability of an organization to outperform relatively others in the same industry or market in terms of various performance criteria.

Digital Transformation: The transformation of the organization's way of doing business, customer experience, and business processes with digital technologies to meet changing expectations

Learning organization: Organizations that can provide information from internal and external sources at the right place and time, use it appropriately at the organizational scale in response to environmental changes, and produce knowledge again for sustainable competitive advantage.

Pandemic: It is the general name that defines epidemic diseases that spread and affect a very wide area in the world.

Post-Covid19 Era: The era, which includes the new dynamics and understandings brought by the Covid 19 pandemic, is the "new normal".

VUCA: It consists of the initials of the following four words in English (Volatility, Uncertainty, Complexity Ambiguity). VUCA expresses the context of an organization's current and future situations in its planning and management processes.

Chapter 11
Gender Differences in the Entrepreneurial Orientation Dimensions in the Middle East:
Evidence From Palestine

Nidal A. Darwish
Al-Quds University, Palestine

Mohammed A. Bayyoud
Al-Quds University, Palestine

ABSTRACT

The research aims to explore and describe to what extent there is gender difference across the entrepreneurial orientation dimensions (risk-taking, innovativeness, proactiveness, competitiveness, and autonomy) in the Middle East. To achieve this goal, the authors employed a descriptive quantitative research design where 60 male and female entrepreneurs in Palestine were surveyed through a closed-ended questionnaire. The study findings indicate that males are more entrepreneurial-oriented than females, but to a relatively small extent. Moreover, the results showed that male entrepreneurs have a higher mean in risk-taking, competitiveness, and innovativeness, whereas females have a higher mean in proactiveness and autonomy. Additionally, the study showed that the traditions and customs prevalent in Palestine were the most critical restrictions for females to become entrepreneurs. Moreover, female entrepreneurs face different restrictions, including society's perception toward women, lack of funds, and legislation obstacles such as registration.

DOI: 10.4018/978-1-6684-7509-6.ch011

INTRODUCTION

Entrepreneurs have the most important effect on driving innovation in an economy. Such businesses were the primary source of change in traditional markets. Small businesses helped the economies to transform and embrace change by exploring new business opportunities. However, the concept of entrepreneurship in the Schumpeter period was different from the classical era. The Schumpeter entrepreneurs were innovators and change agents (Schumpeter 1954), while the classical entrepreneurs were risk-takers, capitalists, and rational and maximizing agents (Shane & Venkataraman, 2000).

The role played by gender on entrepreneurial behavior became an essential component of academic conversations around entrepreneurship. In recent years, an increasing number of studies focused on female entrepreneurship. In this regard, a long-lasting debate follows the entrepreneurial literature concerning gender roles in shaping entrepreneurial behavior. The increased participation of females in businesses by starting small independent businesses in different countries directed the academic investigators' attention as well as an international regulator to ensure diversity and equality. Preliminary findings reported that women make up approximately half of the global population (50%), but their ownership, participation, and management of international businesses are significantly low compared to men (Kim, 2007). Several reasons identified in the existing research such las ower women entrepreneurs include less activeness among women to develop new ends means frameworks, lack of entrepreneurial talent, social stereotypes, and lack of opportunities (Kim, 2007; Kelley et al., 2016). However, from a scientific point of view, the study of female entrepreneurship as a distinct area of inquiry is legitimate because women's entrepreneurship presents several distinctive characteristics that differentiate it from men's entrepreneurship.

Besides, the entrepreneurial behavior of women investigated the relationship with wealth formation, employment decisions, human capital development, labor market forces at work, and other factors. Researchers such as (Tsyganova & Shirokova, 2010; Johnson & Powell, 1994; Ayub et al., 2013) shed the light on the increased participation of males in entrepreneurial activities can be attributed to the differences in the levels of entrepreneurial orientations (EO) between the two genders. EO refers to "the processes, practices, and decision-making activities used by entrepreneurs that lead to the initiation of an entrepreneurial firm" (Lumpkin & Dess, 1996; p.135). Therefore, beyond the simple gender perspective, it is vital to investigate and understand the differences in EO for both genders to see how these can affect female management of their entrepreneurial ventures.

Most literature on gender entrepreneurship is drawn from developed countries, and there is a lack of studies that focus on countries like Middle Eastern countries. The society in the Middle East is characterized by specific gender roles where women are supposed to be running a business or be on top of the firm's management. It makes the Middle East different and unique in the context. Palestine is no alien, so it is vital to investigate the phenomenon. Palestinian women face significant challenges in setting up independent small businesses and managing them in competition with their male counterparts. To date, there is a lack of research that investigates the differences in the perceptions of EO of Palestinian females and males. The current study aims to bridge this gap.

The current study aims to investigate and explore to what extent the perceptions of entrepreneurial orientation (EO) of females are different from those of their male counterparts. And to shed the light on the obstacles and challenges women entrepreneurs encounter while establishing their ventures. The study focuses on the gender differences in five EOs: risk-taking, innovativeness, pro-activeness, competitiveness, and autonomy for comparison between the two groups. Consequently, the current study is an attempt to answer the following research questions:

- To what extent do perceptions of entrepreneurial orientation (EO) of females differ from those of their male counterparts in the middle east?
- What are the main constraints that affect female entrepreneurs launching their businesses in the Middle East?

To address this research question, we need an appropriate theory to explore the difference between the perceptions of entrepreneurial orientation (EO) of females and their male counterparts. Shinnar et al. (2012) stressed gender differences in entrepreneurial abilities, intentions, and other entrepreneurial attributes. Hence, we chose gender theory because Gender theory postulates that men and women have different approaches in managing their businesses (Quaye et al., 2015).

The contribution of this study is twofold: First, it contributes to the entrepreneurship literature, there was a growing interest and research that focused on women's entrepreneurship (e.g., Boyd, 2005; Bruni et al., 2004; Brush et al., 2006; Lerner & Pines, 2010; Pines, 2002; Pines & Schwartz, 2008). Second, it attempts to enrich the gender theory by understanding the difference between male and female entrepreneurial behavior. Indeed, research on women's entrepreneurship in the context of the Middle East is scarce and this study can provide an overview of the obstacles and the support required for the development of women's entrepreneurship in this region. (Ghouse et al., 2019).

The chapter is structured as follows: an introduction to the theoretical background. Then, the methodological approach of this study is described. Finally, the findings are provided, followed by a discussion of the study's implications for theory and practice.

LITERATURE REVIEW

Women Entrepreneurship

Global interest in women entrepreneurs has been growing (Marlow & McAdam, 2013) as there is recently a significant increase in female entrepreneurs (Hughes et al., 2012). According to the emerging literature, women can contribute significantly to entrepreneurial activity (Noguera et al., 2013), economic development (Kelley et al., 2017; Hechevarra et al., 2019), job creation and GDP growth (Bahmani-Oskooee et al., 2013; Ayogu & Agu, 2015), with positive effects on poverty reduction (Langowitz & Minniti, 2007; Rae, 2015). However, the percentage of women who choose to pursue an entrepreneurial career is lower than that of men (Elam et al., 2019), and this difference becomes more pronounced as the country's level of development rises (Coduras & Autio, 2013). As the number of women starting new businesses grows, significant efforts have been made to investigate the impact of gender on entrepreneurship (Braches & Elliott, 2016; Henry et al., 2016). Women still face more difficulties and pressures when managing their businesses (Bui et al., 2018). For example, the entrepreneur stereotype includes masculine characteristics such as assertiveness, risk-taking, opportunity recognition, and economic growth (Ahl, 2006).

Women's businesses, on average, are smaller and more likely to be organized as sole proprietorships than corporations, in lower occupational status sectors, grow more slowly, have fewer sales, and are less profitable (Marlow & Patton, 2005; Powell & Eddleston, 2013). Moreover, property rights facilitate access to resources, and in many institutional contexts, women are particularly limited in their access to the economic resources required for entrepreneurship (Brush et al., 2009), as entrepreneurs must rely more on informal networks that are typically dominated by men (Brush et al., 2009). Furthermore, men can be more effective in dealing with government officials due to gender-defined social positioning (Bardasi et al., 2011). However, there is empirical evidence that a woman's decision to start a business is influenced by her sociocultural background (Ahl, 2006) due to gender stereotypes. Ahl (2004) discovered that in all of the texts reviewed in her study of how academics contribute to perpetuating stereotypes about female entrepreneurship, women entrepreneurs were considered secondary to men. The reasons for this "negative representation" continue to be the subject of international debate, with no expected outcomes. This stereotypical and male-centered vision discourages some women from participating in business activities, which may also impact people who interact with women in the community, creating an additional barrier (Langowitz & Morgan, 2003).

According to the findings of Sullivan and Meek's (2012) systematic analysis, the attributions of society and the various socialization processes relating to men and women may create barriers for women due to unequal distribution of assets and services, educational objectives, and daily life activity expectations. It appears critical to increase the percentage of women in entrepreneurship, which has sparked political interest in recent years, by emphasizing the potential economic benefits (Carter et al., 2015), claiming that gender equality contributes to economic growth. The "global gender gap" is at the heart of EU policy, as it identifies a clear economic logic for encouraging women to become self-employed (Carter et al., 2015; Sorgner et al., 2017). Finally, according to Boyd (2016), a critical counterweight must be added to the public debate. There is no collective questioning among all actors working in various fields to understand gender-related discrimination, which is required for long-term development (Cardella et al.,2020).

Women Entrepreneurs in the Middle East

Women entrepreneurship in developing countries is difficult due to a lack of opportunities, limited resources, and unique challenges (Panda & Dash, 2014, 2016; Panda, 2018; Verheul et al., 2006). According to the literature, one of the significant challenges faced by women entrepreneurs in the Middle East is access to financial resources (Jamali, 2009; Halkias et al., 2011; Maden, 2015; Naguib & Jamali, 2015; Ramadani et al., 2015). However, the number of women entrepreneurs in the Middle East is increasing, providing more opportunities for women to start, shape, and manage their businesses (Tlaiss, 2015; Dechant & Lamky, 2005). Middle Eastern countries are male-dominated societies where gender roles are strictly defined and differentiated. Men are expected to be decisive, whereas women are expected to be intuitive and focused on relationship building and quality of life (Hofstede, 1994).

Moreover, Middle Eastern societies are also highly collectivist: members are expected to adjust their aspirations to meet or fulfill the group's goals, emphasizing group conformity (Hofstede, 2001). Moreover, men are expected to provide financial support for their families, while women are expected to care for the home and family. Such a culture promotes the idea that a woman's proper place is in her home (Sultan, 2016). No law in the Middle East prohibits women from working or owning a business. However, the business environment is heavily skewed toward men. Women entrepreneurs face various challenges and constraints that limit their economic participation and, as a result, contribute at a lower rate than men (Hisrich & ztürk, 1999). Consequently, women's entrepreneurship rates in the Middle East are the lowest in the world, and their enterprises are small and focused primarily on 'feminine' sectors (World Economic Forum, 2011).

Women in many Middle Eastern countries, including Palestine, struggle against inequality and restrictive practices in economic participation and are constrained by family roles (Hattab, 2012). Many of these unfair practices and limitations originate from local cultural traditions (Haber & Reichel, 2007). For Example, women entrepreneurs in Palestine encounter external barriers such as a lack of financing, exclusion from male-dominated informal networks, and social perception that business ownership is a male activity. These barriers are primarily informal, based on cultural norms, values, and customs (Mohsen, 2007). However, there is little research on the problems experienced by women entrepreneurs in the Middle East, as the majority of research on women entrepreneurs has been conducted in Western or developed economies context (Al-Dajani & Marlow, 2013).

Entrepreneurial Orientation

Entrepreneurship is a "behavior in which an individual or group of individuals takes a risk to start a new business and owning it" (Brush et al., 2009). Entrepreneurship is more about the processes, methods, and styles individuals adopt to practice their Entrepreneurship. It also acts as a market force to drive economic and social development in an economy. It helps people to personally develop and fulfill their needs on a self-basis without depending on anyone. Developed and developing countries showed a significant increase in entrepreneurial activities in the past decade. However, entrepreneurial firms contribute to the growth and progress of society and the welfare of the citizens (Bruton et al., 2013; Dana, 2000).

Over the years, there is an increase in the academic literature on the need for small and medium-sized enterprises (SMEs) to be entrepreneurial, if they want to survive and grow (Martin & Javalgi, 2016; Lumpkin & Dess, 1996; Rauch et al., 2009; Wales et al., 2013). This entrepreneurial trend is referred to in academic literature as entrepreneurial orientation (EO). EO is closely related to the propensity to take advantage of business opportunities, which has a positive effect on firm performance (Yoon, 2012; Radipere, 2013). EO is defined by Lumpkin and Dess (1996) as "the processes, practices, and decision-making activities used by entrepreneurs that lead to the initiation of an entrepreneurial firm." EO is also viewed as the strategic processes, practices, and decisions that key decision-makers of business use to enact their firm's organizational purpose, sustain its vision, and create a competitive advantage (Bazile, 2012; Taylor, 2013; Wiklund & Shepherd, 2003). Mahmood and Hanafi (2013) mentioned that EO is an important factor for business success. Rauch et al. (2009) and Fatoki (2014) emphasize that EO is a significant component of business success and profitability. Also, Radipere (2013) and Van Geenhuizen et al. (2008) observed that EO is a source of competitive advantage and thus acts as a remedy to the problems facing businesses that desire to achieve a sustained competitive advantage. Furthermore, studies (e.g., Wiklund & Shepherd, 2005; Rauch et al., 2009) showed that businesses that have high EO are more willing to take a risk, more innovative, and highly proactive toward unexploited opportunities in the marketplace and opt for new mass of buyers and thus are better positioned to manage the impact of the macroeconomic shocks on their business activities.

Miller (1983) first conceptualized Entrepreneurial Orientation (EO) The concept of entrepreneurial orientation where he categorized EO using three dimensions (innovativeness, pro-activeness, and risk-taking). Miller elucidated that the three dimensions of EO act together to form a basic unidimensional strategic orientation and thus should be combined into a single scale in entrepreneurship research. Subsequent theorization by Lumpkin and Dess (1996) introduced two more formal dimensions (autonomy and competitive aggressiveness). These researchers believe that the EO dimensions can vary independently of each other and thus can be conceptualized as a multi-dimensional scale. Nonetheless, in spite of the huge opinion differences on the methodological and measurement issues of EO by researchers (Cassia & Minola, 2012; Covin & Wales, 2011; Tang et al., 2009; Hughes & Morgan, 2007) the EO construct proved to its reliability and validity (Runyan et al., 2012; Kreiser et al., 2002). For the purpose of this study, the five dimensions of EO – namely, innovativeness, pro-activeness, risk-taking, autonomy, and competitiveness as developed by Lumpkin and Dess (1996) will be used.

Entrepreneurship Orientation Dimensions

Innovativeness

Lumpkin and Dess (1996: 142) define innovativeness as the tendency of a business "to engage in and support new ideas, novelty, experimentation, and creative processes that may result in new products, services, or technological processes." Kropp et al. (2006) identify innovativeness as an important success factor for new businesses. Studies on the gender differences in innovation by De Vita et al. (2014) reveal that female entrepreneurs are less innovative than their male counterparts, thus less inclined to expand and export orientation. Research by Verheul et al. (2006) pointed out that while women entrepreneurs have a greater tendency to innovate on their products despite getting fewer growth expectations, male entrepreneurs, on the other hand, tend to focus on the development of new markets that can enhance the growth of their businesses. Furthermore, several studies (Masona et al., 2015; Soininen et al., 2012; Hameed & Ali, 2011) established a positive relationship between innovativeness and firms' performance.

Autonomy

Autonomy can be defined as an individual's independent aptitude to bring forth an idea or a vision and see it through to its completion. Callaghan and Venter (2011) view autonomy as the concept of free and independent action and decisions taken by the entrepreneur. Sexton and Bowman-Upton's (1990) study on female and male entrepreneurs reveal that female entrepreneur scored significantly higher on the traits related to autonomy than male entrepreneurs. Concerning performance, while Awang et al. (2009) found a positive relationship between autonomy and performance, other studies like Casillas and Moreno, 2010; Hughes and Morgan, 2007, fail to find any significant relationship between autonomy and performance.

Proactiveness

Proactiveness is an opportunity-seeking behavior that characterizes an entrepreneur's quest for pursuing and exploiting new business opportunities, such as introducing new products/services before competitors (Martin & Javalgi, 2013). Jalali et al. (2014) pointed out that proactive firms are innovative and thus can achieve a competitive advantage. Craig et al. (2014) observed that proactive businesses are usually far ahead of their competitors in identifying profitable opportunities and taking initiatives that enhance their businesses' performances. In addition, studies (Masona et al., 2015; Lumpkin & Dess, 2001) revealed a positive relationship between pro-activeness and firm performance. Concerning gender and pro-activeness, Tan (2008) established that women entrepreneurs are more proactive than men as they are more willing to take bolder decisions to move into risky and untried ventures when compared to their male counterparts.

Competitiveness

Competitiveness refers to how a business "relates to competitors and responds to trends and demand that already exist in the marketplace" (Lumpkin & Dess, 1996: 147). Schillo (2011) views competitive aggressiveness as a business way of engaging with its competitors. Studies on gender differences in competitiveness have mainly focused on the experiment. Shurchkov (2012) observed that women are significantly more likely to compete when task stereotypes and time constraints are absent but will be more often stay away from the competition if both sources of pressure are present. Furthermore, the nexus between competitiveness and a firm's performance seems to produce mixed results. Some studies (Masona et al., 2015; Le Roux & Bengesi, 2014) found a positive relationship between competitiveness and a firm's performance. In other studies, Casillas and Moreno (2010) fail to find any relationship.

Risk-Taking Propensity

Tang and Tang (2007) define risk-taking propensity as an individual's current inclination to take or avoid risks. Risk-taking is considered an essential part of entrepreneurship because an entrepreneur cannot know whether the desired product or service can be produced if it will meet the needs and expectations of potential customers; and whether it will generate profit. Risk-taking enhances the profitability of a business (Miller & Le Bruton-Miller, 2011). Jalali et al. (2014) believe that entrepreneurs partake in risk-taking activities when anticipating an expected return. In addition, Masona et al. (2015) found a positive relationship between risk-taking and performance. With regards to gender differences in terms of risk-taking, studies (Sexton & Bowman-Upton, 1990; Kepler & Shane, 2007; Wagner, 2007) established that there is a significant difference between men and women, with women being more risk-averse than men. The fear of failure, the low tolerance for uncertainty, and the ability to identify opportunities limits their abilities to start their businesses and thus account for the lower existence of female entrepreneurship (Minniti & Nardone, 2007). Conversely, Furdas and Kohn (2010) did not find any significant gender differences in the risk tolerance behavior of entrepreneurs in Germany. However, Tan (2008) found that women entrepreneurs participate in more risky ventures than their male counterparts.

The Relationship Between Gender and Entrepreneurial Orientation

Research on female entrepreneurs is increasing rapidly, but little academic literature focused on gender differences in entrepreneurs (Yordanova & Alexandrova-Boshnakova, 2010). This may be due to undersized conceptualization in the milieu of female entrepreneurship (Brindley, 2005). Johnson and Powell (1994) emphasized on the significance of differences between male and female entrepreneurial behavior on the success of businesses because of their entrepreneurial orientation in decision contexts. Gender differences in behavior might be caused by gender differences in entrepreneurial orientation preferences, but they might also be caused by situational factors such as options provided to females and the advice they receive. Empirical research in business and finance reveals that females and males differ in their entrepreneurial orientation. Numerous studies approached gender differences in the contexts of risk orientation (Jianakopolos & Bernasek, 1998; Williams & Narendran, 1999; Croson & Gneezy, 2009) which is for the most part a central dimension of entrepreneurial orientation. For instance, Powell and Ansic (1997) stated that females have less risk preferences than males.

Furthermore, Gustafson (1998) validated the thought discussed above by revealing females' and males' differences in risk perceptions both in qualitative and quantitative terms. The analysis of EO according to gender was not the subject of many studies. Indeed, few academic studies focused on the differences between the EO of women and men (Yordanova, Alexandrova-Boshnakova 2010). According to Ayub et al. (2013), research on woman entrepreneurs is increasing rapidly, but little is known about the gender differences between entrepreneurs. This can be due to a lack of conceptualization of the female entrepreneurship sphere (Brindley, 2005). Yet gender studies can enrich theoretical knowledge in the entrepreneurial field (Chasserio et al., 2016).

However, the five dimensions of entrepreneurship related to gender were studied by researchers in different studies, such as the disparity in risk preferences observed between women and men explains the differences in EO (Jianakopolos & Bernasek 1998; Williams & Narendran 1999; Croson & Gneezy 2009). Moreover, Fellnhofer et al. (2016) emphasize that gender inequalities are present in every organization and exist at various organizational levels. Thus, women and men evaluate their EO levels differently within the same organization (Wales et al. 2011).

Gender Theory and Entrepreneurship

Recently, advocates and scholars paid more attention to gender issues because of the growing correlation between gender and entrepreneurship success. In this sense, some authors have defined gender as socially constructed rules, relationships, and learned behaviors of males and women (Dejene, 2007). According to Orhan (2000), when gender theory and entrepreneurship are compared, two distinct gender frameworks—psychological and constructivism—emerge. According to constructivist scholars, the flexibility of entrepreneurship attracts entrepreneurs (especially women) more than the constraints of traditional employment. The psychological school of thinking contends that being an entrepreneur can be a lifestyle decision. Additionally, studies examined how discrimination against women affects their personal life and the growth of the national economy (DeMartino & Barbato, 2003). DeMartino and Barbato (2003) aimed to evaluate gender differences and how these differences could be used for entrepreneurship-based national development.

According to Fischer et al. (1993), looking at feminism through the lens of entrepreneurship reveals distinctions between male and female entrepreneurs. The socialization process and overt discrimination against women are the main causes of this discrepancy. Some scholars suggested relationships between entrepreneurial orientation and several other variables, including performance. Others have utilized entrepreneurial orientation as a moderating factor for variables such as business performance (Su et al., 2011), sales growth (Chaston & Sadler-Smith, 2012), and firm strategy growth (Moreno & Casillas, 2008). Some of this research identified several dimensions of entrepreneurial orientation were revealed in some of these studies.

Research Methodology

Research Approach

In the current study, we employ a descriptive research approach as we aim to describe, clarify and explain its inner relationships and properties (Huczynski & Buchana, 1991). Descriptive research will portray an accurate profile of people, events, or situations (Robson, 1993). Descriptive research in contrast with exploratory research defines questions, people surveyed, and the method of analysis prior to the beginning of data collection. In other words, descriptive research defines the research aspects, who, what, where, when, why and sometimes how of the research. Therefore, the study follows the descriptive approach to achieve the aim of the study (Yin, 1994), which was to examine the gender differences regarding entrepreneurial orientation dimensions.

To achieve the study's objective deductive method was adopted by using the survey as the primary tool for gathering data from the sample of male and female entrepreneurs that would help understand the differences between genders and other dimensions regarding entrepreneurial orientation in Palestine. The same will also assist in identifying what are the constraints that affect female entrepreneurs in launching their businesses. Therefore, the study adopted a quantitative approach for collecting and analysing the data gathered from the sample of the research population (Saunders, et al, 2009). For the purpose of the study, we took a purposive sample. The quantitative measures were made on a five-point Likert scale ranging from 1 (strongly disagree) to 5 (strongly agree).

Table 1. Adjustment mean scale

Low Degree	1.00-2.66
Middle Degree	2.67-3.66
High Degree	3.67-5.00

Data Collection

The primary data was collected through a closed-ended questionnaire via phone calls and personal meetings to fulfill the questionnaires and by communicating with the district's chambers of industry and commerce in West Bank to help identify a list of women and men entrepreneurs and support the fulfillment of the questionnaires. Closed-ended questions help to arrive at opinions about a product or service, and sometimes, about a company, in a more efficient manner (Saunders et al., 2009). We also employed open-ended questions. The questionnaires were distributed to over 75 entrepreneurs, and only 60 questionnaires were retrieved to be analysed statistically. Hence, the data collection process consisted of three steps. Where in the first step, the researcher had personal meetings with entrepreneurs. In the second step, questionnaires were fulfilled by phone. In the third step, the researcher communicated with the Industrial and Commercial Chambers around the west bank to make the process more official.

Data Analysis

The data collected through the closed-ended survey questionnaire were analysed through statistical tools including the percentages, the averages, and the standard deviations.

RESULTS

The study's findings can be divided into three sections. First, we will present the findings from the first research question. In addition, the main study hypothesis is tested in the second section. Finally, in the third section, we present the answer to the second research question.

Results of the First Research Question

Different statements were analysed under the question to determine the level of entrepreneurial dimension in males and females concerning risk-taking, innovativeness, competitiveness, proactivity, and autonomy. As shown in Table 2, the degree of entrepreneurial orientation in males is higher in innovativeness with (3.97 mean) than in females with (3.89 mean), this is could be because males encourage their employees to explore and develop new ideas. However, females are more innovative toward seeking new marketing methods whereas males seek out new ways that add value to the product/service. In a similar way, when it comes to risk-taking for males is higher with (3.92 mean) compared to female entrepreneurs where the mean is (3.7). Therefore, male entrepreneurs tend to be more risk-takers than female entrepreneurs.

The competitiveness means of both show that male entrepreneurs are more competitive with average means of (3.71) than females with average means of (3.51), as they adopt more aggressive competition tools toward their competitors. Moreover, the Proactivity dimension of males (3.69 mean) and females (3.56 mean) are similar in terms of monitoring the market trends and identifying the future needs of customers. On the other hand, female entrepreneurs have a higher mean of autonomy (3.83 mean) than males having a (3.68) mean implying that females prefer having the freedom toward anything necessary in their work and do not ask for help in making decisions. In total, the average mean for males of the entrepreneurial orientation (EO) is (3.79 mean) which is higher than for female entrepreneurs with an average mean (3.7). Given that, we can conclude that male entrepreneurs are more entrepreneurial-oriented than females but to a limited degree in the Arab world.

Table 2. Mean and standard deviation of male and female entrepreneurial orientation (EO)

Standard Deviation	Mean	Number	Gender	EO
0.59	3.97*	29	Male	Innovativeness
0.52	3.89	31	Female	Innovativeness
0.42	3.92*	29	Male	Risk Taking
0.39	3.70	31	Female	Risk Taking
0.57	3.71*	29	Male	Competitiveness
0.51	3.51	31	Female	Competitiveness
0.6	3.69*	29	Male	Proactivity
0.53	3.56	31	Female	Proactivity
0.46	3,68	31	Male	Autonomy
0.53	3.83*	29	Female	Autonomy
0.54	3.79*	29	Male	Total
0.35	3.70	31	Female	Total

Hypotheses Testing

Main hypothesis: There were no significant differences at α=0.05 of the level of the extent perceptions of entrepreneurial orientation (EO) of females' difference compared to those of their male counterparts.

We used a t-test to test hypotheses for the differences in the level of the extent perceptions of entrepreneurial orientation (EO) of female's difference compared to those of their male counterparts according to gender, as follows:

Table 3. The results of (T-test) for the differences in the level of the extent perceptions of entrepreneurial orientation (EO) of female's difference compared to those of their male counterparts

	Gender	Number	Mean	Std. Deviation	DF	T	Sig
Risk Taking	Male	29	3.92	0.42	58	1.993	0.051
	Female	31	3.70	0.39			
Innovativeness	Male	29	3.97	0.59	58	0.544	0.589
	Female	31	3.89	0.52			
Proactivity	Male	29	3.69	0.60	58	0.907	0.368
	Female	31	3.56	0.53			
Competitiveness	Male	29	3.71	0.57	58	1.449	0.153
	Female	31	3.51	0.51			
Autonomy	Male	29	3.68	0.53	58	-1.109	0.272
	Female	31	3.83	0.46			
Average value	Male	29	3.81	0.41	58	1.056	0.296
	Female	31	3.70	0.35			

The results of the analysis in the table above indicate that there were no significant differences at α=0.05 for the level of the extent perceptions of entrepreneurial orientation (EO) of females difference compared to those of their male counterparts according to the gender. This is the core objective of the study, when we can say from the results that there are no significant differences between male and female entrepreneurs in all dimensions in general, but there are differences in a number of dimensions. This means that the managerial and intellectual circumstances and environment for both genders encourage both genders toward adopting all dimensions and being an entrepreneur. We believe that both genders have the same opportunities toward adopting and applying the entrepreneurial dimensions, but with conservations related to females, in which they face some social and economic obstacles.

Results of the Second Research Question

The second research question is: what are the main constraints that affect female entrepreneurs launching their businesses in the Middle East?

Table 4. Mean and standard deviation for the questions of the study as ordered with their importance

	Statement	Mean	Std. Deviation	Degree
8	Traditions and customs prevalent in Palestine put a lot of restrictions on the women	3.94	1.09	High
9	Women in Palestine hack awareness about their potential	3.90	1.04	High
13	You obtain support from your spouse toward running your project	3.84	1.06	High
2	I have difficulties securing a fund for my business	3.77	0.66	High
11	I face a lot of competition from men	3.68	0.87	High
10	Society is dominated by males	3.65	0.91	Middle
5	Balancing between business and family life is difficult.	3.58	0.95	Middle
3	I always struggle to be taken seriously	3.58	1.05	Middle
1	I face social obstacles as a woman entrepreneur	3.55	1.12	Middle
12	Women are easily cheated in the market	3.16	1.00	Middle
4	It is hard for me to build an extensive and supportive network	3.03	1.01	Middle
7	I suffer from a negative view of the society	2.94	1.23	Middle
6	I don't have enough support from the family	2.81	1.35	Middle
	Average	3.49	0.54	Middle

Table 4 indicates that the traditions and customs prevalent in Palestine form the most critical restrictions among females toward being entrepreneurs. Also, women in Palestine lack awareness of their competencies. Moreover, married women in Palestine, are the most supported by their husbands, but they face a lot of competition from men, this is related to the Eastern community which prevents women from doing all things that men can do, such as work, and innovativeness. But at the same time, the Palestinian community created an environment for women with the ability to achieve their objectives, the same as men. This reflects in the middle average and degree sentence, in which the women do not have enough support from their families.

Furthermore, we posed an open question to female entrepreneurs: "what are the main constraints you faced when you started your business as a woman?". When starting their businesses, all women entrepreneurs who responded to this question faced a variety of challenges, some related to society and others to managerial, financial, and other issues, as follows:

Table 5. Main obstacles faced by women toward being entrepreneurs

Number	Statement	Number of responses	Valid percent
1	Lack of funds.	16	18.6
2	Society's perception of the woman.	10	11.6
3	Legislation obstacles	9	10.4
4	Inequity between both genders.	7	8.1
5	Adaptation between family and work.	7	8.1
6	The masculinity of the society.	5	5.8
7	Administrative Obstacles	4	4.6
8	Traditions of the society	3	3.5
9	Family objection toward woman's work.	3	3.4
10	Woman's perception of herself	2	2.3

Table 5 indicates the most critical obstacles among females, which are society's perception of women; however, the other two barriers faced by both women and men together toward being entrepreneurs are lack of funds and legislation obstacles such as registration. These obstacles ensure that women and men also fail to be an entrepreneur. Palestine has many points of failure in laws that prohibit women from registering and doing all legislative issues, while men are not. Indeed, it is worth mentioning that the Palestinian and Arabian communities are the main obstacle against women, with old traditions and thoughts regarding women who must stay at home to care for children, which is not acceptable in the contemporary world.

DISCUSSION

The findings of the questionnaire showed that there is a difference in risk-taking, innovativeness, and competitiveness entrepreneurial dimension between male and female entrepreneurs. Risk-taking is identified in the literature as one of the most important attributes of entrepreneurs. Risk-taking attribute mainly leads to business success. The findings of the study are similar to the finding of the literature where Tsyganova and Shirokova (2010) indicated that due to the male gender attribute, male entrepreneurs are more risk-taking than females. Dana (2000) argued that female entrepreneurs are less likely to take risks. However, findings related to innovation are different from the literature as Brush et al. (2009) identified that female entrepreneurs are more innovative than male. Innovation is one of the key determinants of a successful enterprise. An entrepreneur should be able to encourage and adopt innovative ideas in order to improve business performance and gain market share in the industry.

As far as competitiveness is concerned, literature such as Dana (2000) found that male and female entrepreneurs both can be equally competitive. Competitiveness is another important attribute of the entrepreneur because competitiveness boosts innovation in identifying the consumers' needs and fulfilling them accordingly. The current study found that both male and female entrepreneurs are competitive in their own sphere thereby they both possess competitiveness attributes.

Autonomy is also important for effective entrepreneurship because it helps in making them work according to their own goals, values, tastes, and beliefs. The current study findings show that females are more autonomous than male entrepreneurs, as female entrepreneurs enjoy freedom in decision-making whereas male entrepreneurs like to consult other employees. Tsyganova and Shirokova (2010) identified that autonomy can be effective in entrepreneurship to some extent only. However, too much autonomy can be risky for the success of the enterprise.

Moreover, the findings of the study showed that the managerial and intellectual circumstances and environment for both genders encourage both genders toward adopting all dimensions and being an entrepreneur. It implies that both genders have the same opportunities toward adopting and applying the entrepreneurial dimensions, but with conservations related to females, in which they face some social and economic obstacles. These findings are similar to the findings of Brush et al. (2009) that found that male and female managerial circumstances determine how both genders adopt entrepreneur attributes. Male entrepreneurs, although, are likely to have more entrepreneurial attributes, and female entrepreneurs share the same level of attributes in risk-taking, proactive approach, autonomy, competitiveness, and innovativeness regardless of age and gender difference.

FUTURE RESEARCH DIRECTIONS AND CONCLUSION

The primary purpose of the current study is to explore and describe whether and to what extent there are gender differences across the EO dimensions (risk-taking, innovativeness, proactiveness, competitiveness, and autonomy). Therefore, the central research question is, "to what extent do perceptions of entrepreneurial orientation (EO) of females differ from those of their male counterparts in the middle east?" To achieve this goal, we employed a descriptive quantitative research design where 60 male and female entrepreneurs in Palestine were surveyed through a closed-ended questionnaire. The study findings indicate that males are more entrepreneurial-oriented than females but to a relatively small extent. Moreover, the results showed that male entrepreneurs have a higher mean in risk-taking, competitiveness, and innovativeness, whereas females have a higher mean in proactiveness and autonomy.

The second research question is, "what are the main constraints that affect female entrepreneurs launching their businesses in the Middle East? Findings indicate that the traditions and customs prevalent in Palestine form the most critical restrictions among females toward being entrepreneurs. Moreover, the results indicate that essential obstacles among females are society's perception toward women, lack of funds, and legislation obstacles such as registration.

Both male and female entrepreneurs have low levels of innovativeness, competitive aggressiveness, and proactiveness, indicating the importance of developing these competencies among Middle Eastern entrepreneurs because these EO dimensions can significantly improve the performance of their businesses. Furthermore, entrepreneurs and managers can improve their businesses' overall EO posture by empowering their employees to act entrepreneurially through entrepreneurial skill development. Furthermore, risk-taking and proactiveness are widely recognized for influencing business performance and growth. However, this study found significant gender differences in these two factors, with men being risk-takers and females being more proactive. As a result, they are forming gender-balanced partnerships that will allow business owners and managers to have optimal levels of both factors to improve their company's performance and growth.

Based on the conclusion, it is recommended that the governments, decision-makers, and politicians in developing countries, particularly Palestine, work on updating the laws toward giving women more rights in the social and economic aspects of life. It is also important to engage both women and men in entrepreneurial education to develop the right abilities, skills, and competencies critical for women to make vital contributions through entrepreneurial ventures. More attention should be paid to women's economic and social empowerment to change the community's perspectives against women. The current study also recommends that women should be promoted as entrepreneurs. It should also be ensured that women have access to education at all levels. Dedicated women's business centers should be developed, offering essential business information, networks, knowledge sharing, training, and mentoring.

The study also recommends allocating programs that support women's entrepreneurship to encourage more women to become entrepreneurs and change the gendered entrepreneurship discourse. Such programs are critical for women to achieve their personal and economic goals (Marlow & Patton, 2005). According to Hanson (2009), a greater emphasis on empowering women entrepreneurs within support programs will enable women to challenge gender structures. Women entrepreneurs must network more to become more successful, establishing that women, not structures, must change (Hughes et al., 2012). However, governments of emerging economies, policymakers, and international donor organizations embraced entrepreneurship as a strategic tool for economic growth and social advancement (Al-Dajani et al., 2015). Therefore, they should support women entrepreneurs, especially in emerging and developing economies, and they should believe that women are good at entrepreneurship and that entrepreneurship is good for women.

The gendered experiences of women entrepreneurs and the effects on their enterprises in various country contexts, particularly in developing countries, both during and after COVID-19, may thus be explored in future research using qualitative methodologies. We would also encourage such research to undertake longitudinal analyses to explore these impacts and uncover women's creative responses to business recovery.

REFERENCES

Ahl, H. (2004). *The Scientific Reproduction of Gender Inequality; A Discourse Analysis of Research Texts on Women's Entrepreneurship*. Copenhagen Business School Press.

Ahl, H. (2006). Why research on women entrepreneurs needs new directions. *Entrepreneurship, 30*, 595–621.

Al-Dajani, H., Carter, S., Shaw, E., & Marlow, S. (2015). Entrepreneurship among the Displaced and Dispossessed: Exploring the Limits of Emancipatory Entrepreneuring. *British Journal of Management, 26*(4), 713–730. doi:10.1111/1467-8551.12119

Al-Dajani, H., & Marlow, S. (2013). Empowerment and entrepreneurship: A theoretical framework. *International Journal of Entrepreneurial Behaviour & Research, 19*(5), 503–524. doi:10.1108/IJEBR-10-2011-0138

Awang, A., Khalid, S. A., Kassim, K. M., Ismail, M., Zain, R. S., & Madar, A. R. S. (2009). Entrepreneurial orientation and performance relations of Malaysian Bumiputera SMEs: The impact of some perceived environmental factors. *International Journal of Business and Management*, *4*(9), 84–94. doi:10.5539/ijbm.v4n9p84

Ayogu, D. U., & Agu, E. O. (2015). Assessment of the contribution of women entrepreneur towards entrepreneurship development in Nigeria. *International Journal of Current Research and Academic Review*, *3*, 190–207.

Ayub, A., Razzaq, A., Aslam, S. M., & Iftekhar, H. (2013). Gender effects on entrepreneurial orientation and value innovation: Evidence from Pakistan. *European Journal of Business and Social Sciences*, *2*(1), 82–90.

Bahmani-Oskooee, M., Kutan, M. A., & Xi, D. (2013). The impact of economic and monetary uncertainty on the demand for money in emerging economies. *Applied Economics*, *45*(23), 3278–3287. doi :10.1080/00036846.2012.705430

Bardasi, E., Sabarwal, S., & Terrel, K. (2011). How do female entrepreneurs perform? Evidence from three developing regions. *Small Business Economics*, *37*(4), 417–441. doi:10.100711187-011-9374-z

Basile, A. (2012). Entrepreneurial orientation in SMEs: Risk taking to enter international markets. *Far East Journal of Psychology and Business*, *7*(2), 1–21.

Boyd, G. G. D. (2016). The girl effect: A neoliberal instrumentalization of gender equality. *Consilience*, *15*, 46–180.

Boyd, R. L. (2005). Race, gender, and survival entrepreneurship in large northern cities during the Great Depression. *Journal of Socio-Economics*, *34*(3), 331–339. doi:10.1016/j.socec.2004.09.018

Braches, B., & Elliott, C. (2016). Articulating the entrepreneurship career: A study of German women entrepreneurs. *International Small Business Journal*, *35*(5), 535–557. doi:10.1177/0266242616651921

Brindley, C. (2005). Barriers to women achieving their entrepreneurial potential: Woman and risk. *International Journal of Entrepreneurial Behaviour & Research*, *11*(2), 144–161. doi:10.1108/13552550510590554

Bruni, A., Gherardi, S., & Poggio, B. (2004). Doing gender, doing entrepreneurship: An ethnographic account of intertwined practices. *Gender, Work and Organization*, *11*(4), 406–429. doi:10.1111/j.1468-0432.2004.00240.x

Brush, C., Carter, N. M., Gatewood, E. J., Greene, P. G., & Hart, M. M. (2006). *Women and Entrepreneurship: Contemporary Classics*. Edward Elgar.

Brush, C., de Bruin, A., & Welter, F. (2009). A gender-aware framework for women's entrepreneurship. *International Journal of Gender and Entrepreneurship*, *1*(1), 8–24. doi:10.1108/17566260910942318

Bruton, G. D., Ketchen, D. J. Jr, & Ireland, R. D. (2013). Entrepreneurship as a solution to poverty. *Journal of Business Venturing*, *28*(6), 683–689. doi:10.1016/j.jbusvent.2013.05.002

Bui, H. T. M., Kuan, A., & Chu, T. T. (2018). Female entrepreneurship in patriarchal society: Motivation and challenges. *Journal of Small Business and Entrepreneurship*, *30*(4), 325–343. doi:10.1080/08276331.2018.1435841

Cardella, G. M., Hernandez-Sanchez, B. R., & Sanchez-Garcıa, J. C. (2020). *Women entrepreneurship: a systematic review to outline the boundaries of scientific literature* (Vol. 11). Frontiers in Psychology Frontiers Media S.A.

Carter, S., Mwaura, S., Ram, M., Trehan, K., & Jones, T. (2015). Barriers to ethnic minority and women's enterprise: Existing evidence, policy tensions and unsettled questions. *International Small Business Journal*, *33*(1), 49–69. doi:10.1177/0266242614556823

Casillas, J. C., & Moreno, A. M. (2010). The relationship between entrepreneurial orientation and growth: The moderating role of family involvement. *Entrepreneurship and Regional Development*, *22*(3-4), 265–291. doi:10.1080/08985621003726135

Cassia, L., & Minola, T. (2012). Hyper-growth of SMEs: Toward a reconciliation of entrepreneurial orientation and strategic resources. *International Journal of Entrepreneurial Behaviour & Research*, *18*(2), 179–197. doi:10.1108/13552551211204210

Chasserio, S., Poroli, C., & Redien-Collot, R. (2016). French women entrepreneurs' leadership practices and well-being in a high-growth context. In M. L. Connerley & J. Wu (Eds.), *Handbook on well-being of working women* (pp. 243–260). doi:10.1007/978-94-017-9897-6_15

Chaston, I., & Sadler-Smith, E. (2012). Entrepreneurial cognition, entrepreneurial orientation and firm capability in the creative industries. *British Journal of Management*, *23*(3), 415–432.

Coduras, A., & Autio, E. (2013). Comparing subjective and objective indicators to describe the national entrepreneurial context: The global entrepreneurship monitor and the global competitiveness index contributions. *Investig. Regionales*, *26*, 47–74.

Covin, J. G., & Wales, W. J. (2011). The measurement of entrepreneurial orientation. *Entrepreneurship Theory and Practice*, *1*(1), 1–26.

Craig, J. B., Dibrell, C., & Garrett, R. (2014). Examining relationships among family influence, family culture, flexible planning systems, innovativeness and firm performance. *Journal of Family Business Strategy*, *5*(3), 229–238. doi:10.1016/j.jfbs.2013.09.002

Croson, R., & Gneezy, U. (2009). Gender differences in preferences. *Journal of Economic Literature*, *47*(2), 448–474. doi:10.1257/jel.47.2.448

Dana, L. P. (2000). *Economies of the Eastern Mediterranean Region: economic miracles in the making*. World Scientific. doi:10.1142/4567

Dechant, K., & Lamky, A. A. (2005). Towards an understanding of Arab women entrepreneurs in Bahrain and Oman. *Journal of Developmental Entrepreneurship*, *10*(2), 123–140. doi:10.1142/S1084946705000100

Dejene, Y. (2007). Promoting women's economic empowerment in Africa. *Proceedings of the Singapore Economic Review Conference*, 1-20.

DeMartino, R., & Barbato, R. (2003). Differences between women and men MBA entrepreneurs: Exploring family flexibility and wealth creation as career motivators. *Journal of Business Venturing*, *18*(6), 815–832. doi:10.1016/S0883-9026(03)00003-X

Elam, A. B., Brush, C. G., Greene, P. G., Baumer, B., Dean, M., & Heavlow, R. (2019). *Global Entrepreneurship Monitor 2018/2019 Women's Entrepreneurship Report*. Babson College: Smith College and the Global Entrepreneurship Research Association.

Fatoki, O. O. (2014). The Entrepreneurial Orientation of Micro Enterprises in the Retail Sector in South Africa. *Journal of Sociology and Social Anthropology*, *5*(2), 125–129. doi:10.1080/09766634.2014.11885616

Fellnhofer, K., Puumalainen, K., & Sjögrén, H. (2016). Entrepreneurial orientation and performance – are sexes equal? *International Journal of Entrepreneurial Behaviour & Research*, *22*(3), 346–374. doi:10.1108/IJEBR-12-2015-0286

Fischer, E., Reuben, R. A., & Dyke, L. S. (1993). A theoretical overview and extension of research on sex, gender, and entrepreneurship. *The Journal of Business*, 8151–8168.

Furdas, M., & Kohn, K. (2010). What's the Difference?! Gender, Personality, and the Propensity to Start a Business. *IZA Discussion Paper No. 4778.*

Ghouse, S. M., McElwee, G., & Durrah, O. (2019). Entrepreneurial success of cottage-based women entrepreneurs in Oman. *International Journal of Entrepreneurial Behaviour & Research*, *25*(3), 480–498. doi:10.1108/IJEBR-10-2018-0691

Gustafson, P. E. (1998). Gender differences in risk perception: Theoretical and methodological perspectives. *Risk Analysis*, *18*(6), 805–811. doi:10.1023/B:RIAN.0000005926.03250.c0 PMID:9972583

Haber, S., & Reichel, A. (2007). The cumulative nature of the entrepreneurial process: The contribution of human capital, planning and environmental resources to small venture performance. *Journal of Business Venturing*, *22*(1), 119–145. doi:10.1016/j.jbusvent.2005.09.005

Halkias, D., Nwajiuba, C., Harkiolakis, N., & Caracatsanis, S. M. (2011). Challenges facing women entrepreneurs in Nigeria. *Management Research Review*, *34*(2), 221–235. doi:10.1108/01409171111102821

Hameed, I., & Ali, B. (2011). Impact of Entrepreneurial Orientation, Entrepreneurial Management and Environmental Dynamism on Firm's Financial Performance. *Journal of Economics and Behavioral Studies*, *3*(2), 101–114. doi:10.22610/jebs.v3i2.260

Hanson, S. (2009). Changing Places through Women's Entrepreneurship. *Economic Geography*, *85*(3), 245–267. doi:10.1111/j.1944-8287.2009.01033.x

Hattab, H. (2012). Towards understanding female entrepreneurship in Middle Eastern and North African countries. *Education, Business and Society*, *5*(3), 171–186. doi:10.1108/17537981211265561

Hechevarría, D., Bullough, A., Brush, C., & Edelman, L. (2019). High-growth women's entrepreneurship: Fueling social and economic development. *Journal of Small Business Management*, *57*(1), 5–13. doi:10.1111/jsbm.12503

Henry, C., Foss, L., & Ahl, H. (2016). Gender and entrepreneurship research: A review of methodological approaches. *International Small Business Journal, 34*(3), 217–241. doi:10.1177/0266242614549779

Hisrich, R. D., & Ayse Öztürk, S. (1999). Women entrepreneurs in a developing economy. *Journal of Management Development, 18*(2), 114–124. doi:10.1108/02621719910257639

Hofstede, G. (1994). The business of international business *is culture. International Business Review, 3*(1), 1–14. doi:10.1016/0969-5931(94)90011-6

Hofstede, G. (2001). *Culture's Consequences: Comparing Values, Behaviors, Institutions and Organizations across Nations* (2nd ed.). Sage.

Huczynski, A., & Buchanan, D. (1991). *Organizational Behavior*. Prentice-Hall.

Hughes, K. D., Jennings, J. E., Brush, C., Carter, S., & Welter, F. (2012). Extending Women's Entrepreneurship Research in New Directions. *Entrepreneurship Theory and Practice, 36*(3), 429–442. doi:10.1111/j.1540-6520.2012.00504.x

Hughes, M., & Morgan, R. E. (2007). Deconstructing the relationship between entrepreneurial orientation and business performance at the embryonic stage of firm growth. *Industrial Marketing Management, 36*(5), 651–661. doi:10.1016/j.indmarman.2006.04.003

Jalali, A., Jaafar, M., & Ramayah, T. (2014). Entrepreneurial orientation and performance: The interaction effect of customer capital. *World Journal of Entrepreneurship, Management and Sustainable Development, 10*(1), 48–68. doi:10.1108/WJEMSD-05-2013-0030

Jamali, D. (2009). Constraints and opportunities facing women entrepreneurs in developing countries: A relational perspective. *Gender in Management, 24*(4), 232–251. doi:10.1108/17542410910961532

Jianakoplos, N. A., & Bernasek, A. (1998). Are women more risk averse? *Economic Inquiry, 36*(4), 620–630. doi:10.1111/j.1465-7295.1998.tb01740.x

Johnson, J. E. V., & Powell, P. L. (1994). Decision Making, Risk and Gender: Are Managers Different? *British Journal of Management, 5*(2), 123–138. doi:10.1111/j.1467-8551.1994.tb00073.x

Kelley, D. J., Baumer, B. S., Brush, C., Greene, P. G., Mahdavi, M., Majbouri, M., & Heavlow, R. (2017). *Women's entrepreneurship 2016/2017 report.* Global Entrepreneurship Research Association.

Kepler, E., & Shane, S. (2007). *Are male and female entrepreneurs really that different?* US Small Business Administration.

Kim, J. C., Watts, C. H., Hargreaves, J. R., Ndhlovu, L. X., Phetla, G., Morison, L. A., Busza, J., Porter, J. D. H., & Pronyk, P. (2007). Understanding the impact of a microfinance-based intervention on women's empowerment and the reduction of intimate partner violence in South Africa. *American Journal of Public Health, 97*(10), 1794–1802. doi:10.2105/AJPH.2006.095521 PMID:17761566

Kreiser, P., Marino, L., & Weaver, K. (2002). Assessing the psychometric properties of the entrepreneurial scale: A multi-country analysis. *Entrepreneurship Theory and Practice, 26*(4), 71–92. doi:10.1177/104225870202600405

Kropp, F., Lindsay, N., & Shoham, A. (2006). Entrepreneurial, market, and learning orientations and international entrepreneurial business venture performance in South African firms. *International Marketing Review*, *23*(5), 504–523. doi:10.1108/02651330610703427

Langowitz, N., & Minniti, M. (2007). The entrepreneurial propensity of women. *Entrepreneurship*, *31*, 341–364.

Langowitz, N., & Morgan, C. (2003). Women entrepreneurs: breaking through the glass barrier. In J. Butler (Ed.), *New Perspectives on Women Entrepreneurs* (pp. 101–119). Information Age Publishing.

Le Roux, I., & Bengesi, M. K. (2014). Dimensions of entrepreneurial orientation and small and medium enterprise performance in emerging economies. *Development Southern Africa*, *31*(4), 606–624. doi:10.1080/0376835X.2014.913474

Lerner, M., & Malach-Pines, A. (2011). Gender and culture in family business: A ten-nation study. *International Journal of Cross Cultural Management*, *11*(2), 11. doi:10.1177/1470595811399190

Lumpkin, G. T., & Dess, G. G. (1996). Clarifying the entrepreneurial orientation construct and linking it to performance. *Academy of Management Review*, *21*(1), 135–172. doi:10.2307/258632

Lumpkin, G. T., & Dess, G. G. (2001). Linking two dimensions of entrepreneurial orientation to firm performance: The moderating role of environment and industry life cycle. *Journal of Business Venturing*, *16*(5), 429–451. doi:10.1016/S0883-9026(00)00048-3

Maden, C. (2015). A gendered lens on entrepreneurship: women entrepreneurship in Turkey. *Gender in Management: An International Journal*, *30*(4), 312-331.

Mahmood, R., & Hanafi, N. (2013). Entrepreneurial Orientation and Business Performance of Women-Owned Small and Medium Enterprises in Malaysia: Competitive Advantage as a Mediator. *International Journal of Business and Social Science*, *4*(1), 82–90.

Marlow, S., & McAdam, M. (2013). Gender and entrepreneurship: Advancing debate and challenging myths – exploring the mystery of the under-performing female entrepreneurship. *International Journal of Entrepreneurial Behaviour & Research*, *19*(1), 114–124. doi:10.1108/13552551311299288

Marlow, S., & Patton, D. (2005). All Credit to Men? Entrepreneurship, Finance, and Gender. *Entrepreneurship Theory and Practice*, *29*(6), 717–735. doi:10.1111/j.1540-6520.2005.00105.x

Martin, S., & Javalgi, R. (2016). Entrepreneurial orientation, marketing capabilities and performance: The Moderating role of Competitive Intensity on Latin American International New Venture. *Journal of Business Research*, *69*(6), 2040–2051. doi:10.1016/j.jbusres.2015.10.149

Masona, C. M. (2015). Understanding the impact of entrepreneurial orientation on SMEs' Performance. The role of the financing structure. *Procedia Economics and Finance*, *23*, 1649–1661. doi:10.1016/S2212-5671(15)00470-0

Miller, D. (1983). The correlates of entrepreneurship in three types of firms. *Management Science*, *29*(7), 770–791. doi:10.1287/mnsc.29.7.770

Miller, D., & Breton-Miller, I. L. (2011). Governance, Social Identity, and Entrepreneurial Orientation in Closely public Companies. *Entrepreneurship Theory and Practice*, *35*(5), 873–894. doi:10.1111/j.1540-6520.2011.00457.x

Minniti, M., & Nardone, C. (2007). Being in Someone Else's Shoes: Gender and Nascent Entrepreneurship. *Small Business Economics Journal*, *28*(2-3), 223–239. doi:10.100711187-006-9017-y

Mohsen, D. (2007), —Arab women entrepreneurs and SMEs: Challenges and realities. *Masress*. https://www.masress.com/en/dailynews/109630

Moreno, A. M., & Casillas, J. C. (2008). Entrepreneurial orientation and growth of SMEs: A causal model. *Entrepreneurship Theory and Practice*, *32*(3), 507–528. doi:10.1111/j.1540-6520.2008.00238.x

Naguib, R. & Jamali, D. (2015). Female entrepreneurship in the UAE: a multi-level integrative lens. *Gender in Management: An International Journal*, *30*(2), 135-161.

Noguera, M., Álvarez, C., & Urbano, D. (2013). Socio-cultural factors and female entrepreneurship. *The International Entrepreneurship and Management Journal*, *9*(2), 183–198. doi:10.100711365-013-0251-x

Orhan, M. (2000). A new model for analysing female entrepreneurship. *Proc. Int. Conf. Small Bus.* (http://www.sbaer.uca.edu/Research/2000/ICSB/index.html

Panda, S. (2018). Constraints faced by women entrepreneurs in developing countries: Review and ranking. *Gender in Management*, *33*(4), 315–331. doi:10.1108/GM-01-2017-0003

Panda, S. & Dash, S. (2014). Constraints faced by entrepreneurs in developing countries: a review and assessment. *World Review of Entrepreneurship, Management and Sustainable Development*, *10*(4), 405-421.

Panda, S. & Dash, S. (2016). Exploring the venture capitalist–entrepreneur relationship: evidence from India. *Journal of Small Business and Enterprise Development*, *23*(1), 64-89.

Pines, A. M. (2002). The female entrepreneur: Burnout treated using a psychodynamic existential approach. *Clinical Case Studies*, *1*(2), 171–181. doi:10.1177/1534650102001002005

Pines, A. M., & Schwartz, D. (2008). Now you see them, now you don't: Gender differences in entrepreneurship. *Journal of Managerial Psychology*, *23*(7), 811–832. doi:10.1108/02683940810896358

Powell, G. N., & Eddleston, K. A. (2013). Linking family-to-business enrichment and support to entrepreneurial success: Do female and male entrepreneurs experience different outcomes? *Journal of Business Venturing*, *28*(2), 261–280. doi:10.1016/j.jbusvent.2012.02.007

Powell, M., & Ansic, D. (1997). Gender Differences in Risk Behaviour in Financial Decision-Making: An Experimental Analysis. *Journal of Economic Psychology*, *18*(6), 605–628. doi:10.1016/S0167-4870(97)00026-3

Quaye, D., Acheampong, G., & Asiedu, M. (2015). Gender differences in entrepreneurial orientation: Evidence from Ghana. *European Journal of Business and Management*, *7*(12), 128–140.

Radipere, N. S. (2013). *Analysis of local and immigrant entrepreneurship in the South African small enterprise sector (Gauteng province)*. [Thesis, University of South Africa, Pretoria].

Rae, D. (2015). *Opportunity-Centred Entrepreneurship*. Palgrave McMillan. doi:10.1007/978-1-137-47410-0

Ramadani, V., Hisrich, R.D., & Gërguri-Rashiti, S. (2015). Female entrepreneurs in transition economies: insights from Albania, Macedonia and Kosovo. *World Review of Entrepreneurship, Management and Sustainable Development, 11*(4), 391-413.

Rauch, A., Wiklund, J., Lumpkin, G. T., & Frese, M. (2009). Entrepreneurial orientation and business performance: An assessment of past research and suggestions for the future. *Entrepreneurship Theory and Practice, 33*(3), 761–787. doi:10.1111/j.1540-6520.2009.00308.x

Robson, P. (1993). The New Regionalism and the Developing Countries. *Journal of Common Market Studies, 31*(3), 329–348. doi:10.1111/j.1468-5965.1993.tb00467.x

Runyan, R., Ge, B., Dong, B., & Swinney, J. (2012). Entrepreneurial orientation in cross-cultural research: Assessing measurement invariance in the construct. *Entrepreneurship Theory and Practice, 36*(4), 819–836. doi:10.1111/j.1540-6520.2010.00436.x

Saunders, M., Lewis, P., & Thornhill, A. (2009). *Research Methods for Business Students* (5th ed.). Pearson Education.

Schillo, S. (2011). Entrepreneurial Orientation and Company Performance: Can the Academic Literature Guide Managers? *Technology Innovation Management Review, 20*(2), 20–25. doi:10.22215/timreview/497

Schumpeter, J. A. (1954). History of economic analysis. Oxford University Press.

Sexton, L. D., & Bowman-Upton, N. (1990). Female and male entrepreneurs: Psychological characteristics and their role in gender related. *Journal of Business Venturing, 5*(1), 29–36. doi:10.1016/0883-9026(90)90024-N

Shane, S., & Venkataraman, S. (2000). Entrepreneurship as a field of research: The promise of entrepreneurship as a field of research. *Academy of Management Review, 26*(1), 13–17. doi:10.5465/amr.2001.27879269

Shinnar, R. S., Giacomin, O., & Janssen, F. (2012). Entrepreneurial perceptions and intentions: The role of gender and culture. *Entrepreneurship Theory and Practice, 36*(3), 465–493. doi:10.1111/j.1540-6520.2012.00509.x

Shurchkov, O. (2012). New Elites and Their Influence on Entrepreneurial Activity in Russia. *Journal of Comparative Economics, 40*(2), 240–255. doi:10.1016/j.jce.2011.12.003

Soininen, J., Puumalainen, K., Sjögrén, H., & Syrjä, P. (2012). The impact of global economic crisis on SMEs: Does entrepreneurial orientation matter? *Management Research Review, 35*(10), 927–944. doi:10.1108/01409171211272660

Sorgner, A., Bode, E., & Krieger-Boden, C. (2017). *Women20 Study. The Effects of Digitalization on the Gender Equality in the G20 Economies*. Kiel Institute for the World Economy.

Su, Z., Xie, E., & Li, Y. (2011). Entrepreneurial Orientation and Firm Performance in New Ventures and Established Firms. *Journal of Small Business Management*, *49*(4), 558–577. doi:10.1111/j.1540-627X.2011.00336.x

Sullivan, D. M., & Meek, W. R. (2012). Gender and entrepreneurship: A review and process model. *Journal of Managerial Psychology*, *27*(5), 428–458. doi:10.1108/02683941211235373

Sultan, S. S. (2016). Women entrepreneurship working in a conflict region: The case of Palestine. *World Review of Entrepreneurship, Management and Sustainable Development*, *12*(2–3), 149–156. doi:10.1504/WREMSD.2016.074970

Tan, J. (2008). Breaking the 'bamboo curtain' and the 'glass ceiling': The experience of women entrepreneurs in high-tech industries in an emerging market. *Journal of Business Ethics*, *80*(3), 547–564. doi:10.100710551-007-9454-9

Tang, J., & Tang, Z. (2007). The relationship of achievement motivation and risk-taking propensity to new venture performance: A test of the moderating effect of entrepreneurial munificence. *International Journal of Entrepreneurship and Small Business*, *4*(4), 450–472. doi:10.1504/IJESB.2007.013691

Tang, Z., Kreiser, P. M., Marino, L., Dickson, P., & Weaver, K. M. (2009). A Hierarchical Perspective of the Dimensions of Entrepreneurial Orientation. *The International Entrepreneurship and Management Journal*, *5*(2), 181–201. doi:10.100711365-008-0097-9

Taylor, P. (2013). The effect of entrepreneurial orientation on the internationalization of SMEs in developing countries. *African Journal of Business Management*, *7*(19), 1927-1937.

Tlaiss, H. A. (2014). Women's entrepreneurship, barriers and culture: Insights from the United Arab Emirates. *The Journal of Entrepreneurship*, *23*(2), 289–320. doi:10.1177/0971355714535307

Tsyganova, T., & Shirokova, G. (2010). Gender differences in entrepreneurship: Evidence from gem data. *Organizations and Markets in Emerging Economies*, *1*(1), 120–141. doi:10.15388/omee.2010.1.1.14309

Van Gelderen, M., Brand, M., van Praag, M., Bodewes, W., Poutsma, E., & Van Gils, A. (2008). Explaining entrepreneurial intentions by means of the theory of planned behaviour. *Career Development International*, *13*(6), 538–559. doi:10.1108/13620430810901688

Verheul, I., Stel, A.V. and Thurik, R. (2006). Explaining female and male entrepreneurship at the country level. *Entrepreneurship and Regional Development*, *18*(2), 151-183.

Wagner, J. (2007). What a Difference a Y Makes – Female and Male Nascent Entrepreneurs in Germany. *Small Business Economics*, *28*(1), 1–21. doi:10.100711187-005-0259-x

Wales, W., Monsen, E., & McKelvie, A. (2011). The organizational pervasiveness of entrepreneurial orientation. *Entrepreneurship Theory and Practice*, *35*(5), 895–923. doi:10.1111/j.1540-6520.2011.00451.x

Wales, W. J., Gupta, V. K., & Mousa, F. T. (2013). Empirical research on entrepreneurial orientation: An assessment and suggestions for future research. *International Small Business Journal*, *31*(4), 357–383. doi:10.1177/0266242611418261

Wiklund, J., & Shepherd, D. (2003). Knowledge-based resources, entrepreneurial orientation, and the performance of small and medium sized businesses. *Strategic Management Journal, 24*(13), 1307–1314. doi:10.1002mj.360

Wiklund, J., & Shepherd, D. (2005). Entrepreneurial orientation and small business performance: A configurational approach. *Journal of Business Venturing, 20*(1), 71–91. doi:10.1016/j.jbusvent.2004.01.001

Williams, S., & Narendan, S. (1999). Determinants of managerial risk: Exploring personality and cultural influences. *The Journal of Social Psychology, 139*(1), 102–125. doi:10.1080/00224549909598365

World Economic Forum. (2011). *Accelerating entrepreneurship in the Arab world.* WEF. www3.weforum.org/docs/WEF_YGL_Accelerating Entrepreneurship Arab World_Report_2011.pdf (accessed 24 December 2012).

Yin, R. K. (1994). *Case study research: Design and methods* (2nd ed.). Sage Publications.

Yoon, H. (2012). The Performance Effects of Entrepreneurial Orientation: Evidence from South Korean Start-ups. *International Journal of Arts and Commerce, 1*(4), 248–254.

Yordanova, D. I., & Alexandrova-Boshnakova, M. I. (2011). Gender effects on risk-taking of entrepreneurs: Evidence from Bulgaria. *International Journal of Entrepreneurial Behaviour & Research, 17*(3), 272–295. doi:10.1108/13552551111130718

Chapter 12
Strategy Development With Future Scenarios:
Brainstorming for the Future of a University

Mehmet Ertem
Yozgat Bozok University, Turkey

ABSTRACT

In this chapter, a university's story of conducting a "brainstorming session for strategy development with future scenarios" process and the steps of this process are presented and examined, in detail. This chapter aims to help managers and scholars know how to conduct a brainstorming session for producing future scenarios for their organizations by explaining the process with a lived example. For this purpose, "Narrative Research Design," which is one of the qualitative research designs, is chosen for this research study. Consequently, a brief theoretical framework and a step-by-step guide are presented for the related parties.

INTRODUCTION: FIGHTING FIRE WITH FIRE

In 1975, H. Igor Ansoff discarded the notion of developing universal strategic formulas, opting instead to discern faint indications of future developments in order to anticipate unforeseeable events (Ansoff, 1975). In 1998, Richard D'Aveni woke up to a new era of Hypercompetition (D'Aveni, 1998). In 2007, Gary Hamel believed that management and organization were falling behind in various areas of progress and innovation and pondered the future of management (Hamel & Breen, 2007). While these authors acknowledged the rapidity of change and lamented the challenges of coping with it, many of the technological advances that exist today (which are both means and ends of change) may have only existed in the imaginations of a few special minds at their times. Today, the speed and depth of change are truly out of hand.

DOI: 10.4018/978-1-6684-7509-6.ch012

Throughout human history, the source of change is the boundless imagination power of free and developed minds all over the world, so change is limited by only the limits of human imagination. While there are various strategic management and long-term planning tools that can assist organizations in navigating change, these tools are limited in their effectiveness. As a result, organizations often rely on the collective imagination of internal or external "bright minds" to anticipate and prepare for the future. To remain competitive in an ever-changing environment, it seems that organizations have no choice but harnessing this collective imagination. The concept of creating strategies based on future scenarios or revising and strengthening existing strategies with these scenarios stems from this idea (Wilkinson et al., 2013; Burt et al., 2017; Bradfield et al., 2005).

Universities are widely recognized as important centers for development, change, and learning, throughout history. This distinction places high expectations on universities to adapt and respond to change effectively. To meet these expectations, universities must continuously renew and transform themselves more urgently than other institutions. In this context, the senior management of X University, a young and growing university in Türkiye, has determined that new strategies and updating existing ones are necessary to keep pace with rapid change. To accomplish this goal, the university's leadership has decided to use the method of "Planning with Future Scenarios" along with other methods. This study, which you are currently reading, is one of the results of this decision, made as part of the university's efforts to improve quality and transform the institution.

The aim of this chapter is to share the process of brainstorming for future scenarios of a developing university, conducted with a group of experts, including academics from diverse fields such as physics, medicine, engineering, business management, and sociology (Chase, 2005; Clandinin & Connelly, 2000). In sharing this experience, the goal is for readers who are considering conducting a brainstorming session for creating future scenarios for their own organization to know the necessary steps and points to be careful of without needing additional resources. To achieve these objectives, an interpretive perspective (Creswell et al., 2007; Riessman, 2008) and the "Narrative Research Design" were chosen among qualitative research designs for this chapter.

The narrative research design essentially entails the narration of the experiences of researchers or other individuals who have lived through an event, phenomenon, or concept that is important and meaningful to them (Wang, 2020, Mücevher, 2020). The researcher examines the experience chronologically in a storytelling language and analyses this narrative from an interpretive point of view. The reason for presenting the subject in the form of a "story" rather than another format is that stories have been the most natural, simple, and memorable way for people to share events and feelings with others, as well as make sense of the world around them, since the earliest times of mankind.

In narrative research, researchers collect stories from people through interviews, documents, or observations, then analyze them by focusing on the content and facts behind the scenes and attaching importance to the contexts in which the events unfold (Creswell et al., 2007; Riessman, 2008). In this narrative research, data was obtained through observations made during a meeting on creating future scenarios for X University and through the analysis of the scenarios created during the meeting, using a qualitative perspective.

MAIN FOCUS OF THE CHAPTER

In this chapter, the focus is on examining the concept of developing strategies with future scenarios, providing readers with a basic level of knowledge on the subject to enhance understanding of the process as whole. The details of the brainstorming technique for creating scenarios are shared, including a specific example. In the final section, recommendations are provided for managers and academics who plan to conduct similar scenario creation studies.

The story of X University, which is the focus of this chapter, and the stages of the scenario planning process utilizing brainstorming, will be explained in detail in the following sections. Before delving into the details of the scenario creation process, the author thought that it would be more useful to provide a brief overview of X University's change story so that readers can better understand the process.

A University's Brief Change Story: The Background of the Change

X university began operations as a branch of an older and larger university in 1996. Later, it became an independent university and entered the higher education market of Türkiye independently as one of the younger universities in the region. After the first (founding) rector, three rectors (head of university) changed, and it is currently in the period of the fourth rector. This story of change includes the change process within the last months of the third rector and the process of change during the entire time of the last one, until today.

When the last rector took the office, the university's position in Türkiye's and the world's university rankings was quite low, and it was still declining. Accordingly, the numbers of academic publications, patents, utility models, scientific, and entrepreneurial projects were either not growing or rapidly decreasing. Moreover, although there was an operating strategic planning committee in the university before, the vision and mission of the institution and its strategy were not clearly revealed and explained to the entire university. The organization had the appearance of a university that was advancing slowly and blindly under the harsh conditions of the higher education market in Türkiye.

On the other hand, the quality, and the strategic planning processes, which were being imposed by Turkish Council of Higher Education (YÖK) on all the universities in Türkiye including X University, had started but were not progressing as expected. In this regard, when the fourth Rector took the office, he began leading a university that was in serious need of change. Additionally, the pandemic came into the scene in his management's first year, and the environment around the university started to change drastically. Under these harsh conditions, the senior management of the university initiated the following processes of change in the managerial and educational structure of the university:

- Starting a strategic planning process and accordingly a quality management process.
- Completing EU Bologna Process and initiating the transition to distant education due to the pandemic.

These two processes, managerial and educational, had to be carried out simultaneously, making things more difficult for the top management. Under these conditions, the top management of the university established four different change teams (commissions) to lead and supervise the change in these two main fields. Three vice-rectors were assigned to lead the teams which were consisting of academicians and professional managers, and they began to carry out the mentioned change processes. Today, it can be said that a very important distance has been taken in all these change processes. The future scenario development process that is presented in this study was carried out within the quality management activities, and the whole process was based on the question of how the university can be more ready for the future.

Strategic Planning with Future Scenarios

Since the early days of the field of strategic management, a large number of planning instruments, such as matrices, charts, and checklists, have been presented to facilitate the work of researchers and management practitioners. These instruments have been criticized for having no practical value, particularly by management practitioners (Jarkabowsky & Kaplan, 2015; Timilsina et al., 2020). However, scenario planning emerges as a method that has proven its usefulness in various ways, such as in guiding decision making, risk management and long-term strategy development. This method is one of the basic methodologies for strategy development along with the strategic planning process. The concept of scenario here refers to thought experiments used to cope with the uncertain possibilities of future. These thought experiments are used as participatory and interactive strategy tools for creating future scenarios to see what cannot be foreseen under normal circumstances. These scenarios are used to determine what actions should be taken today to prepare for any of the possible future outcomes foreseen (Berkhout & Hertin, 2002; Ramirez & Selsky, 2014; Broo et al., 2021; Barbosa et al., 2022).

Planning with scenarios as a strategy development tool refers to creating time and space where management teams or experts can share their ideas, predictions, hopes and, concerns without worrying about being judged, ridiculed, or insulted. Basic goal of this activity is creating ideas to deal with the uncertainty of future, the complexity of external environment and the difficulty of adapting to these rapidly changing conditions (Burt et al., 2017; Docherty & McKiernan, 2008). As a result of the opportunity provided, participants are expected to think deeply for creating future scenarios, that are expected to be the products of collective mind, knowledge, creativity, and imagination of the entire group. These scenarios should focus on predicting and -perhaps- shaping the future (Van Der Heijden et al., 2002; Bishop et al., 2007). Then, the planning team analyses the scenarios and discusses what the organization/enterprise will experience, if any of the scenarios come true and what is needed to be done today for being ready for those future projections. In the last step, the team starts the planning part of the activity (or revision of existing plans) according to the different versions of the future that were pictured in the scenarios. Consequently, the purpose of planning with future scenarios is to make the uncertainty of the future predictable to a certain extent, to be able to develop strategies, and thus to ensure that the organization's strategy maintains its validity and meaningfulness over time (Oliver & Parrett, 2018).

There are a variety of methods to gather people, both from within and outside an organization, for the purpose of scenario planning. Among these methods, the brainstorming technique applied in this study, stands out as an effective technique. The following section provides a detailed examination of the brainstorming technique.

Brainstorming

The concept of "Brainstorming" first appeared in the book by American advertising company executive Alex Faickney Osborn (1953) entitled "Applied Imagination". In his work, Osborn primarily used the concept as a verb, as in the sentence "I brainstormed on this topic" (Osborn, 1956). Soon after, the technique became popular and was used as a method for producing creative solutions to problems in various fields such as business management, politics, international relations, public management, and communication (Delbecq et al., 2004; King, Horrocks, & Brooks, 2018; Brown, 1968; AlMutairi, 2015).

Brainstorming entails bringing groups of people together to generate new and creative ideas. The basic mechanism is that individuals are brought together in groups and these groups produce new and creative ideas that may sound illogical or even unconventional at first glance. During the brainstorming process, individuals are encouraged to express their ideas freely, without the influence of anxieties of others' prejudices, fear of being judged, or fear of making mistakes (Wilson, 2013).

During a brainstorming session, the moderator establishes a clear and specific question or set of questions for the participants. The question forms the foundation of the brainstorming session, and participants are expected to produce as many and as creative answers or ideas as possible in response to the question within the given time frame. Then comes the process of evaluating, eliminating, and classifying the generated ideas, and transforming them into a set of useful knowledge on the targeted topic (Brahm & Kleiner, 1996; Sinha, 2003).

Basic Rules and Steps of Brainstorming

It is important to note that there are certain guidelines that must be adhered to facilitate effective brainstorming sessions. Boddy (2012) lists these guidelines as follows (Boddy, 2012, s. 4-6):

- The ideas put forward should not be met with a critical or humiliating attitude.
- Participants in brainstorming are encouraged to express their ideas freely, without fear of judgment.
- Participants are asked to generate as many ideas as possible, without limiting themselves in any way.

These rules are essential for maximizing the output of the brainstorming activity. However, proper implementation of these rules is achieved by following certain steps and practices. Brainstorming sessions are typically implemented in three steps (Ven & Delbeco, 1971; AlMutairi, 2015):

- Preparation of the environment and the participants
- Performing brainstorming
- Analyzing and presenting the results

Although these main steps of the process can be expanded into more detailed steps, the foundation of brainstorming consists of these three main phases. The first of these is the preparation phase. During this phase, the environment and participants are prepared for the brainstorming session. It is essential to ensure that the potential participants are fully aware of the subject and purpose of the brainstorming. The second phase is the implementation of the brainstorming session itself. In the final stage, the ideas generated during the brainstorming session are processed and analyzed, and decisions are made, and actions are taken in line with these ideas (AlMutairi, 2015).

Creating a Future Scenarios for a University

For creating scenarios for the future of X University, a team-based brainstorming workshop was carried out on 09.11.2022, in which 15 experts of different academic titles from almost all fields of science at the university voluntarily took part. The meeting was carried out in three phases in line with the relevant literature:

- Preparation
- Application
- Analysis

It must be emphasized that according to the X University's experience, there are other phases of the process before and after these stages mentioned. The one before these phases is preparing the minds of the team who is responsible for the brainstorming activity and the one after the phases is learning from the brainstorming experience for the future. Although these steps are invisible, it is well-known to the professionals who specialize in such applications that they are very important for brainstorming technique applications. Along with these visible and invisible phases, the whole process of creating future scenarios with brainstorming was carried out over a total period of 35 days.

Preparation Phase

In the preparation phase, the future scenarios team came together to carefully plan the upcoming future scenarios meeting. This included determining the most suitable method for conducting the meeting, which was ultimately decided to be a brainstorming session. To ensure that the brainstorming sessions are as productive as possible, it was decided that the meetings will be held face-to-face, and that participation will be voluntary. Furthermore, to foster a creative and open environment, it was decided to minimize the participation of top management in the meeting. Instead, it was recommended that the brainstorming sessions be led and participated by individuals who are passionate about the topic and willing to actively contribute ideas. This way, participants would be able to share their ideas without fear of criticism or ridicule. Additionally, it was determined that the meeting's focus will be on the next five years as a timeframe, in alignment with the university's 2021 strategic plan. By doing so, the results of the future scenarios meeting will not only contribute to refining and improving the existing strategic plan but also contribute to the ongoing efforts in quality management.

The date, location, and agenda for the future scenarios meeting were officially announced to the entire university via email and official documents approximately two weeks prior to the meeting (on October 27, 2022). The announcement included an explanation of the purpose and goals of conducting future scenario planning as well as a description of the specific methods that will be used during the brainstorming sessions, including the steps and content of the brainstorming activity, to inform those who have never participated in a brainstorming session before.

Implementation Phase

During the implementation phase, 15 academicians (10 male and 5 female) from different fields of expertise voluntarily participated in the meeting. First, a short presentation was made to the participants about planning scenarios and how the meeting would be carried out with the steps of the brainstorming session.

It was emphasized in the presentation that no one was allowed to ridicule or humiliate anyone while expressing an opinion during brainstorming, and that all the work was for unleashing their creative potential to make the university more competitive in the future. The presentation also included information on the main (abstract) subjects and the future time interval focus of the scenario meeting. Afterwards, the moderator started the session.

An inductive and interpretive perspective was taken as the basis for the brainstorming practice. In line with this approach, the practice was not limited to certain topics, so that participants could share their ideas freely without any limitations. The first direct idea generation was started with the following question: What great and important changes - predictable or unpredictable - can occur in the next five years, in the world and in Türkiye? The second important question was then asked, and the brainstorming continued: What should the university do to be ready for this picture of future?

The details of the brainstorming session and the important issues to be careful about are explained in "Table-1" as the content of the "Recommendations" section of the chapter. However, in line with the relevant literature (Ven & Delbeco, 1971; AlMutairi, 2015), the implementation phase of the brainstorming application was conducted with the following steps:

- **Step 1:** Moderator's icebreaker session.
- **Step 2:** Free idea generation and note-taking by participants.
- **Step 3:** Participants share their ideas loudly with the moderator and the rest of the group and the moderator writes these ideas on the board.
- **Step 4:** Grouping the ideas written on the board under specific topics.
- **Step 5:** Group discussion on how ideas in each topic can be turned into a scenario.
- **Step 6:** Discussion with the group about what measures the university should take in case of future events in each topic.
- **Step 7:** Summing up and closing the meeting.

It was originally intended to proceed to the brainstorming session after the presentation, but despite the preliminary information the participants received, it is decided to begin with an icebreaker session. This was because it's observed that the participants were a little nervous and prejudiced because they had not participated in a meeting of future scenarios or brainstorming before. Then, the free brainstorming took place on the two basic questions mentioned before. During the free brainstorming, the participants were observed to be a bit shy and reserved about sharing their opinions freely. In order to overcome this state of the participants and encourage them to be more creative, the moderator loudly shared some of his own "crazy" or "illogical" ideas, including even some conspiracy theories. Then participants began to share their ideas willingly and the statements containing their future predictions were collected. The statements containing the participants' predictions of future events were subsequently compiled and grouped under the following main headings:

- Internet and Information Technologies
- Health and Natural Sciences
- Social and Cultural Developments
- International Politics

In this section, the heading of "Internet and Information Technologies" and the scenario created under this heading will be shared. The reason for sharing only this heading and the scenario related to it is due to the constraints imposed by the scope of this chapter and the high level of public interest in the subject matter of this heading. The list of future predictions collected in the context of internet and information technologies is as follows:

- The international network structure and the internet will experience a significant disruption.
- Virtual and augmented reality will become widespread.
- The importance of big data will increase significantly.
- We will be surrounded by blockchain technology. Electronic currencies will be more prevalent.
- Artificial intelligence will provide significant benefits.
- It may be necessary to take measures to prevent artificial intelligence from gaining too much autonomy.
- All organizations will become virtual organizations.
- Digital political movements, parties, and citizenship issues will be taken into greater consideration.
- Our perception of reality will become blurred. It will be increasingly difficult to distinguish between what is virtual and what is real.
- Teleportation will become a normalized means of transportation.
- Machine Learning will evolve at a rapid pace.
- Robotic Technologies will experience significant advancements, and humanoid robots will be increasingly present in business settings as employees.

After the brainstorming stages, the scenario planning team worked on the generated ideas that were classified under these titles, and transformed them into complete scenarios, paying attention to the literary aspect of the text. Then, they shared the scenarios with the participants via e-mail, adding the titles of "The Dominant Forces Shaping This Scenario" and "The Questions to be Considered" to the scenario text. Within the e-mails, the participants were asked to provide feedback on the scenario, and the scenario was finalized with the feedback received. The final version of the scenario was presented to the university senate, the top management of the organization. These scenarios were discussed by the senate, including the deans and other senior executives in the university, and decisions were made to take serious actions related to the managerial and educational structure of the university. In the following section, one of the four scenarios created by the brainstorming participants and the planning team will be presented. This scenario focuses on the possible future developments in the field of internet and information technologies. A series of key questions under two titles were added to the scenario to assist the decision-making process of the university's top management. When considering the scenario, (1) what are the key forces driving the change, (2) what external and/or internal developments could impact this scenario? Then, a related questions section was added to the text, and the process was finalized.

Technology is Changing Universities: Next Five Years

In line with the rapid advancement in information technologies, the development of artificial intelligence and big data technologies is radically changing higher education as well as every other field of life. Thanks to artificial and augmented reality applications and neuroscience research developing in parallel with these technologies, a greater part of education is moving to the virtual environment and the number of higher education institutions that do not have a physical space and exist in a completely virtual environment with their courses, teachers, students, and classes increases unexpectedly. This situation forces classical higher education institutions to reconsider the conventional education, training, and examination practices they are accustomed to, even if they are not prepared or willing. The reason for this is the rapid shift in the expectations of internal and external stakeholders of the universities from them. Now their expectations are so much different and high that the old practices are increasingly becoming meaningless.

Correspondingly, the educational content of the departments and programs is changing. Higher education institutions and their departments are looking for ways to provide their lecturers and students with education opportunities in areas such as information literacy, software, data security, big data analysis, artificial intelligence, machine learning, and blockchain applications, regardless of their fields. The expectations of students and academics from higher education institutions are also shaped in this direction because it is becoming increasingly difficult for those who cannot develop competencies in these subjects to find a place for themselves in the world of business and science, and people do not want to lose their jobs or become underqualified for the job market. The rapid change in information technologies does not only affect technical areas such as engineering. Other research areas such as Sociology, Psychology, Social Psychology, Business Management, Health Sciences, Sports Sciences, increasingly require such knowledge for producing meaningful and commercializable information and projects.

On the other hand, the private sector and state institutions, which are external stakeholders of universities, demand different qualities from higher education institutions. The need for qualified employees who possess the ability to effectively utilize artificial intelligence, big data and blockchain applications in sectors such as manufacturing, services and utilities is at an extreme level. Recent graduates, who have knowledge of these subjects, even at the most superficial level, are being almost grabbed in the air by the private sector and government institutions all over the world.

Within this picture, the large and developed universities with advanced financial resources plan and implement very serious investment projects for developing human resources and the necessary infrastructure for computer and information technologies. Other smaller universities, which have more limited monetary, human, and technological resources, are trying to benefit from the infrastructure, educational technological and scientific research facilities of larger universities by establishing national and international collaborations. In this way, smaller developing universities are trying to choose certain niche areas in the field of computer and information technologies as specializing in a narrower field for being able to catch up with the change without pushing their own financial sources to the limits.

This environment brings new problems and threats to universities as well as to all other institutions and organizations. The prominence of information technologies and the data and physical infrastructure security issues forced universities to take serious precautions into account to be ready for possible threats such as hackers and cyber-attacks.

Dominant Forces Shaping the Change

In this scenario, the key factors driving change are the rapid advancements in information technology, including the internet, artificial intelligence, machine learning, big data, blockchain, and software technologies related to neuroscience.

Factors Impacting the Scenario

It is a well-established fact that people began avoiding crowded places and group activities due to the pandemic. Though the pandemic has largely come to an end, people continue to avoid congregating in large groups. Thus, higher education institutions have had to develop their own distance education infrastructure in Türkiye and around the world, due to the conditions brought about by the pandemic.

The pandemic forced people to stay home and rely on the internet and electronic devices to access a wide range of services, including shopping, education, and, in some cases, healthcare. This situation has led to a widespread use of the internet and information technologies and electronic devices such as computers and smartphones in society.

The number of private and government organizations investing in research and development (R&D) projects related to technologies such as artificial intelligence, big data, machine learning, and blockchain applications is rapidly increasing worldwide.

The fast and inexpensive communication capabilities provided by the rapidly advancing internet and associated technologies also present new opportunities for education and research in universities.

Questions

To make the most of this scenario, consider the following questions and try to answer them:

- Can such an environment be considered as a sustainable climate for the higher education sector?
- What key factors will allow the university to differentiate and excel in this system?
- What actions should the university take to increase competitiveness in the fields of education, science, and entrepreneurship?
- What areas of education and educational technologies should be invested in today to ensure that graduates and members of the university (academics, administrative staff, and students) are competitive in the business and scientific world in the future?
- What measures should be taken today to address potential threats that this future may bring? For example, what skills should be developed among members (staff and students) of the university?

SOLUTIONS AND RECOMMENDATIONS

Generating future scenarios is one of the main methodologies to develop strategies and long-term plans for organizations (Timilsina et al., 2020 Barbosa et al., 2022; Broo et al., 2021). On the other hand, brainstorming seems to be a very effective method, which is a collective way of creative thinking, to induce the process of generating future scenarios (Akram et al., 2020). However, for this kind of collective creative thinking practices to be successful, it is crucial that participation should be mostly or fully voluntary. It is experienced by the author that when participation is voluntary, individuals become more likely to overcome their anxiety about sharing ideas with others face-to-face. Potential participants can be motivated to participate voluntarily in the brainstorming session as using appropriate incentives.

While the group size did result in a high level of creativity, it also led to tension and interpersonal conflicts, making it difficult for the group to maintain focus on the task at hand. It is recommended that in cases where there are more than 7-8 participants, it may be more beneficial to divide them into smaller groups for the brainstorming process.

Another important issue is the necessity to establish a scenario planning team before the brainstorming session. The team should include strategy experts (scholars, practitioners etc.) with an interpretive and qualitative perspective to process the raw data of random future predictions in terms of strategy.

Without an interpretive perspective, the roughly outlined scenarios created with the collected raw ideas will not be useful enough for developing strategies and, thus the targeted benefits from this work may not be fully obtained. It is suggested that organizations willing to perform future scenarios planning with brainstorming sessions should consider receiving external consultancy or forming a team up to manage this practice within the organization and educate them to make them gain an interpretive perspective, to learn how to conduct brainstorming sessions and to learn how to write future scenarios. As a result of the this experience, "Table 1" has been provided below to guide researchers and practitioners about the process step by step and as detailed as possible.

Within the table above the column titled "General Brainstorming Phase" refers to the three main phases of brain storming. The second column titled "Steps of the Relevant Phase" refers to the steps to be taken within the main phases of the brainstorming session. The Last column of the table titled "Considerations and Recommendations" refers directly to the recommendations and evaluations of the author which are derived from the X University's planning with future scenarios experience.

CONCLUSION

The scenario outlined above, which has been followed in detail, is the product of one of the very first future scenarios planning studies ever conducted by a university in Türkiye. The most significant conclusion that can be drawn from this experience with brainstorming-based future scenarios planning is that this type of creative thinking can be a valuable tool for organizations. Especially those organizations that are resistant to change in management, in terms of maintaining the relevance of their strategies and continually improving themselves, can benefit from this tool for their strategy development processes.

REFERENCES

Akram, W., Adeel, S., Tabassum, M., Jiang, Y., Chandio, A., & Yasmin, I. (2020). *Scenario Analysis and Proposed Plan for Pakistan Universities – COVID – 19: Application of Design Thinking Model.* Cambridge Open Engage., doi:10.33774/coe-2020-ql1w6

AlMutairi, A. N. (2015). The Effect of Using Brainstorming Strategy in Developing Creative Problem Solving Skills among male Students in Kuwait: A Field Study on Saud Al-Kharji School in Kuwait City. *Journal of Education and Practice*, *6*(3), 136–146.

Ansoff, H. I. (1957). Strategies for Diversification. *Harvard Business Review*, *35*(5), 113–124.

Ansoff, H. I. (1975). Managing Strategic Surprise by Response to Weak Signals. *California Management Review*, *18*(2), 21–33. doi:10.2307/41164635

Barbosa, C. E., Lima, Y. O., Costa, L. F., Santos, H. S., Lyra, A., Argôlo, M., & Souza, J. M. (2022). Future of work in 2050: Thinking beyond the COVID-19 pandemic. *European Journal of Futures Research*, *10*(25), 25. doi:10.118640309-022-00210-w

Berkhout, F., & Hertin, J. (2002). Foresight futures scenarios: Developing and applying a participative strategic planning tool. *Greener Management International, 2002*(37), 37–52. doi:10.9774/GLEAF.3062.2002.sp.00005

Bishop, P., Hines, A., & Collins, T. (2007). The current state of scenario development: An overview of techniques. *Foresight, 9*(1), 5–25. doi:10.1108/14636680710727516

Boddy, C. (2012). The Nominal Group Technique: An aid to Brainstorming ideas in research. *Qualitative Market Research, 15*(1), 6–18. doi:10.1108/13522751211191964

Bradfield, R., Wright, G., Burt, G., Cairns, G., & Heijden, K. V. (2005). The origins and evolution of scenario techniques in long range business planning. *Futures, 37*(8), 795–812. doi:10.1016/j.futures.2005.01.003

Brahm, C., & Kleiner, B. H. (1996). Advantages and disadvantages of group decision-making approaches. *Team Performance Management, 2*(2), 30–35. doi:10.1108/13527599610105538

Broo, D. G., Lamb, K., Ehwi, R. J., Pärn, E., Koronaki, A., Makri, C., & Zomer, T. (2021). Built environment of Britain in 2040: Scenarios and strategies. *Sustainable Cities and Society*, 65.

Brown, B. B. (1968). *Delphi Process: A Methodology Used for the Elicitation of Opinions of Experts*. RAND Corp.

Burt, G., Mackay, D. J., Heijden, K., & Verheijdt, C. (2017). Openness disposition: Readiness characteristics that influence participant benefits from scenario planning as strategic conversation. *Technological Forecasting and Social Change, 124*, 16–25. doi:10.1016/j.techfore.2016.11.024

Chase, S. (2005). Narrative Inquiry. In N. K. Denzin, & Y. S. (Eds.), The sage handbook of qualitative research. Sage Publications.

Chermack, J., & Coons, L. M. (2015). Scenario planning: Pierre Wack's hidden messages. *Futures, 73*, 187–193. doi:10.1016/j.futures.2015.08.012

Clandinin, D. J., & Connelly, F. M. (2000). *Narrative Inquiry: Experience and Story in Qualitative Research*. Jossey-Bass, Inc.

Creswell, J. W., Hanson, W. E., Clark, V. L., & Morales, A. (2007). Qualitative Research Designs: Selection and Implementation. *The Counseling Psychologist, 35*(2), 236–264. doi:10.1177/0011000006287390

D'Aveni, R. A. (1998). Waking up to the new era of hypercompetition. *The Washington Quarterly, 21*(1), 183–195. doi:10.1080/01636609809550302

Delbecq, A. L., Ven, A. H., & Gustafson, D. H. (2004). *Group Techniques for Program Planning: A Guide to Nominal Groups and Delphi Process*. Green Briar Press.

Docherty, I., & McKiernan, P. (2008). Scenario planning for the Edinburgh city region. *Environ. Plann. C, 26*(7), 982–997. doi:10.1068/c0665r

Hagen, M., Bernard, A., & Grube, E. (2016, March). Do It All Wrong! Using Reverse-Brainstorming to Generate Ideas, Improve Discussions, and Move Students to Action. *Management Teaching Review, 1*(2), 85-90. www.creatingminds.org: http://creatingminds.org/tools/reverse_brainstorming.htm

Hamel, G., & Breen, B. (2007). *The Future of Management*. Harvard Business Press.

Iacucci, G., & Kuutti, K. (2002). Everyday Life as a Stage in Creating and Performing Scenarios for Wireless Devices. *Personal and Ubiquitous Computing*, *6*(6), 299–306. doi:10.1007007790200031

Jarkabowsky, P., & Kaplan, S. (2015). Strategy Tools-In-Use: A Framework for Understanding "Technologies Rationality" In Practice. *Strategic Management Journal*, (36), 537–558.

King, N., Horrocks, C., & Brooks, J. (2018). *Interviews in Qualitative Research*. Sage Pub.

Lacucci, G., & Kuutti, K. (2002). Everyday Life as a Stage in Creating and Performing Scenarios for Wireless Devices. *Personal and Ubiquitous Computing*, (6), 299–306.

Mücevher, M. H. (2020). Anlatı ve Hayat Hikayesi Araştırmaları. *Süleyman Demirel Üniversitesi İİBF Dergisi*, *25*(3), 277–295.

Oliver, J. J., & Parrett, E. (2018). Managing future uncertainty: Reevaluatingthe role of scenario planning. *Business Horizons*, *61*(2), 339–352. doi:10.1016/j.bushor.2017.11.013

Osborn, A. F. (1956). *Applied Imagination: Principles and Procedures of Creative Thinking*. Charles Scribner's Sons.

Ramirez, R., & Selsky, J. W. (2014). Strategic Planning in Turbulent Environments: A Social Ecology Approach to Scenarios. *Long Range Planning*, *49*(1), 90–102. doi:10.1016/j.lrp.2014.09.002

Riessman, C. K. (2008). *Narrative Methods for the Human Sciences*. Sage Pub.

Schoemaker, P. J., Day, G. S., & Snyder, S. A. (2013). Integrating organizational networks, weak signals,strategic radars and scenario planning. *Technological Forecasting and Social Change*, *80*(4), 815–824. doi:10.1016/j.techfore.2012.10.020

Sinha, R. (2003, February 24). *Beyond cardsorting: Free-listing methods to explore user categorizations*. Boxes and Arrows. www.boxesandarrows.com: https://boxesandarrows.com/beyond-cardsorting-free-listing-methods-to-explore-user-categorizations/

Smedt, P. D., Borch, K., & Fuller, T. (2013). Future scenarios to inspire innovation. *Technological Forecasting and Social Change*, *80*(3), 432–443. doi:10.1016/j.techfore.2012.10.006

Timilsina, R. R., Nakagawa, Y., & Kotani, K. (2020). Exploring the Possibility of Linking and Incorporating Future Design in Backcasting and Scenario Planning. *Sustainability*, *12*(23), 12. doi:10.3390u12239907

Van Der Heijden, K., Bradfield, R., Burt, G., Cairns, G., & Wright, G. (2002). *The Sixth Sense: Accelerating Organizational Learning with Scenarios*. John Wiley & Sons Ltd.

Ven, A. V., & Delbeco, A. L. (1971). Nominal versus Interacting Group Processes for Committee Decision-Making Effectiveness. *Academy of Management Journal*, *14*(2), 203–212. doi:10.2307/255307

Wang, L. (2020). Entrepreneurial narratives and concept teaching and learning. *Industry and Higher Education*, *34*(1), 24–35. doi:10.1177/0950422219878986

Wilkinson, A., Kupers, R., & Mangalagiude, D. (2013). How plausibility-based scenario practices are grappling with complexity to appreciate and address 21st Century Challenges. *Technological Forecasting and Social Change*, *80*(4), 699–710. doi:10.1016/j.techfore.2012.10.031

Wilson, C. (2013). *Brainstorming and Beyond: A User-Centered Design Method.* Elsevier.

KEY TERMS AND DEFINITIONS

Brainstorming: A group creativity technique used to generate a large number of ideas for solving a problem or generating new ideas. It encourages participants to share and build on each other's ideas in an open and non-judgmental environment.

Narrative Inquiry: A research approach that focuses on the collection and analysis of stories, experiences, or narratives of individuals or groups. It aims to understand the meaning and context of these experiences and how they shape people's understanding of the world.

Planning with Future Scenarios: A method of strategic planning that involves creating multiple possible future scenarios and then developing strategies to prepare for and respond to each one. It is an important tool for organizations to mitigate risks and capitalize on opportunities in an uncertain future.

Strategy Development: The process of creating a plan of action for achieving specific goals and objectives. It involves analyzing the current situation, identifying opportunities and threats, and determining the resources needed to execute the plan. It is a continuous process that is essential for the success of any organization.

Turkish Council of Higher Education (YÖK): A state institution which is the government agency responsible for coordinating and supervising all higher education institutions in Türkiye. Its main role is to ensure the quality and relevance of higher education in the country and to develop policies for the higher education sector.

Chapter 13

Mastering the Chaos: Data-Driven and AI-Based Change Management as an Answer to Challenges in Unprecedented Times

Jens M. Sorg
CGI Deutschland B.V. & Co. KG, Germany

Karen Hodge Cunningham
CGI, Canada

Assia Stoyanova
CGI, USA

ABSTRACT

You know that change endeavors are highly complex. You know that decision-making can be extremely challenging. Today, change capacities are more important than ever. This holds even more true in unprecedented times. What if it is possible to handle change endeavors with +1000, +10.000, and even +5 million affected stakeholders and indefinite challenges? Sounds too good to be true? It is the sound of the future. CGI is harnessing the velocity of change and is making the complex simple. The authors will give insights into the current field of data-driven and AI-based strategic change management (SCM) consulting. The focus of the chapter is the challenges the authors currently facing in elaborating a data-driven and AI-based consulting approach for SCM.

For AI-based consulting, one must master change management before one masters change.

DOI: 10.4018/978-1-6684-7509-6.ch013

INTRODUCTION

Accelerating the Pace of Change Screaming for Scaled-Up Change Management

While setting up projects, the focus is on technical aspects. Sure, you will not initialize a change endeavor just for the sake of change. With your project, you follow a certain goal – e.g., to make workflows more robust, you standardize or automate processes; to gain efficiencies, you implement a new IT system, or to achieve better project results and to be more client-oriented, you introduce agile project management.

As other research and the project experience of the authors are showing is that the technical part of a project is usually set up very well. Often, the intended solution is quite smart, and technically all functionalities work. However, the solution also often does not achieve the intended business case. In some cases, it completely fails due to, what is common knowledge the neglect of proper change management (Gartner, 2020; Keller & Aiken, 2009; Nur-e Rahman, 2014). However, many organizations lack access to first-class change management consulting skills and services. This neglect is often related to the lack of resources – financial or qualified personnel. Many organizations – especially small and medium enterprises (SME), social entrepreneurs, or women-owned businesses do not have the financial or human resource to make use of strategic change management (SCM). SMEs are not the only enterprises impacted – multinational companies (MNC) also often do not utilize the full potential of SCM when integrating the practice into major projects. Often due to initial cost savings while setting up projects or programs, the development and integration of change measures are frequently taken out of initial proposals and scope. The focus is on the technical installation, not on the human aspects of the endeavor.

As a result, the gap between the calculated business case for the future state and the achieved outcome is already predictable. Research shows that about 65% of the project and the related project benefits are 99% to 100% people-dependent (Prosci, 2014) and only 20% of executives investing in digital transformation are achieving the expected results (CGI, 2022). That means to achieve the upfront calculated business case the technical solution plays a minimal role in making the project a success. The research reveals that it is the ability of the affected stakeholders to change.

On one hand, CGI's goal is to [...] "chart a path to a more inclusive and sustainable world" (CGI, 2021) and to enable under represented economic groups – such as SMEs, social entrepreneurs, and women-owned businesses – to utilize SCM for their business success. On the other hand, CGI – as one of Canada' leading AI service providers – and its innovation teams are keen to work on data-driven and AI-based approaches to achieve better decisions and to drive the future of management consulting (IDC, 2022).

Data-driven and AI-based SCM consulting – as AI systems in general (Waardenburg et al., 2021a) – make use of machine learning algorithms and self-learning mechanisms, which can learn using big data. As a result, the data-driven and AI-based SCM system will be able to independently come up with effective change measures and new suggestions sustainably implementing the change, decisions, or predictions for the future state.

Change management (e.g. Lauer, 2021; Stolzenberg, 2022; Vernooij et al., 2022), management consulting (e.g. Armbrüster, 2006; Kipping, 2003; Kipping & Clark, 2013), and AI (Barbey et. al., 2021; DiMatteo et al., 2022; Frankish & Ramsey, 2014) are well-researched disciplines. All three have their field of research and sub-disciplines, and students can get a specific university degree. AI is researched around the globe (Munoz & Maurya, 2022) and often discussed in the field of law (e.g. Burchard, 2018;

Wischmeyer & Rademacher, 2019), sociology, and philosophy (Schönecker & Kim, 2022). Further, implanting AI and data in business and decision-making processes is one of the mage trends for change management (Ryder, 2019; Taulli, 2019). However, data-driven and AI-based change management consulting – meaning applying AI and data to a change management consulting approach – is one of the white spots in the scientific community. The content analyses of the SSCI and IDC databases came up with four results. All results are not addressing the authors' perspective of applying AI in the field of change management consulting.[1]

Engel et al. (2021) empirically explore [...] "the Cause-Effect Relationships of AI Characteristics, Project Management Challenges, and Organizational Change" (p. 166). The article analysis the implementation of implementing AI in organizations. The research focuses on the failure of implementing AI in organizations and the challenges regarding the experimental character, context sensitivity, black box character, and learning requirements of AI rather than the application of AI to facilitate change management consulting (Engel et al., 2021). Naz et al. (2013) focus on the "Effective Usage of AI Technique for Requirement Change Management Practices" (p 1). However, Naz et al. (2013) use change management in the meaning of the IT service management discipline (Naz et al., 2013). In this context, change management ensures that standardized methods and procedures, such as Information Technology Infrastructure Library (ITIL) are used for an efficient and prompt change to IT infrastructure and software. O'Leary (2021) focuses on contract life-cycle management and AI-centric marketing. He gives insights into how enterprises are leveraging AI within the contract lifecycle management, containing US-only data (O'Leary, 2021). Sozinova et al. (2022) neither address AI nor change management. Here, it is referenced to AI as a period (Sozinova et al., 2022).

The purpose of the chapter is to give insights into the current field of application of data-driven and AI-based SCM consulting. Since the application of AI in strategic change management is at its very beginning, the article rather focuses the challenges of the application of AI in the field of human-centered consulting approaches. The authors, Dr. Jens M. Sorg, Karen Hodge Cunningham, and Assia Stoyanova have worked for many decades in the field of change management consulting and are the founding members of CGI's global Change Management Think Tank.

OMNIPRESENCE OF CHANGE AND ITS EVER-INCREASING COMPLEXITY

The COVID-19 pandemic magnified the vulnerable nature of our highly integrated national and regional economies. The collapse of the world supply chains – accompanied by the current war in Ukraine – is on everyone's minds. The images of shipping vessels parked at sea and the de facto imprisoned sailor on these ships are still vivid in our minds. The threat of another hard lockdown of the world production hubs and the deadlock of the major product lines is omnipresent.

Ever Increasingly Complex Change Impacts Disproportionately Smaller Organizations

Also, the COVID-19 pandemic quickly tested and transformed many business models. The transition to virtual education, telehealth, and connected supply chains in consumer goods accelerated the digital transformation from years to months. Many of the – literally – overnight installed measures changed the way of working – maybe even living – of millions. And one thing is for sure, many of them will stay until they are suspended by a better version during "the ever-accelerating [AI and big-driven] digital revolution" (Burchard, 2018, p. 16).

In a recent interview with the Guardian, founder of the XPrize Foundation and famed engineer, Peter Diamandis, talked about the accelerating pace of change in today's society. He stated, that in the next 10 years, every industry on this planet is going to be reinvented (The Guardian, 2020), and according to artificial intelligence scientist Toby Walsh, the whole society will change due to the application of AI by 2050 (Healey, 2020). The talk of the town is now hyper-automation, data economy, the future of work, and AI (Waardenburg et al., 2021b). With that, change in organizations becomes continuous for employees and the question is how do we work with daily work changing too fast, too often? Implementing AI alone will bring significant change to 63% of the 2000+ organizations MIT Sloan Management Review surveyed (MIT, 2020). Successful adaptation is highly unlikely without a sustained change management effort and strategic concepts. Not only that but that effort can no longer be carried by a few change experts every now and then. There is an increasing demand for scaling up current change management approaches.

As the pace of change causes great anxiety and poses tough challenges to organizations, change projects also become more complex. They bring a more complex multifaceted change to employees' ways of working. According to Harvey Nash/KPMG, 61% of surveyed CIOs say projects are becoming more and more complex, and 58% say they are more ambitious than just five years ago. This trend has continued, and with complex projects come compound changes for both the business and the IT teams (Harvey Nash/KPMG, 2017). In 2018 Prosci estimated 89% of projects bring process change and 65% bring job role change. Undoubtedly, the impact of that change has significantly increased in recent years (Prosci, 2018). And because multiple changes compile, even small change has a bigger impact on how employees are performing their day-to-day work.

Change initiatives force process and behavioral shifts across organizations, large and small. Within larger organizations, the impact can be vast but not as burdensome. Within smaller enterprises, however, change initiatives can cause major disruptions on top of often already tough business landscapes. Why does this matter? 99% of the world's companies – SMEs, including social entrepreneurs, and women-owned businesses – employ approx. 60% of the world population and contribute over 50% of the world's net added value. These companies are not represented by mass media as presented above (Bundesministerium für Wirtschaft, 2019; Bundesverband mittelständische Wirtschaft, 2022; Government of Canada, 2021; Organisation for Economic Co-operation and Development, 2021; Office of the US Trade Representatives, 2021; US Small Business Administration, 2021; World Bank, 2021).

As Tennin (2022) shows, during crises – such as the COVID-19 pandemic – SMEs, social entrepreneurs, and women-owned businesses are most vulnerable. Tennin states: "Filing an application for funding to remain open by paying operating expenses and employees shouldn't be the only option for companies" (Tennin, 2022). Instead, Tennin is asking if "[...] aspects of change management [could] be applied to assist? [...] What about applying change management strategies for the short-term to remain open, for the long-term to mitigate risk and prove the company against future catastrophes and unpreparedness, but also for the long-term because the length of a catastrophic economical event is typically unknown? Businesses help economies not only exist but to survive and thrive" (Tennin, 2022).

The Inherent Complexity of Change

With change omnipresent in organizations and layering fast, new change approaches are necessary for addressing these challenges. However, it is not frameworks such as ADKAR, Prosci's Change Triangle (PCT) People-Centered Implementation (PCI), or the Standard of the Association of Change Management Practitioners (ACMP), nor phase models such as Kotter, Lewin, or Senge that alone are the solution for the given challenges (Association of Change Management Professionals [ACMP], 2019; Changefirst, 2022; Kotter, 1996; Lewin, 1947; Prosci, 2022a; 2022b; Senge, 1990). The answer also does not reside in single methodologies or tools. It lies in the experience and expertise of a change professional. Let's explore why:

A change…

- is initiated by various triggers – sometimes by various synchronous triggers *(agile transformation, compliance, digitization, leadership, process automation, strategy…).*
- affects different stakeholders *(employees, management, executive board, customers, shareholders).*
- occurs with varying intensity *(facts: directly measurable, can be influenced straightly; emotions: hardly directly measurable, can be influenced indirectly)*
- occurs at different times *(stakeholders are at different stages of the change curve).*
- varies stakeholder's requirements to lower resistance and compensate for the loss of performance *(involvement, empowerment, communication, appreciation).*
- can vary over time (*at different stages of the change curve).*

This means the standard aspect of change management can be minimal. You need a master to lead in this high pace, highly complex, chaotic environment. A successful change manager can structure such an environment while influencing oppositional factions. With these skills, change professionals are of high value for any business in today's ever-shifting environment (Sorg et al., in press).

The challenge becomes that change professionals who can effectively master highly complex environments are rare. This makes change management practitioners a precious asset – and rare and precious goods can be costly.

Putting aside that leaders may often be blind to the need to deliberately manage the impact of change, organizations are also now challenged to acquire skilled change managers or – as in the case of many SMEs - are unable to make such a large investment. Even so, smaller organizations may still be able to reap the benefits of certain change management activities if we look for innovative ways to do so.

In the following, the authors will lay out key questions that have to be addressed for data-driven and AI-based SCM consulting to be such an innovative way.

SOLUTIONING DATA-DRIVEN AND AI-BASED SCM CONSULTING

CGI's SCM team and change management think tank engage these challenges head-on with an evidence-based approach leveraging data-driven and AI-based SCM approach. Finally, the authors want to contribute to initial cost-reduction during change projects, opening the professional service of SCM consulting to currently excluded stakeholders such as SMEs, women-owned businesses, and social entrepreneurs, but also supporting MNEs making better use of available data, generating smarter decisions and achieving sustainable change and transformation.

Where to Start: Key Questions to Ask

To kick off the development of a data-driven, AI-based approach, the team asked two questions – how can we lower the cost and how can we advance the decision-making process and achieve better change results?

First, how can we lower the cost? The goal is to significantly reduce the preliminary cost of SCM during the initial required phase to diagnose the change endeavor. The initial data intake and data processing are inevitable since without it, the change practitioners and stakeholders would not know the why, what, and how of the change, who is impacted, and what the actual extent of that impact is. To effectively drive a change endeavor, not putting the future state at risk, one must know 'what is in the box'. Only with this information, effective change measures – often 'outside the box' – can be defined.

Only meaningful change measures anchor the change in the minds of the affected stakeholders. Without this understanding, the change endeavor is more of a blind flight of a supersonic aircraft. The intended future state will only be reached by chance – and putting the desired outcomes at risk right from the beginning is probably not intended. The earlier we discover and diagnose, the better the chances for a strong change management approach. Highly complex, systemic challenges can be identified right from the beginning, risks can be lowered, the resulting gap can be further closed, the chance to successfully implement change is amplified, and the return on investment of the change is increased (Sorg, n,d.; Prosci, 2022c; Prosci, 2022d) So, streamlining and automating that first step of the change planning process will allow lower startup costs and enable earlier change planning start.

Second, how can we advance the decision-making process and achieve better change results, especially in what the authors call experimental environments? Experimental environments in the decision-making process are characterized by a high number of stakeholders involved (+1000, +10.000, or even +5 million) and final authority is not necessarily identifiable at the beginning of the change process (Sorg, 2021). Combined with the general complexity of change, this high number of individual variables increases the risk of failure and must be supported by data science and AI.

In addition, in increasingly unpredictable and experimental environments, leaders must make complex decisions faster. Usually, these decisions are focused on operations and less on creating meaningful value for the organization. Today and in the future, this will no longer be enough (Wallace, 2022)

Four Challenges to Tackle

The authors have identified four main challenges to address when implemeting a change project:

1. First, the change endeavor is highly complex. Due to too many variables, it cannot be approached by a classical waterfall approach and a simple decision tree. The change project must follow an iterative approach.
2. The second challenge is related to the first. To follow an iterative approach in an experimental environment, the project sponsor a) must be open to such an approach, b) must be able to master uncertainty, and c) has to trust the change professional. This alone is often already a change project since people want to know what the result will look like.

3. Third, during the intake or discovery and diagnosis phase, a lot of information is generated. Deeper insights into the triggers of change are generated. The cause that initiates the change becomes clear – e.g. the new strategy, the intended future organizational design, or the new methodology to be implemented, such as agile. It is revealed what the current organizational culture looks like. It becomes clear who is going to be affected by the change and information about the past as well as the current change experience of the organization is collected.
4. Finally, the data collected is processed – still in the phase of discovery and diagnosis. Now, one begins to understand how the organizational culture works, how disruptive the impact will be, and finally how both the individual and corporate culture will be affected – all necessary knowledge to go the next step.

Shaping the Solution for Ever-Increasing Complexity

When tackling complex change projects, and addressing the first challnage, CGI's change management professionals utilize the iterative Strategic Change Management (iSCM) approach. As with most other frameworks, this approach is based on basic change management frameworks and the most current change management research. However, by its baked-in iterative design, iSCM significantly differs from more stages and waterfall-oriented frameworks such as Kotter, ADKAR, the ACMP Standard, etc. The iSCM approach addresses the need for iteration from the very beginning. That allows change professionals applying iSCM to systemically reconsider the change endeavors' impact. On one hand, the purpose of this approach is to have a standardized method, which easily can be replicated. On the other hand, iSCM is flexible enough to take unforeseen events and identified obstacles into account, by not neglecting the previous efforts of the change project.

Figure 1. iterative strategic change management (iSCM)

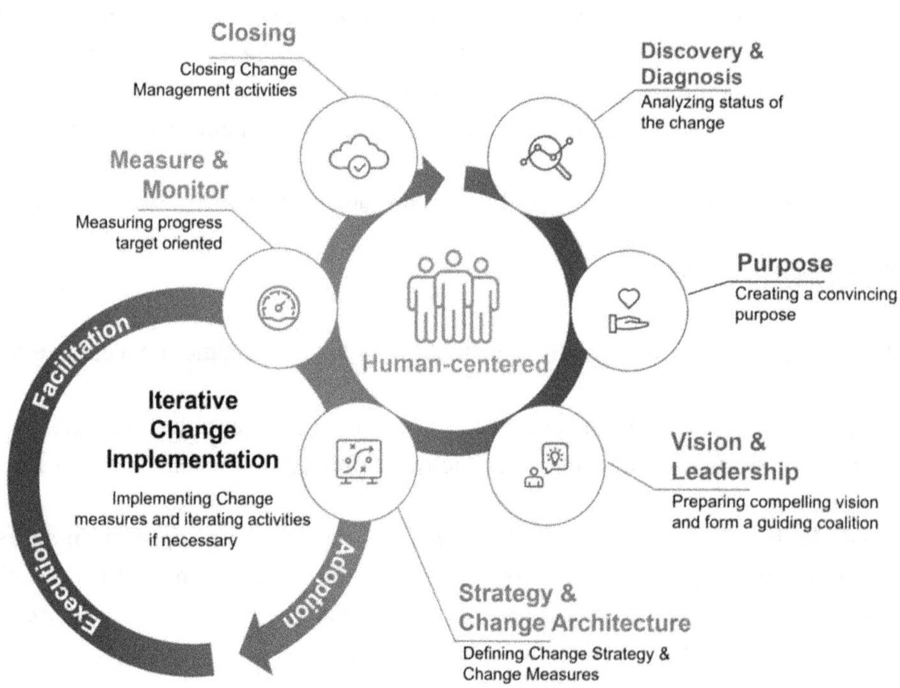

The second challenge – supporting the change sponsor – is addressed by coaches inside and outside of CGI. Since we talk of a mindset shift, most decision-makers need the support of a professional coach to master uncertainty and to be open to iterative approaches.

The third and fourth challenge – data intake and data processing – is the tricky part. Today, change professionals are capable of gathering and processing data. However, if this part is scaled up, it becomes more and more difficult to manage the influx of data. In all of the cases – which today are often sold as data-driven change management – change professionals simply try to slice it in smaller pieces. Usually, this is approached by a kind of work breakdown structure (WBS) or an objective and key result (OKR)-based approach. These are very basic approaches in change management – which is more an art and not magic as some in the field would like you to think. Sometimes this approach is supported by computerized data aggregation, e.g. Roadmap Pro[2], Autodesk[3], or Proxima[4]. However, if supported by computerized data aggregation or not, it can be a time-consuming task (data collection, aggregation, and cleansing), and, due to the pure mass of data, one cannot be sure to cover all important aspects.[5]

At that stage, one can understand every project sponsor not being willing to spend too much money on change management, especially if resources and time are precious. The sponsor – usually not a highly trained change professional – must have faith in the promise that applying change measures keep the performance up (or not), shortens the time of the change endeavor (or not), lowers the costs of the project (or not), and finally reaches the intended business case (or not) – quite a challenging demand from the authors perspective.

Even with sustaining progress in methodologies, data science, AI, and reporting technologies, gaining trustworthy insights for strategic decision-making is still a small fraction of the value gained from advanced analytics. More than ever – especially in times in unprecedented times – organizations and their leaders must enable decision-makers with data-driven and AI-based decision-making processes. Decisions can be visualized and simulated. This is what CGI calls 'value in motion' (CGI, 2022: p. 2).

However, enablement is only one aspect. Besides having data and AI support, leaders and decision-makers have to be prepared to make use of the insights provided and to act fast to respond to events such as a global pandemic or direct and indirect effects of war. This is what CGI calls 'sense and respond instinct' (CGI, 2022: p. 2).

DATA-DRIVEN AND AI-BASED CHANGE MANAGEMENT

To further elaborate on how to approach the challenges, the authors provide insights into the current stage of research and the practical implementation CGI seeks to achieve. They hope to give useful insights to the business and academic community by providing opportunities for discourse on the topic of data-driven and AI-based change management consulting.

Start with a Narrow Model and Iterate

In the current stage, together with CGI AI experts, the authors develop a narrow AI model – which is only the tip of the iceberg. The goal for the first iteration is to have an MVP of a data model and decision tree based on standard indications, e.g. how precise and understandable the change definition for the impacted stakeholders is, if resources are available to achieve the change benefits, or if change leaders act according to the future state and are seen as role-models for the change.

Already the very first steps reveal the aspiration of AI-based and data-driven change management consulting. On one hand, the data model and decision tree must master the inherent complexity of change as presented above itself. The initial model must cover unknown and various triggers of change – even if they appear synchronously. It also must include all affected stakeholders – equally and weighted. On the other hand, the data model and decision tree must reflect the intensity of the specific change which varies from stakeholder to stakeholder. It must also cover the stakeholder's requirements to lower resistance and compensate for the loss of performance which – again – can vary. Finally, the model also needs to cover the aspect of time, since a sample is always time-bound – for AI-based change management consulting, one must master change management before one masters change.

The latter shall be addressed by the second iteration. It will comprise the suggestion of standard methodologies and tools to drive the change endeavor. To achieve the needed commitment this includes instructions on how to facilitate the methodologies and tools in the areas of involvement, e.g. context-sensitive feedback and co-creative strategy definition, enablement, such as classroom sessions and training on the job, appreciation by meaningful recognition and rewards, and change communication.

By taking these steps, organizations are enabled to strategically implement change. In other words, the authors are currently creating a narrow AI model similar to Deep Blue.

Deep Blue became famous in 1997 defeating the Chess Grand Master, Gary Kasparov. The concept is based on a brute force algorithm, which is a straightforward technique to solve problems systematically by calculating all possible solutions, utilizing the problem statement and given definitions (Qureshi, 2018) The authors already know today that this is not sufficient for SCM so this step is more of a learning phase. In parallel, they seek to create a second prototype. This prototype will be based on an artificial neural network (ANN). Still being a narrow AI, the ANN can calculate more solutions. Based on the data available – the organizational demographics, the trigger of change, and change measures – the ANN is trained to identify the best possible solutions within the quadrant of involvement, enablement, appreciation, and communication, to keep performance up and shorten the time of the change endeavor. An ANN – Google's DeepMind[6] – became famous in 2015 and 2016 in defeating the Go champions Fan Hui and Lee Se-dol (Chen, 2022; CNN, 2019; Silver et al., 2016). Already this step would be a major milestone for today's change management practice.

Both, Deep Blue and DeepMind make clear what challenges are lying ahead for AI-based and data-driven change management consulting. While the game-tree complexity of chess (Deep Blue) is already resulting in 10^{120} possible solutions (Shannon Number), Go has a game-tree complexity of approximately 10^{360} (DeepMind) (Allis, 1994; Shannon, 1950). While chess and Go or other games can be considered as a "micro world [...] in which common-sense knowledge and natural languages are not relevant" (Allis, 1994: p. 4) change management addresses exactly these aspects of (corporate) culture.

In this sense, AI-based and data-driven change management consulting is still in the 18th century, when Wolfgang von Kempelen demonstrated his mechanical chess player, the *Schachtürke* in 1796. Today there are tools such as Roadmap Pro, Autodesk, or Proxima to support change professionals with data aggregation. There are also tools such as Pandatron[7] claiming AI as an integral part of their approach, "and yet, in most of these games, humans are (still) superior to their artificial counterparts" (Allis, 1994: p. 4).

However, for the authors – as well as for the whole change management and the AI community – this is not the limit. The next step could go in the direction of IBM's Watson.[8] Still being a narrow AI – the approach will only work in the predefined parameter of SCM – it can analyze natural language and understand the context. Integrating spoken language and the understanding of connoted meaning,

AI-based SCM will be able to integrate the first aspects of culture and unwritten laws – one of the core elements of change management.

Data-driven and AI-based change management consulting will finally leave the surface and dive deeper.

Icebergs Ahead: Ethical AI, Data Governance, and Decision-Making

Diving deeper raises further challenges with the application of a data-driven and AI-based SCM consulting approach. Besides others, such as data aggregation, acquiring training data, the authors focus on ethics, data governance, and decision-making.

Ethics

Ethics is one of the hot topics in AI (Healey, 2020). Jobin et al. (2019) identified 84 ethics guidelines for AI – including industry-led as well as civil society and academia-led initiatives. Especially for change management – not only utilized to mitigate risks in a project but strategically applied to strive for better outcomes – ethical standards are important. The authors argue that contemporary guidelines, such as the Standard for Change Management and ACMP Change Management Code of Ethics must be enhanced or combined with ethical guidelines for AI (ACMP, 2019).

When AI is the "bedrock for decision-making in future-ready organizations" (CGI, 2022: p. 7), it seems not to be sufficient to call upon the responsibility for adding value and ethically contributing to the success of organizations. It is rather necessary to reconsider the mechanics and the decision design. According to Wallace, this starts with diagnosing critical decisions linked to the organization's value and working back to what type of insights and data is needed to understand the context. This process is supported by creating a decision-making framework based on a joint understanding of the values and key business imperatives (Wallace, 2022). According to ACMP, the responsibility for adding value and ethically contributing to the success of organizations is deeply connected with the change practitioner's responsibility for his or her decisions and actions (ACMP, 2019). But what will happen to this responsibility when a machine is creating the decision-making framework and making the respective decisions? Who will have the ultimate responsibility? Therefore, it is imperative that an AI used in SCM consulting is designed with hard-wired ethics, including a code of conduct and focus on human-centered decisions related to the company's decision-making process. These ethics must also uphold while mitigating risks, since already today, very experienced change professionals have the capabilities to channel decision-making processes (CGI, 2022: p. 7).

Discussing ethics in change management is highly complex and the way of communicating during the decision-making process is characterized by multiple layers. For instance, following the ACMP standards and ethics of honesty. How does an AI conduct change communication considering truth, sincerity, and candor, but also having a feeling for the situation and not just bluntly laying out the facts? How often do we as change professionals need to tweak our communication during a concrete situation, such as a client workshop, not endangering the intended change benefits but at the same time not overstepping the red line of dishonesty and insincerity? The change story has not just to be logically understandable. It is as important that it is emotionally justifiable. AI must have this imprinted.

Data Governance and Decision-making

While discussing ethics in change management another question arises regarding the use of AI: is it lawful, to utilize AI during a change process? Or must a change professional always be present, similar to a driver at the steering wheel of a self-driving car?

According to Hoffmann-Riem (2019), "[t]he law must ensure good digital governance [...]" (p. 2). In front of the saying 'Every change is different', particularly the question of machine learning is highly relevant. For instance, a machine learns during a change that the change measures of compensation for job loss and job application support have positive effects on the affected stakeholders to commit to the unavoidable change. However, even if two people have the same preconditions at the first glance – both could settle their housing loan and get a new job immediately – the change might still be more impactful for one of them. Person A and B might be very happy about settling the housing loan. However, person B loses all her social relations, since all her relations are connected to her working environment. After a while person, B realizes this and falls into deep depression (staggered impact). This becomes even more problematic in cases of hidden (unwittingly) or masked (willingly) discrimination, when the collection or aggregation of data is flawed or normative unresponsive. Ensuring accountability, responsibility, transparency, and the capability of integrating lessons learned is of great difficulty but important for AI (European Commission, 2020; Hoffmann-Riem, 2019; Tischbirek, 2019). However – as it is for AI – these aspects are paramount for a trust-building SCM approach. By that, it is inevitable to discuss and find answers to these questions.

Another question for the change processes is: can AI neglect or forget data on purpose? And will this AI ever be strong? In making human-centered decisions related to the company's decision-making process an AI must be able to decide which data is to be used for the respective decision in the change process – again, hidden or masked discrimination is a paramount challenge here. The specific use case could be a change project resulting in laying-off staff. What data – the AI has in principle available or could acquire, e.g. health data or surveillance data, – will be used to come to decisions and adequate change measures? And what if the data available, but not being allowed to use, would lead to better change benefits for all affected stakeholders?

Again, does the AI decide the principles of which data is to be used? Will this decision remain with the human individual and the AI stays weak? Will the decision be made by a strong AI? Or will a potential superior AI responsible for ethical decision-making within decisions contribute to the final change measures?

This becomes further relevant when entering the field of data privacy. "Artificial intelligence, big data analytics, and machine learning challenge the current law [...]" (Marsch, 2019: p 34) and existing legislation (European Parliament, 2020) – or vice versa. According to the General Data Protection Regulation (GDPR), those affected by an automated decision-making process have the right to receive meaningful information about the logic involved in the decision (Art. 20, h GDPR). In addition, the traditional basic concept of data protection law strictly limits the use of AI. Limiting the processing of personal data is one of the cornerstones of the GDPR. The use of AI conflicts with this (Marsch, 2019).

However, current discussions assume that an AI-based decision-making process using so-called Explainable Artificial Intelligence (XAI) – considerably enhances the potential field of application. XAI aims to explain the decision-making parameters of an AI system. With so-called Local Interpretable Model Agnostic Explanations (LIME) variations for the original data set can be generated and the reaction of an AI can be observed. The input parameters for the AI algorithm are derivable and LIME makes the AI-based decisions explainable (Klöker, 2020). According to the European Commission proposals regulating the flow of data is essential, since "citizens and businesses alike need to be able to trust the technology they interact with, have a predictable legal environment and rely on effective safeguards protecting fundamental rights and freedoms" (European Commission, 2018: p. 14). "Trustworthy AI is key to reaping AI's [and change] benefits" (Organisation for Economic Co-operation and Development, 2019: p 16). For SCM this aspect is as important. It is paramount to explain transparently the 'why' of a decision to gain trust for the change endeavor and into the future state.

Still, all the questions presented are not yet fully answered. But to stop scratching the surface and go deeper, these questions must be answered in the future by a whole set of scientific disciplines, above all philosophy, law, sociology, psychology, political science, and ethics, but also by economics, business studies, data science, and informatics.

CONCLUSION: A LONG WAY TO GO

This research is motivated by the goal to contribute to better exploring the field of applied AI. The article laid out that AI-based and data-driven SCM consulting is an uncharted field of research – and application. It provided some answers but also raised new questions. With their current approach, the authors are at the forefront of the research and an early stage of AI maturity. A simple, rule-based approach with scripts and macros is elaborated. That clearly shows that for AI-based and data-driven SCM consulting a long and probably bumpy road lies ahead.

However, the authors intend to induce further scientific research in the field of applied AI, strategy consulting and change management. Besides the obstacles presented, shaping and accompanying AI-based and data-driven SCM consulting, the authors strongly believe it is the most promising path supporting SMEs, social entrepreneurs, or women-owned businesses as well as MNCs. Unprecedented times, rising complexity, and ever-prevailing change will always be present. For that, it is necessary to make better use of data and the possibilities AI is giving to the consulting industry.

Also, the authors' imagination is not limited to what is known today but is buoyed by the fact they are driven by the unknown. Crossing the line to strong AI, the authors can imagine two inclusive possibilities for the future. On the one hand, future AI-based SCM consulting will not only optimize the change endeavor. Simultaneously it will continuously optimize the future state and intended change benefits – a true continuous change. On the other hand, the model will not only apply to change management. It will be possible to change the rules of the game and integrate other areas of problem-solving and consulting. AI will not only apply to one problem. It will apply its intelligence to any problem.

To achieve a fruitful and extensive study environment, the authors not only appeal to scholars to drive their research in the field of applied AI and consulting but also upon leaders and labor representatives to be open and allow experiments with AI-based and data-driven consulting approaches. Today these approaches have to be controlled by change professionals. However, since complicated change projects of the past became increasingly complex change endeavors of today, the future change and transformation aspirations will probably include chaotic environments with an unmanageable mass of unstructured data and the ethical utilization of AI will be inevitable to get change and transformation right.

To lay the foundation the authors also call upon change practitioners utilizing today's data-driven tools to create data for further research and model design.

However, there is one very important aspect not mentioned yet. Introducing and implementing data-driven and AI-based consulting in an organization must be accompanied by SCM. And again, SMEs as well as women-owned businesses and social entrepreneurs face most barriers to implementing AI, similar to that hampering digitization (European Parliament, 2020). And women-owned businesses are affected in a particular way by the implementation of AI (Collett, 2022). That needs to be reflected in SCM consulting endeavors (Donald, 2019), as have the competencies needed in an AI-based future (Bounfour, 2022).

With that outlook, the authors close the article with the words of Robert J. Kennedy: "Some men see things as they are and say why. I dream things that never were and say why not."

REFERENCES

Allis, L. V. (1994). *Searching for Solutions in Games and Artificial Intelligence*. Rijksuniversiteit Limburg. doi:10.26481/dis.19940923la

Armbrüster, T. (2006). *The economics and sociology of management consulting*. Cambridge University Press. doi:10.1017/CBO9780511488467

Association of Change Management Professionals. (2019). *Standard for Change Management and ACMP Change Management Code of Ethics*. Association of Change Management Professionals.

Barbey, A. K., Karama, S., & Haier, R. J. (2021). *The Cambridge handbook of intelligence and cognitive neuroscience*. Cambridge University Press. doi:10.1017/9781108635462

Bounfour, A. (2022). *Platforms and Artificial Intelligence: The Next Generation of Competences*. Springer International Publishing AG. doi:10.1007/978-3-030-90192-9

Bundesministerium für Wirtschaft. (2019). *Wirtschaftsmotor Mittelstand - Zahlen und Fakten zu den deutschen KMU*. Bundesministerium für Wirtschaft.

Bundesverband mittelständische Wirtschaft. (2022). *Der Mittelstand ist Garant für Stabilität und Fortschritt*. BVMW. https://www.bvmw.de/themen/mittelstand/zahlen-fakten/

Burchard, C. (2018). Artificial intelligence and law. In B. Wolff (Ed.), *Whither artificial intelligence? Debating the policy challenges of the upcoming transformation*. Mercator Science-Policy Fellowship-Programme.

CGI. (2022). *Value in motion: Driving forward data-driven decision making*. CGI. https://www.cgi.com/sites/default/files/2021-11/cgi-data-driven-decision-making-value-in-motion-white-paper.pdf

CGI. (2021). *Our commitment to a more inclusive and sustainable world. Corporate Social Responsibility Report 2021*. CGI.

Changefirst (2022). *People-centered Implementation (PCI)*. Changefirst. https://www.changefirst.com

Chen, B. (2022). *Opinion: Can AI be creative? AI can create new content but does not understand its creations*. https://highschool.latimes.com/diamond-bar-high-school/opinion-can-ai-be-creative/

CNN. (2019). *Korean Go master quits the game because AI 'cannot be defeated'*. CNN. https://edition.cnn.com/2019/11/27/tech/go-master-google-intl-hnk-scli/index.html

Collett, C., Neff, G., & Gomes, L. G. (2022). The effects of AI on the working lives of women. UNESCO, Inter-American Development Bank, & Organisation for Economic Co-operation and Development (OECD). doi:10.18235/0004055

DiMatteo. L.A./Poncibò, C./Cannarsa, M. (2022). The Cambridge handbook of artificial intelligence: global perspectives on law and ethics. Cambridge University Press.

Donald, M. (2019). *Leading and Managing Change in the Age of Disruption and Artificial Intelligence.* ProQuest. doi:10.1108/9781787563674

Engel, C., Ebel, P., & van Giffen, B. (2021). *Empirically Exploring the Cause-Effect Relationships of AI Characteristics, Project Management Challenges, and Organizational Change, Wirtschaftsinformatik 2021 Proceedings, Track 10: Design, management and impact of AI-based systems. 3.* University of St. Gallen.

European Commission (2018). *Artificial Intelligence for Europe.* COM(2018) 237. European Commission.

European Commission. (2020) *On Artificial Intelligence - A European approach to excellence and trust, White Paper.*

European Parliament. (2020) *Opportunities of artificial intelligence, Brussels.* European Parliament. https://data.europa.eu/doi/10.2861/692222

Frankish, K., & Ramsey, W. (2014). *The Cambridge handbook of artificial intelligence.* Cambridge University Press. doi:10.1017/CBO9781139046855

Gartner. (2020). *Gartner Top Strategic Predictions for 2019 and Beyond.* Gartner.

Government of Canada. (2021). *Key Small Business Statistics.* https://www.ic.gc.ca/eic/site/061.nsf/vwapj/KSBS_2021.pdf/$FILE/KSBS_2021.pdf

Nash, H. & KPMG (2017). *Harvey Nash/KPMG CIO Survey: Navigation Uncertainly.* KPMG. https://assets.kpmg/content/dam/kpmg/xx/pdf/2017/07/harvey-nash-kpmg-cio-survey-2017.pdf

Healey, J. (2020). *Artificial Intelligence.* The Spinney Press.

Hoffmann-Riem, W. (2019). Artifcial Intelligence as a Challenge for Law and Regulation. In T. Wischmeyer & T. Rademacher (Eds.), *Regulating Artificial Intelligence.* Springer International Publishing AG.

IDC. (2022). *IDC MarketScape: Canadian AI Services 2022 Vendor Assessment.* IDC. https://www.idc.com/research/viewtoc.jsp?containerId=CA48060822

Jobin, A., Ienca, M., & Vayena, E. (2019). The global landscape of AI ethics guidelines. *Nature Machine Intelligence*, *1*(9), 389–399. doi:10.103842256-019-0088-2

Keller, S., & Aiken, C. (2009). *The Inconvenient Truth About Change Management. Why it isn't working and what to do about it.* McKinsey & Company.

Kipping, M. (2003). *Management consulting: emergence and dynamics of a knowledge industry*. Oxford University Press.

Kipping, M., & Clark, T. (2013). *The Oxford handbook of management consulting*. Oxford University Press.

Klöker, A. (2020). Explainable AI verschiebt Grenzen der KI-Nutzung. *vb Versicherungsbetriebe*, 2/2020.

Kotter, J. P. (1996). *Leading the Change*. Harvard Business School Press.

Lauer, T. (2021). *Change Management: Fundamentals and Success Factors*. Springer. doi:10.1007/978-3-662-62187-5

Lewin, K. (1947). Frontiers in group dynamics. Concept, method and reality in social science. Social equilibria and social change. *Human Relations*, *1*(1), 5–41. doi:10.1177/001872674700100103

Marsch, N. (2019). Artifcial Intelligence and the Fundamental Right to Data Protection: Opening the Door for Technological Innovation and Innovative Protection. In T. Wischmeyer & T. Rademacher (Eds.), *Regulating Artificial Intelligence*. Springer International Publishing AG.

MIT. (2020). *How AI Changes the Rules for Management.* https://sloanreview.mit.edu/sponsors-content/infographic-how-ai-changes-the-rules-for-management/

Munoz, J.M./Maurya, A. (2022). *International perspectives on artificial intelligence*. Anthem Press.

Naz, H., Motla, Y. H., Asghar, S., Abbas, M. A., & Khatoon, A. (2013). Effective Usage of AI Technique for Requirement Change Management Practices, *5th International Conference on Computer Science and Information Technology (CSIT),* Amman, Jordan. 10.1109/CSIT.2013.6588769

Nichols, N. (2014). Why Change Management Often Fails: The People. *Forbes.* https://www.forbes.com/sites/sungardas/2014/05/20/the-dirty-side-of-change-management/?sh=70c9fa516297

O'Leary, R. (2021). *Contract Life-Cycle Management Software AI-Centric Marketing: A Reflection of Reality?* IDC. https://www.idc.com/getdoc.jsp?containerId=US48266921&pageType=PRINTFRIENDLY

Office of the US Trade Representatives. (2021). *Small- and Medium-Sized Enterprises (SMEs).* USTR. https://ustr.gov/trade-agreements/free-trade-agreements/transatlantic-trade-and-investment-partnership-t-tip/t-tip-12

Organisation for Economic Co-operation and Development. (2019). *Artificial Intelligence in Society.* OECD. https://ebookcentral.proquest.com/lib/senc/detail.action?docID=6410013

Organisation for Economic Co-operation and Development. (2021). *Financing SMEs and Entrepreneurs 2020: An OECD Scoreboard.* OECD. https://www.oecd-ilibrary.org/finance-and-investment/financing-smes-and-entrepreneurs-2020_061fe03d-en

Prosci (2014). ROI of Change Management Webinar.

Prosci (2018). *Best Practices in Change Management 2018 Edition*, https://www.prosci.com/hubfs/367443/2.downloads/research/2018-Best-Practices-Executive-Summary.pdf?hsLang=en-ca

Prosci (2022a). *The Prosci ADKAR Model*. https://www.prosci.com/methodology/adkar

Prosci (2022b), *Prosci Change Triangle (PCT)*. https://www.prosci.com/methodology/pct-model

Prosci (2022c). *Defining the Value of Change Management*, https://www.prosci.com/resources/webinars/defining-the-value-of-change-management

Prosci (2022d). *Cost-benefit analysis of change management*. https://www.prosci.com/hubfs/367443/2.downloads/thought-leadership/Cost-Benefit-Analysis-TL.pdf?hsLang=en-us

Qureshi, K. (2018). *Advanced Concepts of Information Technology*. Educreation Publishing.

Ryder, A. (2019). *Big Data: artificial intelligence and business strategy. Three steps to implement AI.* https://sloanreview.mit.edu/article/three-steps-to-implement-ai/

Schönecker, D., & Kim, H. (2022). *Kant and Artificial Intelligence*. De Gruyter.

Senge, P. (1990). *The Fifth Discipline: The Art and Practice of the Learning Organization*. Random House.

Shannon, C. E. (1950). Programming a Computer for Playing Chess. *Philosophical Magazine*, *41*(314), 256–275.

Silver, D., Huang, A., Maddison, C. J., Guez, A., Sifre, L., van den Driessche, G., Schrittwieser, J., Antonoglou, I., Panneershelvam, V., Lanctot, M., Dieleman, S., Grewe, D., Nham, J., Kalchbrenner, N., Sutskever, I., Lillicrap, T., Leach, M., Kavukcuoglu, K., Graepel, T., & Hassabis, D. (2016). Mastering the game of Go with deep neural networks and tree search. *Nature*, *529*(7587), 484–489. doi:10.1038/nature16961 PMID:26819042

U. S. Business Administration (2021). *2021 Small Business Profile*. CDN. https://cdn.advocacy.sba.gov/wp-content/uploads/2021/08/30143723/Small-Business-Economic-Profile-US.pdf

Sorg, J. M. (2021). *Experimentalist Regional Goverance. Policy Analysis in Geographic-Functional Regions*. Peter Lang. doi:10.3726/b17629

Sorg, J.M. (n.d.): *Strategic change management. A methodology to calculate the ROI of change*. [unpublished research paper].

Sorg, J. M., Hodge Cunningham, K., & Stoyanova, A. (in press). *Why every CxO should have a court jester. A different introduction to change management*. [unpublished research paper].

Sozinova, A. A., Litvinova, T. N., Kurilova, A., & Morozova, I. A. (2022). Fight against climate change and sustainable development based on ecological economy and management in the AI era. In Frontiers in Environmental Science, 10. doi:10.3389/fenvs.2022.1091149

Stolzenberg, K. (2022). *Change Management: Successfully Shaping Change Processes – Mobilizing Employees. Vision, Communication, Participation, Qualification*. Springer. doi:10.1007/978-3-662-65396-8

Tannin, K. (2022). *Call for Chapters: Change Management During Unprecedented Times*. IGI Global. https://www.igi-global.com/publish/call-for-papers/call-details/6098?

Taulli, T. (2019). Implementing AI The Right Way. *Forbes*. https://www.forbes.com/sites/tomtaulli/2019/04/13/implementing-ai-the-right-way/?sh=5583ee5d57e4

The Guardian. (2020). Interview by Zoë Corbyn. Peter Diamandis: 'In the next 10 years, we'll reinvent every industry'. *The Guardian*. https://www.theguardian.com/technology/2020/jan/25/peter-diamandis-future-faster-think-interview-ai-industry

Tischbirek, A. (2019). Artifcial Intelligence and Discrimination: Discriminating Against Discriminatory Systems. In T. Wischmeyer & T. Rademacher (Eds.), *Regulating Artificial Intelligence*. Springer International Publishing AG.

Vernooij, C., Stuijt, J., Hendriks, M., /Have, W./Have, S. (2022). *Organizational Behaviour and Change Management: The impact of cognitive*, Taylor & Francis Group.

Waardenburg, L., Huysman, M., & Agterberg, M. (2021a). Introduction to managing AI wisely. In L. Waardenburg, M. Huysman, & M. Agterberg (Eds.), *Managing AI wisely: from development to organizational change in practice*. Edward Elgar Publishing. doi:10.4337/9781800887671.00010

Waardenburg, L., Huysman, M., & Agterberg, M. (2021b). Changing work. In L. Waardenburg, M. Huysman, & M. Agterberg (Eds.), *Managing AI wisely: from development to organizational change in practice*. Edward Elgar Publishing. doi:10.4337/9781800887671.00017

Wallace, C. (2022). *Rethinking the mechanics of data-driven decision-making to fuel business value*. CGI. https://www.cgi.com/en/blog/advanced-analytics/rethinking-mechanics-data-driven-decision-making-fuel-business-value

Wischmeyer, T., & Rademacher, T. (2019). *Regulating Artificial Intelligence*. Springer International Publishing AG.

World Bank. (2021). *Small and Medium Enterprises (SMEs) Finance*. World Bank. https://www.worldbank.org/en/topic/smefinance

ENDNOTES

1 International Data Corporation 2022: A query with the advanced search resulted in 0 results for a title search (change management) AND (artificial intelligence), 1 result a title search (change management) AND (AI); Social Sciences Citation Index 2022. A query with the advanced search resulted in 0 results for a title search (TI=(change management)) AND TI=(artificial intelligence); 3 results for a title search (TI=(change management)) AND TI=(artificial intelligence).

2 www.changefirst.com.

3 www.autodesk.com.

4 www.prosci.com/solutions/proxima

5 E.g., during past research to fully understand decision processes and the change behind and +5 million affected stakeholders, around 40 GB of data (approx. 14.000 files) with about 150.000 pages of qualitative data were gathered (Sorg, 2021). Alone the data intake and processing took over 2 years. This means, that just to come to the start line of a change endeavor, can be very time consumptive and expensive.

6 www.deepmind.com.

7 https://pandatron.ai

8 www.ibm.com/watson.s

Chapter 14
Unleashed, Harnessed, and Empowered:
The Potential of Women in the Change Management and Leadership of Crises

Catherine Hayes
University of Sunderland, UK

ABSTRACT

This chapter provides an insight into the challenges faced specifically by women in relation to the agency they are afforded within the context of change management in crisis situations and responses. This is contextualised within global higher education and examined through theoretical perspectives such as neoliberalism, which have impacted so much on the context specificity of change management and the cultures within which it has influenced so greatly. The recent global COVID-19 pandemic is used as a vehicle by which to drive thinking around concepts, which have had such an impact on women during this time, such as emotional labour and inequality. The chapter concludes with a consideration of organisational structures and the agency that this has afforded women both historically and within the leadership challenges they currently face.

INTRODUCTION

'There is nothing wrong with change if it is in the right direction...'

Winston Churchill (1874-1965)

The impact of the COVID-19 pandemic has ensured not only that humanity has dealt with a sudden and harsh reminder of its own position relative to the risks man lives with on an everyday basis, but also the opportunities to initiate and manage the change that these bring, specifically for women in business (Peters et al, 2020). The existential crisis facing Higher Education Institutions as a direct consequence of 2020 has served as a lens through which other facets of ambiguity and contingency also influence

DOI: 10.4018/978-1-6684-7509-6.ch014

meta-thinking concerning their strategic governance and operationalization of policies in practice (Pellegrini et al, 2020). Facing ethical dilemmas, institutional leaders also must grapple with compounding intraneous and extraneous variables which exacerbate the current crisis situations HEIs now face (Rapanta et al, 2020).

BACKGROUND

Whereas the majority of HEIs across the globe work within specific methodological and management methodologies, the capacity for flexible adaptation, creativity, and innovation in crisis, arguably manifests more commonlamongst women leaders than their male counterparts (El-Besomey, 2020). The gender balance and diversity that women bring to executive leadership positions during times of crisis provide a correspondingly more diversified epistemic standpoint through which crises can be considered (Aldrich & Lotito, 2020). These often subtle but diverse differences in knowledge positionality serve to be more transformative than transactional and as such are often more contextually and situationally relevant to immediately pressing issues, offering a wider lens through which to present, frame and articulate considered solutions (Martinez-Leon et al., 2020). Crises impact upon the theoretical underpinnings of the institutional rationales, designs, and operations of these contexts – within HEI and in parallel fields of praxis, where women have been witnessed at executive leadership levels, coping better and more appropriately than their male peers, almost as if facing a hypothetical wartime battle (Benziman, 2020; Maas et al., 2020).

THEORETICAL BACKGROUND

The malalignment of the theoretical framework of HEI relative to the disciplinary perspectives of education has long been annotated as an issue for address (Barnett, 1990), however this was framed at a particularly politically volatile time as a means of highlighting larger ethical issues of concern, rather than crisis as an independent concept (Jandrić et al, 2020). The most recent challenge, presented by COVID-19, is to ensure that pedagogic practice across HEIs can adapt to new teaching and assessment methodologies, whilst at the same time ensuring an optimal quality and student experience for those joining academic programmes of study at HEIs (Rapanta et al., 2020) These experiences will potentially form the foundational bedrock which will ultimately underpin their future careers, lives and capacity for wider civic societal contributions.

Media reports that women in leadership roles have greatly outperformed men in the strategic management of the implications of COVID-19 globally, have become an everyday source of interest and intrigue. The positive lauding of female prime ministers, presidents and politicians has also been counterbalanced by accounts from women with more standard positions on career trajectories, for whom home working, home schooling and the attempted continuance of everyday norms amidst a global pandemic are, by their very nature, far more routine and mundane prospects (Whitty-Collins, 2020). On an even more negative and resonant note, the media have reported on the increased incidence and prevalence rates of domestic violence crimes committed against women, which further detail the challenges that some women (and their children) in 21st Century society also face (Wenham, Smith, & Morgan, 2020).

MAIN FOCUS OF THE CHAPTER

The scope and parameters of this chapter do not permit a consideration of all issues that all women face, rather this chapter provides an insight into the agentic roles of women leaders in global crises, which have ensured their credibility and dependability in times of greatest challenge to the context of Higher Education (HE) leadership across the world. A collective insight into the roles of women leaders within the COVID-19 pandemic has been featured widely in the international press, where multi-agency perspectives on their actions and reactions have been largely positive (Trent, 2020). However, this media frenzy lies a far deeper debate in just how representative these women leaders are of those working within diverse HE leadership contexts and settings and how far transferable their situational leadership skills are (Henley & Roy, 2020).

The individual positionality of all women is equally important to those who operate as strategic heads of state and whose lives are largely characterised by the privilege of hierarchical positions and the status accompanying them (Bright, Acosta, & Parker, 2020; Inman, 2020)). This chapter aims to provide an insight into the existing evidence base of how women leaders in Higher Education during a global pandemic, such as COVID-19, cope in reality. Not only does this illuminate the reality of concepts such as emotional labor, mental health and well-being and authenticity, it also serves to delineate the personhood of women from the professional roles they occupy across our global societies, within the situational specificity of Higher Education (Tshivhase, 2020).

In its entirety, this chapter also serves to deconstruct the characteristic and agentic qualities of women leaders amidst global crises, which are also reflected in the traits of women managing in more recognizable and relatable leadership roles in the context of Higher Education leadership (Thomas, 2020). The core acknowledgments that on a global level the impact of crises inevitably leads to a disproportionate impact on women, a lack of prioritization of global impetus to address levels of gender inequality, and the embedded role of gender equity in relation to human progression and development on a macro level is apparent (Power, 2020; WHO, 2020). This global perspective illuminates the inequalities that women educators face and the impact that this has on the broader scope of professional development through educational impact (Barba & Iraizoz, 2020). Whilst situational specificity is significant in terms of the context of HE leadership, the universality of human experience underpinning them remains the connecting thread, which enables the deconstruction of meaning-making in applied educational leadership experiences.

ROOTING PROACTIVE RESPONSE IN CRISIS

Crisis management of any variety necessitates a proactive response, rooted in complex ambiguity, which is non-conventional and is underpinned by active application of cognition, metacognition, and epistemic cognition to practice. In terms of temporal issues, response times can necessitate an immediacy of thinking and correspondingly rapid response, all of which may have potentially long-term consequences, necessitating leaders to be both accountable and responsible for their actions. Parallel to this lies Mezirow's (2009) Perspective Transformation Theory, posited by Mezirow, in relation to transformative learning as,

"... the epistemology of how adults learn to reason for themselves - advance and assess reasons for making a judgement - rather than act on the assimilated beliefs, values, feelings and judgements of others..."

In terms of overall cognitive processing in the contexts of crisis, how gender is of direct relevance is rooted in the increased capacity women have, relative to men, to think flexibly, adaptably and with compassion (Villiers, 2019). This is not to denigrate the gender attributable skill sets of male employees across HEIs but to acknowledge that how people problem solve and react can often have its basis in concepts which are adjuncts to, rather than facets of gender. Whereas men are geared towards objective problem solving in binary 'black and white' fashions as opposed to the capacity to think in shades of grey, which women more clearly demonstrate, what is clear, is that situation and context are the pivotal deciding variables in terms of the need for immediacy of action (Cahdriyana, et al., 2019). These problematic frames of reference, described by Mezirow in the context of education, serve to explain how humans monitor their problem-solving capacities, once engaged in contexts and settings of complex ambiguity, where contingency planning comes to the fore (Mezirow, 2009).

THE IMPACT OF COMPLEX AND DISRUPTIVE AMBIGUITY

Within the context of complex and disruptive ambiguity in crisis, the capacity for both critical reflection and critical reflexivity are paramount. Self-awareness features highly as one of the core aspects of being able to undertake either optimally and effective action, since how responsive behaviour's may be viewed by others, and the interrelationship of this with the alternative perspective of others can be indicators of potential success in crisis management. Illuminating this awareness enables a further conceptual consideration of the gender delineation occurring naturally because of the agentic qualities and attributes of women in the context of crisis management.

What is pivotal in these incidences is the capacity for and subsequent integration of tacit knowledge to practice, which stems from not only an extant evidence base but also experiential learning and wisdom, rather than any certainty or concretization of new knowledge (Dewey, 1933). It is this which is transformational rather than transactional in terms of application and use in leadership praxis and aligns directly with the traditional gender traits of women and men in executive leadership positions, respectively. Through the advancement of the body of work in cognitive psychology at the turn of the 21st century, and the understanding of epistemic assumptions, models such as 'the reflective judgment model' posited by King and Kitchener (2004) (see Table 1 overleaf) lend themselves to adapted application in relation to gender delineation. Whilst all of these are evidence based on the extant literature, the issues of situational specificity and context are pivotal in any consideration of complex ambiguity in crisis, not least because of the relative certainty of knowledge within them.

Table 1. A Gender delineation adaptation of the King and Kitchener (2004) reflective judgement model

Thinking Stage	Potential Impact on Agentic Qualities
Stage 1 ***Pre-reflective***	Knowledge is absolute and concrete, no reason to ask why, I believe only what I have seen and thus know it to be true-single category belief system – exposure to diversity of thinking.
Stage 2 ***Pre-reflective***	Knowledge is absolutely certain but not readily available to everyone, the right person in authority needs to be sought– some people hold right beliefs and some people hold wrong beliefs - similar to Perry's dualism observed or taught by an authority figure.
Stage 3 ***Pre-reflective***	Knowledge is assumed to be absolutely certain or temporarily uncertain and believe that absolute truth will be manifest in concrete data sometime in the future. Implicitly they maintain that ultimately all problems have solutions.
Stage 4 ***Quasi-reflective***	Knowledge is no longer certain, there is always a layer of ambiguity, limitations of the knower are acknowledged and without certainty knowledge cannot be validated. Well-structured problems such as arithmetic can be described completely, and ill-structured problems are afforded legitimacy at this stage.
Stage 5 ***Quasi-reflective***	Knowledge is contextual and subjective, interpretations are different, so knowledge is different.
Stage 6 ***Reflective***	Knowing is uncertain and knowledge must be understood in relation to the context from which it was derived. Knowledge is constructed through evaluation, comparing knowledge and opinions across contexts, an initial basis for forming judgement/solutions to ill-structured problems.
Stage 7 ***Reflective***	Knowing is uncertain and subject to interpretation and epistemically justifiable claims can be made about the best solution to the problem. Knowledge as an outcome and a process of evaluation. Re-evaluation, new methods of inquiry, or new perspectives become available over time.

GENDER-BASED CAPACITY FOR PROCESSES OF CRITICAL REFLEXIVITY

Axiologically identifiably fixed and typically white male, middle-aged, middle-class mindsets have shaped the society within which corporate leadership operates, with global Higher Education Institutions being no exception. The perspectives these fixed mindsets are rooted in, stems not only from professional bias, but the constraints of cultures which seek to categorise, label and define men and women in relation to biology rather than their capacity to function as leaders, where gender is and ought to be regarded as matterless. What is evident is that the characteristic agentic qualities of both genders differ but what is equally clear is that these have been socially constructed over the course of lifetimes and it is a change in the fixed mindset of modern society that is gradually enabling recognition and acknowledgement of this. Sadly, whilst the COVID-19 pandemic may increase access to educational opportunities and potentially widen participation, the economic effects will have a greater negative impact, restricting even basic access to educational opportunity. In May 2020 the World Bank estimated that 60 million people at risk of being pushed into extreme poverty worldwide as a result of Covid; erasing all progress made to alleviate poverty over the past 3 years. This will likely adversely impact upon women in particular.

Tversky & Kahneman (1974) provided some of the first insights into how judgements under uncertainty, which primarily rely on three heuristics are made. The first, is the probability or likelihood of something, the second is the plausibility of it occurring at all and finally the capacity to develop dual process thinking. Considering all three in the context of the COVID-19 pandemic, has necessitated an instinctual and emotional response, which fits into Tversky and Kahneman's definitive System 1 thinking, whereas System 2 has a tendency to engage logic and systematic thinking. The agentic qualities of women and men, although attributable to societal construction correspond with these Systems of duality. What enables coping in crisis situations, is not actually an innate capacity to cope, but the recognition and address of complex ambiguity. Where the agentic qualities of women are an advantage here, is that they have a tendency for relationality and transformation as opposed to the functionalism and transactional approaches traditionally adopted by men.

WOMEN'S LEADERSHIP IN THE CONTEXT OF HIGHER EDUCATION

Despite HEI's making formal recognition of barriers to women reaching senior management positions across their organisational hierarchies, their executives have done relatively little to address issues of structure and agency in relation to antiquated practices that perpetuate these identified inequities (O'Connor, 2020). The situational and contextual backdrops which influence these inequities globally are, of course, largely defined by subcultures and contexts at macro, micro and meso levels – the ecological perspectives of where change has been lost in translation in an effort to quite often tokenistically address gender inequity in the workplace are often clearly tangible (Grimson and Grimson, 2019). However authentic approaches to tackling the provision of opportunities for women are rooted too, in wider societal actions and agencies which women respond to prior to and in the early development of establishing a professional identity. The perpetuation of an underrepresentation of women in senior management positions within the labour market generally, and the higher education senior leadership market specifically, is an issue for address. The commonality of issues surrounding women in HEI leadership positions within and between diverse countries, is widely reported as something which transcends cultural barriers and contextual specificities. What unites the relative framing and positioning of these roles is the inflexibility of organisational infrastructures to accommodate diversity beyond feminist tokenism, which contributes directly to a lack of accessibility to leadership roles for women. This is a historical legacy characterised predominantly by dated approaches to the integration of women into the labour market at executive leadership levels (O'Connor, 2019). Remuneration levels are all too often aligned with this inequity and what is evident is that whereas globally most institutions are making moves to close the gender pay gap, they are doing relatively little to change the infrastructure and support for potential women leaders, which impacts on the degree of opportunity afforded to them during their career trajectories (Heymann et al, 2019; Taylor et al, 2017). These career trajectories, by virtue of biological function, are still inevitably interrupted by maternity leave and caring responsibilities to a larger extent than the careers of their male counterparts. Equality and diversity initiatives at national levels in the UK, now ensure that many organisations are designated the status of equal opportunities employers, which have seen the rise of initiatives such as the Athena Swann mark emblazoned across HEI provider websites, reflecting their articulated capacity to advocate and support equal opportunities in the workplace. Whether this impacts authentically on these wider issues of structures and agency is something only longer-term evaluation will reveal.

Whilst equality proofing quality initiatives serve well in the identification of the impact of policies which have unintentionally negative impacts on women in practice, one key challenge is being able to identify and filter out the factors underpinning them. In the context of wider professional practice measures these can potentially serve to identify unintended policy impacts but serve neither to identify mechanisms to monitor or reverse the ongoing masculinisation of HEI provision. It ought to be expected that those countries which implement these policy initiatives (e.g., UK, New Zealand, Australia and Sweden) have a greater degree of success in their levels of equal opportunity for women in HEIs but the published research evidence actually points to countries such as Turkey, Portugal and Cyprus having better success rates despite having no formal nationally applied gender based equality initiatives in formal operation (Tanova et al, 2008; Reay, 2004).

THE IMPACT OF NEOLIBERALISM ON HIGHER EDUCATION AND WOMEN LEADERS

Neoliberalism has had an extraordinary impact on the structure and agency of HEIs, with the commodification of education necessitating a new wave of managerialism which has been equally entrenched with misogyny as an integral part of the realms of traditional academia (Meyers, 2013). Characterized by a culture of often toxic masculinity, the tangible and lasting impact, which actively disadvantages women leaders, is well reported in the existing published evidence base surrounding this issue (Canaan & Shumar, 2008). On a global level, this impact varies in relation to the extent of the emergence of managerialism in HEIs, where female academic presence is predominant in humanities and those disciplines perceived as 'soft' in comparison to their overtly male-led empirical science disciplines. The interrelationship with poor opportunities for external research funding across these female-dominated academic disciplines has provided a now historically visible delineation between the genders, with the motivational climate for progression being negatively affected since there is little to no opportunity for the development and integration of creativity and imagination (Bagilhole, 2019).

This has not only had an impact at a disciplinary level for women, it also directly impacts on their future likelihood of being able to gain full professorships, a pathway which is often necessary to gain an academic senior management position in reputable and credible HEIs. Since the relative number of women operating at the professorial level is significantly different across countries, and particularly in countries such as Ireland, which has the least proportion of women employed at either professorial or associate professorial levels, then it is also still evident that these women have least opportunity for promotion to executive roles in HEIs (Bailes & Guthery, 2020). As an adjunct to these statistics, is the fact that women also are far more likely to shoulder additional responsibilities in relation to caring for children, elderly relatives. This, alongside having to continually make a stand against the gender stereotyping which characterises 21st Century HEI workplaces paints a picture, which to some women leaders can be perceived as overwhelming and not worth the additional effort needed to challenge them. By continually instilling and reinforcing this culture into the contexts and settings of where women work in academia, these women often also begin to recognise that the gate keeping which prevents their progression in organisations, also ensures that their perception of a career trajectory at professorial level and consequently in executive management is fundamentally illusory to them (ibid, 2008).

To move beyond the tokenism that characterises male hegemony in HEIs globally, a key issue for address is the minimal representation of women within senior management positions. The challenges faced by women who do venture into these positions often serves to further highlight the extent of male domination at senior management level that exists within these HEIs. This tokenism has also ensured that women are not in positions where they can actively challenge either toxic masculinity or the supplementary structure and agency that prevail in today's HEI workplaces and which continue to resonate in the context of HEI women leadership (Wheaton & Kezar, 2019).

SIGNATURE PEDAGOGIES-DRIVERS OF GENDER EQUITY IN HIGHER EDUCATION

The longevity of male dominance in particular disciplinary subjects such as mathematics, science and engineering has done little to positively enhance the quality and duration of HEI women leaders' career trajectories. An evidence-based insight into this reveals a clear deficit of female professors across these disciplines, which bears witness to the corresponding longevity and history of education locally, nationally and globally. One of the first steps to deconstructing this inequality is, as the STEM initiative in the UK has focused upon, to encourage equity and new awareness of careers available in traditionally male dominated professions (Fitzgerald, 2020). Where gendered organisational culture and processes are evident in favour with male employees, it is apparent from the literature that, conformity is also more widely valued than attributes of creativity, and, as a by-product, innovation. This has been both historically and contemporaneously apparent in the body of literature available but amidst crisis with the advent of the COVID-19 pandemic, has never been more relevant.

In HEIs which have demonstrably lower levels of women at senior executive levels across their organisations, this brings into question the purist epistemic assumptions which are clearly non diverse and non-aspirational in terms of equality, diversity and as a consequence creativity. The exponential reach afforded by a clear capacity for a diverse workforce, not merely constructed of ideological representation, but one of operationalised knowledge and skill, is immeasurable and has been clearly evidenced by the progression of parallel fields of practice (Evidence Here). As an active consequence of these dilemmas which have pervaded organisations for the best part of half a century, issues of gatekeeping, the impact of gendered cultures and infrastructures policies and initiatives are at last beginning to feature mechanisms of moving forward positively but they also indicate the extreme way to go that organisation have to correct these systemic imbalances. What is clear is that if central policy does not change to reflect these needs, the governments, which also reflect an imbalance in the representation of women in executive roles, will persist in influencing the macro levels of society at which meso and micro levels are then by default poised to remain indefinitely.

TRADITIONALIST LEGACIES IN HIGHER EDUCATION

Research has been conducted which conclusively identifies that senior managers of HEI organizations believe or hold assumptions that women, from a signature pedagogy perspective, are far more likely to work in the context of disciplines such as the social sciences, arts and humanities - those often termed 'soft subjects' or those which are responsible in health and medical care in the remit of 'caring' such as nursing (Dilnot, 2018; Henderson et al., 2018). They also perceived those empirical sciences due to the cultural necessity of maintaining the status quo of daily operations would potentially be interrupted by career breaks and the accommodation of caring responsibilities.

In contrast to this perspective though, remains the fact that women's choice of study during school and university years also demonstrates that relatively few young women wish to study subjects such as science, technology, engineering and mathematics and as the current initiatives in UK educational settings indicate, this has become an identified area for redress in terms of changing the misconceptions that girls have about academic study in the post-compulsory sector (Lannelli & Duta, 2018). At a macro level, the labour market dictates the value of subject disciplines by leaders of global societies, where the representation of women leadership is also comparatively low. Reflective of this, is the fact that a corresponding hierarchy of subjects and disciplines exist, which is positively reinforced by the masculine perspectives driving their need. Because of this, fewer women follow maths, technology and sciences in preference to the arts, humanities and social sciences. Aligned with the capacity for maximal earning capacity in the labour market are the opportunities to work in disciplines of these empirical studies, hence widening the gap between men and women in the potential to gain highly paid roles.

Again, the redress of this balance would serve to close the gender income gap which characterizes global economies. Research also highlights that those disciplines with which women more readily engage, also contribute widely to the development of the skill sets that men are known to lack. Gender segregation in the early stages of student learning at school can be regarded as a key cause of the gender gap, both economically and in terms of leadership opportunities that women experience throughout their academic careers. Where these are of greatest concern is in relation to the concepts of citizenship, which HEIs often claim to incorporate as an integral part of their organizational strength across global communities. Within this context, diversity and equality are two issues upon which the capacity for citizenship and capacity for active civic reach, can hinge.

POLITICS

The delineating features of women who have dominated as successful political leaders, both historically and contemporaneously, can be aligned with the agentic qualities associated with the concept of stereotypical gender stereotyping. In European contexts, two of the most typical examples are Baroness Margaret Thatcher and Angela Merkel. What these distinguished women reveal, upon analysis is a capacity for both the transactional autocratic style characterised by professional positionality and a task-oriented approach, usually associated with male hegemony alongside an equally desirable skill set which is linked not only with strategic success but also social justice in a truly transformative sense. The transformative leadership usually associated with successful female leadership echoes and reinforces the theoretical perspectives of Mezirow. This capacity for remaining person-centred alongside the strength and resilience associated with making decisions which are not always palatable for a wider collective benefit remains at the heart of realising that organisational factors such as gender comparison, situation, context, and hierarchy are all important moderators of leadership style in practice. All these agentic qualities are still confounded with the concept of gender.

The active delineation of leadership from management is important. It was perhaps best operationally defined for the context of HEIs by Gardner (1995), when he defined it, accounting for both task and relationship dimensionality, as

'The ability to influence, either directly or indirectly, the behaviour, thoughts and actions of a significant number of individuals'

Since temporality, situation and context are inherently dynamic and altered at any given point, it can be stated that there is no such thing as definably perfect leadership. It is optimal leadership and not management which is the greatest determinant of organisational success. This was a key mechanism for solving both public and private sector challenges, often many of which are politically underpinned in the context of HEI settings.

In times of societal crisis, the words of Fitzgerald (2003) resonate harshly in the culture and climate of today's HEI organisations, when the assertion 'Conceptualisations of leadership without full account of both gender and ethnicity are futile'. Recent impacting factors on how we consider all leaders, not merely on the basis of their gender, add an extra dimension to how best crisis ought to be managed and how long held assumptions and pre-suppositions can be actively challenged in practice.

Critical to this is the capacity for self-reflection and the desire to implement critical reflexivity at the heart of crisis environments. Mezirow's now seminal work on transformative learning can be seen as the keystone that enables all people to be seen as more than simply a collection of qualifications and experience, towards knowing people who know themselves. This is arguably one of the few mechanisms of being able to claim true and authentic approaches to the leadership and management of self, alongside organisations and institutions whose infrastructures serve to permeate wider society as an integral part of their civic contribution to society.

DEBUNKING THE DEFICIT MODEL MYTH

Within longstanding published literature it is well established that the skills that leading in the context of HEIs entails are not actually gendered at all (Burke & Crozier, 2014). More recently it has been recognized that these skills are centered around the capacity and capability for endurance in relation to hard work, strategic vision, evidence of reputational impact in research, the courage to manage in the context of taking measured risk and the resilience and integrity to operationalize what is necessary for success (Meletiadou, 2022). From an axiological standpoint, it is more often the case that the value placed upon what women leaders do, stems from the value of the disciplinary perspectives from which they emerge, rather than any overt judgment surrounding gender (Jamali et al., 2022). Within the context of male senior management there are far more likely to be male academics from traditionally masculine subjects such as science and engineering, whereas, due to the historical legacies and patterns of humanities and caring professions, women are far less likely to have worked with and alongside them (Bauer & Taylor, 2022).

New public governance of organizations has meant that a strategic revamp of most of the organizational structuring has taken place across HEIs globally, however whilst these have shifted things predominantly towards a consumer-led market perspective, the impact on the gendered leadership in HEIs has arguably been only vaguely considered. Therefore, these axiological standpoints are often little more than tokenism in relation to the practical application of values based strategic vision to practice. Arguably the best starting point for axiological underpinnings to be addressed, lies at the heart of organizational structures and cultures, which enable the authentic agency of women to flourish and to be genuinely valued (Tiwary & Gupta, 2022). Since core values lie at the credibility of every HEI across the globe, these remain ongoing areas for address and further research.

Women leaders are far more likely to express a capacity for collective and relationship behavioural approaches in practice, than male leaders, who are more likely to adopt purely transactional leadership strategies and operationalize these in practice. As a consequence of this approach, women are often deemed to be less effective since their capacity to deal with complex ambiguity often entails detailed critical thinking as opposed to the binary decision-making associated with transactional approaches (O'Connor et al., 2022). This is wholly dependent on the situational specificity of organizational contexts, which ultimately provides a platform for leadership execution and the ethos evident within it, in relation to differing leadership styles and approaches (Ruben, Mahon, & Shapiro, 2022).

Pyramidal Organisational Hierarchies and Gender Constraint in Leadership

The formal administration structures of HEIs have altered little in a century. Still featuring a pyramidal structure where women notoriously occupy the bottom rung of the organizational hierarchy, remains a typical profile for the majority of global HEIs. In European and American HEIs, initiatives aimed specifically at addressing gender equity in education, are thriving, which aim to provide transformational leadership opportunities and development for women. These provide bespoke training, education and progression pathways for those who wish to further their academic career trajectories but are limited in availability and opportunity to access them is often lacking in equity of opportunity. The central issue of capacity for women leaders in HEIs is not actually the number of women in HEIs across the globe but rather the positions they occupy, which tend to be traditionally clustered at the bottom of the organizational hierarchy with minimal degrees of representation at higher levels.

As a consequence, women rarely progress to the level of Dean, but do occupy their subordinate positions as Associate Deans, Directors or Pro Vice Chancellors, rather than linchpin positions at the top. This is a source of blocking women's access to powerful positions and thus exerting a vision for the next generation of female leaders. Perhaps the greatest danger in this dynamic is the sheer invisibility of organizational and gender-based bias, which serves to block female progression. As a key aspect of social justice and equity in action, as both process and goal this is a fundamental area for address across the globe where untapped potential and the provision of opportunity warrant redress (McNair, Bensimon, & Malcom-Piqueux, 2020; Okoli et al., 2020).

Men are far more likely to attribute the underrepresentation or lack of women in executive-level positions to the breaks they necessarily take in relation to family caring responsibilities, career interruptions due to pregnancy and their comparative and relative lack of research impact in HEI praxis. In contrast women's perceptions of the same experience are littered with reports of actively overt and covertly demonstrated workplace discrimination, fuelled by the basis of their gender. Unlike the successes of Merkel and Thatcher in a political setting, where transformative learning is valued, the opposite has been found to be largely true in the context of HEI settings, where the higher women climb within the organizational hierarchy, the more they assume the character traits represented by male leaders, where they become deliberately and overly transactional (Allen & Flood, 2018).

As a direct consequence of this, they progressively develop the same perspectives, that recruitment on the basis of gender is something that ought to be tokenistic rather than something actually addressed in HEI professional practice. These deficit models are potentially damaging, but even more so where this is often unintentionally reinforced by members of their own gender as a consequence of the cultural normalization of gender stereotyping (Teelken & Deem, 2013). Göransson, et al. (2008) stated that gendered organizational cultures are in turn linked to gendered knowledge, which means the naturally occurring agentic qualities with which women are wired to lead, are often masked by the bureaucracy and culture of organizations, rather than anything else. As a consequence, the hegemonic and often toxic masculinity which drives organizations pervades into the wider cultural climate and becomes entrenched and difficult to address. At the heart of addressing these issues is the nature of recruitment and the nature of actively retaining women through to the point where they have visibly recognizable opportunities to apply for promotion or at least seek a career trajectory reflective of their capacity and capability. This is apparent across many professional disciplines in the context of Higher Education (Hayes & Graham 2020; Bellini et al., 2019). The nature of women's participation is also an issue, since they need the basis of equity and inclusivity to participate on an equal footing with their male counterparts. Those pragmatic issues which serve as barriers to this, are often found in the institutional operational policies within which all staff are required to work, regardless of academic or professional discipline (Cardel et al., 2020).

ACTIVE PARTICIPATION VERSUS VISIBLE REPRESENTATION OF GENDER IN HEIS

The agentic qualities that women do bring to the context of executive leadership within the context of HEIs are based around their capacity for creativity and as a direct consequence the bridge to innovation that this secures (Lipton, 2015). They are also widely reported as enhancing capacity for effective communication and an authentic approach to dealing with both the professional and personal needs of others.

Perhaps dwelling overly on long-held debates of both the metaphorical glass ceiling and glass escalator ought to be diminished by the consideration of women, who whilst largely atypical of female representativeness across HEIs, provide important lessons surrounding the agentic qualities which have underpinned their success (Arriaga, Stanley, & Lindsey, 2020).

Presenting these women as exemplars, however runs two distinct risks which have important implications for professional practice (Jameson, 2019). Firstly, the situations and contexts within which all women operate as leaders are largely unique and therefore the opportunity to emulate success is limited and secondly, women who are unable to transfer approaches into the context of their own workplace have an increased potential to perceive they will fail. Actually, in relation to the concept of failure, there are far wider independent variables and contextual issues at play, which correspondingly align with the far wider cultural challenges of organisational norms (Benslimane & Moustaghfir, 2020).

SOLUTIONS AND RECOMMENDATIONS

One of the most insightful set of perspectives are those presented by Syed (2019) whose perspective on the need for accuracy rather than creativity in the progressive development of change on major world issues such as feminism. His debate that during COVID-19 some leaders have demonstrated a clear capacity to pivot between leadership styles via the integration of both diverse views and binary decision-making processes.

FUTURE RESEARCH DIRECTIONS

Reconciling the perceived tension that arises when seeking to increase diversity within established meritocracies remains a pivotal debate in any consideration of women and their opportunities to use innate agency within the crisis. Doubtless this will prevail, although the pandemic has provided a forum for the illumination of not just exceptional women from the higher echelons of society but all those coping in more everyday settings of the home, the office and beyond.

CONCLUSION

This chapter has explored the fundamental impact of how gendered leadership in Higher Education Institutions can shape culture, context, and the civic progression of women's roles across professional contexts. The chapter has provided a theoretical insight into how the gender balance and diversity that women bring to leadership positions can strategically influence recovery from the crisis. It has been possible to consider how traditional signature pedagogies and disciplinary perspectives can often serve to stereotype and create assumptions about the need for leadership styles which are traditionalist, outmoded and lacking in creativity. The agentic roles occupied by women, as outlined in the chapter enable the illumination of workplace issues such as emotional labor and mental health to highlight core issues in the professional context of Higher Education Institutes. The proactivity that global responses to crisis necessitate have ensured that the universality of human experience, is now an integral part of not only the dynamic management of crisis but also recovery from it.

Gender delineation and theoretical consideration of how the crisis impacts on the agentic qualities of leadership in crisis has been a fundamental part of considering how best to address progressive thinking in the context of future progression in educational leadership in this chapter, within which capacity for critical reflexivity is essential. It is here that the relational capacity of women and their ability to undertake processes of metacognition which not only impact on functional responses but the potential impact of them, can be considered. Creativity and innovation that stems from unlocked diversity of thought will be sorely needed to address both the educational delivery challenges presented by the COVID-19 and adaptations necessary to deal with its long-lasting economic impact. The ongoing challenge for women, is to engage these as opportunities to be grappled with, as opposed to avoiding them for any perceived lack of confidence, knowledge and skill which has arisen from the projection of wrong assumption and traditional-dominated organizational cultures and climates.

REFERENCES

Aldrich, A. S., & Lotito, N. J. (2020). Pandemic performance: Women leaders in the Covid-19 crisis. *Politics & Gender*, *16*(4), 1–9. doi:10.1017/S1743923X20000549

Allen, T. G., & Flood, C. T. (2018). The experiences of women in higher education: Who knew there wasn't a sisterhood? *Leadership and Research in Education*, *4*, 10–27.

Arriaga, T. T., Stanley, S. L., & Lindsey, D. B. (2020). *Leading while female: A culturally proficient response for gender equity*. Corwin.

Bagilhole, B. (2019). Against the odds: Women academics' research opportunities. In Gender, Teaching and Research in Higher Education (pp. 46-56). Routledge.

Bailes, L. P., & Guthery, S. (2020). Held down and held back: Systematically delayed principal promotions by race and gender. *AERA Open*, *6*(2), 2332858420929298. doi:10.1177/2332858420929298

Barba, I., & Iraizoz, B. (2020). Effect of the great crisis on sectoral female employment in Europe: A structural decomposition analysis. *Economies*, *8*(3), 64. doi:10.3390/economies8030064

Barnett, R. (1990). The idea of higher education. McGraw-Hill education (UK).

Bauer, N. M., & Taylor, T. (2022). Selling them short? Differences in news coverage of female and male candidate qualifications. *Political Research Quarterly*, 10659129221086024.

Bellini, M. I., Graham, Y., Hayes, C., Zakeri, R., Parks, R., & Papalois, V. (2019). A woman's place is in theatre: Women's perceptions and experiences of working in surgery from the Association of surgeons of Great Britain and Ireland women in surgery working group. *BMJ Open*, *9*(1), e024349. doi:10.1136/bmjopen-2018-024349 PMID:30617103

Benslimane, M., & Moustaghfir, K. (2020). Career development practices and gender equity in higher education. *International Journal of Management Education*, *14*(2), 183–211.

Benziman, Y. (2020). "Winning" the "battle" and "beating" the COVID-19 "enemy": Leaders' use of war frames to define the pandemic. *Peace and Conflict*, *26*(3), 247–256. doi:10.1037/pac0000494

Bright, A., Acosta, S., & Parker, B. (2020). Humility matters: Interrogating our positionality, power, and privilege through collaboration. In *Handbook of Research on Diversity and Social Justice in Higher Education* (pp. 19–40). IGI Global. doi:10.4018/978-1-7998-5268-1.ch002

Burke, P. J., & Crozier, G. (2014). Higher education pedagogies: Gendered formations, mis/recognition and emotion. *Journal of Research in Gender Studies*, *4*(2), 52.

Cahdriyana, R. A., Richardo, R., Fahmi, S., & Setyawan, F. (2019, March). Pseudo-thinking process in solving logic problem. []. IOP Publishing.]. *Journal of Physics: Conference Series*, *1188*(1), 012090. doi:10.1088/1742-6596/1188/1/012090

Canaan, J. E., & Shumar, W. (Eds.). (2008). *Structure and agency in the neoliberal university* (Vol. 15). Routledge. doi:10.4324/9780203927687

Cardel, M. I., Dhurandhar, E., Yarar-Fisher, C., Foster, M., Hidalgo, B., McClure, L. A., & Willig, A. L. (2020). Turning chutes into ladders for women faculty: A review and roadmap for equity in academia. *Journal of Women's Health*, *29*(5), 721–733. doi:10.1089/jwh.2019.8027 PMID:32043918

Dewey, J. (1933). *How we think a restatement of the relation of reflective thinking to the educative process*. Heath & Co Publishers.

Dilnot, C. (2018). The relationship between A-level subject choice and league table score of university attended: The 'facilitating', the 'less suitable', and the counter-intuitive. *Oxford Review of Education*, *44*(1), 118–137. doi:10.1080/03054985.2018.1409976

El-Besomey, D. A. M. (2020). The contemporary vision of universal strategic planning for facing (COVID-19) crisis in the field of higher education via virtual learning-training. *European Journal of Education*, *3*(2), 151–164. doi:10.26417/869dvb85y

Fitzgerald, T. (2020). Mapping the terrain of leadership: Gender and leadership in higher education. *Irish Educational Studies*, *39*(2), 1–12. doi:10.1080/03323315.2020.1729222

Gardner, H. (1995). *Leading minds*. Harper Collins.

Göransson, K. E., Ehnfors, M., Fonteyn, M. E., & Ehrenberg, A. (2008). Thinking strategies used by registered nurses during emergency department triage. *Journal of Advanced Nursing*, *61*(2), 163–172. doi:10.1111/j.1365-2648.2007.04473.x PMID:18186908

Grimson, J., & Grimson, W. (2019). Eliminating gender inequality in engineering, industry, and academia. In *The Engineering-Business Nexus* (pp. 315–339). Springer. doi:10.1007/978-3-319-99636-3_15

Hayes, C., & Graham, Y. N. (2020). Prophylaxis in action: # MeToo for women of medical and surgical disciplines. In *Gender Equity in the Medical Profession* (pp. 270–279). IGI Global. doi:10.4018/978-1-5225-9599-1.ch019

Henderson, M., Sullivan, A., Anders, J., & Moulton, V. (2018). Social class, gender and ethnic differences in subjects taken at age 14. *Curriculum Journal*, *29*(3), 298–318. doi:10.1080/09585176.2017.1406810

Henley, J., & Roy, E. A. (2020). Are female leaders more successful at managing the coronavirus crisis. *Guardian, 25th April* https://www. theguardian. com/world/2020/apr/25/why-do-femal e-leadersseem-to-be-more-successful-at-managing-the-coronavi rus-crisis *(accessed 04/09/2020).*

Heymann, J., Levy, J. K., Bose, B., Ríos-Salas, V., Mekonen, Y., Swaminathan, H., ... Darmstadt, G. L. (2019). Improving health with programmatic, legal, and policy approaches to reduce gender inequality and change restrictive gender norms. *Lancet*, *393*(10190), 2522–2534. doi:10.1016/S0140-6736(19)30656-7 PMID:31155271

Inman, A. G. (2020). Culture and positionality: Academy and mentorship. *Women & Therapy*, *43*(1-2), 112–124. doi:10.1080/02703149.2019.1684678

Jamali, A., Bhutto, A., Khaskhely, M., & Sethar, W. (2022). Impact of leadership styles on faculty performance: Moderating role of organizational culture in higher education. *Management Science Letters*, *12*(1), 1–20. doi:10.5267/j.msl.2021.8.005

Jameson, J. (Ed.). (2019). *International perspectives on leadership in higher education: Critical thinking for global challenges*. Routledge. doi:10.4324/9781315122410

Jandrić, P., Hayes, D., Truelove, I., Levinson, P., Mayo, P., Ryberg, T., & Jackson, L. (2020). Teaching in the age of Covid-19. *Postdigital Science and Education*, 1-162.

King, P. M., & Kitchener, K. S. (2004). Reflective judgment: Theory and research on the development of epistemic assumptions through adulthood. *Educational Psychologist*, *39*(1), 5–18. doi:10.120715326985ep3901_2

Lannelli, C., & Duta, A. (2018). Inequalities in school leavers' labour market outcomes: Do school subject choices matter? *Oxford Review of Education*, *44*(1), 56–74. doi:10.1080/03054985.2018.1409970

Lipton, B. (2015). A new" ERA" of women and leadership: The gendered impact of quality assurance in Australian higher education. *Australian Universities Review*, *57*(2), 60–70.

Maas, B., Grogan, K. E., Chirango, Y., Harris, N., Liévano-Latorre, L. F., McGuire, K. L., & Primack, R. B. (2020). Academic leaders must support inclusive scientific communities during COVID-19. *Nature Ecology & Evolution*, *4*(8), 1–2. doi:10.103841559-020-1233-3 PMID:32493950

McNair, T. B., Bensimon, E. M., & Malcom-Piqueux, L. (2020). *From equity talk to equity walk: Expanding practitioner knowledge for racial justice in higher education*. John Wiley & Sons. doi:10.1002/9781119428725

Meletiadou, E. (2022). The lived experiences of female educational leaders in higher education in the UK: Academic resilience and gender. In *Handbook of Research on Practices for Advancing Diversity and Inclusion in Higher Education* (pp. 1–19). IGI Global. doi:10.4018/978-1-7998-9628-9.ch001

Meyers, M. (2013). The war on academic women: Reflections on post-feminism in the neoliberal academy. *The Journal of Communication Inquiry*, *37*(4), 274–283. doi:10.1177/0196859913505619

Mezirow, J. (2009). Transformative learning theory. In J. Mezirow & E. W. Taylor (Eds.), *Transformative Learning in Practise: Insights from Community, 39 Workplace, and Higher Education* (pp. 18–32). Jossey Bass.

Milovanović, A., Kostić, M., Zorić, A., Đorđević, A., Pešić, M., Bugarski, J., Todorović, D., Soković, N., & Josifovski, A. (2020). Transferring COVID-19 challenges into learning potentials: Online workshops in architectural education. *Sustainability*, *12*(17), 7024. doi:10.3390u12177024

O'Connor, P. (2019). Gender imbalance in senior positions in higher education: What is the problem? What can be done? *Policy Reviews in Higher Education*, *3*(1), 28–50. doi:10.1080/23322969.2018.1552084

O'Connor, P. (2020). Creating gendered change in Irish higher education: Is managerial leadership up to the task? *Irish Educational Studies*, *39*(2), 139–155. doi:10.1080/03323315.2019.1697951

O'Connor, P. J., Jimmieson, N. L., Bergin, A. J., Wiewiora, A., & McColl, L. (2022). Leader tolerance of ambiguity: Implications for follower performance outcomes in high and low ambiguous work situations. *The Journal of Applied Behavioral Science*, *58*(1), 65–96. doi:10.1177/00218863211053676

Okoli, G. N., Moore, T. A., Thomas, S. L., & Allen, T. T. (2020). Minority women in educational leadership. *Handbook on Promoting Social Justice in Education*, 1711-1727.

Pellegrini, M., Uskov, V., & Casalino, N. (2020). Reimagining and re-designing the post-COVID-19 higher education organizations to address new challenges and responses for safe and Effective Teaching Activities. Law and Economics Yearly Review Journal-LEYR, Queen Mary University, London, UK, 9(part 1), 219-248.

Peters, M. A., Rizvi, F., McCulloch, G., Gibbs, P., Gorur, R., Hong, M., & Quay, J. (2020). Reimagining the new pedagogical possibilities for universities post-Covid-19: An EPAT collective project. *Educational Philosophy and Theory*, 1–44.

Power, K. (2020). The COVID-19 pandemic has increased the care burden of women and families. *Sustainability: Science. Practice and Policy*, *16*(1), 67–73.

Rapanta, C., Botturi, L., Goodyear, P., Guàrdia, L., & Koole, M. (2020). Online university teaching during and after the Covid-19 crisis: Refocusing teacher presence and learning activity. *Post-digital. Science and Education*, 1–23.

Reay, D. (2004, January). Cultural capitalists and academic habitus: Classed and gendered labour in UK higher education. []. Pergamon.]. *Women's Studies International Forum*, *27*(1), 31–39. doi:10.1016/j.wsif.2003.12.006

Ruben, B., Mahon, G., & Shapiro, K. (2022). Academic leader selection, development, evaluation, and recognition: Four critical higher education challenges. In *International Perspectives on Leadership in Higher Education* (Vol. 15, pp. 115–138). Emerald Publishing Limited. doi:10.1108/S1479-362820220000015007

Syed, M. (2019). Rebel Ideas: The power of diverse thinking. Hachette UK.

Tanova, C., Karatas-Özkan, M., & Inal, G. (2008). The process of choosing a management career: Evaluation of gender and contextual dynamics in a comparative study of six countries: Hungary, Israel, North Cyprus, Turkey, UK and the USA. *Career Development International*, *13*(4), 291–305. doi:10.1108/13620430810880790

Taylor, L. L., Beck, M. I., Lahey, J. N., & Froyd, J. E. (2017). Reducing inequality in higher education: The link between faculty empowerment and climate and retention. *Innovative Higher Education*, *42*(5-6), 391–405. doi:10.100710755-017-9391-1

Teelken, C., & Deem, R. (2013). All are equal, but some are more equal than others: Managerialism and gender equality in higher education in comparative perspective. *Comparative Education*, *49*(4), 520–535. doi:10.1080/03050068.2013.807642

Thomas, S. (2020). Women in higher education administration leadership and the role of institutional support. In *Accessibility and Diversity in the 21st Century University* (pp. 234–249). IGI Global. doi:10.4018/978-1-7998-2783-2.ch012

Tiwary, A. R., & Gupta, T. (2022). Stereotypical barriers affecting women aspiring high-ranking leadership role in higher education. In *Role of Leaders in Managing Higher Education* (Vol. 48, pp. 99–116). Emerald Publishing Limited. doi:10.1108/S2055-364120220000048007

Trent, R. J. (2020). *Women's perspectives on the role of organizational culture in their career advancement to leadership positions: A generic inquiry* [Doctoral dissertation, Capella University].

Tshivhase, M. (2020). Personhood: Implications for moral status and uniqueness of women. Handbook of African Philosophy of Difference, 347-360.

Tversky, A., & Kahneman, D. (1974). Judgment under uncertainty: Heuristics and biases. *science*, *185*(4157), 1124-1131.

Villiers, C. (2019). Boardroom culture: An argument for compassionate leadership. *European Business Law Review*, *30*(2), 253–278. doi:10.54648/EULR2019012

Wenham, C., Smith, J., & Morgan, R. (2020). COVID-19: The gendered impacts of the outbreak. *Lancet*, *395*(10227), 846–848. doi:10.1016/S0140-6736(20)30526-2 PMID:32151325

Wheaton, M. M., & Kezar, A. (2019). Interlocking systems of oppression: Women navigating higher education leadership. In *Challenges and opportunities for women in higher education leadership* (pp. 61–83). IGI Global. doi:10.4018/978-1-5225-7056-1.ch005

Whitty-Collins, G. (2020). *Why men win at work:...and How to make inequality history*. Luath Press Ltd.

World Health Organization. (2020). COVID-19 and violence against women: what the health sector/system can do, 7 April 2020 (No. WHO/SRH/20.04). World Health Organization.

ADDITIONAL READING

Annarelli, A., & Nonino, F. (2016). Strategic and operational management of organizational resilience: Current state of research and future directions. *Omega*, *62*, 1–18. doi:10.1016/j.omega.2015.08.004

Dabrowski, V. (2021). 'Neoliberal feminism': Legitimising the gendered moral project of austerity. *The Sociological Review*, *69*(1), 90–106. doi:10.1177/0038026120938289

Kusa, R., Duda, J., & Suder, M. (2022). How to sustain company growth in times of crisis: The mitigating role of entrepreneurial management. *Journal of Business Research*, *142*, 377–386. doi:10.1016/j.jbusres.2021.12.081

Lalonde, C., & Roux-Dufort, C. (2013). Challenges in teaching crisis management: Connecting theories, skills, and reflexivity. *Journal of Management Education*, *37*(1), 21–50. doi:10.1177/1052562912456144

Miceli, A., Hagen, B., Riccardi, M. P., Sotti, F., & Settembre-Blundo, D. (2021). Thriving, not just surviving in changing times: How sustainability, agility and digitalization intertwine with organizational resilience. *Sustainability*, *13*(4), 2052. doi:10.3390u13042052

Purnomo, E. N., Supriyanto, A., & Dami, Z. A. (2021). The effectiveness of principal leadership styles in crisis management. *Pedagogika, 141,* p. 5-25.

Sedlack, R. (2021). Crisis Management in a Pandemic: Voices from the field. *Issues of Educational Leadership: Crisis Management During Challenging Times*, 21.

Soares, S. E., & Sidun, N. M. (2021). Women leaders during a global crisis: Challenges, characteristics, and strengths. *International Perspectives in Psychology : Research, Practice, Consultation*, *10*(3), 130–137. doi:10.1027/2157-3891/a000020

Šumonja, M. (2021). Neoliberalism is not dead–On political implications of Covid-19. *Capital and Class*, *45*(2), 215–227. doi:10.1177/0309816820982381

KEY TERMS AND DEFINITIONS

Crisis: A time of intense difficulty or danger, when the immediacy of decision-making and strategic leadership is paramount.

Critical Reflection: A process of identifying, questioning, and assessing our deeply held assumptions.

Critical Reflexivity: The capacity to see one's own perspective and assumptions and understand how one's perspective, assumptions, and identity are socially constructed through critical reflection.

Emotional Labour: The management of emotional response to present the outward image of control and reassurance to continue interaction with other people in a certain way while doing a job in stressful circumstances.

Inequality: Inequality in this chapter refers to the phenomenon of unequal and/or unjust distribution of resources and opportunities among members of a given society, in this instance female leaders.

Neoliberalism: Neoliberalism is a political philosophical term used to signify the political reappearance of 19th-century ideas associated with free-market capitalism, and in this chapter refers to the commodification of global Higher Education provision.

Positionality: Refers to the social and political context that creates your identity in terms of race, class, gender, sexuality, and ability status.

Signature Pedagogy: Refers to the forms or styles of teaching and instruction that are common to specific disciplines, areas of study, or professions and as such can unintentionally define and constrain them.

Chapter 15
Perspectives on Socio-Ecological Innovation Management Models

José G. Vargas-Hernandez
Instituto Tecnológico Mario Molina, Mexico

Teresa I. Salazar-Echeagaray
Universidad Autonoma de Sinaloa, Mexico

Omar C. Vargas-González
Tecnológico Nacional de México, Ciudad Guzmán, Mexico

ABSTRACT

This study has the aim to analyze the different perspectives on socio-ecological innovation management models. The analysis departs if socio-ecological innovation initiatives connect to resources and capabilities, culture, creativity, tacit, and formal knowledge between nurtured entrepreneurship and different domains of innovation management models that become supply factors to determine the production potential and based on this assumption to analyze the ability to economic growth. The method used is the meta-analytic reflection based on theoretical and empirical literature review. It is concluded that the socio-ecological thinking and collaborative knowledge production takes the natural environmental resources for socio-ecological management innovation relevant for the transition towards the analytical framework for innovation management models This is a crucial factor that contributes to economic development of the internal and external environments full of a range of threats and opportunities because the interactions of biological diversity.

DOI: 10.4018/978-1-6684-7509-6.ch015

INTRODUCTION

Research and development of integrated economic and socio-ecological dynamic models aimed to forecast. And, to control the dynamics of innovation economy based on analysis of complicated conditions of instability and crises. The model of innovation is a feasible method to tackle challenges of global warming. Through the knowledge and know-how focusing on the socio-ecological exchange and transfer of knowledge in specific nation-state situations (Barth, 2011).

BACKGROUND

An integral analysis of socio-ecological innovation considers the complexity of transitions based on structural resources, cognitive and material dimensions of innovation processes. A key concept is the historical socio-ecological transition. Which is defined in two parts: first as the results from long-term dynamic spatial and functional energy metabolism in connections and disconnections of changes in energy metabolism (natural resources, land uses, local governance, etc.) affecting local social-ecological regimes. Secondly, as a process of spatial, temporal, and functional-dysfunctional connection and disconnection of industrial complexes to combine or decouple urban metabolism from local natural resources.

In a complex world variety of assets, competencies, strategies, and opportunities enable transitions to socio agroecological arrangements of production, contexts of biophysical, socio-ecological, and socio-economic resources. The global geographical distributional of natural resources reflect the disparities that demand creation and dissemination of socioecological innovation to anticipate the needs and adapt to future changes of humanity.

Common ground for global, national, and local scales for environmental sustainability and socio-ecological changes by embedding markets within the communities leading to lower the ecological footprint of energy and material resources and goods leading to shortening the supply chains (Quilley, 2019).

During the 70s took place an impetus for the national innovation systems based on governmental institutions and agencies. Those organizations had devoted resources aimed to promote the creation, dissemination and application of scientific knowledge and technological innovation for basic inputs. Also, they had capital with ambitious programs of economic policy aimed to achieve industrial self-sufficiency and scientific and technological autonomy (Melo, 2001; Abreu, 1992). The national innovation systems devoted resources and capabilities to: 1) development; and 2) the consolidation of a system of science and technology. Both aimed to overcome the scientific and technological dependency in strategic industrial sectors.

This study is divided in six parts. It starts with the analysis of socio-ecological innovation models. Secondly, a relationship with the knowledge model. Thirdly, a view related with the resource-based and capabilities model. Fourthly, a link with the cultural environment. Fifthly, the perspective of the triple and quintuple helix innovation models. Sixthly, the socio-ecological innovation model applies to innovation management. Finally, this analysis presents some relevant conclusions.

MAIN FOCUS OF THE CHAPTER

The increased complexity of production interconnected information, requires learning about the internal cognitive. Also, needs socio-ecological resources with external resources and, network linkages. Resources, units, users, and governance systems interact in complex socio-ecological systems to produce outcomes despite of being separated (Ostrom, 2009).

The distinction between the capacious and the conventional innovation models is the different policy implications. In this way a modeling calibration may reveal the differences in development patterns. A spatial socio-ecological innovation model can implement innovative policy methodologies and instruments. Those implementations aimed to address the growth of land use related to emission. Meaning that controlling the growth zone will mitigate emissions.

The purpose of research is therefore to find out what is known about the socio-ecological innovation models. There are a variety of perspectives related to this idea. When reviewing the different perceptions, it can be observe that it has an interdisciplinary and multidimensional character with the potential to encompass social, biogeophysical and ecological aspects. The socio-ecological innovation models are a contributing factor to the continued economic development of the internal and external environments. Therefore, it is threatened by interactions with biological diversity. However, it is also given opportunities, because all the innovations in technology need to receive continuous improvements in both resources and capabilities.

SOCIO-ECOLOGICAL INNOVATION MODELS

Innovation narratives are emerging. They are not depending from conventional economic growth machinery to be classified as socio-ecological models of innovation (Healy & Morgan 2012; Truffer & Coenen, 2012; Marques et al., 2018; Todtling & Trippl, 2018). In the long-term economic growth, wealth is the base of an economy. While sustainable growth and development is supported by a comprehensive and inclusive concept of wealth based on material assets and natural resources capital. Increasing economic growth on a finite planet resource threatens the socio-ecological thresholds. This situation may not be reversible, undermining the delivery of ecosystem services to humanity (Farley, 2016).

Proposals of socioecological models counting on the expertise. And contributes to pressing the construction and development of knowledge towards achieving more stabilized, contested, and trusted environmental scenarios. The nation-state leads to develop new knowledge and innovations to meet the challenges in sustainable development in different fields in the future under the global warming. A key concept is sustainable development. Which is conceptualized as the development of industrial enterprises related to the components with the environment, the economic, social, and ecological. It is characterized by sustainable factors of land, energy and non-energy resources, natural resources, etc., involved in the production processes.

The socio-ecological innovation model bridges with knowledge and innovation production in natural environments of economy and society (Carayannis and Campbell, 2010). Innovation knowledge and learning stress a regional innovation policy to be applied to all cases. Taking into considerations the specific regional and local needs, demands, resources, and potential. It's starting from the scratch and it's driven by innovation of agglomeration processes to reduce investments.

Socio-ecological innovation models are constructed using processes of data collection. Then they are manipulated. They make a calibration of behavioral preferences and socio-economic functions, urban structures, and development patterns. The socio-ecological innovation modeling system should be structured around the needed systematic data for statistical analysis. Which is used to determine causal relationships, mechanisms, and patterns. The innovative use of databases in a comparative socio-ecological innovation modeling approach helps to identify improvement opportunities for climate action plans.

Urban innovation science parameters and socio-ecological innovation modeling approaches can be combined to analyze the improvements of climate action planning by comparing gas emissions and sources. The socio-ecological innovation modeling can innovate planning and policy instruments to mitigate the urban gas emissions. The socio-ecological innovation model approach contributes with its ability to test innovative urban planning and policy instruments to mitigate gas emissions at urban level. Socio-ecological innovation models can compare the relationships between urban gas emissions, land uses, climate changes, and other factors. Growth control zoning policies derive from socio-ecological innovation modeling that adds to the behavioral interventions in climate action planning at urban levels.

Innovative socio-ecological policy instruments for urban growth control and urban zoning are tested through the socio-ecological model. They aimed to determine the effectiveness of interventions extensive the urban methods. And they aimed to develop a socio-ecological framework as an emerging paradigm in complex urban socio-ecological systems and urban sustainability policies (Pan et al., 2019, 2018b; Urbaniec et al., 2018; Yang et al., 2013; Yu et al., 2019).

KNOWLEDGE MODELS OF SOCIO-ECOLOGICAL INNOVATION

The knowledge process captures results in the conceptual socio-ecological innovation model development. It is aimed to design development of prototypes of natural context to interact through the environmental goals. The socio-ecological innovation model approach is a context-specific, low reusability and transferability across other different applications (Banos-González et al., 2015; Hong et al., 2009). Socio-ecological innovation models in context-heavy can be combined with analysis techniques. This will generate complex and sound solutions useful for policymaking in urban planning. And it will analyze the cause and effects of urban gas emissions supporting the climate action planning. It is assumed that socio-ecological innovation initiatives connect to knowledge, creativity, tacit and formal knowledge between nurtured entrepreneurship and different domains.

Open socio-ecological innovation networks allow broad participation in creation, development, and transferability of knowledge. Socio-ecological analysis of agroecological sustainability transitions requires the creation and development of new knowledge. Also, needs skills and material practices at individual, firms, and sectors. Among other agroecological policies, there are the ones proposed to improve agro-food productivity. Through the biodiversification of crop rotation, subsidy payments, establishing new metrics and measures based on ecological innovation knowledge. Sustainable development referred in global warming leads to nation-state involved in world economy and politics. It is determined by the societal balance of knowledge, innovation, and know-how. It focuses on the coevolution of knowledge economy and society (Dubina et al., 2012).

The models of knowledge creation and innovation creativity are the traditional university research established by peers. Models with an emphasis on coevolution and coexistence. Models with diversity of knowledge and plural with interdisciplinary and transdisciplinary applications (Carayannis & Campbell, 2012; Gibbons et al., 1994; Carayannis & Campbell, 2010; Carayannis & Campbell, 2006). Local University Innovation System proposes to create the local innovation systems. As a requirement for the evolution of an institutional model and, the economic and social paradigm based on the strategic knowledge-based innovation.

RESOURCE-BASED AND CAPABILITIES INNOVATION MODEL

The case of socio-agroecology is an example of a long-term research process. It analyzed environmental and socio-ecological resources of innovation behaviors within contextual transition processes. And in most of the cases do not function in isolation. An integrated resource-based approach to the socio-ecological innovation model must capture the complexity to analyze patterns of the risky events. Also, it must facilitate communication and execution of biodiversity conservation and territories (Wolf & Primmer, 2006). The resource-based approach allows to identify the enabling and constraining transitional factors to socio-agroecological production (Wolf & Primmer, 2006).

Productivity based on knowledge guarantees the conditions of competitiveness in a dynamic global context (Porter, 1998). Also, ensures the creation of an environment through infrastructure, resources, and capabilities to support the increasing levels of productivity. This is achieved through competition at microeconomic basis. The potential returns of innovation projects may be underestimated by providers of financial resources who lack of skills to assess the risks involved (OECD, 1997b).

Provision of resources to firms is prioritized by fostering cooperation through technological innovation mechanisms. Such as, training with some funds to specific technologies aimed to achieve satisfactory results. A key concept is the technological capability. Which is defined as the ability to develop technological components on the market and assess their value (Meyer-Stamer, 1994). Technological capability is a skill possessed by producers and decision makers. It is a prerequisite for technological innovation developments and transfers that complement each other.

An integrated analysis of: a) socio-ecological dimensions; b) cognitive and material; c) structural environmental resources; and, d) constraints of innovation processes must be considered in the complexity environmental sustainability transitions. New domains in innovation transition emerge from industrial commons. Such as, sustainable innovation, the collective research and development, and the engineering capabilities (Foray, 2015). Sustainable innovation is the socioecological innovation and sustainable environmental development. A paradigm developed from the union of the resource and capability based theory, and the sustainability and innovation theories. Social variability is an aspirational capability in shaping prospects attributable to material wealth as a relevant factor to prospect futures.

Geography is uneven in natural and investment resources in socio-ecological innovation (Braun, 2015). A crucial assumption on resources that become supply factors to determine the production potential. And based on this assumption it is analyzed the ability to grow and the economic growth (Hausman, 2007), achieving balanced growth formed in endogenous internal market characterized by sustainable development.

Promotion of local innovation systems is an instrument present to best practices. It is valid as innovation policy. Although it must be consolidated in many regions because the requirements to have universities and research institutions, political support, resources and capabilities development, financial and legal institutions. There are institutions that provide resources to finance the various stages of firms. The mechanisms supporting the flow of innovation are the direct support instruments for projects and firms. They have components in public sources of resources, seed capital fund, community of angel investors and venture capital industry.

Firms that lack specific technological capabilities try to take advantage of other firms. With the objective to leverage technology if they have absorptive capacity and equity capital. Other component of innovation strategies for the development of technological capabilities of start-ups is the development of social capital of firms and their environments. Technological capabilities and social capital are developed together to take advantage of start-ups. The level of social capital appropriate to each level of technological capability depends on the firms depending on the level of technological capital limited by the social capital to make a positive contribution.

Firms are forced to combine their internal technological strengths with those of other firms. As costs of research and development increase and the technological dynamics get more complex. Firms can accelerate development of their capabilities through learning alliances to exploit the developed knowledge. In current technological environment only, the firm can reach technological capabilities induced by learning alliances (Vanhaverbeke et al., 2015).

The anchor of the university has security with respect to public resources in the continuity of proposals due to organizing and coordinating force. The local innovation system university base incorporated to the incubator and innovation parks. This incorporation of resources, partners, and services, in innovation projects supports innovation in entrepreneurship. The innovation system university-based is the institution with most permanent character of local innovation systems. It has a capacity to offer information and human resources. It can consolidate the system. It performs as the reticulation agency to create ties and maintain negotiations. It defines the appropriate government structure aimed to satisfy the needs and interests of the involved actors and agents.

Government innovation policymaking must provide support to private sector. This will lead the development and share the risks of innovation initiatives for local systems. As consequence it will commit and guarantee resources and capabilities. Government policies are directed towards the promotion of innovation environments. They are conducive to the generation of skills and capabilities for competitive technology innovation-based firms (Porter, 2001).

An agency of sources of entrepreneurship and innovation and research resources relates to emerging firms and processes of interaction between the university, research institutes and technological innovation partners. Which support the innovative flow. The main elements of an innovation system are: the incubators; innovation centers; technology partner's companies; providers of specialized resources; and graduated companies.

Diffusion of technological innovation is a social process. It occurs through learning processes with tacit and explicit technology knowledge and innovation. It requires investments, equipment and intangibles in research and development resources and capabilities. Then, the knowledge spread is absorbed and transferred from the location where it is generated (de Melo, 2001). The best practices in innovation technology diffusion are focusing on the needs for firms and market. They are covering diverse types of technology. They are including transfer of platform and sophisticated technologies under diffusion schemes. They aimed to provide expertise and services between the involved and interested actors (including networking, training, and developing links). And they are promoting collaboration under the assumptions that have sufficient resources, leverage and links to articulate with other firms (OECD, Secretariat, 1997c).

Transitions to socio-agroecology usually requires alternative resources. Those resources are from private service providers with specific knowledge in production, distribution, and consumption (Wolf,

1995; Wolf & Nowak, 1995). The transition toward environmental sustainability leads toward critical changes in economic growth. It is built on the finite natural resources and fossil fuels. This generates necessary job losses in some economic sectors related to the emission-intensive industries. And generates job creation in sectors such as renewable energy (Gouverneur & Netzer, 2014). Implementation of innovations requires sufficient supportive work and dedication of resources. Specially to become phenomenally successful in practicability and diffusion of the sustainable socioecological development.

Application of public resources as a complement to social capital in technological training of firms-based. It is aimed to share the creation of resources and capabilities in emerging innovation firms' technology-based. This technology-based firms are the priority in university-based local innovation system. And they can be promoted by the components of technological enablement innovation strategies. Other component of the technological innovation strategies is, the identification and support of shareable training elements. As is the case of motivated and structured cooperation. As well as, the collective efficiencies and specific technologies. This enables public investments capable to internalize resources. And it fosters cooperation between firms to complement innovation technologies sharing resources by public investment.

Technology-based firms must face challenges. They are in a reality which should be contemplated in healthy forms of public policies by the government agencies. Those institutions must be seeking to avoid wasting public resources and capabilities. They must be implementing with intervention forms appropriated to the structure of technology-based companies. Including universities and research institutes, and other actors and agents coexisting and reflecting the reality of the same context and the environmental demand. Technological innovation policies for the provision of public goods are relevant for: 1) practices in technology diffusion; 2) human resources development; 3) creation and development of scientific knowledge; and 4) technological innovation. This is important for research and developed university based and research institutions, for the policies aimed to organize, coordinate and convening, etc. (de Melo, 2001).

An important concept is the public innovation policies. They are a form of state intervention in the local economy of the environment. They are applied to promotion context of the local innovation systems based on the university. And they have substantial public resources and capacities in research infrastructure and training. The environment of the local innovation system university based can support the non-financial resources and attract government agencies to provide financial resources.

CULTURAL ENVIRONMENTAL INNOVATION MODEL

The socio-ecological base of cultures can serve as a vital source for regional landscapes and livelihoods, cultural resources, etc. (Watkins, 2015a, 2015b). Regional diversification refers to the development of productive activity based on regional resources and assets.

An environmental communication proposed in a new cultural model with concerns in constructing narratives. It is appealing to emerging environmental values for socio-ecological transformation. And it is invoking new conceptions of knowledge, governance, agency, and time (Delanty & Mota, 2017). The value retention mechanism needs to be defined. Especially in the entrepreneurship and innovation model for the environment in innovation. Which work with the research and studies center in the promotion of technology transfer, commercialization, and training programs.

Innovation theory and new tools can foster adaptive strategies. It will account for coupled socio-ecological dynamics and epidemiological models. Meaning, it will change sensitivity predictive outcomes of socioeconomic and biotic conditions, shifting landscapes, and recovery efforts. And it will become into disaster adaptive response strategies, post-trauma reassembles, etc. Theoretical development and observational trauma-prone areas (or post-trauma conditions) lead to model implementation and validation. Combining socio-ecological and epidemiological models may mitigate efforts to improve efficacy. Despite the modeling advances in applications.

THE TRIPLE AND QUINTUPLE HELIX INNOVATION MODELS

The Triple Helix innovation model focuses on university-industry and government relations. It is acknowledged higher education for knowledge production and innovation. Meaning it is compatible with knowledge economy. While in the Quadruple Helix, the media-based and culture-based public and civil society are together. And they encourage the knowledge society and democracy in coevolution with knowledge production and innovation. However, in the Quintuple Helix innovation model it adds the socio-ecological transition. Which is more sensitive to natural environments of society and economy. It drivers for knowledge production and innovation framed with the knowledge economy. Transformations between socio-ecology, knowledge and innovation develop synergies between economy, society, and democracy.

The Quintuple Helix innovation model is a socio-ecological transition. It is oriented toward sustainable development. It is creating incentives for knowledge and innovation production. It is located in the context of knowledge economy and society or knowledge democracy and natural environmental sustainability of society (Carayannis & Campbell, 2012; Etzkowitz & Leydesdorff, 2000; and Danilda et al., 2009). In the quintuple helix model, innovation and the natural environment are interrelated (Carayannis & Campbell, 2010).

Government incentives to networks as an instrument of innovation policies are relevant in innovation technology environments. They serve as sponsor and catalyst to provide financial resources, skills, and other tools. This develops social infrastructure. It addresses collective the needs of industry. And, it evaluates the expected policy results (Rosenfeld, 1997). Incentives for technology innovation should be provided by government agencies in a structured way. By joining public and private capabilities with resources. They are capable to be mobilized and to be articulated according to shared conditions and objectives with the national and local science, technology, and innovation system.

Start-ups in initial stages are not extremely attractive to private venture capital model. Which is based on the income on mechanisms of administration expenses on the invested amount that has a lower value than advanced stages. A model of consolidation of networks in environments of firms already in operation that need support to develop innovations (Dias, de Melo & Rosenthal, 2000).

The socio-ecological transition of economy and society has been identified as the mayor challenge of development. It is represented by the global warming. It is supported by the Quintuple Helix innovation model stressing the natural environments. Which focus on interactions, ecodevelopment and coevolution of economy and society (Carayannis & Campbell, 2010). Global warming is a challenge of quintuple Helix model adopted as sustainable development. Knowledge innovation models are resources created through combinations of creative and productive processes available for society (Carayannis & Campbell, 2010).

INNOVATION MANAGEMENT

Innovation management is a factor that contributes to human capital, intellectual abilities, and ingenuity. In the economic development of the internal and external environments full of a range of threats and opportunities (Popkov, 2007). Industrial ecology optimizes resource management interactions between stakeholders in a common geographic area.

The socio-ecological innovation model is constructed for specific spatial-explicit cases. It can test innovative socio-ecological policy instruments. It stimulates changes of land use patterns in relation to climate action planning. It address urban planning and socioeconomic growth management policies residential and commercial building choices, community demands, etc. As factors coupled between human and nature systems (Keesstra et al., 2018; Pan et al., 2019, 2018a; Urbaniec et al., 2018; Yu et al., 2019; Anthony, 2004; Robinson et al., 2005).

Subsystem management for growth and conservation as a goal of sustainability may threatens to collapse the entire system. It needs an adequate infrastructure, physical facilities, structure for management consulting, and business creation. Furthermore, it needs development and innovation, provision services and development of plans, promotions of events aimed to establish and strengthen the links between participant entrepreneurs with the financial investment community.

The analytical framework of innovation management theory and collaborative knowledge production takes the natural environmental resources for socio-ecological innovation (Carayannis & Campbell, 2010, 2012). Radical innovation approach includes the components and procedural requirements of redirecting change to sustainability. It experiments with diversity approaches of policy innovation. And it shares the burdens for transformation to connect innovation capacities to requirements of boundary resource use (Leach et al., 2012).

Forms of sustainability brokering and dimensions of diversity, distribution and direction guides the analysis of decision making to safe guard the natural resources of the planet (Leach et al., 2012). University technology and innovation centers in universities have the objective to act between the technical and managerial units. And to instruct people in the application of scientific knowledge and technological innovation to the common purposes of life, in educational and training of entrepreneurs (Dias, de Melo, & Rosenthal, 2002). Managerial and technological training of firms emerge as a challenge for policymaking innovation.

Socio-ecological processes need of innovation change, transformation, and development of social behaviors in social groups with different interests in natural resources management and environmental sustainability policies. The innovation parks promote innovation. They provide support to researchers and academics in relation to technical and legal support, intellectual property, and commercialization of modern technologies. And they aim of retaining economic value generated by developed technologies using university research facilities and resources.

Innovation parks must have a policy for environmental management. It must be governed by environmental regulations affecting the technologies used by local firms. And it must be regulated by a Development Standards Agreement aimed to guarantee the development standards. Innovation parks offer firms: 1. access to physical infrastructure; 2. knowledge assets; and, 3. human resources in research-intensive communities aimed to increase the economic growth, social value, and sustainable development (Porter, 2001).

Technology-based firms need to recognize the need to enhance their innovative dynamics in technological capacity. It will represent an increase in their economic gains. Although training in innovative technology may not lead necessarily into economic benefits and social value. Because there are some other limitations such as managerial capabilities.

Management and conservation of natural resources has the need of innovations. Particularly, for a more sustainable livelihood development with the potential to find better solutions for land use development. Causing to promote and to improve the livelihood for people and the development of local economies (Nautiyal, 2011). The local innovation systems are a negotiated agreement among the links and relationships of actors. This agreement has the aim to provide conditions for the anticipation and implementation economic, social, managerial, and technical changes necessary for survival in times of uncertain and turbulent environments.

The transition management approach is a participative governance concept and reflexive. It influences the direction change and the speed for attempting to manage transformative societal change in sustainable development. This is made by combining long-term thinking with short-term action through processes of searching for visions, and cycles of experimenting, learning, and adapting. Transition management experiments are conducted at iconic projects tactical and operational levels with an elevated risk and a potential large innovation. Transition Management Approach is based on: 1. a complex systems analysis (Rotmans & Lorbach, 2009); 2. an innovation Systems Approach (Jacobsson & Bergek, 2011); and, 3. a Viennese Socio-metabolic Transitions Approach (Fischer-Kowalski & Haberl, 2007).

Agroecological practices have an ability to reawaken the experimental methods of ethic of care sense of environmental goals brought to inform households management (Buck, 2017; Davies & Doyle, 2015). Socio-ecological thinking is relevant for the transition of socio agroecological innovation management because the interactions of biological diversity.

The transition management approach is practical. It is supported by political trend to achieve sustainable transitions. Comparing to the Viennese socio-metabolic approach that is a theoretical framework applied to analyze national and local communities to initiate. The socio-ecological transition is the term used by the Viennese socio-metabolic transition and the transition management approaches. Societal transitions that result from sustainability transitions. They reinforce socio-ecological and other forms. For example, socio-technical changes leading to sustainability transitions using combinations of concepts between management and socio-metabolic transitions (Squazzoni, 2008).

Reindeer development management is a socio-ecological innovation and a national brand. It becomes a policy recommendation (Lerner 2003; Lessing 2003; Forbes et al. 2004). The adaptive flexibility may be combined in some specific cases with a conservative culture to be effectively managed and leveraged. Enhancing resources through organic bottom-up. Reindeer management is not categorized in modern culture making difficult for outsiders to get influence in outside culture (Hukkinen et al., 2002). In reindeer management, institutional and environmental problems cause internal conflicts leading to the disruption of cultures in communities.

In the socio-ecological model the public sector delivers services of socio-economic value. This is an answer to sustainable resource management and societal challenges in aspects as demographic ageing, risk of poverty, social exclusion, healthcare services, governance, etc (Foray, D. et al., 2012; (European Commission, 2012). Failure in the public sector innovation can be a disaster for management. Feedback and failure face obstacles in public sector innovations. They are difficult to manage even through mechanism such as the introduction of whistleblower laws (Coenen, 2018). The public sector needs to allocate resources, spaces, and time to policy experimentalism. Also to learn from monitoring and evaluation (Smeds & Acuto, 2018).

The governance structure as a function refers to the regulations and practices related to issues of governance as are: the innovation center and park; management of the value of the innovation system for each involved agent and actor; development of trust; social capital; and, relationships of cooperation arrangements. The regulations and practices are made with responsibility in their relationships and interactions. As well as from learning and from cooperation of the environment. In addition of informal and voluntary relationships strengthened by a reticulation process. It is responsibility and commitment of government agencies, the task of mobilizing resources and capabilities to achieve the strategic objectives on technological innovation.

A Board of Trustees advice the President in decision making affecting the common institutional purposes. However only the President should approve the issues of resource planning, investment approval, equipment acquisition, conflicts of interest, etc. The consolidation of governance is defined by socio-ecological criteria and the achievement of objectives of the system that provide conditions for the implementation of social, technical, and managerial changes. Allowing actors in the system to assimilate the impact of constant evolutive changes in a turbulent environment.

Strategic guidelines are determining elements of public policies. They can guide actions aimed to achieve the objectives institutionally required to face the challenges of science, technology, and innovation systems. Some of these strategic guidelines are the implementation of science, technology, and innovation system. They increase the competitiveness of firms with sustainable investments. As a consequence, it expands and modernizes training systems. As well as, it diversifies and consolidates research capacities, institutions and procedures for management policies and articulation mechanisms. Also, it promotes education for knowledge and innovation society. And, it explores new opportunities for cooperation and it expands strategic dimensions of Science, Technology and Innovation activities.

Public policies are necessaries in local contexts to reflect the environments. They generate indirect mechanisms of support through investments in infrastructure. As a result, they yield shared benefits in increasing the cooperation between firms. All of this in terms of multiplier effects of the rational use of public resources and reduce technological interference in the public sector in technological innovation training. As an initiative of active participation of involved actors depends on the coordination mechanisms compatible to different values and convergence of the system objectives (de Melo, 1997, 2002).

The strategic niche management is related to the multi-level perspective (Kemp, Schot, & Hoogma, 1998). Socio-ecological innovation models explain urban spatial changes. They affect gas emissions, and they inform climate action planning on growth planning and management strategies (Deal et al., 2017b, 2017a; Pan & Deal, 2020). Socio-ecological models of disturbance ensure responses to catastrophes. They do this through transformation of post-trauma reassembly intended to sustain recovery and shifting dynamics. The socio-ecological innovation model improves the assessment of gas emissions impacts of urban land use change. This occurs by determining the urban growth in residential buildings and single-family houses. Because they are sources of gas emissions and carbon sink losses. And they generate implications on travel demands and transportation changes (Wang et al., 2018; Yang & Zhang, 2016; Hankey & Marshall, 2010).

Socio-ecological analysis of disturbance and reassembly along-side the landscape and population conditions lead to outcomes in terms of post-trauma landscape management and population displacements, etc.

Labor is the human activities consciously performed to create social development. This happens when meeting personal and social needs. It must be adding ecological development of natural and spiritual benefits. And it must be including economic development, meaning capital, innovation, the consumption of labor in services and goods, and the information management. Also, it must be considered machines and how they represent an expansion. They are a complement of the functions of man, employees and management. And they can be included in the same principle.

There is a mismatch between the need of socio-ecological innovation in structural weak regions. Because they have a low absorptive capacity to manage funding (Hassink & Marques, 2016; Marques & Morgan, 2018; Muscio, Reid, & Rivera Leon, 2015; Oughton, Landabaso, & Morgan, 2002; Papamichail, Rosiello, & Wield, 2019). This type of state is assumed to be benevolent. It is well-endowed with resources and capabilities to coordinate collective action. And it acknowledges assumed diversity and differences across nations and regions (Mazzucato, 2015).

The challenge posed by the applications of the scientific research on knowledge economy has received funding resources. It aimed to transform the scientific research on products with economic value. However, it leaded to questionable results. The innovation funding related to the mission-oriented approach recognizes the value of innovation. It goes beyond the economic value. It leads to societal challenges such as climate change, refugee crises, aging societies, food poverty, etc. Situations that remain as predicated on the notion of an entrepreneurial state.

The institutional mission and the strategic objectives of the cultural innovation park must emphasize in the entrepreneurship and innovation. They must function as a bridge between technological innovation resources available at the University and research centers. Including the units in the local innovation systems and the business incubators, technological parks, technology transfer and marketing. This must be achieved without diverging from institutional principles and their autonomy. Given the dispersion of the institutional multiplicity, it makes necessary to define the superior instance. For it to act as the guardian of the integrity values and compromising the identity of the innovation system. And to be activated in critical situations capable of affecting the purposes of the involved institutions.

Incentives have direct and indirect formats. They are characterized by being sources of funds aimed to contribute to the construction of long-term science, technology, and innovation. They are to encourage technological innovation development appropriate to the needs of investments. These mechanisms have been introduced to firms with more opportunistic responses than planned. The recipients of funds motivate them. As a consequence of an absence of structuring and mobile objectives because there is a lack of commitment of responsible government agencies of formulation and implementation of innovation policies. Other causes are the lack of financial resources, management training, ability of cooperation, rentier-type positions, and direct support to companies.

The socio-ecological investment management results in a reduced exposure to negative externalities. And incorporates socio-ecological externalities and the possibility to identify market opportunities (Porter & Kramer, 2011). Public ventures usually provide management and strategic financial advice. Venture capital tends to maximize private participation with the government agencies gradually withdraw. A measurement system is used to reframe the system of social finances. It places emphasis on creating a social investments portfolio to manage risk and creating change for building the complex socio-ecological systems.

SOLUTIONS AND RECOMMENDATIONS

Socio-economic and socio-ecological evaluation of the efficiency of potential of existing innovations for their applicability to solve complexities of natural resources management and livelihood options.

They avoid resultant social conflicts (Rogers, 2003). Collaboration and social capital are factors that emphasize and enhance trust in relationships. They manage complexity and absorb uncertainties inherent to the innovation process (Lastres et al., 1999). Collaborative innovations give support to urban living labs to manage socio-ecological innovation practices. Evaluation of various implemented innovations under the perspective of sustainable development and environmental sustainability. they relate to management for sustainable resource use and community participation linked to conservation and human needs (Manuel-Navarrete et al., 2006).

FUTURE RESEARCH DIRECTIONS

Collaboration and social capital are factors that emphasize and enhance trust in relationships to manage complexity and absorb uncertainties inherent to the innovation process (Lastres et al., 1999). Trust relationships are more likely to be develop in environments that enhance the socio-cultural identity as the consequence of collaboration between the agents involved (OECD, 2001c; Nahapiet & Ghoshal, 1998) facilitating trust leading to establish the competitive innovation environment.

CONCLUSION

This study aimed to analyze the different perspectives on socio-ecological innovation management models. It departed from the assume that socio-ecological innovation initiatives connect to resources and capabilities. And they connect with the knowledge, culture, creativity, tacit and formal knowledge. This happens between nurtured entrepreneurship and different domains of innovation management models. They become supply factors to determine the production potential and based on this assumption to analyze the ability to economic growth.

The socio-ecological thinking and collaborative knowledge production take natural environmental resources for socio-ecological management innovation. Which is relevant for the transition towards the analytical framework for innovation management models. A crucial factor that contributes to economic development of the internal and external environments. And it is full of a range of threats and opportunities because the interactions of biological diversity.

Technological innovation requires continuous improvement of resources and capabilities with the induction of modern technologies, goods, and services. When expanding technological innovation research bases, infrastructure, institutional resources and capabilities. Also are expanding interactions among regions. And they are having an effective collaboration in actions among the involved actors. Those are some of the requirements of science, technology, and innovation processes. That lead to improve, consolidate, and modernize institutional development as a base to support the involvement of society. Institutions and capabilities are necessary to make happen the responsible research and innovation to the public and voices.

The innovation institutes act in line with institutional values and the objective of the university innovation. Which is based as crossover for governance structure of the environment. And it becomes the access mechanism for entrepreneurs to the university innovation resources. Ethics and social responsibility are essential for the development and preservation of social capital. This is between the members of the groups in activities of innovation. It leads to the establishment of mechanisms in innovation environments facilitating the access of firms and other agents and actors involved in the local innovation systems to innovation resources and entrepreneurship without conflict of interests.

The analysis of the technological innovation and the constant search for sources and resources must lead to achieve the competitive advantage of firms. The implicit socio-ecological innovation model as the research and innovation strategies deserves to become more prominent. Due to its different ends of economic competitiveness to make more significant the ends of human needs and ecological integrity. Strategies and policies for sustainability governance includes the urban sustainability considering that have socioecological disadvantages and advantages to use natural resources, energy, materials, and spaces efficiently.

The socio-ecological models of innovation involve interactive knowledge and learning with less transactional and more explicitly transformational relationships. Socio-ecological models of innovation process move beyond the knowledge exploration and exploitation recognizing innovation as deliberative and collective problem-solving.

Findings of research on innovation support to evaluate the potential to resolve strategies and developing the socioeconomic improvements and conservation of natural resources. Socio-ecological transformation calls on society to limit consumption of natural and renewable resources and energy. And to reduce climate change and pollution through the innovation processes. Human–ecological relations are aimed to achieve a productive, innovative, and a low carbon society. By using natural resources efficiently and recognizing the limits of environmental sustainability.

Interlinkages and changes in the elements of the socio-technical system transition contribute to the sustainability transition and in the transition management approach. A shared management system between the participation of the various levels of government, universities and research institutions, technical associations and chambers, the private productive sector, etc., lead to the establishment of science, technology, and innovation policies to be formulated and implemented.

The allocation of public research resources and capabilities must strength innovation systems. Through granting funds to foster innovation environments. Through encourage communication between local agencies and local business, universities and research institutions and other support institutions. External socio-ecological innovation knowledge must be at reach of actors.

Government innovation policymaking must provide support to private sector to lead the development and sharing the risks of innovation initiatives for local systems. It must commit and guarantee resources and capabilities. Policymaking must ensure the entrepreneurial critical mass and capacity building. It must commit public resources to consolidate initiatives aimed to create local innovation systems. Government agencies support must address venture capital issues for seed-stage and start-up firms.

REFERENCES

Abreu, M. P. (Ed.). (1992). *A Ordem do Progresso: cem anos de política econômica republicana*. Editora Campus.

Anthony, J. (2004). Do state growth management regulations reduce sprawl? *Urban Affairs Review*, *39*(3), 376–397. doi:10.1177/1078087403257798

Banos-González, I., Martínez-Fernández, J., & Esteve-Selma, M. Á. (2015). Dynamic integration of sustainability indicators in insular socio-ecological systems. *Ecological Modelling, 306*, 130–144. doi:10.1016/j.ecolmodel.2014.08.014

Barth, T. D. (2011). The idea of a green new deal in a Quintuple Helix Model of knowledge, know-how and innovation. *International Journal of Social Ecology and Sustainable Development, 1*(2), 1–14. doi:10.4018/jsesd.2011010101

Braun, B. (2015). Futures: Imagining socioecological transformation—An introduction. *Annals of the Association of American Geographers, 105*(2), 239–243. doi:10.1080/00045608.2014.1000893

Buck, I. (2017). The Cost of High Prices: Embedding an Ethic of Expense into the Standard of Care (September 6, 2016). 58 B.C. L. Rev. 101 (2017), *University of Tennessee Legal Studies Research Paper No. 309*. https://ssrn.com/abstract=2835816

Carayannis, E. G., & Campbell, D. F. (2010). Triple Helix, Quadruple Helix and Quintuple Helix and How Do Knowledge, Innovation and the Environment Relate To Each Other? A Proposed Framework for a Trans-disciplinary Analysis of Sustainable Development and Social Ecology. *International Journal of Social Ecology and Sustainable Development, 1*(1), 41–69. doi:10.4018/jsesd.2010010105

Carayannis, E. G., & Campbell, D. F. J. (2006). Knowledge creation, diffusion, and use in innovation networks and knowledge clusters. A comparative systems approach across the United States, Europe, and Asia (pp. 1–25). Praeger, Westporti.

Carayannis, E. G., & Campbell, D. F. J. (2012). *Mode 3 Knowledge Production in Quadruple Helix Innovation Systems*. Springer New York. doi:10.1007/978-1-4614-2062-0

Danilda, I., Lindberg, M., & Torstensson, B.-M. (2009). *A Quattro Helix Innovation System on the European Agenda*. Women Resource Centres. http:// www.hss09.se/own_documents/Papers/3-11%20-%20Danilda %20Lindberg% 20&%20Torstensson%20-%20paper.pdf. 2

Davies, A., & Doyle, R. (2015). Transforming household consumption: From backcasting to HomeLabs experiments. *Annals of the Association of American Geographers, 105*(2), 425–436. doi:10.1080/000 45608.2014.1000948

de Melo, A. (2001). *The Innovation Systems of Latin America and the Caribbean*. Inter-American Development Bank. Agosto.

de Melo, M. A. C. (1997). *Processo de Planejamento e as Inovações Tecnológicas e Sociais: uma perspectiva sócio-ecológica*. Anais do 5o. Seminário de Modernização Tecnológica.

de Melo, M.A.C. (2002). Inovação e Modernização Tecnológica e Organizacional nas MPMEs: o domínio interorganizacional. *Seminário Internacional: Políticas para Sistemas Produtivos Locais de MPME*: 2002.

Deal, B., Pan, H., Pallathucheril, V., & Fulton, G. (2017). Urban resilience and planning support systems: The need for sentience. *Journal of Urban Technology, 24*(1), 29–45. doi:10.1080/10630732.2017.1285018

Deal, B., Pan, H., Timm, S., & Pallathucheril, V. (2017). The role of multidirectional temporal analysis in scenario planning exercises and Planning Support Systems. *Computers, Environment and Urban Systems, 64*, 91–102. doi:10.1016/j.compenvurbsys.2017.01.004

Delanty, G., & Mota, A. (2017). Governing the Anthropocene: Agency, Governance, Knowledge. *European Journal of Social Theory, 20*(1), 9–38. doi:10.1177/1368431016668535

Dias, A.B., de Melo, M.A.C & Rosenthal, D. (2002). *Enriquecendo a Atuação de Incubadora de Empresas. Tecnologia e Inovação: experiências de gestão nas micro e pequenas empresas.* PGT/USP.

Dias, A. B., Rosentha, L. D., & de Melo, M. A. C. (2000) Enriquecendo a Atuação de Incubadoras de Empresas. XXI Simpósio de Gestão da Inovação Tecnológica. Co-autores: Adriano Batista Dias e David Rosenthal. São Paulo.

Dubina, I. N., Carayannis, E. G., & Campbell, D. F. J. (2012). Creativity economy and a crisis of the economy? Coevolution of knowledge, innovation, and creativity, and of the knowledge economy and knowledge society. *Journal of the Knowledge Economy, 3*(1), 1–24. http://www.springerlink.com/content/t5j8l12136h526h5/ 10.1007/s13132-011-0042-y. doi:10.100713132-011-0042-y

Farley, J., & Voinov, A. (2016). Economics, socio-ecological resilience and ecosystem services. *Journal of Environmental Management, 183*(2), 389–398. https://www.sciencedirect.com/science/article/pii/S0301479716305023. doi:10.1016/j.jenvman.2016.07.065 PMID:27480914

Fischer-Kowalski, M., & Haberl, H. (2007). *Socioecological Transitions and Global Change.* Edward Elgar. doi:10.4337/9781847209436

Foray, D., David, P. A., & Hall, B. H. (2009). Smart specialisation: The concept. In E. Commission (Ed.), *Knowledge for growth: Prospects for science, technology, and innovation* (pp. 25–29). European Commission. DG Research.

Hankey, S., & Marshall, J. D. (2010). Impacts of urban form on future US passenger-vehicle greenhouse gas emissions. *Energy Policy, 38*(9), 4880–4887. doi:10.1016/j.enpol.2009.07.005

Hassink, R., & Marques, P. (2016). The regional innovation paradox revisited. In U. Hilpert (Ed.), *Routledge Handbook of politics and technology* (pp. 120–131). Routledge.

Hausman, D. M. (2007). *The Philosophy of Economics: An Anthology* (3rd ed.). Cambridge University Press. doi:10.1017/CBO9780511819025

Healy, A., & Morgan, K. (2012). Spaces of innovation: Learning, proximity, and the ecological turn. *Regional Studies, 46*(8), 1041–1053. doi:10.1080/00343404.2012.672725

Heikkinen, H. (2002) *Sopeutumisen mallit. Poronhoidon adaptaatio jälkiteolliseen toim-intaympäristöön Suomen läntisellä poronhoitoalueella 1980–2000 (in Finnish; models of adaptation – adaptation of Reindeer Herding to the post-industrial envi-ronment in the Western Finnish reindeer herding area 1980–2000).* [Doctoral dissertation, University of Oulu, Suomalaisen Kirjallisuuden Seura, Helsink].

Hong, B., Limburg, K. E., Erickson, J. D., Gowdy, J. M., Nowosielski, A. A., Polimeni, J. M., & Stainbrook, K. M. (2009). Connecting the ecological-economic dots in human-dominated watersheds: Models to link socio-economic activities on the landscape to stream ecosystem health. *Landscape and Urban Planning, 91*(2), 78–87. doi:10.1016/j.landurbplan.2008.11.012

Itkowitz, H., & Leydesdorff, L. (2000). The dynamics of innovation: From National Systems and "Mode 2" to a Triple Helix of university–industry–government relations. *Research Policy, 29*(2), 109–123. https://www.sciencedirect.com/science/article/pii/S0048733399000554. doi:10.1016/S0048-7333(99)00055-4

Jacobsson, S., & Bergek, A. (2011). Innovation system analyses and sustainability transitions: Contributions and suggestions for research. *Environmental Innovation and Societal Transitions, 1*(1), 41–57. doi:10.1016/j.eist.2011.04.006

Keesstra, S., Nunes, J., Novara, A., Finger, D., Avelar, D., Kalantari, Z., & Cerdà, A. (2018). The superior effect of nature based solutions in land management for enhancing ecosystem services. *The Science of the Total Environment, 610*, 997–1009. doi:10.1016/j.scitotenv.2017.08.077 PMID:28838037

Kemp, R., Schot, J., & Hoogma, R. (1998). Regime Shifts to Sustainability Through Processes of Niche Formation: The Approach of Strategic Niche Management. *Technology Analysis and Strategic Management, 10*(2), 175–196. doi:10.1080/09537329808524310

Lastres, H. M. M. (orgs.). (1999). *Globalização e Inovação Localizada: experiências.*

Lastres, H. M. M., Cassiolato, J. E., Lemos, C. Maldonado, j.

Leach, M. J., Rockström, P., Raskin, I., Scoones, A. C., Stirling, A., Smith, J., Thompson, J., Millstone, E., Ely, A., Arond, E., Folke, C., & Olsson, P. (2012). Transforming innovation for sustainability. *Ecology and Society, 17*(2), 11. doi:10.5751/ES-04933-170211

Lerner, L. (2003) *Renman-tutkimusprojekti suosittelee parannuksia – maankäyttö.*

Manuel-Navarrete, D., Slocombe, S., & Mitchell, B. (2006). Science for place-based socioecological management: Lessons from the Maya Forest (Chiapas and Petén). *Ecology and Society, 11*(1), 8. https://www.ecologyandsociety.org/vol11/iss1/art8/. doi:10.5751/ES-01608-110108

Marques, P., & Morgan, K. (2018). The heroic assumptions of smart specialisation: A sympathetic critique of regional innovation policy. In A. Isaksen, R. Martin, & M. Trippl (Eds.), *New avenues for regional innovation systems-theoretical advances, empirical cases, and policy lessons* (pp. 275–293). Springer. doi:10.1007/978-3-319-71661-9_14

Marques, P., Morgan, K., & Richardson, R. (2018). Social innovation in question: The theoretical and practical implications of a contested concept. *Environment and Planning C. Politics and Space, 36*(3), 496–512.

Mazzucato, M. (2015). *The Entrepreneurial State: Debunking Public vs. Private Sector Myths.* PublicAffairs.

Muscio, A., Reid, A., & Rivera Leon, L. (2015). An empirical test of the regional innovation paradox: Can smart specialisation overcome the paradox in Central and Eastern Europe? *Journal of Economic Policy Reform, 18*(2), 153–171. doi:10.1080/17487870.2015.1013545

Nahapiet, J. E., & Ghoshal, S. (1998). Social Capital, Intellectual Capital, and the Organizational Advantage. *Academy of Management Review, 33*(2), 242–266. doi:10.2307/259373

Nautiyal, S. (2011). Can conservation and development interventions in the Indian Central Himalaya ensure environmental sustainability? A socioecological evaluation. *Sustainability Science*, *6*(2), 151–167. doi:10.100711625-011-0126-4

OECD. (1997b). Government Venture Capital for Technology-Based Firms. Ducument OCDE/GD (97), 201. Paris: OECD, 1997b.

OECD. (1997c). Diffusion Technology to Industry: Government Policies and Programmes. Document OCDE/GD (97)60. Paris: 1997c.

OECD. (2001c). *Innovative Networks: co-operation in national innovation systems*. OECD.

Ostrom, E. (1990). *Governing the commons: the evolution of institutions for collective action*. Cambridge University Press. doi:10.1017/CBO9780511807763

Oughton, C., Landabaso, M., & Morgan, K. (2002). The regional innovation paradox: Innovation policy and industrial policy. *The Journal of Technology Transfer*, *27*(1), 97–110. doi:10.1023/A:1013104805703

Pan, H., & Deal, B. (2020). Reporting on the performance and usability of planning support systems—Towards a mutual understanding. *Applied Spatial Analysis and Policy*, *13*(1), 137–159. doi:10.100712061-019-09296-5

Pan, H., Deal, B., Chen, Y., & Hewings, G. (2018). A Reassessment of urban structure and land-use patterns: Distance to CBD or network-based? —evidence from Chicago. *Regional Science and Urban Economics*, *70*, 215–228. doi:10.1016/j.regsciurbeco.2018.04.009

Pan, H., Deal, B., Destouni, G., Zhang, Y., & Kalantari, Z. (2018b). Sociohydrology modeling for complex urban environments in support of integrated land and water resource management practices. *Land Degradation & Development*, *29*(10), 3639–3652. doi:10.1002/ldr.3106

Pan, H., Zhang, L., Cong, C., Deal, B., & Wang, Y. (2019). A dynamic and spatially explicit modeling approach to identify the ecosystem service implications of complex urban systems interactions. *Ecological Indicators*, *102*, 426–436. doi:10.1016/j.ecolind.2019.02.059

Papamichail, G., Rosiello, A., & Wield, D. (2019). Capacity-building barriers to S3 implementation: An empirical framework for catch-up regions. *Innovation (Abingdon)*, *32*(1), 66–84. doi:10.1080/13511610.2018.1537844

Popkov, M. V. V. (2007). Sustainable economic development in the context of globalization and the knowledge economy: The conceptual foundations of the theory and practice scientific publication. *Economy*, *2007*, 295.

Porter, M. (1998). Clusters and the new economics of competition. *Harvard Business Review*, Nov-Dez: 1998.

Porter, M. (2001). *Clusters of Innovation: regional foundations of U. S competitiveness. Council on Competitiveness*. Monitor Group.

Porter, M., & Kramer, M. (2011). Creating shared value: How to reinvent capitalism – and unleash a wave of innovation and growth. *Harvard Business Review*, *89*(1–2), 62–77.

Quilley, S. (2019). Green Politics and the Right: Possible Alliance? In *Proceedings of the 12th Biennial Conference of the Canadian Society for Ecological Economics*, Waterloo, ON, Canada.

Robinson, L., Newell, J. P., & Marzluff, J. M. (2005). Twenty-five years of sprawl in the Seattle region: Growth management responses and implications for conservation. *Landscape and Urban Planning*, *71*(1), 51–72. doi:10.1016/j.landurbplan.2004.02.005

Rosenfeld, S. (1997). *Clustering, Networking, and Industrial Modernization*. Regional Technology Strategies<http://www.cherry.gatech.edu/sim/slides/rosenfeld.html.

Rotmans, J., & Lorbach, D. (2009). Complexity and transition management. *Journal of Industrial Ecology*, *13*(2), 184–196. doi:10.1111/j.1530-9290.2009.00116.x

Smeds, E., & Acuto, M. (2018). Networking cities after Paris: Weighing the ambition of urban climate change experimentation. *Global Policy*, *9*(4), 549–559. doi:10.1111/1758-5899.12587

Squazzoni, F. (2008). A (computational) social science perspective on societal transitions. *Computational & Mathematical Organization Theory*, *14*(4), 266–282. doi:10.100710588-008-9038-y

Tödtling, F., & Trippl, M. (2018). Regional innovation policies for new path development – beyond neo-liberal and traditional systemic views. *European Planning Studies*, *26*(9), 1779–1795. doi:10.1080/09654313.2018.1457140

Truffer, B., & Coenen, L. (2012). Environmental innovation and sustainability transitions in regional studies. *Regional Studies*, *46*(1), 1–21. doi:10.1080/00343404.2012.646164

Urbaniec, K., Mikulčić, H., Wang, Y., & Duić, N. (2018). System integration is a necessity for sustainable development. *Journal of Cleaner Production*, *195*(10), 122–132. doi:10.1016/j.jclepro.2018.05.178

Vanhaverbeke W., Belderbos, R., Duysters G., Beerkens B. (2015). Technological performance and alliances over the industry life cycle: evidence from the ASIC industry *The journal of product innovation management*, *32*(4), 556-573. doi:10.1111/jpim.12253

Wang, C., Wang, Y., Wang, R., & Zheng, P. (2018). Modeling and evaluating land-use/land-cover change for urban planning and sustainability: a case study of Dongying city, China

Watkins, C. (2015a). African oil palms, colonial socioecological transformation and the making of an Afro-Brazilian landscape in Bahia, *Brazil. Environ. Hist*, *21*(1), 13–42. doi:10.3197/096734015X14183179969700

Watkins, C. (2015b). *An Afro-brazilian Landscape: African Oil Palms and Socioecological Change in Bahia, Brazil*. Baton Rouge PhD dissertation.

Wolf, S. (1995). Cropping systems and conservation policy: The roles of agrichemical dealers and independent crop consultants. *Journal of Soil and Water Conservation*, *50*, 263–269.

Wolf, S., & Nowak, P. (1995). Development of information intensive agrichemical management services in Wisconsin. *Environmental Management*, *19*(3), 371–382. doi:10.1007/BF02471979

Wolf, S., & Primmer, E. (2006). Between incentives and action: A pilot study of biodiversity conservation competencies for multifunctional forest management in Finland. *Society & Natural Resources*, *19*(9), 845–861. doi:10.1080/08941920600835601

Yang, T., & Zhang, X. (2016). Benchmarking the building energy consumption and solar energy trade-offs of residential neighborhoods on Chongming Eco-Island. *China Appl. Energy*, *180*, 792–799. doi:10.1016/j.apenergy.2016.08.039

Yang, W., Liu, W., Viña, A., Tuanmu, M.-N., He, G., Dietz, T., & Liu, J. (2013). Nonlinear effects of group size on collective action and resource outcomes. *Proceedings of the National Academy of Sciences of the United States of America*, *110*(27), 10916–10921. doi:10.1073/pnas.1301733110 PMID:23776222

Yu, H., Wang, Y., Li, X., Wang, C., Sun, M., & Du, A. (2019). Measuring ecological capital: State of the art, trends, and challenges. *Journal of Cleaner Production*, *219*, 833–845. doi:10.1016/j.jclepro.2019.02.014

KEY TERMS AND DEFINITIONS

Public innovation policies: a form of state intervention in the local economy of the environment. They are applied to promotion context of the local innovation systems based on the university. And they have substantial public resources and capacities in research infrastructure and training.

Socio-ecological transition: The results from long-term dynamic spatial and functional energy metabolism in connections and disconnections of changes in energy metabolism (natural resources, land uses, local governance, etc.) affecting local social-ecological regimes. Secondly, as a process of spatial, temporal, and functional-dysfunctional connection and disconnection of industrial complexes to combine or decouple urban metabolism from local natural resources.

Sustainable development: Which is conceptualized as the development of industrial enterprises related to the components with the environment, the economic, social, and ecological.

Chapter 16
Understanding the Implementation of Lean Philosophy in Warehouse Management

Vanessa Amorim
ISCAP, Polytechnic of Porto, Portugal

Orlando Lima Rua
Center for Organisational and Social Studies (CEOS), ISCAP, Polytechnic of Porto, Portugal & Research Center of Business Sciences (NECE), Portugal

Bruno de Sousa Lopes
University of Aveiro, Portugal

ABSTRACT

The core of the lean concept is expressed not only in eliminating waste and losses but also in the pursuit of continual improvement and creating greater value. Although lean management is commonly linked with industrial production processes, this research illustrates the application of lean techniques to optimize warehouse management operations. In this context, the research in an SME of the Import and Export sector in Portugal intends to describe the use of lean tools in warehouse optimization. The outcomes of the lean tool deployment meet the specified objectives and emphasize the need to integrate various approaches to achieve a better pursuit of the optimization strategy. The organization can respond to customer needs more effectively and efficiently through improved warehouse flow and continuous improvement.

DOI: 10.4018/978-1-6684-7509-6.ch016

INTRODUCTION

Lean thinking was developed in Japan at Toyota Motor Corporation, by engineer Taiichi Ohno, due to the scarcity of resources and the particularities of the Japanese economy at the time. From his visits to factories in the United States (US), he realized that he would have to make adaptations because American methods would not work in Japan. The American production method was based on large amounts of stock stored in large warehouses, produced by large machinery with rigorous processes. While US factory managers were not overly concerned with process efficiency, Ohno analyzed the waste that existed in each process, aiming to reduce overproduction, eliminate defects in production processes, create a linear production flow, reduce inventories and intermediate products, and meet customer requirements, thus seeking a multidimensional standard of perfection by promoting continuous improvement, making it possible to compete with automobile companies from Western countries (Howell, 1999). The success of the Toyota production method resulted in the wide dispersion of the lean philosophy and its respective practice, having been used first in automotive companies in Western countries and later in other industries, sectors, and countries (Anđelković et al., 2016).

The learning gained through the successful example of Toyota allowed us to define that the goal of a lean system is to optimize its performance according to the customer's unique requirements, creating a continuous flow by eliminating waste (Howell, 1999). Lean thinking has become widely recognized in the last 20 years, and its techniques have been applied to different areas and industries, namely to warehouse process management.

Warehouses play a crucial role in supply chains, mainly defining business success, namely the company's competitiveness in terms of cost levels and customer service capability. The versatility and adaptability of the lean concept allow establishing that implementing this concept can be an excellent strategy in warehouse optimization (Phogat, 2013).

In this sense, this study, developed in an SME in the Import and Export sector, aims to describe the implementation of lean tools in the optimization of storage activities, having as overall objectives the reduction and elimination of existing waste and the increase of value for the customer. Regarding the specific objectives, they consist of the elimination of unnecessary movements and empty runs, the reduction of the distances covered by employees, greater control of the physical location of products, the reduction of picking errors, the reduction of lead time, the increase of customer satisfaction and the ability to provide greater well-being to the company's employees.

BACKGROUND

Lean Concept

The lean concept represents the ability to do more with less, using minimal effort, energy, equipment, time, floor space, materials, and capital - while providing customers exactly what they want (Womack & Jones, 1996).

Despite the evolution of the concept, its original definition remains clear, reflecting the importance of creating a production system that can produce a customized product after the customer's order, reducing or eliminating intermediate stocks, through the following basic principles: identify and deliver value to the customer, eliminating what does not add value; organize production as a continuous flow; refine the product and create a reliable flow, removing the existence of inventories; distribute information for decision making; and continuously seek perfection, providing a product that meets the customer's requirements (Howell, 1999).

Lean principles first define the product's value as perceived by the customer, followed by aligning the flow with it, striving for perfection through continuous improvement to eliminate waste, and classifying value-added and non-value-added activities (Sundar et al., 2014). Activities that do not add value are considered waste, where waste represents a vital obstacle to value creation. According to Taiichi Ohno, there are seven types of waste: transportation, inventories, movements, waiting, overprocessing, overproduction, and product defects (Womack & Jones, 1996). However, Womack and Jones (1996) add an eighth waste: goods and services that do not meet customer needs, and other authors also consider the underutilization of people's capabilities.

Management Tools

Value Stream Mapping (VSM)

The author's Rother and Shook (2003) consider that the VSM aims to allow an overview of a product's value stream, from the acquisition of raw materials to the shipment of the final product. VSM is a tool for waste detection, representing support for implementing lean philosophy, making it possible to use it in the most distinct activity sectors. The use of VSM is essential for any company, as it allows the visualization of material and information flows and the sources of waste in the value stream to identify and eliminate them (Rewers et al., 2016). It is also an effective way to record delivery times, setup times, and other indicators so a system's performance can be visualized (Oliveira et al., 2017).

According to Oliveira et al. (2017), the application of the VSM methodology implies the pursuit of a set of steps, namely: 1) selection of the product or family of products to be used as the focus of improvement; 2) design of the representation of the current state; 3) representation of the future state, without the inefficiencies, previously pointed out and 4) preparation of a work plan to achieve the future state. The VSM is a graphical method that uses icons to represent each critical element of the value chain. All procedures have their respective times. It is possible to calculate the time of value-added and non-value-added activities by adding up the times of each activity typology (Rohac & Januska, 2015).

The second phase of the VSM is to design a future state map based on the improvement plan. The availability of information from the VSM facilitates and validates the decision to implement lean tools and can also motivate the company during implementation to achieve the desired results (Sundar et al., 2014).

Spaghetti Diagram

The spaghetti diagram is a methodology that allows visualizing the movement of an object in a system using lines. The object in motion can refer to an employee of a company or a product, and the system in which this object moves can represent any area (Senderská et al., 2017). Using this diagram allows the trajectory of movement of any object or person to be established, and it is possible to use different colors for various objects (or people) and to establish the movement at different times. After analyzing the diagram, it is possible to identify the lengths of the movements, the number of movements, the time required for each movement, the overlapping and cross movements, and their characteristics. Applying the diagram result can identify inefficient movements and areas and change work organization or workplace layout (Senderská et al., 2017).

5S

The 5S tool was developed in Japan by Sakichi Toyoda, Kishiro Toyoda, and Taiichi Ohno in the 1960s (Oliveira et al., 2017). The 5S consists of a methodology for creating and maintaining well-organized, clean, highly efficient, high-quality workplaces. Eliminating equipment failures and breakdown losses also improves quality and safety at work (Filip & Marascu-Klein, 2015; Pasale & Bagi, 2013). The 5S method is one of the lean strategy's most widely adopted tools today. It is a fundamental concept that establishes the operational stability needed to make and sustain continuous improvements (Filip & Marascu-Klein, 2015).

This method consists of the sequential implementation of five steps: **Seiri (Sort)** - removal of everything that is considered unnecessary, i.e., the workplace should only contain what is necessary to perform the respective activities; **Seiton (Set in order)** - everything must have a place, and that space must be designated for it, which results in the quick and visual identification of tools and areas, saving time and facilitating processes; **Seizo (Shine)** - cleanliness of the work area is essential, reducing the risk of accidents, improving health and the work environment, and helping with different checks; **Seiketsu (Standardize)** - to optimize the first three S's, standards must be created and followed; **Shitsuke (Sustain)** - the last step consists in developing a method (usually 5S audits) to ensure that the 5S technique is followed continuously, which requires discipline and focus. The 5S provides several benefits for a company, the most relevant being the decrease in waste of time and space (Oliveira et al., 2017; Rewers et al., 2016).

The 5S audit allows for periodic review and verification of the 5S methodology. The development, implementation, and continuous monitoring of the 5S implementation are the responsibility of the different employees and not of the quality auditor. After a 5S audit, the auditor can analyze whether improvements or setbacks have occurred from the previous audit (Filip & Marascu-Klein, 2015).

Swimlane

The swimlane or functional diagram allows the visualization of processes as a set of sequenced internal activities that can be performed by a company, the defining characteristic of the swimlane being the indication of the steps involved in the different phases of the process. The sequence of activities is conveyed using arrows, which usually connect the activities so that the entire process can be followed from a start to an end. The diagram can optionally represent delays between activities. This type of diagram also serves as a validation tool by which the accuracy and completeness of processes can be determined. Because processes are usually cross-functional, elements from multiple departments can be included (Jeyaraj & Sauter, 2014).

Visual Management

Visual management is fundamental to the communication process that drives lean strategies. One of the critical factors learned from Toyota's production system is that everyone involved could view and fully understand the different aspects of the process and its status at any given time. The transparency of the process allowed for immediate feedback on the current status and indicated where adjustments might be needed to enable a strategy to meet customer specifications (Parry & Turner, 2006).

In today's corporate world, visual management is a management system that seeks to improve organizational performance by connecting and aligning organizational vision, core values, goals, and culture with other management systems, work processes, workplace elements, and stakeholders through stimuli, which directly address one or more of the five human senses. These stimuli communicate quality information (necessary, relevant, correct, immediate, easy to understand, and stimulating), which helps people quickly understand the organizational context (Tezel et al., 2009).

Authors Oliveira et al. (2017) concluded that visual management consisted of a self-ordered, self-explanatory, self-regulating, and self-enhancing work environment using visual devices. Visual management is considered the basis of several other lean tools, such as 5S and standard work, aiming to empower employees to manage their work environment, reducing errors and other forms of waste.

Pull and Push System

A push system seeks to start the production of a given product based on the ability to meet the expected future demand, i.e., according to information in history (updated weekly or monthly), being fundamental to the detailed scheduling for the acquisition of materials for the production of goods. Thus, future demand periods are prepared for the company's products (Singh & Ahuja, 2012). The push system can be further defined as a system in which control information flow is in the same direction as the flow of materials (Bonney et al., 1999).

On the other hand, in a pull system, the production of a particular product is initiated with the demand or request made by the buyer. The product's customer pulls the last link in the supply chain; this, in turn, pulls the previous one, and so on. Authors Singh and Ahuja (2012) describe that there is a certain amount of inventory in each process, in which the subsequent process requests and withdraws the parts from the previous process only at the rate and at the time it has consumed all the parts and then the last process is produced only when the subsequent process withdraws the parts. The pull system can also be presented as a system in which the flow of information is opposite to the flow of materials (Bonney et al., 1999).

Warehouse Management

A warehouse is an element of a logistics network where goods are temporarily stored or redirected to another location in the network. It is an integral part of a logistics system where products are temporarily deposited between the origin and the point of consumption. Its main functions are to store, move, and transfer information. A warehouse can also provide assembly, sorting, labeling, and packaging functions.

Warehouses play a fundamental role in supply chains, defining to a large extent the success of the business, that is, the company's competitiveness in terms of cost levels and customer service capacity. Despite the high costs associated with inventories, warehouses respond to the variability of supply and demand, making them a necessary element in today's supply chains. The high costs associated with warehouses pose the challenge of simultaneously achieving low-cost warehousing and a high level of customer satisfaction (Phogat, 2013). Lean thinking has become widely recognized in the last 20 years. Its techniques have been applied to different areas, and industries, proving the concept's versatility and adaptability and supporting that lean implementation in warehouse management can succeed (Phogat, 2013).

The concept of lean warehousing implies constant, systematic, sustainable, and measurable improvement of the entire process, with the full participation of all employees. In addition, the warehouse is responsible for adding value to the customer by creating utility in time and place. Still, it is also an area of logistics that can cause many types of waste. Authors Anđelković et al. (2016) note that lean warehousing can also be defined as reducing the concept of waste in the upstream or downstream logistics chain, depending on the location and function of warehouses in the supply chain to serve the right customer at the right time and place.

Since warehouse operations represent not only a source of cost but also a source of competitive advantage through a higher level of service, the acceptance of lean culture in this area will contribute to higher value and lower costs. Lean warehousing aims to increase responsiveness to market demands and reduce total costs by simplifying distribution operations (Anđelković et al., 2016). Lean warehousing focuses on minimizing and reducing non-value-added activities in all warehouse operations: goods receiving, warehousing, picking and order preparation, and shipping operations.

Identifying possible waste in a warehouse allows validation that this is an ideal area for implementing a lean strategy, which will be reflected in eliminating losses and, therefore, minimizing warehouse costs. Optimizing warehouse management through lean implementation will allow for obtaining an increasing source of competitive advantages, establishing effective and efficient responses to customer requests through a better flow in the warehouse, and its continuous improvement (Anđelković et al., 2016).

CASE STUDY

The company under study was established in 1984 and has dedicated itself to Import and Export activity since its foundation. It is based in Porto – Portugal, and currently operates in the national and international markets, selling several ranges and product lines according to the seasonality of commercial campaigns in the business-to-business segment. The headquarters is composed of four warehouses with a total area of 2400 m^2, a showroom that has 350 m^2, and three offices with a total area of 130 m^2, which represents a total area of 2880 m^2.

Regarding the layout of the storage area, a U-shaped flow can be considered, which allows the establishment of several advantages, namely: the reduction of the average travel distance and the reduction of the space needed for receiving/shipping - since this space is joint for the two activities and a more accessible organization of storage areas based on volume and volume in motion (demanded by the customers). The activities performed as part of the warehouse operations are described in Table 1.

Table 1. Description of the activities in the case study warehouses

Activities	Description
Reception of goods	- Reception and discharge of vehicles. - Control and checking of delivered goods. - Decision on the locations of the goods.
Storage	- Place the goods in their locations. - Confirm in the management system the location used. - Dispatch the goods to supply the picking area.
Picking	- Collect/select items from stock for order fulfillment.
Consolidation	- Sort and/or consolidate goods by load/destination or order.
Shipping	- Shipping and loading of vehicles. - Preparation of transport documentation.

Source: Own elaboration (2021)

The strategy of the company under study is based on a model of combining products from suppliers with different origins - National, European, and Far Eastern, where the consolidation of loads for customers is carried out according to the selection of products that make up their orders, as shown in Figure 1.

Figure 1. Example of the product mix model in the case study
Source: Own elaboration (2021)

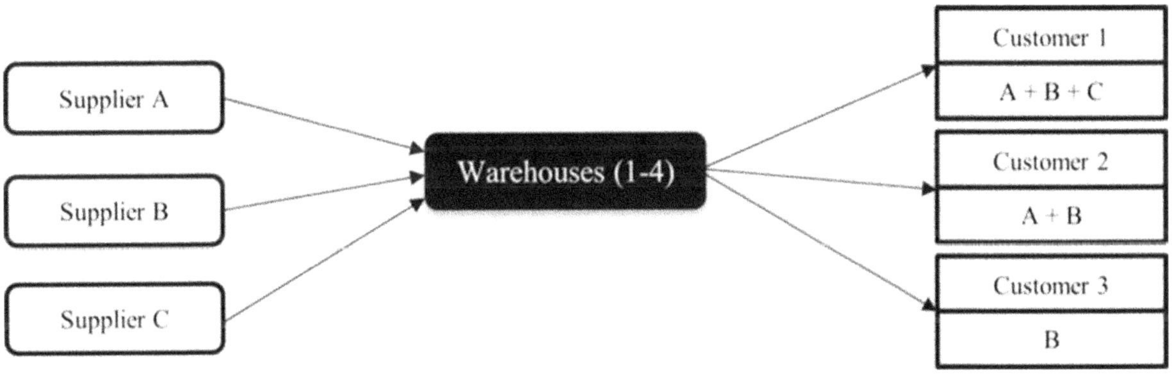

METHODOLOGY

The work encompassed the practices inherent to warehouse management, implementing the lean concept to provide a greater flow of value to the customer and simultaneously eliminate existing waste. The incorporation and sequenced implementation of lean elements are fundamental for successfully implementing an optimization system for warehouse management.

To improve the operational conditions of the warehouses under study, several lean techniques were adopted and applied in three distinct areas: 1) process identification, 2) waste identification, reduction, and elimination, and 3) operations planning. Initially, the warehouse processes were identified using a Swimlane; later, to identify waste to reduce or eliminate it, the VSM, the 5S, and the Spaghetti Diagram were used; and finally, in the scope of warehouse operations planning, Visual Management, and the Pull-Push Integrated System were integrated.

The study was developed following four main and distinct phases. In the first stage, a brief literature review of lean and warehouse management was performed to frame the work to be developed, mainly through analyzing scientific articles. The second stage involved analyzing warehouse operations to identify processes, waste, problems, and planning needs. Then, in the third stage, the theoretical concepts were applied to support the practical work to analyze and evaluate possible lean tools applicable to the case study. In the last stage, the results consisted of the applicability and analysis of the lean tools, establishing possible solutions, recommendations, and conclusions.

RESULTS

Swimlane

The swimlane elaborated in Figure 2 allows the visualization of the connections of the different processes that make up the set of internal operational activities of the storage area, structured sequentially. This tool aims to validate the accuracy and integrity of warehouse processes, allowing for a better understanding of the overall functioning of the process.

Figure 2. Swimlane of warehouse activities
Source: Own elaboration (2021)

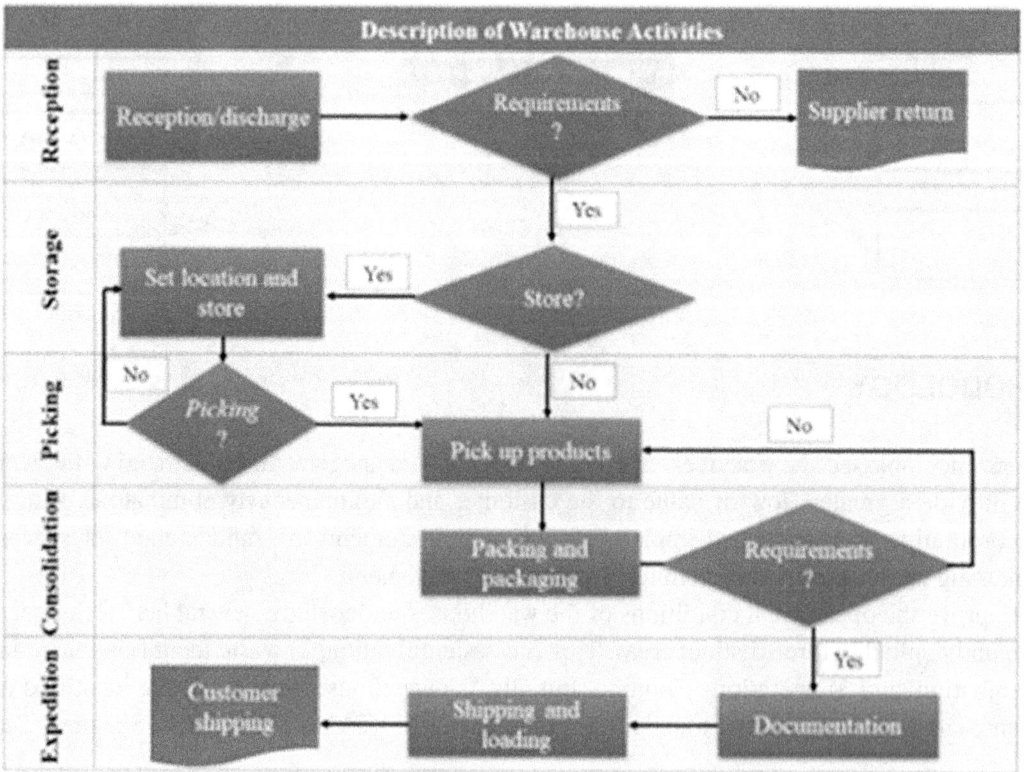

The functional diagram defined with the description of warehouse activities can also be applied together with the table of activities defined daily for each employee, which facilitates the overall understanding of the steps of the different processes, as well as allows optimization in the execution of different tasks, thus contributing to the reduction and elimination of waste associated with time and processes, which helps to highlight the internal flows of the company, adding more outstanding value for the end customer.

Value Stream Mapping (VSM)

The VSM tool aims to allow an overview of the information and material flows of the company, having been developed in this case study in the storage area. Thus, through the analysis of this tool, it will be possible to detect waste, representing support to the implementation of lean philosophy, to the extent that value activities and activities that do not represent value are identified.

The general objectives of the VSM in the case study are represented by the following: 1) understand the current state of the storage processes; 2) recognize the waste through the activities that generate value and those that do not generate value; 3) reduce or eliminate the existing waste; and 4) define strategies to optimize the process.

Figure 3. Current representation of a VSM in the case study
Source: Own elaboration (2021)

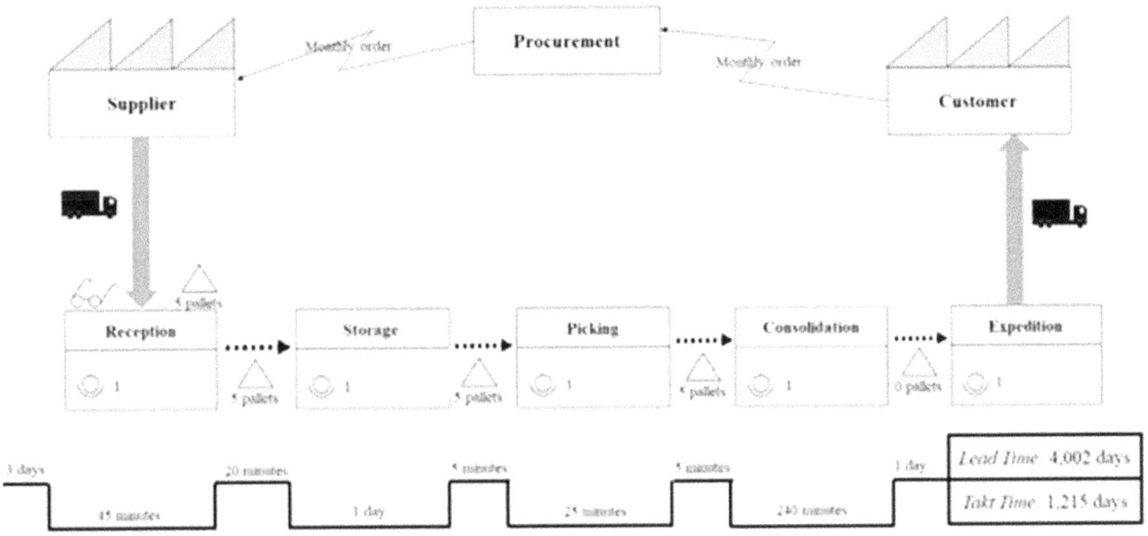

The schematized representation in Figure 3 allows the previously identified analysis and evaluation of the objectives. Thus, it is possible to visualize the information flows in a supply situation determined by a customer's request belonging to a chain of hypermarkets and the consequent request to the European supplier. Regarding the material flows, they are defined through the different phases of storage activity in warehouse 1, reflecting the number of employees involved, stock movement, processing time, and lead time, making it possible to visualize the entire system's performance.

The activities performed in the process can be considered value-adding. However, waste is associated, namely, the time factor that occurs in the different activities of storage, picking, consolidation, and shipping. Thus, optimizing the process to reduce the processing time and lead time of customer orders is essential by analyzing the movements made by employees, the respective time elapsed in these movements, and the work environment definition.

Regarding the representation of the future state of the process, Figure 4 shows the VSM with the following Kaizen opportunities: 1) eliminate manual transports within the warehouse and organization of the workplace through the 5S's, which allows for achieving greater efficiency and reduction of processing time; 2) eliminate unnecessary movements and reduce the distances traveled, using the Spaghetti Diagram; it also becomes essential to have greater control over product locations through the management program, reducing possible picking errors; 3) organize the consolidation area with all the necessary materials and tools so that no time is wasted in accessing the resources needed for the packaging of goods; and 4) increase daily shipping capacity through the completion of a more significant number of orders, provided by the overall reduction of processing times in all daily orders, which will reduce lead time and increase customer satisfaction.

Figure 4. Future representation of a VSM in the case study
Source: Own elaboration (2021)

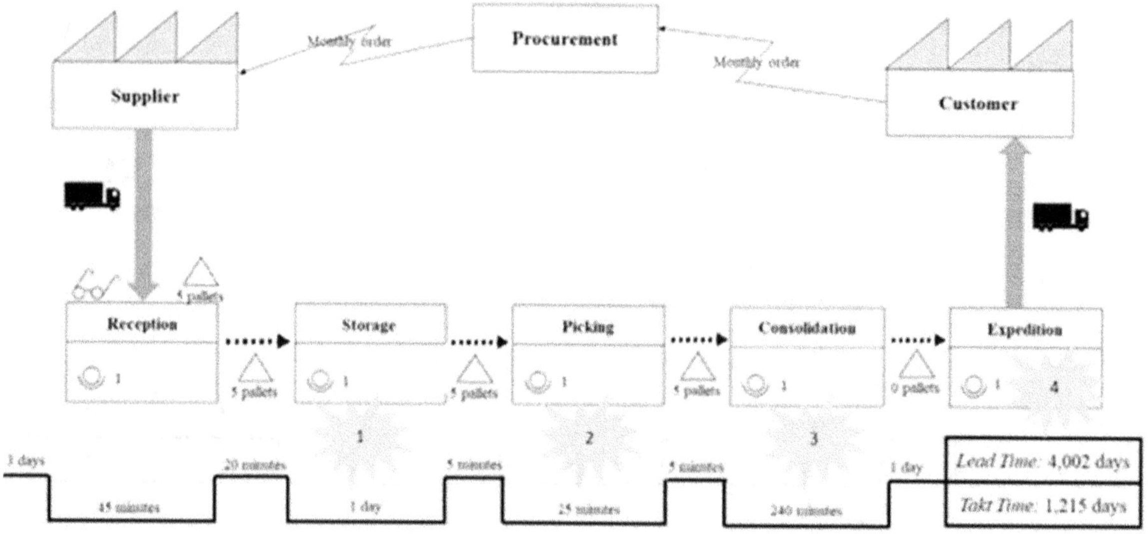

Spaghetti Diagram

Initially, it is necessary to specify the basic parameters of the analysis, namely, its objective, the required input data, the analysis of the process itself, and the analysis from the employee's point of view (Senderská et al., 2017). The case study aimed to analyze an employee's movements to pick an order composed of 10 items from different locations in two of the four warehouses. Through a draft of the layouts of the four warehouses, without dimensional data, the authors proceeded to the analysis of the workplace in the entire operation, followed by the movements of the employee from the office where she collected the picking request, the access to equipment and materials needed, the collection of products along the various points of the warehouse, ending her journey in the order consolidation area, where another employee will proceed to its proper packaging. During the described process, the time and distance factor was introduced to quantify the distance traveled and the time elapsed between the collection of the picking order and the final movement to the order consolidation area. In Figure 5, it is possible to visualize the spaghetti diagram obtained.

Figure 5. Spaghetti Diagram for an illustrative picking request
Source: Own elaboration (2021)

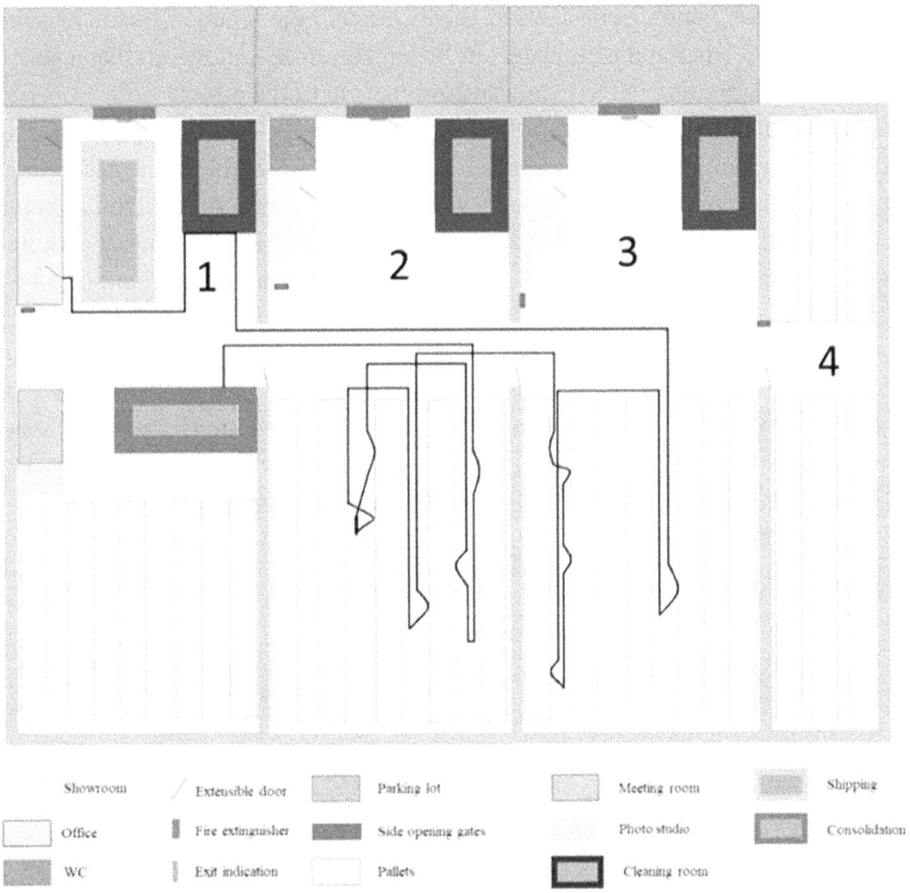

The spaghetti diagram of the process accounted for the time spent on the picking operation and the total distance traveled by the employee, totaling 18 minutes and approximately 260 meters. The analysis of the employee's movements in the above diagram allowed us to conclude that movements and distances traveled were unnecessary, leading to increased order preparation and lead time. Also, given the employee's lower control of product locations, the possibility of errors associated with the picking was potentiated.

Thus, the need to implement changes to product management became evident, so a global inventory of the different families of products was carried out in a table, which was introduced in the respective product reference location. This data was later imported into the system's product sheets.

Customer orders are placed through the company's online store or pre-sales software used by the sales team. After synchronizing the orders in the management system, the sorting represented the follow-up of product selection by the customer, which did not necessarily reflect a sorting logic for the best picking strategies. Thus, a development was made to the system in which, after synchronizing the orders, the references were automatically sorted in the document, following as parameters the sorting by the respective families and sub-families described in the sheets of each product. This ordering will be more compatible with the organization of goods in the different warehouses. However, it was imperative to add a field in the picking order that shows the locations of the products entered by the inventory, with the indication of the respective warehouse, which, in turn, offers the location of the products on the respective pallets, which are represented by a letter and a number. The order, therefore, follows an increasing ordering of warehouses from 1 to 4, according to the letters and numbering of the pallets.

The spaghetti diagram allowed a very contributive analysis for the optimization of the displacements of employees in the collection of picking orders, having verified a decrease in the average time of order preparation by 23% in the period between March and May 2021 when compared to the same period the previous year, reducing the waste associated with the time factor, reflected in the reduction of lead time and, consequently, in the increase of added value for the customer and its satisfaction.

5S

The implementation of 5S in the warehouse operations area of this case study aimed to create and maintain well-organized and clean workplaces and to create efficiency and quality standards. The steps and description of the implementation process of the 5S tool are described in Table 2.

Table 2. Description of the implementation of the 5S tool in the case study

5S Stages	Description
Sorting	- In the order consolidation area, the reception/shipping dock, and storage of equipment and materials, the classification into tools necessary or unnecessary for performing the activities of the different posts was carried out. - Unnecessary tools were removed.
Set in order	- Definition of the order processes required in each work area, according to the logic of frequency of use and accessibility of tools and materials. - Elaboration of the toolkits needed for specific tasks. - Less frequently used tools and materials were also organized but placed further away from the sphere of frequent use. - The different areas in the warehouses were delineated according to a color code to which a specific area corresponds (Figure 6). - Quick visual identification of all areas and tools/materials.
Shine	- Prompt and regular cleaning in the different work areas allows the identification and elimination of clutter and keep the workplace clean. - During cleaning, the tools/materials and the workplace are checked.
Standardize	- Obtaining photographic records to define the pattern of order and organization. - Through the delineation and organization of the different areas, it was possible to achieve standardization, simplify the work environment, decrease the time spent looking for tools and materials, and obtain higher levels of efficiency and excellent safety.
Sustain	- Encouraging motivation to maintain the different sites according to the pre-established organization. - Conducting monthly audits to monitor the sites according to a checklist developed for each work area.

Source: Own elaboration (2021)

Figure 6. Delineation of the different areas in the warehouse
Source: Own elaboration (2021)

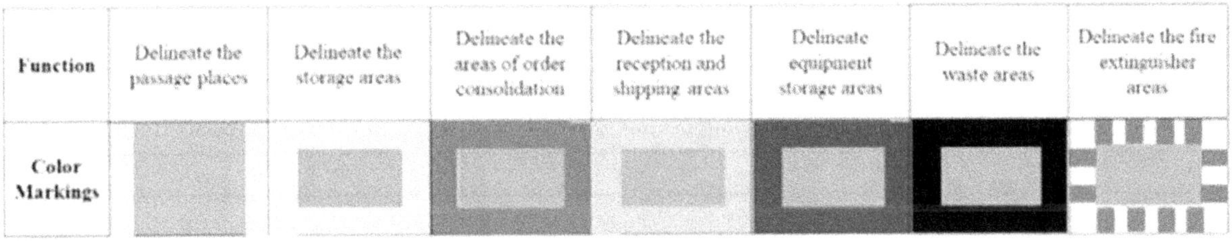

The monthly audits carried out in the company allow verification of compliance with the different components of the 5S but add the possibility of creating continuous improvement through feedback from the different employees. They can indicate new actions for the different places and workstations. The initial results of the 5S audits demonstrated the need to continue to improve workplace organization, promoting the encouragement of continuous improvement of each space. Currently, the organization and maintenance practices of the different areas are well-defined in the company's culture, reflected in the positive results of the audits.

Visual Management

Besides the additions provided by the 5S, visual management in the company under study is also established through a simple board located in the office of warehouse one that encompasses all the daily activities to be performed by indicating the responsible employee in the respective quadrant. The information is presented and makes it possible to visualize the progress of the different processes. In the board shown in Figure 7, only the activities that add value to the warehouse's daily activities management process are included. The advantages of using this table of activities are:

- the ease of use;
- the ease of visualization of information;
- the reduction of wasted time due to the extensive visual control;
- the ease, on the part of the manager, of monitoring all tasks, which helps the team to achieve its daily work goals and allows the work team to be organized, avoiding repetition of tasks; and
- the access of all employees to new learning and techniques, which fosters teamwork and facilitates communication.

Figure 7. Table of warehouse activities per employee
Source: Own elaboration (2021)

Process: Warehouse Activities by Employee							
Employee	Goods Receipt	Storage	*Picking*	Order consolidation	Shipping	After-sales service	Completion of tasks
A							
B							
C							
D							
Responsible Manager:							
Date:							

Pull-Push Integrated System

Pull and push systems are rarely used exclusively and independently, so several studies propose combining both approaches in an integrated pull-push strategy, as shown in this case study (Lyonnet & Toscano, 2014).

The pull system is demand-based, with the purchasing process dependent on customer requirements and market inputs. This strategy is applicable within the company when the suppliers of the products demanded by customers are from the National or European market, and it is possible to have the products of these suppliers in the sales catalog, which leads the company to make production orders to the respective suppliers only when its customers make orders. Thus, given the geographical proximity between the company and its suppliers, it is possible to reduce the delivery times of goods from suppliers. This makes possible the zero inventories of these products because only customer demand establishes the need for purchase. This system also has the advantage of increasing customer satisfaction, as it is possible to present them with a greater variety of choices, as well as the possibility of delivering more customized products according to their requirements.

Sales forecasting is a crucial issue for companies, involving the proper use of many techniques, both quantitative and qualitative. Quantitative methods use historical data to project future demand, while qualitative approaches are based on studies to obtain the forecast (Lyonnet & Toscano, 2014).

The push strategy is applicable in the scope of the Far Eastern suppliers through quantitative techniques that project future demand based on the sales profile of the products, i.e., based on the history, the detailed scheduling of imports is initiated, establishing the production and purchase orders of the different products for the various seasonal campaigns. The viability of using this strategy stems from the possibility of controlling the pace of production at suppliers in the Far East and, given the low uncertainty and the long-term contractual relationships with customers of hypermarket chains.

CONCLUSION

SMEs are groups of companies with several specificities. For this, the author Jedynak (2015) established a set of factors highlighting the supporting and limiting capabilities of implementing a lean strategy. Thus, it can be seen that the implementation of lean strategies in the case study is in line with the supporting factors described in the literature, namely: ease of communication, faster decision-making processes, the existence of a unified organizational culture, the trend towards greater flexibility, the ability to respond more quickly to customer needs, and support in initiatives associated with innovation and continuous improvement. However, there are some impeding factors, such as limited financial resources, which pose challenges to lean implementation, including the acquisition of warehouse mobility software, which would allow the optimization of logistics processes in terms of picking activities through greater accessibility to documents relating to orders, improving the time spent by employees in their movements, avoiding the occurrence of errors, reducing the consumption of resources, and would also allow the maintenance of inventories more efficiently.

The results of lean implementation in the case study refer to a significant improvement in waste and more excellent value creation, achieving a more continuous flow and the search for perfection. However, the authors highlight the possibility of implementing Hoshin Kanri, which emerged in the Japanese culture in the 1960s, as an integrative approach to management processes, combining total quality control and management by objectives (Witcher & Butterworth, 2000). Thus, its high applicability in the warehouse operating system is verified, being started through the strategic plan and goals by top management, which is subsequently transmitted to the different hierarchical levels of the company and all employees, ensuring the knowledge and understanding of the company's strategy by all its elements, as well as it is possible to establish the individual contribution to the pursuit of the same, resulting in an alignment of the company's strategic objectives with the individual objectives, which are reflected in a stable growth (Rewers et al., 2016).

Poka-Yoke is an error prevention method, which eliminates many control operations, minimizes the number of defects, and reduces the need for attention on the part of the employee, allowing them to identify other possible improvements and ultimately control the process (Rewers et al., 2016). In this sense, although the implemented methods have led to a reduction in picking errors, their total elimination is sought, which allows identifying the acquisition of a warehouse mobility system as a possible future direction. The warehouse mobility systems use devices that read the European Article Numbers (EANs), which in turn, receive the picking request and define the best route to be taken by the employee. Subsequently, the employee performs his movements in the warehouses to collect the products, which is necessary to validate the products collected by reading their EANs. Thus, if the employee selects the product incorrectly, the error is detected by the equipment alerting him immediately, avoiding the preparation of incorrect documents, the passing of defects to the customer, the creation of waste, and customer dissatisfaction.

The Kaizen philosophy is represented by Rewers et al. (2016) as the concept of continuous improvement, which assumes the constant search for improvements in all company areas. Therefore, in this case, the involvement of all the company's employees stands out. The introduction of lean culture seeks to permanently reduce or eliminate wasteful activities, having as a guideline the possibility of adding value through continuous improvement.

The present study allows us to conclude that lean management, encompassing various tools, offers companies significant benefits if properly implemented. Using lean tools is a simple way to involve and empower employees for greater productivity, competitiveness, and quality, considering continuous improvement and eliminating and reducing waste throughout the organization.

Taking into consideration the principles of warehouse management that consist of using space efficiently, minimizing movements, controlling flows, and minimizing human and material risks, it is possible to conclude that lean management and its tools are perfectly adapted to the principles of warehouse management, aiming to guarantee better quality, fewer failures and errors, lower costs, increased reliability, and customer satisfaction, motivating work environments, through its organization and efficiency, and fundamentally, the increase of value in all its aspects.

ACKNOWLEDGMENT

This work is financed by national funds through the FCT – Foundation for Science and Technology, I. P., under the project with the reference UI/BD/152804/2022.

REFERENCES

Anđelković, A., Radosavljević, M., & Panić, D. S. (2016). Effects of Lean Tools in Achieving Lean Warehousing. *Economic Themes*, *54*(4), 517–534. doi:10.1515/ethemes-2016-0026

Bonney, M. C., Zhang, Z., Head, M. A., Tien, C. C., & Barson, R. J. (1999). Are Push and Pull Systems Really So Different? *International Journal of Production Economics*, *59*(1-3), 53–64. doi:10.1016/S0925-5273(98)00094-2

Filip, F. C., & Marascu-Klein, V. (2015, June 17-20). The 5S Lean Method is a Tool of Industrial Management Performances [Paper Presentation]. *Modern Technologies in Industrial Engineering (ModTech2015),* Mamaia, Romania.

Howell, G. (1999, July 26-28). *What is Lean Construction* [Paper Presentation]. *7th Annual Conference of the International Group for Lean Construction*, University of California.

Jedynak, P. (2015). Lean Management Implementation: Determinant Factors and Experience. *Jagiellonian Journal of Management*, *1*(1), 51–64. doi:10.4467/2450114XJJM.15.004.3811

Jeyaraj, A., & Sauter, V. L. (2014). Validation of Business Process Models Using Swimlane Diagrams. *Journal of Information Technology Management*, *25*(4), 27–37.

Lyonnet, B., & Toscano, R. (2014). Towards an Adapted Lean System – A Push–pull Manufacturing Strategy. *Production Planning and Control*, *25*(4), 346–354. doi:10.1080/09537287.2012.702867

Oliveira, J., Sá, J. C., & Fernandes, A. (2017). Continuous Improvement Through "Lean Tools": An Application in a Mechanical Company. *Procedia Manufacturing*, *13*, 1082–1089. doi:10.1016/j.promfg.2017.09.139

Parry, G. C., & Turner, C. E. (2006). Application of Lean Visual Process Management Tools. *Production Planning and Control*, *17*(1), 77–86. doi:10.1080/09537280500414991

Pasale, R. A., & Bagi, J. S. (2013). 5S Strategy: A Workplace Improvement Lean Tool. *Journal of Engineering and Technology Research*, *1*(1), 100–107.

Phogat, S. (2013). An Introduction to Applicability of Lean in Warehousing. *International Journal of Latest Research in Science and Technology*, *2*(5), 105–109.

Rewers, P., Trojanowska, J., & Chabowski, P. (2016, June 28-30). Tools and Methods of Lean Manufacturing - A Literature Review [Paper Presentation*]. 7th International Technical Conference (Technological Forum 2016),* Prague, Czech Republic.

Rohac, T., & Januska, M. (2015). Value Stream Mapping Demonstration on Real Case Study. *Procedia Engineering*, *100*, 520–529. doi:10.1016/j.proeng.2015.01.399

Rother, M., & Shook, J. (2003). *Learning to See - Value-Stream Mapping to Create Value and Eliminate MUDA*. The Lean Enterprise Institute.

Senderská, K., Mares, A., & Václav, S. (2017). Spaghetti Diagram Application for Workers' Movement Analysis. *U.P.B. Scientific Bulletin - Series D*, *79*(1), 139–150.

Singh, G., & Ahuja, I. S. (2012). Just-in-time Manufacturing: Literature Review and Directions. *International Journal of Business Continuity and Risk Management*, *3*(1), 57–98. doi:10.1504/IJBCRM.2012.045519

Sundar, R., Balaji, A. N., & Satheesh-Kumar, R. M. (2014). A Review on Lean Manufacturing Implementation Techniques. *Procedia Engineering*, *97*, 1875–1885. doi:10.1016/j.proeng.2014.12.341

Tezel, B. A., Koskela, L. J., & Tzortzopoulos, P. (2009, January). The Functions of Visual Management [Paper Presentation]. *International Research Symposium*, Salford, UK.

Witcher, B., & Butterworth, R. (2000). Hoshin Kanri at Hewlett-Packard. *Journal of General Management*, *25*(4), 70–85. doi:10.1177/030630700002500405

Womack, J. P., & Jones, D. T. (1996). *Lean Thinking - Banish Waste and Create Wealth in Your Corporation*. Free Press, Simon & Schuster, Inc.

KEY TERMS AND DEFINITIONS

5S: It represents a lean tool whose objectives are the organization of the workplace, the standardization of work processes efficiently, and the transformation of employees' attitudes, values, and behavior.

Kaizen: It indicates the continuous improvement of production processes by permanently introducing minor improvements to reduce costs, improve quality, increase productivity, and, consequently, efficiency.

Lean Management: It aims to create value and eliminate waste through the involvement of all employees of the organizations to promote permanent continuous improvement.

Spaghetti Diagram: This lean tool is intended to perform layout definition for industrial or administrative purposes, using the analysis of the distance covered by employees.

Swimlane: It corresponds to a classic tool, which contains the graphical representation of a process, allowing the understanding of the information transition in an accessible and prompt manner.

Value Stream Mapping: It constitutes a lean tool, which allows the identification of the flow of materials and information along the value chain to identify the activities that generate value and the activities that do not create value and thus propose improvements with a view to the future.

Visual Management: A lean tool that helps employees identify their tasks and when to perform them through visual resources. Thus, it provides a faster understanding of the information and allows the standardization and maintenance of the processes by constantly updating them.

Waste: It refers to what does not add value for the customer. From the organization's perspective, it is composed of overproduction, waiting times, unnecessary transport and handling, process waste, excess stock, and defects.

Compilation of References

Abdelgawad, S. G., Zahra, S. A., Svejenova, S., & Sapienza, H. J. (2013). Strategic Leadership and Entrepreneurial Capability for Game Change. *Journal of Leadership & Organizational Studies*, *20*(4), 394–407. doi:10.1177/1548051813475484

Abraham, R. (2000). Organizational cynicism: Bases and consequences. *Genetic, Social, and General Psychology Monographs*, *126*(3), 269–292. PMID:10950198

Abreu, M. P. (Ed.). (1992). *A Ordem do Progresso: cem anos de política econômica republicana*. Editora Campus.

Acar, Y. (2020). Yeni Koronavirüs (Covid-19) Salgını ve Turizm Faaliyetlerine Etkisi. *Güncel Turizm Araştırmaları Dergisi*, *4*, 7–21. doi:10.32572/guntad.703410

Acharya, A., Singh, S. K., Pereira, V., & Singh, P. (2018). Big data, knowledge co-creation, and decision making in fashion industry. *International Journal of Information Management*, *42*, 90–101. doi:10.1016/j.ijinfomgt.2018.06.008

ACMP. (2019, March). *Standard for Change Management*. Standard for Change Management© ACMP Change Management Code of Ethics. https://cdn.ymaws.com/www.acmpglobal.org/resource/resmgr/files/ACMP_Standard_2019_03_21.pdf

Adams, J. S., Taschian, A., & Shore, T. H. (1996). Ethics in family and non-family owned firms: An exploratory study. *Family Business Review*, *9*(2), 157–170. doi:10.1111/j.1741-6248.1996.00157.x

Adams-Prassl, A., Boneva, T., Golin, M., & Rauh, C. (2020). Inequality in the impact of the coronavirus shock: Evidence from real-time surveys. *Journal of Public Economics*, *189*, 104245. doi:10.1016/j.jpubeco.2020.104245

AERA. (n.d.). *Teaching Behaviors and Student Differences: Lecture Organization and Test Anxiety*. The Annual Meeting of the American Educational Research Association, San Francisco, CA.

Aghina, W., De Smet, A., Lackey, G., Lurie, M., and Muraka, M. (2018). The five trademarks of agile organizations. *McKinsey & Company Report*.

Aghina, W., Handscomb, C., Ludolph, J., Róna, D., & West, D. (2020). *Enterprise agility: Buzz or business impact?* McKinsey. https://www.mckinsey.com/business-functions/people-and-organizational-performance/our-insights/enterprise-agility-buzz-or-business-impact

Aghina, W., Handscomb, C., Salo, O., & Thaker, S. (2021). *The impact of agility: How to shape your organization to compete* avaliable at: https://www.mckinsey.com/business-functions/people-and-organ izational-performance/our-insights/the-impact-of-agility-how -to-shape-your-organization-to-compete# Aliber,M., Danoesastro, M., Kinderen,T., Djavdan,P., Hildebrandt,P. & Lenhard,E. (2022) *What 11,500 Employees Say About Agile Transformation.* BCG. https://www.bcg.com/publications/2022/what-employees-say-abo ut-agile-transformations

Agrawal, A., & Joglekar, A. (2013). Role of Women in 21 st Century. *Age*, *18*(26, 40).

Ahl, H. (2004). *The Scientific Reproduction of Gender Inequality; A Discourse Analysis of Research Texts on Women's Entrepreneurship.* Copenhagen Business School Press.

Ahl, H. (2006). Why research on women entrepreneurs needs new directions. *Entrepreneurship*, *30*, 595–621.

Akhtar, V., Gupta, G., & Kotter, J. P. (2021). *Change: How organisations achieve hard-to-imagine results in uncertain and volatile times.* Wiley.

Akram, W., Adeel, S., Tabassum, M., Jiang, Y., Chandio, A., & Yasmin, I. (2020). *Scenario Analysis and Proposed Plan for Pakistan Universities – COVID – 19: Application of Design Thinking Model.* Cambridge Open Engage., doi:10.33774/coe-2020-ql1w6

Akter, S., Bhattacharyya, M., Wamba, S., & Aditya, S. (2016). How does Social Media Analytics create value? *Journal of Organizational and End User Computing*, *28*(3), 1–9. doi:10.4018/JOEUC.2016070101

Al Ahbabi, S., Singh, S. K., Gaur, S. S., & Balasubramanian, S. (2017). A knowledge management framework for enhancing public sector performance. *International Journal of Knowledge Management Studies*, *8*(3–4), 329–350. doi:10.1504/IJKMS.2017.087076

Albukhitan, S. (2020). Developing digital transformation strategy for manufacturing. *Procedia Computer Science*, *170*, 664–671. doi:10.1016/j.procs.2020.03.173

Al-Dajani, H., Carter, S., Shaw, E., & Marlow, S. (2015). Entrepreneurship among the Displaced and Dispossessed: Exploring the Limits of Emancipatory Entrepreneuring. *British Journal of Management*, *26*(4), 713–730. doi:10.1111/1467-8551.12119

Al-Dajani, H., & Marlow, S. (2013). Empowerment and entrepreneurship: A theoretical framework. *International Journal of Entrepreneurial Behaviour & Research*, *19*(5), 503–524. doi:10.1108/IJEBR-10-2011-0138

Aldrich, A. S., & Lotito, N. J. (2020). Pandemic performance: Women leaders in the Covid-19 crisis. *Politics & Gender*, *16*(4), 1–9. doi:10.1017/S1743923X20000549

Ali, B. J., & Anwar, G. (2021). The mediation role of change management in employee development. *Ali, BJ, & Anwar, G.(2021). The Mediation Role of Change Management in Employee Development. International Journal of English Literature and Social Sciences*, *6*(2), 361–374. doi:10.22161/ijels.62.52

Alicke, K., Gupta, R., & Trautwein, V. (2020) *Resetting supply chains for the next normal.* McKinsey. https://www.mckinsey.com/business-functions/operations/our-i nsights/resetting-supply-chains-for-the-next-normal

Allen, T. G., & Flood, C. T. (2018). The experiences of women in higher education: Who knew there wasn't a sisterhood? *Leadership and Research in Education*, *4*, 10–27.

Allis, L. V. (1994). *Searching for Solutions in Games and Artificial Intelligence*. Rijksuniversiteit Limburg. doi:10.26481/dis.19940923la

Alloy, L. B., & Ahrens, A. H. (1987). Depression and pessimism for the future: Biased use of statistically relevant information in predictions for self-versus others. *Journal of Personality and Social Psychology*, *52*(2), 366–378. doi:10.1037/0022-3514.52.2.366 PMID:3559896

AlMutairi, A. N. (2015). The Effect of Using Brainstorming Strategy in Developing Creative Problem Solving Skills among male Students in Kuwait: A Field Study on Saud Al-Kharji School in Kuwait City. *Journal of Education and Practice*, *6*(3), 136–146.

Alqatawenah, A. S. (2018). Transformational leadership style and its relationship with change management. *Verslas: TeorijaIrPraktika/Business. Theory into Practice*, *19*(0), 17–24. doi:10.3846/btp.2018.03

Alsamhi, M. H., Al-Ofairi, F. A., Farhan, N. H. S., Al-ahdal, W. M., & Siddiqui, A. (2022). Impact of Covid-19 on firms' performance: Empirical evidence from India. *Cogent Business & Management*, *9*(1), 2044593. doi:10.1080/23311975.2022.2044593

Altekar, A. S. (1956). *The position of women in Hindu civilization, from prehistoric times to the present day*. Motilal Banarsidass Publ.

Ambergh. (2020). The Arab world. *Ambergh*. http://www.ambergh.com/learn-arabic/the-arab-world

Aminova, M., Mareef, S., & Machado, C. (2020). Entrepreneurship Ecosystem in Arab World: The status quo, impediments and the ways forward. *International Journal of Business Ethics and Governance*, 1–13.

Amis, J., & Greenwood, R. (2020). Organisational change in a (post-) pandemic world: Rediscovering interests and values. *Journal of Management Studies*. doi:10.1103/PhysRevD.101.055025

Amrhein, V., Trafimow, D., & Greenland, S. (2019). Inferential statistics as descriptive statistics: There is no replication crisis if we don't expect replication. The American Statistician, 73(sup1), pp.262-270. doi:10.3390ym12010019

Anđelković, A., Radosavljević, M., & Panić, D. S. (2016). Effects of Lean Tools in Achieving Lean Warehousing. *Economic Themes*, *54*(4), 517–534. doi:10.1515/ethemes-2016-0026

Andersson, L. M., & Bateman, T. S. (1997). Cynicism in the workplace: Some causes and effects. *Journal of Organizational Behavior*, *18*(5), 449–469. doi:10.1002/(SICI)1099-1379(199709)18:5<449::AID-JOB808>3.0.CO;2-O

Ansoff, H. I. (1957). Strategies for Diversification. *Harvard Business Review*, *35*(5), 113–124.

Ansoff, H. I. (1975). Managing Strategic Surprise by Response to Weak Signals. *California Management Review*, *18*(2), 21–33. doi:10.2307/41164635

Anthony, J. (2004). Do state growth management regulations reduce sprawl? *Urban Affairs Review*, *39*(3), 376–397. doi:10.1177/1078087403257798

Anwer, S., Wen, L., & Wang, Z. 2019. A systematic approach for identifying requirement change management challenges: Preliminary results. *Proceedings of the Evaluation and Assessment on Software Engineering*, (pp. 230-235). ACM. 10.1145/3319008.3319031

Appel, G., Grewal, L., Hadi, R., & Stephen, A. T. (2020). The future of social media in marketing. *Journal of the Academy of Marketing Science*, *48*(1), 79–95. doi:10.100711747-019-00695-1 PMID:32431463

Ardelt, M. (2005). How wise people cope with crises and obstacles in life. *ReVision*, *28*(1), 7–19. doi:10.3200/REVN.28.1.7-19

Argyris, C. (1999). *On organizational learning*. Blackwell.

Armbrüster, T. (2006). *The economics and sociology of management consulting*. Cambridge University Press. doi:10.1017/CBO9780511488467

Armenakis, A. A., & Harris, S. G. (2009). Reflections: Our journey in organizational change research and practice. *Journal of Change Management*, *9*(2), 127–142. doi:10.1080/14697010902879079

Armenakis, A. A., Harris, S. G., Cole, M. S., Fillmer, J. L., & Self, D. R. (2007a). A Top Management Team's Reactions to Organizational Transformation: The diagnostic Benefits of Five Key Change Sentiments. *Journal of Change Management*, *7*(3), 273–290. doi:10.1080/14697010701771014

Armenakis, A. A., Harris, S. G., & Mossholder, K. W. (1993). Creating Readiness for Organizational Change. *Human Relations*, *46*(6), 681–703. doi:10.1177/001872679304600601

Armenakis, A., Bernerth, J. B., Pitts, J. P., & Walker, H. J. (2007b). Organizational Change Recipients' Beliefs Scale: Development of an instrument. *The Journal of Applied Behavioral Science*, *43*(4), 481–505. doi:10.1177/0021886307303654

Arriaga, T. T., Stanley, S. L., & Lindsey, D. B. (2020). *Leading while female: A culturally proficient response for gender equity*. Corwin.

Asch, S. E. (1951). Effects of group pressure upon the modification and distortion of judgments. In H. Guetzkow (Ed.), *Groups, leadership and men; research in human relations* (pp. 177–190). Carnegie Press.

Association of Change Management Professionals. (2019). *Standard for Change Management and ACMP Change Management Code of Ethics*. Association of Change Management Professionals.

Astrachan, J. H. (2004). Organizational departures: The impact of separation anxiety as studied in mergers and acquisitions simulation. *The Journal of Applied Behavioral Science*, *40*(1), 91–110. doi:10.1177/0021886304263850

Aucejo, E. M., French, J., Araya, M. P. U., & Zafar, B. (2020). The impact of COVID-19 on student experiences and expectations: Evidence from a survey. *Journal of Public Economics*, *191*, 104271. doi:10.1016/j.jpubeco.2020.104271 PMID:32873994

Auray, S., & Eyquem, A. (2020). The macroeconomic effects of lockdown policies. *Journal of Public Economics*, *190*, 104260. doi:10.1016/j.jpubeco.2020.104260 PMID:32863463

Austin, J. R., & Bartunek, J. M. (2006). Theories and practices of Organizational Development. Gallos, J. V (ed): Organization Development. San Francisco, CA. Jossey-Bass.

Avey, J. B., Wernsing, T. S., & Luthans, F. (2008). Can Positive Employees Help Positive Organizational Change? Impact of Psychological Capital and Emotions on Relevant Attitudes and Behaviors. *The Journal of Applied Behavioral Science*, *44*(1), 48–70. doi:10.1177/0021886307311470

Awang, A., Khalid, S. A., Kassim, K. M., Ismail, M., Zain, R. S., & Madar, A. R. S. (2009). Entrepreneurial orientation and performance relations of Malaysian Bumiputera SMEs: The impact of some perceived environmental factors. *International Journal of Business and Management*, *4*(9), 84–94. doi:10.5539/ijbm.v4n9p84

Axelos. (2017). *Managing successful projects with PRINCE2*. TSO.

Ayadurai, D. (1987). *The Employer, the Employee, and the Law in Malaysia*. Butterworth-Heinemann.

Ayogu, D. U., & Agu, E. O. (2015). Assessment of the contribution of women entrepreneur towards entrepreneurship development in Nigeria. *International Journal of Current Research and Academic Review*, *3*, 190–207.

Ayub, A., Razzaq, A., Aslam, S. M., & Iftekhar, H. (2013). Gender effects on entrepreneurial orientation and value innovation: Evidence from Pakistan. *European Journal of Business and Social Sciences*, *2*(1), 82–90.

Bagilhole, B. (2019). Against the odds: Women academics' research opportunities. In Gender, Teaching and Research in Higher Education (pp. 46-56). Routledge.

Bahmani-Oskooee, M., Kutan, M. A., & Xi, D. (2013). The impact of economic and monetary uncertainty on the demand for money in emerging economies. *Applied Economics*, *45*(23), 3278–3287. doi:10.1080/00036846.2012.705430

Bailes, L. P., & Guthery, S. (2020). Held down and held back: Systematically delayed principal promotions by race and gender. *AERA Open*, *6*(2), 2332858420929298. doi:10.1177/2332858420929298

Baldwin, R., & Mauro, B. (2020). *Economics in the time of COVID-19* (R. Baldwin & B. W. di Mauro, Eds.). CEPR Press.

Baligh, H. H. (2011). *Organisation structures: Theory and design, analysis and prescription.* Springer.

Balogun, J., & Hailey, V. H. (2004), *Exploring Strategic Change.* Prentice Hall/Financial Times, Harlow.

Bamford, D. R., & Forrester, P. L. (2003). Managing planned and emergent change within an operations management environment. *International Journal of Operations & Production Management*, *23*(5), 546–564. doi:10.1108/01443570310471857

Bandura, A. (1997), *Self-efficacy: The exercise of control.* W H Freeman/Times Books/ Henry Holt & Co.

Banos-González, I., Martínez-Fernández, J., & Esteve-Selma, M. Á. (2015). Dynamic integration of sustainability indicators in insular socio-ecological systems. *Ecological Modelling*, *306*, 130–144. doi:10.1016/j.ecolmodel.2014.08.014

Barach, J. A. (1984). Is there a cure for the paralyzed family board? *Sloan Management Review*, *26*(1), 3–12.

Barakat, H. (1987). The Arab Family and The Challenge of Social Transformation. *Al-Raida Journal*, 6–7.

Baraldi, S., Jawaid Kalyal, H., Berntson, E., Näswall, K., & Sverke, M. (2010). The Importance of Commitment to Change in Public Reform: An Example from Pakistan. *Journal of Change Management*, *10*(4), 347–368. doi:10.1080/14697017.2010.516482

Barba, I., & Iraizoz, B. (2020). Effect of the great crisis on sectoral female employment in Europe: A structural decomposition analysis. *Economies*, *8*(3), 64. doi:10.3390/economies8030064

Barbey, A. K., Karama, S., & Haier, R. J. (2021). *The Cambridge handbook of intelligence and cognitive neuroscience.* Cambridge University Press. doi:10.1017/9781108635462

Barbosa, C. E., Lima, Y. O., Costa, L. F., Santos, H. S., Lyra, A., Argôlo, M., & Souza, J. M. (2022). Future of work in 2050: Thinking beyond the COVID-19 pandemic. *European Journal of Futures Research*, *10*(25), 25. doi:10.118640309-022-00210-w

Bardasi, E., Sabarwal, S., & Terrel, K. (2011). How do female entrepreneurs perform? Evidence from three developing regions. *Small Business Economics*, *37*(4), 417–441. doi:10.100711187-011-9374-z

Bargain, O., & Aminjonov, U. (2020). Trust and compliance to public health policies in times of COVID-19. *Journal of Public Economics*, *192*, 104316. doi:10.1016/j.jpubeco.2020.104316 PMID:33162621

Barlatier, P., & Mention, A. (2020). How social media can fuel innovation in businesses: A strategic roadmap. *The Journal of Business Strategy*, *41*(2), 11–18. doi:10.1108/JBS-12-2018-0197

Barnes, L. B., & Hershon, S. A. (1994). Transferring power in the family business. *Family Business Review*, *7*(4), 377–392. doi:10.1111/j.1741-6248.1994.00377.x

Barnett, R. (1990). The idea of higher education. McGraw-Hill education (UK).

Barratt-Pugh, L., Bahn, S., & Gakere, E. (2012). Managers as change agents. Implications for human resource managers engaging with culture change. *Journal of Organizational Change, 26*(4), 748–764. doi:10.1108/JOCM-Feb-2011-0014

Barreira, P., Basilico, M., & Bolotnyy, V. (2018). *Graduate student mental health: Lessons from American economics departments*. Harvard University. https://scholar.harvard. edu/sites/scholar.harvard.edu/files /bolotnyy/files/bbb_mentalhealth_paper.pdf

Barr, P. S., Stimpert, J. L., & Huff, A. S. (1992). Cognitive Change, Strategic Action and Organizational Renewal. *Strategic Management Journal, 27*(S1), 489–510. doi:10.1002mj.4250131004

Barth, T. D. (2011). The idea of a green new deal in a Quintuple Helix Model of knowledge, know-how and innovation. *International Journal of Social Ecology and Sustainable Development, 1*(2), 1–14. doi:10.4018/jsesd.2011010101

Bartik, A. W., Bertrand, M., Cullen, Z., Glaeser, E. L., Luca, M., & Stanton, C. (2020). The impact of COVID-19 on small business outcomes and expectations. *Proceedings of the National Academy of Sciences of the United States of America, 117*(30), 17656–17666. doi:10.1073/pnas.2006991117 PMID:32651281

Bartunek, J. M., Krim, R., Necochea, R., & Humphries, M. (1999). Sense-making, Sense Giving and Leadership in Strategic Organizational Development. In J. Wagner (Ed.), *Advanced in Qualitive Organizational Research, 4,37-71.*

Bartunek, J. M., Walsh, K., & Lacey, C. A. (2000). Dynamics and Dilemmas of Women Leading Women. *Organization Science, 11*(6), 589–610. doi:10.1287/orsc.11.6.589.12531

Barwa, S. D. (2003). *Impact of Start Your Business (SYB) training on women entrepreneurs in Vietnam.* ILO Office in Vietnam.

Basco, R. (2017). Epilogue: The multiple embeddedness of family firms in the Arab world. In Family Businesses in the Arab World (pp. 247–256). Springer.

Basile, A. (2012). Entrepreneurial orientation in SMEs: Risk taking to enter international markets. *Far East Journal of Psychology and Business, 7*(2), 1–21.

Bass, B. M., & Avolio, B. J. (1990). The Implications of Transactional and Transformational Leadership for Individual, Team and Organisational Development. In *Pasmore, W. A. and Woodman, R. W. Organisational Change and Development* (Vol. 4, pp. 231–272). JAI Press Inc.

Bateson, G. (1972). Steps to an ecology of mind. Chandler Publishing Company

Bauer, N. M., & Taylor, T. (2022). Selling them short? Differences in news coverage of female and male candidate qualifications. *Political Research Quarterly*, 10659129221086024.

Beaudry, P., & Portier, F. (2006). Stock prices, news, and economic ñuctuations. *The American Economic Review, 96*(4), 1293–1307. doi:10.1257/aer.96.4.1293

Beer, M., Eisenstat, R. A., & Spector, B. (1990). *The Critical Path to Corporate Renewal*. Harvard Business School Press.

Bellini, M. I., Graham, Y., Hayes, C., Zakeri, R., Parks, R., & Papalois, V. (2019). A woman's place is in theatre: Women's perceptions and experiences of working in surgery from the Association of surgeons of Great Britain and Ireland women in surgery working group. *BMJ Open, 9*(1), e024349. doi:10.1136/bmjopen-2018-024349 PMID:30617103

Bennis , W., Nanus, B. (1985). Leaders: Strategies for Taking Charge. Harper & Row

Bennis, W. G. (1966). *Changing Organizations*. McGraw-Hill.

Bennis, W. G., & Nanus, B. (2003). *Leaders: Strategies for taking charge*. HarperCollins.

Benslimane, M., & Moustaghfir, K. (2020). Career development practices and gender equity in higher education. *International Journal of Management Education*, *14*(2), 183–211.

Benziman, Y. (2020). "Winning" the "battle" and "beating" the COVID-19 "enemy": Leaders' use of war frames to define the pandemic. *Peace and Conflict*, *26*(3), 247–256. doi:10.1037/pac0000494

Berger, P., & Luckmann, T. (1966). *The Social Construction of Reality*. Anchor Books.

Berkhout, F., & Hertin, J. (2002). Foresight futures scenarios: Developing and applying a participative strategic planning tool. *Greener Management International*, *2002*(37), 37–52. doi:10.9774/GLEAF.3062.2002.sp.00005

Bernstein, B. B. (1970). A Socio-Linguistic Approach to Social Learning. Sebeok, T. (ed) Language and Poverty. Markham, London.

Bhimani, H., Mention, A., & Barlatier, P. (2019). Social media and innovation: A systematic literature review and future research directions. *Technological Forecasting and Social Change*, *144*, 251–269. doi:10.1016/j.techfore.2018.10.007

Bichler, B. F., Kallmuenzer, A., Peters, M., Petry, T., & Clauss, T. (2022). Regional entrepreneurial ecosystems: How family firm embeddedness triggers ecosystem development. *Review of Managerial Science*, *16*(1), 15–44. doi:10.100711846-020-00434-9

Bigelow, J. (1992). Developing managerial wisdom. *Journal of Management Inquiry*, *1*(2), 143–153. doi:10.1177/105649269212008

Binder, C. (2020). Coronavirus fears and macroeconomic expectations. *The Review of Economics and Statistics*, *102*(4), 721–730. doi:10.1162/rest_a_00931

Birdthistle, N. (2006). Training and learning strategies of family businesses: An Irish case. *Journal of European Industrial Training*, *30*(7), 550–568. doi:10.1108/03090590610704402

Bishop, P., Hines, A., & Collins, T. (2007). The current state of scenario development: An overview of techniques. *Foresight*, *9*(1), 5–25. doi:10.1108/14636680710727516

Blackburn, S., LaBerge, L., O'Toole, C., & Schneider, J. (2020). *Digital strategy in a time of crisis*. McKinsey. https://www.mckinsey.com/business-functions/mckinsey-digital/our-insights/digital-strategy-in-a-time-of-crisis

Boddy, C. (2012). The Nominal Group Technique: An aid to Brainstorming ideas in research. *Qualitative Market Research*, *15*(1), 6–18. doi:10.1108/13522751211191964

Boden, R. J. Jr, & Nucci, A. R. (2000). On the survival prospects of men's and women's new business ventures. *Journal of Business Venturing*, *15*(4), 347–362. doi:10.1016/S0883-9026(98)00004-4

Bolanowski, W. (2005). Anxiety about professional future among young doctors. *International Journal of Occupational Medicine and Environmental Health*, *18*(4), 367–374. PMID:16617853

Bonesso, S., Gerli, F., & Scapolan, A. (2014). The individual side of ambidexterity: Do individuals' perceptions match actual behaviors in reconciling the exploration and exploitation trade-off? *European Management Journal*, *32*(3), 392–405. doi:10.1016/j.emj.2013.07.003

Bonney, M. C., Zhang, Z., Head, M. A., Tien, C. C., & Barson, R. J. (1999). Are Push and Pull Systems Really So Different? *International Journal of Production Economics*, *59*(1-3), 53–64. doi:10.1016/S0925-5273(98)00094-2

Bono, R., Arnau, J., Alarcón, R., & Blanca, M.J. (2019). Bias, precision, and accuracy of skewness and kurtosis estimators for frequently used continuous distributions. *Symmetry, 12*(1), 19. 10.25/eydgfi201931.222

Borah, P., Iqbal, S., & Akhtar, S. (2022). Linking social media usage and SME's sustainable performance: The role of digital leadership and innovation capabilities. *Technology in Society, 68*, 101900. doi:10.1016/j.techsoc.2022.101900

Bordia P, Restubog, S.L.D, Jimmieson N.L., & Irmer, B.E. (2011). Haunted by the past: effects of poor change management history on employee attitudes and turnover. *Group & Organization Management, 36*, 191–222. doi:10.1177/1059601110392990

Bordia, P., Hobman, E., Jones, E., Gallois, C., & Callan, V. J. (2004). Uncertainty during organizational change: Types, consequences, and management strategies. *Journal of Business and Psychology, 18*(4), 507–532. doi:10.1023/B:JOBU.0000028449.99127.f7

Born, B., Mu¨ller, G. J., Schularick, M., & Sedlacek, P. (2019). The costs of economic nationalism: Evidence from the brexit experiment. *Economic Journal (London), 129*(623), 2722–2744. doi:10.1093/ej/uez020

Bostan, S., Erdem, R., Öztürk, Y. E., Kılıç, T., & Yılmaz, A. (2020). The Effect of Covid-19 Pandemic on the Turkish Society. *Electronic Journal of General Medicine, 17*(6), em237. doi:10.29333/ejgm/7944

Boudon, R., & .... (1999). Szociológiai lexikon. *Budapest: Corvina*. 154-155, Boulding, K. E., (1969) 'A rendszerelmélet mint szemléletmód. In *Kindler J. -Kiss I. (szerk.), Rendszerelmélet* (pp. 113–130). KJK.

Bounfour, A. (2022). *Platforms and Artificial Intelligence: The Next Generation of Competences*. Springer International Publishing AG. doi:10.1007/978-3-030-90192-9

Boutaud, N., Agarwal, A., Postel, E. A., & Pericak-Vance, M. A. (2005). Complement Factor H Variant Increases the Risk of Age-Related Macular Degeneration. *Science, 308*(5720), 419–421. doi:10.1126cience.1110359 PMID:15761120

Bovey, W.H, Hede, A. (2001), Resistance to organisational change: the role of defence mechanisms, *Journal of Managerial Psychology, 16*(7), 534-548.

Boyd, B., Royer, S., Pei, R., & Zhang, X. (2015). Knowledge transfer in family business successions: Implications of knowledge types and transaction atmospheres. *Journal of Family Business Manage.*

Boyd, G. G. D. (2016). The girl effect: A neoliberal instrumentalization of gender equality. *Consilience, 15*, 46–180.

Boyd, R. L. (2005). Race, gender, and survival entrepreneurship in large northern cities during the Great Depression. *Journal of Socio-Economics, 34*(3), 331–339. doi:10.1016/j.socec.2004.09.018

Bozkurt, N. (2004). Bir Grup Üniversite Öğrencisinin Depresyon ve Kaygı Düzeyleri ile Çeşitli Değişkenler Arasındaki İlişkiler. *Eğitim ve Bilim, 29* (133), 1300-1337, http://egitimvebilim.ted.org.tr/index.php/EB/article/view/5095/1179

Braches, B., & Elliott, C. (2016). Articulating the entrepreneurship career: A study of German women entrepreneurs. *International Small Business Journal, 35*(5), 535–557. doi:10.1177/0266242616651921

Bradfield, R., Wright, G., Burt, G., Cairns, G., & Heijden, K. V. (2005). The origins and evolution of scenario techniques in long range business planning. *Futures, 37*(8), 795–812. doi:10.1016/j.futures.2005.01.003

Bradley, S. P., & Nolan, R. L. (1998). *Sense and Respond: Capturing Value in the Network Era.* Harvard Business School Press.

Brahm, C., & Kleiner, B. H. (1996). Advantages and disadvantages of group decision-making approaches. *Team Performance Management, 2*(2), 30–35. doi:10.1108/13527599610105538

Brandstätter, H. (2011). Personality aspects of entrepreneurship: A look at five meta-analyses. *Personality and Individual Differences*, *51*(3), 222–230. doi:10.1016/j.paid.2010.07.007

Brandwatch. (2022). Buying habits and trends for the consumer packaged goods industry. *Brandwatch*. https://www.brandwatch.com/reports/cpg-consumer-trends/view/

Braun, B. (2015). Futures: Imagining socioecological transformation—An introduction. *Annals of the Association of American Geographers*, *105*(2), 239–243. doi:10.1080/00045608.2014.1000893

Bridges, S. (n.d.). *Bridges Transition Model*. William Bridges Associates. https://wmbridges.com/about/what-is-transition/

Bright, A., Acosta, S., & Parker, B. (2020). Humility matters: Interrogating our positionality, power, and privilege through collaboration. In *Handbook of Research on Diversity and Social Justice in Higher Education* (pp. 19–40). IGI Global. doi:10.4018/978-1-7998-5268-1.ch002

Brindley, C. (2005). Barriers to women achieving their entrepreneurial potential: Woman and risk. *International Journal of Entrepreneurial Behaviour & Research*, *11*(2), 144–161. doi:10.1108/13552550510590554

Broo, D. G., Lamb, K., Ehwi, R. J., Pärn, E., Koronaki, A., Makri, C., & Zomer, T. (2021). Built environment of Britain in 2040: Scenarios and strategies. *Sustainable Cities and Society*, 65.

Brosseau, D., Ebrahim, S., Handscomb, C., & Thaker, S. (2019). *The journey to an agile organization*. McKinsey. www.mckinsey.com%2F~%2Fmedia%2FMcKinsey%2FBusiness%2520Functions%2FOrganization%2FOur%2520Insights%2FThe%2520journey%2520to%2520an%2520agile%2520organization%2FThe-journey-to-an-agile-organization-final.pdf&clen=1232003&chunk=true.

Brown, B. B. (1968). *Delphi Process: A Methodology Used for the Elicitation of Opinions of Experts*. RAND Corp.

Brown, C., Kulik, T., Cregan, C., & Metz, I. (2017). 5) Understanding The Change– Cynicism Cycle: The Role Of HR. *Human Resource Management*, *56*(1), 5–24. doi:10.1002/hrm.21708

Bruin, T. d. (2005). *Understanding the main phases of developing a maturity assessment model*. Academia. https://www.academia.edu/66533016/Understanding_the_Main_Phases_of_Developing_a_Maturity_Assessment_Model

Bruni, A., Gherardi, S., & Poggio, B. (2004). Doing gender, doing entrepreneurship: An ethnographic account of intertwined practices. *Gender, Work and Organization*, *11*(4), 406–429. doi:10.1111/j.1468-0432.2004.00240.x

Brush, C., Carter, N. M., Gatewood, E. J., Greene, P. G., & Hart, M. M. (2006). *Women and Entrepreneurship: Contemporary Classics*. Edward Elgar.

Brush, C., de Bruin, A., & Welter, F. (2009). A gender-aware framework for women's entrepreneurship. *International Journal of Gender and Entrepreneurship*, *1*(1), 8–24. doi:10.1108/17566260910942318

Bruton, G. D., Ketchen, D. J. Jr, & Ireland, R. D. (2013). Entrepreneurship as a solution to poverty. *Journal of Business Venturing*, *28*(6), 683–689. doi:10.1016/j.jbusvent.2013.05.002

Bryan, J. (2022). Building workplace resilience in a changing environment. *Workplace Insight Magazine*. https://workplaceinsight.net/building-resilience-in-a-changing-environment/

Bryan, M., & Venkatu, G. (2001). *The Curiously Different Inflation Perspectives of Men and Women*. Federal Reserve Bank of Cleveland.

Bryan, J. (2021). *Leading People in Change: A Practical Guide*. Hero Publishing.

Buber, M. (2004). *I and Thou.* Continuum.

Buck, I. (2017). The Cost of High Prices: Embedding an Ethic of Expense into the Standard of Care (September 6, 2016). 58 B.C. L. Rev. 101 (2017), *University of Tennessee Legal Studies Research Paper No. 309.* https://ssrn.com/abstract=2835816

Bui, H. T. M., Kuan, A., & Chu, T. T. (2018). Female entrepreneurship in patriarchal society: Motivation and challenges. *Journal of Small Business and Entrepreneurship, 30*(4), 325–343. doi:10.1080/08276331.2018.1435841

Bundesministerium für Wirtschaft. (2019). *Wirtschaftsmotor Mittelstand - Zahlen und Fakten zu den deutschen KMU.* Bundesministerium für Wirtschaft.

Bundesverband mittelständische Wirtschaft. (2022). *Der Mittelstand ist Garant für Stabilität und Fortschritt.* BVMW. https://www.bvmw.de/themen/mittelstand/zahlen-fakten/

Burchard, C. (2018). Artificial intelligence and law. In B. Wolff (Ed.), *Whither artificial intelligence? Debating the policy challenges of the upcoming transformation.* Mercator Science-Policy Fellowship-Programme.

Burch, J. J., Burch, G. F., Heller, N. A., & Batchelor, J. H. (2015). Rethinking family business education. *Journal of Family Business Management, 5*(2), 277–293. doi:10.1108/JFBM-02-2015-0007

Burke, P. J., & Crozier, G. (2014). Higher education pedagogies: Gendered formations, mis/recognition and emotion. *Journal of Research in Gender Studies, 4*(2), 52.

Burlew, L. D., Pederson, J. E., & Bradley, B. (1994). The reactions of managers to the pre-acquisition stage of a corporate merger: A qualitative study. *Journal of Career Development, 21*, 11–22.

Burnes, B. (1996). No such thing as . . . a "one best way" to manage organizational change. *Management Decision, 34*(10), 11–18. doi:10.1108/00251749610150649

Burnes, B. (2004). *Managing Change:A Strategic Approach to Organizational Dynamics* (4th ed.). Prentice Hall.

Burns, J. M. (1978). *Leadership.* Harper & Row.

Burns, P. (2011). *Entrepreneurship and small business.* Palgrave Macmillan Limited. doi:10.1007/978-0-230-20848-3

Burns, T., & Stalker, G. M. (1961). *The Management of Innovation.* Tavistock.

Burt, G., Mackay, D. J., Heijden, K., & Verheijdt, C. (2017). Openness disposition: Readiness characteristics that influence participant benefits from scenario planning as strategic conversation. *Technological Forecasting and Social Change, 124*, 16–25. doi:10.1016/j.techfore.2016.11.024

By, R. T. (2005). Organizational Change management: A critical approach. *Journal of Change Management, 5*(4), 369–380. doi:10.1080/14697010500359250

Byrne, S. (2011). Does individual locus of control matter in a JIT environment? *Journal of Applied Management Accounting Research, 9*(1), 37–57.

Cabrera-Suarez, K., De Saa-Perez, P., & Garcia-Almeida, D. (2001). The Succession Process from a Resource- and Knowledge-based View of the Family Firm. *Family Business Review, 14*(1), 37–47. doi:10.1111/j.1741-6248.2001.00037.x

Cahdriyana, R. A., Richardo, R., Fahmi, S., & Setyawan, F. (2019, March). Pseudo-thinking process in solving logic problem. [). IOP Publishing.]. *Journal of Physics: Conference Series, 1188*(1), 012090. doi:10.1088/1742-6596/1188/1/012090

Caillois, R. (1961). The definition of play. *The Game Design Reader: A Rules of Play Anthology*, 123–128.

Caldwell, R. (2003). Change leaders and change managers: Different or complementary? *Leadership and Organization Development Journal, 24*(5), 285–293. doi:10.1108/01437730310485806

Cameron, E., & Green, M. (2012). *Making Sense of Change Management: A Complete Guide to the Models, Tools, and Techniques of Organisational Change*. Kogan Page.

Cameron, E., & Green, M. (2015). *Making Sense of Change Management: A Complete Guide to the Models, Tools and Techniques of Organizational Change* (4th ed.). Kogan Page Publishers.

Canaan, J. E., & Shumar, W. (Eds.). (2008). *Structure and agency in the neoliberal university* (Vol. 15). Routledge. doi:10.4324/9780203927687

Cao, W., Fang, Z., Hou, G., Han, M., Xu, X., Dong, J., & Zheng, J. (2020). The psychological impact of the COVID-19 epidemic on college students in China. *Psychiatry Research, 287*, 112934. doi:10.1016/j.psychres.2020.112934 PMID:32229390

Carayannis, E. G., & Campbell, D. F. J. (2006). Knowledge creation, diffusion, and use in innovation networks and knowledge clusters. A comparative systems approach across the United States, Europe, and Asia (pp. 1–25). Praeger, Westporti.

Carayannis, E. G., & Campbell, D. F. (2010). Triple Helix, Quadruple Helix and Quintuple Helix and How Do Knowledge, Innovation and the Environment Relate To Each Other? A Proposed Framework for a Trans-disciplinary Analysis of Sustainable Development and Social Ecology. *International Journal of Social Ecology and Sustainable Development, 1*(1), 41–69. doi:10.4018/jsesd.2010010105

Carayannis, E. G., & Campbell, D. F. J. (2012). *Mode 3 Knowledge Production in Quadruple Helix Innovation Systems.* Springer New York. doi:10.1007/978-1-4614-2062-0

Cardella, G. M., Hernandez-Sanchez, B. R., & Sanchez-Garcıa, J. C. (2020). *Women entrepreneurship: a systematic review to outline the boundaries of scientific literature* (Vol. 11). Frontiers in Psychology Frontiers Media S.A.

Cardel, M. I., Dhurandhar, E., Yarar-Fisher, C., Foster, M., Hidalgo, B., McClure, L. A., & Willig, A. L. (2020). Turning chutes into ladders for women faculty: A review and roadmap for equity in academia. *Journal of Women's Health, 29*(5), 721–733. doi:10.1089/jwh.2019.8027 PMID:32043918

Cardon, M. S., & Patel, P. C. (2015). Is stress worth it? Stress-related health and wealth trade-offs for entrepreneurs. *Applied Psychology, 64*(2), 379–420. doi:10.1111/apps.12021

Cardoso, S. (2020). *Google Ads - Adquira os clientes certos para o seu negócio*. Webinar organizado pela NEST - Centro de Inovação do Turismo.

Carnevale, J. B., & Hatak, I. (2020). Employee adjustment and well-being in the era of COVID-19: Implications for human resource management. *Journal of Business Research, 116*, 183–187. doi:10.1016/j.jbusres.2020.05.037 PMID:32501303

Carr, R. (2012) Family Business: Setting a Benchmark. *Vision.* http://vision.ae/articles/ family_business_setting_a_benchmark

Carter, C., & Scarbrough, H. (2001). Towards a second generation of KM? The people management challenge. *Education + Training, 43*(4), 215–224. doi:10.1108/EUM0000000005483

Carter, S., Mwaura, S., Ram, M., Trehan, K., & Jones, T. (2015). Barriers to ethnic minority and women's enterprise: Existing evidence, policy tensions and unsettled questions. *International Small Business Journal, 33*(1), 49–69. doi:10.1177/0266242614556823

Cascio, J. (2020, April 29). Facing the Age of Chaos. We are in an age of chaos, an era that... | by Jamais Cascio. *Medium*. https://medium.com/@cascio/facing-the-age-of-chaos-b00687b1f51d

Cascio, W., & Montealegre, R. (2019, January 17). *How Technology Is Changing Work and Organizations*. Research Gate. https://www.researchgate.net/publication/299400943_How_Technology_Is_Changing_Work_and_Organizations .

Casillas, J. C., & Moreno, A. M. (2010). The relationship between entrepreneurial orientation and growth: The moderating role of family involvement. *Entrepreneurship and Regional Development, 22*(3-4), 265–291. doi:10.1080/08985621003726135

Cassia, L., & Minola, T. (2012). Hyper-growth of SMEs: Toward a reconciliation of entrepreneurial orientation and strategic resources. *International Journal of Entrepreneurial Behaviour & Research, 18*(2), 179–197. doi:10.1108/13552551211204210

Castrillon, C. (2019). Why more women are turning to entrepreneurship. *Forbes*, (December), 20.

Cawsey, T., Deszca, G., & Ingols, C. (2012): Organizational Change: An action –oriented toolkit. Sage Publications.

CGI. (2021). *Our commitment to a more inclusive and sustainable world. Corporate Social Responsibility Report 2021*. CGI.

CGI. (2022). *Value in motion: Driving forward data-driven decision making*. CGI. https://www.cgi.com/sites/default/files/2021-11/cgi-data-driven-decision-making-value-in-motion-white-paper.pdf

Change Management Institute. (2014). *The Effective Change Manager: The Change Management Body of Knowledge*. Vivid Publishing.

Changefirst (2022). *People-centered Implementation (PCI)*. Changefirst. https://www.changefirst.com

Chase, S. (2005). Narrative Inquiry. In N. K. Denzin, & Y. S. (Eds.), The sage handbook of qualitative research. Sage Publications.

Chasserio, S., Poroli, C., & Redien-Collot, R. (2016). French women entrepreneurs' leadership practices and well-being in a high-growth context. In M. L. Connerley & J. Wu (Eds.), *Handbook on well-being of working women* (pp. 243–260). doi:10.1007/978-94-017-9897-6_15

Chaston, I., & Sadler-Smith, E. (2012). Entrepreneurial cognition, entrepreneurial orientation and firm capability in the creative industries. *British Journal of Management, 23*(3), 415–432.

Chaturvedi, S., Rizvi, I. A., & Pasipanodya, E. T. (2019). How Can Leaders Make Their Followers to Commit to the Organization? the Importance of Influence Tactics. *Global Business Review, 20*(6), 1462–1474. doi:10.1177/0972150919846963

Chauviere, K., Maritz, B., & van Halder, J. (2016, November 17). *The role of the transformation office*. McKinsey. https://www.mckinsey.com/capabilities/rts/our-insights/the-role-of-the-transformation-office

Chen, B. (2022). *Opinion: Can AI be creative? AI can create new content but does not understand its creations*. https://highschool.latimes.com/diamond-bar-high-school/opinion-can-ai-be-creative/

Chen, H. C., & Yeh, C. W. (2021). Global financial crisis and COVID-19: Industrial reactions. *Finance Research Letters, 42*, 101940. doi:10.1016/j.frl.2021.101940 PMID:34566533

Chen, J., & Wang, L. (2007). Locus of control and the three components of commitment to change. *Personality and Individual Differences, 42*(3), 503–512. doi:10.1016/j.paid.2006.07.025

Chermack, J., & Coons, L. M. (2015). Scenario planning: Pierre Wack's hidden messages. *Futures*, *73*, 187–193. doi:10.1016/j.futures.2015.08.012

Cherniss, C., & Goleman, D. (2001). The emotionally intelligent workplace: how to select for, measure, and improve emotional intelligence in individuals, groups, and organizations. Jossey-Bass, NY.

Cheval, S., Mihai Adamescu, C., Georgiadis, T., Herrnegger, M., Piticar, A., & Legates, D. R. (2020). Observed and potential impacts of the COVID-19 pandemic on the environment. *International Journal of Environmental Research and Public Health*, *17*(11), 4140. doi:10.3390/ijerph17114140 PMID:32532012

Child, J. (1984). *Organisation: A guide to problems and practice*. SAGE Publications. doi:10.4135/9781446280348

Chlewinski, Z. (1994). PrzyszioSC swiata w aspekcie szans i zagrozen. Psychologiczne badania studentow: 1992 rok. [The future of the world in view of the chances and threats, Psychological research on students]. *Przegląd Psychologiczny*, *37*, 51–63.

Choi, M., & Ruona, W. E. A. (2013). Individual Readiness for Organizational Change. In Leonard, H. S., Lewis, R., Freedman A. M., and Passmore (eds.), The Wiley-Blackwell Handbook of the Psychology of Leadership, Change, and Organizational Development. J. John Wiley and Sons, Ltd.

Choi, M., & Ruona, W. E. A. (2011). Individual Readiness for Organisational Change and Its Implications for Human Resource and Organisation Development'. *Human Resource Development Review*, *10*(1), 46–73. https://psycnet.apa.org/doi/10.1002/9781118326404.ch16. doi:10.1177/1534484310384957

Choi, Y., Kim, J. Y., & Yoo, T. (2016). 'A study on the effect of learning organisation readiness on employees' quality commitment: The moderating effect of leader–member exchange'. *Total Quality Management & Business Excellence*, *27*(3-4), 325–338. doi:10.1080/14783363.2014.981072

Chrisman, J. J., Chua, J. H., & Sharma, P. (2003). Current trends and future directions in family business management studies: Toward a theory of the family firm. *Coleman White Paper Series*, *4*, 1-63.

Chrisman, J. J., Chua, J. H., & Sharma, P. (2005). Trends and directions in the development of a strategic management theory of the family firm. *Entrepreneurship Theory and Practice*, *29*(5), 555–576. doi:10.1111/j.1540-6520.2005.00098.x

Chua, J. H., Chrisman, J. J., & Bergiel, E. B. (2009). An agency theoretic analysis of the professionalized family firm. *Entrepreneurship Theory and Practice*, *33*(2), 355–372. doi:10.1111/j.1540-6520.2009.00294.x

Chua, J. H., Chrisman, J. J., & Sharma, P. (1999). Defining the family business by behavior. *Entrepreneurship Theory and Practice*, *23*(4), 19–40. doi:10.1177/104225879902300402

Churchill, N. C., & Hatten, K. J. (1997). Non-market-based transfers of wealth and power: A research framework for family business. *Family Business Review*, *10*(1), 53–67. doi:10.1111/j.1741-6248.1997.00053.x

Chu, S. (2011). Viral advertising in social media: Participation in Facebook groups and responses among college-aged users. *Journal of Interactive Advertising*, *12*(1), 30–43. doi:10.1080/15252019.2011.10722189

Clampitt, P. G., DeKoch, R. J., & Cashman, T. (2000). A strategy for communicating about uncertainty. *The Academy of Management Perspectives*, *14*(4), 41–57. doi:10.5465/ame.2000.3979815

Clandinin, D. J., & Connelly, F. M. (2000). *Narrative Inquiry: Experience and Story in Qualitative Research*. Jossey-Bass, Inc.

CNN. (2019). *Korean Go master quits the game because AI 'cannot be defeated'*. CNN. https://edition.cnn.com/2019/11/27/tech/go-master-google-intl-hnk-scli/index.html

Coch, L., & French, J. R. P. Jr. (1948). Overcoming resistance to change. *Human Relations, 1*(4), 512–532. doi:10.1177/001872674800100408

Coduras, A., & Autio, E. (2013). Comparing subjective and objective indicators to describe the national entrepreneurial context: The global entrepreneurship monitor and the global competitiveness index contributions. *Investig. Regionales, 26*, 47–74.

Coduras, A., de la Vega, I., & Salman, M. B. (2018). Entrepreneurial Ecosystems in Arabic Countries: A Recent Overview. In N. Faghih & M. R. Zali (Eds.), *Entrepreneurship Ecosystem in the Middle East and North Africa (MENA): Dynamics in Trends, Policy and Business Environment* (pp. 283–302). Springer International Publishing. doi:10.1007/978-3-319-75913-5_9

Coffman, K., & Lutes, K. (2007). Change Management: Getting User Buy-In. Management of Change, USA.

Cohen, L., Manion, L., & Morrison, K. (2007). Research Methods in Education (6th ed.). London and New York, NY: Routledge doi:10.4324/9780203029053

Cole, M., & Higgins, J. (2022). *Leadership Unravelled: the faulty thinking behind modern management*. Routledge.

Coleman, J. S. (1990). *Foundations of social theory*. Harvard University Press, Belknap Press.

Collett, C., Neff, G., & Gomes, L. G. (2022). The effects of AI on the working lives of women. UNESCO, Inter-American Development Bank, & Organisation for Economic Co-operation and Development (OECD). doi:10.18235/0004055

Collins, L., Grisoni, L., Seaman, C., Graham, S., Fakoussa, R., & Otten, D. (2012). *The Modern Family Business: Relationships, Succession and Transition*. Palgrave Macmillan. doi:10.1057/9781137001337

Colquitt, J. A., Greenberg, J., & Zapata-Phelan, S. P. (2005). What is organizational justice? A historical overview. In J. Greenberg & J. A. Colquitt (Eds.), *Handbook of organizational justice* (pp. 3–56). Erlbaum.

Conway, E., & Monks, K. (2008). HR practices and commitment to change: An employee-level analysis. *Human Resource Management Journal, 18*(1), 72–89. doi:10.1111/j.1748-8583.2007.00059.x

Cope, J. (2005). Towards a dynamic learning perspective of entrepreneurship. *Entrepreneurship Theory and Practice, 29*(4), 373–399. doi:10.1111/j.1540-6520.2005.00090.x

Covernton, G. A., Pearce, C. M., Gurney-Smith, H. J., Chastain, S. G., Ross, P. S., Dower, J. F., & Dudas, S. E. (2019). Size and shape matter: A preliminary analysis of microplastic sampling technique in seawater studies with implications for ecological risk assessment. *The Science of the Total Environment, 667*, 124–132. doi:10.1016/j.scitotenv.2019.02.346 PMID:30826673

Covin, J. G., & Wales, W. J. (2011). The measurement of entrepreneurial orientation. *Entrepreneurship Theory and Practice, 1*(1), 1–26.

Craig, M. (2020, August 20). *IT capability maturity framework (IT-CMF) – Pittsburgh change ...* Pittsburgh Change Management Professionals. https://pitcmp.org/2020/08/20/it-capability-maturity-framework-it-cmf/

Craig, J. B., Dibrell, C., & Garrett, R. (2014). Examining relationships among family influence, family culture, flexible planning systems, innovativeness and firm performance. *Journal of Family Business Strategy, 5*(3), 229–238. doi:10.1016/j.jfbs.2013.09.002

Creswell, J. W., Hanson, W. E., Clark, V. L., & Morales, A. (2007). Qualitative Research Designs: Selection and Implementation. *The Counseling Psychologist, 35*(2), 236–264. doi:10.1177/0011000006287390

Critchley, B., King, K., & Higgins, J. (2007). *Organisational consulting: a relational perspective*. Middlesex University Press.

Croson, R., & Gneezy, U. (2009). Gender differences in preferences. *Journal of Economic Literature*, *47*(2), 448–474. doi:10.1257/jel.47.2.448

Cuellar, R., Augustine, S., & Scheere, A. (2021). *From PMO to VMO: Managing for value delivery*. Berrett-Koehler Publishers.

Cummings, T., & Worley, C. (2015). *Organization development and change* (10th ed.). Thomson/South-Western.

Cunningham, G. B. (2006). The relationships among commitment to change, coping with change, and turnover intentions. *European Journal of Work and Organizational Psychology*, *15*(1), 29–45. doi:10.1080/13594320500418766

D'Allura, G. M. (2017). Bringing emotions into family firms: The business theatre as a tool for management coaching. *Academy of Management Proceedings*, *2017*(1), 11006. doi:10.5465/AMBPP.2017.11006abstract

D'Aveni, R. A. (1998). Waking up to the new era of hypercompetition. *The Washington Quarterly*, *21*(1), 183–195. doi:10.1080/01636609809550302

Dafne's story. (n.d.). Cherie Blair Foundation for Women. https://cherieblairfoundation.org/impact/her-stories/dafne-adapting-to-covid19/

Daly, J. P., & Geyer, P. D. (1994). The role of fairness in implementing large-scale change: Employee evaluations of process and outcome in seven facility relocations. *Journal of Organizational Behavior*, *15*(7), 623–638. doi:10.1002/job.4030150706

Dana, L. P. (2000). *Economies of the Eastern Mediterranean Region: economic miracles in the making*. World Scientific. doi:10.1142/4567

Daniels, H., Edwards, A., Engeström, Y., Gallagher, T., & Ludvigsen, S. R. (2013). *Activity theory in practice: Promoting learning across boundaries and agencies*. Routledge. doi:10.4324/9780203609439

Danilda, I., Lindberg, M., & Torstensson, B.-M. (2009). *A Quattro Helix Innovation System on the European Agenda*. Women Resource Centres. http:// www.hss09.se/own_documents/Papers/3-11%20-%20Danilda%20Lindberg% 20&%20Torstensson%20-%20paper.pdf. 2

Danoesastro, M., Rehberg, B., Ritter, D., Krishna, A., Hildebrandt, P., & Islam, M. (2020). *When the Ground Shifts, It Pays to Be Agile*. BCG.https://www.bcg.com/publications/2020/understanding-why-agile-will-help-move-the-needle-post-covid-19

Davidson, R., Goodwin-Stewart, J., & Kent, P. (2005). Internal Governance Structures and Earnings Management. *Accounting and Finance*, *45*(2), 241–267. doi:10.1111/j.1467-629x.2004.00132.x

Davies, A., & Doyle, R. (2015). Transforming household consumption: From backcasting to HomeLabs experiments. *Annals of the Association of American Geographers*, *105*(2), 425–436. doi:10.1080/00045608.2014.1000948

de Jong, T., Wiezer, N., de Weerd, M., Nielsen, K., Mattila-Holappa, P., & Mockałło, Z. (2016). The impact of restructuring on employee well-being: A systematic review of longitudinal studies. *Work and Stress*, *30*(1), 91–114. doi:10.1080/02678373.2015.1136710

De Massis, A., & Kotlar, J. (2015). Learning resources for family business education: A review and directions for future developments. *Academy of Management Learning & Education*, *14*(3), 415–422. doi:10.5465/amle.2014.0246 de Melo, M. A. C. (1997). *Processo de Planejamento e as Inovações Tecnológicas e Sociais: uma perspectiva sócio-ecológica.* Anais do 5o. Seminário de Modernização Tecnológica.

de Melo, M.A.C. (2002). Inovação e Modernização Tecnológica e Organizacional nas MPMEs: o domínio interorganizacional. *Seminário Internacional: Políticas para Sistemas Produtivos Locais de MPME*: 2002.

de Melo, A. (2001). *The Innovation Systems of Latin America and the Caribbean.* Inter-American Development Bank. Agosto.

De Wit, B., & Meyer, R. (2005). *Strategy Synthesis: Resolving Strategy Paradoxes to Create Competitive Advantage* (2nd ed.). Thomson Learning.

Deal, B., Pan, H., Pallathucheril, V., & Fulton, G. (2017). Urban resilience and planning support systems: The need for sentience. *Journal of Urban Technology, 24*(1), 29–45. doi:10.1080/10630732.2017.1285018

Deal, B., Pan, H., Timm, S., & Pallathucheril, V. (2017). The role of multidirectional temporal analysis in scenario planning exercises and Planning Support Systems. *Computers, Environment and Urban Systems, 64*, 91–102. doi:10.1016/j.compenvurbsys.2017.01.004

Dechant, K., & Lamky, A. A. (2005). Towards an understanding of Arab women entrepreneurs in Bahrain and Oman. *Journal of Developmental Entrepreneurship, 10*(2), 123–140. doi:10.1142/S1084946705000100

Dejene, Y. (2007). Promoting women's economic empowerment in Africa. *Proceedings of the Singapore Economic Review Conference*, 1-20.

Del Giudice, M. (2011). Knowledge Management and Family Business. In *Knowledge and Family Business. Innovation, Technology, and Knowledge Management* (Vol. 7). Springer.

Delaini, S. (2022, June 27). *How Microsoft used change management best practices to launch a new business intelligence platform - Inside Track Blog.* Microsoft. https://www.microsoft.com/insidetrack/blog/how-microsoft-used-change-management-best-practices-to-launch-a-new-business-intelligence-platform/

Delanty, G., & Mota, A. (2017). Governing the Anthropocene: Agency, Governance, Knowledge. *European Journal of Social Theory, 20*(1), 9–38. doi:10.1177/1368431016668535

Delbecq, A. L., Ven, A. H., & Gustafson, D. H. (2004). *Group Techniques for Program Planning: A Guide to Nominal Groups and Delphi Process.* Green Briar Press.

DelSole, T., & Tippett, M. K. (2021). Correcting the corrected AIC. *Statistics & Probability Letters, 173*, 109064. doi:10.1016/j.spl.2021.109064

DeMartino, R., & Barbato, R. (2003). Differences between women and men MBA entrepreneurs: Exploring family flexibility and wealth creation as career motivators. *Journal of Business Venturing, 18*(6), 815–832. doi:10.1016/S0883-9026(03)00003-X

Denrell, J., & March, J. G. (2001). Adaptation as information restriction: The hot stove effect. *Organization Science, 12*(5), 523–538. doi:10.1287/orsc.12.5.523.10092

Desai, D. (2019). Digital marketing: A review. *International Journal of Trend in Scientific Research and Development*, 196-200.

Dewey, J. (1933). *How we think a restatement of the relation of reflective thinking to the educative process.* Heath & Co Publishers.

Dhawan, S. (2020). Online Learning: A Panacea in the Time of COVID-19 Crisis. *Journal of Educational Technology Systems, 49*(1), 5–22. doi:10.1177/0047239520934018

Dias, A. B., Rosentha, L. D., & de Melo, M. A. C. (2000) Enriquecendo a Atuação de Incubadoras de Empresas. XXI Simpósio de Gestão da Inovação Tecnológica. Co-autores: Adriano Batista Dias e David Rosenthal. São Paulo.

Dias, A.B., de Melo, M.A.C & Rosenthal, D. (2002). *Enriquecendo a Atuação de Incubadora de Empresas. Tecnologia e Inovação: experiências de gestão nas micro e pequenas empresas.* PGT/USP.

Diaz-Moriana, V., Hogan, T., Clinton, E., & Brophy, M. (2019). Defining Family Business: A Closer Look at Definitional Heterogeneity. In E. Memili & C. Dibrell (Eds.), *The Palgrave Handbook of Heterogeneity among Family Firms* (pp. 333–374). Springer International Publishing. doi:10.1007/978-3-319-77676-7_13

Dietrich, A. M., Kuester, K., Müller, G. J., & Schoenle, R. C. (2020). *News and uncertainty about Covid-19: Survey evidence and short-run economic impact.* Federal Reserve Bank of Cleveland, Working Paper No. 20-12. 1 doi:0.26509/frbcwp-202012

Digman, J. M. (1990). Personality structure: Emergence of the five-factor model. *Annual Review of Psychology, 41*(1), 417–440. doi:10.1146/annurev.ps.41.020190.002221

Dilnot, C. (2018). The relationship between A-level subject choice and league table score of university attended: The 'facilitating', the 'less suitable', and the counter-intuitive. *Oxford Review of Education, 44*(1), 118–137. doi:10.1080/03054985.2018.1409976

DiMatteo. L.A./Poncibò, C./Cannarsa, M. (2022). The Cambridge handbook of artificial intelligence: global perspectives on law and ethics. Cambridge University Press.

Dobák, M. (2002). *Szervezeti formák és vezetés.* KJK – Kerszöv.

Docherty, I., & McKiernan, P. (2008). Scenario planning for the Edinburgh city region. *Environ. Plann. C, 26*(7), 982–997. doi:10.1068/c0665r

Doern, R., Williams, N., & Vorley, T. (2019). Special issue on entrepreneurship and crises: Business as usual? An introduction and review of the literature. *Entrepreneurship and Regional Development, 31*(5-6), 400–412. doi:10.1080/08985626.2018.1541590

Donald, M. (2019). *Leading and Managing Change in the Age of Disruption and Artificial Intelligence.* ProQuest. doi:10.1108/9781787563674

Donthu, N., & Gustafsson, A. (2020). Effects of COVID-19 on business and research. *Journal of Business Research, 117*, 284–289. doi:10.1016/j.jbusres.2020.06.008 PMID:32536736

Drucker, P. F. (1993). *Management: Tasks, responsibilities, practices.* HarperCollins.

Dubina, I. N., Carayannis, E. G., & Campbell, D. F. J. (2012). Creativity economy and a crisis of the economy? Coevolution of knowledge, innovation, and creativity, and of the knowledge economy and knowledge society. *Journal of the Knowledge Economy, 3*(1), 1–24. http://www.springerlink.com/content/t5j8l12136h526h5/ 10.1007/s13132-011-0042-y. doi:10.100713132-011-0042-y

Dunphy, D., Griffith, A., & Benn, S. (2007). *Organizational change for corporate sustainability. A guide for leaders and change agents of the future* (2nd ed.). Routledge.

Dunphy, D., & Stace, D. (1993). The strategic management of corporate change. *Human Relations, 46*(8), 905–918. doi:10.1177/001872679304600801

Dwivedi, Y., Ismagilova, E., Hughes, D., Carlson, J., Filieri, R., Jacobson, J., Jain, V., Karjaluoto, H., Kefi, H., Krishen, A., Kumar, V., Rahman, M., Raman, R., Rauschnabel, P., Rowley, J., Salo, J., Tran, G., & Wang, Y. (2021). Setting the future of digital and social media marketing research: Perspectives and research propositions. *International Journal of Information Management, 59*, 102168. doi:10.1016/j.ijinfomgt.2020.102168

Dzenopoljac, V., Alasadi, R., Zaim, H., & Bontis, N. (2018). Impact of knowledge management processes on business performance: Evidence from Kuwait. *Knowledge and Process Management, 25*(2), 77–87. doi:10.1002/kpm.1562

Eckert, P. (1993). *The school as a community of engaged learners*, [unpublished manuscript].

Eddleston, K. A., & Kellermanns, F. W. (2007). Destructive and productive family relationships: A stewardship theory perspective. *Journal of Business Venturing, 22*(4), 545–565. doi:10.1016/j.jbusvent.2006.06.004

Effects of the coronavirus (COVID-19) pandemic on 'high-contact' industries . (n.d.). Office for National Statistics. https://www.ons.gov.uk/economy/grossvalueaddedgva/articles/effectsofthecoronaviruscovid19pandemiconhighcontactindustries
/2022-05-06

Eggers, F. (2020). Masters of disasters? Challenges and opportunities for SMEs in times of crisis. *Journal of Business Research, 116*, 199–208. doi:10.1016/j.jbusres.2020.05.025 PMID:32501306

Elali, W. (2021). The importance of strategic agility to business survival during corona crisis and beyond. *International Journal of Business Ethics and Governance, 4*(2), 1–8. doi:10.51325/ijbeg.v4i2.64

Elam, A. B., Brush, C. G., Greene, P. G., Baumer, B., Dean, M., & Heavlow, R. (2019). *Global Entrepreneurship Monitor 2018/2019 Women's Entrepreneurship Report*. Babson College: Smith College and the Global Entrepreneurship Research Association.

El-Besomey, D. A. M. (2020). The contemporary vision of universal strategic planning for facing (COVID-19) crisis in the field of higher education via virtual learning-training. *European Journal of Education, 3*(2), 151–164. doi:10.26417/869dvb85y

Elias, N. (2000). *The Civilizing Process*. Blackwell.

Elrod, P. D. III, & Tippett, D. D. (2002). The "death valley" of change. *Journal of Organizational Change Management, 15*(3), 273–291. doi:10.1108/09534810210429309

Emsza, B., Eliyana, A., & Istyarini, W. (2016). The relationship between self-efficacy and readiness for change: The mediator roles of employee empowerment. *Mediterranean Journal of Social Sciences, 7*(3), 201–206. doi:10.5901/mjss.2016.v7n3s1p201

Engel, C., Ebel, P., & van Giffen, B. (2021). *Empirically Exploring the Cause-Effect Relationships of AI Characteristics, Project Management Challenges, and Organizational Change, Wirtschaftsinformatik 2021 Proceedings, Track 10: Design, management and impact of AI-based systems. 3*. University of St. Gallen.

Engeström, Y. (1999). Activity theory and individual and social transformation. *Perspectives on Activity Theory, 19*(38).

Ensley, M. D., Pearson, A. W., & Sardeshmukh, S. R. (2007). The negative consequences of pay dispersion in family and non-family top management teams: An exploratory analysis of new venture, high-growth firms. *Journal of Business Research, 60*(10), 1039–1047. doi:10.1016/j.jbusres.2006.12.012

Erdogan, S., & Yucalar, F. (2009, July). *A questionnaire based method for cmmi level 2 maturity assessment*. Academia.edu. https://www.academia.edu/16827112/A_questionnaire_based_method_for_cmmi_level_2_maturity_assessment

Erikson, E. H. (1982). *The life cycle completed* (1st ed.). Norton.

Errington, E. (2003). *Developing scenario-based learning: Practical insights for tertiary educators.* Dunmore Press.

Esmanech, T. (2018, July 19). *The purpose of a business is to create and keep a customer.* LinkedIn. https://www.linkedin.com/pulse/purpose-business-create-keep-customer-tommaso-esmanech/

European Commission (2018). *Artificial Intelligence for Europe.* COM(2018) 237. European Commission.

European Commission. (2020) *On Artificial Intelligence - A European approach to excellence and trust, White Paper.*

European Parliament. (2020) *Opportunities of artificial intelligence, Brussels.* European Parliament. https://data.europa.eu/doi/10.2861/692222

EY. (2022). EY NextGen. *EY.* https://www.ey.com/en_gl/next-generation Last accessed: 18.10.2022

EY. (2022). Family enterprise. *EY.* https://www.ey.com/en_vn/family-enterprise Last accessed: 22.10.2022

Fahrenkrog, S. L. (n.d.). *OPM3 - Successful execution of organisational strategies.* PMI. https://www.pmi.org/learning/library/organizational-strategies-outcomes-improvements-8398

Fakoussa, R., & Collins, L. (2017). Socioemotional Approach: Exploring Women's Guilt in an All-Female Egyptian Family Business. In *Family Businesses in the Arab World* (pp. 107–130). Springer. doi:10.1007/978-3-319-57630-5_7

Fakoussa, R., O'Leary, S., & Salem, S. (2020). An exploratory study on social entrepreneurship in Egypt. *Journal of Islamic Accounting and Business Research, 11*(3), 694–707. doi:10.1108/JIABR-02-2017-0023

Fama, E. F., & Jensen, M. C. (1983). Separation of ownership and control. *The Journal of Law & Economics, 26*(2), 301–325. doi:10.1086/467037

Fang, C., Lee, J., & Schilling, M. A. (2009). Balancing Exploration and Exploitation Through Structural Design: The Isolation of Subgroups and Organizational Learning. *Organization Science, 21*(3), 625–642. doi:10.1287/orsc.1090.0468

Farley, J., & Voinov, A. (2016). Economics, socio-ecological resilience and ecosystem services. *Journal of Environmental Management, 183*(2), 389–398. https://www.sciencedirect.com/science/article/pii/S0301479716305023. doi:10.1016/j.jenvman.2016.07.065 PMID:27480914

Farouk, H. (2013). Cited in Grant Thornton: The Rules of Engagement for Family-Owned Businesses. *Grant Thorton.* http://www. grantthornton.ae/page/the-rules-of-engagement-for-family-owned-businesses

Fatoki, O. O. (2014). The Entrepreneurial Orientation of Micro Enterprises in the Retail Sector in South Africa. *Journal of Sociology and Social Anthropology, 5*(2), 125–129. doi:10.1080/09766634.2014.11885616

Favaretto, J., & Meirelles, F. (2015, March). Nolan's stage level measurement of information and communication technology in modern organizations. *Research Gate.* https://www.researchgate.net/publication/311966074_Nolans_stage_level_measurement_of_Information_and_Communication_Technology_in_modern_organizations

FBCG. (2022). Our work and your success begin with education *The FBG.* https://www.thefbcg.com/what-we-do/presentations-workshops/

Felin, T., Foss, N. J., Heimeriks, K. H., & Madsen, T. L. (2012). Microfoundations of routines and capabilities: Individuals, processes, and structure. *Journal of Management Studies, 49*(8), 1351–1374. doi:10.1111/j.1467-6486.2012.01052.x

Feliu, N., & Botero, I. C. (2016). Philanthropy in Family Enterprises: A Review of Literature. *Family Business Review, 29*(1), 121–141. doi:10.1177/0894486515610962

Fellnhofer, K., Puumalainen, K., & Sjögrén, H. (2016). Entrepreneurial orientation and performance – are sexes equal? *International Journal of Entrepreneurial Behaviour & Research, 22*(3), 346–374. doi:10.1108/IJEBR-12-2015-0286

Fernandes, N. (2020). *Economic effects of coronavirus outbreak (COVID-19) on the world economy.* SSRN. https://papers.ssrn.com/sol3/papers.cfm?abstract_id=3557504

Ferrari, F. (2019). Everything must change, because nothing changes. A history of organizational change in Italian bank sector, in Hamlin R.G., Ellinger A:D., & Jones J. (Eds). Evidence-Based Initiatives for Organizational Change and Development. IGI-Global Publishing.

Ferrari, F. (2019a). Facing organizational change. Seven challenges for practitioners, in Hamlin R.G., Ellinger A:D., & Jones J. (Eds). Evidence-Based Initiatives for Organizational Change and Development. IGI-Global Publishing. doi:10.4018/978-1-5225-6155-2.ch017

Ferrari, F. (2020). A Theoretical Approach Exploring Knowledge Transmission Across Generations in Family SMEs. In M. Khosrow-Pour D.B.A. (Eds.), Encyclopedia of Organizational Knowledge, Administration, and Technology (pp. 1531-1550). IGI Global. doi:10.4018/978-1-7998-3473-1.ch105

Ferrari, F. (2022). Skills mismatch and change confidence: the impact of training on change recipients' self-efficacy. *European Journal of Training and Development.* doi:10.1108/EJTD-06-2021-0072

Ferrari, F., & Emiliani, E. (2010), Lo sviluppo delle competenze. Fondamenti teorici ed esperienze pratiche per l'apprendimento di una professione, Roma: Carocci.

Ferrari, F. (2017). Human Resource Management and Organizational Reliability: Coordination Mechanisms, Training Models, and Diagnostic Systems for Contingency Management. In B. Christiansen & H. Chandan (Eds.), *Handbook of Research on Industrial and Organizational Psychology in the Modern Workforce.* Igi-Global Publishing. doi:10.4018/978-1-5225-2250-8.ch003

Ferrari, F. (2017a). *The impact of skill-mismatch on readiness to change: empirical research in the Italian Bank sector.* WOA - XVII Workshop dei Docenti e dei Ricercatori di Organizzazione Aziendale.

Fielden, S. L., Davidson, M. J., Dawe, A. J., & Makin, P. J. (2003). Factors inhibiting the economic growth of female owned small businesses in North West England. *Journal of Small Business and Enterprise Development, 10*(2), 152–166. doi:10.1108/14626000310473184

Filip, F. C., & Marascu-Klein, V. (2015, June 17-20). The 5S Lean Method is a Tool of Industrial Management Performances [Paper Presentation]. *Modern Technologies in Industrial Engineering (ModTech2015),* Mamaia, Romania.

Fischer, E., Reuben, R. A., & Dyke, L. S. (1993). A theoretical overview and extension of research on sex, gender, and entrepreneurship. *The Journal of Business,* 8151–8168.

Fischer-Kowalski, M., & Haberl, H. (2007). *Socioecological Transitions and Global Change.* Edward Elgar. doi:10.4337/9781847209436

Fitzgerald, T. (2020). Mapping the terrain of leadership: Gender and leadership in higher education. *Irish Educational Studies, 39*(2), 1–12. doi:10.1080/03323315.2020.1729222

Five Levels of Change Management Maturity. (n.d.). Prosci. https://www.prosci.com/resources/articles/change-management-maturity-model

Foray, D., David, P. A., & Hall, B. H. (2009). Smart specialisation: The concept. In E. Commission (Ed.), *Knowledge for growth: Prospects for science, technology, and innovation* (pp. 25–29). European Commission. DG Research.

Forbes.com. (2022). Why Change Management Fails. *Forbes*. https://www.forbes.com/sites/victorlipman/2013/09/04/new-study-explores-why-change-management-fails-and-how-to-perhaps-succeed/?sh=4daf34347137

Ford, H., & Crowther, S. (2014). *My Life And Work*. CreateSpace Independent Publishing Platform.

Forte, A. (2005). Locus of control and the moral reasoning of managers. *Journal of Business Ethics*, *58*(1-3), 65–77. doi:10.100710551-005-1387-6

Foss, N. J. (2011). Why micro-foundations for resource-based theory are needed and what they may look like. *Journal of Management*, *37*(5), 1413–1428. doi:10.1177/0149206310390218

Frankish, K., & Ramsey, W. (2014). *The Cambridge handbook of artificial intelligence*. Cambridge University Press. doi:10.1017/CBO9781139046855

Freeman, M. A., Staudenmaier, P. J., Zisser, M. R., & Andresen, L. A. (2019). The prevalence and co-occurrence of psychiatric conditions among entrepreneurs and their families. *Small Business Economics*, *53*(2), 323–342. doi:10.100711187-018-0059-8

French, J. R. P. Jr., & Raven, B. (1959). The bases of social power. In D. Cartwright (Ed.), Studies in social power (pp. 150–167). University of Michigan.

Frese, M., Garst, H., & Fay, D. (2007). Making things happen: Reciprocal relationships between work characteristics and personal initiative in a four-wave longitudinal structural equation model. *The Journal of Applied Psychology*, *92*(4), 1084–1102. doi:10.1037/0021-9010.92.4.1084 PMID:17638467

Fried, Y., Tiegs, R. B., Naughton, T. J., & Ashforth, B. E. (1996). Managers' reactions to a corporate acquisition: A test of an integrative model. *Journal of Organizational Behavior*, *17*(5), 401–427. doi:10.1002/(SICI)1099-1379(199609)17:5<401::AID-JOB774>3.0.CO;2-R

Fugate, M., Harrison, S., & Kinicki, A. J. (2011). Thoughts and Feelings About Organizational Change: A Field Test of Appraisal Theory. *Journal of Leadership & Organizational Studies*, *18*(4), 421–437. doi:10.1177/1548051811416510

Fugate, M., Kinicki, A., & Prussia, G. (2008). Employee coping with organizational change: An examination of alternative theoretical perspectives and models. *Personnel Psychology*, *61*(1), 1–36. doi:10.1111/j.1744-6570.2008.00104.x

Fugate, M., Prussia, G. E., & Kinicki, A. J. (2012). Managing Employee Withdrawal During Organizational Change: The Role of Threat Appraisal. *Journal of Management*, *38*(3), 890–914. doi:10.1177/0149206309352881

Furdas, M., & Kohn, K. (2010). What's the Difference?! Gender, Personality, and the Propensity to Start a Business. *IZA Discussion Paper No. 4778.*

Galbraith, J. (1997). *The Good Society: The Humane Agenda*. Houghton Mifflin.

Galbraith, J. R. (1973). *Designing Complex Organizations*. Addison- Wesley.

Gallo, M. A., & Sveen, J. (1991). Internationalizing the family business: Facilitating and restraining factors. *Family Business Review*, *4*(2), 181–190. doi:10.1111/j.1741-6248.1991.00181.x

Gandolfo, G. (1998). *International trade theory and policy*. Springer Berlin Heidelberg. doi:10.1007/978-3-642-61680-8

Gardner, D. G., Dunham, R. B., Cummings, L. L., & Pierce, J. L. (1987). Employee focus of attention and reactions to organizational change. *The Journal of Applied Behavioral Science*, *23*(3), 351–370. doi:10.1177/002188638702300305

Gardner, H. (1995). *Leading minds*. Harper Collins.

Garland, P. (2014). What can the work of Habermas offer educational researcher development programmes? *Studies in Higher Education*, *39*(1), 87–101. doi:10.1080/03075079.2011.644785

Gartner. (2020). *Gartner Top Strategic Predictions for 2019 and Beyond*. Gartner.

Gartner, J. D. (2008). *The hypomanic edge: the link between (a little) craziness and (a lot of) success in America*. Simon and Schuster.

Garvin, D. A. (2007). Teaching executives and teaching MBAs: Reflections on the case method. *Academy of Management Learning & Education*, *6*(3), 364–374. doi:10.5465/amle.2007.26361626

Gaver, W., Boucher, A., Pennington, S., & Walker, B. (2004). Cultural probes and the value of uncertainty. *Interactions-Funology*, *11*(5), 53–56. doi:10.1145/1015530.1015555

Gerwing, C. (2016). *Meaning of Change Agents within Organizational Change, Journal of Applied Leadership and Management*. University of Applied Sciences. https://www.journal-alm.org/article/view/17107

Gherardi, S., & Nicolini, D. (2004). *Apprendimento e conoscenza nelle organizzazioni*. Carocci.

Ghouse, S. M., McElwee, G., & Durrah, O. (2019). Entrepreneurial success of cottage-based women entrepreneurs in Oman. *International Journal of Entrepreneurial Behaviour & Research*, *25*(3), 480–498. doi:10.1108/IJEBR-10-2018-0691

Giddens, A. (1984). *The construction of society*. University of California Press.

Gilley, A. (2005). *The manager as change leader*. Praeger.

Gilligan, C. (1993). *In a different voice: Psychological theory and women's development*. Harvard University Press. doi:10.4159/9780674037618

Gittings, L., Toska, E., Medley, S., Cluver, L., Logie, C. H., Ralayo, N., Chen, J., & Mbithi-Dikgole, N. (2021). 'Now my life is stuck!': Experiences of adolescents and young people during COVID-19 lockdown in South Africa. *Global Public Health: An International Journal for Research, Policy and Practice*, *16*(6), 947–963. doi:10.1080/17441692.2021.1899262 PMID:33750269

Goedhart, M., Levy, C., & Morgan, P. (2015, November 1). *A better way to understand internal rate of return*. McKinsey. https://www.mckinsey.com/capabilities/strategy-and-corporate-finance/our-insights/a-better-way-to-understand-internal-rate-of-return

Goldman, S., Nagel, R., & Preiss, K. (1995). *Agile Competitors and Virtual Organizations*. Van Nostrand Reinhold.

Goldman, S., Nagel, R., Preiss, K., & Dove, R. (1991). *21st Century Manufacturing Enterprise Strategy: An Industry Led View*. Iacocca Institute, Lehigh University.

Goleman, D. (2002). *The New Leaders: Transforming the Art of Leadership into the Science of Results*. Time Warner Books.

Gonsalves, E., & Fakoussa, R. (2018). Playfulness - a novel approach to learning about family-owned business dynamics. In *Proceedings of 3E– ECSB Entrepreneurship Education Conference (vol. 7, pp. 43)*, Gothenburg, Sweden: ECSB Press.

Gonsalves, E., & Zamora, R. (2015). RETS-MICA: An Entrepreneurial Learning workshop tool for MBA & MA programs. In *Proceedings of ABS Learning, Teaching & Student Experience Conference,* (vol. 4), York, UK.

Gonsalves, E., & Zamora, R. (2017). Ludic Executives: The Case For Play in Entrepreneurial Learning Design. In P. Jones & L. Pittaway (Eds.), *Entrepreneurship Education: New Perspectives on Research, Policy and Practice* (pp. 213–233). Emerald Publishing Ltd. doi:10.1108/S2040-724620170000007014

Gonsalves, E., & Zamora, R. (2020). Ludens Familias: Playful Learning for the Entrepreneurial Family. In A. O. Ayandibu (Ed.), *Reshaping Entrepreneurship Education With Strategy and Innovation.* IGI Global Publishing Ltd.

Gonzalez, C., & Bush, R. O. (2020). *Instrument for the assessment of maturity in the digital economy.* Academia. https://www.academia.edu/85920803/Instrument_for_the_assessment_of_maturity_in_the_digital_economy

Göransson, K. E., Ehnfors, M., Fonteyn, M. E., & Ehrenberg, A. (2008). Thinking strategies used by registered nurses during emergency department triage. *Journal of Advanced Nursing, 61*(2), 163–172. doi:10.1111/j.1365-2648.2007.04473.x PMID:18186908

Gorgievski, M. J., Bakker, A. B., Schaufeli, W. B., van der Veen, H. B., & Giesen, C. W. M. (2010). Financial problems and psychological distress: Investigating reciprocal effects among business owners. *Journal of Occupational and Organizational Psychology, 83*(2), 513–530. doi:10.1348/096317909X434032

Government of Canada. (2021). *Key Small Business Statistics.* https://www.ic.gc.ca/eic/site/061.nsf/vwapj/KSBS_2021.pdf/$FILE/KSBS_2021.pdf

Grama, B., & Todericiu, R. (2017). Change, Resistance to Change and Organizational Cynicism. *Studies in Business and Economics, 11*(3), 47–54. doi:10.1515be-2016-0034

Grave, J. (2019). What KPIs Are Key. Evaluating Performance Metrics for Social Media Influencers. *Social Media + Society, 5*(3), 1–9. doi:10.1177/2056305119865475

Greene, V. (2013). *Dancing in the Rain.* West Brow Press.

Greenwood, R., & Hinings, C. R. (1993). Understanding Radical Organizational Change: Bringing Together the Old and the New Institutionalism. *Academy of Management Review, 21*(4), 1022–1054. doi:10.2307/259163

Greiner, L. (1972). Evolution and revolution as organizations grow. [Haines, J. L., Hauser, M. A., Schmidt, S., Scott, W. K., Olson, L. M., Gallins, P., Spencer, K. L., Shu, Y. K., Noureddine, M., Gilbert, J. R., Schnetz]. *Harvard Business Review,* (July-August), 37–46. PMID:10179654

Grimson, J., & Grimson, W. (2019). Eliminating gender inequality in engineering, industry, and academia. In *The Engineering-Business Nexus* (pp. 315–339). Springer. doi:10.1007/978-3-319-99636-3_15

Grint, K. (2000). *The Art of Leadership.* Oxford University Press.

Gustafson, P. E. (1998). Gender differences in risk perception: Theoretical and methodological perspectives. *Risk Analysis, 18*(6), 805–811. doi:10.1023/B:RIAN.0000005926.03250.c0 PMID:9972583

Haber, S., & Reichel, A. (2007). The cumulative nature of the entrepreneurial process: The contribution of human capital, planning and environmental resources to small venture performance. *Journal of Business Venturing, 22*(1), 119–145. doi:10.1016/j.jbusvent.2005.09.005

Hagel, J. I., & Brown, S. (2003). *The agile dance of architectures—reframing IT enabled business opportunities.* SAP Design Guild, Edition on Composite Applications.

Hagen, M., Bernard, A., & Grube, E. (2016, March). Do It All Wrong! Using Reverse-Brainstorming to Generate Ideas, Improve Discussions, and Move Students to Action. *Management Teaching Review, 1*(2), 85-90. www.creatingminds.org: http://creatingminds.org/tools/reverse_brainstorming.htm

Halkias, D., Nwajiuba, C., Nicholas, H., & Caracatsanis, S. M. (2011). Challenges facing women entrepreneurs in Nigeria. *Management Research Review, 34*(2), 221–235. doi:10.1108/01409171111102821

Hall, S., Lovallo, D., & Musters, R. (2012, March 1). *How to put your money where your strategy is.* McKinsey. https://www.mckinsey.com/capabilities/strategy-and-corporate-finance/our-insights/how-to-put-your-money-where-your-strategy-is

Hameed, I., & Ali, B. (2011). Impact of Entrepreneurial Orientation, Entrepreneurial Management and Environmental Dynamism on Firm's Financial Performance. *Journal of Economics and Behavioral Studies, 3*(2), 101–114. doi:10.22610/jebs.v3i2.260

Hamel, G., & Breen, B. (2007). *The Future of Management.* Harvard Business Press.

Hamilton, A. B., & Finley, E. P. (2019). Qualitative methods in implementation research: An introduction. *Psychiatry Research, 280*, 112516. doi:10.1016/j.psychres.2019.112516 PMID:31437661

Hamilton, E. (2011). Entrepreneurial learning in family business: A situated learning perspective. *Journal of Small Business and Enterprise Development, 18*(1), 8–26. doi:10.1108/14626001111106406

Hammad, M. A. (2016). Future Anxiety and its Relationship to Students' Attitude toward Academic Specialization. *Journal of Education and Practice, 7*(15). https://files.eric.ed.gov/fulltext/EJ1103253.pdf

Hankey, S., & Marshall, J. D. (2010). Impacts of urban form on future US passenger-vehicle greenhouse gas emissions. *Energy Policy, 38*(9), 4880–4887. doi:10.1016/j.enpol.2009.07.005

Hanson, S. (2009). Changing Places through Women's Entrepreneurship. *Economic Geography, 85*(3), 245–267. doi:10.1111/j.1944-8287.2009.01033.x

Harapko, S. (2021). *How COVID-19 impacted supply chains and what comes next.* EY. https://www.ey.com/en_gl/supply-chain/how-covid-19-impacted-supply-chains-and-what-comes-next

Harrison, R., Fischer, S., Walpola, R. L., Chauhan, A., Babalola, T., Mears, S., & Le-Dao, H. (2021). Where do models for change management, improvement and implementation meet? A systematic review of the applications of change management models in healthcare. *Journal of Healthcare Leadership, 13*, 85–108. doi:10.2147/JHL.S289176 PMID:33737854

Harvey, M., & Evans, R. E. (1994). The Impact of Timing and Mode of Entry on Successor Development and Successful Succession. *Family Business Review, 7*(3), 221–236. doi:10.1111/j.1741-6248.1994.00221.x

Hassink, R., & Marques, P. (2016). The regional innovation paradox revisited. In U. Hilpert (Ed.), *Routledge Handbook of politics and technology* (pp. 120–131). Routledge.

Hattab, H. (2012). Towards understanding female entrepreneurship in Middle Eastern and North African countries. *Education, Business and Society, 5*(3), 171–186. doi:10.1108/17537981211265561

Hausman, D. M. (2007). *The Philosophy of Economics: An Anthology* (3rd ed.). Cambridge University Press. doi:10.1017/CBO9780511819025

Hayes, C., & Graham, Y. N. (2020). Prophylaxis in action: # MeToo for women of medical and surgical disciplines. In *Gender Equity in the Medical Profession* (pp. 270–279). IGI Global. doi:10.4018/978-1-5225-9599-1.ch019

Headings, S. (n.d.). *Unit-III-Women Entrepreneur: Nature, Definition, Features and in Indian perspectives.* CCS University.

Healey, J. (2020). *Artificial Intelligence.* The Spinney Press.

Healy, A., & Morgan, K. (2012). Spaces of innovation: Learning, proximity, and the ecological turn. *Regional Studies, 46*(8), 1041–1053. doi:10.1080/00343404.2012.672725

Hechanova, M. R. M., Caringal-Go, J. F., & Magsaysay, J. F. (2018). Implicit change leadership, change management, and affective commitment to change: Comparing academic institutions vs business enterprises. *Leadership and Organization Development Journal, 39*(7), 914–925. doi:10.1108/LODJ-01-2018-0013

Hechevarría, D., Bullough, A., Brush, C., & Edelman, L. (2019). High-growth women's entrepreneurship: Fueling social and economic development. *Journal of Small Business Management, 57*(1), 5–13. doi:10.1111/jsbm.12503

Heikkinen, H. (2002) *Sopeutumisen mallit. Poronhoidon adaptaatio jälkiteolliseen toim-intaympäristöön Suomen läntisellä poronhoitoalueella 1980–2000 (in Finnish; models of adaptation – adaptation of Reindeer Herding to the post-industrial envi-ronment in the Western Finnish reindeer herding area 1980–2000).* [Doctoral dissertation, University of Oulu, Suomalaisen Kirjallisuuden Seura, Helsink].

Henderson, M., Sullivan, A., Anders, J., & Moulton, V. (2018). Social class, gender and ethnic differences in subjects taken at age 14. *Curriculum Journal, 29*(3), 298–318. doi:10.1080/09585176.2017.1406810

Henley, J., & Roy, E. A. (2020). Are female leaders more successful at managing the coronavirus crisis. *Guardian, 25th April* https://www. theguardian. com/world/2020/apr/25/why-do-femal e-leadersseem-to-be-more-successful-at-managing-the-coronavi rus-crisis *(accessed 04/09/2020).*

Henry, C., Foss, L., & Ahl, H. (2016). Gender and entrepreneurship research: A review of methodological approaches. *International Small Business Journal, 34*(3), 217–241. doi:10.1177/0266242614549779

Herold, D. M., Fedor, D. B., Caldwell, S., & Liu, Y. (2008). The effects of transformational and change leadership on employees' commitment to a change: A multilevel study. *The Journal of Applied Psychology, 93*(2), 346–357. doi:10.1037/0021-9010.93.2.346 PMID:18361637

Heron, J., & Reason, P. (1997). A Participative Inquiry Paradigm. *Qualitative Inquiry, 3*(3), 274–294. doi:10.1177/107780049700300302

Herscovitch, L. (1999). *Employee commitment to organizational change. Extension and evaluation of a three componente model.* [Unpublished master's thesis, University of Western Ontario].

Heymann, D. L., & Shindo, N. (2020). Covid-19: What is next for public health? *The Lancet.*

Heymann, J., Levy, J. K., Bose, B., Ríos-Salas, V., Mekonen, Y., Swaminathan, H., ... Darmstadt, G. L. (2019). Improving health with programmatic, legal, and policy approaches to reduce gender inequality and change restrictive gender norms. *Lancet, 393*(10190), 2522–2534. doi:10.1016/S0140-6736(19)30656-7 PMID:31155271

Hindle, K., Eva, M., Rollason, C., & Turner, P. (2014). Business analysis (D. Paul, J. Cadle, & D. Yeates, Eds.). BCS, The Chartered Institute for IT.

Hinduan, Z. R., Wilson-Evered, E., Moss, S., & Scannell, E. (2009). Leadership, work outcomes and openness to change following an Indonesian bank merger. *Asia Pacific Journal of Human Resources, 47*(1), 59–78. doi:10.1177/1038411108099290

Hisrich, R. D., & Ayse Öztürk, S. (1999). Women entrepreneurs in a developing economy. *Journal of Management Development, 18*(2), 114–124. doi:10.1108/02621719910257639

Hjorth, D. (2005). Organizational Entrepreneurship: With de Certeau on Creating Heterotopias (or Spaces for Play). *Journal of Management Inquiry, 14*(4), 386–398. .

Hjorth, D., Strati, A., Drakopoulou Dodd, S., & Weik, E. (2018). *Organizational creativity, play and entrepreneurship: Introduction and framing*. SAGE Publications.

Hoffmann-Riem, W. (2019). Artifcial Intelligence as a Challenge for Law and Regulation. In T. Wischmeyer & T. Rademacher (Eds.), *Regulating Artificial Intelligence*. Springer International Publishing AG.

Hofstede, G. (1994). The business of international business *is culture. International Business Review, 3*(1), 1–14. doi:10.1016/0969-5931(94)90011-6

Hofstede, G. (2001). *Culture's Consequences: Comparing Values, Behaviors, Institutions and Organizations across Nations* (2nd ed.). Sage.

Hollander, B. S., & Elman, N. S. (1988). Family-owned businesses: An emerging field of inquiry. *Family Business Review, 1*(2), 145–164. doi:10.1111/j.1741-6248.1988.00145.x

Holland, J. (1992). Genetic algorithms. *Scientific American, 267*(1), 66–72. doi:10.1038cientificamerican0792-66

Holliday, G., Statler, M., & Flanders, M. (2007). Developing practically wise leaders through serious play. *Consulting Psychology Journal, 59*(2), 126–134. doi:10.1037/1065-9293.59.2.126

Holmqvist, M., & Pessi, K. (2006). Agility through scenario development and continuous implementation: A global aftermarket logistics case. *European Journal of Information Systems, 15*(2), 146–158. doi:10.1057/palgrave.ejis.3000602

Holt, D. T., Armenakis, A. A., Feild, H. S., & Harris, S. G. (2007). Readiness for Organizational Change: The Systematic Development of a Scale. *The Journal of Applied Behavioral Science, 43*(2), 232–255. doi:10.1177/0021886306295295

Holt, D. T., Pearson, A. W., Payne, G. T., & Sharma, P. (2018). Family Business Research as a Boundary-Spanning Platform. *Family Business Review, 31*(1), 14–31. doi:10.1177/0894486518758712

Hong, B., Limburg, K. E., Erickson, J. D., Gowdy, J. M., Nowosielski, A. A., Polimeni, J. M., & Stainbrook, K. M. (2009). Connecting the ecological-economic dots in human-dominated watersheds: Models to link socio-economic activities on the landscape to stream ecosystem health. *Landscape and Urban Planning, 91*(2), 78–87. doi:10.1016/j.landurbplan.2008.11.012

Hornung, S., & Rousseau, D. M. (2007). Active on the job—proactive in change: How autonomy at work contributes to employee support for organizational change. *The Journal of Applied Behavioral Science, 43*(4), 401–426. doi:10.1177/0021886307307555

Howell, G. (1999, July 26-28). *What is Lean Construction* [Paper Presentation]. *7th Annual Conference of the International Group for Lean Construction*, University of California.

Huczynski, A., & Buchanan, D. (1991). *Organizational Behavior*. Prentice-Hall.

Hughes, K. D., Jennings, J. E., Brush, C., Carter, S., & Welter, F. (2012). Extending Women's Entrepreneurship Research in New Directions. *Entrepreneurship Theory and Practice, 36*(3), 429–442. doi:10.1111/j.1540-6520.2012.00504.x

Hughes, M., & Morgan, R. E. (2007). Deconstructing the relationship between entrepreneurial orientation and business performance at the embryonic stage of firm growth. *Industrial Marketing Management, 36*(5), 651–661. doi:10.1016/j.indmarman.2006.04.003

Hutton, D. (1994). *The change agents' handbook. A survival guide for quality improvement champions*. ASQC Quality Press.

Iacucci, G., & Kuutti, K. (2002). Everyday Life as a Stage in Creating and Performing Scenarios for Wireless Devices. *Personal and Ubiquitous Computing*, *6*(6), 299–306. doi:10.1007007790200031

IDC. (2022). *IDC MarketScape: Canadian AI Services 2022 Vendor Assessment*. IDC. https://www.idc.com/research/viewtoc.jsp?containerId=CA48060822

IIBA. (2015). *BABOK V3*. The international institute of business analysis.

ILO. (2020). *ILO Monitor: COVID-19 and the world of work*. ILO.

Inman, A. G. (2020). Culture and positionality: Academy and mentorship. *Women & Therapy*, *43*(1-2), 112–124. doi:10.1080/02703149.2019.1684678

Islam, D. M. Z., Khalid, N., Rayeva, E., & Ahmed, U. (2020). COVID-19 and financial performance of SMEs: Examining the nexus of entrepreneurial self-efficacy, entrepreneurial resilience and innovative work behavior. *Revista Argentina de Clínica Psicológica*, *29*(3), 587.

Itkowitz, H., & Leydesdorff, L. (2000). The dynamics of innovation: From National Systems and "Mode 2" to a Triple Helix of university–industry–government relations. *Research Policy*, *29*(2), 109–123. https://www.sciencedirect.com/science/article/pii/S0048733399000554. doi:10.1016/S0048-7333(99)00055-4

Ivanov, D. (2020). Viable supply chain model: Integrating agility, resilience and sustainability perspectives-lessons from and thinking beyond the COVID-19 pandemic. *Annals of Operations Research*. doi:10.100710479-020-03640-PMID:32836614

Jabeen, F., Ahmad, S. Z., & Alkaabi, S. (2016). The Internationalization Decision-Making of United Arab Emirates Family Businesses [Chapter]. Handbook of Research on Impacts of International Business and Political Affairs on the Global Economy. IGI Global.

Jacobsson, S., & Bergek, A. (2011). Innovation system analyses and sustainability transitions: Contributions and suggestions for research. *Environmental Innovation and Societal Transitions*, *1*(1), 41–57. doi:10.1016/j.eist.2011.04.006

Jalali, A., Jaafar, M., & Ramayah, T. (2014). Entrepreneurial orientation and performance: The interaction effect of customer capital. *World Journal of Entrepreneurship, Management and Sustainable Development*, *10*(1), 48–68. doi:10.1108/WJEMSD-05-2013-0030

Jamali, A., Bhutto, A., Khaskhely, M., & Sethar, W. (2022). Impact of leadership styles on faculty performance: Moderating role of organizational culture in higher education. *Management Science Letters*, *12*(1), 1–20. doi:10.5267/j.msl.2021.8.005

Jamali, D. (2009). Constraints and opportunities facing women entrepreneurs in developing countries: A relational perspective. *Gender in Management*, *24*(4), 232–251. doi:10.1108/17542410910961532

Jamal, M. (1991). Job stress, satisfaction, and mental health: An empirical examination of self-employed and non-self-employed Canadians. *Journal of Small Business Management*, *35*(4), 48–58.

Jameson, J. (Ed.). (2019). *International perspectives on leadership in higher education: Critical thinking for global challenges*. Routledge. doi:10.4324/9781315122410

Jandrić, P., Hayes, D., Truelove, I., Levinson, P., Mayo, P., Ryberg, T., & Jackson, L. (2020). Teaching in the age of Covid-19. *Postdigital Science and Education*, 1-162.

Jarkabowsky, P., & Kaplan, S. (2015). Strategy Tools-In-Use: A Framework for Understanding "Technologies Rationality" In Practice. *Strategic Management Journal*, (36), 537–558.

Jayatilleke, S., & Lai, R. (2018). A systematic review of requirements change management. *Information and Software Technology*, *93*, 163–185. doi:10.1016/j.infsof.2017.09.004

Jedynak, P. (2015). Lean Management Implementation: Determinant Factors and Experience. *Jagiellonian Journal of Management*, *1*(1), 51–64. doi:10.4467/2450114XJJM.15.004.3811

Jeffrey, G. J., Stone, C. C., Zegeye, A., & Charles, T. A. (2009). How much math do students need to succeed in business and economics statistics? An ordered probit analysis. *Journal of Statistics Education : An International Journal on the Teaching and Learning of Statistics*, *17*(3), 3. doi:10.1080/10691898.2009.11889532

Jennings, J. E., Dempsey, D., & James, A. E. (2018). Bifurcated HR practices in family firms: Insights from the normative-adaptive approach to stepfamilies. *Human Resource Management Review*, *28*(1), 68–82. doi:10.1016/j.hrmr.2017.05.007

Jessop, D. C., Herberts, C., & Solomon, L. (2005). The impact of financial circumstances on student health. *British Journal of Health Psychology*, *10*(3), 421–439. doi:10.1348/135910705X25480 PMID:16238857

Jessop, D., Reid, M., & Solomon, L. (2020). Financial concern predicts deteriorations in mental and physical health among university students. *Psychology & Health*, *35*(2), 196–209. doi:10.1080/08870446.2019.1626393 PMID:31181966

Jeyaraj, A., & Sauter, V. L. (2014). Validation of Business Process Models Using Swimlane Diagrams. *Journal of Information Technology Management*, *25*(4), 27–37.

Jianakoplos, N. A., & Bernasek, A. (1998). Are women more risk averse? *Economic Inquiry*, *36*(4), 620–630. doi:10.1111/j.1465-7295.1998.tb01740.x

Jobin, A., Ienca, M., & Vayena, E. (2019). The global landscape of AI ethics guidelines. *Nature Machine Intelligence*, *1*(9), 389–399. doi:10.103842256-019-0088-2

Johnson, J. E. V., & Powell, P. L. (1994). Decision Making, Risk and Gender: Are Managers Different? *British Journal of Management*, *5*(2), 123–138. doi:10.1111/j.1467-8551.1994.tb00073.x

Jovanov, T., & Stojanovski, M. (2012). Marketing knowledge and strategy for SMEs: Can they live without it? Thematic Collection of papers of international significance. *Reengineering and entrepreneurship under the contemporary conditions of enterprise business,* 131-143.

Judge, T. A., Thoresen, C. J., Pucik, V., & Welbourne, T. M. (1999). Managerial coping with organizational change: A dispositional perspective'. *The Journal of Applied Psychology*, *84*(1), 107–122. https://psycnet.apa.org/doi/10.1037/0021-9010.84.1.107. doi:10.1037/0021-9010.84.1.107

Junusi, R. (2020). Digital marketing during the pandemic period; A study of islamic perspective. *Journal of Digital Marketing and Halal Industry*, *2*(1), 150–28. doi:10.21580/jdmhi.2020.2.1.5717

Kafel, T. (2021). *Multidimensional public sector organisations digital maturity model*. Academia. https://www.academia.edu/88263663/Multidimensional_public_sector_organizations_digital_maturity_model

Kalaycı, Ş. (2016). *SPSS Uygulamalı Çok Değişkenli İstatistik Teknikleri.*

Kamdar, R. (2019). The inattentive consumer: Sentiment and expectations, meeting paper from Society for Economic Dynamics. *Economic Dynamics.* https://economicdynamics.org/meetpapers/2019/paper_647.pdf

Kanikani, I. (2022). Whitepaper: Building change maturity. *Academia*. https://www.academia.edu/96126468/Whitepaper_Building_Organisational_Change_Maturity

Kanikani, I. (2022, October 25-10-22). *The change maturity report*. Linkedin. https://www.linkedin.com/pulse/draft/AgHwKO0tvNXsFwAAAYQplOQry0J7WDmNtjplc2tw2Pgrzfqlg_PCJHAWR2dAiP3r0laagtA

Kanikani, I. (2022, September 21). *ChangeOps*. LinkedIn. https://www.linkedin.com/post/edit/7000346460504358912/

Kanter, R. M., Stein, B., & Jick, T. (1992). *The Challenge of Organizational Change: How Companies Experience it and Leaders Guide it*. Free Press/Maxwell Macmillan Canada/Maxwell Macmillan International.

Karrie, J., Craig, K., Brown, J., & Andrew, B. (2000). *Environmental factors in the etiology of anxiety neuropsychopharmacology: The fifth generation of progress*. ANCP. http://www.acnp.org/g4/GN401000127/Default.htm

Katai, L. (2018). 3 Reasons why audio will conquer all social media. *Adweek*. https://www.adweek.com/performance-marketing/3-reasons-why-audio-will-conquer-social-media/

Kaushik, M., & Guleria, N. (2020). The Impact of Pandemic COVID -19 in Workplace. *European Journal of Business and Management*, *12*(5), 9–18.

Keesstra, S., Nunes, J., Novara, A., Finger, D., Avelar, D., Kalantari, Z., & Cerdà, A. (2018). The superior effect of nature based solutions in land management for enhancing ecosystem services. *The Science of the Total Environment*, *610*, 997–1009. doi:10.1016/j.scitotenv.2017.08.077 PMID:28838037

Kegan, R., & Lahey, L. (2016). *An Everyone Culture: Becoming a Deliberately Developmental Organization*. Harvard Business Review Press.

Keller, S., & Aiken, C. (2009). *The Inconvenient Truth About Change Management. Why it isn't working and what to do about it*. McKinsey & Company.

Kelley, D. J., Baumer, B. S., Brush, C., Greene, P. G., Mahdavi, M., Majbouri, M., & Heavlow, R. (2017). *Women's entrepreneurship 2016/2017 report*. Global Entrepreneurship Research Association.

Kelly, D., & Amburgey, T. L. (1991). Organizational Inertia and Momemtum: A Dynamic Model of Strategic Change. *Academy of Management Journal*, *34*(3), 591–612. doi:10.2307/256407

Kemper, T. D. (1978). *A social interactional theory of emotions*. Wiley.

Kemp, R., Schot, J., & Hoogma, R. (1998). Regime Shifts to Sustainability Through Processes of Niche Formation: The Approach of Strategic Niche Management. *Technology Analysis and Strategic Management*, *10*(2), 175–196. doi:10.1080/09537329808524310

Kepler, E., & Shane, S. (2007). *Are male and female entrepreneurs really that different?* US Small Business Administration.

Kets de Vries, M. F. R., & Korotov, K. (2007). Creating transformational executive education programs. *Academy of Management Learning & Education*, *6*(3), 375–387. doi:10.5465/amle.2007.26361627

Kets de Vries, M. F. R., Miller, D., & Noël, A. (1993). Understanding the leader-strategy interface: Application of the strategic relationship interview method. *Human Relations*, *46*(1), 5–22. doi:10.1177/001872679304600102

Khurana, K., & Sharma, S. (2013). A comparative analysis of association rule mining algorithms. International Journal of Scientific and Research Publications, 3(5), 0.

Kidd, P. T. (2000). *Agile manufacturing enterprise strategy*. Cheshirenbury.

Kiebler, J., & Stewart, A. J. (2022, April). Student experiences of the COVID-19 pandemic: Perspectives from first-generation/lower-income students and others. *Analyses of Social Issues and Public Policy (ASAP)*, *22*(1), 198–224. doi:10.1111/asap.12288

Kiefer, T. (2005). Feeling bad: Antecedents and consequences of negative emotions in ongoing change. *Journal of Organizational Behavior*, *26*(8), 875–897. doi:10.1002/job.339

Kim, D., Kim, M., & Shim, M. (2021). The macroeconomic consequences of stimulating offline consumption during COVID-19. *Global Economic Review*, *50*(1), 20–42. doi:10.1080/1226508X.2021.1875868

Kim, J. C., Watts, C. H., Hargreaves, J. R., Ndhlovu, L. X., Phetla, G., Morison, L. A., Busza, J., Porter, J. D. H., & Pronyk, P. (2007). Understanding the impact of a microfinance-based intervention on women's empowerment and the reduction of intimate partner violence in South Africa. *American Journal of Public Health*, *97*(10), 1794–1802. doi:10.2105/AJPH.2006.095521 PMID:17761566

Kim, T. Y., Bateman, T. S., Gilbreath, B., & Andersson, L. M. (2009). Top management credibility and employee cynicism: A comprehensive model. *Human Relations*, *62*(10), 1435–1459. doi:10.1177/0018726709340822

King, K., & Higgins, J. (2010). *Organizational consulting @ the edges of possibility*. Faringdon: Libri.

King, K., & Higgins, J. (2014). *The change doctors: reimagining organisational practice*. Faringdon: Libri.

King, N., Horrocks, C., & Brooks, J. (2018). *Interviews in Qualitative Research*. Sage Pub.

King, P. M., & Kitchener, K. S. (2004). Reflective judgment: Theory and research on the development of epistemic assumptions through adulthood. *Educational Psychologist*, *39*(1), 5–18. doi:10.120715326985ep3901_2

Kipping, M. (2003). *Management consulting: emergence and dynamics of a knowledge industry*. Oxford University Press.

Kipping, M., & Clark, T. (2013). *The Oxford handbook of management consulting*. Oxford University Press.

Klapwijk, H. P. (2004). *Economics Reconfigured - A vision on tomorrow's Value Chains*. (Inaugural Speech): University Nyenrode

Klöker, A. (2020). Explainable AI verschiebt Grenzen der KI-Nutzung. *vb Versicherungsbetriebe*, 2/2020.

Knotek, E. S., Schoenle, R. S., Dietrich, A. M., Kuester, K., Müller, G. J., Myrseth, K. O. R., & Webe, M. (2020). *Consumers and Covid-19: A real-time survey*. Federal Reserve Bank of Cleveland. doi:10.26509/frbc-ec-202008

Koellinger, P., Minniti, M., & Schade, C. (2008). *Seeing the world with different eyes: Gender differences in perceptions and the propensity to start a business*. Research Gate.

Koiranen, M., & Chirico, F. (2006). *Family Firms as Arenas for Trans-generational Value Creation: A Qualitative and Computational Approach*. University of Jyvaskyla Press.

Konopaski, M., Jack, S., & Hamilton, E. (2015). How family business members learn about continuity. *Academy of Management Learning & Education*, *14*(3), 347–364. doi:10.5465/amle.2014.0244

Kontinen, T., & Ojala, A. (2010). The internationalization of family businesses: A review of extant research. *Journal of Family BusinessStrategy*, *1*(2), 97–107. doi:10.1016/j.jfbs.2010.04.001

Korchagina, E., Desfonteines, L., Ray, S., & Strekalova, N. (2022). Digitalization of Transport Communications as a Tool for Improving the Quality of Life. *In International Scientific Conference on Innovations in Digital Economy* (pp. 22-34). Springer, Cham. 10.1007/978-3-031-14985-6_2

Kotler, P., Keller, K. L., Koshy, A., & Jha, M. (2013). *Marketing management: a South Asian perspectives*. Scientific Research Publishing.

Kotter, J. P. (1999) A Változások Irányítása Kossuth Kiadó, Budapest, Kotter, John P. Heskett, J. L.(1992). Corporate Culture and Performance, The Free Press, New York.

Kotter, J. P. (1995). Leading Change. *Why Transformation Effort Fail in Harvard Business Review*, *73*(March-April), 59–67.

Kotter, J. P. (1996). *Leading the Change*. Harvard Business School Press.

Kotter, J. P. (2012). *Leading change*. Harvard Business Review Press.

KPI.ORG. (2022). What is a Key Performance Indicator (KPI)? *KPI*. https://kpi.org/KPI-Basics

Kramer, D. (2000). Wisdom as a classical source of human strength: Conceptualization and empirical inquiry. *Journal of Social and Clinical Psychology*, *19*(1), 1. doi:10.1521/jscp.2000.19.1.83

Kreiser, P., Marino, L., & Weaver, K. (2002). Assessing the psychometric properties of the entrepreneurial scale: A multi-country analysis. *Entrepreneurship Theory and Practice*, *26*(4), 71–92. doi:10.1177/104225870202600405

Kroll, A., & Pasha, O. (2019). Managing change and mitigating reform cynicism. *Public Money & Management*. Advance online publication. doi:10.1080/09540962.2019.1683982

Kropp, F., Lindsay, N., & Shoham, A. (2006). Entrepreneurial, market, and learning orientations and international entrepreneurial business venture performance in South African firms. *International Marketing Review*, *23*(5), 504–523. doi:10.1108/02651330610703427

Kübler-Ross, E. (1969). *On Death and Dying*. Macmillan.

Labrum, M. (n.d.). *Multiple candles: Mike Labrum*. Unsplash. https://unsplash.com/@labrum777

Lane, S., Astrachan, J. H. H., Keyt, A., & McMillan, K. (2006). *Guidelines for family business boards of directors. Family Business Review, 19(2), 147-167. Lawrence, P., & Lorsch, J. (1967). Organization and its Environment*. Harvard University Press.

Langowitz, N., & Minniti, M. (2007). The entrepreneurial propensity of women. *Entrepreneurship*, *31*, 341–364.

Langowitz, N., & Morgan, C. (2003). Women entrepreneurs: breaking through the glass barrier. In J. Butler (Ed.), *New Perspectives on Women Entrepreneurs* (pp. 101–119). Information Age Publishing.

Lannelli, C., & Duta, A. (2018). Inequalities in school leavers' labour market outcomes: Do school subject choices matter? *Oxford Review of Education*, *44*(1), 56–74. doi:10.1080/03054985.2018.1409970

Lansberg, I., & Gersick, K. (2015). Educating Family Business Owners: The Fundamental Intervention. *Academy of Management Learning & Education*, *14*(3), 400–413. doi:10.5465/amle.2014.0254

Lastres, H. M. M. (orgs.). (1999). *Globalização e Inovação Localizada: experiências*.

Lastres, H. M. M., Cassiolato, J. E., Lemos, C. Maldonado, j.

Lauer, T. (2021). *Change Management: Fundamentals and Success Factors*. Springer. doi:10.1007/978-3-662-62187-5

Lave, J. (1993). The practice of learning. In *S. Chaiklin, J. Lave (1993), Understanding practice. Perspective on activity and context*. Cambridge University Press. doi:10.1017/CBO9780511625510.002

Lave, J., & Wenger, E. (1991). *Situated Learning: Legitimate Peripheral Participation.* Cambridge University Press. doi:10.1017/CBO9780511815355

Lawrence, P. R., & Lorsch, J. W. (1967). *Organization and Environment.* Harvard Business School Press.

Lazarus, R. S. (1991). *Emotion and Adaptation.* Oxford University Press.

Le Breton–Miller, I., Miller, D., & Steier, L. P. (2004). Toward an Integrative Model of Effective FOB Succession. *Entrepreneurship Theory and Practice, 28*(4), 305–328. doi:10.1111/j.1540-6520.2004.00047.x

Le Roux, I., & Bengesi, M. K. (2014). Dimensions of entrepreneurial orientation and small and medium enterprise performance in emerging economies. *Development Southern Africa, 31*(4), 606–624. doi:10.1080/0376835X.2014.913474

Leach, M. J., Rockström, P., Raskin, I., Scoones, A. C., Stirling, A., Smith, J., Thompson, J., Millstone, E., Ely, A., Arond, E., Folke, C., & Olsson, P. (2012). Transforming innovation for sustainability. *Ecology and Society, 17*(2), 11. doi:10.5751/ES-04933-170211

Leduc, S., & Liu, Z. (2016). Uncertainty shocks are aggregate demand shocks. *Journal of Monetary Economics, 82*, 20–35. doi:10.1016/j.jmoneco.2016.07.002

Lee, M. S., & Rogoff, E. G. (1996). Research note: Comparison of small businesses with family participation versus small businesses without family participation: An investigation of differences in goals, attitudes, and family/business conflict. *Family Business Review, 9*(4), 423–437. doi:10.1111/j.1741-6248.1996.00423.x

Leifer, R. (1989). Understanding organizational transformation using a dissipative structural model. *Human Relations, 42*(10), 899–916. doi:10.1177/001872678904201003

Lerner, L. (2003) *Renman-tutkimusprojekti suosittelee parannuksia – maankäyttö.*

Lerner, M., Brush, C., & Hisrich, R. (1997). Israeli women entrepreneurs: An examination of factors affecting performance. *Journal of Business Venturing, 12*(4), 315–339. doi:10.1016/S0883-9026(96)00061-4

Lerner, M., & Malach-Pines, A. (2011). Gender and culture in family business: A ten-nation study. *International Journal of Cross Cultural Management, 11*(2), 11. doi:10.1177/1470595811399190

Leutner, F., Ahmetoglu, G., Akhtar, R., & Chamorro-Premuzic, T. (2014). The relationship between the entrepreneurial personality and the Big Five personality traits. *Personality and Individual Differences, 63*, 58–63. doi:10.1016/j.paid.2014.01.042

Levinson, H. (1971). Conflicts that plague family businesses. *Harvard Business Review, 49*(2), 90–98.

Lewin, (1975). *Csoportdinamika Közgazdasági és Jogi Kiadó*, Budapest, Lewin, K (1944). Problems of Research in Social Psychology. *D. Cartwright (Ed.) Field theory in social science.* London: Social Science Paperbacks.

Lewin, K. (n.d.). *Frontiers in group dynamics.* Sage Journals. https://journals.sagepub.com/doi/10.1177/001872674700100103

Lewin, K. (1947). Frontiers in group dynamics. Concept, method and reality in social science. Social equilibria and social change. *Human Relations, 1*(1), 5–41. doi:10.1177/001872674700100103

Lewin, K. (1972). *Mezőelmélet A Társadalomtudományban Gondolat*, Budapest, Lewitt, B.March, J. G (1988) Organizational Learning. *Annual Review of Psychology, 14*, 319–340.

Lewin, K., Lippitt, R., & White, R. K. (1939). Patterns of Aggressive Behaviour in Experimentally Created Social Environments. *The Journal of Social Psychology, 10*(2), 271–299. doi:10.1080/00224545.1939.9713366

Liang, H., Wang, N., Xue, Y., & Ge, S. (2017). Unraveling the Alignment Paradox: How Does Business-IT Alignment Shape Organizational Agility? *Information Systems Research*, *28*(4), 863–879. doi:10.1287/isre.2017.0711

Li, J. Y., Sun, R., Tao, W., & Lee, Y. (2021). Employee coping with organizational change in the face of a pandemic: The role of transparent internal communication. *Public Relations Review*, *47*(1), 101984. doi:10.1016/j.pubrev.2020.101984 PMID:36568504

Liker, J. K. (2004). *The Toyota way*. McGraw-Hill Education.

Lim, A. (2020, November 5). *The real purpose of business: Why does your business exist? | ariel lim consulting*. Ariel Lim. https://ariel-lim.com/blog/real-purpose-of-business-why-exist/

Lin, C.-Y. (2020). Social reaction toward the 2019 novel coronavirus (COVID-19). *Social Health Behavior*, *3*(1), 1. doi:10.4103/SHB.SHB_11_20

Linkedin.com. (2022). *How to make change management work in Asia*. Linkedin. [https://www.linkedin.com/pulse/how-make-change-management-work-asia-anthony-liu]

Lipton, B. (2015). A new" ERA" of women and leadership: The gendered impact of quality assurance in Australian higher education. *Australian Universities Review*, *57*(2), 60–70.

Liu, Y., & Perrewé, P. L. (2005). Another look at the role of emotion in the organizational change: A process model. *Human Resource Management Review*, *15*(4), 263–280. doi:10.1016/j.hrmr.2005.12.001

Li, Y., & Xie, Y. (2019). Is a picture worth a thousand words? An empirical study of image content and social media engagement. *JMR, Journal of Marketing Research*, *57*(1), 1–19. doi:10.1177/0022243719881113

Li, Y., Zhao, J., Ma, Z., McReynolds, L. S., Lin, D., Chen, Z., Wang, T., Wang, D., Zhang, Y., Zhang, J., Fan, F., & Liu, X. (2021). Mental health among college students during the COVID-19 pandemic in China: A 2-wave longitudinal survey. *Journal of Affective Disorders*, *281*, 597–604. doi:10.1016/j.jad.2020.11.109 PMID:33257043

Luciano, M. M., Nahrgang, J. D., & Shropshire, C. (2020). Strategic leadership systems: Viewing top management teams and boards of directors from a multiteam systems perspective. *Academy of Management Review*, *45*(3), 675–701. doi:10.5465/amr.2017.0485

Ludwig, A. M. (1992). Creative achievement and psychopathology: Comparison among professions. *American Journal of Psychotherapy*, *46*(3), 330–356. doi:10.1176/appi.psychotherapy.1992.46.3.330 PMID:1530096

Luecke, R. (2003). *Harvard Business Essentials. Managing Change and Transition*. Harvard Business School Press.

Lumpkin, G. T., & Dess, G. G. (1996). Clarifying the entrepreneurial orientation construct and linking it to performance. *Academy of Management Review*, *21*(1), 135–172. doi:10.2307/258632

Lumpkin, G. T., & Dess, G. G. (2001). Linking two dimensions of entrepreneurial orientation to firm performance: The moderating role of environment and industry life cycle. *Journal of Business Venturing*, *16*(5), 429–451. doi:10.1016/S0883-9026(00)00048-3

Lyfe. (2019). 12 Social media KPIs you should not ignore. *Lyfe Marketing*. https://www.lyfemarketing.com/blog/social-media-kpis/

Lyonnet, B., & Toscano, R. (2014). Towards an Adapted Lean System – A Push–pull Manufacturing Strategy. *Production Planning and Control*, *25*(4), 346–354. doi:10.1080/09537287.2012.702867

Maas, B., Grogan, K. E., Chirango, Y., Harris, N., Liévano-Latorre, L. F., McGuire, K. L., & Primack, R. B. (2020). Academic leaders must support inclusive scientific communities during COVID-19. *Nature Ecology & Evolution*, *4*(8), 1–2. doi:10.103841559-020-1233-3 PMID:32493950

MacLeod, A., Williams, J. M., & Bekerian, D. A. (1991). Worry is reasonable: The role of explanations in pessimism about future personal events. *Journal of Abnormal Psychology*, *100*(4), 478–486. doi:10.1037/0021-843X.100.4.478 PMID:1757661

Maden, C. (2015). A gendered lens on entrepreneurship: women entrepreneurship in Turkey. *Gender in Management: An International Journal*, *30*(4), 312-331.

Madkor, O. R. E., Elsorady, K. E., Abdelhady, D. H., AbdulJawad, P., & Aly El Gabry, D. (2021). COVID-19 life events-anxiety inventory (C-19LAI): Development, reliability, and validity study on Egyptian population. *Middle East Curr Psychiatry*, *28*(1), 21. doi:10.118643045-021-00101-z

Madsen, S. R., Miller, D., & John, C. R. (2005). Readiness for organizational change: Do organizational commitment and social relationships in the workplace make a difference? *Human Resource Development Quarterly*, *16*(2), 213–234. doi:10.1002/hrdq.1134

Mahajan, S. (2013). Women entrepreneurship in India. *Global Journal of Management and Business Studies*, *3*(10), 1143–1148.

Mahmood, R., & Hanafi, N. (2013). Entrepreneurial Orientation and Business Performance of Women-Owned Small and Medium Enterprises in Malaysia: Competitive Advantage as a Mediator. *International Journal of Business and Social Science*, *4*(1), 82–90.

Mainemelis, C., Altman, Y., & Sandelands, L. (2010). The play of change. *Journal of Organizational Change Management*. 23(I 1), 71-86

Malecki, E. J. (2018). Entrepreneurship and entrepreneurial ecosystems. *Geography Compass*, *12*(3), e12359. doi:10.1111/gec3.12359

Mandal, P. (2019). Public policy issues in direct and digital marketing - concerns and initiatives: Public policy in direct and digital marketing. *International Journal of Public Administration in the Digital Age*, *6*(4), 54–71. doi:10.4018/IJPADA.2019100105

Mansaray, H. E. (2019). The role of leadership style in organisational change management: A literature review. *Journal of Human Resource Management*, *7*(1), 18–31. doi:10.11648/j.jhrm.20190701.13

Manuel-Navarrete, D., Slocombe, S., & Mitchell, B. (2006). Science for place-based socioecological management: Lessons from the Maya Forest (Chiapas and Petén). *Ecology and Society*, *11*(1), 8. https://www.ecologyandsociety.org/vol11/iss1/art8/. doi:10.5751/ES-01608-110108

March, J. G. (1991). Exploration and exploitation in organizational learning. *Organization Science*, *2*(1), 71–87. doi:10.1287/orsc.2.1.71

March, J. G. (Ed.). (2015). *Handbook of organizations*. Routledge.

Marlow, S., & McAdam, M. (2013). Gender and entrepreneurship: Advancing debate and challenging myths – exploring the mystery of the under-performing female entrepreneurship. *International Journal of Entrepreneurial Behaviour & Research*, *19*(1), 114–124. doi:10.1108/13552551311299288

Marlow, S., & Patton, D. (2005). All Credit to Men? Entrepreneurship, Finance, and Gender. *Entrepreneurship Theory and Practice*, *29*(6), 717–735. doi:10.1111/j.1540-6520.2005.00105.x

Marques, P., & Morgan, K. (2018). The heroic assumptions of smart specialisation: A sympathetic critique of regional innovation policy. In A. Isaksen, R. Martin, & M. Trippl (Eds.), *New avenues for regional innovation systems-theoretical advances, empirical cases, and policy lessons* (pp. 275–293). Springer. doi:10.1007/978-3-319-71661-9_14

Marques, P., Morgan, K., & Richardson, R. (2018). Social innovation in question: The theoretical and practical implications of a contested concept. *Environment and Planning C. Politics and Space*, *36*(3), 496–512.

Marquis, C., & Tilcsik, A. (2013). Imprinting: Toward a Multilevel Theory. *The Academy of Management Annals*, *7*(1), 195–245. doi:10.5465/19416520.2013.766076

Marsch, N. (2019). Artifcial Intelligence and the Fundamental Right to Data Protection: Opening the Door for Technological Innovation and Innovative Protection. In T. Wischmeyer & T. Rademacher (Eds.), *Regulating Artificial Intelligence*. Springer International Publishing AG.

Martin, N. (2019). Why utilizing data in your digital marketing strategy is so essential. https://www.forbes.com/sites/nicolemartin1/2019/10/22/why-utilizing-data-in-your-digital-marketing-strategy-is-so-essential/?sh=4821dbedd525

Martin, A. J., Jones, E. S., & Callan, V. J. (2005). The role of psychological climate in facilitating employee adjustment during organizational change. *European Journal of Work and Organizational Psychology*, *14*(3), 263–283. doi:10.1080/13594320500141228

Martin, S., & Javalgi, R. (2016). Entrepreneurial orientation, marketing capabilities and performance: The Moderating role of Competitive Intensity on Latin American International New Venture. *Journal of Business Research*, *69*(6), 2040–2051. doi:10.1016/j.jbusres.2015.10.149

Mason, A., Narcum, J., & Mason, K. (2021). Social media marketing gains importance after Covid-19. *Cogent Business & Management*, *8*(1), 1870797. doi:10.1080/23311975.2020.1870797

Masona, C. M. (2015). Understanding the impact of entrepreneurial orientation on SMEs' Performance. The role of the financing structure. *Procedia Economics and Finance*, *23*, 1649–1661. doi:10.1016/S2212-5671(15)00470-0

Mattar, D. M. (2021). An Organizational Change With Quarantined Members. *SAGE Open*, *11*(1). Advance online publication. doi:10.1177/2158244020988851

Mavrot, C., Hadorn, S., & Sager, F. (2019). Mapping the mix: Linking instruments, settings and target groups in the study of policy mixes. *Research Policy*, *48*(10), 103614. doi:10.1016/j.respol.2018.06.012

Mazzucato, M. (2015). *The Entrepreneurial State: Debunking Public vs. Private Sector Myths*. PublicAffairs.

McCann, G., DeMoss, M., Dascher, P., & Barnett, S. (2003). Educational needs of family businesses: Perceptions of university directors. *Family Business Review*, *16*(4), 283–291. doi:10.1177/08944865030160040601

McCollom, M. E. (1988). Integration in the family firm: When the family system replaces controls and culture. *Family Business Review*, *1*(4), 399–417. doi:10.1111/j.1741-6248.1988.00399.x

McConaughy, D. L., & Phillips, G. M. (1999). Founders versus descendants: The profitability, efficiency, growth characteristics and financing in large, public, founding-family-controlled firms. *Family Business Review*, *12*(2), 123–131. doi:10.1111/j.1741-6248.1999.00123.x

McCrae, R. R., & Costa Jr, P. T. (2008). Empirical and theoretical status of the five-factor model of personality traits.

McGowan, P., Redeker, C. L., Cooper, S. Y., & Greenan, K. (2012). Female entrepreneurship and the management of business and domestic roles: Motivations, expectations and realities. *Entrepreneurship and Regional Development, 24*(1-2), 53–72. doi:10.1080/08985626.2012.637351

McGregor, D. V. (1960). *The Human Side of Enterprise*. McGraw-Hill Books Co.

McKinsey & Co. (2022). *Risk and Resilience*. McKinsey & Co. https://www.mckinsey.com/capabilities/risk-and-resilience/our-insights/covid-19-implications-for-business

McKinsey 7S Model - Overview, Structure and application, example. (2022, October 27). Corporate Finance Institute. https://corporatefinanceinstitute.com/resources/management/mckinsey-7s-model/

McNair, T. B., Bensimon, E. M., & Malcom-Piqueux, L. (2020). *From equity talk to equity walk: Expanding practitioner knowledge for racial justice in higher education*. John Wiley & Sons. doi:10.1002/9781119428725

McNiff, J. (2013). Becoming cosmopolitan and other dilemmas of internationalisation: Reflections from the Gulf States. *Cambridge Journal of Education, 43*(4), 501–515. doi:10.1080/0305764X.2013.831033

Mead, G. H. (1934). *Mind, Self and Society*. University Press.

Meletiadou, E. (2022). The lived experiences of female educational leaders in higher education in the UK: Academic resilience and gender. In *Handbook of Research on Practices for Advancing Diversity and Inclusion in Higher Education* (pp. 1–19). IGI Global. doi:10.4018/978-1-7998-9628-9.ch001

MenaHerald. (2019). Family Business Council – Gulf and PwC publish a guide on managing shareholder exits in family businesses. *MenaHerald*. https://www.menaherald.com/en/business/events-services/family-business-council-%E2%80%93-gulf-and-pwc-publish-guide-managing-shareholder

Meyer, J. P., & Allen, N. J. (1991). A three-component conceptualization of organizational commitment. *Human Resource Management Review, 1*(1), 61–89. doi:10.1016/1053-4822(91)90011-Z

Meyer, J. P., & Herscovitch, L. (2001). Commitment in the workplace: Toward a general model. *Human Resource Management Review, 11*(3), 299–326. doi:10.1016/S1053-4822(00)00053-X

Meyer, J. P., Srinivas, E., Lal, J., & Topolnytsky, L. (2007). Employee commitment and support for an organizational change: Test of the three-component model in two cultures. *Journal of Occupational and Organizational Psychology, 80*(2), 185–211. doi:10.1348/096317906X118685

Meyer, J. P., Stanley, D. J., Herscovitch, L., & Topolnytsky, L. (2002). Affective, Continuance, and Normative Commitment to the Organization: A Meta-analysis of Antecedents, Correlates, and Consequences. *Journal of Vocational Behavior, 61*(1), 20–52. doi:10.1006/jvbe.2001.1842

Meyer, J., & Hamilton, L. (2013). Commitment to organizational change: Theory, research, principles, and practice. In S. Oreg, A. Michel, & R. By (Eds.), *The Psychology of Organizational Change: Viewing Change from the Employee's Perspective* (pp. 43–64). Cambridge University Press. doi:10.1017/CBO9781139096690.005

Meyers, M. (2013). The war on academic women: Reflections on post-feminism in the neoliberal academy. *The Journal of Communication Inquiry, 37*(4), 274–283. doi:10.1177/0196859913505619

Meyler, A., & Reiche, L. (2021). Making sense of consumers' inflation perceptions and expectations – the role of (un)certainty. *ECB Economic Bulletin*, https://www.ecb.europa.eu/pub/economic-bulletin/articles/2021/html/ecb.ebart202102_02~32e2ff1af1.en.html

Meythaler, A., & Röber, B. (2020). *Organizational Agility as Competitive Factor*. Viewer. https://viewer.joomag.com/goetzpartners-publications-agile-performer-index-2/0283980001575907006?short

Mezirow, J. (2009). Transformative learning theory. In J. Mezirow & E. W. Taylor (Eds.), *Transformative Learning in Practise: Insights from Community, 39 Workplace, and Higher Education* (pp. 18–32). Jossey Bass.

Michaelis, B., Stegmaier, R., & Sonntag, K. (2009). Affective commitment to change and innovation implementation behavior: The role of charismatic leadership and employees' trust in top management. *Journal of Change Management*, *9*(4), 399–417. doi:10.1080/14697010903360608

Michaelis, B., Stegmaier, R., & Sonntag, K. (2010). Shedding light on followers' innovation implementation behavior: The role of transformational leadership, commitment to change, and climate for initiative. *Journal of Managerial Psychology*, *25*(4), 408–429. doi:10.1108/02683941011035304

Mihaylov, E., Mizen, P., Parker, N., Renault, T., Smietanka, P., & Thwaites, G. (2020). Economic uncertainty before and during the COVID-19 pandemic. *Journal of Public Economics*, *191*, 104274. Advance online publication. doi:10.1016/j.jpubeco.2020.104274 PMID:32921841

Milgram, S. (1974). *Obedience to authority: An experimental view*. Harper & Row: New York.

Miller, D. (1983). The correlates of entrepreneurship in three types of firms. *Management Science*, *29*(7), 770–791. doi:10.1287/mnsc.29.7.770

Miller, D., & Breton-Miller, I. L. (2011). Governance, Social Identity, and Entrepreneurial Orientation in Closely public Companies. *Entrepreneurship Theory and Practice*, *35*(5), 873–894. doi:10.1111/j.1540-6520.2011.00457.x

Miller, D., Steier, L., & Le Breton-Miller, I. (2003). Lost in time: Intergenerational succession, change, and failure in family business. *Journal of Business Venturing*, *18*(4), 513–531. doi:10.1016/S0883-9026(03)00058-2

Milovanović, A., Kostić, M., Zorić, A., Đorđević, A., Pešić, M., Bugarski, J., Todorović, D., Sokolović, N., & Josifovski, A. (2020). Transferring COVID-19 challenges into learning potentials: Online workshops in architectural education. *Sustainability*, *12*(17), 7024. doi:10.3390u12177024

Mink, O. G., Esterhuysen, P. W., Mink, B. P., & Owen, K. Q. (1993). *Change at Work*. Jossey-Bass.

Minniti, M., & Nardone, C. (2007). Being in Someone Else's Shoes: Gender and Nascent Entrepreneurship. *Small Business Economics Journal*, *28*(2-3), 223–239. doi:10.100711187-006-9017-y

Mintzberg, H., Ahlstrand, B., & Lampel, J. (2008). *Strategy Safari: The complete guide through the wilds of strategic management*. FT Publishing.

Mishra, A. K., & Spreitzer, G. M. (1998). Explaining how survivors respond to downsizing: The roles of trust, empowerment, justice, and work redesign. *Academy of Management Review*, *23*(3), 567–588. doi:10.2307/259295

Mishra, P., Pandey, C. M., Singh, U., Gupta, A., Sahu, C., & Keshri, A. (2019). Descriptive statistics and normality tests for statistical data. *Annals of Cardiac Anaesthesia*, *22*(1), 67. doi:10.4103/aca.ACA_157_18 PMID:30648682

MIT. (2020). *How AI Changes the Rules for Management*. https://sloanreview.mit.edu/sponsors-content/infographic-how-ai-changes-the-rules-for-management/

Mitchell, M. (1996). *An Introduction to Genetic Algorithms*. MIT Press.

Mohsen, D. (2007), —Arab women entrepreneurs and SMEs: Challenges and realities. *Masress*. https://www.masress.com/en/dailynews/109630

Moon, M. J. (2020). Fighting Against COVID-19 with agility, transparency, and participation: Wicked policy problems and new governance challenges. *Public Administration Review, 80*(4), 651–656. doi:10.1111/puar.13214 PMID:32836434

Moran, J. W., & Brightman, B. K. (2001). Leading organizational change. *Career Development International, 6*(2), 111–118.

Moran, J., & Brightman, B. (2000). Leading organizational change. *Journal of Workplace Learning, 12*(2), 66–74. doi:10.1108/13665620010316226

Moreno, A. M., & Casillas, J. C. (2008). Entrepreneurial orientation and growth of SMEs: A causal model. *Entrepreneurship Theory and Practice, 32*(3), 507–528. doi:10.1111/j.1540-6520.2008.00238.x

Morgan, G. (2006). *Images of Organization*. Sage.

Morris, M. H., Williams, R. O., Allen, J. A., & Avila, R. A. (1996). Correlates of success in family business transitions. *Journal of Business Venturing, 12*(5), 385–401. doi:10.1016/S0883-9026(97)00010-4

Mücevher, M. H. (2020). Anlatı ve Hayat Hikayesi Araştırmaları. *Süleyman Demirel Üniversitesi İİBF Dergisi, 25*(3), 277–295.

Mundra, S., & Sharma, J. (2013). A Comparative Analysis of the Status of Women Entrepreneurship: India Vs. Global. *Research Journal of Social Science & Management, 3*(4).

Munoz, J.M./Maurya, A. (2022). *International perspectives on artificial intelligence*. Anthem Press.

Muscio, A., Reid, A., & Rivera Leon, L. (2015). An empirical test of the regional innovation paradox: Can smart specialisation overcome the paradox in Central and Eastern Europe? *Journal of Economic Policy Reform, 18*(2), 153–171. doi:10.1080/17487870.2015.1013545

Mustapha, J. O., Adedokun, K. A., & Nasir, I. A. (2020). Public health preparedness towards COVID-19 outbreak in Nigeria. *Asian Pacific Journal of Tropical Medicine, 13*(5), 197–198. doi:10.4103/1995-7645.279650

Naguib, R. & Jamali, D. (2015). Female entrepreneurship in the UAE: a multi-level integrative lens. *Gender in Management: An International Journal, 30*(2), 135-161.

Nahapiet, J. E., & Ghoshal, S. (1998). Social Capital, Intellectual Capital, and the Organizational Advantage. *Academy of Management Review, 33*(2), 242–266. doi:10.2307/259373

Nandi, S., Sarkis, J., Hervani, A. A., & Helms, M. M. (2021). Redesigning supply chains using blockchain-enabled circular economy and COVID-19 experiences. *Sustainable Production and Consumption, 27*, 10–22. doi:10.1016/j.spc.2020.10.019 PMID:33102671

Nandy, S., & Kumar, S. (2014). Women Entrepreneurship in 21st Century India. *Global Journal of Finance and Management, 6*(9), 967–976.

Nash, H. & KPMG (2017). *Harvey Nash/KPMG CIO Survey: Navigation Uncertainly*. KPMG. https://assets.kpmg/content/dam/kpmg/xx/pdf/2017/07/harvey-nash-kpmg-cio-survey-2017.pdf

Nauheimer, H. (2007). Change Management Toolbook. *Creative Commons Attribution-Share-Alike 3.0 Unported License.*

Nautiyal, S. (2011). Can conservation and development interventions in the Indian Central Himalaya ensure environmental sustainability? A socioecological evaluation. *Sustainability Science, 6*(2), 151–167. doi:10.100711625-011-0126-4

Naz, H., Motla, Y. H., Asghar, S., Abbas, M. A., & Khatoon, A. (2013). Effective Usage of AI Technique for Requirement Change Management Practices, *5th International Conference on Computer Science and Information Technology (CSIT),* Amman, Jordan. 10.1109/CSIT.2013.6588769

NBBJ. (2022). *Social media is evolving quickly, and your business needs to also*. NBBJ. https://www.northbaybusinessjournal.com/article/industrynews/social-media-is-evolving-quickly-and-your-business-needs-to-also/

Nehru, J., & Bhardwaj, S. (2013). Women Entrepreneurship in India: Issues & Problems "You can tell the condition of a Nation by looking at the Status of its Women". Spectrum. *Journal of Multidisciplinary Research*, *2*(7), 8–16.

Nelson, K. (1983). Differences in graduate and undergraduate performance in a core research course. *Journal of Education for Social Work*, *19*(2), 77–84.

Nelson, L. (2003). A case study in organizational change: Implications for theory. *The Learning Organization*, *10*(1), 18–30. doi:10.1108/09696470310457478

Nelson, R. R., & Winter, S. G. (1982). *An Evolutionary Theory of Economic Change*. Belknap Press.

Neves, P. (2009). Readiness for change: Contributions for employee's level of individual change and turnover intentions. *Journal of Change Management*, *9*(2), 215–231. doi:10.1080/14697010902879178

Nichols, N. (2014). Why Change Management Often Fails: The People. *Forbes*. https://www.forbes.com/sites/sungardas/2014/05/20/the-dirty-side-of-change-management/?sh=70c9fa516297

Nikolaou, I., Gouras, A., Vakola, M., & Bourantas, D. (2007). Selecting change agents: Exploring traits and skills in a simulated environment. *Journal of Change Management*, *7*(3-4), 291–313. doi:10.1080/14697010701779173

Noguera, M., Álvarez, C., & Urbano, D. (2013). Socio-cultural factors and female entrepreneurship. *The International Entrepreneurship and Management Journal*, *9*(2), 183–198. doi:10.100711365-013-0251-x

O'Connor, P. (2019). Gender imbalance in senior positions in higher education: What is the problem? What can be done? *Policy Reviews in Higher Education*, *3*(1), 28–50. doi:10.1080/23322969.2018.1552084

O'Connor, P. (2020). Creating gendered change in Irish higher education: Is managerial leadership up to the task? *Irish Educational Studies*, *39*(2), 139–155. doi:10.1080/03323315.2019.1697951

O'Connor, P. J., Jimmieson, N. L., Bergin, A. J., Wiewiora, A., & McColl, L. (2022). Leader tolerance of ambiguity: Implications for follower performance outcomes in high and low ambiguous work situations. *The Journal of Applied Behavioral Science*, *58*(1), 65–96. doi:10.1177/00218863211053676

O'Leary, R. (2021). *Contract Life-Cycle Management Software AI-Centric Marketing: A Reflection of Reality?* IDC. https://www.idc.com/getdoc.jsp?containerId=US48266921&pageType=PRINTFRIENDLY

Obschonka, M., Schmitt-Rodermund, E., Silbereisen, R. K., Gosling, S. D., & Potter, J. (2013). The regional distribution and correlates of an entrepreneurship-prone personality profile in the United States, Germany, and the United Kingdom: A socioecological perspective. *Journal of Personality and Social Psychology*, *105*(1), 104–122. doi:10.1037/a0032275 PMID:23586410

OECD Network.. (2021, March 31). *What impact has COVID-19 had on women entrepreneurs and what can governments and policy makers do to put gender equality at the heart of global recovery?* The OECD Forum Network. https://www.oecd-forum.org/posts/what-impact-has-covid-19-had-on-women-entrepreneurs-and-what-can-governments-and-policy-makers-do-to-put-gender-equality-at-the-heart-of-global-recovery

OECD. (1997b). Government Venture Capital for Technology-Based Firms. Ducument OCDE/GD (97), 201. Paris: OECD, 1997b.

OECD. (1997c). Diffusion Technology to Industry: Government Policies and Programmes. Document OCDE/GD (97)60. Paris: 1997c.

OECD. (2001c). *Innovative Networks: co-operation in national innovation systems*. OECD.

Office of the US Trade Representatives. (2021). *Small- and Medium-Sized Enterprises (SMEs)*. USTR. https://ustr.gov/trade-agreements/free-trade-agreements/transatlantic-trade-and-investment-partnership-t-tip/t-tip-12

Okan, Z. (2003). Edutainment: Is learning at risk? *British Journal of Educational Technology*, *34*(3), 255–264. doi:10.1111/1467-8535.00325

Okoli, G. N., Moore, T. A., Thomas, S. L., & Allen, T. T. (2020). Minority women in educational leadership. *Handbook on Promoting Social Justice in Education*, 1711-1727.

Okumus, F., & Hemmington, N. (1998). Barriers and resistance to change in hotel firms: An investigation at unit level. *International Journal of Contemporary Hospitality Management*, *10*(7), 283–288. doi:10.1108/09596119810240906

Oliveira, J., Sá, J. C., & Fernandes, A. (2017). Continuous Improvement Through "Lean Tools": An Application in a Mechanical Company. *Procedia Manufacturing*, *13*, 1082–1089. doi:10.1016/j.promfg.2017.09.139

Oliver, J. J., & Parrett, E. (2018). Managing future uncertainty: Reevaluatingthe role of scenario planning. *Business Horizons*, *61*(2), 339–352. doi:10.1016/j.bushor.2017.11.013

Online Visual Paradigm. (2022). *Understanding Lewin's Change Management Model*. Visual Paradigm Online. https://online.visual-paradigm.com/knowledge/business-design/understand-lewins-change-management-model/.

Oosterhout Marcel Van, Waarts Eric & Axelsson R. (2007). Business Agility: Need, Readiness and Alignment with IT Strategies, Agile Information Systems: Conceptualization. *Construction Manager*, *44*, 52–69.

Oosterhout, M. V., Waarts, E., & Hillegersberg, J. V. (2006). Change Factors Requiring Agility and Implications for IT. *European Journal of Information Systems*, *15*(2), 132–145. doi:10.1057/palgrave.ejis.3000601

Oreg, S., Vakola, M., & Armenakis, A. (2011). Change Recipients' Reactions to Organizational Change: A 60-Year Review of Quantitative Studies. *The Journal of Applied Behavioral Science*, *47*(4), 461–524. doi:10.1177/0021886310396550

Organisation for Economic Co-operation and Development. (2019). *Artificial Intelligence in Society*. OECD. https://ebookcentral.proquest.com/lib/senc/detail.action?docID=6410013

Organisation for Economic Co-operation and Development. (2021). *Financing SMEs and Entrepreneurs 2020: An OECD Scoreboard*. OECD. https://www.oecd-ilibrary.org/finance-and-investment/financing-smes-and-entrepreneurs-2020_061fe03d-en

Orhan, M. (2000). A new model for analysing female entrepreneurship. *Proc. Int. Conf. Small Bus.* (http://www.sbaer.uca.edu/Research/2000/ICSB/index.html

Orlikowski, W. J., & Hofman, D. J. (1997). An Improvizational Model for Change Management: The Case of Groupware Technologies. *Sloan Management Review*, *38*(2), 11–21.

Osborn, A. F. (1956). *Applied Imagination: Principles and Procedures of Creative Thinking*. Charles Scribner's Sons.

Osteen, K., & Subramanian, R. (2013, September). *Assessment maturity model for competency mapping -A talent management enabler*. Academia.edu. https://www.academia.edu/5321331/Assessment_Maturity_Model_for_Competency_Mapping_A_Talent_Management_Enabler

Ostrom, E. (1990). *Governing the commons: the evolution of institutions for collective action.* Cambridge University Press. doi:10.1017/CBO9780511807763

Ouedraogo, N., & Ouakouak, M. L. (2020). Antecedents and outcome of employee change fatigue and change cynicism. *Journal of Organizational Change Management, 34*(1), 158–179. doi:10.1108/JOCM-05-2019-0141

Oughton, C., Landabaso, M., & Morgan, K. (2002). The regional innovation paradox: Innovation policy and industrial policy. *The Journal of Technology Transfer, 27*(1), 97–110. doi:10.1023/A:1013104805703

Overby, E., Bharadwaj, A., & Sambamurthy, V. (2006). Enterprise agility and the enabling role of information technology. *European Journal of Information Systems, 15*(2), 120–131. doi:10.1057/palgrave.ejis.3000600

Overview of the organisation maturity index (OMI) — ODTI. (n.d.). OrgCMF.

Özatay, F., & Sak, G. (2020). Kovid-19'un Ekonomik Sonuçlarını Yönetebilmek İçin Ne Yapılabilir? *Türkiye Ekonomi Politikaları Araştırma Vakfı,* https://www.tepav.org.tr/upload/files/1585023057-6. Covid_19un_Ekonomik_Sonuclarini_Yonetebilmek_Icin_Ne_Yapilabilir.pdf

Ozcelik, S.K., Havva O., & Bahcecik A.N. (2020). Effects of organisational restructuring of hospitals on nurses. *Journal of Nursing Management, 28*(7); 1740-1747. doi:10.1111/jonm.13133

Ozkeser, B. (2019). Impact of training on employee motivation in human resources management. *Procedia Computer Science, 158*, 802–810. doi:10.1016/j.procs.2019.09.117

Paddeu, D., Parkhurst, G., & Shergold, I. (2020). Passenger comfort and trust on first-time use of a shared autonomous shuttle vehicle. *Transportation Research Part C, Emerging Technologies, 115*, 102604. doi:10.1016/j.trc.2020.02.026

Palaiologos, G., & Khunaizi, Z. A. (2017). Growing the Arab Family Business (1): Hybrid Organizational Arrangements. *Journal of Entrepreneurship and Business Innovation, 4*(1), 25. doi:10.5296/jebi.v4i1.10819

Panda, S. & Dash, S. (2014). Constraints faced by entrepreneurs in developing countries: a review and assessment. *World Review of Entrepreneurship, Management and Sustainable Development, 10*(4), 405-421.

Panda, S. & Dash, S. (2016). Exploring the venture capitalist–entrepreneur relationship: evidence from India. *Journal of Small Business and Enterprise Development, 23*(1), 64-89.

Panda, S. (2018). Constraints faced by women entrepreneurs in developing countries: Review and ranking. *Gender in Management, 33*(4), 315–331. doi:10.1108/GM-01-2017-0003

Pan, H., & Deal, B. (2020). Reporting on the performance and usability of planning support systems—Towards a mutual understanding. *Applied Spatial Analysis and Policy, 13*(1), 137–159. doi:10.100712061-019-09296-5

Pan, H., Deal, B., Chen, Y., & Hewings, G. (2018). A Reassessment of urban structure and land-use patterns: Distance to CBD or network-based? —evidence from Chicago. *Regional Science and Urban Economics, 70*, 215–228. doi:10.1016/j.regsciurbeco.2018.04.009

Pan, H., Deal, B., Destouni, G., Zhang, Y., & Kalantari, Z. (2018b). Sociohydrology modeling for complex urban environments in support of integrated land and water resource management practices. *Land Degradation & Development, 29*(10), 3639–3652. doi:10.1002/ldr.3106

Pan, H., Zhang, L., Cong, C., Deal, B., & Wang, Y. (2019). A dynamic and spatially explicit modeling approach to identify the ecosystem service implications of complex urban systems interactions. *Ecological Indicators, 102*, 426–436. doi:10.1016/j.ecolind.2019.02.059

Pantano, E., Pizzi, G., Scarpi, D., & Dennis, C. (2020). Competing during a pandemic? Retailers' ups and downs during the COVID-19 outbreak. *Journal of Business Research*, *116*, 209–213. doi:10.1016/j.jbusres.2020.05.036 PMID:32501307

Papamichail, G., Rosiello, A., & Wield, D. (2019). Capacity-building barriers to S3 implementation: An empirical framework for catch-up regions. *Innovation (Abingdon)*, *32*(1), 66–84. doi:10.1080/13511610.2018.1537844

Parish, J. T., Cadwallader, S., & Bush, P. (2008). Want to, need to, ought to: Employee commitment to change. *Journal of Organizational Change Management*, *21*(1), 32–52. doi:10.1108/09534810810847020

Parker, M. (2018). *Shut down the Business School*. Pluto Press. doi:10.2307/j.ctvqhtj8

Park, S., & Kim, E.-J. (2015). Revisiting knowledge sharing from the organizational change perspective. *European Journal of Training and Development*, *39*(9), 769–797. doi:10.1108/EJTD-06-2015-0042

Parry, G. C., & Turner, C. E. (2006). Application of Lean Visual Process Management Tools. *Production Planning and Control*, *17*(1), 77–86. doi:10.1080/09537280500414991

Pasale, R. A., & Bagi, J. S. (2013). 5S Strategy: A Workplace Improvement Lean Tool. *Journal of Engineering and Technology Research*, *1*(1), 100–107.

Pataki, B. (1999). Technológiaváltások menedzselése – a változásmenedzsment alkalmazása a technológiamenedzsment területén. Műszaki Könyvkiadó, Budapest, Pokhrel, Sumitra., Chhetri, Roshan. (2021). A Literature Review on Impact of COVID-19 Pandemic on Teaching and Learning. *Higher Education for the Future*, *8*(1), 133–141.

Patzelt, H., & Shepherd, D. A. (2011). Negative emotions of an entrepreneurial career: Self-employment and regulatory coping behaviors. *Journal of Business Venturing*, *26*(2), 226–238. doi:10.1016/j.jbusvent.2009.08.002

Paulk, M., Chrissis, M. B., Curtis, B., & Weber, C. (1993, August). Capability maturity model version 1.1. *Research Gate*. https://www.researchgate.net/publication/3246910_Capability_Maturity_Model_Version_11

Pellegrini, M., Uskov, V., & Casalino, N. (2020). Reimagining and re-designing the post-COVID-19 higher education organizations to address new challenges and responses for safe and Effective Teaching Activities. Law and Economics Yearly Review Journal-LEYR, Queen Mary University, London, UK, 9(part 1), 219-248.

Pemsel, S., Wiewiora, A., Muller, R., Aubry, M., & Brown, K. (2014). A conceptualization of knowledge governance in project-based organizations. *International Journal of Project Management*, *32*(8), 1411–1422. doi:10.1016/j.ijproman.2014.01.010

People, process, technology: The PPT framework, explained. (2022, March 8). Plutora. https://www.plutora.com/blog/people-process-technology-ppt-framework-explained

Perry, E. (2018). Meet HearMeOut: the social media platform looking to bring audio back into the mainstream. *HearMeOut*. https://tinyurl.com/y8yxbzah

Peters, T., & Waterman, R. (2019, December 31). *Enduring ideas: 7-S Framework*. YouTube. https://www.mckinsey.com/capabilities/strategy-and-corporate-finance/our-insights/enduring-ideas-the-7-s-framework# PMI. .

Peters, A., McEwen, B. S., & Friston, K. (2015). Uncertainty and stress: Why it causes diseases and how it is mastered by the brain. *Progress in Neurobiology*. Advance online publication. doi:10.1016/j.pneurobio.2017.05.004 PMID:28576664

Peters, M. A., Rizvi, F., McCulloch, G., Gibbs, P., Gorur, R., Hong, M., & Quay, J. (2020). Reimagining the new pedagogical possibilities for universities post-Covid-19: An EPAT collective project. *Educational Philosophy and Theory*, 1–44.

Peters, T., & Waterman, R. (1982). *In search of excellence: Lessons from America's best-run companies*. Harper & Row.

Pettigrew, A. M., Woodman, R. W., & Cameron, K. S. (2001). Studying organizational change and development: Challenges for future research. *Academy of Management Journal*, *44*(4), 697–713. doi:10.2307/3069411

Phogat, S. (2013). An Introduction to Applicability of Lean in Warehousing. *International Journal of Latest Research in Science and Technology*, *2*(5), 105–109.

Pho, K. H., Ly, S., Ly, S., & Lukusa, T. M. (2019). Comparison among Akaike information criterion, Bayesian information criterion and Vuong's test in model selection: A case study of violated speed regulation in Taiwan. *Journal of Advanced Engineering and Computation*, *3*(1), 293–303. doi:10.25073/jaec.201931.220

Piccarozzi, M., Silvestri, C., & Morganti, P. (2021). COVID-19 in management studies: A systematic literature review. *Sustainability*, *13*(7), 3791. doi:10.3390u13073791

Piderit, S. K. (2000). Rethinking resistance and recognizing ambivalence: A multidimensional view of attitudes toward an organizational change. *Academy of Management Review*, *25*(4), 783–794. doi:10.2307/259206

Pierce, C. (2016) What's Holding Back Family Businesses in the GCC? *Gulf News*. https://gulfnews.com/business/sme/what-s-holding-back-family-businesses-in-the-gcc-1.1870272

Pines, A. M. (2002). The female entrepreneur: Burnout treated using a psychodynamic existential approach. *Clinical Case Studies*, *1*(2), 171–181. doi:10.1177/1534650102001002005

Pines, A. M., & Schwartz, D. (2008). Now you see them, now you don't: Gender differences in entrepreneurship. *Journal of Managerial Psychology*, *23*(7), 811–832. doi:10.1108/02683940810896358

Pinheiro, J., Farias, T., & Abe-Lima, J. (2013). Painel de especialistas e estratégia multimétodos: Reflexões, exemplos, perspectivas. *PSICO*, *44*(2), 184–192.

Pittino, D., Visintin, F., & Lauto, G. (2018). Fly Away From the Nest? A Configurational Analysis of Family Embeddedness and Individual Attributes in the Entrepreneurial Entry Decision by Next-Generation Members. *Family Business Review*, *31*(3), 271–294. doi:10.1177/0894486518773867

Pittman, M., & Reich, B. (2016). Social media and loneliness: Why an Instagram picture may be worth more than a thousand twitter words. *Computers in Human Behavior*, *62*, 155–167. doi:10.1016/j.chb.2016.03.084

Popkov, M. V. V. (2007). Sustainable economic development in the context of globalization and the knowledge economy: The conceptual foundations of the theory and practice scientific publication. *Economy*, *2007*, 295.

Porras, J. I., & Robertson, P. J. (1987). Organization Development Theory: A Typology and Evaluation. In R. W. Woodman & W. A. Pasmore (Eds.), Research in Organizational Change and Development, Greenwich, CT: JAI Press, 1, 1–57.

Porras, J. I., & Robertson, P. J. (1992). Organizational Development: Theory, Practice, Research. In M. D. Dunnette and L. M. Hough (Eds.), Handbook of organizational psychology Palo Alto, CA: Psychology Press, 3, 719–822.

Porter, M. (1998). Clusters and the new economics of competition. *Harvard Business Review*, Nov-Dez: 1998.

Porter, M. (2001). *Clusters of Innovation: regional foundations of U. S competitiveness. Council on Competitiveness*. Monitor Group.

Porter, M., & Kramer, M. (2011). Creating shared value: How to reinvent capitalism – and unleash a wave of innovation and growth. *Harvard Business Review, 89*(1–2), 62–77.

Powell, G. N., & Eddleston, K. A. (2013). Linking family-to-business enrichment and support to entrepreneurial success: Do female and male entrepreneurs experience different outcomes? *Journal of Business Venturing, 28*(2), 261–280. doi:10.1016/j.jbusvent.2012.02.007

Powell, M., & Ansic, D. (1997). Gender Differences in Risk Behaviour in Financial Decision-Making: An Experimental Analysis. *Journal of Economic Psychology, 18*(6), 605–628. doi:10.1016/S0167-4870(97)00026-3

Power, K. (2020). The COVID-19 pandemic has increased the care burden of women and families. *Sustainability: Science. Practice and Policy, 16*(1), 67–73.

Poza, E. J. (2010). *Family Business.* Thomson South-Western.

Preiss, K. J., & McCrohan, D. (2006). *GEM global summary 2006: United Arab Emirates.* London School of Economics/Babson.

Primary sponsor's role and importance. (n.d.). Prosci. https://www.prosci.com/resources/articles/primary-sponsors-role-and-importance

Project management maturity model (PMMM) in educational organisations. (2010). Academia. https://www.academia.edu/42143101/Project_Management_Maturity_Model_PMMM_in_educational_organizations

Prosci (2014). ROI of Change Management Webinar.

Prosci (2018). *Best Practices in Change Management 2018 Edition*, https://www.prosci.com/hubfs/367443/2.downloads/research/2018-Best-Practices-Executive-Summary.pdf?hsLang=en-ca

Prosci (2022a). *The Prosci ADKAR Model.* https://www.prosci.com/methodology/adkar

Prosci (2022b), *Prosci Change Triangle (PCT).* https://www.prosci.com/methodology/pct-model

Prosci (2022c). *Defining the Value of Change Management*, https://www.prosci.com/resources/webinars/defining-the-value-of-change-management

Prosci (2022d). *Cost-benefit analysis of change management.* https://www.prosci.com/hubfs/367443/2.downloads/thought-leadership/Cost-Benefit-Analysis-TL.pdf?hsLang=en-us

Prosci. (n.d.). *What is change management and how does it work?* Prosci. https://www.prosci.com/resources/articles/what-is-change-management-and-how-does-it-work

PWC. (2017) *Global Family Business Survey.* PWC. https://assets.kpmg/content/dam/kpmg/bh/pdf/gcc-family-business-survey-2017.pdf html Last accessed: 25.10.2022

Qiu, J., Shen, B., Zhao, M., Wang, Z., Xie, B., & Xu, Y. (2020). A nationwide survey of psychological distress among Chinese people in the Covid-19 epidemic: Implications and policy recommendations. *General Psychiatry, 33*(2), e100213. doi:10.1136/gpsych-2020-100213 PMID:32215365

Quaye, D., Acheampong, G., & Asiedu, M. (2015). Gender differences in entrepreneurial orientation: Evidence from Ghana. *European Journal of Business and Management, 7*(12), 128–140.

Queiroz, M., Tallon, P. P., Sharma, R., & Coltman, T. (2018). The role of IT application orchestration capability in improving agility and performance. *The Journal of Strategic Information Systems, 27*(1), 4–21. doi:10.1016/j.jsis.2017.10.002

Quilley, S. (2019). Green Politics and the Right: Possible Alliance? In *Proceedings of the 12th Biennial Conference of the Canadian Society for Ecological Economics*, Waterloo, ON, Canada.

Quinn, R. E., Spreitzer, G. M., & Brown, M. V. (2000). Changing others through Changing Ourselves: The Transformation of Human systems. *Journal of Management Inquiry, 9*(2), 47–164. doi:10.1177/105649260092010

Qureshi, K. (2018). *Advanced Concepts of Information Technology.* Educreation Publishing.

Radipere, N. S. (2013). *Analysis of local and immigrant entrepreneurship in the South African small enterprise sector (Gauteng province).* [Thesis, University of South Africa, Pretoria].

Rae, D. (2015). *Opportunity-Centred Entrepreneurship.* Palgrave McMillan. doi:10.1007/978-1-137-47410-0

Rafferty, A. E., & Griffin, M. A. (2006). Perceptions of organizational change: A stress and coping perspective. *The Journal of Applied Psychology, 91*(5), 1154–1162. doi:10.1037/0021-9010.91.5.1154 PMID:16953776

Rafferty, A. E., & Restubog, S. L. D. (2010). The impact of change process and context on change reactions and turnover during a merger. *Journal of Management, 36*(5), 1309–1338. doi:10.1177/0149206309341480

Rahim, A. (1996). Stress, strain, and their moderators: An empirical comparison of entrepreneurs and managers. *Journal of Small Business Management, 34*(1), 46.

Rajagopalan, N., & Spreitzer, G. M. (1996). Towards a Theory of Strategic Change: A Multi-Lens Perspective and Integrative Framework. *Academy of Management Review, 22*(1), 48–79. doi:10.2307/259224

Ramadani, V., Hisrich, R.D., & Gërguri-Rashiti, S. (2015). Female entrepreneurs in transition economies: insights from Albania, Macedonia and Kosovo. *World Review of Entrepreneurship, Management and Sustainable Development, 11*(4), 391-413.

Ramirez, R., & Selsky, J. W. (2014). Strategic Planning in Turbulent Environments: A Social Ecology Approach to Scenarios. *Long Range Planning, 49*(1), 90–102. doi:10.1016/j.lrp.2014.09.002

Randerson, K., Dossena, G., & Fayolle, A. (2016). The futures of family business: Family entrepreneurship. *Futures, 75*, 36–43. doi:10.1016/j.futures.2015.10.008

Randøy, T., & Goel, S. (2003). Ownership structure, founder leadership, and performance in Norwegian SMEs: Implications for financing entrepreneurial opportunities. *Journal of Business Venturing, 18*(5), 619–637. doi:10.1016/S0883-9026(03)00013-2

Rao, L. (2017). Instagram copies Snapchat once again with face filters. *Fortune.* https://tinyurl.com/ybcuxxdv

Rapanta, C., Botturi, L., Goodyear, P., Guàrdia, L., & Koole, M. (2020). Online university teaching during and after the Covid-19 crisis: Refocusing teacher presence and learning activity. *Post-digital. Science and Education*, 1–23.

Rauch, A., Wiklund, J., Lumpkin, G. T., & Frese, M. (2009). Entrepreneurial orientation and business performance: An assessment of past research and suggestions for the future. *Entrepreneurship Theory and Practice, 33*(3), 761–787. doi:10.1111/j.1540-6520.2009.00308.x

Ray, S. (2021). "Ifs" and "Buts" in Poverty and Developmental Economics. Perspectives of Entrepreneurial University Model in Counervailing Effects. *Beneficium*, (2 (39)), 55–60.

Reason, P. (1988). *Human inquiry in action: developments in new paradigm research.* Sage.

Reay, D. (2004, January). Cultural capitalists and academic habitus: Classed and gendered labour in UK higher education. []. Pergamon.]. *Women's Studies International Forum, 27*(1), 31–39. doi:10.1016/j.wsif.2003.12.006

Recchi, E., Ferragina, E., Helmeid, E., Pauly, S., Safi, M., Sauger, N., & Schradie, N. (2020). The "Eye of the Hurricane" paradox: An unexpected and unequal rise of well-being during the Covid-19 lockdown in France. *Research in Social Stratification and Mobility, 68*, 100508. Advance online publication. doi:10.1016/j.rssm.2020.100508 PMID:32834344

Reichers, A. E., Wanous, J. P., & Austin, J. T. (1997). Understanding and managing cyni cism about organizational change. *The Academy of Management Executive, 11*(1), 48–59. doi:10.5465/ame.1997.9707100659

Reitz, M., & Higgins, J. (2022). Leading in an age of employee activism. *Sloan Review*. https://sloanreview.mit.edu/article/leading-in-an-age-of-employee-activism/

Reitz, M., & Higgins, J. (2019). *Speak-up: say what needs to be said and hear what needs to be heard.* FT Publishing.

Ren, J., Yusuf, Y. Y., & Burns, N. D. (2009). A decision-support framework for agile enterprise partnering. *International Journal of Advanced Manufacturing Technology, 41*(1-2), 180–192. doi:10.100700170-008-1443-3

Rewers, P., Trojanowska, J., & Chabowski, P. (2016, June 28-30). Tools and Methods of Lean Manufacturing - A Literature Review [Paper Presentation*]. 7th International Technical Conference (Technological Forum 2016),* Prague, Czech Republic.

Ricciardi, F., Zardini, A., & Rossignoli, C. (2018). Organizational integration of the IT function: A key enabler of firm capabilities and performance. *Journal of Innovation & Knowledge, 3*(3), 93–107. doi:10.1016/j.jik.2017.02.003

Rieber, L. P. (2001). Designing learning environments that excite serious play. *Annual Meeting of the Australasian Society for Computers in Learning in Tertiary Education,* Melbourne, Australia.

Rieley, J. B., & Clarkson, I. (2001). The impact of change on performance. *Journal of Change Management, 2*(2), 160–172. doi:10.1080/714042499

Riessman, C. K. (2008). *Narrative Methods for the Human Sciences*. Sage Pub.

Rietveld, R., Dolen, W., Mazloom, M., & Masoud, M. (2019). What You Feel, Is What You Like influence of message appeals on customer engagement on Instagram. *Journal of Interactive Marketing, 49*(1), 20–53. doi:10.1016/j.intmar.2019.06.003

Robbins, S. P., & Judge, T. A. (2013). *Organisational Behavior* (15th ed.). Pearson.

Robinson, L., Newell, J. P., & Marzluff, J. M. (2005). Twenty-five years of sprawl in the Seattle region: Growth management responses and implications for conservation. *Landscape and Urban Planning, 71*(1), 51–72. doi:10.1016/j.landurbplan.2004.02.005

Robson, P. (1993). The New Regionalism and the Developing Countries. *Journal of Common Market Studies, 31*(3), 329–348. doi:10.1111/j.1468-5965.1993.tb00467.x

Roczniewska, M., Puchalska-Kamińska, M., & Łądka-Barańska, A. (2020). Facing education reform: Change-related self-efficacy is linked to job insecurity via appraisal. *Economic and Industrial Democracy*. Advance online publication. doi:10.1177/0143831X20975479

Rohac, T., & Januska, M. (2015). Value Stream Mapping Demonstration on Real Case Study. *Procedia Engineering, 100*, 520–529. doi:10.1016/j.proeng.2015.01.399

Roldán. J. L., Leal-Rodríguez, A., L.& Felipe, C. (2015*)* Information systems capabilities and organizational agility: understanding the mediating role of absorptive capacity when influenced by a hierarchy culture. In *2nd International Symposium on Partial Least Squares Path Modeling - The Conference for PLS Users.*, Seville, Spain

Romano, C. A., Tanewski, G. A., & Smyrnios, K. X. (2001). Capital structure decision making: A model for family business. *Journal of Business Venturing*, *16*(3), 285–310. doi:10.1016/S0883-9026(99)00053-1

Roomi, M. A., Harrison, P., & Beaumont-Kerridge, J. (2009). Women-owned small and medium enterprises in England: Analysis of factors influencing the growth process. *Journal of Small Business and Enterprise Development.*

Rosenbaum, D., More, E., & Steane, P. (2018). Planned organisational change management: Forward to the past? An exploratory literature review. *Journal of Organizational Change Management*, *31*(2), 286–303. doi:10.1108/JOCM-06-2015-0089

Rosenfeld, S. (1997). *Clustering, Networking, and Industrial Modernization*. Regional Technology Strategies<http://www.cherry.gatech.edu/sim/slides/rosenfeld.html.

Roskil, J. (2022) *Demonstrates Its Staying Power* avaliable at: https://www.forbes.com/sites/forbestechcouncil/2022/01/14/2022-prediction-agility-demonstrates-its-staying-power/?sh=2e3
1f24f32c3

Rothblum, E. D., Solomon, L. J., & Murakami, J. (1986). Affective, cognitive, and behavioral differences between high and low procrastinators. *Journal of Counseling Psychology*, *33*(4), 387–394. doi:10.1037/0022-0167.33.4.387

Rother, M., & Shook, J. (2003). *Learning to See - Value-Stream Mapping to Create Value and Eliminate MUDA*. The Lean Enterprise Institute.

Rotmans, J., & Lorbach, D. (2009). Complexity and transition management. *Journal of Industrial Ecology*, *13*(2), 184–196. doi:10.1111/j.1530-9290.2009.00116.x

Rozier, C. K., & Thompson, M. (1998). Female entrepreneurs in a female-dominated health profession: An exploratory study. *Journal of Developmental Entrepreneurship*, *3*(2), 149.

Ruben, B., Mahon, G., & Shapiro, K. (2022). Academic leader selection, development, evaluation, and recognition: Four critical higher education challenges. In *International Perspectives on Leadership in Higher Education* (Vol. 15, pp. 115–138). Emerald Publishing Limited. doi:10.1108/S1479-362820220000015007

Rudd, J., Hooley, G., Piercy, N., & Nicoulaud, B. (2017). *Marketing strategy and competitive positioning*. Pearson.

Runyan, R., Ge, B., Dong, B., & Swinney, J. (2012). Entrepreneurial orientation in cross-cultural research: Assessing measurement invariance in the construct. *Entrepreneurship Theory and Practice*, *36*(4), 819–836. doi:10.1111/j.1540-6520.2010.00436.x

Rutherford, M. W., Muse, L. A., & Oswald, S. L. (2006). A New Perspective on the Developmental Model for Family Business. *Family Business Review*, *19*(4), 317–333. doi:10.1111/j.1741-6248.2006.00079.x

Ryder, A. (2019). *Big Data: artificial intelligence and business strategy. Three steps to implement AI*. https://sloanreview.mit.edu/article/three-steps-to-implement-ai/

Sabi, A. (2015) The Succession Challenge in GCC Family Business. http: //globalriskinsights.com/2015/11/the-succession-challenge-in-gcc-family-businesses/ .

Sak, R. (2018). Gender Differences in Turkish Early Childhood Teachers' Job Satisfaction, Job Burnout and Organizational Cynicism. *Early Childhood Education Journal, 46*(6), 643–653. doi:10.100710643-018-0895-9

Saleh, M. A. K. (2019). Review of the challenges facing family businesses in the Arab Region. *Next Generation Tools: Future Roadmap for Business and Industry*. https://www.academia.edu/44467706/Review_of_the_challenges_facing_family_businesses_in_the_Arab_Region

Salvato, C., Sharma, P., & Wright, M. (2015). From the guest editors: Learning patterns and approaches to family business education around the world—Issues, insights, and research agenda. Academy of Management Briarcliff Manor, NY.

Samara, G. (2020). Family businesses in the Arab Middle East: What do we know and where should we go? *Journal of Family Business Strategy, 12*(3), 100359. doi:10.1016/j.jfbs.2020.100359

Sambamurthy, V., Bharadwaj, A., & Grover, V. (2003). Shaping agility through digital options: Reconceptualizing the role of information technology in contemporary firms. *Management Information Systems Quarterly, 27*(2), 237–263. doi:10.2307/30036530

Sandelands, L. (2010). The play of change. *Journal of Organizational Change Management, 23*(1), 71–86. doi:10.1108/09534811011017216

Sandhu, N., Hussain, J., & Matlay, H. (2012). Barriers to finance experienced by female owner/managers of marginal farms in India. *Journal of Small Business and Enterprise Development, 19*(4), 640–655. doi:10.1108/14626001211277442

Sandhu, N., Hussain, J., & Matlay, H. (2012). Entrepreneurship education and training needs of family businesses operating in the agricultural sector of India. *Education + Training, 33*(4), 727–743. doi:10.1108/00400911211274855

Sarker, S., & Sarker, S. (2009). Exploring Agility in Distributed Information Systems Development Teams: An Interpretive Study in an Offshoring Context. *Information Systems Research, 3*(20), 440–461. doi:10.1287/isre.1090.0241

Saunders, D., & Severn, J. (1999). *Simulation and games for strategy and policy planning, The International Simulation and Gaming Research Yearbook* (Vol. 7). Psychology Press.

Saunders, M., Lewis, P., & Thornhill, A. (2009). *Research Methods for Business Students* (5th ed.). Pearson Education.

Sayeed, A., Kundu, S., Hasan Al Banna, M., Tasdik Hasan, M., Begum, R. M., & Shafiqul Islam Khan, M. (2020). Mental health outcomes during the COVID-19 and perceptions towards the pandemic: Findings from a cross-sectional study among Bangladeshi students. *Children and Youth Services Review, 119*, 105658. doi:10.1016/j.childyouth.2020.105658 PMID:33518861

Schilling, M. A., & Phelps, C. (2007). Interfirm collaboration networks: The impact of large scale network structure on firm innovation. *Management Science, 53*(7), 1113–1126. doi:10.1287/mnsc.1060.0624

Schillo, S. (2011). Entrepreneurial Orientation and Company Performance: Can the Academic Literature Guide Managers? *Technology Innovation Management Review, 20*(2), 20–25. doi:10.22215/timreview/497

Schoemaker, P. J., Day, G. S., & Snyder, S. A. (2013). Integrating organizational networks, weak signals,strategic radars and scenario planning. *Technological Forecasting and Social Change, 80*(4), 815–824. doi:10.1016/j.techfore.2012.10.020

Schönecker, D., & Kim, H. (2022). *Kant and Artificial Intelligence*. De Gruyter.

Schuman, A., Stutz, S., & Ward, J. (2010). *Family business as paradox*. Springer. doi:10.1057/9780230291768

Schumpeter, J. A. (1954). History of economic analysis. Oxford University Press.

Schweiger, D. M., & Denisi, A. S. (1991). Communication with employees following a merger: A longitudinal field experiment. *Academy of Management Journal, 34*(1), 110–135. doi:10.2307/256304

Science. (2020). The effect of travel restrictions on the spread of the 2019 novel coronavirus (Covid-19) outbreak. *Science, 368*(6489), 395-400.

Self, D., Armenakis, A., & Schraeder, M. (2007). Organizational change content, process and context: A simultaneous analysis of employee reactions. *Journal of Change Management, 7*(2), 211–229. doi:10.1080/14697010701461129

Senderská, K., Mares, A., & Václav, S. (2017). Spaghetti Diagram Application for Workers' Movement Analysis. *U.P.B. Scientific Bulletin - Series D, 79*(1), 139–150.

Senge, P. (1990). *The Fifth Discipline: The Art and Practice of the Learning Organization.* Random House.

Senior, B. (2002). *Organisational Change* (2nd ed.). Prentice Hall.

Sexton, L. D., & Bowman-Upton, N. (1990). Female and male entrepreneurs: Psychological characteristics and their role in gender related. *Journal of Business Venturing, 5*(1), 29–36. doi:10.1016/0883-9026(90)90024-N

Shahid, M. Z., & Li, G. (2019). Impact of Artificial Intelligence in Marketing: A Perspective of Marketing Professionals of Pakistan. *Global Journal of Management and Business Research, 19*(2), 27–33.

Shane, S., & Venkataraman, S. (2000). Entrepreneurship as a field of research: The promise of entrepreneurship as a field of research. *Academy of Management Review, 26*(1), 13–17. doi:10.5465/amr.2001.27879269

Shannon, C. E. (1950). Programming a Computer for Playing Chess. *Philosophical Magazine, 41*(314), 256–275.

Sharifi, H., & Zhang, Z. (1999). A Methodology for Achieving Agility in Manufacturing Organizations: An Introduction. *International Journal of Production Economics, 62*(1-2), 7–22. doi:10.1016/S0925-5273(98)00217-5

Sharma, P., Hoy, F., Astrachan, J. H., & Koiranen, M. (2007). The practice-driven evolution of family business education. *Journal of Business Research, 60*(10), 1012–1021. doi:10.1016/j.jbusres.2006.12.010

Sharma, P., Leung, T. Y., Kingshott, R. P., Davcik, N. S., & Cardinali, S. (2020). Managing uncertainty during a global pandemic: An international business perspective. *Journal of Business Research, 116*, 188–192. doi:10.1016/j.jbusres.2020.05.026 PMID:32501304

Shearer, C. S., Hames, D. S., & Runge, J. B. (2001). How CEOs Influence Organizational Culture following Acquisitions. *Leadership and Organization Development Journal, 22*(3), 105–113. doi:10.1108/01437730110389256

Sherehiy, B., Karwowski, W., & Layer, J. K. (2007). A Review of Enterprise Agility: Concepts, Frameworks, and Attributes. *International Journal of Industrial Ergonomics, 5*(37), 445–460. doi:10.1016/j.ergon.2007.01.007

Sheth, J. (2020). Impact of Covid-19 on consumer behavior: Will the old habits return or die? *Journal of Business Research, 117*, 280–283. doi:10.1016/j.jbusres.2020.05.059 PMID:32536735

Shinnar, R. S., Giacomin, O., & Janssen, F. (2012). Entrepreneurial perceptions and intentions: The role of gender and culture. *Entrepreneurship Theory and Practice, 36*(3), 465–493. doi:10.1111/j.1540-6520.2012.00509.x

Shrum, S., Chrissis, M. B., & Konrad, M. (2003). *CMMI: Guidelines for process integration and product improvement.* Addison-Wesley.

Shurchkov, O. (2012). New Elites and Their Influence on Entrepreneurial Activity in Russia. *Journal of Comparative Economics, 40*(2), 240–255. doi:10.1016/j.jce.2011.12.003

Siddiqui, A. B. (2012). Problems Encountered by Women Entrepreneurs in India. *International Journal of Applied Research & Studies*, *I*(II), 1–11.

Sidhu, R., Smith, R., Skelsey, D., King, D., & APMG (Eds.). (2014). *The effective change manager's handbook: Essential guidance to the change management body of knowledge*. Kogan Page.

Silver, D., Huang, A., Maddison, C. J., Guez, A., Sifre, L., van den Driessche, G., Schrittwieser, J., Antonoglou, I., Panneershelvam, V., Lanctot, M., Dieleman, S., Grewe, D., Nham, J., Kalchbrenner, N., Sutskever, I., Lillicrap, T., Leach, M., Kavukcuoglu, K., Graepel, T., & Hassabis, D. (2016). Mastering the game of Go with deep neural networks and tree search. *Nature*, *529*(7587), 484–489. doi:10.1038/nature16961 PMID:26819042

Singh, G., & Ahuja, I. S. (2012). Just-in-time Manufacturing: Literature Review and Directions. *International Journal of Business Continuity and Risk Management*, *3*(1), 57–98. doi:10.1504/IJBCRM.2012.045519

Sinha, R. (2003, February 24). *Beyond cardsorting: Free-listing methods to explore user categorizations.* Boxes and Arrows. www.boxesandarrows.com: https://boxesandarrows.com/beyond-cardsorting-free-listing-methods-to-explore-user-categorizations/

Sintema, E. J. (2020). Effect of COVID-19 on the Performance of Grade 12 Students: Implications for Stem Education. *Eurasia Journal of Mathematics, Science and Technology Education*, *16*(7), 1–6. doi:10.29333/ejmste/7893

Sirmon, D. G., & Hitt, M. A. (2003). Managing Resources: Linking Unique Resources, Management, and Wealth Creation in Family Firms. *Entrepreneurship Theory and Practice*, *27*(4), 339–358. doi:10.1111/1540-8520.t01-1-00013

Smeds, E., & Acuto, M. (2018). Networking cities after Paris: Weighing the ambition of urban climate change experimentation. *Global Policy*, *9*(4), 549–559. doi:10.1111/1758-5899.12587

Smedt, P. D., Borch, K., & Fuller, T. (2013). Future scenarios to inspire innovation. *Technological Forecasting and Social Change*, *80*(3), 432–443. doi:10.1016/j.techfore.2012.10.006

Smollan, R. K. (2015). Causes of stress before, during and after organizational change: A qualitative study. *Journal of Organizational Change Management*, *28*(2), 301–314. doi:10.1108/JOCM-03-2014-0055

Social (2021), Social media marketing trends for 2022. https://www.zoho.com/social/journal/social-media-marketing-trends-2022.html

Soininen, J., Puumalainen, K., Sjögrén, H., & Syrjä, P. (2012). The impact of global economic crisis on SMEs: Does entrepreneurial orientation matter? *Management Research Review*, *35*(10), 927–944. doi:10.1108/01409171211272660

Sommet, N., & Morselli, D. (2021). Keep calm and learn multilevel linear modeling: A three-step procedure using SPSS, Stata, R, and MPlus. *Revue Internationale de Psychologie Sociale*, *34*(1), 24. doi:10.5334/irsp.555

SonobeT.TakedaA.YoshidaS.TruongH. T. (2021). *The impacts of the Covid-19 pandemic on micro, small, and medium enterprises in Asia and their digitalization responses.* ADBI Working Paper 1241. https://ssrn.com/abstract=3912355 or doi:10.2139/ssrn.3912355

Sorg, J. M., Hodge Cunningham, K., & Stoyanova, A. (in press). *Why every CxO should have a court jester. A different introduction to change management.* [unpublished research paper].

Sorg, J.M. (n.d.): *Strategic change management. A methodology to calculate the ROI of change.* [unpublished research paper].

Sorg, J. M. (2021). *Experimentalist Regional Goverance. Policy Analysis in Geographic-Functional Regions.* Peter Lang. doi:10.3726/b17629

Sorgner, A., Bode, E., & Krieger-Boden, C. (2017). *Women20 Study. The Effects of Digitalization on the Gender Equality in the G20 Economies*. Kiel Institute for the World Economy.

Sormaz, J., Kuzmanovic, M., & Jeremic, V. (2019). Customer preferences towards digital marketing strategies. In *Economics of Digital Transformation*, 507-526.

Sortino, J. (n.d.). *Lights in single direction: Joshua Sortino. Unsplash.* https://unsplash.com/@sortino

Sozinova, A. A., Litvinova, T. N., Kurilova, A., & Morozova, I. A. (2022). Fight against climate change and sustainable development based on ecological economy and management in the AI era. In Frontiers in Environmental Science, 10. doi:10.3389/fenvs.2022.1091149

Spector, P. E. (1982). Behaviour in organizations as a function of employee's locus of control. *Psychological Bulletin*, *91*(3), 482–297. doi:10.1037/0033-2909.91.3.482

Spitzer, R. L., Kroenke, K., Williams, J. B., & Löwe, B. (2006). A brief measure for assessing generalized anxiety disorder: The GAD-7. *Arch Intern Med. 22*, *166*(10), 1092-1097. . doi:10.1001/archinte.166.10.1092

Squazzoni, F. (2008). A (computational) social science perspective on societal transitions. *Computational & Mathematical Organization Theory*, *14*(4), 266–282. doi:10.100710588-008-9038-y

Stajkovic, A., & Luthans, F. (1998a). Self-efficacy and work-related performance: A meta analysis. *Psychological Bulletin*, *124*(2), 240–261. doi:10.1037/0033-2909.124.2.240

Stajkovic, A., & Luthans, F. (1998b). Social cognitive theory and self-efficacy. *Organizational Dynamics*, *26*(4), 62–74. doi:10.1016/S0090-2616(98)90006-7

Stang, S. (2021). *Impact Of The Coronavirus Pandemic On Businesses And Employees By Industry*. BLS. https://www.bls.gov/spotlight/2021/impact-of-the-coronavirus-pandemic-on-businesses-and-employees-by-industry/home.htm

Stanley, D. J., Meyer, J. P., & Topolnytsky, L. (2005). Employee Cynicism and Resistance to Organizational Change. *Journal of Business and Psychology*, *19*(4), 429–459. doi:10.100710869-005-4518-2

Starchcr, D. C. (1996). *Women entrepreneurs: Catalysts for transformation.* European Bahá'í Business Forum.

Statista.com. (2020). [Data Sett]. *Statista.* https://www.statista.com/chart/22027/startup-sme-financial-situation-india/

Statista.com. 2022a. *Change management in organisations based on project and culture*. Statista. https://www.statista.com/statistics/1085414/enterprise-change-management-worldwide/

Statista.com. 2022b. *Tech start-up business investment value from 2017 to 2020 in Southeast Asia*. Statista. https://www.statista.com/statistics/1251921/sea-value-of-tech-startup-funding/

Statista.com. 2022c. *Lack of knowledge and skills of leaders for handling technological application*. Statista. https://www.statista.com/statistics/1248921/challenges-to-technology-transformation-in-companies/#:~:text=Challenges%20of%20technology%20transformations%20in%20companies%202020&text=The%20majority%20of%20the%20surveyed,changing%20their%20technology%20operating%20models

Statler, M., Heracleous, L., & Jacobs, C. D. (2011). Serious play as a practice of paradox. *The Journal of Applied Behavioral Science*, *47*(2), 236–256. doi:10.1177/0021886311398453

Steier, L. (2003). Variants of agency contracts in family-financed ventures as a continuum of familial altruistic and market rationalities. *Journal of Business Venturing*, *18*(5), 597–618. doi:10.1016/S0883-9026(03)00012-0

STEP. 2022. Advanced Certificate in Family Business Governance Accessed online: https://www.step.org/qualifications-courses/advanced-certificate-family-business-governance. Last accessed: 22.10.2022

Stephan, U., & Roesler, U. (2010). Health of entrepreneurs versus employees in a national representative sample. *Journal of Occupational and Organizational Psychology*, *83*(3), 717–738. doi:10.1348/096317909X472067

Stephen, E. (n.d.). *How microsoft uses the ADKAR model to improve customer success.* Prosci. Retrieved November 20, 2022, from https://www.prosci.com/blog/how-microsoft-uses-the-adkar-model-to-improve-customer-success

Stolzenberg, K. (2022). *Change Management: Successfully Shaping Change Processes – Mobilizing Employees. Vision, Communication, Participation, Qualification*. Springer. doi:10.1007/978-3-662-65396-8

STRATEGIC ADVANTAGE | English meaning. (2022, November 16). Cambridge Dictionary. https://dictionary.cambridge.org/dictionary/english/strategic-advantage

Strike, V. M. (2012). Advising the family firm: Reviewing the past to build the future. *Family Business Review*, *25*(2), 156–177. doi:10.1177/0894486511431257

Sudarsanam, S. K. (2017). Social media metrics. In R. Raghavendra (Ed.), *Social media listening and monitoring for business applications* (pp. 131–149). IGI Global. doi:10.4018/978-1-5225-0846-5.ch007

Sullivan, D. M., & Meek, W. R. (2012). Gender and entrepreneurship: A review and process model. *Journal of Managerial Psychology*, *27*(5), 428–458. doi:10.1108/02683941211235373

Sultan, S. S. (2016). Women entrepreneurship working in a conflict region: The case of Palestine. *World Review of Entrepreneurship, Management and Sustainable Development*, *12*(2–3), 149–156. doi:10.1504/WREMSD.2016.074970

Sundar, R., Balaji, A. N., & Satheesh-Kumar, R. M. (2014). A Review on Lean Manufacturing Implementation Techniques. *Procedia Engineering*, *97*, 1875–1885. doi:10.1016/j.proeng.2014.12.341

Suoniemi, S., Meyer-Waarden, L., Munzel, A., Zablah, A. R., & Straub, D. (2020). Big data and firm performance: The roles of market-directed capabilities and business strategy. *Information & Management*, *57*(7), 103365. https://www.sciencedirect.com/science/article/am/pii/S0378720620303037. doi:10.1016/j.im.2020.103365

Su, Z., Xie, E., & Li, Y. (2011). Entrepreneurial Orientation and Firm Performance in New Ventures and Established Firms. *Journal of Small Business Management*, *49*(4), 558–577. doi:10.1111/j.1540-627X.2011.00336.x

Syed, M. (2019). Rebel Ideas: The power of diverse thinking. Hachette UK.

Tagiuri, R., & Davis, J. (1996). Bivalent attributes of the family firm. *Family Business Review*, *9*(2), 199–208. doi:10.1111/j.1741-6248.1996.00199.x

Tajfel, H., Billig, M. G., Bundy, R. P., & Flament, C. (1971). Social categorization and intergroup behaviour. *European Journal of Social Psychology*, *1*(2), 149–178. doi:10.1002/ejsp.2420010202

Tajfel, H., & Turner, J. C. (1979). An integrative theory of intergroup conflict. In W. G. Austin & S. Worchel (Eds.), *The social psychology of intergroup relations* (pp. 33–37). Brooks/Cole.

Tang, J., & Tang, Z. (2007). The relationship of achievement motivation and risk-taking propensity to new venture performance: A test of the moderating effect of entrepreneurial munificence. *International Journal of Entrepreneurship and Small Business*, *4*(4), 450–472. doi:10.1504/IJESB.2007.013691

Tang, Z., Kreiser, P. M., Marino, L., Dickson, P., & Weaver, K. M. (2009). A Hierarchical Perspective of the Dimensions of Entrepreneurial Orientation. *The International Entrepreneurship and Management Journal*, *5*(2), 181–201. doi:10.100711365-008-0097-9

Tan, J. (2008). Breaking the 'bamboo curtain' and the 'glass ceiling': The experience of women entrepreneurs in high-tech industries in an emerging market. *Journal of Business Ethics*, *80*(3), 547–564. doi:10.100710551-007-9454-9

Tannenbaum, R., & Schmidt, W. H. (1958). How to Choose a Leadership Pattern. *Harvard Business Review*, (March-April), 162–180.

Tannin, K. (2022). *Call for Chapters: Change Management During Unprecedented Times*. IGI Global. https://www.igi-global.com/publish/call-for-papers/call-details/6098?

Tanova, C., Karatas-Özkan, M., & Inal, G. (2008). The process of choosing a management career: Evaluation of gender and contextual dynamics in a comparative study of six countries: Hungary, Israel, North Cyprus, Turkey, UK and the USA. *Career Development International*, *13*(4), 291–305. doi:10.1108/13620430810880790

Taulli, T. (2019). Implementing AI The Right Way. *Forbes*. https://www.forbes.com/sites/tomtaulli/2019/04/13/implementing-ai-the-right-way/?sh=5583ee5d57e4

Tawse, A., Patrick, V. M., & Vera, D. (2019). Crossing the chasm: Leadership nudges to help transition from strategy formulation to strategy implementation. *Business Horizons*, *62*(2), 249–257. doi:10.1016/j.bushor.2018.09.005

Taylor, P. (2013). The effect of entrepreneurial orientation on the internationalization of SMEs in developing countries. *African Journal of Business Management*, *7*(19), 1927-1937.

Taylor, L. L., Beck, M. I., Lahey, J. N., & Froyd, J. E. (2017). Reducing inequality in higher education: The link between faculty empowerment and climate and retention. *Innovative Higher Education*, *42*(5-6), 391–405. doi:10.100710755-017-9391-1

Teacher, L. (November 2013). Role of Promoters in Company Establishment. *Law Teacher*. https://www.lawteacher.net/free-law-essays/business-law/role-of-promoters-in-company-establishment-business-law-essay.php?vref=1

Teelken, C., & Deem, R. (2013). All are equal, but some are more equal than others: Managerialism and gender equality in higher education in comparative perspective. *Comparative Education*, *49*(4), 520–535. doi:10.1080/03050068.2013.807642

Telli, S & Altun, D (2020). Coronavirüs ve Çevrimiçi (Online) Eğitimin Önlenemeyen Yükselişi. *Üniversite Araştırmaları Dergisi, 3*, 25-34

Temmen, M. (2021, February 7). *BANI vs VUCA— a new acronym for a new world*. Marian Temmen. Retrieved November 23, 2022, from https://marian-temmen.medium.com/bani-vs-vuca-a-new-acronym-for-a-new-world-59c7be2dddce

Tezel, B. A., Koskela, L. J., & Tzortzopoulos, P. (2009, January). The Functions of Visual Management [Paper Presentation]. *International Research Symposium*, Salford, UK.

Thakhathi, A., le Roux, C., & Davis, A. (2019). Sustainability leaders' influencing strategies for institutionalisingorganisational change towards corporate sustainability: A strategy-as-practice perspective. *Journal of Change Management*, *19*(4), 246–265. doi:10.1080/14697017.2019.1578985

Thakur, H. (2022, September 2). *Gartner business intelligence maturity model*. 121 Business Ideas. https://121businessideas.com/business-model/gartner-business-intelligence-maturity-model/

Thakur, V., & Mangla, S. K. (2019). Change management for sustainability: Evaluating the role of human, operational and technological factors in leading Indian firms in home appliances sector. *Journal of Cleaner Production*, *213*, 847–862. https://pearl.plymouth.ac.uk/bitstream/handle/10026.1/14932/BDAJCPR203March2019+%20SKM.docx?sequence=2. doi:10.1016/j.jclepro.2018.12.201

The Guardian. (2020). Interview by Zoë Corbyn. Peter Diamandis: 'In the next 10 years, we'll reinvent every industry'. *The Guardian*. https://www.theguardian.com/technology/2020/jan/25/peter-diamandis-future-faster-think-interview-ai-industry

The World Bank. (2021). *How COVID-19 is Affecting Companies Around the World*. https://www.worldbank.org/en/news/infographic/2021/02/17/how-covid-19is-affecting-companies-around-the-world

Thomas, S. (2020). Women in higher education administration leadership and the role of institutional support. In *Accessibility and Diversity in the 21st Century University* (pp. 234–249). IGI Global. doi:10.4018/978-1-7998-2783-2.ch012

Tilman, L. M. (2019). *Agility: How to navigate the unknown and seize opportunity in a world of disruption*. Missionday.

Timilsina, R. R., Nakagawa, Y., & Kotani, K. (2020). Exploring the Possibility of Linking and Incorporating Future Design in Backcasting and Scenario Planning. *Sustainability*, *12*(23), 12. doi:10.3390u12239907

Tischbirek, A. (2019). Artifcial Intelligence and Discrimination: Discriminating Against Discriminatory Systems. In T. Wischmeyer & T. Rademacher (Eds.), *Regulating Artificial Intelligence*. Springer International Publishing AG.

Tiwary, A. R., & Gupta, T. (2022). Stereotypical barriers affecting women aspiring high-ranking leadership role in higher education. In *Role of Leaders in Managing Higher Education* (Vol. 48, pp. 99–116). Emerald Publishing Limited. doi:10.1108/S2055-364120220000048007

Tlaiss, H. A. (2014). Women's entrepreneurship, barriers and culture: Insights from the United Arab Emirates. *The Journal of Entrepreneurship*, *23*(2), 289–320. doi:10.1177/0971355714535307

Tödtling, F., & Trippl, M. (2018). Regional innovation policies for new path development – beyond neo-liberal and traditional systemic views. *European Planning Studies*, *26*(9), 1779–1795. doi:10.1080/09654313.2018.1457140

Toussaint, A., Hüsing, P., Gumz, A., Wingenfeld, K., Härter, M., Schramm, E., & Löwe, B. (2020). Sensitivity to change and minimal clinically important difference of the 7-item generalized anxiety disorder questionnaire (GAD-7). *Journal of Affective Disorders*, *265*, 395–401. doi:10.1016/j.jad.2020.01.032 PMID:32090765

Trent, R. J. (2020). *Women's perspectives on the role of organizational culture in their career advancement to leadership positions: A generic inquiry* [Doctoral dissertation, Capella University].

Truffer, B., & Coenen, L. (2012). Environmental innovation and sustainability transitions in regional studies. *Regional Studies*, *46*(1), 1–21. doi:10.1080/00343404.2012.646164

Tshivhase, M. (2020). Personhood: Implications for moral status and uniqueness of women. Handbook of African Philosophy of Difference, 347-360.

Tsuchiya, S. (1998). Simulation/gaming as an essential enabler of organizational change. *Simulation & Gaming*, *29*(4), 400–408. doi:10.1177/104687819802900403

Tsyganova, T., & Shirokova, G. (2010). Gender differences in entrepreneurship: Evidence from gem data. *Organizations and Markets in Emerging Economies*, *1*(1), 120–141. doi:10.15388/omee.2010.1.1.14309

Tucker, H. (2020). Coronavirus Bankruptcy Tracker: These Major Companies Are Failing Amid The Shutdown. *Forbes*. https://www.forbes.com/sites/hanktucker/2020/05/03/coronavirus-bankruptcy-tracker-these-major-companies-are-failing-amid-the-shutdown/?sh=4882bad13425 URL1:https://trends.google.com.tr/trends/explore?date=all&q=agile%20transformation

Tushman, M. L., & Romanelli, E. (1985). Organizational Evolution: A Metamorphosis Model Of Convergence And Reorientation. In: L Cummings – B. M. Staw (Eds) Research in Organizational Behavior Greenwich, CT:JAI Press, 7,171-222.

Tversky, A., & Kahneman, D. (1974). Judgment under uncertainty: Heuristics and biases. *science, 185*(4157), 1124-1131.

Tversky, A., & Kahneman, D. (1973). Availability: A heuristic for judging frequency and probability. *Cognitive Psychology*, *5*(2), 207–232. doi:10.1016/0010-0285(73)90033-9

U. S. Business Administration (2021). *2021 Small Business Profile*. CDN. https://cdn.advocacy.sba.gov/wp-content/uploads/2021/08/30143723/Small-Business-Economic-Profile-US.pdf

Understanding and using maturity driven improvement with the Org-CMF — ODTI. (n.d.). OrgCMF. https://orgcmf.com/en-gb/pages/knowledge/org-cmf/maturity/

United Nations Industrial Development Organization. (2003). *Developing Rural and Women Entrepreneurship*.

Urbaniec, K., Mikulčić, H., Wang, Y., & Duić, N. (2018). System integration is a necessity for sustainable development. *Journal of Cleaner Production*, *195*(10), 122–132. doi:10.1016/j.jclepro.2018.05.178

Uzzi, B., & Spiro, J. (2005). Collaboration and creativity: The small world problem. *American Journal of Sociology*, *111*(2), 447–504. doi:10.1086/432782

Vakola, M., Armenakis, A., & Oreg, S. (2013). Reactions to organizational change from an individual differences perspective: A review of empirical research. In S. Oreg, A. Michel, & R. By (Eds.), *The Psychology of Organizational Change: Viewing Change from the Employee's Perspective* (pp. 95–122). Cambridge University Press. doi:10.1017/CBO9781139096690.008

Van de Ven, A. H., & Poole, M. S. (1995). Explaining Development and Change in Organizations. *Academy of Management Review*, *20*(3), 510–540. doi:10.2307/258786

Van der Duin, P., & De Graaf, R. (2010, August). The connection between innovation and the future. *Research gate*. https://www.researchgate.net/figure/The-connection-between-innovation-and-the-future_fig2_233527052

Van Der Heijden, K., Bradfield, R., Burt, G., Cairns, G., & Wright, G. (2002). *The Sixth Sense: Accelerating Organizational Learning with Scenarios*. John Wiley & Sons Ltd.

Van Gelderen, M., Brand, M., van Praag, M., Bodewes, W., Poutsma, E., & Van Gils, A. (2008). Explaining entrepreneurial intentions by means of the theory of planned behaviour. *Career Development International, 13*(6), 538–559. doi:10.1108/13620430810901688

van Gilst, E., Schalk, R., Kluijtmans, T., & Poell, R. (2020). The Role of Remediation in Mitigating the Negative Consequences of Psychological Contract Breach: A Qualitative Study in the Banking Sector. *Journal of Change Management, 20*(3), 264–282. doi:10.1080/14697017.2020.1737180

Van Haren Publishing (Ed.). (2017). *It-cmf: A management guide - Based on the it capability maturity framework.* Van Haren Publishing.

Van Oosterhout, M. P. A. (2010). *Business Agility and Information Technology in Service Organizations (No. EPS-2010-198-LIS).* Erasmus Research Institute of Management. http://hdl.handle.net/1765/19805

Vanhaverbeke W., Belderbos, R., Duysters G., Beerkens B. (2015). Technological performance and alliances over the industry life cycle: evidence from the ASIC industry *The journal of product innovation management, 32*(4), 556-573. doi:10.1111/jpim.12253

Vaterlaus, J. M., Spruance, A., & Patten, E. V. (2021). COVID-19 pandemic and social distancing in the United States: A mixed-methods study on lived experiences and well-being. *The Social Science Journal*, 1–13. doi:10.1080/03623319.2020.1852856

Ven, A. V., & Delbeco, A. L. (1971). Nominal versus Interacting Group Processes for Committee Decision-Making Effectiveness. *Academy of Management Journal, 14*(2), 203–212. doi:10.2307/255307

Verheul, I., Stel, A.V. and Thurik, R. (2006). Explaining female and male entrepreneurship at the country level. *Entrepreneurship and Regional Development, 18*(2), 151-183.

Verma, S., & Gustafsson, A. (2020). Investigating the emerging COVID-19 research trends in the field of business and management: A bibliometric analysis approach. *Journal of Business Research, 118*, 253–261. doi:10.1016/j.jbusres.2020.06.057 PMID:32834211

Vernooij, C., Stuijt, J., Hendriks, M., /Have, W./Have, S. (2022). *Organizational Behaviour and Change Management: The impact of cognitive*, Taylor & Francis Group.

Vijayakumar, A., & Jayachitra, S. (2013). Women entrepreneurs in India-Emerging issues and challenges. *International Journal of Developmental Research, 3*(4), 12–17.

Vijayakumar, T., & Naresh, B. (2013). Women entrepreneurship in India-Role of women in small and medium enterprises. [TAJMMR]. *TRANS Asian Journal of Marketing & Management Research, 2*(7), 13–25.

Villiers, C. (2019). Boardroom culture: An argument for compassionate leadership. *European Business Law Review, 30*(2), 253–278. doi:10.54648/EULR2019012

Vinodh, S., Devadasan, S. R., Vasudeva Reddy, B., & Ravichand, K. (2010a). Agility index measurement using multi-grade fuzzy approach integrated in a 20 criteria agile model. *International Journal of Production Research, 48*(23), 7159–7176. doi:10.1080/00207540903354419

Vinodh, S., Sundararaj, G., Devadasan, S. R., Kuttalingam, D., & Rajanayagam, D. (2010b). Amalgamation of mass customisation and agile manufacturing concepts: The theory and implementation study in an electronics switches manufacturing company. *International Journal of Production Research, 48*(7), 2141–2164. doi:10.1080/00207540802456257

Voelpel, S. C., Dous, M., & Davenport, T. H. (2005). Five steps to creating a global knowledge-sharing system: Siemens' ShareNet. *The Academy of Management Executive, 19*(2), 9–23. doi:10.5465/ame.2005.16962590 von Bertalanffy, L. (1979). *Adalék Egy Általános Rendszertanhoz: A Szervezet, Mint Rendszer Szerkesztő: Bleicher, Knut Dr.* Közgazdasági És Jogi Kiadó.

Vygotsky, L. S. (1962). *Thought and Language.* MIT Press. doi:10.1037/11193-000

Vygotsky, L. S. (1967). Play and its role in the mental development of the child. *Social Psychology, 5*(3), 6–18.

Waardenburg, L., Huysman, M., & Agterberg, M. (2021a). Introduction to managing AI wisely. In L. Waardenburg, M. Huysman, & M. Agterberg (Eds.), *Managing AI wisely: from development to organizational change in practice.* Edward Elgar Publishing. doi:10.4337/9781800887671.00010

Waardenburg, L., Huysman, M., & Agterberg, M. (2021b). Changing work. In L. Waardenburg, M. Huysman, & M. Agterberg (Eds.), *Managing AI wisely: from development to organizational change in practice.* Edward Elgar Publishing. doi:10.4337/9781800887671.00017

Waddell, D., Creed, A., Cummings, T., & Worley, C. (2014). *Organizational change: Development and transformation* (5th ed.). Cengage Learning Australia.

Wagner, J. (2007). What a Difference a Y Makes – Female and Male Nascent Entrepreneurs in Germany. *Small Business Economics, 28*(1), 1–21. doi:10.100711187-005-0259-x

Wales, W. J., Gupta, V. K., & Mousa, F. T. (2013). Empirical research on entrepreneurial orientation: An assessment and suggestions for future research. *International Small Business Journal, 31*(4), 357–383. doi:10.1177/0266242611418261

Wales, W., Monsen, E., & McKelvie, A. (2011). The organizational pervasiveness of entrepreneurial orientation. *Entrepreneurship Theory and Practice, 35*(5), 895–923. doi:10.1111/j.1540-6520.2011.00451.x

Wallace, C. (2022). *Rethinking the mechanics of data-driven decision-making to fuel business value.* CGI. https://www.cgi.com/en/blog/advanced-analytics/rethinking-mechanics-data-driven-decision-making-fuel-business-value

Walter, A. T. (2020). *Organizational agility: ill-defined and somewhat confusing? A systematic literature review and conceptualization.* Management Review Quarterly. doi:10.100711301-020-00186-6

Wang, C., Wang, Y., Wang, R., & Zheng, P. (2018). Modeling and evaluating land-use/land-cover change for urban planning and sustainability: a case study of Dongying city, China

Wangari's story. (n.d.). Cherie Blair Foundation for Women. https://cherieblairfoundation.org/impact/her-stories/hv-kenya-wangari/

Wang, L. (2020). Entrepreneurial narratives and concept teaching and learning. *Industry and Higher Education, 34*(1), 24–35. doi:10.1177/0950422219878986

Wang, Y., Hong, A., Li, X., & Gao, J. (2020). Marketing innovations during a global crisis: A study of China firms' response to COVID-19. *Journal of Business Research, 116*, 214–220. doi:10.1016/j.jbusres.2020.05.029 PMID:32501308

Wanous, J. P., Reichers, A. E., & Austin, J. T. (2000). Cynicism about organizational change: Measurement, antecedents, and correlates. *Group & Organization Management, 25*(2), 132–153. doi:10.1177/1059601100252003

Ward, J. L. (1997). Growing the Family Business: Special Challenges and Best Practices. *Family Business Review, 10*(4), 323–337. doi:10.1111/j.1741-6248.1997.00323.x

Watkins, C. (2015b). *An Afro-brazilian Landscape: African Oil Palms and Socioecological Change in Bahia, Brazil.* Baton Rouge PhD dissertation.

Watkins, C. (2015a). African oil palms, colonial socioecological transformation and the making of an Afro-Brazilian landscape in Bahia, *Brazil. Environ. Hist*, *21*(1), 13–42. doi:10.3197/096734015X14183179969700

Watson, J. (2003). Failure rates for female-controlled businesses: Are they any different"? *Journal of Small Business Management*, *41*(3), 262–277. doi:10.1111/1540-627X.00081

Watts, S. (2020, February 19). *CMMI: An introduction to capability maturity model integration*. BMC Software. https://www.bmc.com/blogs/cmmi-capability-maturity-model-integration/

Watzlawick, P., Weakland, J. H., & Fisch, R. (1974). *Change: Principles of Problem Formation and Problem Resolution*. W. W. Norton.

Watzlawick, P., Weakland, J., & Fisch, R. (2011). *Change: Principles of Problem Formation and Resolution*. WW Norton & Co.

Weber, C. V. (1995). *The capability maturity model: Guidelines for improving the software process* (M. C. Paulk, M. B. Chrissis, C. V. Weber, & B. Curtis, Eds.). Addison-Wesley.

Weforum.org. (2022). *Training for improving leadership*. WeForum. https://www.weforum.org/agenda/2021/06/which-countries-are-most-invested-in-professional-develeopment/ [accessed on: 15.09.2022]

Weick, K. E. (1993). The collapse of sensemaking in organizations: The Mann Gulch disaster. *Administrative Science Quarterly*, *8*(4), 628–652. doi:10.2307/2393339

Weick, K. E. (1995). *Sensemaking in Organizations*. Sage.

Weick, K. E., & Quinn, R. E. (1999). Organizational Change and Development. *Annual Review of Psychology*, *50*(1), 361–386. doi:10.1146/annurev.psych.50.1.361 PMID:15012461

Weick, K. E., & Sutcliffe, K. M. (2005). *Managing the unexpected. Resilient performance in an age of uncertainty*. Wiley.

Weick, K. E., Sutcliffe, K. M., & Obstfeld, D. (1999). Organizing for high reliability: Processes of collective mindfulness. In B. M. Staw & L. L. Cummings (Eds.), *Research in organizational behavior* (Vol. 21, pp. 81–123). JAI Press.

Weiner, B. J. (2009), A theory of organizational readiness for change, *Implementation science*, *4*(1), 67. doi:10.1186/1748-5908-4-67

Wenham, C., Smith, J., & Morgan, R. (2020). COVID-19: The gendered impacts of the outbreak. *Lancet*, *395*(10227), 846–848. doi:10.1016/S0140-6736(20)30526-2 PMID:32151325

Wheaton, M. M., & Kezar, A. (2019). Interlocking systems of oppression: Women navigating higher education leadership. In *Challenges and opportunities for women in higher education leadership* (pp. 61–83). IGI Global. doi:10.4018/978-1-5225-7056-1.ch005

Whitty-Collins, G. (2020). *Why men win at work:...and How to make inequality history*. Luath Press Ltd.

WHO. (2020b). *Mental health & COVID-19*. WHO/ https://www.who.int/teams/mental-health-and-substance-use/covid-19.

Wieman, J. M., & Giles, H. (1997): Az interperszonális kommunikáció In: Szociálpszichológia szerk.: Hewstone,- Stroebe,– Codol,– Stephenson. KJK, Budapest, 1997.221-244.

Wiens, K., & Rowell, D. (2018), How to Embrace Change Using Emotional Intelligence, *Harvard Business Review*. https://hbr.org/2018/12/how-to-embrace-change-using-emotional-intelligence

Wiklund, J., Hatak, I., Lerner, D. A., Verheul, I., Thurik, R., & Antshel, K. (2020). Entrepreneurship, clinical psychology, and mental health: An exciting and promising new field of research. *The Academy of Management Perspectives, 34*(2), 291–295. doi:10.5465/amp.2019.0085

Wiklund, J., & Shepherd, D. (2003). Knowledge-based resources, entrepreneurial orientation, and the performance of small and medium sized businesses. *Strategic Management Journal, 24*(13), 1307–1314. doi:10.1002mj.360

Wiklund, J., & Shepherd, D. (2005). Entrepreneurial orientation and small business performance: A configurational approach. *Journal of Business Venturing, 20*(1), 71–91. doi:10.1016/j.jbusvent.2004.01.001

Wilkinson, A., Kupers, R., & Mangalagiude, D. (2013). How plausibility-based scenario practices are grappling with complexity to appreciate and address 21st Century Challenges. *Technological Forecasting and Social Change, 80*(4), 699–710. doi:10.1016/j.techfore.2012.10.031

Williams, S., & Narendan, S. (1999). Determinants of managerial risk: Exploring personality and cultural influences. *The Journal of Social Psychology, 139*(1), 102–125. doi:10.1080/00224549909598365

Wilson, C. (2013). *Brainstorming and Beyond: A User-Centered Design Method*. Elsevier.

Wiltbank, R., Read, S., Dew, N., & Sarasvathy, S. D. (2009). Prediction and control under uncertainty: Outcomes in angel investing. *Journal of Business Venturing, 24*(2), 116–133. doi:10.1016/j.jbusvent.2007.11.004

Wincent, J., Örtqvist, D., & Drnovsek, M. (2008). The entrepreneur's role stressors and proclivity for a venture withdrawal. *Scandinavian Journal of Management, 24*(3), 232–246. doi:10.1016/j.scaman.2008.04.001

Wischmeyer, T., & Rademacher, T. (2019). *Regulating Artificial Intelligence*. Springer International Publishing AG.

Witcher, B., & Butterworth, R. (2000). Hoshin Kanri at Hewlett-Packard. *Journal of General Management, 25*(4), 70–85. doi:10.1177/030630700002500405

Wolf, S. (1995). Cropping systems and conservation policy: The roles of agrichemical dealers and independent crop consultants. *Journal of Soil and Water Conservation, 50*, 263–269.

Wolf, S., & Nowak, P. (1995). Development of information intensive agrichemical management services in Wisconsin. *Environmental Management, 19*(3), 371–382. doi:10.1007/BF02471979

Wolf, S., & Primmer, E. (2006). Between incentives and action: A pilot study of biodiversity conservation competencies for multifunctional forest management in Finland. *Society & Natural Resources, 19*(9), 845–861. doi:10.1080/08941920600835601

Womack, J. P., & Jones, D. T. (1996). *Lean Thinking - Banish Waste and Create Wealth in Your Corporation*. Free Press, Simon & Schuster, Inc.

Women Entrepreneurs: Surviving the Pandemic & Beyond. (n.d.). Cherie Blair Foundation for Women. https://cherieblairfoundation.org/what-we-do/research/2020-annual-audit/

Wong-Mcdonald, A., & Gorsuch, R. L. (2000). Surrender to God: An Additional Coping Style? *Journal of Psychology and Theology, 28*(2), 149–161. doi:10.1177/009164710002800207

World Bank. (2021). *Small and Medium Enterprises (SMEs) Finance.* World Bank. https://www.worldbank.org/en/topic/smefinance

World Economic Forum. (2011). *Accelerating entrepreneurship in the Arab world.* WEF. www3.weforum.org/docs/WEF_YGL_Accelerating Entrepreneurship Arab World_Report_2011.pdf (accessed 24 December 2012).

World Health Organization. (2014). Mental health: A state of well-being. WHO. https://www.who.int/features/factfiles/mental_health/en/

World Health Organization. (2020). COVID-19 and violence against women: what the health sector/system can do, 7 April 2020 (No. WHO/SRH/20.04). World Health Organization.

Wu, H., Xu, Z., & Skare, M. (2022). How do family businesses adapt to the rapid pace of globalization? A bibliometric analysis. *Journal of Business Research, 153*, 59–74. doi:10.1016/j.jbusres.2022.08.022

Xiao, C. (2020). A novel approach of consultation on 2019 novel coronavirus (COVID-19)- Related psychological and mental problems: Structured letter therapy. *Psychiatry Investigation, 17*(2), 175–176. doi:10.30773/pi.2020.0047 PMID:32093461

Yang, S. Y. (2013). Wisdom and good lives: A process perspective. *New Ideas in Psychology, 31*(3), 194–201. doi:10.1016/j.newideapsych.2013.03.001

Yang, T., & Zhang, X. (2016). Benchmarking the building energy consumption and solar energy trade-offs of residential neighborhoods on Chongming Eco-Island. *China Appl. Energy, 180*, 792–799. doi:10.1016/j.apenergy.2016.08.039

Yang, W., Liu, W., Viña, A., Tuanmu, M.-N., He, G., Dietz, T., & Liu, J. (2013). Nonlinear effects of group size on collective action and resource outcomes. *Proceedings of the National Academy of Sciences of the United States of America, 110*(27), 10916–10921. doi:10.1073/pnas.1301733110 PMID:23776222

Yayavaram, S., & Ahuja, G. (2008). Decomposability in knowledge structures and its impact on the usefulness of inventions and knowledge-base malleability. *Administrative Science Quarterly, 53*(2), 333–362. doi:10.2189/asqu.53.2.333

Yıkılmaz, İ. (2021a). Digital transformation and organizational agility -Dijital dönüşüm ve örgütsel çeviklik. İ.Erdoğan Tarakçı& B. Göktaş (Eds.) in İşletmecilikte Dijital Dönüşüm (425-442). Efe Akademi,İstanbul.

Yıkılmaz, İ. (2021b). Covid-19 Pandemic As A Digital Transformation Catalyst. In M. Meciar & H. Şimşek (Eds.), *The Social And Economic Impact Of Covid-19* (pp. 119–138). IJOPEC Publication Limited.

Yin, R. K. (1994). *Case study research: Design and methods* (2nd ed.). Sage Publications.

Yoon, H. (2012). The Performance Effects of Entrepreneurial Orientation: Evidence from South Korean Start-ups. *International Journal of Arts and Commerce, 1*(4), 248–254.

Yordanova, D. I., & Alexandrova-Boshnakova, M. I. (2011). Gender effects on risk-taking of entrepreneurs: Evidence from Bulgaria. *International Journal of Entrepreneurial Behaviour & Research, 17*(3), 272–295. doi:10.1108/13552551111130718

Yu, H., Wang, Y., Li, X., Wang, C., Sun, M., & Du, A. (2019). Measuring ecological capital: State of the art, trends, and challenges. *Journal of Cleaner Production, 219*, 833–845. doi:10.1016/j.jclepro.2019.02.014

Zabala, R. A. (2019). The family business as a clan: Resources and uniqueness. *Dimensión Empresarial, 17*(4), 9.

Zabit, M. N. M. (2010). Problem-Based Learning on Students' Critical Thinking Skills in Teaching Business Education in Malaysia: A Literature Review. *American Journal of Business Education, 3*(6), 19–32. doi:10.19030/ajbe.v3i6.436

Zahra, S. A. (2005). Entrepreneurial Risk Taking in Family Firms. *Family Business Review*, *18*(1), 23–40. doi:10.1111/j.1741-6248.2005.00028.x

Zaidi, S. (n.d.). *Lines of light: Sohib Zaidi*. Unsplash. https://unsplash.com/@msohebzaidi

Zaleski, Z. (1996). Future anxiety, concept, measurement, and preliminary research. *Personality and Individual Differences*, *21*(2), 165–174. doi:10.1016/0191-8869(96)00070-0

Zamora, R. (2012). *A model of collaboration in complexity for management in times of uncertainty and change*. Lulu Press.

Zelbst, P. J., Green, K. W., Sower, V. E., & Abshire, R. D. (2011, Fall). Radio Frequency Identification Technology Utilization and Organizational Agility. *Journal of Computer Information Systems*, 24–33.

Zhang, Z., & Sharifi, H. (2007). Towards theory building in agile manufacturing strategy-a taxonomical approach. *IEEE Transactions on Engineering Management*, *54*(2), 351–370. doi:10.1109/TEM.2007.893989

Zhao, H., & Feng, Z. (2020). Staggered release policies for COVID-19 control: Costs and benefits of relaxing restrictions by age and risk. *Mathematical Biosciences*, *326*, 108405. doi:10.1016/j.mbs.2020.108405 PMID:32565231

Zou, P., Huo, D., & Li, M. (2020). The impact of the COVID-19 pandemic on firms: A survey in Guangdong Province. China. *Global Health Research and Policy*, *5*(1), 41. doi:10.118641256-020-00166-z PMID:32885048

About the Contributors

Kyla L. Tennin, DM, MBA, is an industry practitioner and DM in Management and Organizational Leadership. She focuses on Change Management and mixed methods empirical research for continuous improvement, business transformation, and recovery during and after internal/external crisis to nations, institutions, and individual's lives. She is a leader in various roles at investment forums where she works with Presidents of Nations, Heads of Banks, Prime Ministers, High Commissioners, and Chambers of Commerce and other business leaders to strategize and make business decisions to help businesses start-up, advance, and/or scale to improve economic development, promote social justice, and create jobs in various nations. At the World Business Angels Investment Forum (WBAF), affiliated partner of the G20 Global Partnership for Financial Inclusion (GPFI), this vision is to promote social justice, create jobs, financial inclusion, and innovative financial instruments for innovators, startups, and SMEs, helping them to scale. Dr. Tennin is also affiliated with the International Monetary Fund, World Bank Group, and Parliamentary Network to enhance economies and various forms of businesses. She is an OB/GYN MD track turned DM (doctor) with background in biology, biotechnology, and organic and biochemistry, with major emphasis in women and gender studies, has project management and lean six sigma certifications, a Master of Business Administration (MBA), and is a Ph.D. Fellow at the Global Peace Institute, headquartered in the United Kingdom. She contributed to the accreditation process at the University of Phoenix College of Doctoral Studies and completed additional studies (to launch and scale corporations) at Harvard, Stanford, Yale, University of Cape Town, and University of Glasgow to name a few. She has personally written approximately 18 books, 3 book chapters with colleagues, 3 patents, several other intellectual properties, and nearly 85 research reports, later conceptualized into products and services for global businesses. Dr. Tennin has presented research and posters in practitioner and academic conferences, workshops, and international webinars. She has professional experience in the financial services and investments, hospitality, restaurant, consumer products/beauty, and healthcare industries, with 95% of her experience spent in financial services and higher education. Dr. Tennin has 23 years of experience in higher education and 17 years owning her own global conglomerate corporation, which she built while homeless, to recover for self-sufficiency, to recover financially, and create jobs for people. Operating in 31 countries, with 24 locations, on 6 continents, and 2 world headquarters. She was awarded over 30 corporate awards, mentored entrepreneurs for 22 years with global organizations and world-renowned corporations and banks as sponsors, and currently owns a business academy, women's entrepreneurship academy, and women's entrepreneurship bootcamp program where entrepreneurship, resilience, finance, pricing and tax strategy, research methodology and data analysis for consultants, digital transformation, property ownership, and other courses are taught. Her areas of expertise and research interests are strategy, entrepreneurship, cosmeceuticals, economic development, emerging markets, multinationals, corporate governance, well-being/burnout, and women's empowerment.

***

Vanessa Amorim is a Business and Economics Ph.D. student at the University of Aveiro - Portugal. She has a master's in Organizational Management - Specialization: Business Management, and a Post-Graduation in Management Tools for Business Competitiveness from the Porto Accounting and Business School - Polytechnic of Porto - Portugal. She has participated in various national and international conferences and is the author and co-author of several book chapters and articles. Her main research interests are Innovation, Entrepreneurship, Marketing, and Management.

Mohammed Bayyoud is a part of Department of Banking & Finance, Al-Quds University, Palestine. a Director of Bayyoud's Financial & Consultancy Services, London, UK, Senior Consultant for RBC (Royal Bank of Canada), Head of Finance & Banking Department Al Quds University, Jerusalem, Restructurer and consultant of Business, Director and Operational Manager CANAR Technical Services Inc., Toronto, Canada, Certified Residential Underwriter (CRU) the Real Estate of Canada, Certificate in Mortgage Lending for Residential Housing (CMC) and Accredited Financial Analyst AFA, by the Global Management and Finance, USA.

Raktima Bharadwaj is an aspiring and passionate psychologist, who completed her graduation from Amity University Kolkata with a Bachelor's Degree in Applied Psychology. She is pursuing a Postgraduate in Clinical Health Psychology from Queen's University Belfast and have a burning desire to contribute to the mental health and well-being of society. A keen observer and a good listener who is highly enthusiastic about spreading positive energy among people.

Jennifer Bryan is a published author, global speaker and Managing Director of Change and Leadership, who has worked with over 40 different organisations across multiple industries. She is also a Vice President of the ACMP (Association of Change Management Professionals) UK Chapter. She believes in helping people - in whatever capacity she can - by making sure people are thought of first, last and throughout change projects and programmes. Her written work includes the book "Leading People in Change: A Practical Guide," and articles in multiple industry journals. She can be heard at TEDx and on several independent podcasts sharing her thoughts on leading people centric change ().

Oindrila Chakraborty is a gold medalist in her MBA programme from University of Calcutta. She has 14 years of teaching experience in management education. She has completed her PhD from University of Calcutta and has several publications to furnish in National and International Journals of high repute.

Nidal Darwish was born in Palestine. He received a Ph.D. degree in economics and management of technology from the University of Bergamo in Italy and a master's degree in business administration from Al-Quds University in Palestine. He has a bachelor's degree in business administration from Bethlehem University in Palestine. Currently, he is an assistant professor at Al-Quds University, Palestine. His research interests are entrepreneurship, family business, developing countries, international business, high-growth firms, and marketing. Moreover, he has a great deal of experience in teaching since he has worked in this field for more than ten years and taught more than 20 different courses in management, marketing, and entrepreneurship. He teaches Advance Marketing Management, International Business, Global Marketing, Advanced Topics in Entrepreneurship, Entrepreneurship, and Business Essentials. He also supervises the thesis of master students.

Rajoshi Das is an aspiring psychologist who graduated from Amity University Kolkata with a Bachelor's degree in Applied Psychology. Das had the opportunity to complete various internships during the undergraduate years, the most prominent of which was at Apollo Gleneagles Hospital, where Das worked in the Child Developmental Center. Das is now pursuing for a Masters degree in Applied Psychology at Amity University in Kolkata. Das' areas of interest include scholarly activities. Along with research, there is also a special interest in sports Psychology.

Mehmet Ertem is a scholar of Management and Strategy focused on Strategic Decision Making, Change Management, and Commitment to Change. He uses mostly qualitative research methods in research studies including grounded theory, conceptual content analysis, and phenomenology. He has an academic position at Yozgat Bozok University of Türkiye as an assistant professor.

Rebecca Fakoussa Senior Lecturer in Business Entrepreneurship, University of Northampton, Marketing & Entrepreneurship Centre for Sustainable Business Practices.

Silvia Fernandes is an Assistant Professor at the Faculty of Economics of the University of Algarve. Holds a PhD from this university and is member of Cinturs (Research Centre for Tourism, Sustainability and Well-being). Lectures Information Technology/Systems and Innovation Management in undergraduate and master courses. Has several publications in books and journals, and communications in international conferences in themes such as: enterprise information systems, smart tourism, open innovation, etc.

Filippo Ferrari holds a Bachelor degree in Work and Organizational Psychology and a Masters degree in Adult Training and Education. He currently serves as a Lecturer at Bologna University, School of Economics, Management and Statistics, where he teaches Organizational Behaviour and Design and Leadership. His fields of interests are International Human Resources Management, Organizational Reliability, Change Management, Adult Training.

Ramazan Gökbunar, completed his undergraduate education in the Department of Finance and his graduate education in the Department of Finance at Dokuz Eylül University. He started to work as a research assistant at Manisa Celal Bayar University in 1992 and still continues his duty.

Edward Gonsalves is a Senior Fellow of the Higher Education Academy and a European Entrepreneurship Education Fellow He is Associate Professor at ESADE Business & Law School (Barcelona) and Visiting Professor of Entrepreneurship & Human Resources at Toulouse Business School (Barcelona) . He was previously Pathway Leader for the MA Entrepreneurship Program at Regents University, London. His research interests and recent publications focus on executive, entrepreneurial and organization play; entrepreneurship and family-business education; strategic management and organizational learning; decision-making in uncertain and ambiguous settings. Edward is Director of the Cooplexity Institute (Oxford & Barcelona). He specializes in the design, development and delivery of senior executive programs for high performance teams in entrepreneurial and large firms. He also holds a number of directorships, advises, consults and publishes in the area of strategic and entrepreneurial learning.

Catherine Hayes qualified in Podiatric Medicine and a Founding Fellow of the Faculty of Podiatric Medicine at the Royal College of Physicians and Surgeons (Glasgow), Catherine Hayes is Professor of Health Professions Pedagogy and Scholarship at the University of Sunderland, where she is Programme Leader for the Professional Doctorate programme pathways to the award of DBA, EdD, DPM and generic DProf degrees.

John Higgins is a widely published author and researcher into all aspects of organizational life, whose work has appeared in both the Harvard Business Review and the Sloan Management Review. His work draws on his long running association with the Ashridge Doctorate and Masters in Organizational Change. He can be heard in conversation with Brene Brown talking about his latest work exploring activism in the workplace ().

Karen Hodge-Cunningham is an accomplished Senior Executive with over twenty (20+) years of growth and performance, who leads with passion and is driven by purpose and integrity. MS. Hodge Cunningham has a proven track record of building and leading teams to high performance, built on a values-first approach. Her record demonstrates that she believes in and stands for results and excellence through the investment and development of people and relationships. She has been leading and coaching C-suite leaders across industries such as financial services, federated associations, military, scientific and research agencies, municipal, federal government agencies and crown corporations navigate their contemporary organizations through today's turbulent environment, so they can modernize, stay relevant and achieve both their cultural and business imperatives. Ms. Hodge Cunningham's approach is firmly rooted in the knowledge and experience that an organization that genuinely lives its values and embraces the talents of its people while driving for excellence, must simultaneously remain nimble to keeping pace with the every-changing environment. An organization must know that knows its purpose, and have it embedded in its fabric in order to succeed. As an experienced Senior Leader, C-suite Advisor and Strategic Culture and Change practitioner, she works in a collaborative fashion leveraging the elements of various change and proven business methodologies from across the spectrum to support the development of a change ready environment, leadership coaching, engagement of stakeholder adoption, organizational behavior and its impact on culture and success, learning and development, and governance. As a founding member of the CGI global think tank for Strategic Culture and Change, and CIO advisory, she has worked to strengthen the knowledge, awareness and increased the understanding of the critical significance of the people defendant nature of all success regardless of industry or project. Through collaboration with international teammates, she has authored a number of articles, blogs, and delivered numerous presentations to mobilize and inform on the necessity of engaging in a strategic culture and change strategy both at an organizational level down through individual initiatives. Ms. Hodge Cunningham is working to demonstrate that change is the support structure in the evolution of new and emerging technologies such as AI, Cyber security and machine learning. Ms. Hodge Cunningham has received National Award of Service Excellence in 2019 for her work done with Canada's largest governmental agency "Employment Services Development Canada" in their transformation and modernization journey. She has been a recipient of CGI's IMPACT aware for her work to increase awareness and develop action direction and action for Diversity in the workplace for the National Capital Region. She has received

Canadian Chief of Defense staff's coin in 2016 for her work and mobilization of community support for the National Capital Region Military Family Resource Centre. Was one of the first nominated women in CGI's "Women of Impact Award in 2021". These awards are just an example of the impact that Ms. Hodge Cunningham has had on the people and organizations she has had the privilege to work with. She is a sought-after author, and speaker delivering numerous key notes, and participated in various international podcasts, and developed various leadership, mentorship and sales enablement curriculum centered around fundamentals of leadership and its direct impact on culture and organizational success.

Isolde Kanikani is a Transformation & Organisational Change management lead, working with decision-makers on a daily basis to realise their digital strategy and transformation stories. As a seasoned professional, Isolde is known to be a driving force and initiator who gets a lot of satisfaction from seeing a job well done. She works on complex global projects focused on organisational development, governance and change maturity building, alongside the technological advancements every organisation is busy with these days. She has the privilege to be a Global board member of the ACMP and join together with all the amazing staff and volunteers working to "lead the way change works". Her search for knowledge and growth through new experiences has led to an MBA, a master's in human resources management and pro bono consultancy in the non-profit sector. As an entrepreneur, Isolde has founded two successful businesses and considers herself a world citizen after many years of extensive professional travel, meeting new cultures and ways of viewing the world. Sparked by mixed roots in New Zealand and the United Kingdom, she has lived in Argentina and Spain, finally putting down roots with her partner Fred in the Netherlands. Isolde has written her first book, has published research and founded the change management best practices innovation group FUTURE:CM. She is passionate about helping new people enter the change profession and innovating current best practices with experienced peers. Isolde is a true believer in building community and the idea that we are stronger together.

Füsun Küçükbay, received her MS in Business Administration from Ege University, Turke in 2004. She received her PHD in Business Administration from Ege University, Turkey in 2009. The name of the PHD thesis is 'Performance measurement in Turkey: An Attempt at modelling for Turkey'. She worked at Ege University between 2002-2004 periods as a research assistant in Faculty of Business Administration at Accounting and Finance Department. She worked in İzmir Ekspres Corporation between 2005-2013 periods as a finance manager. She has been working as an Associate Professor in Faculty of Business Administration, Manisa Celal Bayar University, Turkey since 2013. Her research interests include corporate finance, working capital, performance evaluations problems and portfolio selection problems. She has two daughter. Her names are Ceren and İnci.

Fatima Lampreia holds a PhD from Essex University and is a researcher of CinTurs (Research Centre for Tourism, Sustainability and Well-being). Lectures disciplines related with sustainability and governance and has publications in books, journals and communications in international conferences in themes such as governance, citizenship, and educational policy.

Orlando Lima Rua holds a Habilitation and a Ph.D. in Management. He is an Adjunct Professor of Management at the Porto Accounting and Business School (ISCAP) of the Polytechnic of Porto (Portugal). He is a researcher at the Center for Organizational and Social Studies (CEOS.PP) (Polytechnic of Porto – ISCAP), the Research Center of Business Sciences (NECE) of the University of Beira Interior (UBI), and the Management Applied Research Unit (UNIAG) of the Association of Polytechnic Institutes of Northern Portugal (APNOR). His major research subjects are entrepreneurship, innovation, and strategy, and his papers have been published in several relevant international journals and scientific conferences (JCR/Web of Science and Scopus).

Bruno de Sousa Lopes is a Business and Economics Ph.D. student at the University of Aveiro - Portugal. He has a master's in Human Resource Management and Development and a bachelor's degree in Human Resources from the Institute Polytechnic of Porto, Portugal. His main research interests are Human Resources, Ageing, Career Management, and Business Management.

Anindita Majumdar has completed her PhD in Applied Psychology from University of Calcutta. She is an academician and a Rehabilitation Council of India registered psychologist. She has 11 years of work experience, both in education and corporate sectors. She is associated with Association of Rehabilitation Psychologist & Professionals India and International Benevolent Research Foundation as Life Member. Her areas of teaching and research interest include- Creativity, Expressive arts psychotherapy, Positive Psychology, Clinical & Rehabilitation Psychology, Child & Educational Psychology, Psycho-social & Personality research, and Qualitative Analysis. She has several papers published and presented in these domains.

Samrat Ray is involved as researcher in economics focusing on entrepreneurship and innovation strategies across various verticals.Special interest lies in poverty eradication,inequality,social innovation as well as behavioral psychology behind economic activity.Always looking for research collaboration,joint authorship and publication activities across various verticals in economics and management sciences.

Teresa Salazar is a Research professor at Faculty of Administrative Economic Sciences of Mazatlan.

Jens Sorg is a passionate change and transformation manager. He has more than 15 years of consulting and training experience. In over 100 projects, he has held various management and support positions. As Director Business Consulting at CGI, Jens is leading a consulting team focused on Strategic Change Management. Since the beginning of his professional career, Jens has successfully initiated and accompanied change projects and entire transformations for his customers. The focus was on the introduction of new forms of organization and cooperation models, the implementation of processes, their digitization, and optimization, as well as the introduction of methods from classic and agile project management or the implementation of new compliance guidelines. Jens has also worked on strategic topics for many years. In recent years, his sectoral focus has been on automotive, financial services, governance/administration, and industrial location service management. Jens also has many years of experience in the areas of logistics, telecommunications, and international cooperation and development. In addition to this broad sectoral structure, Jens has extensive cultural experience. He worked in many European countries and Afghanistan, Ethiopia, China, Dubai, the USA, and South Africa. These experiences enable Jens to have a great understanding of diversity and empathy for stakeholders from all cultural backgrounds and hierarchical levels. Jens is also a certified trainer for People-Centered Implementation (PCI®), Certified Change Management Professional™ (CCMP™), and certified in the Capacity Works and Wallbreakers methods. All of them aim in particular at change management and organizational development, but also leadership and collaboration. Jens is also a systemic consultant, executive coach, and Scrum Master. In addition to his work at CGI, Jens is chairman of the board of the German Chapter of the Association for Change Management Professionals (ACMP®), member of the leadership team and chapter coach of the Chapter Formation Committee of ACMP Global, and member of the advisory board of GREEN Finance Consulting e.V., the student management consultancy of Goethe University/Frankfurt.

Assia Stoyanova is senior leader with 25+ years of experience in human-centered business transformation and culture and change management across 10+ industries. As a founding member of CGI's culture and change management practices, Ms. Stoyanova has coauthored and executed repeatable processes and methodologies for successfully assisting large enterprises through organic and inorganic change to realize quantifiable results. As a lead practitioner, Ms. Stoyanova focuses on change management including stakeholder adoption and behavior, culture, communications, training, organizational design, team development, knowledge management, and collaboration, and change program governance. Her client advisory experience spanning various geographies and industries, such as utilities & manufacturing, financial services, healthcare, and life sciences, state and local government, insurance, and telecommunications has enabled her to distill culture and change characteristics and strategies that transcend verticals and locations and focus on the common human psychology traits. In addition to change management, Ms. Stoyanova has significant experience in business process analysis and re-engineering, strategy roadmap and business case development, governance, and PMO. Ms. Stoyanova holds an MBA from MIT Sloan School of Management with major in Financial Management and Economics and minor in Organizational Development under Edgar Schein and Systemic Change under Peter Senge. She also holds a Masters in Computer Technologies, a cross-section of computer science and compute engineering, that allows her to appreciate the impacts that modern technologies bring to the every day workplace. She is certified with Human Synergistics® Organizational Culture Inventory (OCI), Human Synergistics® Organizational Effectiveness Inventory (OEI), Prosci® Change Management and attended specialized trainings in principled negotiations, executive communications, team performance, dispute resolution, covert organizational processes, and behavioral modeling. Ms. Stoyanova is a founding member of CGI's US CSG Women's Forum and a CGI Bridge Builder Award recipient. She is also a member of MIT Club of New York, MIT Sloan Club of New York, Association of MIT Alumnae, and MIT Sloan Women in Management, and an MIT Education Counselor.

Omar Vargas-González is professor and Head of Systems and Computing Department at Tecnologico Nacional de Mexico Campus Ciudad Guzman, professor at Telematic Engineering at Centro Universitario del Sur Universidad de Guadalajara with a master degree in Computer Systems. Has been trained in Innovation and Multidisciplinary Entrepreneurship at Arizona State University (2018) and a Generation of Ecosystems of Innovation, Entrepreneurship and Sustainability for Jalisco course by Harvard University T.H. Chan School of Health. At present conduct research on diverse fields such as Entrepreneurship, Economy, Statistics, Mathematics and Information and Computer Sciences. Has colaborated in the publication of over 20 scientific articles and conducted diverse Innovation and Technological Development projects.

José Vargas-Hernandez is a research professor.

İbrahim Yikilmaz serves as a research assistant at Kocaeli University, Department of Management and Organization. Dr. Yıkılmaz got his Ph.D. degree in Management and Organization (Kocaeli University

2022), master degrees in Management and Organization (Ankara Yıldırım Beyazıt University 2018) and Public Administration (Turkey and Middle East Public Administration Institute 2016) and bachelor degrees in System Engineering (Military Academy 2009). Before starting his career as a research assistant, he held managerial positions in various public institutions. He continues to work on strategic management, leadership, digital transformation, innovation, and agile organizations. He has various publications in national and international congresses and journals. He speaks English at a professional level.

Index

5S 326-327, 329, 332, 334-336, 338-340

A

Activity 19, 27, 29-30, 34-37, 39, 46, 49-50, 72, 159-160, 194, 197, 199-200, 230-232, 249, 255-257, 299, 309, 325, 328, 331
Advocacy 26, 41, 281
Agile Human Resources 227
Agile Transformation 217-221, 227, 270
Ambiguity 1, 4, 12, 92, 94, 99, 191, 194, 206-207, 227, 284, 286-287, 289, 293, 299
Anxiety 10-11, 13, 27, 52, 57, 81-84, 86-87, 89, 91-99, 130, 156, 209, 261, 269
Arab Family Business 186, 191, 203
Artificial Intelligence 79, 259-261, 269, 276, 278-282

B

Big Data Analytics 266, 276
Brainstorming 252-259, 261-263, 265
Business Value 139, 147, 282

C

Capability 93-94, 128-134, 137, 139, 141, 143, 147, 150-151, 153-154, 171, 198, 206-207, 209-210, 212, 214, 217, 219-221, 224, 244, 276, 293-294, 307-308, 324
Challenges 2, 17, 21, 24, 43-44, 47-50, 55, 59, 61, 75, 102, 106, 108, 122, 124, 180-181, 187-188, 191-194, 204-205, 222-223, 226, 229, 231, 239, 244-245, 248, 252, 265-266, 268-271, 273-275, 278-279, 284-285, 290, 292, 295-296, 298-301, 304-305, 309, 312-314, 322, 337
Change 1-11, 13-28, 30-43, 57, 63, 65, 74-75, 77, 79, 83, 87, 92-94, 98, 100-102, 104-108, 110-113, 117, 120-134, 136-137, 139-140, 143, 145-147, 149-161, 163-173, 175, 177, 179-184, 186-188, 191-192, 194-196, 198, 202-205, 207, 209-220, 223, 226-227, 229, 242, 252-255, 259-260, 262-284, 288-289, 291, 295, 298-299, 310-314, 316, 318, 321, 326
Change Agent 7-8, 11-12, 24
Change Commitment 1, 3, 5-6, 8, 12, 24
Change Cynicism 10, 21, 24
Change Management 1-2, 4-5, 10-16, 20-23, 27, 93-94, 100-102, 104-113, 117, 120-129, 131-132, 137, 139-141, 143, 150-159, 161, 163-164, 167-168, 170, 181-183, 188, 198, 202, 204, 219-220, 227, 266-282, 284
Change Management Maturity 128, 139-141, 143, 152, 154
Change Maturity 128-134, 136-137, 139-141, 143, 147, 149-150, 152, 154
Change Recipients 1, 3-6, 8-13, 17, 21, 24
ChangeOps 128-129, 134, 141, 145-147, 149-150, 152, 154
Communication Strategies 75, 77, 100, 109, 121, 127
Competitive Advantage 16, 77, 145, 207, 209-210, 214-215, 217, 219-221, 227, 232-233, 247, 316, 328
Complexity 1-2, 7, 39, 156, 163, 166, 189, 191, 195-196, 205-207, 227, 255, 265, 268, 270-272, 274, 277, 304-305, 307, 315, 321
Concerns 31, 78, 81-84, 86-88, 92-94, 155, 160, 207, 216, 255, 309
Consulting 26, 40, 56, 153, 193, 201, 216, 219, 266-268, 270, 273-275, 277-278, 280, 311
Continuous Improvement 128, 134, 139, 141, 143, 145-146, 149, 154, 210, 217, 315, 323-325, 328, 335, 337-340
Coping Strategies 43, 57, 62, 156-157, 161, 171, 181-182
Covid-19 2, 53-61, 78, 81-99, 106-107, 155-156, 159-161, 183-185, 206-208, 216-217, 220, 222-226, 242, 262, 268-269, 284-286, 288, 291, 295-301
Crisis 3, 55, 58, 62, 82, 92, 94, 102, 122, 155-157, 161, 183, 206, 208-209, 216, 222, 225-226, 249,

284-288, 291, 293, 295-299, 301, 318
Critical Reflection 284, 287, 301
Critical Reflexivity 284, 287-288, 293, 296, 301

D

Data Science 266, 271, 273, 277
Decision-making 33, 132, 150, 187-188, 192, 195-196, 201, 209, 229, 232, 241, 248, 259, 263-264, 266, 268, 271, 273, 275-276, 282, 293, 295, 301, 337
Digital Business 63, 79
Digital Marketing 63-66, 69-70, 73-75, 78-79
Digital Transformation 79, 121, 207, 225-227, 267-268
Dynamic Capability 206-207, 210, 212, 220-221

E

Emotion 4, 8, 19, 25, 297
Emotional Labour 284, 302
Engagement 9, 25-26, 29, 31, 33-36, 39, 42, 63-66, 68-69, 75-79, 101, 197, 200, 217
Entrepreneurial Orientations 229
Executive Learning 186
Expectations 9, 33-34, 37, 59, 81-84, 90-95, 97, 105, 207-212, 214-217, 219-222, 227, 231, 233-234, 253, 260
Extended Epistemology 25-26, 42

F

Female entrepreneurs 43-44, 47-49, 51, 55, 60, 62, 228, 230, 233-241, 243, 246, 249
Framework 13, 37, 39, 52, 65-66, 74, 103, 109, 128, 133-134, 136-137, 139-141, 143, 147, 149-151, 153-154, 165, 167, 169, 184, 199, 224, 226, 242-243, 252, 264, 275, 285, 303, 306, 311-312, 315, 317, 320
Future Scenarios 252-258, 261-262, 264-265

G

Gender 22, 44, 48-50, 55-56, 59-60, 62, 81, 84, 92-93, 112, 126, 163, 228-231, 233-236, 238, 240-251, 285-300, 302
Governance 21, 53, 65, 130-134, 136-137, 139, 143-145, 147, 154, 182, 190-191, 193, 198, 204, 220, 222-223, 248, 275-276, 285, 293, 304-305, 309, 312-313, 315-316, 318, 322
Gross Domestic Product 82, 99

I

I-It 38, 42
Inequality 83, 95, 231, 242, 284, 286, 291, 298, 300-302
Inflation 72, 82, 90-91, 93-94, 96-97, 99
Innovation Management 249, 303-304, 311-312, 315, 321
Inquiry 14, 19, 26, 40-42, 184, 201, 229, 246, 263, 265, 299-300
Integrity 25, 28, 293, 314, 316, 330
Intention To Quit 5, 9-11, 24
Internationalization 186, 188-190, 192, 194, 197-198, 201-202, 250
I-Thou 38, 42

J

Just in Time 323

K

Kaizen 143, 154, 332, 338, 340
Key Performance Indicators (KPI) 65-67, 69-71, 73-74, 78-79

L

Leadership 1, 3, 7-8, 12-13, 15, 17-18, 20, 24-26, 28, 34, 37-42, 48, 77, 100-102, 104, 107-109, 111-113, 117, 120-126, 130-131, 133, 141, 156, 165, 182, 184, 187, 189, 198, 203, 215, 219, 244, 253, 270, 284-290, 292-301
Leadership Strategies 100-102, 104, 107, 109, 111-112, 120-121, 126, 293
Leading 5, 7-8, 11, 21, 25-26, 28-29, 35-41, 65, 72, 76, 98, 125, 152, 156, 182, 193, 211, 254, 267, 279-280, 293, 296-297, 304, 312, 315, 334
Lean 323-331, 337-340
Lean Management 323, 338-340
Lean Tools 323-325, 327, 330, 338-339
Learning Organization 21, 212, 219, 227, 281

M

Machine Learning 259-261, 266-267, 276
Management Strategies 2, 14, 43, 62, 158, 269, 313
Maturity 63, 70-71, 74-75, 128-134, 136-137, 139-141, 143, 147, 149-154, 277
Mental Health 51-52, 56-57, 59, 61, 81-84, 86-95, 97-99, 286, 296

Middle East 97, 187-188, 191, 199, 204, 228-232, 238, 241
Models of Innovation 303, 305, 316

N

Narrative Inquiry 263, 265
Narrative Research Design 252-253
Neoliberalism 284, 290, 301-302

O

Optimization 164, 218, 323-324, 329, 331, 334, 337
Organisational Change Management 109, 123-124, 131, 154-155
Organisational Structure 100, 105, 130, 147
Organizational Agility 206-207, 210-213, 217-221, 223-226
Organizational Reliability 1-4, 7, 17, 24

P

Pandemic 2, 34, 37, 53-56, 58, 61, 74, 76, 78, 81-95, 97-99, 101-102, 106-107, 120, 122-123, 155-156, 159-161, 163, 171-181, 183-184, 206-210, 212, 216-217, 220-221, 223-227, 254, 260-262, 268-269, 273, 284-286, 288, 291, 295-297, 299, 301
Performance 2, 9, 13, 22-24, 30, 43-44, 52-54, 57, 59, 63-67, 69-72, 74-79, 93, 98, 104-105, 107-108, 111, 122, 124, 133, 139-141, 181, 183-184, 203, 206, 213, 218, 220-221, 224, 227, 232-235, 240-241, 243-247, 249-251, 263, 270, 273-274, 296, 298-299, 320-321, 324-325, 327, 332
Planning with Future Scenarios 253, 255, 262, 265
Play 6, 11, 29, 33, 35, 44, 47, 56, 64, 93, 186-188, 193-195, 197-199, 201-205, 207, 215, 220, 295, 324, 327
Positionality 285-286, 292, 297-298, 302
Post-Covid 19 Era 206
Practitioner 26, 38, 42, 192, 275, 299
Praxis 25, 27, 38, 42, 285, 287, 294
Psychosocial Aspect 43, 62
Public Innovation Policies 309, 322
Pull-Push Integrated System 323, 330, 336

R

Reactions 10, 12-14, 17-18, 21-23, 58, 73, 81-84, 87-94, 156, 170, 286
Readiness to Change 4, 9, 17, 24
Relationality 42, 289
Resilience 4-7, 12, 38, 40, 42, 53, 57, 59, 191, 198, 206-207, 217, 223, 292-293, 299, 301, 317-318

S

Signature Pedagogy 291, 302
Situated Learning 7, 18-19
Social Media 51, 63, 65-67, 69-72, 74-80
Social Network 65, 80
Societal Stigma 62
Socio-Ecological Innovation 303-307, 311-316
Socio-Ecological Transition 304, 310, 312, 322
Spaghetti Diagram 323, 325, 329, 332-334, 339-340
Strategy 2-3, 12, 16, 27, 38, 41, 59, 63-65, 69-71, 74-79, 100, 109-110, 112-113, 117, 120-121, 124, 126, 129, 140, 150, 152, 154, 156-160, 163-164, 171, 189-190, 199, 201, 204, 209, 211, 218, 221-223, 235, 244, 252, 254-255, 261-262, 264-265, 270, 272, 274, 277, 281, 323-324, 326-329, 336-337, 339
Strategy Development 252, 255, 262, 265
Students 81-90, 92-94, 96-98, 184, 205, 249, 259-263, 267
Survey 33, 52, 55, 71, 81, 83-84, 86-87, 93-100, 110-112, 119, 126, 161, 191, 203, 236, 279
Sustainable 25-26, 29-30, 35-38, 42, 56, 77, 129-130, 132, 134, 147, 206, 212, 215-216, 219-221, 223, 227, 246, 248-250, 261, 263, 267, 271, 278, 281, 305-307, 309-313, 315, 317, 320-322, 328
Sustainable Development 246, 248-250, 281, 305-307, 310-312, 315, 317, 321-322
Swimlane 326, 329-330, 339-340

T

Transformation 3, 8, 13, 19, 23-24, 28, 39-40, 61, 79, 100, 109, 121, 128, 131-132, 139, 149, 151, 154, 159-160, 163, 168-169, 181, 184, 187, 198, 200, 206-207, 212, 217-221, 225-227, 267-268, 270-271, 277-278, 286, 289, 309, 311, 313, 316-317, 321, 340
Type 1 Change 27, 42
Type 2 Change 27, 42

U

Uncertainty 1, 5-7, 11-12, 14, 21, 23, 35, 39, 56, 92, 94, 96-97, 101, 130-131, 156, 187, 191-192, 194-197, 199, 201, 205-207, 209-211, 213-214, 216-217, 219, 221, 224, 227, 234, 243, 255, 264, 271, 273, 288, 300, 337

V

Value Creation 19, 63, 80, 128, 130, 132, 134, 136, 139, 141, 144, 147, 150, 227, 325, 337
Value Stream Mapping 325, 331, 339-340
Visual Management 326-327, 330, 336, 339-340
Volatility 1, 53, 206-207, 227
VUCA 1-3, 7, 130, 147, 154, 206-207, 210, 227

W

Warehouse Management 323, 327-330, 338
Waste 132, 139, 145, 323-332, 334, 337-340
Workplace 13, 15, 20-21, 30, 33-35, 40-41, 43, 97, 104, 108, 155, 159-160, 171-172, 180-181, 183, 208, 289, 294-296, 299, 326-327, 332-333, 335, 339-340

Ensure Quality Research is Introduced to the Academic Community

Become an Evaluator for IGI Global Authored Book Projects

The overall success of an authored book project is dependent on quality and timely manuscript evaluations.

Applications and Inquiries may be sent to:
development@igi-global.com

Applicants must have a doctorate (or equivalent degree) as well as publishing, research, and reviewing experience. Authored Book Evaluators are appointed for one-year terms and are expected to complete at least three evaluations per term. Upon successful completion of this term, evaluators can be considered for an additional term.

If you have a colleague that may be interested in this opportunity, we encourage you to share this information with them.

www.ingramcontent.com/pod-product-compliance
Lightning Source LLC
LaVergne TN
LVHW062112300926
849161LV00010B/2445
* 9 7 8 1 6 6 8 4 7 5 0 9 6 *